So. California Job Source

Covers the Entire Los Angeles & San Diego Metro Areas
including Orange, San Bernardino and Ventura Counties

Everything You Need to Land The Job of Your Choice in Southern California

• Where to Write • Who to Call • What to Say

So. California Job Source

Over 8,000 Job Contacts, Web Site Addresses & Job Hotlines

for the following categories

- Accounting
- Advertising/Marketing & Sales
- Aerospace & Defense
- Arts & Culture
- Associations/Non-Profit & Public Interest Groups
- Banking & Finance
- Broadcast Media & Communications
- Design & Engineering
- Education
- Entertainment
- Healthcare
- High Tech
- Hospitality
- Insurance
- Largest & Fastest Growing So. California Companies
- Law & Lobbying
- Print Media & Publishing
- Public Relations
- Real Estate
- Sports & Recreation
- Transportation/Travel/Maritime & Utilities
- Federal, State & Local Government

www.JobSourceNetwork.com

Cover Photo provided by Los Angeles Convention & Visitors Bureau and Michele & Tom Grimm

Peter Zakar
2000

THE SOUTHERN CALIFORNIA JOB SOURCE
The Only Source You Need To Land The Job of Your Choice in Southern California

ISBN - 1-89192604-7
$18.95

Jobs/Careers/Business/Job Hunting/Internships/Occupations/
California/Los Angeles/San Diego/Orange County/Southern California

Printed in the United States of America
Series 5, 1st Printing

JOB SOURCE SERIES

- **Baltimore Job Source**   **$15.95**
  Covers the Entire Baltimore Metropolitan Area plus parts of Western and Eastern Maryland

- **South Florida Job Source (New)**   **$18.95**
  Covers all of South Florida including Broward, Brevard, Dade and Palm Beach Counties

- **Pittsburgh Job Source**   **$15.95**
  Covers the Entire Pittsburgh Metropolitan Area plus Western Pennsylvania

- **San Francisco Job Source**   **$18.95**
  Covers the Entire San Francisco Metropolitan Area plus Oakland/East Bay and San Jose/Silicon Valley

- **Southern California Job Source**   **$18.95**
  Covers all of Southern California - Los Angeles, San Diego & Orange County plus San Bernardino, Riverside and Ventura Counties

- **Washington Job Source**   **$16.95**
  Covers the Entire Washington, D.C. Metropolitan Area plus Northern Virginia & Suburban Maryland

TO ORDER, CALL 800-488-4959

Southern California Job Source

The Only Source You Need To Land The Job of Your Choice in Southern California

Lead Author
Mary Louise McMahon
Associate Director for Employer Development
University of Maryland

Co-Authors
Norman Stahl & Jason Wall
Career Counselors
University of California-Los Angeles Career Center

Publisher
Peter Zakar

Managing Editor
Lisa Zakar

Editor
Shannon Scharber

Benjamin Scott Publishing
Pasadena, California

Southern California Job Source

Includes the Counties of:
- Los Angeles
- Orange
- Riverside
- San Bernardino
- San Diego
- Ventura

Publisher	PETER ZAKAR
Managing Editor	LISA ZAKAR
Lead Authors	MARY MCMAHON

Lead Authors

MARY MCMAHON
*Associate Director
for Employer Development*
University of Maryland

NORMAN STAHL & JASON WALL
Career Counselors
**University of California-Los Angeles
Career Center**

Editor SHANNON SCHARBER

Research Coordinator
HARVEY LEW

Market Research
WENDY BEVERIDGE MARGE DELGADO BOBBI VAMTINE

With Special Thanks to:
- Faith Regan Psillas, Dave Neely, Kate Stusrud, & Jen Halpern
- Kathy Sims and the Career Center at UCLA

Southern California Job Source • New for 2001

Benjamin Scott Publishing

20 East Colorado Boulevard
Suite 202
Pasadena, CA 91105
626-449-1339

www.JobSourceNetwork.com

So. California Job Source · Table of Contents

SOUTHERN CALIFORNIA

Preface

For centuries, the best way of landing a job has been by knowing someone. From our own personal experience, we know that any career guide can provide you with company names and addresses--little more than the yellow pages, but the *Job Source Series* goes many steps further. It provides you with that person to contact.

This was the premise behind creating the *Job Source Series*. Give the job-hunter not only the company name and address, but also several job contact names, titles, phone numbers, job hotlines, web site addresses, company descriptions plus much more. By providing so much information, The *Job Source Series* readers will have the upperhand over other job-seekers. And given today's competitive job market, any edge in a job hunt helps.

With more than 8,000 job contacts, job hotlines, web addresses and advice from career counselors and professionals within thirty industries, we truly believe that the *Job Source Series* provides everything you will need to land the internship, entry-level or middle management job of your choice.

It's now your responsibility to get out there and use these contacts to secure your next job. We wish you the best in your job search.

Lisa & Peter Zakar
Publishers

Southern California Job Market

- **Los Angeles**
- **San Bernardino**
- **Orange**
- **Riverside**
- **San Diego**
- **Ventura**

by: Jason Wall & Norman Stahl
University of California-Los Angeles Career Center

So Cal: Defining Cool

Southern California is all about definition. "Definition" in the sense that every year America's coolest and hippest escape the confines of their hometowns and come to Southern California to discover and define themselves. Southern California also almost single-handedly dictates the world's perception of the United States. This is true both literally (as roughly 90% of all movies are filmed in Southern California) and figuratively, as common leisure pursuits such as yoga classes in Malibu, shopping on Melrose in Hollywood and surfing in La Jolla are without a doubt the envy of the nation.

Where else on the planet can you be dining outside (in January) in Chinatown and have a Hispanic waiter (sporting a cell phone and beeper) serve you pizza topped with goat cheese? Without question, Southern California is the reigning heavyweight champion of the world in diversity and opportunity.

Southern California is as unpredictable, beautiful and powerful as the ocean which graces its beaches. Every year literally tens of millions of people come from all over the world to enjoy the Mediterranean-like climate and almost all of them contemplate the notion, "This is gorgeous! Why don't I live here?" In every aspect, Southern California flaunts its diversity in the face of the world. There are few places in the world where you can surf in the morning and ski in the afternoon. Southern Californians have access to the conveniences, shopping and culture of the country's largest cities and the recreational opportunities associated with beaches, mountains and deserts. As time goes by, Southern California's borders are blurring and the aggregate is evolving into an international destination with an unparalleled variety of activities and attractions.

Why Live & Work in California?

In terms of job opportunities, California is stampeding into the 21st century. According to California Employment Development Department (CEDD) in the month of January (2000) alone the state gained 42,300 jobs (nonfarm wage and salary jobs seasonably adjusted), and the unemployment rate fell to 4.7% — the lowest rate since 1969. Combine that with Southern California's 330 days of sunshine every year and the question more appropriately becomes, "Why not live and work in California?"

It is this type of growth which makes Southern California an economic juggernaut. Understandably, Southern California has one of the largest and most diverse regional economies in the world. In fact, according to Los Angeles Economic Development Atlas of Southern California (LAEDC), if Southern California was compared to the rest of the world, it would look something like this:

In terms of population, if Southern California was its own state, it would be the 4th largest state in the U.S.

The cost of living in Southern California is significantly lower than such cities as New York, Boston, Washington D.C. and even Hartford Connecticut.

The total personal income of Southern Californians is greater than the states of Michigan, Florida and New Jersey.

The Gross Product generated by the region (over 400 billion) is greater than those of Switzerland, Mexico and India.

Obviously, with a population and economy of this proportion there are an abundance of job opportunities in a variety of industries. Where, do you ask? Everywhere. Of course there are Southern California's mainstays such as entertainment, international trade and tourism, which drive the economy but there are also the industries of the 21st century, which despite endless media coverage, are still in their infancy and growing rapidly. The Internet, dot-com start-ups, wireless communications and biotechnology are just a few on the forefront. Another low-profile industry is apparel and textile manufacturing. Apparel and manufacturing churned out 4,500 new jobs in California in 1997, and employs more than the computer, electronic component or aircraft industries. Additionally, finance and investing has exploded with exceptionally high nonresidential building permits, and agricultural output surged past $25 billion just prior to Y2K.

A Case Study in Growth & Diversity: San Diego County

In the early 1990s, San Diego County was plagued with a harsh recession as a direct result of military spending cutbacks and the much publicized mergers of aerospace and defens- related industries. At the time, many Southern California residents felt that San Diego was headed for a future filled with unemployment and urban decay. In fewer than 6 years, numerous industries specializing in telecommunications, biotechnology, electronics, computers and manufacturing have been more than happy to move in and fill the void.

This example illustrates the Deloitte & Touche study on "growth" as a strategic direction. "Re-engineering is out; big and getting bigger is in. The current strategic trend favors increased market share and job creation." As a result, The Center for Continuing Study of the California Economy (CCSCE), based in Palo Alto, predicts that San Diego will lead California in employment opportunities into the 21st century.

Statistically Speaking
• LAEDC predicts (nonfarm) employment in California will conservatively increase by 2.8% by late 2000 (about 400,000 new jobs).
• The Southern California entertainment industry and its employees made roughly $7 billion in 1999.
• The average income in Orange County is $33,187.

By 2001 there will be 33,660 new jobs opened for finance-related occupations in Los Angeles County.

The Major Players
Southern California's Hottest Industries

Everyone knows that Southern California is the world headquarters for entertainment, but most people do not realize that the southland is also the nation's leader in international trade and a seed-bed for the communications industry. Additionally, the Center for Demographic Studies at Cal State Fullerton predicts that Orange County will see the majority of its new jobs developed in the areas of financial services, health products, and high-tech manufacturing.

International Trade
From Eggplants to Cell Phones

Although not as glamorous as the entertainment industry (some say the international trade industry in Southern California is the only thing that doesn't have an "image") Southern California's hold on international trade is universally recognized by those who study employment as the muscle behind California's economy. The state of California, conveniently located between Asia and Europe and located at the heart of the Pacific Rim leads the nation by handling approximately 25% of all merchandise traded between the U.S. and the entire world. One fourth of California's approximately $1 trillion (1,000,000,000,000) economy is based on international trade and investment. Additionally, one out of every 10 future jobs will be developed in trade and investment.

Proof Positive
The Alameda Corridor

Southern California is investing $950 million in consolidating over 90 miles of rail with 200 roadway crossings into one 35-mile high capacity intermodal transit corridor which will follow Alameda Street (hence the name Alameda Corridor) through Los Angeles and dramatically improve highway and railroad access to the ports of Los Angeles and Long Beach. What does this mean for Southern California? Briefly stated, 700,000 new jobs and a doubling of the 100 million metric tons of cargo which will mean $314 billion generated for the economy by 2020.

Biotechnology
The New Kid in Town

Stat: California is the world leader in biotech, generating $8.4 billion in revenue

Currently, San Diego County is home to three renowned Biotech commercial research facilities: Scripps Institute, the La Jolla Institute for Allergy and Immunology and The Salk Institute. Additionally, Thousand Oaks (near L.A.) is home to biotech giant Amgen. According to *Business Life*, Pasadena is moving aggressively toward taking a leadership role in the biomedical industry and leading the charge into the 21st century. Home to some of the biggest names in Biotech, Southern California is the headquarters for the leading biomedical companies. In fact, according to *Business Week*, the growth predictions for this industry are so strong that Pasadena city officials are already developing a "Business Growth Referral System" which will allow businesses that require more space than can be accommodated in Pasadena to be smoothly transitioned to neighboring cities.

In 1996, as the result of a Caltech initiative, 10 new biomedical companies opened to fill the needs of this growing industry. In the next 10 years, roughly 100 spin-off companies are expected to emerge. This means a wealth of jobs for everyone.

Entertainment
"Lights...Camera...Opportunity!"

Stat: In 1999, 17 movies grossed more than $100 million

Although a dwarf compared to the dollar figures associated with the international trade industry, it's the field of entertainment which makes Southern California world renowned and fuels California's reputation as arguably the most exciting and stylish place to live in the world. Being involved in entertainment encompasses significantly more than being a starving actor waiting 12 years for the big break. All of the major studios (NBC, Disney, Warner Bros., Universal, DreamWorks, Disney Imagineering, etc.) hire professionals ranging from production assistants, make-up artists, grips, camera operators set designers and about 100 other various entertainment related titles.

Although typically associated with Hollywood, the entertainment industry spans all of southern California with movie sets in San Diego to major studio's home offices located in Burbank. To accommodate the growth of this industry, conservative estimates predict that Burbank will need to add approximately 9 million square feet of new office space in the next several years (roughly 5 football stadiums). Not surprisingly, no single city can accommodate the personnel and space requirements of the entertainment industry. This means more construction, more offices, more work and more jobs for everyone in the entertainment industry.

Computers & Information Technology
Welcome to the Tech Coast

Stat: In the last 5 years the IT industry in San Diego increased 45% with 11,000 new jobs with 500 firms (Source: San Diego Business Directory).

With Y2K being the biggest hoax since Milli Vanilli, and dot-com start-ups multiplying faster than rabbits, the IT industry is booming in Southern California. In 1999, Orange County alone added roughly 3,600 (climbing to 70,100) tech-related jobs. According to the LAEDC, "Driving these gains are advanced communications, networking equipment and software development. The focus of the latter is definitely content, with a surge in the e-commerce firms in the region (Southern California)." With the cost of living going through the roof in Silicon Valley and the rest of Northern California (an average size one bedroom apartment easily costing $1,500 to $1,800 per month) many technology firms are finding living and working in Southern California to be much more appealing and profitable.

Tourism
Polar Bears in San Diego and a Mouse Named Mickey in Burbank

Stat: In 1998, tourism generated roughly $6 billion for the Southern California economy.

According to California Tourism Research, the average household spends approximately $3,900 a year on traveling in the U.S. and abroad. That's twice as much as it spends on health care or on food and beverage combined. Southern California has always been an American Mecca for tourists and recreational activities. Compared to national averages, Southern California's temperature is almost 20 degrees warmer in the winter and 10 degrees cooler in the summer. Combine this with a scant 12 inches of annual rainfall and you have the recipe for non-stop tourism. Locals are so fortunate, they consider a morning with high clouds to be to dreary and will almost certainly cancel beach plans.

When considered as an integrated whole (airlines, hotels, restaurants, etc.), tourism is California's third largest industry. In just one year California entertained 6.4 million international visitors and generated approximately $61.2 billion for the economy. When one considers the diverse attractions situated in Southern California: Sea World, Hollywood Boulevard, surfing, skiing, Disneyland, the San Diego Zoo, The J. Paul Getty museum, Legoland (one of Southern California's newest attractions) and Rodeo Drive in Beverly Hills, just to name a few, the employment opportunities in the hotel, restaurant and travel industry are almost infinite.

A Hollywood Ending

As of March 2000, even with the highly publicized stock market setbacks, the current expansion of the U.S. economy will mark its ninth year of constant growth - the longest period ever recorded in peacetime history. The personal income for the state of California is expected to exceed $1 trillion, easily the largest gain ever. Without a doubt, Southern California is riding this wave of prosperity into the 21st century. The current economic landscape is prime for the first time job seeker and even stronger for newer professionals looking to make the next step (up) in their careers.

Tthe only reason the Southern California economy isn't expanding more is due to the Federal Reserve purposely raising interest rates so the economy doesn't overheat. Even with the stock market see-sawing due to volatile tech stocks, with the government actively regulating the economy, Southern California will be enjoying many years of available jobs and increasing personal income. So, while Southern California's critics (sometimes jealous people who live in cold climates) make unfounded quips regarding the traffic and smog (Houston had lower air quality than Los Angeles in 1999) Southern California is enjoying less per capita crime than such "hot-spots" as Baltimore, Tucson and Albuquerque and a cost of living less than Hartford, CT or Philadelphia.

California is poised to fulfill its destiny of becoming not only a national, but also international, tour de force. We sincerely hope that this guide helps you make sense of the expansive and diverse Southern California economy and that you find the job that's right for you. Happy hunting!

The Gross Product generated by Southern California alone (over 400 billion) is greater than that of Switzerland, Mexico and India.

Landing an Internship in Southern California

By Norman Scott Stahl, Counselor Supervisor, UCLA Career Center

In the not too distant past, internship experiences were limited to college students considering careers in education, government, and the media. Now students can take advantage of internships in many fields, including niche areas like biotechnology, cybernetics, special effects, set design, investment banking, and physical therapy.

Internship opportunities for undergraduates and graduate students at colleges and universities in Southern California are plentiful. According to Dario Bravo, Manager of the UCLA Career Center's EXPO Internship and Study Abroad Services, The last several years have seen many more internships available than there are students willing to accept them. Many of these internships involve paid positions.

While college and high school students remain the population most likely to take advantage of internships, some mid-life career changers have also created internships for themselves to facilitate their career transition. Unfortunately, in some cases, union contracts may limit an employer's ability to offer internships only to persons who are receiving academic credit for their internship. Mid-life career changers generally must initiate the contact directly with the companies with which they want to intern, and pitch a specific proposal emphasizing the benefits that will accrue to the company in exchange for the training and experience they will receive.

Whether you are a student or a career changer, internships allow you to:

• Gain hands-on experience in a career field of interest.
• Demonstrate commitment to the field.
• See if the career fits with your work values and expectations.
• Develop contacts and network with persons in your chosen field.
• Establish an experience base for your resume.

In addition, an internship may lead directly to a full-time position. Companies increasingly use internships as a pre-screening device to determine which interns will make excellent employees, and offer career positions to their best performers.

Because of the many benefits of completing an internship, obtaining one is often very competitive. If you are considering internship as a means of entering your chosen field, you should devote as much effort and preparation to the internship search as you would to a search for a career position. It is important to know the industry, know the firm or institution, and be able to articulate how your skills, interests and experience can contribute to the institution offering the internship.

While it is important to keep the focus on what you can do for the employer, it is also important to ensure that you will receive substantive training and experience. Actions that you can take to increase the likelihood of your internship being a positive experience include getting the employer to clearly define the nature and scope of the training opportunity, ascertaining the degree to which top-level executives are involved in the internship program, and (during the internship) being assertive about achieving the agreed upon training objectives.

During your interview, try to get employer representatives to be very specific about the training offered. Ask if a written training plan exists. If a written plan does not exist, propose one. Whether you write it out or just formulate it in your mind, you should have a clear idea of what you expect to achieve during your internship, and the degree to which the employer will be able to meet those expectations. It is a good idea to ask the employer for a specific breakdown of the training, tasks and duties involved in your internship. Try to get an answer to the following kinds of questions: What percentage of time will be devoted to orientation and formal training activities? What portion of your time will be devoted to working with equipment or practicing skills important to the industry? What percentage of time will be devoted to public contact? What percentage of time will be devoted to receptionist, clerical or administrative tasks?

Determining the degree to which top-level executives are involved in the program is important for two reasons. First, if the boss is genuinely interested in the program, her employees are more likely to make a determined effort to ensure its success. Second, frequent interaction with company executives increases the networking potential of your internship experience. Again, the key is to ask company representatives for specific examples of executive involvement and support. If the responses you receive cause you to doubt the program lacks the active support of top level executives, consider looking for another internship opportunity.

Finally, if during the internship you find that you are not receiving the agreed upon training and experience, speak out. Let your supervisors and mentors know of your dissatisfaction and propose ways of meeting your needs. Volunteer to take on specific responsibilities, or initiate and implement a special project that will benefit the firm.

Today, internships in Southern California are found in all industries from accounting to zoological gardens. Analysis of information provided by JobTrak! indicates the top ten internship categories in Southern California are: Sales & Marketing, Computer & Information Science, Business & Management, Clerical & Secretarial, Accounting & Finance, Engineering & Technology, Customer Service, Social Service and Public Affairs, and Commercial or Food Service industries.

In Los Angeles, Communications and Media internships replace Customer Service in the top ten industries offering internships. In San Diego, Life Science internships replace Customer Service in the top-ten list. Given the preponderance of media and entertainment firms in Los Angeles, and the developing biotechnology industry in San Diego County, the addition of these two fields to Southern California's top-ten internship fields is not surprising.

Common resources for locating internships are college and university career centers, high school counselors, state and local government personnel offices, school district personnel departments, ethnic, religious, and fraternal organizations, social-service agencies, and professional journals. If you have Internet access, one good resource of internship sites is Job Source Network.com.

If you cannot locate an advertised internship in your chosen field, consider creating your own. The following ten steps may be helpful in that endeavor: Thoroughly research the industry to determine the skills, knowledge, attributes and experience required of entry-level employees in that industry. Use the information you gathered in your research to construct a written proposal that details the services that you can provide to a prospective employer in exchange for specified training to be received. Use the yellow pages or the *Southern California Job Source* to identify a list of firms within your commute area that employ persons in your target field. Call the firms and ask for the name and title of the person who heads the department in which you would like to intern. If you are questioned about your reasons for wanting such information, simply respond, "I want to send her a business proposal (your internship proposal is, after all, a business proposal), and I want to make sure I spell her name and title correctly."

Send the department head a letter containing your internship proposal and tell her that you will contact her in the near future to arrange a meeting to discuss your proposal. Prepare and practice a short "sales pitch." Call the firm and confidently ask to speak to the department head by name. When the department head answers, deliver your script, and request a meeting. If you get an affirmative response rejoice silently; if you get a negative response, ask for another name to contact and repeat this cycle until you succeed - Perseverance is the key to success!

Job Search Strategies in the Age of the Internet

by Mary Louise McMahon

As a job seeker today you will find many, many helpful resources on the Internet. In fact there are so many web sites that it may be a bit overwhelming. Even though more and more of the job search occurs virtually with less paper, the sequence of steps you go through for finding a job have remained the same:

Step One: Know Yourself
Step Two: Finding Your Place(s) in the World of Work
Step Three: Put Yourself Out There
Step Four: Presenting Yourself
Step Five: Negotiating the Offer

What does change rapidly are the numbers and types of Internet sites devoted to career issues and novel ways to post your resume, identify job listings and interact with prospective employers. What you will find here are some tips that will help you sort through these resources and offer you advice on the basics of looking for a job effectively. Useful web sites are given along with tips on how to utilize these to assist you in each step of your job search process. Among these is JobSourceNetwork.com (http://www.jobsourcenetwork.com). Developed by the publisher of this book, this multi-faceted web site links you to thousands of career oriented Internet resources. By periodically checking this site you will also be alerted to updates about new sites to help you track the constant additions to career related resources on the World Wide Web. Because the Internet changes every day, it is wise to use the ideas presented here as a launching off point to uncovering the latest web sites to assist

you in your search. It should also be said that there are books and even a web site solely devoted to the topic of job searching using the Internet. Some that you might also want to use as resources include: e-Job Hunting: Planning Your Career and Searching for jobs Online written by Susan Musich and Eric Schlesinger. [Schlesinger, E. & Musich, S. 2000. e-job hunting: *Planning your career and searching for jobs online*. Indianapolis, IN: Macmillan USA.] Researching Companies Online and Web Search Strategies tutorials both created by Debbie Flanagan helps you better understand using search engines and subjective directories. Both can be found at the following web address: http://home/sprintmail.com/~debflanagan/main.html.

Step One: Know Yourself

It is essential to know what you enjoy, what lifestyle you seek and what restrictions - financial, geographic and others you face. Without this focus it is very easy to waste a lot of time and energy and wind up with a job that is a poor match for you. Landing the wrong job may mean you become dissatisfied quickly and start looking for a new job all over again. If you are aware of your strengths and weaknesses and your personality traits it will be much easier for you to figure out what to communicate in a resume, cover letters and interviews. With a focus to guide you, you save time and avoid pursuing jobs and careers that are not a fit.

Assembling Your Job Search "Toolbox"

Here is another way to think about focusing your job search. As you may realize, you are likely to have many different jobs and probably work in a variety of fields during your life. What you do well and your expertise are the contents of your job search "toolbox." This information about yourself is what you use to develop a focus for your job search efforts. Your core skills and what you know are the aspects of your background upon which you build your career. The organizations that provide you on-the-job learning or formal training help you to add to this "toolbox" of experiences and abilities.

Ideally your career path will involve or has involved using a cluster of skills, acquiring new ones, furthering your education, and constantly learning new information which you bring to new fields or industries. Consider this scenario: if you graduate as a business major you might be hired as a financial analyst for a corporation. After a few years you might switch jobs applying your ability to track expenses by working healthcare field with an insurance company, eldercare facility, or hospital administration. Through experiences like these in which you see the connection between healthcare practices and the effects on costs you might be hired as a consultant with a public policy institution that evaluates healthcare issues.

It all begins with identifying what is in your "toolbox" of skills. To figure this out, it can be helpful to ask yourself many questions. What activities do you enjoy? What courses did you enjoy and why? Did you change majors? If so what influenced your decision? How would your friends and family describe you? What types of environments motivate you? What values are most important to you? As you form your answers consider not only what jobs you have had, but also what student clubs, sorority or fraternity involvement, volunteer or sports activities, or even hobbies and recreational interests that illustrate your abilities. Draw examples from paid and part-time positions, internships and co-ops, academic papers and projects for illustrations that enable you to demonstrate your knowledge and competence. Evaluate the skills you have acquired. Did you lead,

teach, persuade, organize, analyze, sell, design, direct or manage? By the way, employers may ask you the same questions that were just listed. The better you understand yourself, the easier it will be to explain what role you may offer to an organization and why you wish to work there.

Using the Internet to Know Yourself

JobSourceNetwork.com links you to several career oriented web sites that offer career advice. Here are some features of just a few of these. "Careers By Design" provides online career counseling and assessment of skills, interests, resumes and interviewing skills. CareerPath.com includes a section called "CareerRX" where job seekers can request career counseling, coaching and testing services. At Monster.com you'll find 1,700 pages of targeted career advice. This site posts times that you can chat with a free agent advisor. At CollegeRecruiter.com there is "Ask the Experts" every Friday during which a panel of experts answers 50 questions submitted by online users.

Step Two: Finding Your Place(s) in the World of Work

Remember that many different types of organizations might employ you. If you are just entering the work world this provides you a wide variety (but not unlimited) of opportunities. (If you have more experience, then skip down to a section with tips written especially for you). Many employers expect someone recently graduating to be in a stage of career exploration. For these reasons don't narrow your career options by making limiting assumptions about your major. One trap is to assume that your major qualifies you for only one kind of job. You have acquired many skills that can be applied to a variety of fields. For example, if you majored in history, you have probably developed the ability to read quickly; analyze and summarize large quantities of data; and communicate your conclusions effectively in written and oral form. With these skills you might find employment as a researcher or analyst in the non-profit, private, or public sectors. If you have quantitative abilities you could also work as a business analyst. In this role you research, evaluate and summarize your findings about the practices and performance of competing organizations (also called benchmarking).

Using the Internet to Find Your Place(s) in the World of Work

Most people will agree that the World Wide Web is the best resource for researching any topic. It is certainly a helpful tool when you are trying to identify jobs, industries and career paths. Comprehensive career web sites like CareerMosaic, JobSourceNetwork.com, and Monster.com connect you to extensive job listings, let you sort information by keywords and industry categories, provide links to company profiles and professional associations. You can gain much helpful information by reading position descriptions. By accessing Internet web sites where many types of jobs are listed you can scan these in order to learn what tasks are involved, skills used and qualifications are required. From this information you can begin to identify what types of jobs require your knowledge, experiences and personal attributes. As you go through this process, you will prefer some web sites over others. You will also discover which web sites most frequently post the type of jobs you are seeking. When you monitor certain web sites regularly it will become clear how often new jobs are added, how many are typically listed at a time and how quickly these opportunities are filled.

Tips for the Career Changer

Switching careers can be stressful. It can be frustrating trying to convince employers in one field that your experience in another field is relevant to them. Nonetheless, more and more people are successful in moving from one kind of job into a very different one. Especially when the economy is strong, employers are even more willing to focus on basic skills like communicating, writing, analyzing, organizing, planning, managing, designing even if these have been applied in a different field.

Your task is to convey your background in such a way that a potential employer will appreciate the value of your prior jobs.

Career counselors encourage career changers to promote their "transferable skills." These are skills that were demonstrated in one field that are useful in an entirely different field. Some examples of transferable skills are the ability to identify and analyze a problem, the ability to design and implement a solution; the ability to successfully respond to an obstacle or set back and persevere; the ability to lead and motivate others; the ability to integrate ideas and create theoretical models or come up with new insights; the ability to quantify data and interpret statistical information; the ability to track processes and project future trends or events. There are many, many more examples of transferable skills, but all of these focus on the functions of your past jobs rather than the setting or industry in which you worked.

Online Resources for Career Changers

You will find many online resources for the experienced employee at JobSourceNetwork.com. There are links to web sites featuring headhunters, executive jobs, MBA and graduate level positions, and employment agencies. One such site, Careerbuilder.com, has a section that addresses transitions, job loss, older and returning workers, and working women. If you have substantial work experience there are web sites like Headhunter.net and the site maintained by the Wall Street Journal that specialize in serving those in this category.

Step Three: Putting Yourself Out There

Creating (or updating) your resume obviously is the critical step to successfully connecting with employers and developing a resume and getting it to the necessary people. You might distribute your resume many ways: through "snail mail" (the slightly irreverent slang for US Postal mail delivery), email, through a posting on an Internet job search site or to a specific company's web site. No matter how you send your resume out, it needs to highlight your experiences and accomplishments. It should contain examples that clearly illustrate the abilities and skills that you know potential employers will value. Include travel experiences, study abroad programs, volunteer activities, leadership development programs, extra-curricular activities, and awards or scholarships. Don't forget to give illustrations of your personality. Most employers want to see examples that demonstrate creativity, independent thinking, an ability to work effectively with others ("teamwork"), an ability to learn quickly, an adaptable and flexible nature, and problem solving skills.

The Resume - Work History Summary

It is not true that you must list all your work experiences on the resume. This fact is often good news for both recent grads and career changers. When looking at resumes of recent graduates, employers are not as concerned about lapses between jobs that took place around a student schedule. If you are a recent graduate you may not have a lot of relevant experience. Creating a section called "Experience" rather than "Employment" enables you to include not just paid jobs but unpaid experiences. You can include internships here. If you have volunteer or extra-curricular activities that demanded significant time and effort consider putting these into your Experience section. Employers are interested in any examples, including these, if they offer concrete examples of your organizational, creative or other skills. Even abstract qualities like perseverance, resourcefulness, or leadership can be communicated here if you describe the obstacles you encounter and how you managed to achieve specific goals. Sometimes unique backgrounds are valued by an employer. Describe travel or study abroad experiences, mention if you worked to pay your own way through school or other personal accomplishments.

A Flexible Resume with Focus

As each employer receives your resume, it needs to illustrate the particular skills that match the jobs being filled. Be-cause you will want to be considered for many jobs your resume needs to be flexible but not lacking a focus. There is another reason why giving your resume a focus is important. Bombarded by resumes, employers simply don't have the time to figure out what you're good at and where exactly you fit in the organization. They expect that you will sort through your activities, academic preparation and jobs and come to some conclusions about what your strengths are and the environment that motivates you to do your best.

How is this accomplished? Career counselors will advise you to describe your responsibilities and accomplishments using "action verbs." A few examples include: analyze, evaluate, strategize, develop, create, design, initiate, propose, plan, manage, implement, promote, quantify, estimate, integrate, advocate, communicate, educate and persuade. These verbs bring life to your resume and are very vivid. Using these can help the person reading your resume to understand the connection between what you have done and what you can do for their organization. Another resume tip is to be really picky about how you describe your work experiences. Forget about mentioning all of your responsibilities involved. Instead think about a particular goal you tried to reach or a situation you tried to improve. You may need more than one sentence to outline a) what you were trying to achieve, b) your role in reaching the goal or making progress towards the goal, c) the skills or traits you demonstrated and d) any results or progress you made towards your goal.

Getting Resume Feedback

To determine if you have developed an effective resume, it is wise to ask others for their feedback. Those who are closest to you are not always able to be objective resume reviewers. Instead ask your friends and family if they can introduce you to people employed in organizations or jobs interesting to you. These individuals can look over your resume and let you know if they find examples of experiences and abilities that will persuade someone to interview you. More and more career web sites offer services where your can submit your resume online and receive a critique from a career advisor or professional from your targeted field or industry. Some of the places you can connect to for this help via the JobSourceNetwork.com web site include: CareerMosaic.com, JobDirect.com, and Monster.com.

More Tips for the Career Changer

Do you have many years of experience? If yes, consider including a "professional summary" on your resume. This highlights for those looking at your resume the particular abilities and accomplishments contained in your career. This section is immediately below your name and address and before any other information. The professional summary usually includes four specific pieces of information about your background: 1) how many years of experience you possess, 2) what level(s) you have reached in an organization, 3) what activities or tasks you have carried out, 4) what industries or fields this background has taken place. Such a sentence might read "Eight years professional experience involving management of staffs of 5-10 people with responsibilities entailing budgeting, forecasting, work flow redesign, and strategic planning in the telecommunications field." You might also include with the summary sentence three or four additional lines that contain concrete examples. These are very brief descriptive statements, which begin with action verbs and describe specific accomplishments. These sentences are laid out in bulleted format and placed just below the summary statement.

If you are switching careers you will need to list all of your experiences without any gaps in the chronology. Today many employees, especially those in the high tech industry, switch jobs frequently. Changing jobs often used to be looked down upon, but this attitude is less common, even in non-technical industries. It is quite acceptable, though, to write at length about one experience compared to what you write about another. When an earlier job enables you to show the skills that a future employer wants, you might describe what you did in several sentences. For other jobs you might only list your title, name of the organization, its location and the dates you were employed without any description about your responsibilities.

Get Rid of Jargon

Although it may be difficult at first, try to remove jargon that was used in your old field of employment. Replace these acronyms and words with words that will be understood by someone who has never worked in that industry. This is very important if you are transitioning from the military or government sector into the private sector. You have excellent skills but this could be lost by your new employer if they don't fully appreciate your examples. For example, don't simply list a military job title. Instead describe how many people reported to you, the full extent of your responsibilities as well as the challenges of dealing with expensive equipment, in dangerous conditions and safeguarding lives.

Posting Your Resume on the Internet

Only a few years ago most career oriented web sites on the Internet were primarily focused on connecting people with computer and engineering skills to positions in the high tech industry or in a technical division of an organization. Although some web sites still focus on this area, there are many, many sites with job opportunities for every kind of interest and background. Some of these include: CareerBuilder.com, CareerMosaic.com, CareerPath.com, CareerSite.com (tailored to postings for positions at small companies), HotJobs.com, JobDirect.com, Jobtrak.com (designed for recent college graduates), JobWeb.org, and Monster.com just to name a few.

If you are not familiar with which sites may best help you JobSourceNetwork.com has job posting web sites organized by many categories including: industry, profession or city as well as by corporate, non-profit, executive jobs or internships. The practice of logging onto career web sites to spot jobs and applying online has become a standard part of looking for employment. In the same way, fewer and fewer job seekers overlook the opportunity to post their resume to online databases maintained by BestJobsUSA, CareerMosaic, Hot Jobs, JobDirect, JobWeb or Monster.com. Not only is someone else marketing this resume database to employers for you, there is the possibility that you might be contacted by a company you had know idea was hiring or was interested in your qualifications.

If you do post your resume to an Internet career or job search web site, you probably don't need to make major changes to it. The traditional resume advice applies to resumes that are distributed through both conventional and high tech methods. Here are just a few tips, however, that you may wish to consider when sending your resume via email, posting to a company website or including in an online pool of resumes.

1) Creating a Key Word Section

"Objective" statements are not recommended for Internet job postings. These are usually only one sentence in length and communicate what type of position you are seeking. It is difficult to write one that has both the flexibility and the focus that you need. There is another approach. Large corporations frequently scan resumes sent by mail into a database. When identifying candidates for a specific job, key words are entered into the computer and those resumes containing these words are considered. To increase the chances of your resume coming up for the jobs you want consider adding a key word section to your resume. To get your creative juices going, write down the key words that you hope to appear in your new job. It may be helpful to look at job descriptions. Label this section "Key Words" and place it just after your name and contact information. List the basic words or phrases that might appear on the job description you are targeting, separate each with a comma.

2) Make It Plain

Fancy graphics can sometimes interfere with transferring the content of your resume over the Internet. Even though there have been many improvements with technology, you are probably better off by keeping your resume very plain. This means removing the bold, italics and other special features. When sending a resume via email to someone, consider cutting and pasting your resume into the email as well as sending it as an attachment. If the recipient can't access the attachment your information will be contained in the email itself. When creating the resume attachment document, it is recommended that you save your resume in a "rich text file." This is usually the easiest type of document to access. If you know how to put your resume into html format this can also increase the number of employers that view it. Should you create your own homepage, you might leave out a street address or phone number as a safety measure. By providing your email address you can be reached quickly and you can determine who receives other more personal information.

3)Developing an Effective Cover Letter

If you are sending your resume via email the text of this message becomes your cover letter. As with any cover letter be brief and focused in your email correspondence. Watch out for typos. Many employers will view these kinds of errors negatively. A cover letter is not always required. For example, some Internet resume databases ask you to key in a personal profile instead of providing a cover letter. This may be the case when you apply to a specific company's online job listings. When sending your resume by mail, though, it is commonly expected that you will send a cover letter and that both your cover letter and resume will be printed on high quality paper.

Here are some tips for those situations when a cover letter is expected. Employers appreciate when you keep your letter to one page. Most people stay within this limit by focusing on the most relevant information. When writing your cover letter, your basic task is to explain to the employer how your experience contains the abilities and background that are desired. Even if you don't have a specific job description, you can describe your strongest skills and mention how you could apply these to benefit the organization. Remember that most employers value creativity, initiative, problem solving and other positive attributes. The most effective cover letters give concrete examples. Cover letter that are interesting to read give specific situations and experiences that demonstrate you have the background, skills and knowledge that the organization needs. Try writing sentences that state what abilities you have and where you have most recently applied that skill or trait. Paid experiences provide stronger examples, but mention projects and activities from social, campus, or academic settings as well. The sample cover letters can offer you some ideas.

Job Source

Sample Cover Letters & Resumes

Southern California Job Source

Seeking Internship Cover Letter

Albert University
Colby Hall, 412
Anytown, NY 10001

Today's Date

Ms. Valerie Chang
Summer Intern Manager
Setchi & Setchi
55 Tremont Street, Ste. 20
Boston, MA   10002

Dear Ms. Chang:

I would like to be employed as a summer intern at Setchi & Setchi's Boston office. I obtained your name from Mr. Nate Daniels, the Human Resource Director in the New York office when I asked him about internship opportunities. As a junior majoring in public relations, I recognize your firm as an innovative leader with Fortune 100 and international clients.

Albert University alumni with public relations careers have described to me the skills that are required to succeed. I have learned that some of these include strong communication and marketing skills, creativity, and the ability to work with a variety of personalities. My leadership and team experiences have demanded that I demonstrate these abilities. For example, as president of a campus organization, I was asked by university officials to inform the student body of new policies regarding alcohol consumption on campus. I gathered committee chairs together and coordinated our efforts. Our organization hosted a "town meeting" with the other fraternities and sororities in which students asked administrators questions and expressed concerns. The event was promoted via campus TV, e-mail, flyers, and phone calls. Over 150 students attended the program.

Not only have my leadership roles taught me the importance of communication and problem solving skills, but I also have learned to work under pressure, handling multiple tasks simutaneously. I maintain a 3.0 grade point average while spending an average of 25 hours a week conducting meetings, tracking committee progress, and volunteering as a tutor.

I would like to apply my initiative, creativity, and interpersonal skills to a public relations firm and learn what makes Setchi and Setchi an industry leader. I can be reached at (508) 555-0000 until May 10th. After this date I will be in the Boston area at (508) 555-5555. If you are interviewing before May 10th, I can travel to Boston to meet with you. I look forward to hearing from you.

Sincerely,

Jason Intern

Jason Intern

Home
45 Chestnut Street
Groton, MA 10324
(508) 555-5555
jintern@jsnetwork.com

Albert University
Colby Hall, Room 412
Anytown, NY 22232
(314) 555-5555 (H)
jintern@albertu.edu

Objective: Seeking internship with public relations firm where I can demonstrate my initiative and apply my organizational and communications skills.

Education
Albert University, Anytown, New York

B.S. Public Relations, *Minor:* Psychology

Leadership Activities

Zeta Zeta Zeta Fraternity, *President, Zeta Chapter,* Albert University
May 2000 - Present

- Oversaw and monitored budget of $30,000 per academic year.
- Managed and coordinated the activities of eight committees. Conducted biweeky meetings.
- Represented fraternity at monthly campus Greek council. Responded to policy issues and participated with student leaders and university officials to provide solutions.
- Successfully organized and implemented philanthropic event which raised over $5,000 for local homeless shelter.

Public Relations Club, *President* , Albert University **September 1999 - May 2000**
- Organized and delivered three programs featuring alumni and other professionals employed in the public relations field. Led team of four club officers in planning sessions and coordinating publicity efforts, logistical arrangements, and budget tracking.

Summer Employment:

Supervisor, **Cinetex Cinema,** Chelmsford, MA
Summers 1998 & 1999

Head Cashier, **A&P,** Groton, MA
Summer 1997

Restaurant Server, **Friendly's Restaurant,** Chelmsford, MA

Computer: WordPerfect, MacWrite, Excel, Lotus

References: Available Upon Request

25

State University
Dorm #249
Street Address
Springfield, WI 55413
(419) 555-5555

Today's Date

Ms. Inez Gutierrez
Vice President
Management Trainee Program
Harrington Corporation
Chicago, IL 10023

Dear Ms. Gutierrez:

I am applying for a position in the June Management Training Program. I learned about this program from Mr. Tom Smith, who is an alumnus from my university and a current Management Trainee at Harrington. From this conversation, I was convinced that Harrington is where I would like to demonstrate my skills and begin my career.

I learned from Mr. Smith that this opportunity provides challenging assignments and rotations in the marketing, finance, human resources, and manufacturing divisions. My own background includes practical business experience. Through my employment with a computer company and information processing firm, I have discovered that I enjoy working in technical environments. My resume provides examples of my ability to organize projects, track financial data, sell products and ideas and supervise others.

In my position as Administrative Assistant, I learned that everyone needs to work toward increasing levels of responsibility. As a Sales Associate, I proved that I like to work hard and exceed expectations whenever possible. In addition, my liberal arts background has developed my writing and pubic speaking skills.

I am very excited by this opportunity to enter the corporate world and prove my abilities. Thank you for considering my application. I look forward to hearing from you as you select your first round of candidates.

Sincerely,

Sally Jobseeker

SALLY JOBSEEKER

#1 Street Address • Springfield, WI 55413 • (419) 555-5555
sallyjob@jsnetwork.com

OBJECTIVE: Seeking a management trainee position at a corporation where I can apply my managing, supervising and organizational skills in business environments.

EXPERIENCE:

Office Manager, Techdata, Inc. - Springfield, WI   May-September 1999
• Managed all office operations. Selected and maintained capital equipment.
• Suggested and implemented upgrade of computer system resulting in improved
   ability to monitor company's financial data.
• Supervised the work assignments of two administrative personnel.
• Oversaw the company's billing activities.
• Tracked accounts payable/receivable.
• Addressed and resolved delayed payment issues.

Floor Supervisor, Marcy's - Springfield, WI   August 1997-May 1999
• Managed, trained, and supervised staff of 27 Sales Associates.
• Prepared payroll and projected operating budgets.
• Participated in budget management sessions. Effective management style
   resulted in consistently top performing sales performance within store,
   lowest employee turnover, and highest quarterly customer satisfaction.
• Promoted from Sales Associate after six months employment in the position.

Administrative Assistant, Datrix, Inc. - Salem, WI   Summers 1995 & 1997
• Reported directly to the CEO of this medium-sized information processing
   firm. Gained understanding of the needs and operations of this field
   through responsibilities including: typing correspondence from company's
   top executive, arranging meetings with key clients and suppliers, creating
   financial spreadsheets and generating financial reports.

EDUCATION :

Bachelor of Arts, Literature
State University, Springfield, WI   May 1997

ACTIVITIES:

University Chorale, President/Member   Sept. 1995-May 1997
• Coordinate with Director of the Department of Performing Arts to schedule
   rehearsals and arrange publicity and logistics for concert events.
Martha's Table (Mobile soup kitchen), Volunteer   Sept. 1995-Present
Michigan Regional Orchestra, Violinist   1994-1998 Seasons

Morgan Technical

Kennedy Towers
216
1531 Wilson Boulevard
Arlington, VA 22201

Home: 703/555-5555 Office: 301/555-9876 e-mail: morgant@jsnetwork.com

---

Today's Date

Mr. Ralph Cavanaugh
President
Equinox, Inc.
45 River Drive
Someplace, Maryland 33333

Dear Mr. Cavanaugh:

I recently attended a breakfast meeting sponsored by the Montgomery High Tech Council, where I met Mr. Stan Wheaton, your Vice President of New Product Development. He described the innovative ways you configure your work teams in order to identify niches in the market. Given your recent surge in business, I wanted to explore opportunities to join your winning team.

I believe I can offer you both strong technical skills and results-oriented managerial and analytical aptitudes. Team members under my management have told me that I anticipate problems, tap the appropriate people, solve problems creatively, and keep a project moving. I enjoy the details of the technical work, but I also like to see how the solutions contribute to the business goals of that office, department, and organization. I would be grateful to bring my exposure and experience in a variety of industries to your organization as it continues to grow.

I have helped many groups transform their processes and operations through creative, technological solutions. I would like to discuss with you what opportunities Equinox may provide. I will call you to see if your schedule would enable us to meet in the next week or two.

Sincerely,

Morgan Technical

Morgan Technical

Kennedy Towers #216 • 1531 Wilson Boulevard • Arlington, VA   22201
Home: 703/555-5555   Office: 301/555-9876
e-mail: morgant@jsnetwork.com

PROFESSIONAL EXPERIENCE

Boze, Alwyn and Harriman, Bethesda, Maryland   April 1999-Present
Business Systems Consultant
• Managed a team of four which analyzed the existing financial system for a Fortune 500 telecommunications client. Led team in the development of a redesign proposal which was reviewed and approved by client's financial executives. System modifications resulted in improved access to corporate financial data and ability to generate quarterly annual reports in shorter timeframe.
• Analyzed user requirements for metropolitan area hospital. Created several tailored designs to better track inventory stocks and lower related costs. Concluded project two weeks ahead of projected schedule.
• Oversaw five person consulting team which modified LAN configuration in the Audit Department in response to company's recent merger. Provided required programming to resolve differences in operating software and to link LANs.

Albertsen Consulting, Washington, DC   May 1998-March 1999
Senior Staff Consultant
• Managed the analysis, design, coding, debugging, testing and document write up of programs for the billing department a national insurance company. Trained users and provided technical support during the installation of a new billing system. Resulted in 25% reduction in administrative costs.
• Supervised staff of seven programmers from Albertsen Consulting and client organization. Coordinated joint efforts to assess and upgrade human resource department database. Developed modifications enabling client to calculate and assess costs associated with various compensation and benefit package offerings.

Prudence Insurance Co., Rockville, Maryland   February 1996-June 1998
Trainer/Assistant Manager, Technical Training Center
• Assisted in the efficient operation of this training facility containing 45 LANed PCs installed with financial and word processing software. Troubleshooted basic hardware problems. Given managerial responsibilities after six months in position. Designed and delivered technical classes.

EDUCATION

The American University, Washington, DC   May 1996
        MBA Concentration: Information Systems
University of Maryland, College Park, Maryland   May 1994
        Bachelor of Science: Computer Science

COMPUTER: BASIC, CICS, COBOL, DB2, dBASE IV, Fortran, Lotus, Excel, MS-DOS, Pascal, QLP, SQL, Word, WordPerfect, Mystat, Paradox

Carla Transitioner

2001 Elm Avenue
Overland Park, Kansas 40023

Today's Date

Mr. Robert Hobbson
Executive Director
National Retired Persons Association
2255 Connecticut Avenue, NW
Washington, DC 20015

Dear Mr. Hobbson:

I am writing to apply for the Eldercare Program Director position. This opening at the National Retired Persons Association would tap my six years of experience in the healthcare field as well as my deep personal interest in the senior population.

My resume illustrates my ability to step in and quickly assume the responsibilities of the Eldercare Program Director. I have a solid understanding of the issues NRPA addresses. As a Healthcare Consultant, I dealt first-hand with rising medical costs, the challenge of bringing new technologies and medications to the public, and the agencies that affect the delivery of services. In addition, my professional contacts at pharmaceutical companies, the FDA and Medicare and Medicaid agencies could serve as helpful information resources when evaluating and recommending policy positions that best serve the NRPA membership. In addition, I would combine this professional knowledge with a network of healthcare professionals and a successful management record.

I believe it is important to describe a personal circumstance that helps to explain why I feel I am so well suited for this position. For two years, I cared for an aging parent with serious health afflictions. During this time, I provided homecare. Later, I explored and chose other healthcare options. Through these experiences I gained personal insight regarding the emotional and financial burdens that friends and families face when addressing the needs of aging loved ones.

I welcome the opportunity to discuss my qualifications in person. I am delighted at the prospect of relocating to Washington, DC. Given my frequent travel to the area, it would not be difficult to interview at your location. I can be reached at 555-1000 during the day or messages can be left at my home number, 555-5555.

Sincerely,

Carla Transitioner

Carla Transitioner

2001 Elm Avenue
Overland Park, Kansas 40035
W (816) 555-1000 H (816) 555-5555
carlat@jsnetwork.com

Summary of Qualifications: Six years experience demonstrating managerial, analytical and problem solving skills in the healthcare field. This includes an understanding of the roles and needs of heathcare providers, pharmaceutical companies, related governmental agencies, and patients, especially the elderly.

PROFESSIONAL EXPERIENCE   *June 1996- Present*

Meditex Consultants, **Healthcare Consultant,** *Kansas City, Missouri*
• Reviewed and assessed individual insurance claims and researched current healthcare policies to secure third party coverage for pharmaceuticals and new medical technology products.
• Promoted pharmaceutical programs and newly FDA approved drugs to patients, physicians, clinics and hospitals for one of the top five pharmaceutical companies in the U.S.

Springvale Pharmacy, Manager (Nights/Weekends), Kansas City, Missouri
• Managed pharmacy and mini-mart, including the training and supervision of seven employees. Troubleshooted scheduling conflicts and effectively addressed employee performance issues.
• Assisted in the installation of a new computerized prescription tracking system. Resulted in improved inventory monitoring and provided an alert to pharmacists regarding potentially dangerous prescription combinations.
• Successfully carried out managerial responsibilities while also earning an MBA full-time.

Waverly Health Center, Administrative Assistant, Lawrence, Kansas
• Collaborated in the creation of an automated performance tracking system to evaluate the performance of nursing staff more effectively.
• Processed paperwork associated with clients' billing. Handled late payment issues and interacted with appropriate agencies to obtain Medicare and Medicaid reimbursements.

EDUCATION:

University of Missouri, Kansas City, Missouri
Masters of Business Administration   *May 1996*

University of Kansas, Larwence, Kansas
Bachelor of Arts, Psychology   *May 1994*

John Professional

210 Oakwood Boulevard · Dayton, Ohio 20012

Today's Date

Mr. Sanjay Gupta
Partner
Pride Waterford
115 Avenue of the Americas
Suite 15
New York, NY 10211

Dear Mr. Gupta:

I recently learned of Pride Waterford's increased number of clients who require asset management consulting. I am enclosing my resume for your review of my credentials and hope you will consider me for any appropriate openings.

I am aware that each week you receive hundreds of inquiries. During my seven years of experience, I have demonstrated two important qualities to my employers and clients that I hope set me apart.

First, I am constantly looking for what is new. As a Consultant or as Asset Manager, my best successes resulted from keeping abreast of the most profitable options. This ability to develop strategies that were financially sound and achieve the best performance comes from monitoring all the financial information resources available. I enjoy the challenge of staying ahead of the curve. My references, which include clients that have profited from my advice, will confirm this aptitude.

Second, I thrive on seeing results. In my attempt to have impact on any project or assignment, I must listen closely to my colleagues and clients. In any crisis or problem presented, I look for the underlying causes or the overlooked resources. This has led to several innovative solutions that maximize financial operations and strategies of various organizations. In addition, I find great pleasure in negotiating. The difficulty in solidifying mutually agreeable business arrangements adds to the reward of making the deal. For this reason, I have a long track record of bringing in and retaining new business.

Joining the ranks of Pride Waterford would mean obtaining an important career goal. I have worked toward acquiring the necessary professional profile to earn a position in your firm. I would greatly appreciate the opportunity to provide additional details regarding my background. I can be reached at the numbers listed above.

Sincerely,

John Professional

John Professional
210 Oakwood Boulevard • Dayton, Ohio 30012

Executive Summary:

Over seven years professional experience in the real estate field as consultant and manager.
- Ability to assess financial activities and resources in order to determine the most advantageous business strategies;
- Identify new business and successfully secure proposed business agreements through effective negotiation methods.

Professional Experience:

Consultant, **Delta Asset Management,** Dayton, Ohio   *10/97-Present*
- Deliver real estate consulting services to individual clients including small business owners and high worth individuals. Evaluate investment opportunities for clients and provide advice in credit workout and settlement negotiations.
- Conduct analysis of client's financial operations to identify opportunities for increased performance. Offer clients effective financial planning strategies.
- Carry out due diligence research to monitor the newest and best high yield investments.

Asset Manager/Acquisitions Analyst, **Dayton Land Co.,** Dayton, Ohio *11/95-9/97*
- Coordinate investment and corporate real estate acquisition and management.
- Conduct market research and financial analysis to support acquisition analyst.
- Negotiate contracts; complete and process title reports, property surveys and appraisal reports; handle mortgage financing and property closings.
- Respond to needs and resolve problems during interactions with property managers, tenants, contractors, and maintenance personnel.

Project Manager, **Williams Contracting, Inc.,** Dayton, Ohio   *6/93-10/95*
- Responsible for providing all cost estimation, financial projections, and budget analysis for construction projects. Projects ranged from $65k to $3.1 million.
- Successfully obtained business by directly soliciting developers and real estate management companies. Negotiated contracts with property owners and subcontractors.
- Managed daily activities; coordinated logistical details; tracked accounting of construction project costs.

Intern/Project Manager, **Kent Phillips & Associates,** Dayton, Ohio *9/92-5/93*
- Approached company president and obtained this internship. Awarded academic credit as a result of real estate experience acquired on the job.
- Conducted feasibility analysis of potential development projects and summarized findings using financial software to present data and recommendations.
- Identified prospective investor sources interested in land acquisition and development projects.

Education: *BBA Real Estate,* **Ohio State University**   *5/92*

Community Affiliations: Dayton Chamber of Commerce, Ohio State Alumni,
Coach, Dayton Little League Association

Phone Etiquette and Tips

Another aspect of the job search is speaking to employers by phone. Even though the Internet has an increased part in connecting to employers, the phone still has its own important role. Many employers screen by phone the candidates they are considering interviewing. During this kind of phone interaction both you and the employer are forming an impression about each other. It can be challenging to pick up the phone and suddenly be in a on-the-spot job interview. Some people leave copies of their resumes or job search notes by their phones that they can look at if an employer calls unexpectedly. Many job seekers are seldom home, however, to receive messages. Cell phones are tools that most of us rely on. If this is not an option, answering services can be arranged with your phone company. This can be a helpful in order to not miss important calls and avoid the frustrating game of "telephone tag."

Step Four: Presenting Yourself

When you reach this stage in the job search your efforts are beginning to be rewarded. This is what you have been working towards. Finally you have a chance to interact with a prospective employer. Usually this interaction occurs in person. This practice is changing. Your initial interview might take place over the phone. You might be interviewed through video-conferencing technology. This is commonly used when there is a distance between you and the recruiter and travel arrangements would be expensive. There are also recruiting events known as "virtual job fairs." All of the activity occurs online. Both the job candidates and the employers post information at a designated web site. The job seekers enter their resume and some other personal profile information. The employers describe their organization and the openings they wish to fill. During the dates of the virtual job fair there is a two-way exchange. Job seekers scan through the position descriptions and direct their resume to employers where they want to apply. Recruiters review the resumes of the candidates and make contact by email or phone.

Despite all the ways an interview can occur, there are fundamental aspects to this interaction with an employer. At the heart of it, the interview focuses on three key questions. Do you have the appropriate qualifications? Do you have the kind of personality that fits with the management style and culture of the organization? Does this position fit into your overall career plans so that you will make a reasonable professional commitment to the organization? Any question, no matter how it's worded addresses one of these three central concerns.

Demonstrating Focus During the Interview

The issue of being focused has been raised at every step of the job search. You've been encouraged to give both your resume and your cover letter focus. When you are interviewing this is again an important goal. Here's why. Interviewers often tell those of us who work in university career offices that they are frustrated, even annoyed, when a candidate says they are willing to work anywhere and able to do anything. From their point of view, you have initiated the process and they are giving you their time and attention. It is your responsibility not theirs, to figure out how you can fit into their organization and contribute to what needs to be done. From the interviewer's perspective, the very best interviews are when a candidate can state exactly why they are interested in the organization and know what type of position they will excel in. Although this may seem contradictory, most interviewers are willing to consider someone that may be switching careers or have unusual background if the job seeker can explain that he or she has the skills required. In the job search process it always comes back to helping the employer understand that you may have had a very different job but the skills applied were the same.

Preparing for the Interview

To prepare for the interview you need to know: 1) what activities and responsibilities the position involves, 2) what specific services or goods the organization provides, 3) who does the organization serve? If it is a non-profit organization, what is its mission? If it is a company, who are its clients or customers? As we all know, the Internet is the ultimate resource for researching information. Career related web sites like JobSourceNetwork.com usually have links to specific fields and industries, to major professional associations and membership organizations, newspapers and large trade journals. Interviewers know that it is now pretty easy to find information. They expect you to be informed and prepared.

Before your interview it may help you to review the key points that you plan to address. For many people, rehearsing your answers with friends and family has many benefits. Practicing your responses can enable you to speak more naturally and confidently in the interview. Typical questions to anticipate include: "Tell me about why you want this position (or what qualifies you for this position)" "What is your most significant accomplishment?" "How does this opportunity fit into your short-term and long-term career goals." "How do you know you can perform the job?" "What are your strengths and weaknesses?" "Describe the kind of management style you prefer." Vault.com and WetFeet Press.com are two companies that specialize in providing (for a fee) information about interviewing to jobseekers. They have comprehensive information about employers that hire business students.

Using the Internet to Present Yourself

All of the career web sites mentioned so far, can also help you prepare for your interviews. Receiving online advice about interviewing could be extremely valuable, especially if you have little prior experience or are not familiar with a U.S. style of interviewing. Of course, the many sites already described that link you to company profiles and industry information enable you to speak knowledgeably about the organization itself and its competitors. As just mentioned above, Vault.com and WetFeet Press.com are outstanding resources to assist with interview preparation. These two sites also provide (for a fee) information about various types of interviews. Here are some general facts you should know.

1) Interview Formats: What to Expect

The interview format, content, and style can vary greatly. Even trends in interviewing methods emerge and change over time. For example "behavioral questioning" is currently popular among recruiters. This practice entails outlining specific scenarios and asking the interviewee to describe how she or he has handled that kind of situation in the past. Difficulties with co-workers, disagreements with supervisors, ethical dilemmas, sensitive problems with clients are the types of issues that might be outlined.

Another practice is to create a task that would be part of one's job description. Someone who recently applied for a marketing position with a consumer products company was asked to design and deliver a marketing presentation on the spot. A prominent international consulting firm asked recent interviewees to scan financial data and provide a detailed explanation of how those numbers should be analyzed, by what methods, in what sequence, to evaluate what factors, and consider what kinds of decisions or recommendations. Another Fortune 500 company expected attendees at a job fair to discuss and elaborate on financial analysis, budgeting, and forecasting models. Likewise, more and more organizations are incorporating personality and aptitude testing as a step in the interview process. This often includes drug testing.

2) Interview Follow-up

Write a thank you note within 24 hours of your interview. Sending this message via email rather than by mail is acceptable. For high tech employers, corresponding via email is preferred. Either way, keep your thank you note brief. Express your appreciation for the opportunity to discuss your qualifications in person. Mention a positive point that emerged during the interview. For example, if the interviewer seemed impressed with a certain work experience, you would be sure to emphasize how that particular position has prepared you for this new opportunity. End the thank you note by restating your interest in this position. Be sure to spell your interviewer's name correctly and include her or his title. Write a slightly different letter to each and every person who formally interviewed you that day. If you send this note by mail, type it and print it on quality stationery.

Always assume that the next step is yours. A week after the interview contact the interviewer and check on the status of the hiring process. Find out whether a final round of candidates have been selected or if any offers have been made. When possible get feedback on how well (or poorly) you interviewed. If you weren't offered the position, what quality or experience did you lack? Use this information to improve your presentation in other interviews. Even if you feel let down or frustrated it is in your interest to set these emotions aside. Let the employer know how much you would like to be considered for other opportunities that may arise in the future. Their first choice may back out or a new position could open up and you could be the first person that is contacted.

Step Five: Negotiate

Congratulations! You have been offered a position! Now it is time to negotiate. For many job seekers this is an exciting but stressful part of the job search process. This is especially true if you are not certain what salary amount is reasonable. In addition, employers in the private sector may offer you a signing bonus, a relocation package, stock options, a year end bonus (usually connected to your individual performance and the company's) if you negotiate for them. Online career sites can provide you the information you need.

A word of caution about the base pay, even though you deserve to ask for the best salary possible don't ignore excellent job opportunities because the salary seems lower than you hoped. Before you write off a position, calculate these factors: what is the dollar value of the health and dental benefits? The annual employer contribution can add up to thousands of dollars. Don't forget to weigh in the vacation and sick leave offered. In addition, professional training, certification, and tuition reimbursement provided by the employer are not only worth money, but make you more marketable.

Using the Internet to Negotiate the Offer

Salary data changes from year to year. Accessing online information can help you learn the latest figures. Here, too, JobSourceNetwork.com provides links sites that will be useful, such as: careerbuilder.com (which has a salary calculator) Exec-U-Net (for positions paying $100,000 and above) and Monster.com and Vault.com. Most career web sites including, CareerPath.com and JobSourceNetwork.com offer you helpful information about relocation issues.

Now it's time to put all these tips to use!

Important Note

Always assume that the next step is yours. A week after the interview contact the interviewer and check on the status of the hiring process.

So. California Job Source

EMPLOYMENT HELP

Job/Support Centers

Special Insights

The Counties of Southern California

Los Angeles, Orange, San Diego, Riverside, San Bernardino
• Chambers of Commerce, Colleges & Universities, Libraries, Local Clubs & Associations •

Internet Job Center

Company Web Sites & Job Hotlines

Alumni Networking

National, State & Local Newspapers & Trade Publications

Industry Associations & Publications

Employment Agencies

• Temporary, Temp-to-Hire, Permanent, Executive Recruiters •

Employment Help

Job/Support Centers

As mentioned in the previous section, getting out there and accepting part-time and some time full-time help will not only pay for rent but allow employers to evaluate your abilities. Many of the job centers listed will help you get a job and review your resume, cover letter and interview skills. A majority of job centers are not-for-profit and may charge small fees for things like mailing resumes or using equipment. It will definitely be worth the price.

California Employment Development Department
www.caljobs.gov

The California Employment Development Department is California's largest employment agency, with a statewide network of service points. Through EDD's automated matching system, they can link employers with qualified job candidates on a local, regional, statewide, and national level.

The Employment Development Department's (EDD) Job Service has a primary mandate to facilitate the match between employers and qualified workers.

While continuing its traditional function as the state's labor exchange, EDD's approach is geared to meet the challenges of the 21st century with increased efficiency and continuously improved customer service. The California Job Openings Browse System, or CalJOBS, plays a vital role in meeting that challenge.

CalJOBS provides an automated, easy-to-use system for personal computers. The system serves employers who want to fill job openings, and individuals seeking employment.

With CalJOBS, you're in control. You decide which aspects of this electronic job-listing and resume system will best suit your needs.

Employers-Enter a job listing and browse resumes of job seekers who meet the specifications of your openings. Job Seekers-Create and store your resume and browse job listings. If you find suitable openings, you can make available a system generated resume for on-line viewing by prospective employers. Agencies in Partnership with EDD-Coordinate and facilitate the match between employers and job seekers.

If you have questions about CalJOBS, you may call (800)758-0398 during regular business hours (Monday through Friday, 8am to 5pm PST) or visit them at www.caljobs.gov

Job Centers

California Employment Development - West Los Angeles
10829 Venice Boulevard
Los Angeles, CA 90034
310-280-2830

Career Encores
3700 Wilshire Boulevard, Suite 200
Los Angeles, CA 90010
800-833-6267

Career Planning Center
1623 South La Cienega Boulevard
Los Angeles, CA 90035
310-273-6633

Chicana Service Action Center
134 East 1st Street
Los Angeles, CA 90012
213-253-5959

City of Los Angeles Employment Office
Personnel Department
700 East Temple Street, Room 100
Los Angeles, CA
213-847-9424
Web Address: www.ci.la.ca.us/dept/PER/ index.htm

City of San Diego
Employment Information Office
1200 3rd Avenue, Suite 300
San Diego, CA 92101
619-236-6467

Rich Snapper, *Personnel Director*

Coastal Job Resource One Stop Center
Coatline Community College
2627 Vista del Oro
Newport Beach, CA 92660
714-718-1212

County of San Diego
Department of Human Resources
1600 Pacific Highway, Room 207
San Diego, CA 92101
619-265-0036
Job Hotline: 619-265-0036
Carol Arauz, *Director of Human Resources*

East County Career Center
924 East Main Street
El Cajon, CA 92021
619-590-3900
Job Hotline: 619-824-3444
Web Address:
  http://eccc.grossmont.k12.ca.us

Forty Plus of Southern California
3450 Wilshire Boulevard, Suite 510
Los Angeles, CA 90010
213-388-2301
Web Address: www.40plussocal.org

Fullerton Job Center
233 East Commonwealth Avenue
Fullerton, CA 92632
714-680-7800

Garden Grove Job Center
11277 Garden Grove Boulevard
Garden Grove, CA 92843
714-741-5020

Goodwill Industries of Southern California
342 San Fernando Road
Los Angeles, CA 90031
213-223-1211

High Desert One-Stop Career Center
Victor Valley College, Student Service Building
18422 Bear Valley Road
Victorville, CA 92392
760-245-4271

Marina Del Ray Career Planning Center
13160 Mindanao Way, Suite 240
Marina Del Ray, CA 90292
310-309-6000

Orange Resource Center
City of Orange
210 North McPhearson Street
Orange, CA 92665
714-633-2753

San Diego Career Center Network
8401 Aero Drive
San Diego, CA 92123
619-974-7620

San Diego Job Corps
1325 Iris Avenue
Imperial Beach, CA 91932
619-429-8500
Gine Dobey, *Human Resource Manager*

San Diego Regional Occupational Program
6401 Linda Vista Road
San Diego, CA 92111
619-292-3758

San Diego Workforce Partnership
1551 4th Avenue, Suite 600
San Diego, CA 92101
619-238-1445
www.workforce.org

San Fernando Job Center
1520 San Fernando Road
San Fernando, CA 91340
818-898-4100

Torrance Job Center
1220 Engracia Avenue
Torrance, CA 90501
310-833-1018

West Covina
933 South Glendora Avenue
West Covina, CA 91790
626-814-8234

West Los Angeles
10829 Venice Boulevard
Los Angeles, CA 90034
310-280-2830

West Orange County One-Stop Career Center
Orange County Private Industry Council
11277 Garden Grove Boulevard, Suite 101-C
Garden Grove, CA 92843
714-741-5020

Special Insights

This section is dedicated to individuals/job seekers who seek special and/or additional assistance and guidance on landing jobs.

GAYS & LESBIANS

Gay Link Chamber of Commerce
2846 Unicornio Street
La Costa, CA 92009

Greater San Diego Business Association -GSDBA-
3737 5th Avenue
San Diego, CA 92104
619-296-4543

Los Angeles Gay & Lesbian Community Services Center
1625 North Schrader Boulevard
Los Angeles, CA 90028
323-993-7480
Web Address: www.gay-lesbian-center.org

MINORITIES

American Indian Chamber of Commerce
4060 30th Street
San Diego, CA 92101

Asian Business Association Chamber of Commerce
4350 Executive Drive Suite 236
San Diego, CA 92121
858-458-6860

Black Business Chamber of Commerce
1201 Civic Center Drive West, Suite 205
Santa Ana, CA 90062
714-547-2646

Black Chamber of Commerce
1727 North Euclid Avenue
San Diego, CA 92105
619-262-2121

Chicana Service Action Center
315 West 9th Street, Suite 101
Los Angeles, CA 90015
213-253-5959

Chinese-American Chamber of Commerce, Orange County
8907 Warner Avenue, #225
Huntington Beach, CA 92647
714-848-0043

Hispanic Chamber of Commerce of Orange County
2323 North Broadway, Suite 305
Santa Ana, CA 92706
714-953-4289

Japanese Chamber of Commerce of South California
244 San Pedro Street, Suite 504
Los Angeles, CA, 90012
213-626-3067

Tom Kamei, *President*

Jewish Vocational Service
6505 Wilshire Boulevard, Suite 303
Los Angeles, CA 90048
323-761-8888
Web Address: www.jvsla.org

Orange County Urban League
12391 Lewis Street, Suite 102
Garden Grove, CA 92640
714-633-2753

Southern California Indian Center
3600 Wilshire Boulevard, Suite 226
Los Angeles, CA 90057
213-387-5772

Southern California Indian Center
3440 Wilshire Boulevard, Suite 904
Los Angeles, CA 90010
213-387-5772

Urban League of Los Angeles
3450 Mount Vernon
Los Angeles, CA 90057
323-299-9660

Vietnamese Chamber of Commerce
9121 Bossa Avenue, Suite 203
Westminster, CA 92683
714-839-2257

PERSONS WITH DISABILITIES

Alliance for the Mentally Ill
213-472-0834

American Foundation for the Blind Hotline
800-232-5463

American Red Cross
213-739-5200

Assisting the Disabled with Employment Placement and Training - ADEPT
213-388-6855

Braille Institute
213-663-1111

Build Rehabilitation Industries
818-898-0020

California Council of the Blind
213-823-4614

California Governor's Committee on Employment of the Handicapped
916-323-3545

Catholic Charities
Employment Services
2301 West Lincoln Avenue, Suite 112
Anaheim, CA 92801
714-635-5230

Center for the Partially Sighted
213-458-3501

Center on Deafness, CSU/Northridge
818-885-2611

City of Los Angeles Department of Aging
2404 Wilshire Boulevard Suite 400
Los Angeles, CA 90057
213-368-4000
TDD: 213-368-7260

City of Santa Monica's Office for the Disabled
213-458-8701

Community Rehabilitation Services
4716 Cesar Chavez Avenue, Building A
Los Angeles, California 90022
323-266-0453
TDD- 323-266-0545

Culver City Disability Services
213-202-5864

Dale McIntosh Center
150 West Cerritos Avenue, Building 4
Anaheim, California 92805
949-772-8285
TDD- 949-772-8366

Darrell McDaniel Independent Living Center
14354 Haynes Street
Van Nuys, California 91401
818-988-9525
TDD- 818-988-3533

Deaf Community Services of San Diego
3788 Park Boulevard
San Diego, CA 92103
619-299-7582

Easter Seal Society
714-545-2033

Goodwill Industries of Orange County
410 North Fairview Street
Santa Ana, CA 92703
714-547-6301
Web Address: www.ocgoodwill.org

Greater Los Angeles Council on Deafness -GLAD
213-383-2220

Hope for Hearing Foundation, UCLA
213-825-5131

Independent Living Center of Southern California
356-B East Avenue, K-4
Lancaster, California 93535
661-945-6602
TDD- 661-945-6604

LA County Commission on Disabilities
213-974-1053
TDD- 213-485-6655

Local State Department of Rehabilitation - Los Angeles
213-736-3904

Local State Department of Rehabilitation - Van Nuys
818-901-5024

Los Angeles City Council on Disability
213-485-6334

Los Angeles County Disability Information Line
213-551-2929

Los Angeles County Mental Health Association
213-629-1529

Los Angeles Mayor's Office for the Handicapped
213-485-4103
TDD- 213-485-6655

Los Angeles Project With Industry
213-644-3894

Los Angeles R.T.D., Disability Hot Line
800-621-7828

Low Vision Council of Southern California
213-395-8231

National Association for Hearing/ Speech Action
800-638-8255

National Council on the Handicapped
202-453-3846

National Organization on Disability
202-293-5960
TDD- 202-293-5968

Occupational Training Services
8799 Balboa Avenue, Suite 100
San Diego, CA 92123
858-560-0411

President's Committee on Employment of the Handicapped
202-653-5010

San Diego Regional Occupational Program
6401 Linda Vista Road
San Diego, CA 92111
858-292-3758

Santa Monica College Disabled Students Services
213-452-9266

Santa Monica West Mental Health Center
213-451-8731

Services Center for Independent Living
480 South Indian Hill Boulevard
Claremont, California 91711
818-621-6722

Southern Calif Projects with Industry
213-869-2075

State Department of Rehabilitation, Santa Monica Office
213-450-2171

State Employment Development Department, Santa Monica Office
213-451-9811

Stroke Program - Santa Monica College
213-452-9267

UCLA Office of Special Services
213-825-1501

West LA Chapter, California Association of the Physically Handicapped -CAPH
213-479-3016

Westside Center for Independent Living -WCIL
213-390-3611
Has a computer training program for the disabled.

Westside Independent Services for the Elderly
213-394-9871

WOMEN in the WORKPLACE

Commission on the Status of Women
250 East 1st Street, Suite 1412
Los Angeles, CA 90012
213-485-6533

Women at Work
50 North Hill Avenue, Suite 300
Pasadena, CA 91106
626-796-6870

Women Helping Women
543 North Fairfax Avenue
Los Angeles, CA 90036
323-655-3807

Women's Focus
210 West Main Street, Suite 204
Tustin, CA 92780
714-731-8992

Important Note

With CalJOBS, you're in control. You decide which aspects of this electronic job-listing and resume system will best suit your needs.

The Counties of Southern California

ADDITIONAL SOURCES FOR JOB LEADS

- Los Angeles
- San Diego
- Orange
- San Bernardino
- Riverside
- Ventura

Many job seekers ignore the incredible tools and resources that surround them in their own community. This chapter is dedicated to offering those additional sources for employment information and job leads. Resources like your local Chamber of Commerce, College or University, City or County Government and libraries offer access to thousands of additional job leads through print and electronic publications.

LOS ANGELES, RIVERSIDE & SAN BERNARDINO COUNTY'S CHAMBERS OF COMMERCE

Alhambra Chamber of Commerce
104 South First Street
Alhambra, CA 91801
626-282-8481

Big Bear Chamber of Commerce
630 Bartlett Road
Big Bear Lake, CA 92315
909-866-4607
Web Address: www.bigbearchamber.com

Burbank Chamber of Commerce
200 West Magnolia Boulevard
Burbank, CA 91502
818-559-4369
Web Address: www.burbankchamber.org

Carson Chamber of Commerce
22010 South Avalon
Bl. Carson, CA 90745
310-522-5595
Web Address: www.carsonchamber.com

Corona Chamber of Commerce
904 East Sixth Street
Corona, CA 92879
909-737-3350
Web Address: www.coronachamber.org

Covina Chamber of Commerce
935 West Badillo Street, Suite 100
Covina, CA 91722(626-967-4191
Web Address: www.covina.org

Culver City Chamber of Commerce
4249 Overland Avenue
Culver City, CA 90230
310-287-3850
Web Address: www.culvercitychamber.com

Glendale Chamber of Commerce
200 South Louise Street
Glendale, CA 91205
818-240-7870

**Greater Riverside
Chamber of Commerce**
3985 University Avenue
Riverside, CA 92501
909-683-7100
Web Address: www.riverside-chamber.com

Hollywood Chamber of Commerce
7018 Hollywood Boulevard
Hollywood, CA 90028
323-469-8311
Web Address: www.hollywoodchamber.net

**Long Beach Area Chamber Of
Commerce**
9900 Talbert Avenue, Suite 300
Fountain Valley, CA 92708

Los Angeles Chamber of Commerce
350 South Bixel Street
Los Angeles, CA 90017
213-580-7500

Malibu Chamber of Commerce
23805 Stuart Ranch Road, Suite 100
Malibu, CA 90265
310-456-9025
Web Address: www.malibu.org

Marina del Rey Chamber of Commerce
9800 South Sepulveda Boulevard, Suite 214
Westchester, CA 90045
310-821-0555
Web Address: www.wlaxchamber.com

Mid Valley Chamber of Commerce
14540 Victory Boulevard, Suite 100
Van Nuys, CA 91411
818-989-0300
Web Address: www.midvalleychamber.com

**Monterrey Park
Chamber of Commerce**
700 El Mercado Avenue
Monterrey Park, CA 91754
626-570-9429
Web Address: www.montereypark.com

Palm Springs Chamber of Commerce
190 West Amado Road
Palm Springs, CA 92262
760-325-1577
Web Address: www.pschamber.org

**Pasadena Chamber of Commerce and
Civic Association**
865 Del Mar Boulevard
Pasadena, CA 91101
626-795-3355
Web Address: www.pasadena-chamber.org

**Rancho Cucamonga Chamber of
Commerce**
8280 Utica Avenue, Suite 160
Rancho Cucamonga, CA 91730
909-987-1012
Web Address: www.ranchochamber.org

**Redondo Beach Chamber of
Commerce**
200 North Pacific Coast Highway
Redondo Beach, California 90277
310-376-6911
Web Address: www.redondochamber.org

San Gabriel Chamber of Commerce
401 West Las Tunas Drive
San Gabriel, California 91776
626-576-2525

**San Pedro Peninsula Chamber of
Commerce**
390 West Seventh Street
San Pedro, CA 90731
310-832-7272
Web Address: www.sanpedrochamber.com

**Santa Clarita Valley Chamber of
Commerce**
23920 Valencia Boulevard, Suite 100
Santa Clarita, CA 91355

**Santa Monica Area Chamber of
Commerce**
501 Colorado Avenue, Suite 150
Santa Monica, CA 90401-2430
310-393-9825
Web Address: www.smchamber.com

Torrance Area Chamber of Commerce
3400 Torrance Boulevard, Suite 100
Torrance, CA 90503
310-540-5858
Web Address: www.torrancechamber.com

West Covina Chamber of Commerce
811 South Sunset Avenue
West Covina, CA 91790
626-338-8496
Web Address: www.westcovinachamber.com

**West Hollywood Chamber of
Commerce**
8278 1/2 Santa Monica Boulevard
West Hollywood, CA 90046
323-650-2688
Web Address: www.wehochamber.org

**Westchester/LAX Chamber of
Commerce**
9800 Sepulvada, Suite 214
Westchester, CA 90045
310-645-5151

For Links to

Thousands of Job Sites

Worldwide, Visit

JobSourceNetwork.com

Employment Help

Anaheim Chamber of Commerce
100 South Anaheim Boulevard
Anaheim, CA 92805
714-758-0222
Web Address: www.anaheimchamber.org

Brea Chamber of Commerce
1 Civic Center Circle
Brea, CA 92821
714-529-4938
Web Address: www.breachamber.com

Fullerton Chamber of Commerce
219 East Commonwealth Avenue
Fullerton, CA 92832-0529
714-871-3100
Web Address: www.fullerton.org

Irvine Chamber of Commerce
17200 Jamboree Road, Suite A
Irvine, CA 92714
714-660-9112

Laguna Niguel Chamber of Commerce
30110 Crown Valley Parkway, Suite 201
Laguna Niguel, CA 92677
949-363-0136

Newport Harbor Area Chamber of Commerce
1470 Jamboree Road
Newport Beach, CA 92660
Web Address: http://newportbeach.com/ nhacc/NHACC.html

Santa Ana Chamber of Commerce
1055 North Main Street, Suite 904
Santa Ana, CA 92701
714-541-5353
Web Address: www.santaanacc.com/

Yorba Linda Chamber of Commerce
17670 Yorba Linda Boulevard
Yorba Linda, CA 92886
714-993-9537

Chula Vista Chamber of Commerce
233 4th Avenue
Chula Vista, CA 91910
619-420-6602
Web Address: www.chulavistachamber.org

Coronado Chamber of Commerce
1224 10th Street
Coronado, CA 92118
619-435-9260
Web Address: www.coronadochamber.com

Del Mar Chamber of Commerce
1104 Camino del Mar
Del Mar, CA 92014
858-793-5292
Web Address: www.delmarchamber.org

El Cajon Chamber of Commerce
201 South Magnolia Avenue
El Cajon, CA 92020
619-440-6161
Web Address: www.eastcountychamber.org

Escondido Chamber of Congress
720 North Broadway
Escondido, CA 92025
760-745-2125
Web Address: www.escondidochamber.com

Golden Triangle Chamber of Commerce
4350 Executive Drive, Suite 200
San Diego, CA 92121
858-558-1744
Web Address: www.goldentrianglechamber.com

Greater San Diego Chamber of Commerce
402 West Broadway, Suite 1000
San Diego, CA 92101
619-232-0124
Web Address: www.sdchamber.org

Oceanside Chamber of Commerce
928 North Coast Highway
Oceanside, CA 92054
760-722-1534
Web Address: www.oceansidechamber.com

Solana Beach Chamber of Commerce
210 West Plaza Street
Solana Beach, CA 92075
858-755-4775

COLLEGES & UNIVERSITIES

Academy Pacific Travel College
1777 North Vine Street, 3rd Floor
Hollywood, CA 90028
323-462-3211

Azusa Pacific University
901 East Alosta Avenue
Azusa, CA 91702
800-825-5278
Web Address: www.apu.edu

Barstow College
2700 Barstow Road
Barstow, CA 92311

Biola University
13800 Biola Avenue
La Mirada, CA 90639
800-652-4652
Web Address: www.biola.edu

California Baptist College
8432 Magnolia Avenue
Riverside, CA 92504
909-689-5771

California Institute of Technology
1200 East California Boulevard
Pasadena, CA 91125
626-395-6811
Web Address: www.caltech.edu

California Institute of the Arts
24700 McBean Parkway
Velencia, CA 91355
661-255-1050
Job Hotline: 661-222-2737
Web Address: www.calarts.edu

California Pacific University
10650 Treena Street, Suite 203
San Diego, CA 92131
858-695-3292

California School of Professional Psychology - Los Angeles
1000 South Fremont Avenue
Alhambra, CA 91803-1360
626-284-2777

California State University, Fullerton
Career Development and Counseling
800 North State College Boulevard
Fullerton, CA 92831-3599
714-278-2011

California State University - Long Beach
1250 Bellflower Boulevard
Long Beach, CA 90840
310-9854111
Web Address: www.csulb.edu

California State University, Los Angeles
Career Planning and Placement
5151 State University Drive
Los Angeles, CA 90032
323-343-3000
Web Address: www.calstatela.edu

California State University, Northridge
Career Center
Northridge, CA 91330
818-885-2381

California State University - San Bernardino
5500 University Parkway
San Bernardino, CA 92407
909-880-5000

Chaffey College
5885 Haven Avenue
Rancho Cucamonga, CA 91737-3002
909-987-1737
Web Address: www.chaffey.cc.ca.us

Chapman University
One University Drive
Orange, California 92866, USA
714-997-2400
Web Address: www.chapman.edu

Claremont Graduate School
171 East 10th Street
Clarement, CA 91711
909-607-3371
Web Address: www.cgs.edu

Coastline Community College
11460 Warner Avenue
Fountain Valley, CA 92708
714-546-7600
Web Address: coastline.cccd.edu

College of Osteopathic Medicine
309 East 2nd Street, College Plaza
Pomona, CA 91766
909-623-6116

Employment Help

Columbia College Hollywood
925 North La Brea Avenue
Hollywood, CA 90038
323-851-0550

Concordia University at Irvine
1530 Concordia West
Irvine, CA 92612-3299
949-854-8002
Web Address: www.cui.edu

Crafton Hills College
11711 Sand Canyon Road
Yucaipa, Ca, 92399
909-794-2161
Web Address: www.sbccd.cc.ca.us/chc/
index.htm

Fashion Careers of California College
1923 Morena Boulevard
San Diego, CA 92110
619-275-4700

Fullerton College
321 East Chapman Avenue
Fullerton, CA 92832-2095
714-992-7000
Web Address: www.fullcoll.edu/

Gemological Institure of America
5345 Armada Deive
Carlsbad, CA 92008
310-829-2991

Golden Gate University
919 South Grand Avenue, Suite 250
Los Angeles, CA 90015-1421
213-623-6000
Web Address: www.ggu.edu

Golden West College
15744 Golden West Street
Huntington Beach, California, 92647-2748
714-892-7711
Web Address: www.gwc.cccd.edu

Hope International University
2500 East Nutwood Avenue
Fullerton, CA 92831
714-879-3901
Web Address: www.hiu.edu/index.html

Irvine Valley College
5500 Irvine Center Drive
Irvine, CA 92618
714-451-5100
Web Address: www.ivc.cc.ca.us

Loma Linda University
Loma Linda, California 92350
909-824-4300
Web Address: www.llu.edu

Los Angeles Trade Technical College
400 West Washington Boulevard
Los Angeles, CA 90015
213-744-9058

National University
11255 North Torrey Pines Road
La Jolla, CA 92037-1011
858-642-8000
Web Address: http://nunic.nu.edu

Nova Institute of Health Technology
3000 South Robertson Boulevard, 3rd Floor
Los Angeles, CA 90034
310-840-5777

Occidental College
1600 Campus Road
Los Angeles, CA 90041
323-259-2500
Web Address: www.oxy.edu

Orange Coast College
2701 Fairview Road
Costa Mesa, CA 92626
714-432-0202
Web Address: www.occ.cccd.edu

Pacific Travel Trade School
3807 Wilshire Boulevard, 3rd Floor
Los Angeles, CA 90010
213-427-1040

Pacific Western University
600 North Sepulveda Boulevard
Los Angeles, CA 90049
310-471-0306

Pepperdine University
24255 Pacific Coast Highway
Malibu, CA 90263
310-456-4000
Web Address: www.pepperdine.edu

Point Loma Nazarene College
3900 Lamaland Drive
San Diego, CA 92106
619-849-2200
Web Address: www.ptloma.edu

San Bernardino Valley College
701 South Mt. Vernon
San Bernardino, CA 92410
909-888-6511
*Web Address: www.sbccd.cc.ca.us/sbvc/
index.htm*

San Diego State University
5500 Campanile Drive
San Diego, CA 92182
619-594-5000
Web Address: www.sdsu.edu

Scripps College
1030 Columbia Avenue
Claremont, CA 91711
Web Address: www.scrippscol.edu

**Southern California College of
Optometry**
2575 Yorba Linda Boulevard
Fullerton, CA 92831
714-870-7226

United States International University
10455 Pomerado road
San Diego, CA 92131
858-271-4300
Web Address: www.usiu.edu

University of California, Irvine
Career Planning and Placement
Irvine, CA 92697
949-824-5011
Web Address: www.uci.edu

University of California, Los Angeles
405 Hilgard Avenue
Los Angeles, CA 90095
310-825-4321
Web Address: www.ucla.edu

University of California, Los Angeles
Career Center
Box 951573
Los Angeles, CA 90095-1573
310-206-1915

University of California Riverside
900 University Avenue
Riverside, CA 92521
909-787-1012
Web Address: www.ucr.edu

University of California, San Diego
Career Services Center
La Jolla, CA 92093
858-534-3750

University of California, San Diego
9500 Gilman Drive
La Jolla, CA 92093
858-534-2230
Web Address: www.ucsd.edu

University of Redlands
1200 East Colton Avenue
Redlands, CA 92373
909-793-2121
Web Address: www.redlands.edu

James R. Appleton, *President*

University of San Diego
5998 Alcala Park
San Diego, CA 92110
619-260-4600
Web Address: www.acusd.edu

University of Southern California
Graduate and Professional Studies
Los Angeles, CA 90089
213-743-2311

University of Southern California
University Park
Los Angeles, CA 90089
Web Address: www.usc.edu

Whittier College
13406 East Philadelphia Street
Whittier, CA 90608
562-907-4200
Web Address: www.whittier.edu

Woodbury University
7500 Glenoaks Boulevard
Burbank, CA 91510
818-767-0888
Web Address: www.woodburyu.edu
Ken Nielsen, *President*

Many job seekers ignore the incredible tools and resources that surround them in their own community. This chapter is dedicated to offering those additional sources for employment information and job leads.

Local Government

Beverly Hills City Hall
455 North Rexford Drive
Beverly Hills, CA 90210

Beverly Hills Community Services
444 North Rexford Drive
Beverly Hills, CA 90210

Chula Vista City Hall
276 Fourth Avenue
Chula Vista CA 91910
619-691-5044

City of Agoura Hills
30101 Agoura Court, #102
Agoura Hills CA 91301
818-597-7300

City of Anaheim
200 South Anaheim Boulevard
Anaheim, CA 92805
714-765-5162

City of Escondido Personnel Office
201 North Broadway, 2nd Floor
760-839-4641

City of Fullerton
303 West Commonwealth
Fullerton, CA 92832
714-738-6317
Web Address: www.ci.fullerton.ca.us

City of Fullerton Personnel Department
303 West Commonwealth
Fullerton, CA 92832
714-738-6378
Job Hotline: 714-738-6378
Web Address: www.ci.fullerton.ca.us/
  noframes/personnel/

City of Long Beach
333 West Ocean Boulevard, 14th floor
Long Beach, California 90802
562-570-6801

Beverly O'Neill, *Mayor*

City of Los Angeles
200 North Spring Street
Los Angeles, CA 90012
213-485-5708
Web Address: www.ci.la.ca.us

City of Newport Beach
3300 Newport Boulevard
Newport Beach, CA 92663-3884
949-644-3309
Web Address: www.city.newport-beach.ca.us

**City of Pasadena -
Human Resources Department**
100 North Garfield Avenue, Room 146
Pasadena, California 91109-7215
626-744-4366
Job Hotline: 626-744-4600

Robert Person, *Director*
Dorothy Kirkland, *Human Resources
  Manager*
Deborah Simms, *Human Resources Manager*

City of San Diego
202 C Street, 11th Floor
San Diego, CA 92101
619-236-6330
Web Address: www.sannet.gov

**City of Santa Monica Personnel
Department**
1685 Main Street, Room 101
Santa Monica, CA 90401
Job Hotline: 310-458-8697
Web Address: www.ci.santa-monica.ca.us/
  personnel/

City of Torrance
Job Hotline: 310-618-2969

City of West Hollywood
8300 Santa Monica Boulevard
West Hollywood, CA 90069
323-848-6400
Web Address: www.ci.west-hollywood.ca.us/

**County of San Bernardino
Human Resources Department**
157 West Fifth Street
San Bernardino, CA 92415-0440
909-387-8304

Glendale
P.O. Box 9653
Glendale 91206-9653
818-548-4844
Web Address: http://glendale-online.com/
  index.html

Larry Zarian, *Mayor*

Glendale Office of Information Services
141 North Glendale Avenue, 3rd Level
Glendale, CA 91206
818-548-3904

Imelda Bickham, *Director*

Glendale Office of Personnel & Employee Relations
613 East Broadway, Suite 100
Glendale, CA 91206-4392
818-548-2168

John F. Hoffman, *Director*

Huntington Beach Personnel Division
2000 Main Street
Huntington Beach, CA 92648
714-536-5492
Job Hotline: 714-374-1570

Los Angeles County
500 West Temple Street
Los Angeles, CA 90012
213-974-1311
Web Address: www.co.la.ca.us

Pomona Department of Human Resources
909-620-2291

Riverside County
4080 Lemon Street
Riverside, CA 92501
909-955-1000
Web Address: www.co.riverside.ca.us

San Bernardino County
351 North Arrowhead Street, 5th Floor
San Bernardino, CA 92415
909-387-2020
Web Address: www.co.san-bernardino.ca.us

San Diego County - Administrative Center
1600 Pacific Highway
San Diego, CA 92101
Job Hotline: 619-236-2191
Web Address: www.co.san-diego.ca.us

San Diego County - Office of Training and Development
3989 Ruffin Road
San Diego, CA 92123
619-694-8770
Job Hotline: 619-236-2191
Web Address: www.co.san-diego.ca.us/cnty/cntydepts/general/human_resources

Santa Monica City Hall
1685 Main Street
Santa Monica, CA 90401

Libraries

Beverly Hills Public Library
444 North Rexford Drive
Beverly Hills, CA 90210

Beverly Hills - Roxbury Senior Adult Library
471 South Roxbury Drive
Beverly Hills, CA 90210

California State University, Long Beach
Web Address: www.csulb.edu/library

California State University, Los Angeles
Web Address: http://web.calstatela.edu/library/

City of Inglewood Public Library
101 West Manchester Boulevard
Inglewood, CA 90301
310-412-5397

City of Los Angeles Central Library
630 West Fifth Street
Los Angeles, CA 90071
213-228-7000

Fontayne Holmes, *Director*

City of San Diego Central Library
Central Library
820 E Street
San Diego, CA 92101-6478
619-236-5800
Web Address: www.sannet.gov/public-library

Rich Snapper, *Personnel Director*

Fullerton Public Library
Main Library
353 West Commonwealth Avenue
Fullerton, CA 92632
714-738-6326

Glendale Public Library
222 East Harvard Street
Glendale, CA 91205-1075
818-548-2030

Laurel Patric, *Director*

Huntington Beach Library
7111 Talbert Avenue
Huntington Beach, CA 92648
714-842-4481

Los Angeles Public Library
Central Library
630 West 5th Street
Los Angeles, CA 90071
213-228-7000
Web Address: www.lapl.org

Newport Beach Public Library
1000 Avocado Avenue
949-717-3800
Web Address: www.city.newport-beach.ca.us/nbpl/

Norman F. Feldheym Library
555 West Sixth Street
San Bernardino, CA 92410-3094
909-381-8201

Orange Public Library
101 North Center Street
Orange, CA 92666
714-288-2400

Pasadena Central Library
285 East Walnut Street
Pasadena, CA 91101
626-744-4052
Web Address: www.ci.pasadena.ca.us/ library

Pomona Public Library
625 South Garey Avenue
Pomona, CA 91766
909-620-2043

Rancho Cucamonga Library
7368 Archibald Avenue
Rancho Cucamonga, CA 91730
909-948-9900

Rosenfeld Business Library-UCLA
Anderson School of Business
University of California, Los Angeles
Los Angeles, CA 90095
310-825-3138
Web Address: www.anderson.ucla.edu/ resources/library/libhome.htm

San Bernardino County Library
104 West Fourth Street
San Bernardino, CA 92415-0035
909-387-5720

San Bernardino Public Library
555 West 6th Stret
San Bernardino, CA 92410
909-381-8201

San Diego County Library System
5555 Overland Avenue, Building 15
San Diego, CA 92123
858-694-2415
Web Address: www.sannet.gov/public-library/

San Diego Public Library
820 East Street
San Diego, CA 92101-6478
619-236-5800

Santa Ana Public Library
26 Civic Center Plaza
Santa Ana, CA 92702
714-647-5250

Torrance Public Library
3301 Torrance Boulevard
Torrance, CA 90503
310-618-5959
Web Address: www.ci.torrance.ca.us/city/ dept/library/torrlib.htm

University of California, Irvine
Web Address: www.lib.uci.edu/

University of California, San Diego
Web Address: www.ucsd.edu/library/ index.html

University of California, Los Angeles - UCLA
Web Address: www.library.ucla.edu/

University of Southern California -USC
Web Address: www.usc.edu/academe/ libraries.html

Ventura County - Camarillo Library
3100 Ponderosa Drive
Camarillo, CA 93010
805-482-1952

FINDING A JOB ON THE INTERNET

- **Browsers & Search Engines**

- **National, State & Local Job & Career Web Sites**

- **Company Web Sites**

- **Alumni Web Sites**

- **National & Local Print Media**

- **Industry Associations, Trade Journals/Magazines**

An easy, new & exciting way of finding a job is through the Internet. With more companies posting jobs on the Internet, job-seekers are finding it easier and response-friendly when applying for jobs over the Internet. Some drawbacks might be that applicant pools for one job might exceed several thousands, thereby raising the level of competition for a particular job. The best way to utilize the Internet is by the wealth of information it provides job-seekers. You can search companies via Internet search engines and obtain important information about the companies' goals & objectives, financial outlook, including annual reports, and their background.

Most addresses can be reached by using browsers like Netscape and/ or Mosaic to surf the Net. These browsers can then connect you to search engines such as Net Search, Lycos, Infoseek, Yahoo and Web Crawler.

HOW • WHERE • WHO

Browsers & Search Engines

Alta Vista	www.atlavista.com	Infoseek	www.infoseek.com
America OnLine	www.aol.com	Lycos	www.lycos.com
Excite	www.excite.com	Snap.com	www.snap.com
Go.com	www.go.com	Webcrawler	//webcrawler.com
	Yahoo	www.yahoo.com	

National & Local Job Web Sites

Academic Employment Network
www.academploy.com

Academic360.com
www.academic360.com
Resources for the academic job hunter focusing on positions in the US, Canada, Australia, and the UK. Has links to job announcements from the HR depts. of nearly 1,800 colleges and universities from around the world and dozens of professional academic associations. Formerly Jobs in Higher Education.

Accessalesjobs.com
www.accessalesjobs.com
A career site dedicated to sales and marketing opportunities.

Accounting Jobs
www.accountingjobs.com

ADG Group
www.adggroup.com
A human resources consulting and career management services firm that works with clients and individuals nationwide.

AdSearch
www.adsearch.com

Adweek Classifieds
www.adweek.com/classifieds

AEC Job Bank
www.aecjobbank.com
Employment resource for the Architectural, Engineering and Construction industries. Absolutely free.

Agency Central
www.agencycentral.co.uk
Offers jobseekers over 90,000 live vacancies, CV submission and distribution, searchable recruitment agency database, discussion forum and free web-based e-mail accounts.

Aggressive Corp.
www.aggressivecorp.com
Provides executive search for mid-to-upper level management executives in manufacturing and H.R.

Alabama International Assistance Project
www.visaus.com/iapa.html
A volunteer organization that provides economic and family orientation assistance to Alabama's new international residents and long-term visitors.

Alexander Advertising
www.education-jobs.co.uk
Web site dedicated to finding education jobs in the United Kingdom

All-Java-Jobs.com
www.all-java-jobs.com
Where Java programmers and Java employers find each other for free

American Society of Association Executives
www.asaenet.org/CareerHeadquarters/index.html

America's HealthCare
www.healthcaresource.com/

Amby's Work Site
www.amby.com/worksite
Comprehensive site that offers info. and support through all stages of the employment process

America's Employers
www.americasemployers.com/

American Jobs
www.AmericanJobs.com/

America's Job Bank
www.ajb.dni.us

American Journalism Review
www.newslink.org/joblink.html

Ardelle Assoc./AA Temps
www.ardelle.com
Washington, D.C. employment agency that offers both permanent and temporary job openings

AreaJobs.com
www.areajobs.com
Focuses on local markets, connecting local candidates with local jobs.

AsiaNet
www.asia-net.com/

Associated Resume Writers
www2.ari.net/fedjobs
Need help landing a Government job? Look no Farther...leading government job site dedicated to assisting job seekers apply and land a government job!

Australian Job Search
www.jobsearch.gov.au

AutoHeadHunter.net
www.autoheadHunter.net
The Automotive industry's premier Internet job board.

Aviation Technical Jobs
www.avtechjobs.com
Employment opportunities for the Aviation Maintenance and Engineering community. Profiles of industry companies and listings of schools that are related to the aviation maintenance and engineering field.

Best Jobs in the USA Today
www.bestjobsusa.com/

BigJobs.net
www.bigjobs.net
Free resource for job seekers and employers to post resumes and open positions.

The Black Collegian
www.black-collegian.com/

Bloomberg.com
www.bloomberg.com/fun/jobs.html

BostonSearch.com
www.bostonsearch.com/

The Canadian Jobs Catalogue
www.kenevacorp.mb.ca/login.htm
Over 3,000 links to employment listings in Canada. Major job banks, specialty job banks, company listings, recruiters and career related information to employment in Canada.

Career Blazers
www.cblazers.com/

CareerBuilder
www.careerbuilder.com/
A Must See! Enter Your Dream Job, Salary, etc. and when their database finds a match, CareerBuilder will E-Mail you.

CareerChangeAbility.com
www.careerchangeability.com
Celia Paul Associates, a career management firm founded in 1980, specializes in career mobility planning for high-level professionals

CareerCity
www.careercity.com

Career.com
www.career.com
The source for thousands of jobs in every field all over the world. Has 7 different ways to narrow down a position: company, hot job, location, newgrad/professional status, international, and many more.

Career Counselors Consortium
careercc.org
Non-profit referral service for people seeking career counselors and Executive Coaches.

Career Exchange
www.careerexchange.com

Career Expo
www.careerexpo.com
An extensive job search database with online conferencing and a "people-match" program to e-mail you new jobs on a daily basis.

Careerhunters.com
www.careerhunters.com
Very comprehensive job and career web site portal. Also features e-resumes, articles, and career profiles.

Career Magazine
www.careermag.com/

CareerMart
www.careermart.com

Career Mosaic
www.careermosaic.com

Careernet
www.careernet.com
Career opportunities, job postings, internships, interview and job search strategies.

CareerNET, Career Resource Center
www.careers.org

CareerOutlook
www.careeroutlook.com
Resume and job posting site that allows jobseekers to submit their resume to prospective employers from anywhere in the world.

CareerOwl
www.careerowl.net
Canadian job site offering a personal search agent to search database of jobs for you!

Career Paradise
www.emory.edu/CAREER/

CareerPath.com
www.careerpath.com/

Careers, Not Just Jobs-The Wall Street Journal
careers.wsj.com

Careers By Design
www.careers-by-design.com
On-line career counseling service. Offers on-line assessments including the well respected Strong Interest Inventory, Myers-Briggs Type Indicator, and FIRO0-B. Also outplacement, interviewing skills and resume review.

Career Sciences
www.careersciences.com
Provides a step-by-step method for finding jobs.

Careersite
www.careersite.com

CareerWeb
www.cweb.com/

Casino Careers On-Line
www.casinocareers.com
The Internet's one stop shop to landing a job in the gaming industry...you can create and post resumes on-line for free.

Catalog-News.com
www.catalog-news.com
Job site for anyone looking for a job with a mail order catalog company

The Catapult
www.jobweb.org/catapult/catapult.htm

CityJobs Worldwide
www.cityjobs.com
UK's leading specialist recruitment web site, specializing in finance, IT, legal, accountancy and media jobs.

Classified Warehouse
www.classifiedwarehouse.com/

ClickITJobs
www.clickITjobs.com
A professional recruitment consultancy firm in India for placements in India, Australia, Singapore, Middle East and in the US.

College and University Job Sites
www.gslis.utexas.edu/~acadres/jobs/

College Grad Job Hunter
www.collegegrad.com/
Comprehensive job site for college grads - offers info on resumes, jobs, employers, networking, interviewing, plus much more!

Colorado Online Job Connection
coloradojobs.com
The premier web site for job seekers in Colorado.

ComputerJobs
www.computerjobs.com
Excellent site...search thousands of computer/high-tech jobs by city or state

ComputerWork
www.computerwork.com

ComputerWorld
www.computerworld.com

Contract Employment Weekly, Jobs Online
www.ceweekly.wa.com/

Cool Works
www.coolworks.com

CPAjobs.com
www.cpajobs.com
Job listings for CPAs at all levels. No fee for job seekers.

Creative Central
www.creativecentral.com
Interactive site for creative professionals in graphic design, marketing, advertising, animation and more.

Cruel World
www.cruelworld.com
A comprehensive job search and career management site. Formerly Career Central.

DatumEurope
www.datumeurope.com
Great site dedicated to anyone seeking a job in Europe

Datum-USA
www.datumeurope.com
Free jobs website for US positions

DGA
www.dga-inc.com
Recruiting firm specializing in placement to the property/casualty insurance market in Canada. Offers permanent, contract and temporary placement services

DriversAgent.com
www.DriversAgent.com
The Truck Drivers' Agent locating the best jobs for the best drivers.

EscapeArtist
www.escapeartist.com/jobs/overseas1.htm
Very comprehensive and helpful web site for the international job seeker

E Jobs: Environmental Jobs and Careers
www.ejobs.org
Great site for job seekers seeking an environmental job - E-Jobs offers a directory of employers in the environmental sector: gov't, companies, law firms, and non-profits.

Emploi Connexion
www.cihr-connexion.com
Recruitment agency specializing in the hospitality industry. Company is based in France but look for opportunities all over the world.

Employers Online
www.employersonline.com
Specializes in sales/marketing, computer/IT, engineering/technical, executive/professional, and medical/health care. Positions are geared toward professionals with salaries from $40k-$150k+ across the nation.

EmployU.com
www.EmployU.com
Recruiting site for college students. Students can search job leads, post resumes and find other helpful career information.

Enforcement Sources, Inc.
enforcementsources.intranets.com
Resources devoted to the law enforcement professional.

Engineer500.com
www.engineer500.com
A job posting web site devoted exclusively to engineers and technical professionals. Designed and maintained by engineers for engineers. Job seekers search the database for free.

EnviroNetwork
www.environetwork.com
Excellent site for anyone seeking an environmental job

The EPages Classifieds
ep.com

Equimax
www.equimax.com
Where jobs and horse people find each other. Online list of jobs and list of candidates. Books faq's and tips on the employment process.

EResumes
www.eresumes.com

E-Span, The Interactive Employment Network
www.espan.com/

Exclusive Search
www.clickITjobs.com
A professional recruitment consultancy firm in India for placements in India, Australia, Singapore, Middle East and in the US.

ExecSearches
www.education-jobs.co.uk
Offers executive and senior level management jobs in the non-profit industry

Exec-U-Net
www.execunet.com
Executive membership organization providing job & salary information, networking meetings, focused newsletters, tips and other resources for the executive making $100K+.

Experience on Demand
www.experienceondemand.com/

FairfieldCountyJobs.com
www.fairfieldcountyjobs.com
Job bank serving Fairfield, CT - including Stamford, Danbury, Bridgeport, and Norwalk. Browse by city, category or company name.

Fast Company
www.fastcompany.com

FINANCIALjobs.com
www.financialjobs.com
Jobs for accounting and finance professionals at all levels. No fee for job seekers. Winner of the "EERIE" Award for Excellence in Electronic Recruiting, Top 100 On-line Sites, from InterBizNet.

Florida Career Link
www.floridacareerlink.com
Job search tool for Orlando, Tampa, Jacksonville, and Miami. Information on FL job fairs, career planning, recruiters, and relocation.

4Work
www.4work.com

Free Resume Clearinghouse
www.mcs.com/~88k/free/index.html

Free Resume Tips
www.free-resume-tips.com
Provides 10 tips to bullet-proof your resume.

Gotajob.com
www.gotajob.com
Job site focusing on part-time, temporary, seasonal, and entry-level positions.

Graystone Partners
www.graystonepartners.com
Serves Global 1000 clients by identifying high-impact, general management and financial executives for key management positions.

GulfJobs
www.gulfjobs.com
Your gateway to career opportunities in the Middle East.

HeadHunter.Net
www.headhunter.net/

Healthcare Consultants Pharmacy Staffing
www.hccrxstaffing.com
Provides full & part-time staffing for the pharmacy industry. Focuses on the southeast US.

Health Care Source
www.HealthCareSource.com/
Very comprehensive healthcare job site...listing job openings nationwide

H.E.A.R.T
www.career.com/

Help Wanted.Com, YSS Inc.
www.helpwanted.com/

The Help Wanted Network
www.Help-Wanted.Net
Search over 2 million job postings from newsgroups, directly crawled jobs, and direct postings.

Hong Kong Jobs
www.hkjobs.com

Hire-Ed
www.hire-ed.org
Comprehensive site listing job opportunities at colleges and universities nationwide

Hireground
www.hireground.com

Hire Quality
www.hire-quality.com/

Hoover's
www.hoovers.com/

Hospital Classifieds
www.hospitalclassifieds.com/
Web site specializing in matching recruiters and job seekers in the fields of nursing, hospital administration, hospital admissions, environmental services, allied health staff, and physician staff.

HotJobs
www.hotjobs.com

HRMjobs.com
www.HRMjobs.com
Job site for HR professionals

The Huntington Group's Career Network
www.hgllc.com

IMCOR
www.imcor.com

Insuranceworks.com
www.insuranceworks.com
Job site focusing on the North American insurance market. Free for candidates to create resumes and cover letters, and search for jobs.

InternJobs.com
www.internjobs.com
Nationwide listing of internships

InternationalJobs.com
www.internationaljobs.com
Excellent directory and resource to international job sites!

Internetjobs.com
www.internetjobs.com
Job site specializing in Internet and web oriented positions.

The Internet Professional Association
www.ipa.com/

iPhysicianNet
wwwiphysiciannet.com
Site details many carreer opportunities available with this company.

JapanSearch
www.japansearch.bigstep.com
Executive search firm specializing in businesses in Japan.

Job & Adverts
www.ja-usa.com/index.html

JobBank USA
www.jobbankusa.com

Jobboard.net
www.jobboard.net
Career links to make finding career related sites easier. You can browse through the general links or select a specific industry of interest.

JobCenter
www.jobcenter.com

JobCircuit
www.JobsCircuit.co.uk
Sports job site located in the UK. Endorsed by Sport England, The National Playing Fields Assoc., The Central Council for Physical Recreation, Nike, Adidas, Reebok, and Dunlop Slazenger.

Jobcue.com
www.jobcue.com
Free resume posting and job finding resources. Has specialized areas for medical and IT positions.

JobDugOut
www.jobdugout.com

Job Engine
www.jobengine.com/

JobFind.com
www.jobfind.com

JobFolder.com
www.jobfolder.com
A free site for posting resumes and jobs for all career paths

JobFinders International, Inc.
www.jobfindersinc.com
Executive marketing firm with over 1,100 open positions on any given day - updated regularly.

Job Finders Online.com
www.jobfindersonline.com
Excellent site for job seekers starting their job search for government, private sector, non-profit or international jobs. Also includes a catalog of over 400 job search resources.

JobHunt:
www.job-hunt.org

Jobs for Bankers
www.bankjobs.com

Job Reference.com
jobreference.com

JobReviews.com
www.jobreviews.com
Specializes in user-generated reviews of different aspects of the job hunting process, including interviews, salaries, and the job position itself.

Job Searching Mining Co.
jobsearch.miningco.com

Jobsearchjunkie
www.jobsearchjunkie.com
Job search advice and humor.

JobSearchPlus
www.jobsearchplus.com/default.asp
Lots of jobs, great search interface, fast response.

Jobseekers
www.jobseekrs.com
Employment opportunities - no fees or registration forms for job seekers. Updated daily.

Job Site.com
www.jobsite.com
The internet's premiere job site specializing in real estate, construction and real estate finance.

JobSmart
www.jobsmart.org

Jobsmart Salary Guides
www.jobsmart.org/tools/salary/index.htm

Job Source Network
www.jobsourcenetwork.com
The Internet's Mega Job Site - scour the major job sites all at once with JSN's two search engines. JSN also list links to thousands of job sites worldwide. They also publish the Job Source Series for Baltimore, Pittsburgh, South Florida, Southern Califorinia, San Francisco and Washington, D.C.

JobsOnTheWeb.com
jobsontheweb.com
A membership cooperative comprised of over 400 professional employment firms and over 200 executive search firms.

Jobs Telecommuting
www.jobs-telecommuting.com

JobTrak
www.jobtrak.com

JobVillage
jobvillage.com
Search jobs from all the major job boards and from over 150,000 corporate human resource pages form one location. Also offers confidential resume database and career resources.

JobWeb
www.jobweb.org

JobWebs.com
www.jobwebs.com
A network of profession specific job sites dedicated to the California market. Offers free job posting, free resume hosting, job searching, news letter, and an automated job application procedure.

JustComputerJobs.com
www.JustComputerJobs.com
A jobsite for technology professionals with numerous technology-niche sites: telephony, networking, Java, etc.

Law Jobs
www.lawjobs.com

Lawoffice.com
www.lawoffice.com
Contains pragmatic, thorough, in-depth information for dealing with legal affairs. All information on Lawoffice.com is provided to users without charge.

LawEnforcementJob.com
www.lawenforcementjob.com
Employment information on municipal police, state police and patrol, sheriff, federal, international, corrections, university and college departments.

LocalHelpWanted.com
www.localhelpwanted.com

Home Page of Malachy
www.execpc.com/~maltoal/

Mancini Technical Recruiting (MTR)
www.m-t-r.com
Provides contingency recruiting services for IT companies nationwide.

Manpower
www.manpower.com/

Manufacturing Marketplace
www.manufacturing.net

Marketing Jobs
www.marketingjobs.com/
Comprehensive job site for anyone seeking a job in Advertising, Marketing and/or Sales

MDJobSite
www.mdjobsite.com
Physician opportunities for the year 2000 and beyond

MedSearch
www.medsearch.com

MediStaff
www.medistaff.com
Specialists in the placement of Medical Professionals

Megajobsites.com
www.megajobsites.com
Over 1,000 unique jobsites for job seekers and employers - 15,000 unique user sessions per day during the first 2 months.

Military Career Guide
www.militarycareers.com

The Monster Board
www.monster.com/

Monster International Zone
international.monster.com
Provides comprehensive career guidance on working and relocating abroad. You can also find jobs throughout the world on this area.

MountainJobs.com
www.mountainjobs.com
A network dedicated to bringing together professionals and mountain resort community employers. The premier resource for career opportunities and lifestyle information in the mountains.

National Association for the Self-Employed
selfemployed.nase.org/NASE/

NationJob Online Job Database
www.nationjob.com

Network of Advanced Home Employment
members.aol.com/sue121/noahe.html
Promotes career advancement opportunities and provides homebased employment solutions. Also offers dental, optical and medical benefits to homebased workers.

NETSHARE
www.netshare.com
A membership service designed to meet the career management needs of executives.

NPO.NET
www.npo.net
A good website for non-profit jobs in the Chicago area.

1-JOBS.com
www.1-jobs.com
Produces over 100 job fairs all across America and Canada.

1-800 People, Irish and International Online Recruitment
www.1-800people.com
Specializes in overseas recruitment and have positions available in Dublin, Vienna, Amsterdam, Sydney, Dusseldorf, New York and New Jersey.

1-2-3 Resume Service
www.thewhiteshouse.com/resume.html
Offers custom resume and cover letters at affordable rates.

Online Career Center
www.occ.com/

Orlando Sentinel
orlandosentinel.com/ClassPrototype/
ClassifiedsMainSearch.htm
The Orlando Sentinel Online is he best source for Orlando Classifieds.

PensacolaJobs
www.pensacolajobs.com
All you need to find a job in Pensacola, Florida.

PennsylvaniaJobs.com
www.PennsylvaniaJobs.com
For businesses and job-seekers in PA. Job posting and closed resume database for businesses. Ask The Professional, free resume posting, relocation and much more for job-seekers.

People, Irish and International Online Recruitment
www.1-800people.com
Specializes in overseas recruitment and have positions available in Dublin, Vienna, Amsterdam, Sydney, Dusseldorf, New York and New Jersey.

Peterson's Education Center: Careers and Jobs
www.petersons.com/career/

Philanthropy Journal
www.philanthropy-journal.org

PhysicianBoard
www.physicianboard.com/
An on-line database to match job-hunting physicians with employment opportunities. Doctors can search for free, and employers or recruiters can post for free.

PlanetEDU.com
www.planetedu.net
New address on the net for students and alumni to connect with entry level jobs and internships.

PlanetResume.com
www.planetresume.com
Premier job site for computer professionals offering technology jobs, resume posting, job searching and career resources.

Planet-Tech
www.planet-tech.net
East Coast connection for quality IT employment

Plumbook
www.access.gpo.gov/plumbook/toc.html

+Jobs Canada
www.canada.plusjobs.com
Canada-wide job database.

ProvenResumes
www.ProvenResumes.com
Resume writing tips, workshops. Teaches job seekers how to control and elevate the image they present in their resumes in order to land more interviews and higher salaries.

ProSearch Recruiters of Cleveland
www.prosearchrecruiters.com
National executive search firm specializing in the areas of Accounting, Automotive, Engineering, IT/MIS, Printing/Packaging, Construction, Chemical, Sales/ Marketing, Legal and Human Resources.

PSE-NET
www.pse-net.com/carerm.htm

Public Sector Jobs
www.publicsectorjobs.com
Comprehensive resource for career and job information in the public and private sectors

PsiSEARCH
www.psisearch.com
Comprehensive On-Line Job Center for computer professionals and employers. Offers easy-to-use service designed to help job seekers quickly find your ideal job!

PursuitNet
www.tiac.net/users/jobs/index.html

QA-JOBS.COM
www.qa-jobs.com
Dedicated to the "Quality Professional": quality assurance, quality control, software quality assurance, quality engineering, quality management, testing automated test development, etc.

RCQ Career Network
www.rcqcareernetwork.com
A job listing service connecting professionals with experience in the Regulatory Affairs, Clinical Research, Quality Assurance and other related areas to career opportunities in the pharmaceutical, medical device and biotechnology industries.

Recruiter's Online Network
www.ipa.com

Recruitinglinks.Com
www.recruiting-links.com

ResortJobs.com
www.resortjobs.com
Finding a job at a major resort hasn't been easier!

RestaurantJobsNetwork.com
www.restaurantjobsnetwork.com
An online employment service for restaurants, restaurant recruitment agencies, and job seekers.

RestaurantManagers.com
www.restaurantmanagers.com
Excellent on-line recruitment source for the restaurant industry.

Scientific Career Transitions
www.harbornet.com/biz/office/sct001.html
Helps scientists, engineers, and other credentialed professionals make a career transition and find appropriate work

Seasonal Employment.com
www.seasonalemployment.com
Great Site providing lot's of job openings for college students/grads

6FigureJobs
www.6figurejobs.com
Confidentially seek and be considered for some of the most prestigious jobs in the country. Also allows Executive Recruiters and employers to advertise positions to high-caliber professionals.

SummerJobs.com
www.summerjobs.com
Comprehensive database of summer jobs - easily search by state

Resumes for Federal Jobs
www2.ari.net/resume/fedgov.html

Rezamaze.com
www.rezamaze.com
Professional resume writing and job search management services/support for IT, MIS, Engineering and Science professionals.

Rifood.com
www.rifood.com
Comprehensive web site for anyone seeking a job in the restaurant and hospitality industry.

Riley Guide
www.dbm.com/jobguide

Robert Half
www.roberthalf.com/jobsRH/

Saludos Web Site
www.saludos.com

Seniorjobbank
www.seniorjobbank.com
Independent non-profit that provides services for senior citizens wishing to re-enter the job marketplace on a PT, temporary or occasional basis.

Seasonal Employment.com
www.seasonalemployment.com
Great Site providing lot's of job openings for college students/grads

Sims Associates
www.simassoc.com
Executive recruiting firm specializing in mid and up per-level management positions in the pharmaceutical, manufacturing and consumer products industries in the CT, NY, and NJ areas.

Snelling Personnel
www.snelling.com
Excellent site for individuals seeking temp jobs nationwide.

Social Work and Social Services Career Guide
128.252.132.4/jobs/index.html

Source Services
www.experienceondemand.com

So. California Job Center
www.so-cal-jobs.com
Offers lots of links, and phone numbers to finding a job in So. California

Spin Control.com
www.spincontrol.com/jobs.html
OnLine Music Industry Jobs Board - specializes in professional positions and internships at major and independent record labels, pr and marketing agencies nationwide.

SportLink
www.sportlink.com
Comprehensive site that offers sports industry job openings.

Staffing World
www.staffingworld.com
Job site designed for all job seekers and HR professionals

StartupNetwork
www.StartupNetwork.com
An on-line recruitment site dedicated exclusively to pre-IPO high tech startups.

SuccessFinder
www.successfinder.com
Guide for information technology professionals searching for career opportunities in Michigan

Texas Workforce Commission
www.twc.state.tx.us/jobs/job.html

ThePavement.com
www.thepavement.com
A comprehensive career-building service for young adults with zero to five years of work experience. Includes database of entry-level and early-career job opportunities and addresses money management, relocation, apartment-hunting, car-buying, etc.

Tiburon Group Inc.
www.tiburongroup.com/
An Internet recruiting consulting firm which specializes in helping e-commerce companies with multiple hiring needs. Services range from job posting administration and advanced resume mining to custom outsourced solutions.

TheWorkSite.com
www.theworksite.com
Impressive free site exclusively for developers and developer employers

Top Jobs in the UK
www.topjobs.net/

Topjobs USA
www.topjobsusa.com/

TriangleJobs
www.trianglejobs.com/

TV Jobs
www.tvjobs.com

TviJobs
www.tvijobs.com
Job site dedicated to the finding jobs for Indians Globally...offers Free confidential resume registration service and job search plus Free e-mail updates on new jobs.

200 Letters for Job Hunters
www.careerlab.com/letters

UK-Top Jobs
www.topjobs.net/

Vermont Jobs
www.vtjobs.com
Vermont's premier job placement service. Temp and permanent placement for technical and non-technical fields.

The Virtual Job Fair
www.vjf.com

Wall Street Journal Careers
careers.wsj.com

Wanted Jobs 98
www.wantedjobs.com
Free software agent searches over 25 top job sites and offers access to over 2 million job listings nationwide

Weddle's Web Guide
www.lawoffice.com

William and Mary, Career Services
www.wm.edu/csrv/career/index.html

Wiredsearch.com
www.wiredsearch.com
High-tech job bank with free resume posting &; job postings.

WorkInBoston.com
www.workinboston.com
A job posting site with internships and job opportunities from organizations all across the metro Boston area.

Work Index
www.workindex.com

Work-Web
www.work-web.com

Working Mothers 100 Best Companies to work for
www.women.com/work/best/

A Write Impression
www.awriteimpression.com
Resume and cover letter writing at affordable prices. Job search and interview tips, career links and more.

The World Wide Web Employment Office
www.harbornet.com/biz/office/annex.html

Yahoo's Classifieds
classifieds.yahoo.com

Yahoo's listings of business employment
www.yahoo.com/Business/Employment

ZD Net Salary Zone
www8.zdnet.com/zdimag/salaryzone/

For More Job and
Career Web-Sites
Visit JobSourceNetwork.com

LOCAL JOB SITES

California Career & Employment Center
http://webcom/~career/welcome.html

California Online Job Network
www.cajobs.com

Federal Government Jobs in California
ftp://ftp.fedworld.gov/pub/jobs/ca.txt

Job Smart Los Angeles
www.jobsmart.org/socal/index.htm

Job Smart San Diego
www.jobsmart.org/sd/index.htm

Los Angeles Times Job Tips/ Classifieds   www.latimes.com

Orange County Careers
www.orangecountycareers.com

Orange County Register Classifieds
www.ocregister.com/ads/classified/
html/employ.htm

San Diego Jobs
www.sandiegojobs.com

San Diego Online
www.sandiego-online.com

San Diego Source
www.sddt.com

San Diego Union-Tribune Interactive Job Listings
www.uniontrib.com/aboutut/

Southern California CityNet
www.city.net/countries/united_states/
california/southern_california

Southern California Job Board
www.gojobs.com/socal/jobsearch.htm

Southern California job Career Helpline
www.so-cal-jobs.com

Technology Job Source
www.sddt.com/jobsource

Virtually Los Angeles
www.virtually.com/los_angeles/

Work Avenue.com
www.workavenue.com

Yahoo Los Angeles
www.layahoo.com

Company Web Sites

A great way to learn more about a company or industry you are interested in is by visiting their web site. Corporate web sites offer everything from mission statements, goals and objectives, financial information, key personnel and addresses to products and services they provide.

Accounting

ADP/Automatic Data Processing
www.adp.com
Alder Green Hasson & Janks
www.aghjcpa.com
Altschuler Melvoin and Glasser
www.amgnet.com
Arthur Andersen
www.arthurandersen.com
Bates Coughtry Reiss & Company
www.bcrcpa.aol.com
BDO Seidman
www.bdo.com
Biggs & Company
www.biggsco.com
Braverman Codron & Company
www.brav.com
Bruno Mack & Barclay
www.bmconsult.com
Cairns Haack Eng Applegate
www.cairns/haack.com
Considine & Considine
www.cccpa.com
Deloitte & Touche
www.dttus.com
Duitch, Franklin & Co.
www.dfco.com
Elliott Lewis Lieber & Stumpf
www.ellscpas.com
Ernst & Young
www.ey.com
Frazer & Torbet
www.msftllp.com
Glenn M. Gelman & Associates
www.gmgcpa.com
Good Swartz & Berns
www.gsbcpa.com
Grant Thornton
www.gt.com
Gursey Schneider & Company
www.gursey.com
Haskell & White
www.hwcpa.com
Kellogg & Andelson Accounting
www.k-a.com
KPMG Peat Marwick
www.kpmg.com
McGladrey & Pullen CPAs & Consultants
www.mcgladrey.com
Moss Adams
www.mossadams.com
Nanas Stern Biers Neinstein & Co.
www.nsbn.com
Ozur Andersen & Radder
www.oarcpa.com/oar
Pacific Computer Systems
www.payrollservices.com
Parks Palmer Turner & Yemenidjian
www.ppty.com

Paychex
www.paychex.com
Price Waterhouse Coopers
www.pwcglobal.com
Stonefield Josephson Accounting.
www.sjaccounting.com
White Nelson & Co CPA & Conslt
www.whitenelson.com
Wiegel Szekel & Walker
www.wsw.cpa.com

Advertising/Marketing

AM Advertising
www.amadvertising.com
Asher & Partners
www.asherpartners.com
Bates USA
www.bates.com
BBDO West
www.bbdo.com
Campbell Ewald
www.campbellewald.com
Casanova Pendrill
www.casanova.com
D'Arcy Masius Benton & Bowles
www.dmbb.com
Dailey & Associates
www.dailey&abs.com
DavisElen
www.daviselen.com
DDB Needham Worldwide
www.ddb.com
Fisher Business Communications
www.fbiz.com
Foote, Cone, & Belding
www.fcb.com
G2 Advertising
www.g2.com
Gavin & Gavin Advertising
www.gavinandgavin.com
Ground Zero
www.groundzero.net
Hunter Barth
www.hunterbarth.com
InterCommunications
www.intercommunications.com
J2 Marketing Services
www.j2marketing.com
McCann-Erickson Los Angeles
www.mccann.com
Ogilvy & Mather
www.ogilvy.com
Rubin Postaer and Associates
www.rpa.com
Saatchi & Saatchi Los Angeles
www.saatchila.com
Seiniger Advertising
www.seiniger.com
TBWA Chiat/Day
www.chiatday.com

Team One Advertising
www.teamoneadv.com
The Gallup Organization
www.gallup.com
The Townsend Agency
www.townsendagency.com
The Verity Group
www.verity-group.com
TMP Worldwide
www.tmp.com

Aerospace & Defense

Aerofit Products
www.aerofit.com
Astech
www.astechmfg.com
Aviation Distributors Incorporated
www.adi-inc.com
Boeing Company
www.boeing.com
Contour Aerospace
www.ccindustries.com
Electrol Manufacturing Co
www.electromfg.com
Hawker Pacific Aerospace
www.hawker.com
Hughes Aircraft
www.hughes.com
Interstate Electronics Corp
www.iehome.com
Kaiser Electroprecision
www.kaiserep.com
Kaynar Technologies
www.kaynar.com
L'Garde
www.lgarde.com
Nellcor Puritan Bennett/Wemac
www.nellcorpb.com
Newmar
www.newmarpower.com
Parker Aerospace
www.parker.com
Southwest Aerospace
www.meggitt.com
Tolo Incorporated
www.tolo.com
Tri-Tech Precision
www.verisurf.com
Weber Aircraft
www.weberair.com
Western Design Howden
www.wd.com
Wills Wing
www.willswing.com

Arts & Culture

Action Video Productions
www.4avideo.com

Association of California School Administrators
www.acsa.org
Fleet, Rueben H., Space Theater and Science Center
www.rhfleet.org
Four Square Productions
www.foursquare.com
Granite Bridge Studio
www.granitebridge.com
Kidspace Museum
http://home.earthlink.net/kidspacem
Los Angeles Children's Museum
www.lacm.org
Los Angeles County Museum of Art
www.lacma.org
Multi Image Productions
www.multiimage.com
Museum of Contemporary Art
www.moca-la.org
Natural History Museum, Balboa Park
www.sdnhm.org
Orange County Museum of Art
www.ocartsnet.org/ocma
Pacific Asia Museum
www.pacasiamuseum.aol.com
Richard Nixon Library/Birthplace
www.nixonfoundation.org
SAIC Video Productions
www.saic.com
San Diego Museum of Contemporary Art
www.mcsd.org
Society of Critical Care Medicine
www.sccm.org
Solar Turbines Corp Video Communications
www.solar.cat.com
Sotheby's
www.sothebys.com
The Bowers Museum/Cultural Art
www.bowers.org
UCLA/Armand Hammer Museum
www.hammerucla.edu

Associations/Non-Profit

Beverly Hills Chamber of Commerce
www.beverlyhillscc.org
Burbank Chamber of Commerce
http://burbank.acityline.com
Catalina Island Visitors Bureau
www.catalina.com
Community Associations Institute
www.caioc.com
Culver City Chamber of Commerce
www.culvercitychamber.org
Easter Seal Society of Southern California
www.essc.org
Hollywood Chamber of Commerce
chamber.hollywood.com
Industry Manufacturers Council
www.ind-chmbr.com
Italy-America Chamber of Commerce West
www.italchambers.net
Pasadena Chamber of Commerce
www.pasadena-chamber.org
Redondo Beach Chamber of Commerce
www.redondochamber.org
San Pedro Peninsula Chamber of Commerce
www.sanpedrochamber.com

Santa Monica Area Chamber of Commerce
www.smchamber.com
Torrance Area Chamber of Commerce
www.torrancechamber.com
West Covina Chamber of Commerce
www.covina.org
Western Growers Association
www.wga.org

Banking & Finance

Aetna Capital Company
www.aetnacapital.com
American First Federal Credit Union
www.amerfirst.org
American Management Systems
www.amsinc.com
American Pacific State Bank
www.apsb.com
Analytic TSA Global Asset Management
www.analytic-tsa.com
Andersen Consulting
www.ac.com
Arthur Andersen
www.arthurandersen.com
Asian Pacific Bank
www.traders.net
Balboa Capitol Corp
www.balboacapital.com
Bank of Commerce
www.bankofcommerce.net
Baxter Credit Union
www.bch.org
BNC Mortgage
www.lonemortgage.com
Broadway Federal Bank
www.broadwayFed.com
BTA Advisory Group
www.standel.com
Cabrillo Federal
www.cabrrillofcu.com
California Korea Bank
www.ckb.net
California State Bank
www.calstatebank.com
Capital Guardian Trust Co.
www.americanfunds.com
Capital Research & Management Company
www.americanfunds.com
Citizens Business Bank
www.cbb.com
City National Bank
www.cityntl.com
Cruttenden Roth Incorporated
www.crut.com
Domain Associates
www.dimensionfunding.com
Downey Savings & Loan
www.downeysavings.com
Drake Beam Morin
www.dbm.com
East-West Bank
www.eastwest.com
Eldorado Bank
www.eldoradobank.com
Electronic Clearing House
www.echo-inc.com
Enterprise Partners
www.ent.com
Ernst & Young
www.ey.com
Evangelical Christian Cred Union
www.eccu.com

EVEREN Securities
www.everensec.com
Executive Service Corps
www.escsc.org
Fallbrook National Bank
www.fallbrooknationalbank.com
Family Savings Bank
www.blkbusiness-expo.com
Financial Federal
www.finacial21.com
First American Trust Company
www.firstam.com
First Quadrant Corp.
www.firstquadrant.com
Foothill Independent Bancorp
www.foothillindbank.com
Gage Marketing Group
www.gage.com
Gardiner & Rauen
www.gardine-raven.com
GBS Financial
www.gbsfinancial.com
Grant Thornton
www.gt.com
Great American Credit Union
www.greatamerican.org
Grossmont Bank
www.grossmontbank.com
Home Savings of America
www.homesavings.com
Impac Funding Corp
www.impaccompanies.com
IMPAC Integrated Systems
www.impac.com
Imperial Bank
www.imperialbank.com
Imperial Thrift & Loan Association
www.imperialthrift.com
Interfirst Capital Corp
www.interfirstcap.com
Itex Corporation
www.itex.com
J.D. Power and Associates
www.jdpower.com
John Hancock Financial Services
www.jhancock.com
Kline Hawkes California LP
www.klinehawkes.com
Koll Co/Strategic HR Services
www.totalemployee.com
Lease Express
www.leasex.com
Lee Hecht Harrison
www.careerlhh.com
Los Angeles National Bank
www.lanatlbank.com
Management Action Programs
www.mapconsulting.com
Manufacturers Bank
www.maubank.com
Marine National Bank
www.marinebank.com
Marwit Capital Corp. LLC
www.marwit.com
McDonnell Douglas Federal Credit Union
www.mdwfcu.org
Media Technology Ventures
www.mtventures.com
Merrill Lynch Private Client
www.merrill-lynch-ml.com
Met Life Pensions
www.metlife.com
Miramar Federal
www.miramarfcu.org
Mission Federal
www.missionfcu.org

National Bank of Southern California
www.scbnk.com
National Pacific Mortgage Corp
www.fha203kexpert.com
Nazarene Credit Union
www.nazarene.com
NWQ Investment Management Co.
www.nwq.com
Orange County Business Council
www.ocbc.org
Orange County Federal Credit Union
www.ocfcu.org
Orange County Teachers Federal
Credit Union
www.octfcu.org
Pacific Crest Capital
www.paccrest.com
Pacific National Bank
www.pacificnationalbank.com
Pacific Thrift & Loan
www.pacthrift.com
PFF Bank & Trust
www.pffb.com
PIMCO Advisors Holdings L.P.
www.pimcoadvisors.com
PLG
www.plg.com
Point Loma Federal
www.plfcu.com
Price Waterhouse Coopers
Consulting
www.pwc.global.com
Provident Investment Counsel
www.provnet.com
Republic Bank California
www.rbca.com
Right Management Consultants
www.right.com
Roger Engemann & Associates
www.secapl.com/rea
Roxbury Capital Management
www.roxcap.com
San Diego County Credit Union
www.sdccu.com
San Diego Teachers' Credit Union
www.sdtcu.org
Scripps Bank
www.scrippsbank.com
Silicon Valley Bank
www.sivio.com
SM&A
www.smawins.com
Smith Barney
www.smithbarney.com
Source Consulting
www.sourcesvc.com
South Western Federal Credit Union
www.swscu.com
Southern California Bank
www.scbank.com
SunAmerica
www.sunamerica.com
Sutro & Co.
www.sutro.com
The First American Financial
Corporation
www.firstam.com
The Geneva Companies
www.genevaco.com
The TCW Group
www.tcw.com
Towers Perrin
www.towers.com
U.S. Trust Company of California
www.ustrust.com
Union Bank of California
www.uboc.com

United Services of America Federal
www.fedcu.org
University & State Employees
www.webmaster.usecu.org
Valutech
www.valutech.com
Waddell & Reed
www.waddell.com
Watson Wyatt Worldwide
www.watsonwyatt.com
Wedbush Morgan Securities
www.wedbush.com
Wescom Credit Union
www.wescom.com
William M. Mercer
www.mercer.com

Media & Communications

AAC Corporation
www.aaccorp.com
ABC Entertainment
www.abc.com
ACC Communications
www.workforceonline.com
Access Television Network
www.AccessTV.com
Antelope Valley Press
www.avpress.com
Applied Digital Access
www.ada.com
Atel Communications
www.atelcommunications.com
BNI Publications
www.bni-books.com
Books on Tape
www.booksontape.com
Brilliant Digital Entertainment
www.bde3.com
Claricom, Inc.
www.claricom.com
Coded Communications Corporation
www.coded.com
ComCast Cable Ad Sales
www.comcast.com
Corridor News
www.pomeradonews.com
Creative Teaching Press
www.creativeteaching.com
Database Publishing Company
www.databasepublishing.com
Day Runner
www.dayrunner.com
Fabians Investment Resource
www.fabian.com
Frames Data
www.framesdata.com
Freedom Communications
www.freedom.com
General Instrument Corporation
www.gi.com
Haas Publishing
www.aptguides.com
Harte-Hanks Pennysaver/Shopper
www.hhinteractive.com
Homebuyers Guide
www.hbg.com
Homes for Sale Magazine
www.homeforsale-socal.com
Installnet
www.ask-inet.com
Investor's Business Daily
www.investors.com
KABC-AM (790)
www.kabc.com
KBNT, Channel 19
www.kbnttv19.com
KBZT-FM

www.gpc.com/gpcc-job.html
KCBS-FM (93)
www.arrowfm.com
Kelley Blue Book
www.kbb.com
KEZY-FM/KORG-AM
www.kezy.com
KFMB-AM/FM & Channel 8
www.760kfmb.com (am),
www.histar.com (fm),
www.kfmbtv8.com (tv)
KFWB-AM (980)
www.kfwb.com
KGB-FM
www.101.kgb.com
KIFM-FM
www.kifm.com
KKBT-FM (92.3)
www.thebeatla.com
KLAC-AM (570)
www.kbig104.com
KLSX-FM (97.1)
www.fmtalk971.com
KMEX Channel 34
www.kmex.com
KMZT-FM (105.1)
www.kmozart.com
KNI Incorporated
www.kninc.com
Knowledge Adventure
www.adventure.com
KNSD-TV, Channel 7
www.nbc739.com
KNX-AM (1070)
www.knx1070.com
KOCE-TV Channel 50
www.koce.com
KPBS-TV, Channel 15
www.kpbs.org
KSDO-AM
www.ksdoradio.com
KTWV-FM (94.7)
www.947wave.com
KYXY-FM
www.kyxy.com
KZLA-FM (93.9)
www.kzla.com
La Opinion
www.laopinion.com
Los Angeles Times
www.latimes.com
Maranatha Music
www.maranathamusic.com
McMullen Publishing
www.mcmullenargus.com
Mitel Telephone Systems
www.mitel.com
North County Times
www.nctimes.com
Orange Coast Magazine
www.orangecoast.com
Orange County Business Journal
www.ocjournal.com
OSI COM Technologies
www.osicom.com
Poway News Chieftain
www.pomeradonews.com
RF Industries Ltd.
www.rfindustries.com
San Diego Business Journal
www.sdbj.com
San Diego Daily Transcript
www.sddt.com
Scoop
www.scoopnews.com
Sea Magazine
www.seamag.com

Siemens Business
Communication Systems
www.siemenscom.com
Sound Source Interactive
www.soundsourceinteractive.com
Standard Tel
www.standardtel.com
Surfer Publications
www.surfermag.com
Teacher Created Materials
www.teachercreated.com
Teldata Voice and Data Communications
www.teldatausa.com
The Anaheim Bulletin
www.ocregister.com
The Orange County Register
www.ocregister.com
The San Diego Union-Tribune
www.uniontrib.com
Thomas Brothers Maps
www.thomas.com
TrialVision
www.trialvision.com
Tustin News
www.ocregister.com
TV/COM
www.tvcom.com
Volt Information Sciences
www.volt-resume.com
XHRM-FM
www.92five.com
XHTZ-FM
www.z90.com
XTRA-AM
www.xtrasports.com
XTRA-FM
www.91x.com

Design & Engineering

AC Martin Partners
www.acmartin.com
Altoon & Porter Architects
www.altoonporter.com
Aref Associates
www.aref.com
Burkett & Wong Engineers
www.burkett-wong.com
Carrier Johnson Wu
www.carrierjohnson.com
Daniel Mann Johnson & Mendenhall
www.dmjm.com
Danielian Associates
www.danielian.com
DMJM Rottet
www.dmjm.com
Ehrlich-Rominger Architects
www.erlich.com
Environetics Group
www.environetics.group
Fluor Corporation
www.fluor.com
Hellmuth Obata & Kassabaum
www.hok.com
HKS Architects
www.hksinc.com
HNTB Corp/West Division
www.hntb.com
Hunsaker & Associates San Diego
www.hunsaker.com
James Leary Architecture &
Planning
www.jlap.com
Janice Stevenor Dale & Associates
www.jsda.com
Johnson Fain Partners
www.jfpartners.com

Klages Carter Vail & Partners
www.kcv.com/kcv
Langdon Wilson Architectural
Planning
www.langdonwilson.com
Leidenfrost/Horowitz & Associates
www.iharchitect.com
McGraw/Baldwin Architects
www.mbarch.com
Montgomery Watson
www.mw.com
Nasland Engineering
www.nasland.com
Neptune-Thomas-Davis
www.ntd.com
Parsons Brinckerhoff
www.pbworld.com
Robert Bein, William Frost &
Associates
www.rbf.com
Rochlin Baran & Balbona
www.rbbinc.colm
TBP Architecture
www.tbparch.com
The Stichler Design Group
www.stichler.com
Wimberly Allison Tong & Goo
www.watg.com
Woodward-Clyde Consultants
www.wcc.com
WWTCOT Morimoto Interiors
www.wwcarch.com
Zimmer Gunsul Frasca Partnership
www.zgf.com

Education

Anaheim City School District
www.acsd.k12.ca.us
Anaheim Union High School District
www.auhsd.k12.ca.us
Antelope Valley Union High School
District
www.avdistrict.org
Azusa Unified School District
www.azusa.usd.k12.ca.us
Bellflower Unified School District
www.busd.k12.ca.us
Bonita Unified School District
www.bonita.k12.ca.us
Brea-Olinda Unified School District
www.ocde.k12.ca.us
California Institute of Technology
www.caltech.edu
California School of Professional
Psychology
www.webcom.com
California State Polytechnic
University
www.csupomona.edu
California State University
Dominguez Hills
www.csudu.edu
California State University, Fullerton
www.fullerton.edu
California State University, Long
Beach
www.csulb.edu
California State University Los
Angeles
www.csula.edu
California State University,
Northridge
www.hrs.csun.edu
California State University, San
Marcos
www.csusm.edu

Capistrano Unified School
District
www.capousd.k12.ca.us
Castaic Union School District
www.castaic.k12.ca.us
Cerritos College
www.cerritos.edu
Chapman Univ/School of Business
www.chapman.edu/sbe
Chapman University
www.chapman.edu
Charter Oak Unified School District
www.cousd.k12.ca.us
Christian Heritage College
www.christianheritage.edu
Coast Community College
www.cccb.edu
Coastline Community College
www.coastline.cccd.edu
Coleman College
www.coleman.edu
College of the Canyons
www.coc.cc.ca.us
Compton Community College
District
www.compton.cc.ca.us
Concordia University
www.cui.edu
Culver City Unified School District
www.ccusd.ca.us
Downey Unified School District
www.dusd.net
Eastside Christian School &
Pre-School
www.eastsidechristian.org
El Camino College
www.elcamino.cc.ca.us
El Monte City School District
www.emcsd.k12.ca.us
El Rancho Unified School District
www.erusd.k12.ca.us
Fairmont Private
www.fairmontschool.org
Fullerton College
www.fullcoll.edu
Fullerton School District
www.fsd.k12.ca.us
Garden Grove Unified School District
www.ggusd.k12.ca.us
Glendale Community College District
www.glendale.cc.ca.us
Glendale Unified School District
www.gusd.jpl.nasa.gov
Glendora Unified School District
www.glendora.k12.ca.us
Golden Gate University
www.ggu.edu
Golden West College
www.gwc.cc.edu
Grossmont College
www.gcccd.cc.ca.us
Hacienda La Puente Unified School
District
www.hlpusd.k12.ca.us
Harbor Day
www.hds.pvt.k12.ca.us
Hawthorne School District
www.hawthornek12.ca.us
Heritage Oak
www.heritageoak.pvt.k12.ca.us
Hughes-Elizabeth Lakes Union
School District
www.helus.org
Huntington Beach Union High
School District
www.hbuhsd.k12.ca.us
Irvine Unified School District
www.iusd.k12.ca.us

Irvine Valley College
www.ivc.cc.ca.us
ITT Technical Institute
www.itttech.com
Kelsey-Jenney College
www.kelsey-jenney.com
Keppel Union School District
www.keppel.k12.ca.us
La Canada Unified School District
www.lcusd.k12.ca.us
La Jolla Country Day School
www.ljcds.pvt.k12.ca.us
La Purisima Elementary
www.ocweb.com/lps
Lancaster School District
www.lancaster.k12.ca.us
Las Virgenes Unified School District
www.lvusd.k12.ca.us
Lawndale School District
www.lawndale.k12.ca.us
Lennox School District
www.lennox.k12.ca.us
Liberty Christian
www.libertychristian.org
Long Beach Community College
District
www.lbcc.cc.ca.us
Los Alamitos Unified School District
www.losalusd.k12.ca.us
Los Angeles City College
www.lacc.cc.ca.us
Los Angeles Community College
District
www.laccd.edu
Los Angeles County Office of
Education
www.lacoe.edu
Los Angeles Trade Technical College
www.lattc.edu
Lowell Joint School District
www.lsw.lacoe.edu
Lutheran High of Orange County
www.lutheranhigh.orange.ca.us
Lynwood Unified School District
www.lynwood.k12.ca.us
MiraCosta College
www.miracosta.cc.ca.us
Montebello Unified School District
www.montebello.k12.ca.us
Mt. San Antonio Community College
District
www.mtsac.edu
National University
www.nu.edu
Newport-Mesa Unified School
District
www.nmusd.k12.ca.us
Norwalk-La Mirada Unified School
District
www.nlmusd.k12.ca.us
Oakridge Tustin
www.oakridgetustin.com
Ocean View School District
www.ovsd.k12.ca.us
Orange Coast College
www.occ.cc.ca.edu
Orange County Christian-CC
www.occs.aol.com
Orange Unified School District
www.orangeusd.k12.ca.us
Our Lady Queen of Angels
www.olga.org
Pacific Christian College
www.pacificcc.edu
Page School of Costa Mesa
www.pageschool.com
Palmdale School District
www.psd.k12.ca.us

Palomar College
www.palomar.edu
Palos Verdes Peninsula Unified
School District
www.pupusd.k12.ca.us
Pasadena Area Community College
District
www.paccd.cc.ca.us
Pasadena Unified School District
www.pasadena.k12.ca.us
Pegasus
www.pegasus.pvt.k12.ca.us
Pepperdine University
www.pepperdine.edu
Placentia-Yorba Linda Unified School
District
www.plyusd.k12.ca.us
Point Loma Nazarene College
www.ptloma.edu
Pomona Unified School District
www.pomona.k12.ca.us
Prentice Day
www.prentice.org
Redondo Beach School District
www.bnet.org
Rio Hondo Community College
www.rhcc.ca.us
Saddleback College
www.saddleback.cc.ca.us
Saddleback Valley Unified School
District
www.svusd.k12.ca.us
Saint Barbara
www.saintbarbara.com
Saint Bonaventure Elementary
www.saintbonaventure.org
Saint John's Lutheran
www.stjohnsluthern.org
Saint Margaret's
www.saintmargarets.org
San Diego City College
www.sdccd.cc.ca.us
San Diego Mesa College
www.sdmesa.sdccd.cc.ca.us
San Diego State University
www.sdsu.edu
Santa Ana Unified School District
www.sausd.k12.ca.us
Santa Margarita Catholic High
www.smhs.org
Santa Monica College
www.smc.edu
Santa Monica-Malibu Unified School
District
www.smmus.org
Saugus Union School District
www.saugus.k12.ca.us
Serra Catholic Elementary
www.serraschool.org
South Orange County Community
College District
www.saddleback.cc.ca.us
Southern California College
www.sccu.edu
Southwestern College
www.swc.cc.ca.us
Sulphur Springs School District
www.ssd.k12.ca.us
The Bishop's School
www.bishops.com
Thomas Jefferson School of
Law
www.jeffersonlaw.edu
United States International
University
www.usiu.edu
University of California at Los
Angeles
www.ucla.edu

University of California Irvine
www.icu.edu
University of California, San Diego
www.admissions.ucsd.edu
University of Phoenix
www.uophx.edu/sandiego
University of San Diego
www.acusd.edu
Walnut Valley Unified School District
— Personal Services
www.walnut-valley.k12.ca.us
Webster University
www.websteruniv.edu
West Los Angeles College
www.wlac.edu
Western State University/Law
www.wsulaw.edu
Westside Union School District
www.westside.k12.ca.us
Whittier Christian High
www.wchs.com
Whittier Law School
www.law.whitier.edu
William S. Hart Union High School
District
www.hart.k12.ca.us
Wilsona School District
www.wison.k12.ca.us

Entertainment

40 Acres & A Mule Filmworks
http://40acres.com
A Band Apart
www.AandE.com
ABC Entertainment
http://abc.com
ABC Pictures
http://abc.com
Abigail Abbott Staffing Svcs
www.abigailabbott.com
Accountants Overload
www.accountantsoverload.com
Bench International
www.benchinternational.com
Buena Vista Productions
www.disney.com
Campus Crusade for Christ
www.campuscrusade.com
Caravan Pictures
www.caravan.com
Castle Rock Entertainment
www.castle-rock.com
CBS Entertainment
www.cbs.com
CDI Corporation-West
www.cdicorp.com
Columbia Pictures
www.spe.sony.com
Columbia Tristar Motion Picture
Group
www.sonypicturesjobs.com
Columbia Tristar Pictures
www.spe.sony.com
Columbia Tristar Television
www.spe.sony.com
Comedy Central
comedycentral.com
Complete Post
www.completepost.com
Crest National Optical Media
www.crestnational.com
Dimension Films
www.dimensionfilms.com
Disney Channel
www.disneychannel.com
DreamWorks SKG
http://showbizjobs.com

E! Entertainment Television
www.eonline.com

Fest of Arts/Pageant of Masters
www.foapom.com

Four Media Company
www.4mc.com

Fox Broadcasting Company
www.foxworld.com

Fox Kids Network
www.foxworld.com

Harpo Films
www.oprah.com

HBO Pictures
www.hbo.com

Hearst Entertainment
www.hearst.com

HRCS
www.hrcs.com

Image Entertainment
www.image-entertainment.com

Imax Corporation
www.imax.com

Irvine Barclay Theatre Operating Company
www.irvinebarclaytheatre.com

Iwerks Entertainment
www.iwerks.com

Jim Henson Company
www.henson.com

Lifetime Television (LA)
www.lifetimetv.com

Marvel Studios
www.marvel.com

McCray & Associates
www.mccray-inc.com

Medcom Trainex
www.medcominc.com

Merv Griffen Productions
www.merv.com

Miramax Films
www.miramax.com

National Geographic Television
www.nationalgeographic.com

NBC Entertainment
http://nbc.com

Netter Digital Entertainment
www.netterdigital.com

New Line Cinema
www.newline.com

New Regency Productions
www.newregency.com

Orange County Performing Arts
www.ocartsnet.org/ocpa

Pacific Ocean Post
www.popstudios.com

Paramount Network Television
www.paramount.com

Paramount Pictures
www.paramount.com

Paramount Television Group
www.paramount.com

Playboy Entertainment Group
www.playboy.com

Polygram Filmed Entertainment
www.reellife.com\pfe

Post Group
www.postgroup.com

Ray & Berndtson
www.rayberndtson.com

Remedy Intelligent Staffing
www.remedystaff.com

Rysher Entertainment
www.rysher.com

Showtime Networks
www.showtimeonline.com

Sony Pictures Entertainment
www.spe.sony.com/

Sony Pictures Imageworks
www.spiw.com

Stanton Chase International
www.stantonchase.com

The Dial Group
www.dialworks.com

Thomas Staffing Services
www.thomas-staffing.com

TLC Services Group
www.tlcsvcsgrp.com

Turner Network Television
www.turner.com

Twentieth Century Fox
www.fox.com

United Artists Pictures
www.mgmua.com

United Paramount Network
www.upn.com

Universal Studios
www.universalstudios.com

USA Networks / Television Group
www.universalstudios.com

Walt Disney Pictures / Touchstone Pictures
www.disney.com

Warner Brothers Feature Animation, Pictures, TV Animation & Prod.
www.warnerbros.com

Yale Video
www.yalevideo.com

Healthcare

Aetna US HealthCare
www.aetna.com/joblink

Allergan
www.allergan.com

Alliance Imaging
www.allianceimaging.com

Applied Cardiac Systems
www.ocsholter.com

ARV Assisted Living
www.arvi.com

Baxter Healthcare Corporation
www.baxter.com

BBI-Source Scientific
www.sourcesci.com

Beckman Instruments
www.beckman.com

Beech Street Corporation
www.beechstreet.com

Beneficial Administration Company
www.bestplans.com

Bergen Brunswig Corporation
www.bergenbrunswig.com

Bio-Orthopedic Lab
www.bio-orthopedic.com

Biosite Diagnostics
www.biosite.com

Blue Cross of California
www.bluecross.ca.com

Blue Shield HMO & Preferred Plan
www.blueshieldca.com

Brea Community Hospital
www.breahospital.com

Capistrano Labs
www.capolabs.com

Capp Care
www.cappcare.com

Chapman Medical Center
www.cmclungctr.com

Chevron Petroleum Technology
www.chevron.com

Children's Hospital & Health Center
www.chsd.org

CIGNA HealthCare of San Diego
www.cigna.com

Coastal Communities Hospital
www.tenethealth.com

CoCensys
www.cocensys.com

COHR
www.cohr-inc.com

Columbia Huntington Beach Hospital
www.tenethealth.com

Columbia Mission Bay Memorial Hospital
www.columbia.com

Columbia West Anaheim Medical Center
www.columbia.net

Community Care Network
www.ccnusa.com

Community Health Group
www.chgsd.com

Comprehensive Care Corporation
http://sternco.com/pr/cmp/cmp.html

Concept Development
www.rtcgroup.com

CORE
www.coreinc.com

Cortex Pharmaceuticals
www.cortexpharm.com

Corvas International
www.corvas.com

CorVel Corporation
www.corvel.com

CR Technology
www.crtechnology.com

CRITO
www.crito.uci.edu

Del Mar Avionics
www.delmarav.com

Diagnostic Solutions
www.teststrip.com

Endocare
www.endocare.com

Energy & Enviro Research Corp
www.eercorp.com

Flex Foot
www.flexfoot.com

Foundation Health Systems
www.fhs.com

Fountain Valley Regional Hospital
www.tenethealth.com

Furon Company
www.furon.com

Garden Grove Hospital
www.tenethealth.com

Gen-Probe
www.gen-brobe.com

Gish Biomedical
www.gishbmed.com

Glidewell Laboratories
www.glidewell-lab.com

Green Hospital of Scripps Clinic
www.scrippsclinic.com

Grossmont Hospital
www.sharp.com

Health Net
www.healthnet.com

HemaCare Corporation
www.hemacare.com

Hoag Memorial Hospital Presbyterian
www.hoag.org

IBRD-Rostrum Global
www.ibrd-rostrum.com

ICN Pharmaceuticals
www.icnpharm.com

Imagyn Medical
www.imagyn.com

Innovation Sports
www.isports.com

Interpore International
www.interpore.com
Irvine Medical Center
www.tenethealth.com
J. Hewitt
www.jhewitt.com
Kaiser Permanente
www.kptx.org
Kaiser Permanente Medical Center
www.ca.kaiser.permanente.org
La Jolla Pharmaceutical Co.
www.ljpc.com
MarDx Diagnostics
www.syntron.net
MBC Applied Enviro Sciences
www.mbcnet.net
Medical Science Systems
www.medscience.com
Medstone International
www.medstone.com
Melles Griot
www.mellegriot.com
Mercy Hospital
www.scrippshealth.org
Metrolaser
www.metrolaserinc.com
Mission Hospital Regional Medical
Center
www.mhrmc.com
Molecular Biosystems
www.mobi.com
NeoTherapeutics
www.neotherapeutics.com
O'Neil Product Development
www.oneilinc.com
Optimum Care Corporation
www.opmc.com
Orthomerica Products
www.orthomerica.com
Pacific Biometrics
www.pacbio.com
Pacific Mutual Holding Co.
www.pacificlife.com
PacifiCare
www.pch.com
PacifiCare Health Systems
www.pacificare.com
PharmaPrint
www.pharmaprint.com
Placentia-Linda Hospital
www.tenethealth.com/
placentialinda
Pomerado Hospital
www.pphs.org
PPO Alliance/OneSource Health
Network/CCN
www.ccn.us.com
Preferred Health Network
www.phn.com
Premier Laser Systems
www.premierlaser.com
Respiratory Systems
www.lifeair.com
Saddleback Memorial Medical Center
www.tenethealth.com
Safeguard Health Enterprises
www.safeguardhealth.com
Scripps Hospital-East County
www.scrippshealth.org
Scripps Memorial Hospital-Chula
Vista
www.scrippshealth.org
Scripps Memorial Hospital-
Encinitas
www.scrippshealth.org
Scripps Memorial Hospital-La Jolla
www.scrippshealth.org
Sentry Medical Products
www.sentrymed.com

Sharp Chula Vista Medical
Center
www.sharp.com
Sharp Coronado Hospital
www.sharp.com
Sharp Metro Hospitals
www.sharp.com
SIBIA Neurosciences
www.sibia.com
SK&A Information Services
www.skainfo.com
Sorin Biomedical
www.sorinbio.com
South Coast Medical Center
www.adventisthealth.com
St. Joseph Hospital of Orange
www.saintjoseph.com
St Jude Medical Center
www.stjude.com
Steri-Oss
www.steri-oss.com
Stratagene
www.stratagene.com
Summit Care Corporation/Fountain
View
www.sumc.com
Survivair
www.survivair.com
Syntron Bioresearch
www.syntron.net
Techniclone Corporation
www.techniclone.com
The Langer Biomechanics Group
www.langerbiomechanics.com
Toshiba America Medical Systems
www.toshiba.com
Tustin Rehabilitation Hospital
www.westernmedical.com
UCSD Medical Center
www.ucsd.edu
UniHealth
www.unihealth.org
Universal Care
www.universalcare.com
Unocal Corp/Agricultural Product
www.unocal.com
Western Medical Center Hosp -
Anaheim
www.westernmedical.com
WestEd Laboratories
www.wested.org
Western Medical Center Santa Ana
www.westernmedical.com
Whitewing Labs
www.whitewing.com

High Tech

3-D Instruments
www.3dinstruments.com
Able Communications
www.able.com
ACCEL Technologies
www.acceltech.com
Accurate Circuit Engineering
www.ace-pcd.com
Acucorp, Inc.
www.acucorp.com
Adaptive Information Systems
www.ais-hitachi.com
Admor Memory Corporation
www.admor.com
Advanced Industrial Systems
www.advancedindustrialsystems.com
Advanced Logic Research
www.alr.com
Advanced Media
www.advancedmedia.com

Advanced Micro Devices
www.amd.com
Advanced Technology Center
www.atc.com
Advantage Memory Corporation
www.advantagememory.com
AeroVironment
www.aerovironment.com
Airshow
www.airshowinc.com
Alpha Microsystems
www.alphamicro.com
Alpha Systems Lab
www.aslrwp.com
Alps Electric USA
www.alpsusa.com
Alton Geoscience
www.altongeo.com
Alyn Corporation
www.alyn.com
Amdahl Corporation
www.amdahl.com
American Computer Hardware
www.achc.com
American Microwave Technology
www.amtinc.com
Amplicon Financial
www.amplicon.com
Amtec Engineering Corporation
www.amtec-eng.com
Anacomp
www.anacomp.com
Anagraph
www.anagraph.com
AnaServe
www.anaserve.com
AOT Electronics
www.shortages.com
Area Electronics Systems
www.areasys.com
Arinc
www.arinc.com
Artios Corporation
www.artioslink.com
ASL Consulting Engineers
www.aslce.com
AST Research
www.ast.com
ATC Associates
www.atc-enviro.com
Aten Research
www.cliffwood.com
ATL Products
www.atlp.com
Atmel Corporation
www.atmel.com
Auspex Systems
www.auspex.com
Auto-By-Tel Corporation
www.autobytel.com
Automated Solutions Group
www.asgsoft.com
Autosplice
http://autosplice.com
Aztek
www.aztek.net
Bambeck Systems
www.bambecksystem.net
Barco Visual Systems
www.barco.com
BAS Micro Industries
www.basmicro.com
Basic Electronics
www.basicinc.com
BCM Advanced Research
www.bcmgvc.com
BE Aerospace/In-Flight Entertainment
www.bear.com

Becwar Engineering
www.becwar.com

Biolase Technology
www.biolase.com

Black & Veatch Engineers/Architects
www.bv.com

Blizzard Entertainment
www.blizzard.com

Bluebird Systems
www.bluebird.com

Boyle Engineering Corporation
www.boyleengineering.com

Broadcom Corporation
www.broadcom.com

Brown & Caldwell
www.brownandcaldwell.com

Business Automation
www.baipro.com

C Hoelzle Associates
www.chainc.com

Cabletron Systems
www.ctron.com

CACI Products Company
www.caciasl.com

Cair Systems Corporation
www.cairsystems.com

Cal Quality Electronics
www.calquality.com

Cal-Tronic's
www.caltronics.com

CalComp Technology
www.calcomp.com

California Analytical Instruments
www.gasanalyzers.com

California Economizer
www.hvaccomfort.com

California IC
www.californiaic.com

California Software Products
www.calsw.com

Calty Design Research
www.calty.com

CAM Data Systems
www.camdata.com

Cambridge Management Corporation
www.cppus.com

Camintonn Corporation
www.camintonn.com

Canon Business Machines
www.canon.com

Canon Computer Systems
www.ccsi.canon.com

CCH
www.prosystemfx.com

CDCE
www.cdce.com

Cedko Electronics
www.cedko.com

Centon Electronics
www.centon.com

Century Computer Corporation
www.centurycomputercorp.com

CET Environmental Service
www.cetenvironmental.com

CG Tech
www.cgtech.com

CH2M Hill
www.ch2m.com

ChatCom
www.jlchatcom.com

CIE America
www.citoh.com

Circuit Image Systems
www.circuitimage.com

Circuit World
www.circuit-world.com

Cirtech
www.cirtech.com

CISD International
www.cisd.com

Clayton Engineering
www.4cei.com

CLS Software
www.maisystems.com

CMD Technology
www.cmd.com

Coast Computer Products
www.purchasepro.com/coast/
computer

Coast Technologies
www.coastech.com

Colorbus
www.colorbus.com

COMARCO
www.cmro.com

Compucable Corporation
www.compucable.com

Compusource Corporation
www.compusource.com

Computer Associates International
www.cai.com

Computer Peripherals International
www.cpinternational.com

ComStream Corporation
www.comstream.com

Continuus Software Corporation
www.continuos.com

**Converse Consultants Orange
County**
www.converseconsultants.com

Copper Clad Multilayer Products
www.ccmpinc.com

Core Dynamics Corporation
www.core-dynamics.com

Corning OCA
www.oca-inc.com

Corollary
www.corollary.com

Cosmotronic Company
www.cosmotronic.com

Coyote Network Systems
www.coyotenetworksystems.com/

Creative Computer Applications
www.ccainc.com

Credentials Services International
www.credentials-net.com

CSS Labs
www.csslabs.com

CSTI
www.celeritysolutions.com

Cyberworks
www.cyberworks.net

D-Link Systems
www.dlink.com

Dainippon Screen Engineering
www.dsea.com

Daniel Measurement & Control
www.danielind.com

Data Color International
www.dci.com

Data Express
www.dataexp.com

Data General Corp/Field Sales
www.dg.com

Data Processing Design
www.dpd.com

**Data Processing Resources
Corporation**
www.dprc.com

Datametrics Corporation
www.datametricscorp.com

Datum
www.datum.com

Davox Corp
www.davox.com

Delphi Components
www.microwavebd.com

Dense-Pac Microsystems
www.dense-pac.com

Details
www.detailsinc.com

Diamond Technologies
www.diamondtech.com

Digital Equipment Corporation
www.digitalinfo.com

Digital West Media
www.dwmi.com

Digital Wizards
www.digwiz.com

DKS Associates
www.dksassociates.com

Document Control Solutions
www.docsolutions.com

Dynamotion
www.elc.sci.com

EIP Microwave
www.eipm.com/index.htm

Electro-Chemical Devices
www.ecdi.com

EMCON
www.emconinc.com

Emulex Corporation
www.emulex.com

Encore Computer Corporation
www.encore.com

ENSR Consulting & Engineering
www.ensr.com

Enterprise Solutions Ltd.
www.csi.esltd.com

EOS International
www.eosintl.com

EQE
www.eqe.com

Equifax National Decision Systems
www.natdecsys.com

ESI/FME
www.esifme.com

Excello Circuits
www.excello.com

Executive Software
www.execsoft.com

Exide Electronics
www.exide.com

Expersoft Corp.
www.expersoft.com

Extron Electronics
www.extron.com

FileNet Corporation
www.filenet.com

Financial Processing Systems
www.fpsnet.com

Fineline Circuits & Technology
www.finelinecircuits.com

FM Systems
www.fmsystems-inc.com

Formula Consultants
www.formula.com

FTG Data Systems
www.ftgdata.com

Future Focus
www.future-focus.com

Gage Babcock & Associates
www.gage-babcock.com

GDE Systems
www.gde.com

**Geac Computers/Hotel
Computer**
www.hotels.geac.com

GEC Plessey Semiconductors
www.gpsemi.com

General Automation
www.genauto.com

General Instrument Corp
www.gi.com
General Monitors
www.generalmonitors.com
General Software Solutions
www.gsscorp.com
Genesis 2000
www/.genesis2000.com
Genisco Tech Corp/Solaris Sys
www.gtc.com
Genovation
www.genovation.com
Gensia Sicor
www.gensiasicor.com
GeoSyntec Consultants
www.geosynthetic.com
GERS Retail Systems
www.gers.com
Golden State Bancorp
www.glenfederal.com
Golden West Circuits
www.gwcircuits.com
Gouvis Engineering California
www.gouvisgroup.com
Graphic Resources Corporation
www.grc.com
GSI
www.gsi-inc.com
Gulton Statham Transducers
www.gulton-statham.com
Harding Lawson Assoc Group
www.harding.com
Hargis + Associates
www.lawinfo.com/biz/hargis
HDR Engineering
www.hdrinc.com
Hirsch Electronics Corporation
www.hirschelectronics.com
Holt Integrated Circuits
www.holtic.com
Horiba Instruments
www.horiba.com
Horizons Technology
www.horizons.com
Hughes Aircraft, Data Systems & Info
Tech Systems
www.hughes.com
Hughes Aircraft/Microelectron
www.raytheon.com
I/Omagic Corporation
www.iomagic.com
ICCI (Intl Circuits/Component)
www.icciusa.com
ICL Retail Systems
www.iclretail.com
Idea
http://eemonline.com/idea
Image & Signal Processing
www.cersnet.com
Imaging Tech
www.imaging.com
iMALL
www.imall.com
IMC Networks
www.imcnetworks.com
Impco Technologies
www.impcotechnologies.com
InCirT Technology
www.incirt.com
IndeNet
www.indenet.com
Infographics Systems Corp
www.infographicsystems.com
Ingram Micro
www.ingrammicro.com
Inline
www.inlineinc.com

Innovative Sensors
www.isi-ph.inter.net
InSight Health Services Corp.
www.insighthealth.com
Inspired Arts
www.inspiredarts.com
Intergraph Corporation
www.intergraph.com
Intermetrics
www.intermetrics.com
International Remote Imaging
Systems
www.proiris.com
International Sensor Technology
www.gotgas.com
International Space Optics SA
www.isorainbow.com
International Technology Corp
www.itcorporation.com
Interplay Productions
www.interplay.com
Iris
www.irisnet.com
Irvine Sensors Corporation
www.irvine-sensors.com
Island Pacific Systems Corp
www.islandpacific.com
Isocor
www.isocor.com
IVID Communications
www.ivid.com
Javelin Systems
www.jvln.com
Jaycor
www.jaycor.com
Jones & McGeoy Sales
www.jonesmcgeoy.com
Jonesville Webs
www.blurtheline.com
KCA Electronics
www.kcamerica.com
KFC USA
www.smilekfc.com
Kimley-Horn & Associates
www.kimleyhorn.com
King Instrument Company
www.kinginstrument.com
Kingston Technology Company
www.kingston.com
Kleinfelder
www.kleinfelder.com
Kofax Image Products
www.kofax.com
Kor Electronics
www.korelec.com
KVB
www.kvb-cems.com
Lantronix
www.lantronix.com
Laser Industries
www.laserindustries.com
Laser Products Corp
www.laserproducts.com
Lasergraphics
www.lasergraphics.com
Leaming Industries
www.leaming.com
Lifetime Memory Products
www.lifetimememory.com
Linfinity Microelectronics
www.linfinity.com
Link SanDiego.Com.
www.sandiego.com
Litronic Industries
www.alliedsignals.com
Live Software
www.livesoftware.com

Lotus Development Corporation
www.lotus.com
MacNeal-Schwendler Corp.
www.macsch.com
Macrolink
www.macrolink.com
Madge Networks
www.madge.com
Magic Software Enterprises
www.magic-sw.com
MAI Systems Corporation
www.maisystems.com
MARCOR Mediation
www.marcor.com
Marway Power Systems
www.marway.com
McCurdy Circuits
www.mccurdy.com
McLaren/Hart
www.mclaren-hart.com
Meade Instruments Corp
www.meade.com
Medata
www.medata.com
MEI (Marcel Electronics Intl)
www.marcelelec.com
Mettler Electronics Corp
www.mettlerelec.com
MGV International
www.mgvgroup.com
Michael Brandman Associates
www.brandman.com
Micro Express
www.microexpress.net
MicroNet Technology
www.micronet.com
Microsemi Corporation
www.microsemi.com
Microsoft Corporation
www.microsoft.com
Mission Geoscience
www.cerfnet.com
Mitsubishi Electronics America
www.mea.com
Monitoring Automation Systems
www.monauto.com
Monroe Systems for Business
www.monroe-systems.com
Montgomery Watson
www.mw.com
MPI Technologies
www.mpitech.com
MTI Technology Corporation
www.mti.com
Multilayer Technology
www.multek.com
Murrieta Circuits
www.murrietta.com
Nadek Computer Systems
www.nadek.com
National Computer Systems
www.ncslink.com
National Steel & Shipbuilding Co.
www.nasco.com
National Technical Systems
www.ntscorp.com
NCCS
www.nccs.com
NCS (National Computer Systems)
www.ncs.com
Net Manage
www.aharmony.com
Network Associates
www.nai.com
Network Intensive
www.ni.net
New Dimension Software
www.ndsoft.com

New Media Corporation
www.newmediacorp.com
NewCom
www.newcominc.com
NewGen Imaging Systems
www.newgen.com
Newport Corporation
www.newport.com
Nexgen SI
www.nexgensi.com
Nichols Research Corporation
www.nichols.com
Ninyo & Moore
www.ninyoandmoore.com
Nova Logic
www.novalogic.com
Novell
www.novell.com
ObjectShare
www.objectshare.com
OC Alphanetics
www.alphanetics.com
OCE' Printing
www.oceprinting.com
Odetics
www.odetics.com
Ogden Environmental & Energy
Services Co.
www.ogdensfo.com
OnVillage Communications
www.onvillage.com
Optical Laser
www.opticallaser.com
OPTUM Software
www.optum.com
Oracle Corporation
www.us.oracle.com
Orange Micro
www.macph.com
OrCad
www.orcad.com
OWEN Group
www.owengroup.com
P&D Consultants
www.cte-eng.com
PairGain Technologies
www.pairgain.com
Palomar Systems
www.elcsci.com
Parsons Transportation Group
www.parsons.com
Pentadyne-Pentaflex
www.pentadyne-pentaflex.com
Perceptronics
www.perceptronics.com
Phase One
www.phase1.com
Phoenix Technologies Ltd.
www.phoenix.com
Photo Research
www.photoresearch.com
Pick Systems
www.picksys.com.
Pinnacle Micro
www.pinnaclemicro.com
Pioneer Circuits
www.pioneercircuits.com
Plaid Brothers Software
www.plaid.com
Plastship Logistics Intl
www.plastship.com
Platinum Software Corporation
www.platsoft.com
Power Circuits
www.powerckts.com
Powerwave Technologies
www.powerwave.com

Precision Glass & Optics
www.precision-glass.com
Presto-Tek Corporation
www.newportinc.com
Printrak International
www.printrakinternational.com
Printronix
www.printronix.com/
Prism Software
www.prism-software.com
Procom Technology
www.procom.com
Productivity Enhancement Products
www.pepinc.com
Professional Service Industries
www.psi.com
Progen Technology
www.progen.com
PSIMED Corporation
www.psi-med.com
PsiTech
www.primenet.com/~psitech
Pulse Engineering
www.pulseeng.com
Puroflow Incorporated
www.puroflow.com
QLogic
www.qlc.com
QLP Laminates
www.qlp.com
QuadraMed Corp.
www.quadramed.com
Quality Systems
www.qsii.com
Quarterdeck Corp.
www.quarterdeck.com
Quest Software
www.quests.com
QuickStart Technologies
www.quickstart.com
Radian International LLC
www.radian.com
Radiant Technology Corporation
www.radianttech.com
Rainbow Technologies
www.rainbow.com
Ram Optical Instrumentation
www.ramoptical.com
Rational Software Corporation
www.rational.com
Reedex
www.robust.com/reedex
Relsys International
www.relsys-inc.com
REMEC
www.remec.com
Research Engineers
www.reiusa.com
Risk Data Corporation
www.riskdata.com
Robert Bein William Frost &
Associates
www.rbf.com
Rockwell International Corporation
www.rockwell.com
ROI Systems
www.roisysinc.com
Ross Systems
www.rossinc.com
Router Solutions
www.rsi-inc.com
Routerware
www.routerware.com
Russell Information Sciences
www.russellinfo.com
Sabtech Industries
www.sabtec.com

Safety Components International
www.safetycomponents.com
SAIC Internet Solutions
www.saic.com
SAS Institute
www.sas.com
Scantron Corporation
www.scantron.com
SCS Engineers
www.scseng.com
Seagate Technology
www.seagate.com
Secure Communication Systems
www.securecomm.com
Seimens Nixdorf Information
Systems
www.intranet.sni-usa.com
Select Software Tools
www.selectst.com
SEMCOR
www.semcor.com
Semicoa
www.semicoa.com
Sensorex
www.sensorex.com
SGS Thomson Microelectronics
www.st.com
Sharp Digital Information Prod
www.sharpsdi.com
Shopping.com
www.shopping.com/ss/
default.asp
Siemens Pyramid Information
Systems
www.pyramid.com
Silicon Graphics Computer Systems
www.sgi.com
Silicon Systems
www.ssi1.com
Simons Li & Associates
www.simonsli.com
Simple Technology
www.simpletech.com
SimpleNet
www.simplenet.com
Simulation Sciences
www.simsci.com
Smartek Educational Technology
www.wordsmart.com
Smartflex Systems
www.smartflex.com
Smith Micro Software
www.smithmicro.com
SMK Electronics Corp USA
www.smkusa.com
SMT Dynamics Corp
www.smtblackfox.com
Soldermask
www.soldermask.com
Soligen Technologies
www.PartsNow.com
Somerset Automation
www.somersetwms.com
Sony Technology Center
www.sgo.sony.com
Source Diversified
www.sourced.com
Southland Micro Systems
www.southlandmicro.com
Space Applications Corp/Information
Systems Division
www.spaceapps.com
Sparta
www.sparta.com
Speedy Circuits
www.speedycircuits.com
SRS Labs
www.srslabs.com

SRS Technologies
www.srs.com
StarBase Corporation
www.starbase.com
State of the Art
www.sota.com
Storage Concepts
www.storageconcepts.com
Storage Technology Corp
www.stortek.com
Subscriber Computing
www.subscriber.com
Sun Microsystems Computer Corp
www.sun.com
Superior Manufacturing Co
www.laxmigroup.com
Symbios Logic
www.symbios.com
Symbol Technologies
www.symbol.com
Symitar Systems
www.symitar.com
Sync Research
www.sync.com
SYS Technology
www.systechnology.com
Syspro Impact Software
www.sysprousa.com
Systems & Software
www.kaiwan.com/nssi/ssi.htmd
T-HQ
www.thq.com
Tait & Associates
www.tait.com
Tanner Research
www.tanner.com
Tayco Engineering
www.taycoeng.com
TCI Management
www.tcisolutions.com
Techmedia Computer Systems
Corporation
www.techmedia.net
Technologic Software
www.technologic.com
Tekelec
www.tekelec.com
Tektronix/Color Printing
www.tek.com
Telecom Solutions
www.tsiusa.com
Tetra Tech
www.tetratech.com
The Cerplex Group
www.cerplex.com
The Flamemaster Corporation
www.flamemaster.com
The Laxmi Group
www.laxmigroup.com
The MacNeal-Schwendler Corp
www.macsch.com
The Park Corporation
www.parkenv.com
The Planning Center
www.planningcenter.com
Tone Software Corporation
www.tonesoft.com
Toshiba America Info Systems
www.toshiba.com
TouchStone Software
Corporation
www.checkit.com
Transitional Technology
www.ttech.com
TRC Environmental Solutions
www.treesi.com
Tri-Star Engineered Products
www.tri-star-epi.com

Triconex Corp
www.triconex.com
TriTeal Corp.
www.triteal.com
Tutor-Saliba Corporation
www.tutorsaliba.com
Unisys Corporation
www.unisys.com
Unit Instruments
www.unit.com
Unitech Research
www.unitech.com
US Sensor Corp
www.ussensor.com
V3I Engineering
www.v3i.com
Vanguard Technology
www.vanguard.com
Velie Circuits
www.velie.com
Viking Components
www.vikingcomponents.com
Virgin Interactive Entertainment
www.vie.com
Vis-A' Vis Communications
www.weedpuller.com
VisiCom Laboratories
www.visicom.com
Vision Solutions
www.visionsolutions.com
VitalCom
www.vitalcom.com
Voice Powered Technology
International
www.vpti.com
Volt Delta Resources
www.volt.com
Wahlco Environmental Systems
www.wahlco.com
Watson General Corp.
www.wgen.com
Wavefunction
www.wavefun.com
Western Data Systems
www.westdata.com
Western Digital Corporation
www.westerndigital.com
Western Pacific Data Systems
www.wpds.com
Western Telematic
www.wti.com
Willdan Associates
www.willdan.com
Wiz Technology
www.wiztech.com
Wonderware Corporation
www.wonderware.com
Woodward-Clyde Intl -Americas
www.wcc.com
Wyle Electronics
www.wyle.com
Wynns International
www.wynns.com
XCD
www.xcd.com
Xicor
www.xicor.com
Xilinx
www.xilinx.com
Xtend Micro Products
www.xmpi.com
XyberNet
www.xyber.net
Xylan Corporation
www.xylan.com
Zenographics
www.zeno.com

ZyXEL Communications
www.zyxel.om

Hospitality

Del Mar Fairgrounds
www.delmarfair.com
Disneyland Hotel
www.disneyland.com
Doubletree Hotel Anaheim/Airport
www.doubletreehotels.com
Doubletree Hotel Pasadena
www.doubletreehotel.com
Embassy Suites La Jolla
www.embassy-suites.com
Fairmont Hotel
www.fairmont.com
Hacienda Hotel
www.haciendahotel.com
Hotel Laguna
www.menubytes.com/
hotellaguna
Hotel Queen Mary
www.queenmary.com
Howard Johnsons Hotel
www.hojoanaheim.com
Hyatt Newporter
www.hyatt.com
Hyatt Regency Hotels
www.hyatt.com
Irvine Marriott Hotel
www.jobshr.com
La Costa Resort, Spa and Country
Club
www.lacosta.com
La Jolla Marriott
www.marriott.com
La Quinta Inn - Irvine
www.laquinta.com
Le Meridan
www.lemeridanbh.com
Loews Coronado Bay Resort
www.loewshotels.com
Marriott's Laguna Cliffs Resort
www.marriott.com
NuOasis Resorts
www.otcfn.com/nuoa
Park Hyatt Los Angeles at Century
City
www.hyatt.com
Radisson Hotel
www.radisson.com
Ramada Inn - Anaheim
www.anaheimramada.com
San Diego Convention Center Corp.
www.sdccc.org
San Diego Marriott Hotels
www.marriott.com
San Diego Mission Valley Hilton
www.hilton.com
San Diego Princess Resort
www.princessresort.com/princess
Seoul Plaza Hotel
www.ramada.com
Sheraton Grande Torrey Pines
www.sheraton-tp.com
Sheraton San Diego Hotel & Marina
www.sandiego-sheraton.com
Sutton Place Hotel
www.travelweb.com/sutton.html
The Anaheim Hilton & Towers
www.hilton.com
The Atrium Hotel
www.atriumhotel.com
The Seal Beach Inn & Gardens
www.sealbeachinn.com
The Waterfront Hilton
www.hilton.com/hilton

The Westin South Coast Plaza
www.westin.com
Town & Country Resort &
Conference Center
www.towncountry.com
Warner Center Marriott
www.marriot.com
Wyndham Hotel
www.wyndham.com

Insurance

Allmarket Insurance Services of
California
www.allmarketinsurance.com
Allstate Insurance Group
www.allstate.com
American Reinsurance Company
www.amre.com
American Sterling Corporation
www.americansterling.com
Amwest Insurance Group
www.farwestservices.com
Aon Risk Services
www.aainsure.com
Argonaut Insurance
www.argonautgroup.com
Armstrong/Robitaille Insurance
Services
www.arinsurance.com
Arrowhead Group of Companies
www.arrowhead.org
Balboa Life & Casualty
www.avco-textron.com
Barney & Barney
www.barney&barney.com
Bliss & Glennon
www.bgsurplus.com
Bolton/RGV Insurance Brokers
http://boltonco.com
Brown & Riding Insurance Services
www.brownandriding.com
California Worker's Compensation
Institute
www.csci.org
Carnet Insurance Agency
www.thecarnet.com
Claim Net
www.claimnet.com
CNA International
www.cnaworldwide.com
Gateway Excess & Surplus Lines
www.gateway.com
Golden Bear Insurance Company
www.goldenbear.com
Hewitt Associates
www.hewittassoc.com
Insurance Educational Association
www.iea.com
Kemper Insurance Companies
www.kemperinsurance.com
Marine Office of America
Corporation
www.moac.com
Murria & Frick Insurance Agency
www.ideafit.com
Pacific Life Insurance Company
www.pacificlife.com
Petersen International Insurance
Brokers
www.picu.org
PHD Insurance Brokers
www.phdins.com
Republic Indemnity of America
www.ri-net.com
Robert F. Driver Co.
www.rfdriver.com

Sullivan & Curits Insurance
www.sullivan-curtis.com
Superior Pacific Insurance
www.superior.com
The Atlantic Mutual Companies
www.atlanticmutualcompanies.com
The Centris Group
www.centrisgroup.com
Total Financial & Insurance Services
www.totalfinancial.com
Western Insurance Information
Service
www.wiis.org
Western Security Surplus Insurance
www.wssib.com

Law & Lobbying

Baker & McKenzie
www.bakerinfo.com
Brobeck Phleger & Harrison
www.brobeck.com
Brown Pistone Hurley VanVlear
www.brownpistone.com
Bryan Cave
www.bryancavellp.com
Buchalter Nemer Fields & Younger
www.buchalter.com
Call Clayton & Jensen
www.ccjlaw.com
Cotkin & Collins
www.cotkincollins.com
Cox Castle & Nicholson
http://ccnlaw.com
Gibson Dunn & Crutcher
http://gdclaw.com
Graham & James
www.gj.com
Greenberg Glusker Fields Claman &
Machtinger
www.ggfcm.com
Hill Farrer & Burrill
www.hf&bllp.com
Irell & Manella
www.irell.com
Jeffer Mangels Butler & Marmaro
www.jmbm.com
Knobbe Martens Olson & Bear
www.kmob.com
Latham & Watkins
www.lw.com
Manatt Phelps & Phillips
www.manatt.com
Marshack & Shulman
www.mglaw.com
McKenna & Cuneo
www.mckennacuneo.com
Milbank Tweed Hadley & McCloy
www.milbank.com
Milberg Weiss Bershad Hynes &
Lerach
www.milberg.com
Morgan Lewis & Bockius
www.mlb.com
Morrison & Foerster
www.mofo.com
O'Melveny & Myers
www.omm.com
Oppenheimer, Wolff & Donneley
www.bruckperry.com
Paone Callahan McHolm & Winton
www.paone.com
Paul Hastings Janofsky & Walker
www.phjw.com
Pillsbury Madison & Sutro
www.pillsburylaw.com
Procopio Cory Hargreaves & Savitch
www.procopio.com

Riordan & McKinzie
www.riordan.com
Rutan & Tucker
www.rutan.com
Seltzer Caplan Wilkins & McMahon
www.scwm.com
Seyfarth Shaw Fairweather &
Geraldson
www.seyfarth.com
Sheppard Mullin Richter & Hampton
www.smrh.com
Sidley & Austin
www.sidley.com
Snell & Wilmer
www.swlaw.com
Walsworth Franklin Bevins/McCall
www.wfbm.com

Public Relations

Berkman Marketing Group
http://bmgmktg.com
Creative Communications Services
www.ccspr.com
Edelman Public Relations Worldwide
www.edelman.com
Fleishman-Hillard
www.fleishman.com
Golin/Harris Communications
www.golinharris.com
Hill & Knowlton
www.hill&knowlton.com
Nelson Communications Group
www.nelsongroup.com
Pondel Parsons & Wilkinson
www.pondel.com
Porter/Novelli
www.porternovelli.com
Shafer Public Relations
www.shafer.net
Stock/Alper & Associates
www.stockalper.com
Stoorza, Ziegaus & Metzger
www.stoorza.com
The Bohle Company
www.bohle.com
The Gable Group
www.gablegroup.com
The Phelps Group
www.phelpsgroup.com
Vista Group
www.vistagroupUSA.com

Real Estate

Alpha Construction Co.
www.alpha.com
Anastasi Construction Company
www.anastasi.com
Asset Management Group
www.assetmanagement.com
Birtcher Real Estate Group
www.birtcher.com
Brock Homes, Ryland Company
www.ryland.com
Business Real Estate Brokerage
Company
www.brecommercial.com
California Pacific Homes
www.calpacific.com
Cannon Constructors
www.cannongroup.com
Capital Commercial/NAI
www.capitalcomm.com
Capital Pacific Holdings
www.cph-inc.com
CB Commercial Real Estate Group
www.cbrichardellis.com

Employment Help

CB Richard Ellis
www.cbc.com
Century 21 All Service Realtors
www.c21asr.com
Century 21 All Star Realty
www.century21allstar.com
Century 21 Award
www.century21award.com
Century 21 First Choice Realty
http://member.aol.com/
c21choice
Century 21/Superstars
www.c21superstars.com
Chicago Title Insurance Company
www.chicagotitle.com
Coldwell Banker Corp/Southern
California
www.coldwellbanker.com
Colliers Iliff Thorn
www.colliers.com
Collins Commercial Corporation
www.collinsve.com
Commonwealth Land Title Company
www.chicagotitle.com
Continental Homes
www.continentalhomes.com
Crown Pacific
www.crownpacific.com
Cushman & Wakefield of California
www.cushwake.com
DAUM Cemmercial Real Estate
Services
www.daum1904.com
Donahue-Schriber
www.donahueschriber.com
Equitable Management/Consulting
www.emcco.com
Fidelity National Financial
www.fnf.com
Fidelity National Title Insurance
Company
www.f&f.com
Fieldstone Communities
www.uniontrib.com
First American Title Company of
Los Angeles
www.fatcola.com
Fu-Lyons Associates
www.fulyons.com
Goldrich & Kest Industries
www.gkind.com
Grant General Contractors
www.grantgc.com
Grubb & Ellis Company
www.grubb-ellis.com
Hanson Realty
www.hansonrealty.com
Holmes & Narver
www.hninc.com
Insignia Commercial Group
www.unitas.net
James Crone & Associates
www.drhorton.com
Janez Properties
www.janezprop.com
John Aaroe & Associates
www.johnarroe.com
John Burnham & Co.
www.johnburnham.com
Koll Construction Co.
www.koll.com
Lyle Parks, Jr.
www.lpj.com
Majestic Realty Co.
www.majesticrealty.com
Marcus & Millichap
www.mmeribc.com

Marcus & Millichap Corp R/E
Services
www.mmreibc.com
MBK Real Estate, Ltd.
www.mbk.com
McCarthy Brothers Company
www.mccarthybldrs.com
Morley Builders
www.morleybuilders.com
Nielsen Dillingham Builders
www.nielsendillingham.com
Nourmand & Associates Realtors
www.nourmand.com
Orange Coast Title Co.
www.octitle.com
Pacific Bay Homes.
www.pacbayhomes.com
Pacific Southwest Realty Services
www.psrs.com
Peck Jones Construction
www.peckjones.com
PM Realty Group
www.pmrg.com
Podley Doan
www.podley.com
Presley Companies
www.presleyhomes.com
Prudential California Realty
www.prudentialcalif.com
R & B Realty Group
www.oakwood.com
R. D. Olson Construction
www.rdolson.com
RE/MAX Executives
www.sandiego-executive.com
RE/MAX of Valencia
http://remax-scv.com
Real Estate Disposition Corp
www.classifiedad.com
Realty Executives Santa Clarita
www.realtyExecs-scv.com
Shea Homes
www.sheahomes.com
Sperry Van Ness
www.svn.com
Standard Pacific Corp
www.dallas.net/~stanpac
Swinerton & Walberg
www.swbuilders.com
Tarbell Realtors
www.tarbell.com
Terra Universal
www.terrauni.com
The 1st American Financial Corp
www.firstam.com
The Eastlake Company
www.eastlakehomes.com
The Irvine Company
www.irvineco.com
The Irving Hughes Group
www.irvinghughes.com
The Mills Corporation
www.millscorp.com
The Prudential-Dunn, REALTORS
www.prudential.com
The Rreef Funds
www.rreff.com
Trammell Crow So. Calif.
www.trammellcrow.com
Turner Construction Co.
www.turnerconstruction.com
Voit Companies
www.voitco.com
Warmington Homes
www.warmingtonhomes.com
Watson Land Co.
www.watsonlandcompany.com

White House Properties
www.whitehouseproperties.com
Willis M. Allen Co.
www.willisallen.com

Sports & Recreation

Aftco Manufacturing Co
www.aftco.com
AMP Research
www.amp-research.com
Anaheim Mighty Ducks
www.nhl.com/teams/ana/
index.htm
Anaheim Sports
www.anaheimangels.com
Balboa Bay Club
www.balboabayclub.com
Bally's Total Fitness
www.ballyfitness.com
Buck Knives
www.buckknives.com
Callaway Golf Company
www.callawaygolf.com
City of Coronado Municipal Golf
Course
www.coronado.ca.us
Cubic Balance Golf Technology
www.cubicbalance.com
Disneyland
www.disney.com
El Camino Country Club
www.coblestone.com
Four Seasons Resort Aviara
www.fhr.com
GT Bicycles
www.gtbicycles.com
Heart Rate
www.heartrateinc.com
Knott's Berry Farm
www.knotts.com
La Costa Resort, Spa and Country
Club
www.lacosta.com
Los Alamitos Race Course
www.losalamitos.com
Marksman Products
www.beeman.com
Master Industries
www.masterindustries.com
Oakley
www.oakley.com
Pala Mesa Resort
www.palamesa.com
Pelican Hill Golf Club
www.pelicanhill.com
Steele Canyon Golf & Country Club
www.steelecanyon.com
Taylor Made Golf Co.
www.taylormadegolf.com
Tectrix Fitness Equipment
www.tectrix.com
The California Angels
www.majorleaguebaseball.com/
al/cal
Unisen
www.startrack.com
Warner Springs Ranch
www.wsranchaol.com
Yamaha Corporation of America
www.yamaha.com

Travel, Transportation & Utilities

Air New Zealand
www.airnz.com

American Airlines
www.aa.com
Associated Travel International
www.traveltron.com
Australian New Zealand Direct Line
www.anzdl.com
Automobile Club of Southern
California
www.aaa-calif.com
Burlington Air Express
www.baxworld.com
Carlson Wagonlit Travel
www.cwtonthegotravel.com
Circle International
www.circleintl.com
Comtrans
www.comtrans.com
Continental Airlines
www.flycontinental.com
First Class Travel Management
www.fctravel.com
Fullerton Municipal Airport
www.ci.fullerton.ca.us
Interstate Consolidation
www.icsla.com
Irvine Ranch Water District
www.irwd.com
Korean Air
www.koreanair.com
Maritz Travel Co.
www.maritz.com
Moulton Niguel Water District
www.mnwd.com
Municipal Water District of OC
www.mwdoc.com
Orange County Water District
www.ocwd.com
Plaza Travel
www.plazatravel.com
Pleasant Holidays
www.pleasantholidays.com
QST Travel
www.qsttravel.com
Service By Air
www.servicebyair.com
Southern California Edison
www.edisonx.com
Southern California Water Company
www.thegasco.com
Southwest Airlines
www.southwest.com
STA Travel
www.statravel.com
Sundance Travel
www.sundancetravel.com
Travel Store
www.travelstore.com
Uniglobe In-World Travel
www.uniglobe.com
World Travel Bureau
www.wtbtvl.com
20th Century Insurance
www.20thcenturyinsurance.com

Largest & Fastest Growing Companies

Aames Financial Corporation
www.aamesfinancial.com
Ace Parking Management
www.aceparking.com
Activision
www.activision.com
Advanced Access
www.advaccess.com
Advanced Marketing Services
www.admsweb.com

AECOM Technology Corp.
www.dmjm.com
Agouron Pharmaceuticals
www.agouron.com
Alaris Medical Systems
www.alarismed.com
Align-Rite International
www.align-rite.com
AlliedSignal Aerospace
www.alliedsignal.com
American Suzuki Motor Corporation
www.suzuki.com
Ameron International Corporation
www.ameron-intl.com
Andataco
www.andataco.com
Anderson Lithograph Company
www.andlitho.com
Applied Micro Circuits Corporation
www.amcc.com
ARB
www.arbinc.com
Artisan
www.artisanpictures.com
Ashworth
www.ashworthinc.com
Atlantic Richfield Company
www.arco.com
Aura Systems
www.aurasystems.com
Balboa Travel
www.balboatravel.com
Barnes Wholesale
www.barneswholesale.com
Bason Computer
www.basoncomputer.com
Belkin Components
www.belkin.com
Bell Industries
www.bellind.com
Big 5 Corp.
www.big5sportinggoods.com
Bob Baker Enterprises
www.bobbaker.com
Bonded Motors
www.bondedmotors.com
Breath Asure
www.breathasure.com
Burnham Pacific Properties
www.bpac.com
Callaway Golf Company
www.callawaygolf.com
CalMat Company
www.calmart.com
Candle Corporation
www.candle.com
CareAmerica Health Plans
www.careamerica.com
COA
www.coaster.com
Compu-D International
www.compu-d.com
Comtrade Electronic
www.comtrade.com
Conterm Consolidation Services
USA
www.conterm.com
Countrywide Credit Industries
www.countrywide.com
Countrywide Home Loans
www.countrywide.com
Coverall Cleaning Concepts
www.coverall.com
CyberMedia
www.cybermedia.com
Dames & Moore
www.dames.com

Dataworks
www.interactive-group.com
DataWorks Corporation
www.dataworks.com
Datron World Communications
www.dtsi.com
DH Technology
www.axiohm.com
Diagnostic Products Corporation
www.dpc.web.com
Dick Clark Productions
www.dickclark.com
Dirt Cheap Car Rental
www.w3m.com/dirtcheap.com
Dole Food Company
www.dole.com
Dura Pharmaceuticals
www.durapharm.com
Dycam
www.dycam.com
EarthLink Network
www.earthlink.net
Easton Sports
www.eastonsports.com
Edison International
www.sce.com
Electro Rent Corp.
www.electrorent.com
En Pointe Technologies
www.enpointe.com
ENCAD
www.encad.com
Epic Solutions
www.epicsolutions.com
Executive Car Leasing
www.executivecarleasing.com
Fedco
www.fedco.com
First Consulting Group
www.scgnet.com
Foodmaker
www.jackinthebox.com
Fountainview
www.sunc.com
FPA Medical Management
www.fpamm.com
Galpin Motors
www.gogalphin.com
Gensia Sicor
www.gensiasicor.com
Glacier Water Services
www.glacierwater.com
Goldmine Software Corporation
www.goldminesw.com
Gray Cary Ware & Freidenrich
www.gcwp.com
Guitar Center
www.musician.com
H.F. Ahmanson & Company
www.homewsavings.com
Hilton Hotels Corp.
www.hilton.com
HNC Software
www.hnc.com
Hughes Electronics Commerce
www.hughes.com
IHOP Corp.
www.ihop.com
Imperial Bancorp
www.imperialbank.com
INCOMNET
www.incomnet.com
Infonet Services
www.infonet.com
Insurance Auto Auctions
www.iaa.com
Interactive Group
www.interactive-group.com

Employment Help

IT NetTrac Corp.
www.nettrac.com
Jenny Craig
www.jennycraig.com
K-Swiss
www.kswiss.com
Kennedy-Wilson
www.kennedywilson.com
Kett Engineering Corp.
www.ketteng.com
Kinetics Technology International
Corp.
www.kticorp.com
Koo Koo Roo
www.kookooroo.com
Kushner Locke Co.
www.kushnerlocke.com
Learning Tree International
www.learningtree.com
Liquid Investments
www.mesadistributing.com
Lithographix
www.lithographix.com
Litton Industries
www.littoncorp.com
Logicon
www.logicon.com
Machinery Sales Co.
www.mchysales.com
Mail Boxes Etc.
www.mbc.com
Marshall Industries
www.marshall.com
Mattel
www.mattel.com
Maxwell Technologies
www.maxwell.com
Mazda Motor of America
www.mazdausa.com
Midern Computer
www.sagernotebook.com
MiniMed
www.minimed.com
Mitake
www.mitake.com
Mitsuba Corp.
www.mitsuba.com
Modern Mold International
www.pens.com
Morrow-Meadows Corp.
www.morrow-meadows.com
MRV Communications
www.nbase.com
Natural Alternatives International
www.nai.online.com
Nestle USA
www.nestle.com
New Century BMW
www.ncbmw.com
New Star Media
www.doveaudio.com
Norm Reeves Honda
www.normreeves.com
NTN Communications
www.ntn.com
O'Melveny & Myers
www.omm.com
Optimal Integrated Solutions
www.optimslis.net
Oriental Motor USA Corp.
www.omusa.com
Osicom Technologies
www.osicom.com
Pacific Theatres Corp.
www.pacifictheatres.com
Pearson Ford Co.
www.pearsonford.com

Peerless Systems Corp.
www.peerless.com
Pinkerton's
www.pinkertons.com
PinnacleOne
www.pinnacle.com
PMR Corp.
www.pmrcorp.com
Pollution Research & Control Corp.
www.dasibi.com
Public Storage
www.publicstorage.com
Qualcomm
www.qualcomm.com
Quidel Corp.
www.quidel.com
R.J. Gordon & Co.
www.rjgordon.com
Realty Income Corp.
www.realtyincome.com
Reliance Steel & Aluminum Co.
www.rsac.com
Rohr
www.rhor.com
Ryan Herco Products Co.
www.ryanherco.com
San Diego Travel Group
www.sdtg.com
Science Applications International
Corp.
www.saic.com
Signature Resorts
www.sunterra.com
Software Dynamics
www.sdinc.com
Software Technologies Corp.
www.stc.com
Southern California Water Co.
www.scwater.com
Southland Industries
www.southlandind.com
Space Electronics
www.spaceelectronics.com
Spatializer Audio Laboratories
www.spatializer.com
Special Devices
www.specialdevises.aol.com
Stac
www.stac.com
Sunkist Growers
www.sunkist.com
Sunrise Medical
www.sunrisemedical.com
Superior Industries International
www.superiorindustries.com
Systems Engineering Associates
www.sea.com
Tetra Tech
www.tetratech.com
The National Dispatch Center
www.ndcwireless.com
The Titan Corp.
www.titan.com
The Walt Disney Company
www.disney.com
ThermoTrex Corp.
www.thermo.com
Ticketmaster Group
www.ticketmaster.com
Times Mirror Co.
www.latimes.com
TransWestern Publishing
www.transwesterpub.com
Trillium Digital Systems
www.trillium.com
TRW Space & Electronics Group
www.trw.com

TV/COM International
www.tvcom.com
University of Southern
California
www.usc.edu
Utility Trailer Manufacturing Co.
www.utilitytrailer.com
Ventura Foods LLC
www.venturafood.com
ViewSonic
www.viewsonic.com
Wavetek Instruments
www.wavetek.com
Webb Automotive Group
www.toyotacerritos.com
WellPoint Health Networks
www.wellpoint.com
Western Atlas
www.univa.com
WGI Solutions
www.wgis.com
Wheb Systems
www.whebsys.com
Xerox
www.zero.com
Xpedx
www.xpedx.com
Zenith National Insurance Corp.
www.znic.com

IMPORTANT TIP

A great way to learn more about a company or industry you are interested in is by visiting their web site. Corporate web sites offer everything from mission statements, goals and objectives, financial information, key personnel and addresses to products and services they provide.

Company Job Hotlines

find more in "Federal, State & Local Government"

Another timely & cost efficient way to hear of current job openings is through company job hotlines. Most are available 24 Hours/Day and provide information and details about job requirements, pay and benefits, plus resume and cover letter contact information.

Advertising/Marketing

DDB Needham Worldwide
310-996-5865
Rubin Postaer and Associates
310-260-4320
Saatchi & Saatchi Los Angeles
310-214-6180
TBWA Chiat/Day
310-314-6685

Associations/Non-Profit

California Science Center
213-630-3059
Santa Monica Area Chamber of Commerce
310-393-9825

Banking & Finance

Andersen Consulting LLP
310-726-2975
Arthur Andersen
213-614-7579
Fallbrook National Bank
888-547-5600
First National Bank
619-233-5395
Grossmont Bank
619-623-3156
Imperial Bank
310-417-5606
Marine Corps West Federal
760-430-7511 ext1058
Mission Federal
619-546-2010
North County Bank
760-737-6677
Northern Trust Bank
213-346-1300
Pacific Thrift & Loan
818-883-6893 x214
Peninsula Bank of San Diego
619-525-7819
Point Loma Federal
619-495-3400
San Diego County
619-453-6941
San Diego National Bank
619-233-1234 x337
San Diego Teachers' Credit Union
619-636-4292

Scripps Bank
619-456-2265
Union Bank
619-230-3771
United Services of America Federal
619-693-9360 x567
University & State Employees CU
619-641-7555
Valle de Oro Bank
619-615-9677

Media & Communications

Applied Digital Access
213-239-7140
AT&T
213-239-7140
Daily Breeze
310-543-6625
Daily News
818-713-3093
Installnet
619-597-1864
KABC-AM (790)
310-557-4222
KBIG-FM (104.3)
800-649-2900
KBZT-FM
704-374-3875
KCBS-FM (93)
213-817-JOBS
KFMB-AM/FM & Channel 8
619-495-8640
KFWB-AM (980)
213-817-JOBS
KGB-FM
619-715-3196
KHTS-FM
619-715-3196
KIFM-FM
704-374-3875
KIOZ-FM
619-715-3196
KKBH-FM
619-715-3196
KKBT-FM (92.3)
800-649-2900
KKLQ-FM
619-715-3196
KLSX-FM (97.1)
213-817-JOBS
Knowledge Adventure
313-793-0599

KNX-AM (1070)
213-817-JOBS
KPBS-FM
619-594-5703
KPBS-TV, Channel 15
619-594-5703
KSON-AM/FM
704-374-3875
KTWV-FM (94.7)
213-817-JOBS
KUSI-TV, Channel 9
619-645-8729
Los Angeles Times
213-237-5700
Press-Telegram
562-499-6239
The San Diego Union-Tribune
619-293-1001
XETV Fox, Channel 6
619-279-6666 x312
XEWT, Channel 12
619-585-9463
XHBJ, Channel 45
619-585-9463
XHKY-FM
619-585-9090
XHTZ-FM
619-585-9090
XHUAA, Channel 57
619-585-9463
XTRA-AM
619-715-3196
XTRA-FM
619-715-3196

Education

Arcadia Unified School District
626-821-8300 x709
Azusa Unified School District
626-858-5066
Beverly Hills Unified School Disctrict
310-277-5900 x119
California Institute of Technology
626-395-4660
California State University Dominguez Hills
310-243-3840
California State University, Long Beach
562-985-5491

Employment Help

California State University Los
Angeles
213-343-3678
California State University,
Northridge
818-677-2087
California State University, San
Marcos
760-750-4410
Cerritos College
562-860-5042
Cerritos Community College
District
562-467-5042
Compton Community College
District
310-900-1605
Compton Unified School
District
310-632-3764
Culver City Unified School
District
310-535-6906
Cuyamaca College
619-644-7000
East Los Angeles College
213-265-8650 x8653
East Whittier City School
District
562-464-9381
El Camino College
310-660-3809
El Monte City School District
626-453-3726
Glendale Unified School
District
2818-47-1384
Grossmont College
619-644-7000
Hermosa Beach City School
District
310-937-5877 x281
La Canada Unified School
District
818-952-8300
Las Virgenes Unified School
District
818-878-5294
Long Beach Community
College District
562-938-4050
Long Beach Unified School
District
562-491-5627
Los Alamitos Unified School
District
562-799-4722
Los Angeles Community
College District
213-891-2099
Los Angeles County Office of
Education
562-401-5540
Los Angeles Harbor College
310-522-8366

Los Angeles Trade Technical
College
213-744-9066
Los Angeles Unified School
District
213-625-5300
Manhattan Beach Unified
School District
310-546-3488 x5993
MiraCosta College
760-795-6868
National University
619-563-7198
Norwalk-La Mirada Unified
School District
562-864-3526
Palomar College
760-744-2199
Pasadena Area Community
College District
626-585-7257
Pepperdine University
310-456-4397
Point Loma Nazarene College
619-849-2212
Pomona Unified School District
909-397-4800 x3188
Rio Hondo Community College
562-692-3677
Rowland Unified School District
626-854-8553
San Diego City College
619-584-6580
San Diego Mesa College
619-584-6580
San Diego Miramar College
619-536-7235
San Diego State University
619-594-5200
Santa Monica College
310-450-5150 x9321
Santa Monica Community
College District
310-452-9336
Santa Monica-Malibu Unified
School District
310-450-8338 x993
Torrance Unified School
District
310-328-2572
University of California at Los
Angeles
310-825-9151
University of San Diego
619-260-4626
West Covina Unified School
District
626-338-3371
West Los Angeles College
310-287-4310
Whittier Union High School
District
562-698-0312

Entertainment

ABC Entertainment
310-557-4222
ABC Pictures
310-557-4222
Castle Rock Entertainment
818-954-5400
Columbia Pictures
310-244-4436
Columbia Tristar Motion Picture
Group
310-244-4436
Columbia Tristar Pictures
310-244-4436
Columbia Tristar Television
310-244-4436
Dimension Films
213-951-4331
DreamWorks SKG
818-733-6100
E! Entertainment Television
213-954-2666
Evie Kreisler & Associates
800-275-3843
Four Media Company
818-840-7378
Fox Broadcasting Company
310-369-1360
Fox Kids Network
310-235-9400
Iwerks Entertainment
818-955-7895
Jim Henson Company
213-960-4096
NBC Entertainment
818-840-4397
New Line Cinema
310-967-6553
North Orange County ROP
776-2170
Pacific Ocean Post
310-458-3300 x5075
Paramount Network Television
213-956-5216
Paramount Pictures
213-956-5216
Paramount Television Group
213-956-5216
Playboy Entertainment Group
310-246-7714
Polygram Filmed Entertainment
310-385-4111
Polygram Television
310-385-4111
Showtime Networks
213-956-5216
Sony Pictures Entertainment
310-244-4436
Sony Pictures Imageworks
310-840-8546
Turner Network Television
310-788-4255
Twentieth Century Fox
310-369-1360

Twentieth Century Fox
Television
310-369-1360
United Artists Pictures
310-449-3569
Universal Studios
818-777-JOBS
Viacom Productions
213-956-5216
Warner Brothers Feature
Animation
818-954-5400
Warner Brothers TV Animation
818-977-8534

Healthcare

Aetna US Healthcare
619-497-4247
Alvarado Hospital Medical
Center
619-224-7100
Blue Shield HMO & Preferred
Plan
800-408-5627
Blue Shield of California
310-670-4040
Chevron Petroleum Technology
415-894-2552
Children's Hospital & Health
Center
619-576-5880
Good Samaritan Hospital
213-977-2300
Green Hospital of Scripps
Clinic
619-554-5627
Grossmont Hospital
619-627-5935
Harbor - UCLA Medical Center
800-970-5478
Health Net
818-676-7236
Hollywood Presbyterian
Medical Center
800-426-6998
Huntington Memorial Hospital
626-397-8504
Kaiser Permanente
714-279-6080
Kaiser Permanente Medical
Center - L.A.
213-857-2615
Martin Luther King Jr.- Drew
Med. Ctr.
213-351-5478
Mercy Hospital
619-554-8400
Mesa Vista Hospital
619-627-5935
Palomar Medical Center
760-739-3960
Paradise Valley Hospital
619-470-4422
Pomerado Hospital
619-485-4680

Prudential HealthCare
800-994-9966
San Pedro Peninsula Hospital
310-540-7373
Scripps Hospital-East County
619-554-8400
Scripps Memorial Hospital-
Chula Vista
619-554-8400
Scripps Memorial Hospital-
Encinitas
619-554-8400
Scripps Memorial Hospital-La
Jolla
619-554-8400
Sharp Chula Vista Medical
Center
619-627-5935
Sharp Coronado Hospital
619-627-5935
Sharp Metro Hospitals
619-627-5935
St. Mary Medical Center
562-491-9844
St. Vincent Medical Center
213-484-7032
The Immune Response Corp.
760-431-3396
Tri-City Medical Center
760-940-5002
UCLA Medical Center
310-794-0526
UCSD Medical Center
619-682-1001
UHP Care
213-955-6923
UniHealth
818-238-6029
Unilab Corporation
818-996-7300 x6680
Universal Care
562-981-9064
VA Medical Center -
Long Beach
562-494-5971

High Tech

Vical
619-646-1143
Autosplice
619-535-0868
Bluebird Systems
800-669-2220
CCH
800-254-7772
Centon Electronics
714-855-2039
Continental Maritime of San
Diego
619-234-8851 #3
Cubic Corporation
619-505-1540
Delta Environmental Consultants
800-988-5819
Emulex Corporation
714-513-8200

GDE Systems
800-545-0506
Ingram Micro
714-566-1000
International Technology Corp
949-660-5434
McLaren/Hart
916-638-3696
Microsoft Corporation
800-892-3181
Mitsubishi Electronics America
714-229-6565
Monroe Systems for Business
562-946-5678
National Steel & Shipbuilding Co.
619-544-8512
Pacific Ship Repair &
Fabrication
619-232-2300 x125
Printronix
714-221-2828
Procom Technology
714-852-1000 x5999
SAS Institute
919-677-8000
SECOR International
619-525-5151
State of the Art
714-759-1222 x4080
The Austin Company
949-453-1000 x263
The Laxmi Group
714-903-5676 x211
Thermeon Corporation
800-232-9191
Toshiba America Info Systems
949-461-4949
TriTeal Corp.
760-827-5509
Wonderware Software Corp
714-727-3200 x7901

Hospitality

Anaheim Marriott Hotel
714-748-2482
Beverly Hilton
310-285-1340
Catamaran Resort Hotel
619-539-7733
Century Plaza Hotel & Tower
310-551-3390
Continental Plaza LA Airport
Hotel
310-649-7049
Country Side Inn Suites
Costa Mesa
714-549-0300 x199
Disneyland Hotel
714-781-1600
DoubleTree Hotel/OC Airport
714-438-4963
Embassy Suites La Jolla
619-453-0400 x547
Hanalei Hotel
619-297-0268

Employment Help

Holiday Inn on the Bay
619-232-3861 x7766
Holiday Inn Torrance
310-781-9100 x578
Hollywood Roosevelt Hotel
213-769-7293
Hotel Inter-Continental
Los Angeles
213-356-4049
Hotel Nikko Beverly Hills
310-246-2074
Hyatt Newporter
704-759-3075
Hyatt Regency Alicante
704-740-6052
Hyatt Regency Irvine
714-225-6716
Hyatt Regency La Jolla
619-552-6058
Hyatt Regency Long Beach
562-624-6090
Hyatt Regency Los Angeles
213-612-3139
Hyatt Regency San Diego
619-687-6000
International Food Service
Executives
714-846-6566
La Costa Resort, Spa and
Country Club
760-433-9675
La Jolla Marriott
619-597-6325
Loews Coronado Bay Resort
619-424-4000 x4480
Loews Santa Monica Beach
Hotel
310-576-3121
Long Beach Marriott
562-627-8000
Los Angeles Airport Hilton &
Towers
310-413-6111
Los Angeles Airport Marriott
310-621-5327
Los Angeles Marriot Downtown
213-617-0788
Marina Beach Marriott
310-448-4850
Marina Village Conference
Center
619-525-2800
Marriott's Laguna Cliffs Resort
714-661-5000 x1111
Miramar Sheraton Hotel &
Bungalows
310-319-3145
New Otani Hotel and Garden
310-617-0368
Omni Los Angeles Hotel and
Center
213-612-3990
Park Hyatt Los Angeles at
Century City
310-284-6521
Radisson Hotel
310-348-4174

Radisson Wilshire Plaza Hotel
213-368-3068
Renaissance Long Beach Hotel
562-499-2518
Renaissance Los Angeles Hotel
888-462-7746
San Diego Concourse
619-525-5151
San Diego Convention Center
619-525-5151
San Diego Hilton Beach &
Tennis Resort
619-275-8994
San Diego Marriott Hotel &
Marina
619-234-1500 x8901
San Diego Mission Valley Hilton
619-543-9441
San Diego Princess Resort
619-581-5902
Sheraton Grande Torrey Pines
619-558-8058
Sheraton San Diego Hotel &
Marina
619-692-2793
Sutton Place Hotel
714-955-5656
The Anaheim Hilton & Towers
714-740-4319
The Atrium Hotel
714-833-2770 x448
The Ritz-Carlton -
Marina del Rey
310-574-4290
The Waterfront Hilton
714-960-7873
Torrance Marriott
310-792-6171
Town & Country Resort &
Conference Center
619-299-2254
Westin Bonaventure Hotel and
Suites
213-612-4845
Westin Horton Plaza San Diego
619-239-2200 x7177
Westin Long Beach
562-499-2056
Wyndham Emerald Plaza
619-515-4541
Wyndham Hotel at Los Angeles
Airport
310-337-6455

Insurance

20th Century Insurance Group
818-704-3760
Arrowhead Group of Companies
619-677-5299
Balboa Life & Casualty
800-654-2826
Fremont Compensation
Insurance
800-646-4478
Pacific Life Insurance Company
714-721-5050

Law & Lobbying

Berger Kahn Shafton, Moss,
Figler, Simon
310-821-9000
Early Maslach Price & Baukol
213-964-8832
Manatt Phelps & Phillips
310-231-5670
Paul Hastings Janofsky &
Walker
213-683-5015
Seltzer Caplan Wilkins &
McMahon
619-685-3127

Public Relations

Cohn & Wolfe
310-226-3015
Paine & Associates
714-755-0400

Real Estate

Century 21/Superstars
800-890-7653
John Burnham & Co.
619-525-2994
Kaufman and Broad Home
Corp.
310-231-4000 x4209
Newhall Land & Farming Co.
805-255-4442
Ninteman Construction Co.
619-294-4474
Snyder Langston Real Estate
714-863-9200
Voit Commercial Brokerage
714-978-7880

Sports & Recreation

Anaheim Sports
818-558-2222
Buck Knives
619-449-1162
City of Coronado Municipal
Golf Course
619-522-7300
Disneyland
714-781-4407
Fountains Executive Course
760-749-3182
Four Seasons Resort Aviara
760-603-6949
Knott's Berry Farm
714-99KNOTT
La Costa Resort, Spa and
Country Club
760-433-9675
Pala Mesa Resort
760-731-6814
Torrey Pines Golf Course
619-236-6467

Warner Springs Ranch
760-782-4234

Travel, Trans & Utilities

Alaska Airlines
206-433-3230
Associated Travel International
800-969-255 x222
Automobile Club of Southern
California
714-850-2888
Continental Airlines
800-444-8414 x6952
Delta Airlines
404-715-2501
Southern California Gas Co
909-394-3600
Southwest Airlines
602-389-3738

Largest & Fastest Growing Companies

Aames Financial Corporation
213-210-5554
Ace Parking Management
619-231-9501
Advanced Access
619-693-1200 x1195
Advanced Marketing Services
800-695-3580 x932010
AlliedSignal Aerospace
310-512-2012
Balboa Travel
619-678-3470
Bank of America
619-515-5514
Boeing North American
818-586-2834
CareAmerica Health Plans
818-228-2400
Cedars-Sinai Medical Center
310-967-8230
Commerce Casino
213-838-3399
Continental Maritime San Diego
619-234-8851
Countrywide Home Loans
800-881-4968
CyberMedia
310-581-6092
Diagnostic Products Corporation
213-776-2609
Dole Food Company
818-874-4999
Edison International
626-302-9850
Environmental Industries
800-224-1024
Foodmaker
619-571-2200
Herbalife International
310-216-5168

Hilton Hotels Corp.
310-205-7692
King Meat
213-582-1813
Mail Boxes Etc.
619-597-8526
Mattel
310-252-3535
Mercury General Corp.
213-857-7198
Nitches
619-625-6230
Pacific Holding
818-847-4999
PMR Corp.
800-866-7677
Public Storage
1-888-477-5627
Qualcomm
619-658-5627
R.J. Gordon & Co.
310-724-6530
Ralphs Grocery/Food 4 Less
310-884-4642
Rohr
619-691-3022
Ryan Herco Products Co.
1-800-597-1141 x569
Smart & Final
800-995-4630
Southern California Water Co.
909-394-3600
Southwest Marine
619-557-4277
Stac
619-794-4576
Sunkist Growers
818-379-7390
Sunrise Medical
760-930-1596
Swatfame
626-961-7928 x193
Ta Chen International Corp.
800-364-8389
The National Dispatch Center
800-439-1896
Ticketmaster Group
310-360-6057
Times Mirror Co.
213-237-6687
TransWestern Publishing
619-467-6067
TRW Space & Electronics
Group
310-814-7500
Virco Manufacturing Corp.
310-533-0474 x220
Welk Resort Center
760-749-3182
WellPoint Health Networks
818-703-3181
Xerox
800-423-3868

Alumni Networking

One of the best ways of getting your foot in the door of a particular industry is to network with alumni from your respective college or university. With the phone numbers and web site addresses provided, you can learn of upcoming events, meetings and job networking services that these organizations might provide.

American University	800-270-ALUM	**Colby Collge**	207-872-3190
www.american.edu		www.colby.edu	
Amherst College	413-542-2313	**Colgate University**	315-824-7433
www.amherst.edu		www.colgate.edu	
Arizona State University	602-965-2586	**Columbia University**	212-870-2530
www.asu.edu		www.columbia.edu	
Auburn University	344-844-2586	**Cornell University**	607-255-2390
www.auburn.edu		www.cornell.edu	
Babson College	617-239-4562	**Dartmouth College**	800-228-1769
www.babson.edu		www.dartmouth.edu	
Bates College	207-786-6127	**Denison University**	614-587-6576
www.bates.edu		denison.edu	
Baylor University	817-755-1121	**Dickinson College**	717-245-1231
www.sicembears.com		www.dickinson.edu	
Bennington College	800-598-2979	**Drexel University**	215-895-2604
www.bennington.edu		www.drexel.edu	
Boston College	800-669-8430	**Duke University**	919-684-5114
www.bc.edu		www.duke.edu	
Boston University	800-800-3466	**Emory University**	404-727-6400
www.bu.edu		www.emory.edu	
Bowdoin College	207-725-3266	**Florida State University**	904-644-2761
www.bowdoin.edu		www.fsu.edu	
Brandeis University	617-736-4100	**Frostburg State University**	301-689-4161
www.brandeis.edu		www.fsu.umd.edu	
Brigham Young University	801-378-4663	**George Mason University**	703-993-8696
www.byu.edu		www.gmu.edu	
Brown University	401-863-3307	**George Washington University**	
www.brown.edu		www.gwu.edu	202-994-6435
Bryn Mawr College	610-526-5227	**Georgetown University**	202-687-1789
www.brynmawr.edu		www.georgetown.edu	
Bucknell University	717-524-3223	**Georgia Tech University**	404-894-2391
www.bucknell.edu		www.gatech.edu	
Carleton College	800-729-2586	**Gettysburg College**	717-337-6518
www.carleton.edu		www.gettysburg.edu	
Carnegie Mellon University	412-268-2060	**Hampden-Sydney College**	804-223-6148
www.cmu.edu		www.hsc.edu	
Case Western University	216-368-2416	**Hampton University**	804-727-5425
www.cwru.edu		www.hamptonu.edu	
Catholic University	800-288-2586	**Harvard University**	617-495-5731
www.cua.edu		www.harvard.edu	
Clark University	508-793-7166	**Hollins College**	540-362-6413
www.clarku.edu		www.hollins.edu	
Clarkson University	315-268-6467	**Holy Cross**	508-793-2418
www.clarkson.edu		www.holycross.edu	
Clemson Univesity	803-656-2345	**Howard University**	202-806-2180
www.clemson.edu		www.howard.edu	

Indiana University	812-855-1711	**Penn State University**	814-865-6516
www.indiana.edu		www.psu.edu	
Iowa State University	515-294-6525	**Pepperdine University**	310-456-4071
www.iastate.edu		www.pepperdine.edu	
Ithaca College	607-274-3194	**Princeton University**	609-258-5816
www.ithaca.edu		www.princeton.edu	
James Madison University	703-568-6234	**Providence College**	401-865-2414
www.jmu.edu		www.providence.edu	
Johns Hopkins University	410-516-0363	**Purdue University**	317-494-5175
www.jhu.edu		www.purdue.edu	
Kansas State University	913-532-6260	**Radford University**	800-782-3174
www.ksu.edu		www.runet.edu	
Kenyon College	614-427-5147	**Randolph Macon College**	804-752-7221
www.kenyon.edu		www.rmc.edu	
Lafayette College	800-LAFAYETTE	**Randolph Macon Woman' College**	
www.lafayette.edu		www.rmwc.edu	804-947-8102
Lehigh University	610-758-3000	**Rice University**	713-527-4057
www.lehigh.edu		www.rice.edu	
Longwood College	804-395-2044	**Roanoke College**	540-375-2238
www.lwc.edu		www.roanoke.edu	
Louisiana State University	318-797-5168	**Rutgers University**	908-932-6774
www.lsu.edu		www.rutgers.edu	
Marquette University	414-288-7441	**Seton Hall University**	201-761-9822
www.marquette.edu		www.shu.edu	
Mary Baldwin College	540-887-7707	**Shepherd College**	304-876-5157
www.mbc.edu		www.shephard.wvnet.edu	
Mary Washington College	800-468-5614	**Shippensburg University**	717-532-1218
www.mwc.edu		www.ship.edu	
Massachusetts Institute of Technology		**Smith College**	413-585-2020
www.mit.edu	617-253-8200	www.smith.edu	
Miami University	513-529-5957	**Southern Methodist University**	
www.miami.edu		www.smu.edu	214-768-4750
Michigan State University	517-355-8314	**Stanford University**	415-723-2021
www.msu.edu		www.stanford.edu	
Middlebury College	802-442-5183	**Sweet Briar College**	804-381-6131
www.middlebury.edu		www.sbc.edu	
Mississippi State University	601-325-2434	**Syracuse University**	315-443-3514
www.msstate.edu		www.syracuse.edu	
Mt. Saint Mary's-MD	301-447-5362	**Temple University**	215-787-7521
www.msmary.edu		www.temple.edu	
New York University	212-998-6888	**Texas A&M University**	409-845-7514
www.nyu.edu		www.tamu.edu	
North Carolina State University		**Texas Christian University**	
www.ncsu.edu	919-515-3375	www.tcu.edu	817-921-7803
Northeastern University	617-437-3186	**Texas Tech University**	806-742-3641
www.northeastern.edu		www.ttu.edu	
Northwestern University	800-682-5867	**Towson State University**	410-830-2234
www.nwu.edu		www.towson.edu	
Oberlin College	216-7758692	**Trinity College**	202-884-9700
www.oberlin.edu		www.trinitydc.edu	
Ohio State University	614-292-2500	**Tulane University**	504-865-5901
www.osu.edu		www.tulane.edu	
Ohio University	614-593-4300	**Tufts University**	800-The-Alum
www.ohiou.edu		www.tufts.edu	
Old Dominion University	804-683-3087	**University of Alabama**	205-348-5963
www.odu.edu		www.ua.edu	
Oklahoma State University	405-744-5368	**University of Arizona**	800-BEAT-ASU
www.okstate.edu		www.arizona.edu	

University of Arkansas	501-575-2801

www.uark.edu

University of California at Berkeley
www.berkeley.edu　　510-642-7026

University of California at Los Angeles
www.ucla.edu　　310-825-3901

University of Chicago	312-702-2150

www.uchicago.edu

University of Colorado	303-492-8484

www.colorado.edu

University of Connecticut	860-486-2240

www.uconn.edu

University of Delaware	302-831-2341

www.udel.edu

University of Florida	904-392-1691

www.ufl.edu

University of Georgia	404-542-2251

www.uga.edu

University of Illinois	217-333-1471

www.illinois.edu

University of Iowa	319-335-3294

www.uiowa.edu

University of Kansas	913-864-4760

www.ku.edu

University of Kentucky	606-257-8905

www.uky.edu

University of Maine	207-581-2586

www.maine.edu

University of Maryland	800-336-8627

www.umd.edu

University of Massachusetts	413-545-2317

www.umass.edu

University of Miami	305-284-2872

www.miami.edu

University of Michigan	313-764-0384

www.umich.edu

University of Minnesota	612-624-2323

www.umn.edu/tc

University of Mississippi	601-232-7375

www.olemiss.edu

University of Missouri
www.missouri.edu

University of Nebraska	402-472-2841

www.unl.edu

University of New Hampshire　603-862-2040
www.unh.edu

University of North Carolina　919-962-1208
www.unc.edu

University of Notre Dame	219-239-6000

www.nd.edu

University of Oklahoma	405-325-1710

www.uoknor.edu

University of Oregon	541-346-5656

www.uoregon.edu

University of Pennsylvania	215-898-7811

www.upenn.edu

University of Pittsburgh	412-624-8222

www.pitt.edu

University of Rhode Island	401-792-2242

www.uri.edu

University of Richmond	804-289-8030

www.urich.edu

University of Rochester	716-275-3684

www.rochester.edu

University of South Carolina　803-777-4111
www.scarolina.edu

University of Southern California
www.usc.edu　　213-740-2300

University of Tennessee	615-974-3011

www.ut.edu

University of Texas	512-471-8839

www.utexas.edu

University of Virginia	804-971-9721

www.virginia.edu

University of Vermont	802-656-2010

www.uvm.edu

University of Washington	206-543-0540

www.washington.edu

University of Wisconsin	608-262-2551

www.wisc.edu

Vanderbilt University	615-322-2929

www.vanderbilt.edu

Vassar College	914-437-5440

www.vassar.edu

Villanova University	215-645-4580

www.vill.edu

Virginia Commonwealth University
www.vcu.edu　　804-367-1227

Virginia Military Institute　540-464-7221
www.vmi.edu

Virginia Tech University	703-231-6285

www.vt.edu

Wake Forest University	910-759-5263

www.wfu.edu

Washington University	314-935-7378

www.wustl.edu

Washington & Lee University　803-463-8464
www.wlu.edu

Wellesley College	617-283-2331

www.wellesley.edu

Wesleyan University	800-685-2000

www.wesleyan.edu

West Virginia University	304-293-4731

www.wvu.edu

William & Mary	804-221-1842

www.wm.edu

Williams College	413-597-4151

www.williams.edu

Yale University	203-432-2586

www.yale.edu

The American College   310-470-2000 x28
www.aiuniv.edu
Armstrong University   510-848-2500
www.armstrong-u.edu
Azusa Pacific University   626-812-3026
www.apu.com
California Institute of Technology
www.caltech.edu   626-395-6361
California Lutheran University   805-493-3170
www.clunet.edu
California State University - Bakersfield
www.csubak.edu   805-664-3211
California State University - Chico
www.csuchico.edu   530-898-6472
California State University - Fresno
www.csufresno.edu   209-278-2586
California State University - Fullerton
www.fullerton.edu   714-CSU-ALUM
California State University - Hayward
www.csuhayward.edu   510-885-3724
California State University - Long Beach
www.csulb.edu
California State University - Los Angeles
www.calstatela.edu   213-343-4980
California State University - Sacramento
www.csus.edu   916-278-6295
California State University - San Bernardino
www.csusb.edu   909-880-5008
California State University - San Marcos
www.csusm.edu
California State University - Stanislaus
www.csustan.edu   209-667-3693
University of California - Berkeley
www.berkeley.edu   510-642-7026
University of California - Davis   916-752-0286
www.ucdavis.edu
University of California - Irvine
www.uci.edu
University of California - Los Angeles
www.ucla.edu   310-206-6052
University of California - Riverside
www.ucr.edu   909-787-4511
University of California - San Diego
www.ucsd.edu   619-534-3900
University of California - Santa Barbara
www.ucsb.edu   805-893-2288
University of California - Santa Cruz
www.ucsc.edu   408-459-2530
Chapman University   714-997-6783
www.chapman.edu
Concordia University - Irvine   949-854-8002
www.cui.edu
City College of San Francisco   415-239-3212
www.ccsf.cc.ca.us
Claremont McKenna College   909-621-8097
www.mckenna.edu

Cuesta College   805-546-3915
www.cuesta.cc.ca.us
Fresno Pacific College   209-453-2058
www.fresno.edu
Golden Gate University   415-442-7824
www.ggu.edu
Harvey Mudd College   www.hmc.edu
Humboldt State University   707-826-3132
www.humboldt.edu
La Pierce College   818-703-0826
www.lapc.cc.ca.us
University of La Verne   909-593-3511
www.ulv.edu
Loyola Marymount University   310-338-3065
www.lmu.edu
Menlo College   650-688-3729
www.menlo.edu
Monterey Institute of International Studies
www.miis.edu   408-647-6600
Occidental College   213-259-2601
www.oxy.edu
University of the Pacific   209-946-2391
www.uop.edu
Pepperdine University   310-456-4348
www.pepperdine.edu
Pomona College   909-621-8110
www.pomona.edu
University of the Redlands   909-335-4011
www.redlands.edu
Saint Mary's College of Ca.   925-631-4200
San Bernardino Valley College   909-888-6511
www.sbccd.cc.ca.us
San Diego State University
www.sdsu.edu
University of San Diego   619-260-4819
San Francisco State University
www.sfsu.edu
University of San Francisco
www.usfca.edu
San Jose State University   408-924-6515
www.sjsu.edu
Santa Clara University   408-554-6800
www.scu.edu
Scripps College   909-621-8054
www.scrippscol.edu
Sonoma State University   707-664-2426
www.sonoma.edu
University of Southern California
www.usc.edu   213-740-2300
Stanford University   650-723-2021
www.stanford.edu
Westmont College   805-565-6056
www.wesmont.edu
Whittier College   www.whittier.edu
Woodbury University   818-767-0888
www.woodburyu.edu

National Newspapers & Publications

National magazines obviously cover a broader range, but the odds are that somewhere or sometime in the last year or so, one of these publications has written stories on local companies. Research back issues at your local library.

NATIONAL BUSINESS MAGAZINES

Business Week
1221 Avenue of the Americas
New York, NY 10020
212-997-1221
Web Address: www.businessweek.com
News on Economy and Industry

Fast Company
77 North Washington Street
Boston, MA 02114
617-973-0300
www.fastcompany.com

Forbes
60 5th Avenue
New York, NY 10011
Web Address: www.forbes.com
News on the Economy and Markets

Fortune
Time Life Building
1271 Avenue of the Americas
New York, NY 10020-1301
212-522-1212
Web Address: www.fortune.com

Inc.
38 Commercial Wharf
Boston, MA 02110
617-248-8000
Web Address: www.inc.com

Million Dollar Directory
Dun & Bradstreet
889 Eaton Avenue
Bethlehem, PA 18025
Listings of Medium and Large Sized Companies

Money
Time Life Building
1271 Avenue of the Americas
New York, NY 10020-1301
212-522-1212
Web Address: www.money.com

USA Today
1000 Wilson Boulevard
Arlington, VA 22201
703-276-3400
Web Address: www.usatoday.com

Wall Street Journal
1025 Connecticut Avenue, N.W.
Washington, D.C. 20036
202-862-9200
Web Address: www.wsj.com

Working Woman
230 Park Avenue
New York, NY 10169
800-234-9675
Publication for Professional Women

NATIONAL TRADE JOURNALS & DIRECTORIES

Adweek Directories
Adweek Agency Directory
1515 Broadway, 12th Floor
New York, NY 10036

Art Job
Western States Arts Federation
236 Montezuma Avenue
Santa Fe, NM 87501
505-988-1166

ArtSEARCH
Theatre Communications Group
355 Lexington Avenue
New York, NY 10017
212-697-5230

Association for Experiential Education
Jobs Clearinghouse
2305 Canyon Boulevard, Suite 100
Boulder, CO 80302
303-440-8844

Athletics Employment Weekly
RDST Enterprises
RR2, Box 140
Carthage, IL 62321
217-357-3615

Aviso
American Association of Museums
1225 I Street, N.W., Suite 200
Washington, D.C. 20005
202-289-1818

Back Stage West
1515 Broadway, 14th Floor
New York, NY 10036
212-764-7300

Book Publishing Career Directory
Gale Research Company
835 Penobscot Building
Detroit, MI 48226

Career Guide: Dunn's Employment Opportunities Directory
Dun and Bradstreet
3 Century Drive
Parsippany, NJ 07054

Career Opportunity News
Garrett Park Press
P.O. Box 190
Garret Park, MD 20896
301-949-2553

Chronical of Philanthropy
Department E
1255 23rd Street, N.W.
Washington, D.C. 20037
800-347-6969

Chronicle of Higher Education
Department E
1255 23rd Steet, N.W.
Washington, D.C. 20037
800-347-6969
Web Address: http://chronical.com

College Placement Annual
National Association of Colleges and Employers Directory
62 Highland Avenue
Bethlehem, PA 18017

Community Jobs
Access/Networking in the Public Interest
50 Beacon Street
Boston, MA 02108
617-720-5627

Consultants and Consulting Organazations Directory
Gale Research Company
835 Penobscot Building
Detroit, MI 48226

Corporate Technology Directory
Corporate Technology Information Services
1 Market Street
Wellesley Hills, MA 02181

Current Jobs in Writing, Editing & Communication
P.O. Box 40550
Washington, D.C. 20016
703-506-4400

Dictionary of Occupational Titles
U.S. Department of Labor
200 Constitution Avenue, N.W.
Washington, D.C. 20210

Directories in Print, Thirteenth Edition
Gale Research Company
835 Penobscot Building
Detroit, MI 48226

Directory of Minority Arts Organizations
Civil Rights Division, National Endowment for the Arts
1100 Pennsylvania Avenue, N.W., Room 812
Washington, D.C. 20506

Directory of Women-Owned Businesses
National Association of Women Business Owners
2000 P Street, N.W., Suite 511
Washington, D.C. 20036

Dun and Bradstreet State Sales Guide
Dun and Bradstreet
430 Mountain Road
New Providence, NJ 07974

Earthwork Hotline
Student Conservation Association
P.O. Box 550
Charlestown, NH 03603
603-543-1700

Encyclopedia of Associations
Gale Research Company
835 Penobscot Building
Detroit, MI 48226

Encyclopedia of Associations: National Organizations of the U.S.
Gale Research Company
835 Penobscot Building
Detroit, MI 48226

Encyclopedia of Business Information Sources
Gale Research Company
835 Penobscot Building
Detroit, MI 48226

Engineering, Science, and Computer Graduates: Peterson's Job Opportunities
Peterson's Guides
202 Carnegie Center
P.O. Box 2123
Princeton, NJ 08543

Entertainment Employment Journal
P.O. Box 7383
Van Nuys, CA 91409
800-335-4335

Environmental Career Opportunities
P.O. Box 560
Standardsville, VA 22973
804-861-0592

Environmental Engineering Selection Guide
American Academy of Environmental Engineers
130 Holiday Court, Suite 100
Anapolis, MD 21401

Equal Employment Opportunity Career Journal
CASS Recrutiment Publications
1800 Sherman Avenue
Evanston, IL 60201
847-475-8800

Fortune Double 500 Directory
Time, Inc.
Rockefeller Building, Rockefeller Center
New York, NY 10020

Gale Directory of Publications and Broadcast Media
Gale Research Company
835 Penobscot Building
Detroit, MI 48226

Grocery Commercial Food Industry Directory
GroCom Group
P.O. Box 10378
Clearwater, FL 34617

Harbinger File
Harbinger Communications
50 Rustic Lane
Santa Cruz, CA 95060

Hispanic Media & Markets Source
Standard Rate & Data Service
3004 Glenview Road
Wilmette, IL 60091

Hoover's Handbook of American Companies
The Reference Press
P.O. Box 140375
Austin, TX 78714

International Advertising Association Membership Directory
342 Madison Avenue
New York, NY 10017

International Career Employment Opportunities
P.O. Box 305
Standardsville, VA 22973
804-985-6444

Job Openings-Publication #510K
Consumer Information Center, Dept G
Pueblo, CO 81009

Job Seeker's Guide to Private and Public Companies
Gale Research Company
835 Penobscot Building
Detroit, MI 48226

Legal Employment Newsletter
Pacific Edition
P.O. Box 36601
Grosse Point, MI 48236
313-961-2023

National Business Employment Weekly
Dow Jones & Company
420 Lexington Avenue
New York, NY 10170
212-808-6792
Web Address: www.enews.com/magazines

National Directory of Addresses and Telephone Numbers
Omnigraphics Inc.
2500 Penobscot Building
Detroit, MI 48226

National Directory of Minority-Owned Business Firms
Business Research Services
4201 Connecticut Avenue, N.W.
Washington, D.C. 20008

National Directory of Women-Owned Business Firms
Business Research Services
4201 Connecticut Avenue, N.W.
Washington, D.C. 20008

National Human Services and Liberal Arts Careers
KB Enterprises
13137 Penndale Lane
Fairfax, VA 22033
703-378-0439

National Trade & Professional Associations of the United States
Columbia Books
1212 New York Avenue, N.W.
Washington, D.C. 20005

O'Dwyer's Directory of Public Relations Firms
J.R. O'Dwyer & Company
271 Madison Avenue
New York, NY 10016

Occupational Outlook Handbook
U.S. Bureau of Labor
200 Consitutional Avenue, N.W.
Washington, D.C. 20210

Opportunity NOC's
The Management Center
870 Market Street, Suite 800
San Francisco, CA 94102
415-362-9735

Peterson's Job Opportunities in Engineering and Technology
Peterson's Guides
202 Carnegie Center
P.O. Box 2123
Princeton, NJ 08543

Recording Industry Sourcebook
Mix Publications
6400 Hollis Street, Suite 10
Emeryville, CA 94608

Sheldon's Retail Directory
Phelon, Sheldon & Marsar
15 Industrial Avenue
Fairview, NJ 07022

Southern California Broadcasters Association Job Alerts
5670 Wilshire Boulevard, Suite 910
Los Angeles, CA 90036
213-938-3100

Technical Employment News
PCI
12416 Hymeadow Drive
Austin, TX 78750
512-250-9023

The African-American Almanac
Gale Research Company
835 Penobscot Building
Detroit, MI 48226

The Almanac of American Employers: A Guide to America's 500 Most Successful Large Corporations
Contemporary Books
180 North Michigan Avenue
Chicago, IL 60601

The National Directory of Magazines
Oxbridge Communications
150 5th Avenue
New York, NY 10011

The Source
Rachel PR Services
500 North Michigan Avenue, Suite 1920
Chicago, IL 60611

Variety
5700 Wilshire Boulevard, Suite 120
Los Angeles, CA 90036
213-857-6600

Ward's Business Directory of U.S. Private and Public Companies
Gale Research Company
835 Penobscot Building
Detroit, MI 48226

Local Newspapers & Publications

Reading the local newspapers & magazines will not only offer numerous job leads but new ideas and approaches to the job search process. The Monday Business Editon of The Los Angeles Times, Orange Register and San Diego Union-Tribune are a must, as are the Business Journals - Book of Lists.

Advertising Age
6500 Wilshire Boulevard
Los Angeles, CA 90048
323-651-3710
Web Address: www.adage.com

Adweek Western Edition
BPI Communications
5055 Wilshire Boulevard, 7th Floor
Los Angeles, CA 90036
323-525-2270

American Cinematographer
P.O. Box 2230
Los Angeles, CA 90078
323-876-5080

Animation Magazine
28024 Dorothy Drive
Agoura Hills, CA 91301
818-991-2884

Architectural Digest
6300 Wilshire Boulevard
Los Angeles, CA 90048
323-965-3700

Back Stage West
5055 Wilshire Boulevard, 6th Floor
Los Angeles, CA 90036
323-525-2356

Billboard -BPI
5055 Wilshire Boulevard
Los Angeles, CA 90036
323-525-2270

California Apparel News
Apparel News Group
110 East 9th Street, Suite A-777
Los Angeles, CA 90079
213-627-3737

California Real Estate Journal
Daily Journal Corporation
915 East 1st Street
Los Angeles, CA 90012
213-229-5300

Daily Variety
5700 Wilshire Boulevard, Suite 120
Los Angeles, CA 90036
323-857-6600
Web Address: www.variety.com

Hollywood Reporter
5055 Wilshire Boulevard, Suite 600
Los Angeles, CA 90036
323-876-1000

Inland Empire Business Journal
8560 Vinyard Avenue, Suite 306
Rancho Cucamonga, CA 91730
909-484-9765

Investor's Business Daily
12655 Beatrice Street
Los Angeles, CA 90066
310-448-6000
Web Address: www.investors.com

William O'Neil, *Publisher*

La Opinion
411 West 5th Street
Los Angeles, CA 90013
213-896-2152

Long Beach Press-Telegram
604 Pine Avenue
Long Beach, CA 90804
562-435-1161

Los Angeles Business Journal
5700 Wilshire Boulevard, Suite 170
Los Angeles, CA 90036
323-549-5225
Web Address: www.labiz.com

Los Angeles Magazine
11100 Santa Monica Boulevard, 7th Floor
Los Angeles, CA 90025
310-312-2200

Music Connection Magazine
4731 Laurel Canyon Boulevard
North Hollywood, CA 91607
818-755-0101
Web Address: www.musicconnection.com

Orange County Business Journal
4590 MacArthur Boulevard, Suite 170
Newport Beach, CA 92660
949-833-8373

Orange County Register
625 Grand Avenue
Santa Ana, CA 92701
714-835-1234

Pasadena Star-News
525 East Colorado Boulevard
Pasadena, CA 91109
626-578-6300

San Diego Business Journal
4909 Murphy Canyon Road, Suite 200
San Diego, CA 92123
858-277-6359

San Diego Sourcebook
San Diego Daily Transcript
2131 3rd Avenue
San Diego, CA 92101
Web Address: www.sddt.com/business

Southern California Business Directory
Database Publishing Company
PO Box 70024
Anaheim, CA 92825
714-778-6400

Reading the local newspapers & magazines will not only offer numerous job leads but new ideas and approaches to the job search process.

The Monday Business Editon of The Los Angeles Times, Orange Register and San Diego Union-Tribune are a must, as are the Business Journals - Book of Lists.

Industry Associations & Publications

Associations & Industry Publications provide numerous job leads. In addition to learning more about the industry in affiliated magazines, most of the associations offer a list of their members which includes addresses and key personnel.

Accounting & Auditing

• Associations •

American Accounting Association
5717 Bessie Drive
Sarasota, Florida 34233
941-921-7747
Web Address: www.aaa-edu.org
Promotes research and education in accounting.

American Institute of Certified Public Accountants
1455 Pennsylvania Avenue, NW, 4th Floor
Washington, DC 20004
202-737-6600
Web Address: www.aicpa.org
Promotes and establishes accounting standards, education, and development.

American Institute of Certified Public Accountants
1211 Avenue of the Americas
New York, New York 10036
212-596-6200
Web Address: aicpa.org
Promotes and establishes accounting standards, education, and development.

American Society of Women Accountants
35 East Wacker Drive
Chicago, Illinois 60601
312-726-9030
Professional society which assists women in accounting careers.

Association of Government Accountants
2200 Mount Vernon Avenue
Alexandria, Virginia 22301
703-684-6931
Web Address: www.agacgfm.org
Professional society of financial managers employed by federal, state, county, and city governments.

Institute of Internal Auditors
P. O. Box 140099
Orlando, Florida 32889
407-830-7600
Professional organization of auditors, accounting, and educators of internal auditing.

Institute of Management Accounting
10 Paragon Drive
Montvale, New Jersey 07645-1760
201-573-9000
Web Address: www.imanet.org
Conducts research on accounting methods and management applications.

National Association of Black Accountants
7249-A Hanover Parkway
Greenbelt, MD 20770
301-474-6222
Promotes academic and professional excellence and student-professional relations.

National Association of Tax Practitioners
720 Association Drive
Appleton, Wisconsin 54914
800-558-3402
Web Address: www.natptax.com
Promotes high standards and provides continuing education.

National Society of Public Accountants
1010 North Fairfax Street
Alexandria, Virginia 22314
703-549-6400
Represents independent practitioners and conducts correspondence courses.

• Publications •

Accountants Directory
American Business Directories, Inc.

Accounting Firms Directory
American Business Directories, Inc.

Accounting Firms & Practitioners
AICPA Directory of Accounting Education
American Institute of Certified Public
Accountants
Harborside Financial Center, Plaza 3
Jersey City, NJ 07311-3881
201-938-3292
Web Address: www.aicpa.org

CPA Journal
200 Park Avenue
New York, New York 10166
Referred Accounting Journal

CPA Letter
1211 Avenue of the Americas
New York, New York 10036

Management Accounting
10 Paragon Drive
Montvale, New Jersey 07645
201-573-9000
Web Address: www.imanet.org
News of Profession

**National Society of Public Accountants
- Yearbook**
National Public Accountant
National Society of Public Accountants
1010 North Fairfax Street
Alexandria, VA 22314-1504
703-549-6400
Association Members and Committees
Articles on Taxes and Accounting Systems

Wendell's Report for Controllers
Warren, Gorham & Lamont, Inc.
31 Saint James Street
Boston MA 02116
617-423-2020
Web Address: www.wgl.com

Who Audits America
Data Financial Press

Advertising & Marketing

• Associations •

Advertising Research Foundation
641 Lexington Avenue
New York, New York 10022
212-751-5656
Promotes effectiveness of advertising.

American Advertising Federation
1101 Vermont Avenue, NW, Suite 500
Washington, D.C. 20005
202-898-0089
Web Address: www.aaf.org
Works to advance advertising.

**American Association of Advertising
Agencies**
405 Lexington Avenue, 18th floor
New York, New York 10174
(212) 682-2500
Fosters development of advertising industry.

American Marketing Association
311 South Wacker Drive, Suite 5800
Chicago, Illinois 60606
800-AMA-1150
Web Address: www.ama.org
Supports research, seminars, and student marketing clubs.

Direct Marketing Association
1120 Avenue of the Americas
New York, NY 10036-6700
212-768-7277
Studies the effectiveness of direct marketing.

International Advertising Association
521 5th Avenue, Suite 1807
New York, New York 10175
212-557-1133
Web Address: www.IAAglobal.org
Demonstrates value of advertising to governments and consumers.

League of Advertising Agencies
2 South End Avenue #4C
New York, New York 10280
212-528-0364
Education in areas of agency administration.

Marketing Research Association
2189 Silas Deane Highway, Suite #5
Rocky Hill, Connecticut 06067
Organization for those involved in Marketing research.

Public Relations Society of America
33 Irving Place
New York, New York 10003
212-995-2230
Web Address: www.prsa.org
Professional development, job referral, and research information center.

The Advertising Council
261 Madison Avenue
New York, New York 10016
212-922-1500
Web Address: *www.adcouncil.org*
Conducts public service advertising campaigns.

World Wide Partners
2280 South Xanadu Way, Suite 300
Aurora, Colorado 80014
303-671-8551

• Publications •

AAAA Roster & Organization
666 Third Avenue, 10th Floor
New York, New York 10017
212-682-2500
Compilation of National Advertising Agencies

Ad Trends
200 North 4th, PO Box 1
Burlington, IA 52601-001
319-752-5415
A monthly report of advertising and merchandise ideas.

Advertising Age
Crain Communications,
740 Rush Street
Chicago, Illinois 60611
312-649-5316
Web Address: *www.adage.com*
News of World Advertising

Advertising Career Directory
Career Press, Inc.
Hawthorne, New Jersey

ADWEEK
1515 Broadway, 12th Floor
New York, New York 10036
212-536-5336
Web Address: *www.adweek.com*
Advertising and Marketing News

American Advertising
1101 Vermont Avenue, N.W., Suite 500
Washington, D.C. 20005
202-898-0089
Journal for the advertising industry.

Brandweek
1515 Broadway
New York, NY 10036
212-536-5336
Covers aspects of brand marketing.

Business Marketing
Crain Communications
740 Rush Street
Chicago, Illinois 60611
312-649-5260

Direct Marketing Magazine
224 7th Street
Garden City, NY 11530
516-746-6700
Magazine of direct marketing which covers lists, brokers, postal issues, and database marketing.

Graphic Design
1556 3rd Avenue, Suite 405
New York, NY 10128
212-534-5500
Advertising Articles

Journal of Marketing
250 South Wacker Drive, Suite 200
Chicago, Illinois 60606
312-648-0536
Web Address: *www.ama.org*
Advances Science and Practice of Advertising

Standard Directory of Advertising Agencies
National Register Publishing Company
121 Chanlon Road
New Providence, New Jersey 07974
800-521-8110
Web Address: *www.reedref.com*

Target Marketing-Who's Who in Direct Marketing
North American Publishing Company
Philadelphia, Pennsylvania

The Gallup Poll Monthly
47 Hulfish Street
P.O. Box 628
Princeton, NJ 08542
609-924-9600
Web Address: *www.gallup.com*
Source of public opinion.

The Marketing News
250 South Wacker Drive, Suite 200
Chicago, Illinois 60606
312-648-0536
Web Address: *www.ama.org*
Articles on Marketing in General

Arts & Entertainment

• Associations •

Academy of Motion Picture Arts and Sciences
8949 Wilshire Boulevard
Beverly Hills, CA 90211
310-247-3000
Web Address: www.ampas.org
Advancement of Arts and Sciences in Motion Pictures.

Academy of Television Arts & Sciences
5220 Lankershim Boulevard
North Hollywood, California 91601
818-754-2800
Web Address: www.emmys.org
Advancement of arts and sciences in television.

Actor's Equity Association
165 West 46th Street
New York, New York 10036
212-869-8530
Represents actors and awards excellence in theatre.

Affiliate Artists
45 West 60th Street
New York, New York 10023
Promotes career development of artists.

American Crafts Council
72 Spring Street
New York, New York 10012
212-274-0630
Works to increase appreciation of American crafts.

American Dance Guild
31 West 21st Street
New York, New York 10010
212-932-2789
Initiates programs of national signifigance.

American Federation of Musicians
1501 Broadway, Suite 600
New York, New York 10036
212-869-1330
Musicians interested in advancing music industry.

American Guild of Musical Artists
1727 Broadway
New York, New York 10019
212-265-3687
Classical and opera singers and related managers.

American Music Center
30 West 26th Street, Suite 1001
New York, New York 10010
212-366-5260
Web Address: www.amc.net
Appreciation and creation of contemporary music.

American Society of Cinematographers
1782 North Orange Drive
Hollywood, CA 90028
323-969-4333

American Society of Composers, Authors & Publishers
1 Lincoln Plaza
New York, New York 10023
212-621-6000
Web Address: www.ascap.com
Clearinghouse of music performing rights.

Americans for the Arts
1 East 53rd Street
New York, New York 10012
212-223-2787
Web Address: www.artsusa.org
Promotes arts and artists.

Dance USA
1156 15th Street N.W., Suite 820
Washington, D.C. 20005
202 833-1717
Web Address: www.danceusa.org/danceusa
Promotes dance and dance programs.

International Documentary Association
1551 South Robertson Boulevard, Suite 201
Los Angeles, CA 90035
310-284-8422
Involved in the promotion of nonfiction film and the support of nonfiction film makers.

International Television Association
6311 North O'Connor Road, Suite 230
Irving, TX 75039
317-816-6269
Web Address: www.itva.org
Working for the advancement of those working in the videotape and nonbroadcast video fields.

Motion Picture Assocation
15503 Ventura Boulevard
Encino, CA 91436
818-995-6600
Web Address: www.mpa.org
Represents the American film industry internationally.

Motion Picture Association of America
1600 Eye Street, N.W.
Washington, D.C. 20006
202-293-1966
Web Address: www.mpaa.org
Represents the main U.S. distributors and producers of motion pictures domestically.

National Artists Equity Association
P.O. Box 28068, Central Station
Washington, D.C. 20038
202-628-9633
Protects rights of visual artists.

National Dance Association
1900 Association Drive
Reston, Virginia 22091
703-476-3464
Advocate for better dance education.

Producers Guild of America
400 South Beverly Drive, Suite 211
Beverly Hills, California 90212
310-557-0807
Association of movie and television producers.

Professional Arts Management Institute
110 Riverside Drive, Suite 4E
New York, New York 10024
212-245-3850
Education for management of performing arts or cultural institutions.

Screen Actors Guild
5757 Wilshire Boulevard
Hollywood, California 90036
General actor assistance.

Society of Motion Picture and Television Engineers
595 West Hartsdale Avenue
White Plains, New York 10607
914-761-1100
Web Address: www.smpte.org
Strives to advance engineering knowledge and practice for television and movies.

Stuntmen's Association of Motion Picture
10660 Riverside Drive, 2nd Floor, Suite E
Toluca, CA 90602
818-766-4334
Web Address: www.stuntnet.com
Members of the Screen Actors Guild or the American Federation of Television and Radio Artists Association who are involved in stunt work in television or motion pictures.

Theatre Communications Group
355 Lexington Avenue
New York, New York 10017
212-697-5230
Web Address: www.tcg.org
Service organization for non-profit theatres, artists, and administrators.

Women in Film
6464 Sunset Boulevard, Suite 1080
Hollywood, CA 90028
323-463-6040
Supporters of women in television and film industry.

• Publications •

American Artist
1515 Broadway
New York, New York 10036
212-764-7300
Artists, Methods, and Problems

Art Business News
Myers Publishing Company
19 Old Kings Highway South
Darien, Connecticut 06820
Fine Art and Picture Framing Industry

Artforum
350 7th Avenue, 19th Floor
New York, New York 10001
212-475-4000
Web Address: www.artforum.com

Artists Market
Writers Digest Books
1507 Dana Avenue
Cincinnati, Ohio 45207
513-531-2222

ArtWeek
2149 Paragon Drive, Suite 100
San Jose, California 95131
408-441-7065

Back Stage
1515 Broadway
New York, New York 10036
212-764-7300
Web Address: www.backstage.com

Billboard
1515 Broadway, 15th Floor
New York, NY 10036
212-536-5167
Web Address: www.billboard.com
Music and Home Entertainment.

Crafts Report
300 Water Street
Wilmington, Delaware 19801
302-656-2209
Web Address: www.craftsreport.com
Business News for Crafts Makers

Creative Black Book
115 5th Avenue, 3rd Floor
New York, New York 10003

Hollywood Reporter
5055 Wilshire Boulevard
Los Angeles, California 90028
323-525-2000
Web Address: www.hollywoodreporter.com

NASAA Directory
National Assembly of State Art Agencies
1029 Vermont Avenue NW, 2nd Floor
Washington, DC 20005
202-347-6352
Web Address: www.nasaa-arts.org

Ross Reports Television
1515 Broadway
New York, NY 10036-8986
718-937-3990

The Academy Players Directories
8949 Wilshire Boulevard
Beverly Hills, California 90211
310-247-3000
Web Address: www.oscar.com

Variety
475 Park Avenue South
New York, New York 10016
News of Entertainment Industry

Women Artist News
300 Riverside Drive
New York, New York 10025
212-666-6990
News for Female Artists

World Broadcast News
9800 Metcalf Avenue
Overland Park, KS 66212
913-341-1300
International Cable and Television News

Banking & Finance

• Associations •

American Finance Association
44 West 4th Street, Suite 9-190
New York, NY 10012
212-998-0370
To study and promote the knowledge about financial economics.

Academy of Marketing Science
University of Miami - School of Business Administration
Coral Gables, Florida 33124
305-284-6673
Advance knowledge and standards of marketing science.

America's Community Bankers
900 19th Street N.W. Suite 400
Washington, D.C. 20006
(202) 857-3100
Web Address: www.acbankers.org
Furthers thrift and home ownership.

American Bankers Association
1120 Connecticut Avenue, N.W.
Washington, DC 20036
202-663-5000
Web Address: www.aba.com
Enhance the role of commercial bankers.

American Business Women's Association
9100 Ward Parkway
P.O. Box 8728
Kansas City, MO 64114-0728
816-361-6621
Web Address: www.abwahq.org
Supports and promotes women in business.

American Financial Services Association
919 18th Street, 3rd Floor
Washington, D.C. 20006
202-296-5544
Web Address: www.americanfinsvcs.com
Encourages financing for useful purposes at reasonable rates.

Associated Credit Bureaus
1090 Vermont Avenue, N.W., No 200
Washington, D.C. 20005-4905
202-371-0910
Web Address: www.acb-credit.com
Maintains and collects credit reports.

Association for Investment Management and Research
560 Ray C. Hunt Drive
Charlottesville, VA 22903-0668
804-951-5499
Web Address: www.aimr.com
Investment analysis.

Bank Administration Institute
1 North Franklin
Chicago, Illinois 60606
800-323-8552
Web Address: www.bai.org
Educational and advisory services for banks.

Bank Marketing Association
1120 Connecticut Avenue, N.W.
Washington, D.C. 20036
800-433-9013
Web Address: www.bmanet.org
Provides marketing education, information, and services to financial services industry.

Banker's Association for Foreign Trade
2121 K Street, N.W., Suite 701
Washington, D.C. 20037
202-452-0952
Promotes and improves international banking and trade.

Center for International Private Enterprise
1155 15th Street NW, Suite 700
Washington DC 20005
202-721-9200
Web Address: www.cipe.org
Promotes international business growth.

Consumers Bankers Association
1000 Wilson Boulevard, Suite 2500
Arlington, VA 22209-3908
703-276-1750
Web Address: www.cbanet.org
Association which sponsors a graduate school at the University of Virginia.

Electronic Funds Transfer Association (EFTA)
950 Herndon Parkway, Suite 390
Herndon, VA 22070
703-435-9800
Web Address: www.efta.org
Provide forum for those involved in Electronic Funds Transfer.

Entrepreneurship Institute
3592 Corporate Drive, Suite 101
Columbus, OH 43231
614-895-1153
Web Address: www.fsti.com/tei/
To provide opportunities for businesses to grow and expand.

Farm Credit Council
50 F Street, N.W., Suite 900
Washington, D.C. 20001
202-626-8710
Web Address: www.fccouncil.com
Makes loans to agricultural and rural America.

Financial Executives Institute
10 Madison Avenue
P.O. Box 1938
Morristown, NJ 07962-1938
973-898-4600
Web Address: www.fei.org
Sponsors financial research activities.

Financial Planning Association
3801 East Florida Avenue, Suite 708
Denver, CO 80210-2571
800-322-4237
Web Address: www.fpanet.org
Provides benefits to certified financial planner licensees nationwide.

Institute of International Bankers
299 Park Avenue, 17th Floor
New York, NY 10171
212-421-1611
Web Address: www.iib.org
Promote the improvement of knowledge in international banking.

Institute of International Finance
2000 Pennsylvania Avenue, NW, Suite 8500
Washington, D.C. 20006-1812
202-857-3600
Web Address: www.iif.com
Seeks to improve the knowledge of financing.

International Association for Financial Planning
5775 Glenridge Drive, NE, Suite B-300
Atlanta, GA 30328-5364
404-845-0011
Web Address: www.fpanet.org
Objective is to promote the education of ethical business financial planning.

International Credit Association
PO Box 15945-314
Lenexa, KS 66285-5945
913-307-9432
Web Address: www.ica-credit.org

International Institute of Investment and Merchant Banking
3104 Q Street, N.W.
Washington, D.C. 20007
202-835-0566
Improve economic growth by eliminating investment barriers and by aiding in the cooperation of investment opportunities.

Independent Community Bankers Association of America
One Thomas Circle, N.W., Suite 400
Washington, D.C. 20005
202-659-8111
Web Address: www.icba.org
Legislative and regulatory information.

Investment Management Consultants Association
9101 East Kenyon Avenue, Suite 3000
Denver, CO 80237
303-770-3377
Web Address: www.imca.org
To promote and protect the interests of investment consulting.

Institute of Financial Education
55 West Mineral, Suite 2800
Chicago, Illinois 60603
312-364-0100

Mortgage Bankers Association of America
1919 Pennsylvania Avenue NW
Washington, DC 20006-3438
202-557-2700
Web Address: www.mbaa.org
Improvement in marketing and servicing of loans.

National Association of Investors Corporation
PO Box 220
Royal Oak, MI 48068
877-275-6242
Web Address: www.better-investing.org
Independent investment groups.

National Association of Real Estate Investment Trusts
1875 Eye Street, NW
Washington, DC 20006
202-739-9400
Web Address: www.nareit.com
Compiles statistics of real estate trusts.

National Council of Real Estate Investment Fiduciaries
180 North Stetson Avenue, Suite 2515
Chicago, IL 60601
312-819-5890
Web Address: www.ncreif.org
Analysis and assesment of investments in real estate.

National Investor Relations Institiute
8045 Leesburg Pike, Suite 600
Vienna, VA 22182
703-506-3570
Web Address: www.niri.org
Improves investment procedures and relations.

National Real Estate Investors Association
89 South Riverview Avenue
Miamiburg, OH 45342
937-866-6200
Investors in real estate.

National Association of Securities Dealers (NASD)
1735 K Street NW
Washington, D.C. 20006
202-728-8000
Web Address: www.nasd.com
Self-regulatory organization for NASDAQ.

National Association of Women Business Owners
1411 K Street NW, Suite 1300
Washington, DC 20005
Web Address: www.nawbo.org
To represent women in business and promote women entrepreneurs.

National Venture Capital Association
1655 North Fort Myer Drive, Suite 700
Arlington, VA 22209
703-351-5269
Web Address: www.nvca.org
To improve investments in new companies.

AAII Journal
625 North Michigan Avenue, Suite 1900
Chicago, IL 60611
312-280-0170
Web Address: www.aaii.com
Personal Finance and Investment.

ABA Banking Journal
1120 Connecticut Avenue, N.W.
Washington, D.C. 20036
800-BANKERS
Web Address: www.aba.com
Trends and Development in Banking

American Bank Directory
6195 Crooked Creek Road
Norcross, Georgia 30092

American Savings Directory
McFadden Business Publications
Norcross, Georgia 30092

Bank Administration
1 North Franklin
Chicago, Illinois 60606
800-323-8552
Web Address: www.bai.org

Bankers Magazine
Park Square Building
31 St. James Avenue
Boston, Massachusetts 02116
617-423-2020
Web Address: www.wgl.com
Specialized Articles on Industry

Bank Marketing Magazine
1120 Connecticut Avenue, N.W.
Washington, D.C. 20036
202-663-5378
Web Address: www.bmanet.org

Barron's National Business and Financial Weekly
World Financial Center
200 Liberty
New York, NY 10281
212-416-2700
Web Address: www.barrons.com
Issues and events which affect the financial community.

Callahan's Credit Union Directory
1001 Connecticut Avenue NW, Suite 1001
Washington, D.C. 20036
202-223-3920
Web Address: www.creditunions.com
Directory of State and Federal Credit Unions

Directory of American Financial Institutions
McFadden Business Publications

Directory of American S&L Associations
T.K. Sanderson
Baltimore, Maryland

Economic Review
925 Grand Boulevard
Kansas City, MO 64198-0001
816-881-2683
Economic journal.

Finance & Development
700 9th Street, N.W.
Washington, DC 20431
202-623-8300

Financial Planning
40 West 57th Street, Suite 802
New York, NY 10019
212-765-5311
Web Address: www.fponline.com
Magazine for Finance Professionals

Futures: The Magazine of Commodities and Options
250 South Wacker Drive, Suite 1150
Chicago, IL 60606
312-977-0999
Magazine for people interested in trading futures and options on commodities.

Investor's Business Daily
12655 Beatrice Avenue
Los Angeles, CA 90066
310-448-6000
Web Address: www.investors.com

Moneyworld
1801 Lee Road, Suite 301
Winter Park, FL 32789-2165
Magazine for investors.

Money Market Directory
Money Market Directories
Charlottesville, Virginia

Moody's Bank & Finance Manual
99 Church Street, 1st Floor
New York, New York 10007
212-553-0300
Web Address: *www.moodys.com*

Mortgage Banking
1125 15th Street, N.W.
Washington, D.C. 20005
202-861-6500
Web Address: *www.mbaa.org*
Real estate financing.

Polk's Bank Directory
1321 Murfree Road
Nashville, Tennessee 37217
615-889-3350

Worth Magazine
575 Lexington Avenue
New York, NY 10022
212-223-3100
Web Address: *www.worth.com*
Magazine for finance and investors.

Broadcast & Print Media

• Associations •

American Federation of Television & Radio Artists
260 Madison Avenue
New York, New York 10016
212-532-0800
Representation of Broadcasters.

American Women In Radio & TV
1595 Spring Hill Road, Suite 330
Vienna, Virginia 22182
703-506-3290
Web Address: *www.awrt.org*
Promotes Women in Broadcasting.

Association of America's Public Television Stations
1350 Connecticut Avenue NW, Suite 200
Washington, D.C. 20036
202-887-1700
Web Address: *www.apts.org*
Organizes Efforts of Public Television Stations.

Association of American Publishers
50 F Street NW, Suite 400
Washington, DC 20001
202-347-3375
Web Address: *www.publishers.org*
Representation of Book Producers.

Association of Independent Video & Filmmakers
304 Hudson Street, 6th Floor North
New York, New York 10013
212-807-1400
Web Address: *www.aivs.org*
Champions Independent Films.

Broadcast Education Association
1771 N Street, NW
Washington, DC 20036
202-429-5355
Web Address: *www.beaweb.org*
Promotes Broadcasting Education.

Communications Workers of America
501 3rd Street, NW
Washington, DC 20001
202-434-1444
Represents Communications Workers.

Magazine Publishers of America
1211 Connecticut Avenue NW, Suite 610
Washington, DC 20036
202-296-7277
Web Address: *www.magazine.org*
Alliance of Magazine Publishers.

Multimedia Telecommunications Association
2500 Wilson Boulevard, Suite 300
Arlington, VA 22201
800-799-MMTA
Web Address: *www.mmta.org*
Association of Telecommunications Providers.

National Association of Broadcasters
1771 N Street NW
Washington, D.C. 20036
202-429-5300
Web Address: *www.nab.org*
Information Resource to Industry.
Job Hotline starts after 6:00 P.M.

National Association of Public Television
1350 Connecticut Avenue NW, Suite 200
Washington, D.C. 20036
202-887-1700
Web Address: *www.apts.org*

National Cable Television Association
1724 Massachusetts Avenue NW
Washington, D.C. 20036
202-775-3550
Web Address: www.ncta.com
Promotes Cable Television.

National Newspaper Association
1010 North Glebe Road
Arlington, Virginia 22201
703-907-7900
Web Address: www.nna.org
Represents Newspaper Producers.

National Newspapers Publishers Association
3200 13th Street NW
Washington, DC 20010
202-588-8764
Aides Newspaper Publishers.

National Press Club
529 14th Street NW, 13th Floor
Washington, D.C. 20045
202-662-7500
Web Address: npc.press.org
Organization for News Media Personnel.

Personal Communication Industry Association
500 Montgomery Street, Suite 700
Alexandria, VA 22314-1561
703-739-0300
Web Address: www.pcia.com
Distribution of Communication and Computer Equipment.

• Publications •

Editor & Publisher International Yearbook
11 West 19th Street
New York, New York 10011
212-675-4380

Radio Resource
14 Inverness Drive East, Suite D-136
Englewood, CO 80112
303-792-2390
Mobile radio systems magazine.

Design & Engineering

• Associations •

American Association of Cost Engineers
209 Prairie Avenue, Suite 100
Morgantown, West Virginia 26501
304-296-8444
Web Address: www.aacei.org
Association for Cost Engineers.

American Association of Engineering Societies
1111 19th Street NW, Suite 403
Washington, DC 20036
202-296-2237
Coordinates Efforts of Member Societies.

American Consulting Engineers Council
1015 15th Street NW
Washington, DC 20005
202-347-7474
Web Address: www.acec.org

American Institute of Architects
1735 New York Avenue NW
Washington, DC 20006
202-626-7300
Web Address: www.aiaonline.com
Education and Training for Members.

American Society for Engineering Education
1818 N Street NW, Suite 600
Washington, D.C. 20036
202-331-3500
Web Address: www.asee.com
Advancement and Quality of Education.

American Society of Civil Engineers
1801 Alexander Bell Drive
Reston, VA 20191
800-548-2723
Web Address: www.asce.org
Association of Civil Engineers.

American Society of Landscape Architects
636 Eye Street, NW
Washington, DC 20001-3736
202-898-2444
Web Address: www.asla.org
Education and Training for Landscape Architects.

Association for Facilities Engineering
8180 Corporate Park Drive, Suite 305
Cincinnati, Ohio 45242
513-489-2473
Web Address: www.afe.org
Association for Plant Engineers and Managers.

National Academy of Engineering
2101 Constitution Avenue, N.W.
Washington, D.C. 20418
202-334-3200
Web Address: www.nae.edu
Advises Government and Honors Excellence.

National Society of Professional Engineers
1420 King Street
Alexandria, Virginia 22314
703-684-2800
Web Address: www.nspe.org
Society of Professional Engineers.

• Publications •

AIA Membership Directory
1735 New York Avenue, N.W.
Washington, D.C. 20006
202-626-7300
Web Address: www.aiaonline.com

Architects Directory
5711 South 86th Circle
Omaha, Nebraska 68127

Design Quarterly
4411 Beard Avenue South
Minneapolis, MN 55410
612-925-9150

Interiors
1515 Broadway, 11th Floor
New York, NY 10036
212-764-7300
Interior design in the commercial field.

Roads & Bridges Magazine
380 East Northwest Highway
Des Plaines, IL 60016-2282
847-391-1008

Education

• Associations •

American Association of Christian Schools
PO Box 1097
Independence, MO 64051
816-252-9900
Web Address: www.aacs.org
Advancement of Christian Schools.

American Federation of School Administrators
1729 21st Street NW
Washington, D.C. 20009
202-986-4209
Established for administrators of education with the intent to promote quality education.

Association of American Universities
1200 New York Avenue, Suite 550
Washington, DC 20005
202-408-7500
Web Address: www.Tulane.edu/~aau
The association assists universities in academic research and professional education.

Cause
4772 Walnut Street, Suite 206
Boulder, CO 80301
303-449-4430
Web Address: www.educause.edu
Established with the intent to improve education with the use of technology based workshops using computers.

National Association of Educational Office Professionals
PO Box 12619
Wichita, KS 67277
316-942-4822
To acknowlege office workers involved in education.

National Association of Women in Education
1325 18th Street NW, Suite 210
Washington, D.C. 20036-6511
202-659-9330
Appreciation and Advancement of Women in Education.

American Association of School Administrators

1801 North Moore Street
Arlington, Virginia 22209
703-528-0700
Web Address: www.aasa.org
Coordinates Efforts of School Administrators.

American Federation of Teachers

555 New Jersey Avenue NW
Washington, DC 20001
202-879-4400
Web Address: www.aft.org
Represents Rights of Teachers.

Association of School Business Officials

11401 North Shore Drive
Reston, Virginia 20190
703-478-0405
Web Address: www.asbointl.org
Improvement of School Business Management.

College & University Personnel Association

1233 20th Street, N.W., Suite 301
Washington, D.C. 20036
202-429-0311
Web Address: www.cupa.org
Promotes Excellence Among University Personnel.

National Association of College Admissions Counselors

1631 Prince Street
Alexandria, Virginia 22314
703-836-2222
Web Address: www.nacac.com

National Association of College & University Business Officials

2501 M Street NW, Suite 400
Washington, DC 20037
202-861-2500
Web Address: www.nacubo.org

National Education Association

1201 16th Street NW
Washington, D.C. 20036
202-833-4000
Web Address: www.nea.org

• Publications •

American Educator

555 New Jersey Avenue, N.W.
Washington, D.C. 20001
202-879-4420
Reports educational news.

American Libraries

50 East Huron Street
Chicago, IL 60611
312-944-6780

American Teacher

555 New Jersey Avenue, N.W.
Washington, D.C. 20001
202-879-4430

Education Week

6935 Arlington Road
Bethesda, MD 20814
301-280-3100
Web Address: www.edweek.org
Elementary and secondary school educators.

Educational Researcher

1230 17th Street NW
Washington, DC 20036-3078
202-223-9485

Instructor

555 Broadway
New York, NY 10012
212-343-6135
Educational magazine.

Review of Educational Research

1230 17th Street NW
Washington, D.C. 20036-3078
202-223-9485
Reviews of educational research literature.

The Chronicle of Higher Education

1255 23rd Street, N.W., Suite 700
Washington, D.C. 20037
202-466-1000
Web Address: chronicle.com

Young Children

1509 16th Street, N.W.
Washington, D.C. 20036
202-232-8777
Educational and developmental journal about children from birth to eight years old.

Washington Higher Education
Association Directory
1307 New York Avenue NW
Washington, D.C. 20005
202-328-5900
Web Address: www.case.org

Healthcare

• Associations •

American Association of Blood Banks
8101 Glenbrook Road
Bethesda, Maryland 20814
301-907-6977
Web Address: www.aabb.org
Enhances Efforts of Blood Banks

American Association of Colleges of Pharmacy
1426 Prince Street
Alexandria, Virginia 22314
703-739-2330
Web Address: www.aacp.org
Promotes Excellence and Standards.

American Association of Dental Schools
1625 Massachusetts Avenue, N.W.
Washington, D.C. 20036
202-667-9433
Web Address: www.aads.edu
Promotes Teaching and Research.

American Association of Health Plans
1129 20th Street, N.W., Suite 600
Washington, D.C. 20036
202-778-3200
Web Address: www.aahp.org

American Association of Medical Assistants
20 North Wacker Drive
Chicago, Illinois 60606
312-899-1500
Accreditation of One and Two Year Programs.

American Chiropractic Association
1701 Clarendon Boulevard
Arlington, Virginia 22209
703-276-8800
Web Address: www.acatoday.com
Promotes Excellence and Standards.

American College of Healthcare Executives
1 North Franklin Street, Suite 1700
Chicago, Illinois 60606-3491
312-424-2800
Web Address: www.ache.org
Updates on Trends and Issues.

American Dental Association
211 East Chicago Avenue
Chicago, Illinois 60611
312-440-2500
Web Address: www.ada.org
Resources for Dental Field.

American Health Care Association
1201 L Street, N.W.
Washington, D.C. 20005
202-842-4444
Web Address: www.ahca.org
Promotes Standards and Quality Care.

American Hospital Association
1 North Franklin Street
Chicago, Illinois 60606
312-422-3000
Strives for Better Service to Patients.

American Nurses Association
600 Maryland Avenue, S.W.
Washington, D.C. 20024
800-274-4ANA
Web Address: www.nursingworld.org
Represents Registered Nurses.

American Pharmaceutical Association
2215 Constitution Avenue, N.W.
Washington, D.C. 20037
202-628-4410
Web Address: www.aphanet.org
Promotes Quality and Standards.

American Physical Therapy Association
1111 North Fairfax Street
Alexandria, Virginia 22314
703-684-2782
Web Address: www.apta.org
Promotes Innovation and Quality.

American Psychiatric Association
1400 K Street, N.W.
Washington, D.C. 20005
202-682-6000
Web Address: www.psych.org
Furthers Study of Mental Disorders.

American Psychological Association
750 First Street, N.E.
Washington, D.C. 20002
202-336-5520
Web Address: www.apa.org
Advances Psychology as a Science.

American Society of Health-System Pharmacists
7272 Wisconsin Avenue
Bethesda, Maryland 20814
301-657-3000
Web Address: www.ashp.org
Placement and Education for Members.

Health Industry Manufacturers Association
1200 G Street, N.W., Suite 400
Washington, D.C. 20005
202-783-8700
Web Address: www.himanet.com
Represents Domestic Manufacturers.

National Medical Association
1012 10th Street, N.W.
Washington, D.C. 20001
202-347-1895
Society of Black Physicians.

National Pharmaceutical Council
1894 Preston White Drive
Reston, Virginia 22091
703-620-6390
Professional Minority Pharmacists.

• Publications •

ADA News
211 East Chicago Avenue
Chicago, IL 60611
312-440-2791
Web Address: www.ada.org/adapco/daily/
today.html
American Dental Association newspaper

Healthcare Executive
1 North Franklin Street, Suite 1700
Chicago, IL 60611
312-424-2800
Healthcare management magazine.

Physician Magazine
8605 Explorer Drive
Colorado Springs, CO 80920
719-548-4575
Magazine for the medical profession.

The American Nurse
600 Maryland Avenue, S.W., Suite 100
Washington, D.C. 20024-2571
202-651-7026
Web Address: www.nursingworld.org/
pub.htm
News of Nursing Profession.

American Medical News
515 North State Street
Chicago, Illinois 60610
312-464-5000
Web Address: www.ama-assn.org

Drug Topics
5 Paragon Drive
Montvale, NJ 07645
201-358-7200
Web Address: www.medec.com

Health Care Executive
1 North Franklin Street, Suite 1700
Chicago, Illinois 60606-3491
312-424-2800
Web Address: www.ache.org

Managed Health Care Directory
1129 20th Street, N.W.
Washington, D.C. 20036
202-778-3200
Web Address: www.aahp.com

Modern Healthcare
740 North Rush Street
Chicago, IL 60611
312-649-5374

High Tech

• Associations •

Aerospace Industries Association of America
1250 I Street, N.W., Suite 1200
Washington, D.C. 20005
202-371-8400
Web Address: www.aia-aerospace.org
Association for Manufacturers

American Institute of Aeronautics & Astronautics
59 John Street
New York, New York 10038
212-349-1120
Web Address: www.aiaa.org
Advancement of Engineering Information

Future Aviation Professionals of America
4959 Massachusetts Avenue
Atlanta, Georgia 30337
Career Planning for Industry

Information Technology Association of America
1616 North Fort Myer Drive, Suite 1300
Arlington, Virginia 22209
703-522-5055
Web Address: www.itaa.org
Companies Offering Software and Services to the Public

National Academy of Engineering
2101 Constitution Avenue, N.W.
Washington, D.C. 20418
202-334-3200
Web Address: www.nae.edu
Advises Government and Honors Excellence

National Aeronautic Association of USA
1815 North Fort Meyer Drive, Suite 500
Arlington, Virginia 22209
703-527-0226
Web Address: www.naa.ycg.org
Development of Aviation

National Society of Professional Engineers
1420 King Street
Alexandria, Virginia 22314
703-684-2800
Web Address: www.nspe.org
Society of Professional Engineers

• Publications •

Aviation Week & Space Technology
1120 Vermont Avenue NW, 12th Floor
Washington, DC 20005

Business & Commercial Aviation
260 Rye Brook
New York, NY 10573

Computerworld
500 Old Connecticut Path
Framingham, MA 01701
508-879-0700
Web Address: www.computerworld.com

Data Communications
1221 Avenue of the Americas
41st Floor
New York, NY 10020
212-512-2000
Web Address: www.data.com

Directory of Engineering Societies
1111 19th Street, Suite 608
Washington, D.C. 20036
202-296-2237

Directory of Engineers in Private Practice
1420 King Street
Alexandria, Virginia 22314
703-684-2800
Web Address: www.nspe.org

EDN Career News
275 Washington Street
Newton, Massachusetts 02158
617-964-3030

Engineering Times
1420 King Street
Alexandria, Virginia 22314
703-684-2800
Web Address: www.nspe.org

InfoWorld
155 Bovet Road, Suite 800
San Mateo, CA 94402-3115
Web Address: www.infoworld.com
A Weekly Publication.

R & D Magazine
2000 Clearwater Drive
Oak Brook, IL 60523
630-320-7000
Reports on research and development.

Hospitality

• Associations •

American Bed and Breakfast Association
P.O. Box 1387
Midlothian, VA 23113-8387
Web Address: www.abba.com

American Hotel & Motel Association
1201 New York Avenue, N.W., Suite 600
Washington, D.C. 20005
202-289-3100
Web Address: www.ahma.com
Promotes Industry through Publicity

American Resort Development Association (ARDA)
1220 L Street, N.W., Suite 500
Washington, D.C. 20005
202-371-6700
Web Address: www.arda.org

Council of Hotel, Restaurant & Institutional Education
1200 17th Street, N.W.
Washington, D.C. 20036
202-331-5990

Hospitality Sales & Marketing Association International
1300 L Street, N.W., Suite 800
Washington, D.C. 20005
202-789-0089

National Restaurant Association (NRA)
1200 17th Street, N.W.
Washington, D.C. 20036
202-331-5900
Web Address: www.restaurant.org

• Publications •

Hotels
1350 East Touhy Avenue
Des Plaines, IL 60018
847-390-2139
Magazine covering hotels and hotel restaurants.

Lodging Magazine
1201 New York Avenue, Suite 600
Washington, D.C. 20005-3931
202-289-3100
Web Address: www.lodgingmagazine.com
Management staff of hotels and motels.

Restaurant Hospitality
1100 Superior Avenue
Cleveland, OH 44114
216-696-7000
Magazine for restaurant managers and owners.

Restaurants USA
1200 17th Street, N.W.
Washington, D.C. 20036-3097
202-331-5900
For restaurant owners and managers.

Insurance

• Associations •

America Insurance Association
1130 Connecticut Avenue, N.W., Suite 1000
Washington, D.C. 20036
202-828-7100
Web Address: www.aiadc.org
Represents Property and Casualty Insurance Providers.

American Council of Life Insurance
1001 Pennsylvania Avenue NW 5th Floor South
Washington, D.C. 20004
202-624-2000
Advancement of Industry

Insurance Information Institute
110 William Street, 24th Floor
New York, NY 10038
212-669-9200
Web Address: www.iii.org
Information and Mass Media for Industry

National Association of Insurance and Financial Advisors
2901 Telestar Court
Falls Church, VA
703-770-8100
Web Address: www.naifa.org/index.html
Promotes Ethical Standards and Goodwill

• Publications •

American Agent & Broker
330 North 4th Street
St. Louis, MO 63102
314-421-5445
Magazine covering for independent insurance agencies in fire, casualty, or surety.

Independent Agent
127 South Peyton Street
Alexandria, VA 22310
703-683-4422
Magazine covering both property/casualty and life/health insurance agencies.

Insurance Almanac
50 East Palisade Avenue
Englewood, NJ 07631
201-569-8808

Insurance Journal
3570 Camino Del Rio North, Suite 200
San Diego, CA 92108
619-584-1100

Insurance Phone Book & Directory
121 Chanlon Road
New Providence, NJ 07974
800-521-8110
Web Address: www.reedref.com

International

• Associations •

American Association of Exporters and Importers
51 East 42nd Street, 7th Floor
New York, NY 10017
212-983-7008
Web Address: www.aaei.org
To promote fair and equal trading of goods and services in the global market.

Banker's Association for Foreign Trade
2121 K Street, N.W., Suite 701
Washington, D.C. 20037
202-452-0952
Promotes and improves international banking and trade

Canada-United States Business Association
100 East Jefferson
Detroit, MI 48266

Czech and Slovak - U.S. Economic Council
1615 H Street, N.W.
Washington, D.C. 20062-2000

Emergency Committee for American Trade
1211 Connecticut Avenue, N.W., Suite 801
Washington, D.C. 20036
202-659-5147
Supports international trade and investment policies.

European - American Chamber of Commerce in the United States
40 West 57th Street, 31st Floor
New York, NY 10019-4092
212-315-2196

Federation of International Trade Associations
11800 Sunrise Valley Drive, Suite 210
Reston, VA 20191
703-620-1588
Web Address: www.fita.org
Works to strengthen the role of local, regional, and national associations.

Institute of International Bankers
299 Park Avenue, 17th Floor
New York, NY 10171
212-421-1611
Web Address: www.iib.org
Promotes the improvement of knowledge in international banking.

Institute of International Finance
2000 Pennslyvania Avenue, N.W., Suite 8500
Washington, D.C. 20006-1812
202-857-3600
Web Address: www.iif.com
Seeks to improve the knowledge of financing.

International Development Research Council
35 Technology Park, Suite 150
Nacross, GA 30092
770-446-8955
Web Address: www.idrc.org

International Institute of Investment and Merchant Banking
3104 Q Street, N.W.
Washington, D.C. 20007
202-835-0566
International investments to improve economic growth by eliminating investment barriers and by aiding in the cooperation of investment opportunities.

International Real Estate Institute (IREI)
1224 North Nokomis
Alexandria, MN 56308
320-763-4648
Web Address: www.iami.org/irei.html

Latin Business Association
5400 East Olympic Boulevard, No. 130
Los Angeles, CA 90022
323-721-4000
Web Address: www.lbausa.com
Established to help promote and develop Latino
business owners and corporations.

Nacore International
440 Columbia Drive, Suite 100
West Palm Beach, FL 33409
561-683-8111
Web Address: www.nacore.org

National Association of Foreign-Trade Zones
1000 Connecticut Avenue, N.W., Suite 1001
Washington, D.C. 20036
202-331-1950
To improve and create foreign trade zones sites to
increase both investment and job opportunites.

National Hispanic Corporate Council
2323 North 3rd Avenue, Suite 101
Phoenix, AZ 85004
602-495-1988
Web Address: www.hispanic.org/nhcc.htm
Promotes the advancement of Hispanic busi-
nesses.

Niagara International Trade Council
300 Main Place Tower
Buffalo, NY 14202
716-852-7160
Web Address: www.niagaraitc.com
To assist businesses with exporting, education,
and investment.

United States Council for International Business
1212 Avenue of the Americas, 21st Floor
New York, NY 10036
212-354-4480
Web Address: www.uscib.org

• Publications •

American Journal of International Law
2223 Massachusetts Avenue, N.W.
Washington, D.C. 20008-2864
202-939-6000

Foreign Affairs
58 East 68th Street
New York, NY 10021
212-734-0400
Web Address: www.cfr.org
Magazine on international affairs such as trade
and economics.

The China Business Review
1818 N Street NW, Suite 200
Washington, D.C. 20036
202-429-0340
Magazine pertaining to international business.

The Brookings Review
1775 Massachusetts Avenue
Washington, D.C. 20036
202-797-6000
Web Address: www.brooks.edu
Magazine which focuses on foreign policy, eco-
nomics, government, and business

The WorldPaper
210 World Trade Center
Boston, MA 02210
617-439-5400
Web Address: www.worldpaper.com
Focuses on global trends and regional issues.

World Broadcast News
9800 Metcalf Avenue
Overland Park, KS 66212
913-341-1300
International cable and television.

World Watch
1776 Massachusetts Avenue, N.W.
Washington, D.C. 20036
202-452-1999
Web Address: www.worldwatch.org
Magazine on ecological protection and economic
development.

Law & Lobbying

• Associations •

American Bar Association
750 North Lake Shore Drive
Chicago, IL 60611
312-988-5000
Web Address: www.abanet.org

Federal Bar Association
2215 M Street NW
Washington, DC 20037
202-785-1614
Web Address: www.fedbar.org
Private and government lawyers and judges in-volved in federal practice

Federal Communications Bar Association
1020 19th Street NW, Suite 325
Washington, D.C. 20036
202-736-8640

National Association of Legal Assistants
1516 South Boston, Suite 200
Tulsa, OK 74119
918-587-6828
Web Address: www.nala.org

National Bar Association (Minority Attorneys)
1225 11th Street, N.W.
Washington, D.C. 20001
202-842-3900

National Conference of Black Lawyers
2 West 125th Street
New York, NY 10027
212-864-4000
Attorneys who represent residents of black and poor communities

National Lawyers Guild
126 University Place, 5th Floor
New York, NY 10003-4538
212-627-2656
Web Address: www.nlg.org
National bar association for legal workers.

• Publications •

ABA Journal
750 North Lake Shore Drive
Chicago, IL 60611-4497
312-988-6018
Web Address: www.abanet.org/journal/
American Bar Association legal magazine.

Corporate Legal Times
656 West Randolph, Suite 500 East
Chicago, IL 60661
312-654-3500

Environmental Law & Management
605 3rd Avenue
New York, NY 10158
212-850-6000
Environmental law and management journal.

The American Lawyer
345 Park Avenue South
New York, NY 10010
212-779-9200
Legal magazine.

The Washington Lawyer
1707 L Street, N.W.
Washington, D.C. 20036
202-331-7700
Legal magazine for the Washington area.

Trial
1050 31st Street, N.W.
Washington, D.C. 20007-4499
202-965-3500
Legal magazine.

Public Relations

• Associations •

Public Relations Society of America
33 Irving Place
New York, New York 10003
212-995-2230
Web Address: www.prsa.org
Professional development, job referral, and research information center.

• Publications •

O'Dwyer's Directory of Public Relations Firms
271 Madison Avenue, Suite 600
New York, NY 10016
212-679-2471

Public Relations Journal Register Issue
33 Irving Place
New York, New York 10003
212-995-2230
Web Address: www.prsa.org

Public Relations News
1201 Seven Locks Road, Suite 300
Potomac, MD 20854
301-340-2100

Employment Help

Real Estate

Building Owners and Managers Association International (BOMA)
1201 New York Avenue, N.W., Suite 300
Washington, D.C. 20005
202-408-2662

Commercial Investment Real Estate Institute (CIREI)
430 North Michigan Avenue
Chicago, IL 60611
312-321-4460
Web Address: www.ccim.com

Institute of Real Estate Management (IREM)
430 North Michigan Avenue
Chicago, IL 60611-4090
312-329-6000
Web Address: www.irem.org

International Association for Financial Planning
5775 Glenridge Drive, N.E., Suite B-300
Atlanta, GA 30328-5364
404-845-0011
Web Address: www.iafp.org
Objective is to promote the education of ethical business financial planning.

International Real Estate Institute (IREI)
1224 North Nikomis
Alexandria, MN 56308
320-763-4648
Web Address: www.iami.org/irei.html

Nacore International
440 Columbia Drive, Suite 100
West Palm Beach, FL 33409
561-683-8111
Web Address: www.nacore.org

National Association of Industrial and Office Properties
2201 Cooperative Way, Woodland Park
Herndon, VA 20171
703-904-7100
Web Address: www.naiop.org

National Association of Real Estate Brokers
1629 K Street, N.W., Suite 602
Washington, D.C. 20006
202-785-4477
Web Address: www.nareb.org

National Association of Real Estate Investment Trusts
1875 Eye Street, NW
Washington, DC 20006
202-739-9400
Web Address: www.nareit.com

National Council of Real Estate Investment Fiduciaries
180 North Stetson Avenue, Suite 2515
Chicago, IL 60601
312-819-5890
Web Address: www.ncreif.com
Analysis and assessment of investments in real estate

National Investor Relations Institiute
8045 Leesburg Pike, Suite 600
Vienna, VA 22182
703-506-3570
Web Address: www.niri.org
Improve investment procedures and relations.

National Real Estate Investors Association
89 South Riverview Avenue
Miamiburg, OH 45342
513-866-6200
Investors in real estate.

Property Management Association (PMA)
7900 Wisconsin Avenue, Suite 204
Bethesda, MD 20814
301-657-9200
Web Address: www.reji.com/reji/associations/
   pma/non-member/data
Promotes the interest and welfare of property owners.

National Association of Realtors
430 North Michigan Avenue
Chicago, IL 60611
312-329-8200
Web Address: www.realtor.com

• Publications •

Real Estate Today
430 North Michigan Avenue
Chicago, IL 60611-4087
312-329-8200

Sports & Recreation

• Associations •

American Junior Golf Association
2415 Steeplechase Lane
Roswell, GA 30076
770-998-4653
Web Address: www.ajga.org
Thirteen to eighteen year old golfers.

American Resort Development Association (ARDA)
1220 L Street, N.W., Suite 510
Washington, D.C. 20005
202-371-6700
Web Address: www.arda.org

Atlantic Coast Conference (ACC)
P.O. Drawer ACC
Greensboro, NC 27419-6199
919-851-8787
Web Address: www.theacc.com
Sponsors competition for collegiate athletes in the Atlantic region.

Big East Conference
56 Exchange Terrace
Providence, RI 02903
401-272-9108
Represents and sponsors athletes in the Big East region.

Big Ten Conference
1500 West Higgins Road
Park Ridge, IL 60068
847-696-1010
Web Address: www.bigten.org
Represents and sponsors athletes in the Big Ten Conference.

Eastern College Athletic Conference
1311 Craigville Beach Road
P.O. Box 3
Centerville, MA 02632
508-771-5060
Web Address: www.ecac.org

Ladies Professional Golf Association
100 International Golf Drive
Daytona Beach, FL 32124-1092
904-274-6200
Web Address: www.lpga.com
Professional women golfers.

National Association of Basketball Coaches of the United States
9300 West 110th Street, Suite 640
Overland Park, KS 66210-1486
913-469-1001
College, university, junior college, and high school level baketball coaches

National Association of Intercollegiate Athletics
6120 South Yale, Suite 1450
Tulsa, OK 74136
918-494-8828
Web Address: www.naia.org
Promotes devlopment of intercollegiate athletic programs.

National Basketball Association
645 5th Avenue, 10th Floor
New York, NY 10022
212-826-7000
Web Address: www.nba.com
Professional Basketball teams.

National Collegiate Athletic Association (NCAA)
Web Address: www.ncaa.org

National Football League
Web Address: www.nfl.com

National Football League Players Association
2021 L Street, N.W., 6th Floor
Washington, D.C. 20036
202-463-2200
Web Address: www.nflplayers.com

Pacific 10 Conference
Web Address: www.pac-10.org
Represents and sponsers athletes in the PAC 10 Conference.

Professional Golfers' Association of America (PGA)
100 PGA Tour Boulevard
Pine Dedra, FL 32082
904-285-3700
Web Address: www.pgatour.com
Associated with professional golfers, tournaments, clubs, and courses.

Southeastern Conference (SEC)
2201 Richard Arrington Boulevard North
Birmingham, AL 35203
205-458-3000
Web Address: www.sec.org
Represents and sponsers athletes in the SEC region.

Southern Conference
Web Address: www.SoConSports.com/
Represents and sponsors athletes in the SC region.

USA Basketball
5465 Mark Dabling Boulevard
Colorado Springs, CO 80918-3842
719-590-4800
Web Address: www.usabasketball.com

US Skiing and Skateboarding Association
1500 Kearns Bouleard, Building F100
Park City, UT 84060
435-649-9090
Official organization for the governing of skiing within the U.S.

United States Golf Association (USGA)
P.O. Box 708
Far Hills, NJ 07931
908-234-2300
Web Address: www.usga.org
Acts as the governing organization for golf within the United States and conducts thirteen national championships annually.

United States Intercollegiate Lacrosse Association
P.O. Box 928
Lexington, VA 24450

United States Professional Tennis Association
3535 Briarpark Drive, Suite 1
Houston, TX 77042
713-978-7782
Web Address: www.uspta.org
To promote tennis instruction in the U.S. whether professional or collegiate.

United States Tennis Association
70 West Red Oak Lane
White Plains, NY 10604
914-696-7000
Web Address: www.usta.com
Seeks to promote the development of tennis throughout the U.S.

University Athletic Association
590 Mount Hope Avenue
Rochester, NY 14620
716-273-5881
Promotes athletic competition for Division III colleges and universities.

Western Athletic Conference
Web Address: www.wac.org
Represents collegiate athletes in WAC region.

World Amateur Golf Council (WAGC)
P.O. Box 708
Far Hills, NJ 07931-0708
908-234-2300

Travel & Transportation

• Associations •

Air Transport Association of America
1301 Pennsylvania Avenue, N.W., Suite 1100
Washington, D.C. 20004
202-626-4000
Web Address: www.air-transport.org

Airline Pilots Association
1625 Massachusetts Avenue, N.W.
Washington, D.C. 20003
202-797-4033
Web Address: www.alpa.org

American Bus Association
1100 New York Avenue, N.W., Suite 1050
Washington, D.C. 20005
202-842-1645

American International Automotive Dealers Association
99 Canal Center Plaza, Suite 500
Alexandria, Virginia 22314
703-519-7800
Web Address: www.aiada.org
Works to preserve free market for automobiles and promote industry.

American Public Gas Association
11094D Lee Highway
Fairfax, Virginia 22030
703-352-3890
Web Address: www.apga.org
Association of public gas providers.

American Public Power Association
2301 M Street, N.W.
Washington, D.C. 20037
202-467-2900
Web Address: www.appanet.org
Association of municipally owned utilities.

American Resort Development Association (ARDA)
1220 L Street, N.W., Suite 510
Washington, D.C. 20005
202-371-6700
Web Address: www.arda.org

American Society of Travel Agents
1101 King Street
Alexandria, Virginia 22314
703-739-2782
Web Address: www.astanet.com
Promotes travel and image of agents.

American Trucking Association
2200 Mill Road
Alexandria, Virginia 22314
703-838-1700
Web Address: www.truckline.com
Works to influence government decisions and promote efficiency.

Institute of Transportation Engineers
525 School Street, S.W., Suite 410
Washington, D.C. 20024
202-554-8050
Web Address: www.ite.org
Representation and education of transport engineers.

National Air Transportation Association
4226 King Street
Alexandria, Virginia 22302
703-845-9000
Represents interests of general aviation companies.

National Motor Freight Traffic Association
2200 Mill Road
Alexandria, Virginia 22314
703-838-1810
Web Address: www.erols.com/nmfta
Promotes professionalism and safety.

Professional Aviation Maintenance Association
500 NW Plaza, Suite 1016
St. Ann, Missouri 63074
Pursues safety and professionalism.

Travel Industry Association of America
1100 New York Avenue, NW, Suite 450
Washington, D.C. 20006
202-408-8422
Web Address: www.tia.org
Representation and promotion of travel industry.

• Publications •

Business Travel News
1515 Broadway, 32nd Floor
Manhasset, NY 11030
212-869-1300
Business travel newspaper.

Corporate Meetings & Incentives
2101 South Arlington Heights Road
Arlington Heights, IL 60005
847-427-9512
Web Address: www.aip.com
Aimed at senior level executives and meeting professionals in corporate America.

Moody's Transportation Manual
99 Church Street
New York, NY 10007
212-553-0300
Web Address: www.moodys.com

Successful Meetings
355 Park Avenue South
New York, NY 10010
212-592-6403
Web Address: www.successmtgs.com
Information on meetings, conventions, and travel industries.

Traffic World Magazine
1230 National Press Building
Washington, D.C. 20045
202-783-1101

Travel Agent
1 Park Avenue, 2nd Floor
New York, NY 10016
212-370-5050
Travel magazine.

Travel Weekly
500 Plaza Drive
Secaucus, NJ 07096
201-902-2000
Travel weekly.

Travelhost
Web Address: www.travelhost.com
Magazine for business and vacation travelers.

Employment Agencies

- Temporary Placement
- Temp-to-hire
- Resume Consulting & Printing
- Permanent Placement
- Executive Recruiters

Working through an employment agency will not only give you valuable work experience, but more importantly, exposure to professionals in your desired field.

CHECK WITH THE FOLLOWING ASSOCIATIONS FOR MORE LISTINGS, LEADS, IDEAS, GUIDANCE AND DIRECTION.

Association of Part-Time Professionals
7700 Leesburg Pike, No.216
Falls Church, VA 22043
703-734-7975
Web Address: www.nbinet.mindbank.com
An association established to aid part-time employees in consultation and job placement.

Association of Executive Search Consultants
500 Fifth Avenue, Suite 930
New York, NY 10110-0900
212-398-9556
Web Address: www.skottedwards.com/aesc.html
To maintain and promote ethical standards of the profession and to encourage the advancement of executive consultants.

Association of Outplacement Consulting Firms International
1200 19th Street, N.W., Suite 300
Washington, D.C. 20036
202-857-1185
Web Address: www.aocfi.org
Provides counsel and job search information to employees who are displaced.

Employee Relocation Council
1720 North Street, N.W.
Washington, D.C. 20036
202-857-0857
Web Address: www.erc.org
To facilitate the relocation of employees and their families.

International Personnel Management Association
1617 Duke Street
Alexandria, VA 22314
703-549-7100
Web Address: www.ipma-hr.org

National Association of Executive Recruiters
222 South Westmonte Drive, Suite 101
Altamonte Springs, FL 32714
312-867-1060
Web Address: www.naer.org
To promote and enhance the profession while serving in the client's best interests.

National Association of Temporary and Staffing Services (NATSS)
119 South Saint Asaph Street
Alexandria, Virginia 22314-3119
703-5460-6287
Web Address: www.natss.org
Promotes and educates consumers to the benefits of their member's services

Employment Agencies

Los Angeles/Orange Counties

A2Z Professional Services
6255 Sunset Boulevard #101
Hollywood, CA 90028
213-461-3217
Tina Martin, *Hiring Contact*

AB Crown Employment
15017 Ventura Boulevard
Sherman Oaks, CA 91403-2442
818-981-4002

A & S Services
1963 West Huntington Drive
Alhambra, CA 91801-1240
626-181-2781

A & S Services
1963 West Huntington Drive
Alhambra, CA 91801-1240
626-281-4397

ABI Employment Services
1711 Sierra Highway
Acton, CA 93510-1896
626-701-7466

Abigail Abbott Staffing Services
18000 Studebaker Road, Suite 610
Cerritos, CA 90703-2679
562-860-1662

Jade Jenkins, *Hiring Contact*

Abigail Abbott Staffing Services
3030 Old Ranch Pky, Suite 230
Seal Beach, CA 90740-2748
562-799-9888

Abigail Abbott Staffing Services
500 South Krumer, Suite 305
Brea, CA 92621
714-671-4200

Abigail Abbott Staffing Services
23832 Rockfield Boulevard, Suite 195
Lake Forest, CA 92630-2805
714-581-6000

Abigail Abbott Staffing Services
1201 Dove Street, Suite 500
Newport Beach, CA 92660-2841
714-756-8000

Abigail Abbott Staffing Services
660 West 1st Street
Tustin, CA 92680-2902
714-731-7757

Abigail Abbott Staffing Services
660 West 1st Street
Tustin, CA 92680-2902
714-731-7711

Account On Us Personnel Svcs
3428 Castlewood Pl
Sherman Oaks, CA 91403-4811
818-506-6121

ACCOUNTANTS 2000
PO Box 3297
San Dimas, CA 91773
818-284-6311

Accountants Exchange Personnel Services
5455 Wilshire Boulevard
Los Angeles, CA 90036
213-933-7411

Accountants, Inc.
4675 MacArthur Ct, Suite 1270
Newport Beach, CA 92660
714-752-2111

Accountants Overload
10990 Wilshire Boulevard, 14th Floor
Los Angeles, CA 90024-3905
310-478-8883
Web Address: www.accountantsoverload.com

Accountants Overload
6 Centerpointe Drive, Suite 250
La Palma, CA 90623-2503
714-562-8899

Accountants Overload
18400 Von Karman Avenue, Suite 130
Irvine, CA 92612
714-475-9640

AccountCORE
6100 Wilshire Boulevard
Los Angeles, CA 90048-5107
213-857-5595

Ken McCollon, *Hiring Contact*

AccountCORE
4000 Macarthur Boulevard, Suite 6300
Newport Beach, CA 92660-2516
714-250-7209

Accountemps
10877 Wilshire Boulevard, Suite 1605
Los Angeles, CA 90024
310-286-6800
Web Address: www.accountemps.com

Accounting Specialists
888 South Figueroa Street, Suite 2020
Los Angeles, CA 90017
213-624-2144

Caroline Delgado, *Hiring Contact*

AccountPros
1800 Avenue of the Stars, Suite 1425
Los Angeles, CA 90067
310-277-7900
Web Address: www.acctpros.com

Laurie Kim, *Hiring Contact*

Accustaff
515 South Figueroa Street, Suite 340
Los Angeles, CA 90071-3301
213-891-0044
Web Address: www.accustaff.com

Yolanda Cuervo, *Hiring Contact*

AccuStaff
8601 Wilshire Boulevard, Suite 100
Beverly Hills, CA 90211
310-289-9999

AccuStaff
16501 Ventura Boulevard., Suite 104
Encino, CA 91436
818-905-5522

AccuStaff Accounting Principals
11845 West Olympic Boulevard, Suite 702
Los Angeles, CA 90064
310-914-4650
Web Address: www.accustaff.com

Acountants On Call
970 West 190th Street, Suite 870
Torrance, CA 90502-1000
310-527-2777

Randy Wagner, *Hiring Contact*

Act Employment services
2130 East 4th Street, Suite 150
Santa Ana, CA 92705
714-245-1895

Act One Personnel Services
18520 Hawthorne Boulevard
Torrance, CA 90504-4515
310-371-2151

Sam Miller, *Hiring Contact*

Adecco
600 Corporate Pointe, Suite 110
Culver City, CA 90230-7624
310-445-8970

Adecco
14408 Hawthorne Boulevard, Suite A
Lawndale, CA 90260-1517
310-219-0650
Web Address: www.adecco.com

Adecco
21250 Hawthorne Boulevard, Suite 155
Torrance, CA 90503-5506
310-792-1334

Adecco
3450 East Spring Street, Suite 103
Long Beach, CA 90806-2440
310-426-0446

Adecco
7120 Hayvenhurst Avenue, Suite 104
Van Nuys, CA 91406-3813
818-782-2830

Adecco
11801 Mississippi Avenue
Los Angeles, CA 90025
310-445-8970

Advance Information Management
900 Wilshire Boulevard, Suite 1424
Los Angeles, CA 90017
213-243-9236
Web Address: www.aimusa.com

Belinda Speth, *Hiring Contact*

Advanced Medical Recruiters
26012 Campeon
Laguna Niguel, CA 92677
714-364-1916

Affiliated Temporary Help
4359 East Florence Avenue
Bell, CA 90201-0124
213-771-1383

Ron Thomas, *Hiring Contact*

AFS Personnel Services
3838 West Carson Street, Suite 300
Torrance, CA 90503-6710
310-316-8266

All Temporaries
14752 Beach Boulevard, Suite 106
La Mirada, CA 90638-4249
714-562-8550

All-Star Agency
205 South Beverly Drive, Suite 214
Beverly Hills, CA 90212-3807
310-271-5217

Mimi Smith, *Hiring Contact*

Allied Staffing
200 East del Mar Boulevard, Suite 214
Pasadena, CA 91105-2544
818-577-9595

ALLYANCE TECHNOLOGIES, LLC
4400 MacArthur Boulevard 5th Fl
Newport Beach, CA 92660
714-955-4940

Alternative Resources Corporation
2400 East Katella Avenue, Suite 1190
Anaheim, CA 92806-5945
714-935-9511

Alternative Resources Corporation
21700 Oxnard Street, Suite 850
Woodland Hills, CA 91367-3642
818-713-0795

Alternative Staffing Group
1801 Avenue of the Stars, Suite 4
Los Angeles, CA 90067
310-788-0911

Lisa Bankhead, *Hiring Contact*

ALVARADO GROUP
1607-D East Lincoln
Orange, CA 92665
714-974-5550

American Metropolitan Consultants
2171 Campus Drive, Suite 320
Irvine, CA 92715-1422
714-252-9393

Amtec Engineering Corp
2749 Saturn Street
Brea, CA 92621-6705
714-993-1713

Anaheim - Arlin
1917 East LaPalma Avenue
Anaheim, CA 92805
714-520-9600

Apple One Temporary Services
327 West Broadway
Glendale, CA 91204-1301
818-240-8688

Application Specific Services
26082 Los Cerros Drive, Suite 11
Laguna Hills, CA 92653-8204
714-831-5359

APR Consulting
17852 East 17th Street, Suite 207
Tustin, CA 92680
714-544-3696

Architectural Staffing
2501 Cherry Avenue, Suite 303
Long Beach, CA 90806
562-989-5550

Dennis Butler, *Hiring Contact*

Arcus Data Staffing
1915 West Orangewood Avenue, Suite 200
Orange, CA 92868
714-939-5550

Associated Home Health Nurses of America
555 East Ocean Boulevard, Suite 203
Long Beach, CA 90802-5003
562-437-5773

Assured Personnel Services
1301 South Beach Boulevard, Suite M
La Habra, CA 90631-6376
562-691-3258
Web Address: www.assured-personnel.com

Jennie Garcia, *Hiring Contact*

Bankers on Call
445 South Figueroa Street, Suite 2600
Los Angeles, CA 90071-1602
213-612-7709

Birl Martin, *Hiring Contact*

BISC, Inc.
21550 Oxnard Street
Woodland Hills, CA 91367
818-222-5736

Black Tie Event Services
628 Venice Boulevard
Venice, CA 90291-4801
310-301-4300

Bracco, Inc.
20942 Osborne Street, Unit B
Canoga Park, CA 91304-1853
818-700-9868

Business & Professional Temporary Services
3255 Wilshire Boulevard, Suite 1732
Los Angeles, CA 90010-1404
213-380-8200

Alex La Peach, *Hiring Contact*

Cal-Staff
20505 East Valley Boulevard. #103
Walnut, CA 91788
714-949-9548

Calcad
23331 El Toro Road, Suite 203
Lake Forest, CA 92630-4891
714-859-1044

California Job Connection
11825 Delamo Boulevard
Cerritos, CA 90703
562-809-7785

Brenda Johnson, *Hiring Contact*

California Professional Employer
955 Carrillo Drive, Suite 105
Los Angeles, CA 90048-5400
213-857-7070

Cameron and Company 'The Pharmacists' Registr
904 Silver Spur Road, Suite 365
Rolling Hills, CA 90274-3800
310-377-4077
Web Address: www.temps-pharmacists.com

Care World
9639 Amigo Avenue
Northridge, CA 91324-1904
818-998-6136

Career Group
1999 Avenue of the Stars, Suite 1150
Los Angeles, CA 90067-6022
310-277-8188

Deborah Pietreface, *Hiring Contact*

Career Quest
1901 Avenue of The Stars, Suite 920
Los Angeles, CA 90067-6001
310-282-8505

Career Quest
1901 Avenue of The Stars, Suite 920
Los Angeles, CA 90067-6001
310-282-8505

Suzanne Aceret, *Hiring Contact*

Carlton Engineer
690 East Green Street, Suite 203
Pasadena, CA 90211
818-796-0972

Cathy Dunn's Associated Personnel Service
800 North Harbor Boulevard, Suite B
La Habra, CA 90631-3102
562-690-6693

Kathy MacIntyre, *Hiring Contact*

CCI
620 Newport Center Drive, 11th Floor
Newport Beach, CA 92660-6420
714-347-8414

CCI
10 Genoa
Laguna Niguel, CA 92677-8933
714-721-6628

Celebrity Partners
11111 Santa Monica Boulevard, Suite 11
Los Angeles, CA 90025
310-268-1710

Cenex Services, L.P. dba Central Casting
3601 West Olive Avenue, Suite 800
Burbank, CA 91505-4603
818-955-6000

Central Line Technical
1427 Via Corta
La Verne, CA 91750-2064
714-593-5446

Champagne Temporary Help
3849 Birch Street
Newport Beach, CA 92660-2616
714-756-1844

Champion Technical Services
111 North LaBrea Avenue, Suite 600
Inglewood, CA 90301
310-673-7742

Chosen Few Personnel Services
911 Wilshire Boulevard, Suite 1880
Los Angeles, CA 90017
213-689-9400

Chrysalis Labor Connection
516 South Main Street
Los Angeles, CA 90013
213-895-7525

Dave McDonough, *Hiring Contact*

CMC Personnel Services
34365 Dana Strand Road, Suite 200
Dana Point, CA 92629
714-717-0625

Cocktail Affair
4482 Barranca Parkway #180-159
Irvine, CA 92604
714-552-1063

Commercial Programming Systems
3250 Wilshire Boulevard, Suite 1212
Los Angeles, CA 90010
213-380-2681
Web Address: www.cpsinc.com

Phil Sawyer, *Hiring Contact*

Computec International Resources
230 North Maryland Avenue, Suite 209
Glendale, CA 91206
818-500-3921

Computer Professionals Unlimited
5942 Edinger Avenue, Suite 113
Huntington Beach, CA 92649
714-891-1244

Coneybear, Inc.
810 French Street
Santa Ana, CA 92701-3718
714-547-8546

Conner Admin
22600-C Lambert Street, Suite 902
Lake Forest, CA 92630
714-458-9331

Consulting Solutions
22647 Ventura Boulevard, Suite 372
Woodland Hills, CA 91364
818-223-8935

Consultis
865 South Figueroa, Suite 3339
Los Angeles, CA 90017
213-533-8900
Web Address: www.consultis.com

Nicole Alix, *Hiring Contact*

CoreLink Staffing Services
18301 Von Karman Avenue, Suite 120
Irvine, CA 92612
714-250-6565

Corestaff
4551 Glencoe Avenue, Suite 155
Marina Del Rey, CA 90292
310-827-0255

Andrea Brammeier, *Hiring Contact*

CORESTAFF Services
6100 Wilshire Boulevard, Suite 150
Los Angeles, CA 90048-5107
213-857-1225

Gina Dusuau, *Hiring Contact*

CORESTAFF Services
9550 East Firestone, Suite 101
Downey, CA 90241
562-928-2531
Web Address: www.corestaff.com

Martha Chavez-Cerda, *Hiring Contact*

CORESTAFF Services
520 North Central AVenue, Suite 710
Glendale, CA 91203
818-246-3961
Web Address: www.corestaff.com

Patty Castellanos, *Hiring Contact*

CORESTAFF Services
1411 West 190th Street, Suite 460
Gardena, CA 90248-4324
310-660-6363
Web Address: www.corestaff.com

Robin Doran, *Hiring Contact*

CORESTAFF Services
5000 East Spring Street, Suite 320
Long Beach, CA 90815-1270
562-420-7616
Web Address: www.corestaff.com

Maria Munoz, *Hiring Contact*

CORESTAFF Services
3040 Saturn Street, Suite 200
Brea, CA 92621-6274
714-572-4200

CORESTAFF Services
4000 MacArthur Boulevard, Suite 6300
Newport Beach, CA 92660
714-752-1443

CORESTAFF Services
18231 Irvine Boulevard, Suite 100
Tustin, CA 92680-3432
714-838-1041

CORESTAFF Services
27405 Puerta Real, Suite 320
Mission Viejo, CA 92691-6314
714-582-3138

CORESTAFF Services
3040 Saturn Street, Suite 200
Brea, CA 92805
714-255-8122

CORESTAFF Services
222 South Harbor Boulevard, Suite 1015
Anaheim, CA 92805-3701
714-956-0701

CORESTAFF Services
2 North Lake Avenue, Suite 560
Pasadena, CA 91101-1858
818-449-7551

CORESTAFF Services
520 North Central Avenue, Suite 710
Glendale, CA 91203-1926
818-246-3961

CORESTAFF Services
16133 Ventura Boulevard, Suite 880
Encino, CA 91436-2403
818-906-2848

CORESTAFF Services
1050 East Garvey Avenue South, Suite 300
West Covina, CA 91790-2924
818-919-1808

CORPORATE CAREERS
1500 Quail Street, Suite 290
Newport Beach, CA 92660-2732
714-476-7007

Cory Associates Agency
1401 Dove Street, Suite 230
Newport Beach, CA 92260
714-261-1988

CoSource Solutions
22800 Savi Ranch Parkway, Suite 214
Yorba Linda, CA 92887
714-282-3832

Courtesy Temporary Service
10 Corporate Park, Suite 120
Irvine, CA 92606
714-251-0866

Courtesy Temporary Service
PO Box 17329
Irvine, CA 92623-7329
714-474-2322

Courtesy Temporary Service
20 East Foothill Boulevard, Suite 100
Arcadia, CA 91006-2335
818-446-8556

Courtesy Temporary Service
935 North Grand Avenue
Covina, CA 91724
818-859-2467

CT Engineering Corp.
2221 Rosecrans Avenue, Suite 131
El Segundo, CA 90245-4910
310-643-8333
Web Address: www.cteng.com

Bob Richardson, *Hiring Contact*

D.P. Specialists
2141 Rosecrans Avenue, Suite 5100
El Segundo, CA 90245
310-416-9846
Web Address: www.dpsla.com

Carole Schlocker, *Hiring Contact*

Dalton Personnel
1401 North Tustin Avenue, Suite 110
Santa Ana, CA 92705-8633
714-558-0800

Data Design Corp.
7777 Center Avenue, Suite 690
Huntington Beach, CA 92647-3067
714-891-2811

Data Processing Resources Corp
4400 McArthur Boulevard, Suite 610
Newport Beach, CA 92660-2037
714-752-9111

Davidson Personnel
2211 Martin, Suite 110
Irvine, CA 92714
714-955-3114

Dec & Associates Healthcare
1601 East Chapman Avenue
Fullerton, CA 92831
714-447-0826

Deemar, Inc.
4004 Tweedy Boulevard
South Gate, CA 90280-6136
213-567-9633

Mara Brown, *Hiring Contact*

Dental Staff
131 South Barranch, Suite 283
West Covina, CA 91791
818-967-2659

Devon & Devon Personnel Services
1601 Dove Street, Suite 130
Newport Beach, CA 92660-2433
714-851-9393

DeZine Search
230 Bethany Road, Suite 302
Burbank, CA 91504-4247
818-846-0555

Discovery, The Staffing Specialists
865 South Figueroa, Suite 3030
Los Angeles, CA 90017
213-362-0755
Web Address: www.discovery-staffing.com

Tina Morales, *Hiring Contact*

Discovery, The Staffing Specialists
1820 Orangewood Avenue, Suite 204
Orange, CA 92868
714-385-8165

DMG Accounting Network
513 Addy Avenue
Placentia, CA 92670-2202
714-524-9222

Doctors Corner Personnel Services
PO Box 1586
Torrance, CA 90505-0586
310-373-0931

DSS Industries
11100 Valley Boulevard # 340-9
El Monte, CA 91731-2533
818-448-8931

Education Technology
844 Moraga Drive
Los Angeles, CA 90049
310-440-3663

Employment Alternatives
PO Box 242
Tustin, CA 92681-0242
714-544-5835

Engineers Exchange
1180 South Beverly Drive, Suite 310
Los Angeles, CA 90035-1153
310-203-0011

Bob Rosen, *Hiring Contact*

ESP Personnel Services
11770 Warner Avenue, Suite 101
Fountain Valley, CA 92708-2659
714-540-8470

Exact Staff
21031 Ventura Boulevard, Suite 501
Woodland Hills, CA 91364
818-348-1100

EXCEL
527 Aspen View Ct
Agoura, CA 91301-3812
818-991-7180

Excel Health Services
3420 South Bristol, Suite 310
Costa Mesa, CA 92626
714-545-0500

Executemp
14172 Livingston Avenue
Tustin, CA 92680-2234
714-730-0119

Executive Nurses
2961 West Macarthur Boulevard, Suite 215
Santa Ana, CA 92704
714-754-2455

EXPRESS PERSONNEL SERVICES
11870 Santa Monica Boulevard, Suite 20
Los Angeles, CA 90025-2201
310-571-2200

Bill Cunningham, *Hiring Contact*

EXPRESS PERSONNEL SERVICES
15725 Hawthorne Boulevard, Suite 101
Lawndale, CA 90260-2641
310-978-6175

Paula Hooks, *Hiring Contact*

EXPRESS PERSONNEL SERVICES
17145 Von Karman Avenue, Suite 104
Irvine, CA 92614
714-833-1550

Finance Diversified Personnel
23945 Calabasas Road
Calabasas, CA 91302-1552
818-222-8367

Fine Howard & Fine Pers Svcs
5959 Topanga Cannon Boulevard., Suite 200
Woodland Hills, CA 91367
818-716-7955

First Call Temporary Services
3511 Pacific Coast Highway, Suite East
Torrance, CA 90505-6600
310-539-2884

Pam Freeley, *Hiring Contact*

Five Star Paralegals
700 South Flower Street, Suite 1100
Los Angeles, CA 90017-4113
213-892-2228

Don Swanson, *Hiring Contact*

Fluor Daniel
333 Michelson Drive
Irvine, CA 92730
714-975-4442

Focus On Temps
16052 Beach Boulevard, Suite 215
Huntington Beach, CA 92647-3801
714-848-6129

Fortune Personnel Consultants
2615 Pacific Coast HIghway, Suite 330
Hermosa Beach, CA 90254
310-376-6964

Mark Casten, *Hiring Contact*

Friedman Personnel Agency
9000 West Sunset Boulevard
Los Angeles, CA 90069-5801
310-550-1002

Glendora Employment Agency
203 South Glendora Avenue
Glendora, CA 91741
818-335-4081

Global Resource Corporation
3250 Cherry Avenue
Long Beach, CA 90807
310-426-2726

Global Telecommunication Resources
1629 Sherwood Village Cir
Placentia, CA 92670-3119
714-502-8298

Group Oliver, LLC
1426 Aviation Boulevard, Suite 101
Redondo Beach, CA 90266
310-798-9313
Web Address: www.groupoliver.com

GW Consulting
810 North Brand Boulevard, Suite 250
Glendale, CA 91203
818-546-2848

H&H Temporary Services
1560 Interlachen Road 66-E
Seal Beach, CA 90740
562-430-0598

Harding Personnel Agency
1150 North Mountain Avenue
Upland, CA 91786-3668
714-985-2020

Harte Enterprises
881 Alma Real Drive, Suite 301B
Pacific Palisades, CA 90272
310-459-0577
Web Address: ww.jobs-socal.com

Heidrick and Struggles
300 South Grand Avenue, Suite 2400
Los Angeles, CA 90071
213-625-8811

Tom Mitchell, *Hiring Contact*

Helpmates Staffing Services
1200 Main Street, Suite B
Irvine, CA 92614
714-752-6888

Helpmates Staffing Services
1203 West Imperial Highway, Suite 100
Brea, CA 92621-3732
714-870-1888

Helpmates Staffing Services
1401 North Batavia Street, Suite 101
Orange, CA 92667-3500
714-288-3500

Helpmates Staffing Services
2780 Skypark Drive, Suite 115
Torrance, CA 90505-5341
310-326-6700

Helpmates Staffing Services
411 North Central Avenue, Suite 350
Glendale, CA 91203-2020
818-265-2890

Helpmates Staffing Services
700 South Flower Street, Suite 1100
Los Angeles, CA 90017-4101
213-892-2275

Helpmates Staffing Services
1200 Main Street 1st Flr, Suite A
Irvine, CA 92614
714-752-6888

Hemingway Personnel
1301 Dove Street, Suite 1070
Newport Beach, CA 92660-2475
714-851-1228

HR Only
6735 Forest Lawn Drive, Suite 218
Los Angeles, CA 90068-1001
213-883-9065
Web Address: ww.hronly.com

Kathy Scouton, *Hiring Contact*

HR Only
12399 Lewis Street, Suite 202
Garden Grove, CA 92840-4697
714-740-7094

Ideal Employee Management
1925 East Vernon Avenue
Los Angeles, CA 90058
213-235-7600
Web Address: www.idealemployee.com

Judith G. Ivanson, *Hiring Contact*

Imperial Staffing, Imperial Home Health Care
17525 Ventura Boulevard, Suite 203
Encino, CA 91316-3843
818-752-2205

IMSC
20 Newcastle Ln
Laguna Niguel, CA 92677
714-496-8008

Inconen, Corp.
6133 Bristol Parkway, Suite 232
Culver City, CA 90230-6614
310-410-1931

Initial Staffing
17800 Castleton Street, Suite 110
Rowland Heights, CA 91748-5720
818-912-0231

Initial Staffing Services
707 Wilshire Road, Suite 450
Los Angeles, CA 90017-5704
213-236-9200
Web Address: www.initial-staffing.com

Initial Talent Tree
12400 Wilshire Boulevard, Suite 1275
Los Angeles, CA 90025-1019
310-207-2555

Initial Talent Tree
21250 Hawthorne Boulevard, Suite 540
Torrance, CA 90503-5506
310-540-1484

Cathy Hamilton, *Hiring Contact*

Insta-Temp
13353 Alondra Boulevard, Suite 102
Santa Fe Springs, CA 90670-5545
562-921-5200
Web Address: www.instatemp.com

Val Fernandez, *Hiring Contact*

INTERIM COURT REPORTING SERVICES
3530 Wilshire Boulevard, Suite 1700
Los Angeles, CA 90010-2328
213-385-4000
Web Address: www.interim.com

INTERIM LEGAL SERVICES
777 South Figueroa Street, Suite 2970
Los Angeles, CA 90017-5800
213-688-8770
Web Address: www.interim.com

Denise Padden, *Hiring Contact*

INTERIM SERVICES
11500 West Olympic Boulevard, Suite 431
West Los Angeles, CA 90064-1524
310-477-2999
Web Address: www.interim.com

Suzanne Weber, *Hiring Contact*

INTERIM SERVICES
6425 East Pacific Coast Highway
Long Beach, CA 90803-4201
562-594-8111

Elizabeth Acosta, *Hiring Contact*

INTERIM SERVICES
16550 Valley View Avenue
La Mirada, CA 90638-5822
714-522-4164

INTERIM SERVICES
910 East Birch Street, Suite 200
Brea, CA 92621-5800
714-990-2441

INTERIM SERVICES
333 South Anita Drive, Suite 855
Orange, CA 92668
714-634-9400

INTERIM SERVICES
2230 West Chapman Avenue, Suite 118
Orange, CA 92668-2647
714-939-1266

INTERIM SERVICES
15401 Red Hill Avenue, Suite C
Tustin, CA 92680-7305
714-259-7787

INTERIM SERVICES
4000 Barranca Pky, Suite 220
Irvine, CA 92714
714-857-3535

INTERIM SERVICES
2192 Dupont Drive, Suite 210
Irvine, CA 92715-1328
714-261-9272

INTERIM SERVICES
18400 Von Karman Avenue, Suite 920
Irvine, CA 92715-1514
714-756-1028

INTERIM SERVICES
15260 Ventura Boulevard, Suite 1220
Sherman Oaks, CA 91403-5307
818-789-8211

INTERIM SERVICES
17861 B Colima Road
City of Industry, CA 91748
818-965-9940

Interim Technologies
4929 Wilshire Boulevard, Suite 500
Los Angeles, CA 90010-3808
213-965-8600

Interim Technologies
333 South Anita Drive, Suite 855
Orange, CA 92668-3320
714-634-9400

International Staffing Consultants
500 Newport Center Drive, Suite 300
Newport Beach, CA 92660-7002
714-721-7990

International Temporaries & Perm
12235 Beach Boulevard 4A
Stanton, CA 90680
714-379-7323

Intertec Personnel Services
6922 Hollywood Boulevard, Suite #211
Los Angeles, CA 90028-6117
213-466-4388

Darian James, *Hiring Contact*

IRI
18552 MacArthur Boulevard, Suite 208
Irvine, CA 92612
714-851-7723

It's ONly Temporary
6922 Hollywood Boulevard, Suite 303
Hollywood, CA 90028-6117
213-467-1790

J. Brown Healthcare Temporaries
375 North Citrus Avenue, Suite 638
Azusa, CA 91702-3909
818-915-0560

J.P.M. & Associates
26060 Acero Drive, Suite 100
Mission Vieja, CA 92691
714-955-2545

Jason Best Temporaries
10940 Wilshire Boulevard, Suite 1210
Los Angeles, CA 90024
310-820-1437

Julie Depoian, *Hiring Contact*

JB Healthcare Temporaries
375 North Citrus Avenue, Suite 638
Azusa, CA 91702-3909
818-335-1101

JEM RESOURCE NETWORK
1775 East Lincoln Avenue, Suite 201
Anaheim, CA 92805-4324
714-776-6797

JMF & Career Resources
16133 Ventura Boulevard, Suite 700
Encino, CA 91436
818-783-1107

Joanne Dunn & Associates
824 Moraga Drive
Los Angeles, CA 90049
310-471-5991

John P. Hazeltine Company
12664 Greenwald Ln
Santa Ana, CA 92705-1498
714-997-9547

Just In Time Temporaries
3525 Lomita Boulevard, Suite 101
Torrance, CA 90505-5016
310-534-5000

Kelly Services
6300 Wilshire Boulevard, Suite 1020
Los Angeles, CA 90048
213-782-8008

Valerie Lipec, *Hiring Contact*

Kibel Green, Inc.
2001 Wilshire Boulevard, Suite 420
Santa Monica, CA 90403-5641
310-829-0255
Web Address: www.kginc.com

Paulette Rua, *Hiring Contact*

Kimco Staffing Services
16832 Red Hill Avenue
Irvine, CA 92606
714-752-6996

Klein & Associates
3510 Torrance Boulevard, Suite 112
Torrance, CA 90503-4814
310-540-3140

Knape And Associates
1201 South Beach, Suite 118
La Habra, CA 90631
562-902-2711

Koll Strategic HR Services, Staffing Division
4343 Von Karman
Newport Beach, CA 92660
714-833-3030

Korn-Ferry International
1800 Century Park East, Suite 900
Los Angeles, CA 90067
310-552-1834
Web Address: www.kornferry.com

Labor Ready
2253 South Atlantic Boulevard
City of Commerce, CA 90040-3955
213-780-1081

Labor Ready
11912 West Washington Boulevard
Los Angeles, CA 90066
310-397-9769

Labor Ready
116 West 7th Street
Long Beach, CA 90813-4345
562-432-3521

Labor Ready
709 South Euclid
Fullerton, CA 92632
714-447-0672

Labor Ready
688 El Camino Real
Tustin, CA 92780-4310
714-444-0464

Labor Ready
2982 South Colorado Street, Suite 102B
Pasadena, CA 91107
818-440-8225

Labor Ready
12226 Victory Boulevard
North Hollywood, CA 91606-3207
818-753-2850

Labor Ready
13900-13902 East Valley Boulevard
La Puente, CA 91746
818-961-8122

Labor Ready
919 Yosemite Boulevard
Modesto, CA 95354
818-440-8225

Lee Hecht Harrison
2415 Campus Drive, Suite 250
Irvine, CA 92612-1527
714-250-9541

Lehman Brothers
601 South Figueroa Street, Suite 4425
Los Angeles, CA 90017
213-362-2550
Web Address: www.lehman.com

Lillian Kaiklian, *Hiring Contact*

Lending Personnel Services
2938 Daimler
Santa Ana, CA 92705
714-250-8133

Life Cycle Consulting
369 Van Ness, Suire 710
Torrance, CA 90501
310-542-5336

Yana Borsky, *Hiring Contact*

Loan Administration Network
1401 Dove Street #400
Newport Beach, CA 92660
714-752-5246

Logical Computer Services
3412 Burbank Boulevard
Burbank, CA 91505
818-845-5656

London Agency
3250 Wilshire Boulevard, Suite 1503
Los Angeles, CA 90010
213-384-8881

MacTemps
6100 Wilshire Boulevard, Suite 410
Los Angeles, CA 90048-5111
213-634-7000
Web Address: www.mactemps.com

MacTemps
4041 Macarthur Boulevard, Suite 240
Newport Beach, CA 92660-2512
714-476-9900

Manpower Inc.
2020 Santa Monica Boulevard, Suite 190
Santa Monica, CA 90404
310-829-2686

Wendy Taufa, *HIring Contact*

Maria America
1608 North Spurgeon Street
Santa Ana, CA 92701-2329
714-564-1747

Markar Associates
940 South Coast Drive, Suite 175
Costa Mesa, CA 92626
714-433-0100

Match-up Employment Agency
19033 Roscoe Boulevard
Northridge, CA 91324-4420
818-701-7021

**Median Personnel Services/
Median Health Care**
23361 El Toro Road, Suite 109
Lake Forest, CA 92630-6922
714-770-1541

Medical Staff Services Res.
628 North Janss Way
Anaheim, CA 92805-2531
714-774-5301

Meridian Office Services
22140 Ventura Boulevard, Suite 1
Woodland Hills, CA 91364-1662
818-703-1234

Meridian Personnel Services
11501 Booker Street, Suite 201
Garden Grove, CA 92840
714-537-7011

Metro Temporary Services
3255 Wilshire Boulevard, Suite 703
Los Angeles, CA 90010-1404
213-385-1703

Alex Olson, *Hiring Contact*

MIDCOM Corporation
4175 East La Palma Avenue, Suite 200
Anaheim, CA 92807
714-579-3000

Min & Associates
4333 Faculty Avenue
Long Beach, CA 90808-1315
714-934-2267

Minute Man
6703 South Atlantic Avenue
Bell, CA 90201-0710
213-771-1776

Rosemary Rodriguez, *Hiring Contact*

Modis
6053 Bristol Parkway
Culver City, CA 90230-6601
310-645-7600

Mortgage and Banking Personnel Services
9363 Wilshire Boulevard, Suite 215
Beverly Hills, CA 90210
310-271-2188

Barbara Collins, *Hiring Contact*

Muse Employment
17750 Camino De Yatasto
Pacific Palisades, CA 90272
310-459-5700

Helen Wilson, *Hiring contact*

National Companies
330 North Azusa Avenue
City of Industry, CA 91744
818-965-1441

NESCO SERVICE COMPANY
2431 North Tustin Avenue, Suite H
Santa Ana, CA 92705
714-973-1303

Norrell Services
4525 Wilshire Boulevard, Suite 120
Los Angeles, CA 90010-3837
213-964-9566

Norrell Services
1020 Wilshire Boulevard, Suite 210
Los Angeles, CA 90024
310-794-0177
Web Address: www.norrellwest.com

Norrell Services
19001 South Western Avenue # A125
Torrance, CA 90509
310 618 4118

Lisa Wagner, *Hiring Contact*

Norrell Services
2377 Crenshaw Boulevard, Suite 156
Torrance, CA 90501-3345
310-782-6436

Stephanie Smith, *Hiring Contact*

Norrell Services
4909 Lakewood Boulevard, Suite 307
Lakewood, CA 90712-2405
562-633-9835

Cathy Son, *Hiring Contact*

Norrell Services
3030 Old Ranch Parkway, Suite 260
Seal Beach, CA 90740-2748
562-799-0080

Nanette Mojica, *Hiring Contact*

Norrell Services
1 Civic Plaza Drive, Suite 370
Carson, CA 90745-2243
310-518-4791

Christine Sanchez, *Hiring Contact*

Norrell Services
940 South Coast Drive, Suite 100
Costa Mesa, CA 92626-1780
714-850-9900

Norrell Services
101 South Kraemer Boulevard, Suite 110
Placentia, CA 92670-6105
714-996-9880

Norrell Services
790 East Colorado Boulevard , Suite 102
Pasadena, CA 91101-2113
818-440-9072

Norrell Services
5950 Canoga Avenue, Suite 219
Woodland Hills, CA 91367-5011
818-340-8810

Now Excel Personnel Agency
127 North Madison Avenue, Suite 210B
Pasadena, CA 91101-1750
818-585-2990

NuCare Agency
1800 East McFadden Avenue, Suite 100
Santa Ana, CA 92705-4736
714-550-0800

Olsten Staffing Services
5750 Wilshire Boulevard, Suite 105
Los Angeles, CA 90036-3697
213-930-0530

Maria Santiago, *Hiring Contact*

Olsten Staffing Services
360 North Sepulveda Boulevard, Suite 1020
El Segundo, CA 90245
310-322-5800

Olsten Staffing Services
18000 Studebaker Road, Suite 280
Cerritos, CA 90703-3678
562924-1185

Lana Kling, *Hiring Contact*

Olsten Staffing Services
18200 Von Karman Avenue, Suite 900
Irvine, CA 92612-1029
714-222-0966

Olsten Staffing Services
3070 Bristol Street, Suite 540
Costa Mesa, CA 92626-3071
714-979-5600

Olsten Staffing Services
17330 Brookhurst Street, Suite 120
Fountain Valley, CA 92708-3759
714-964-1944

Olsten Staffing Services
2300 Katella Avenue, Suite 335
Anaheim, CA 92806
714-937-5327

Olsten Staffing Services
2400 East Katella Avenue, Suite 975
Anaheim, CA 92806
714-978-6640

Olsten Staffing Services
800 East Colorado Boulevard, Suite 120
Pasadena, CA 91101
818-449-1342

Olsten Staffing Services
505 North Brand Boulevard
Glendale, CA 91203
818-500-6750

Olsten Staffing Services
21600 Oxnard Boulevard Main Plz
Woodland Hills, CA 91367
818-593-8080

Olsten Staffing Services
15060 Ventura Boulevard, Suite 201
Sherman Oaks, CA 91403
818-981-9500

Olsten Staffing Services
100 North Citrus Street, Suite 301
West Covina, CA 91791
818-966-1466

Omega Contract Design
5011 Argosy Avenue, Suite 8
Huntington Beach, CA 92649
714-898-8373

On-Demand Resource
1999 West 190th Street, Suite 250
Torrance, CA 90504
310-512-6345
Web Address: www.ondemandresource.com

OutSource International
1200 East Katella Avenue
Anaheim, CA 92805-6623
714-385-1900

P. Murphy Associates
4405 Riverside Drive, Suite 105
Burbank, CA 91505
818-841-2002

Paladin/Los Angeles
11990 San Vicente Boulevard, Suite 350
Los Angeles, CA 90049
310-826-6222
Web Address: www.paladinstaff.com

Lisa Robinson, *Hiring Contact*

PAPPAS
PO Box 71895
Los Angeles, CA 90071
213-483-8796

Paralegal Services
535 North Brand Boulevard, Suite 400
Glendale, CA 91203-1917
818-543-3605

Paralegals for Business & Law
10700 Santa Monica Boulevard, Suite 3
Los Angeles, CA 90025-4715
310-474-1375

Marty Behrendt, *Hiring Contact*

Partridge & Associates
3901 Foothill Boulevard, Suite 106
Glendale, CA 91214
818-957-1988

Pasona, Inc.
777 South Figueroa Street, Suite 2900
Los Angeles, CA 90071-2901
213-489-2989

Maria Escobedo, *Hiring Contact*

Pat Services
8936 Sepulveda Boulevard, Suite 103
Los Angeles, CA 90045
310-649-1471

Pat Services
3878 West Carson Street, Suite 200
Torrance, CA 90503-6707
310-543-0076

PC Pro Temp Personnel
11022 Santa Monica Boulevard, Suite 420
Los Angeles, CA 90025-7513
213-312-6600

PDQ Personnel Services
5900 Wilshire Boulevard, Suite 400
Los Angeles, CA 90036-5013
213-938-3933
Web Address: www.pdqcareers.com

Performance Service
569 North Mountain Avenue, Suite C
Upland, CA 91786-8504
714-946-9066

Persona, Inc.
3900 Birch Street, Suite 103
Newport Beach, CA 92660-2209
714-752-9201

Physicians Search Associates
1224 East Katella Avenue, Suite 202
Orange, CA 92667
714-288-8350

Post Legal Search
8191 Waterspray Drive
Huntington Beach, CA 92646-8542
714-833-1130

Prestige Personnel Services
19069 Colima Road
Rowland Heights, CA 91748-2952
818-964-1082

Primary Source Staffing
3825 Del Amo Boulevard, Suite 200
Torrance, CA 90503-2166
310-214-9175

Prime Technical Services
24102 Brookfield Cir
Lake Forest, CA 92630-3718
714-457-9921

Principal Technical Services
24102 Brookfield Circle
Lake Forest, CA 92630
714-457-9035

Pro Staff Personnel Services
3030 Old Ranch Parkway, Suite 350
Seal Beach, CA 90740
562-795-7700

Pro Staff Personnel Services
225 West Broadway, Suite 103
Glendale, CA 91204
818-551-9145

Professional Employer Services
6464 West Sunset Boulevard, Suite 1030
Los Angeles, CA 90028-8001
213-962-2350

Stuart Grant, *Hiring Contact*

Professional Staffing Services
2361 Campus Drive, Suite 101
Irvine, CA 92612
714-851-5141

Professional Staffing Services
2901 West Macarthur Boulevard, Suite 201
Santa Ana, CA 92704-6910
714-545-2232

Project Professionals
400 Corporate Pointe, Suite 755
Culver City, CA 90230
310-649-6389

PSI Personnel Services
9509 Central Avenue, Suite F
Montclair, CA 91763-2400
714-625-2386

Quantum Technical Solutions
12340 Santa Monica Boulevard, Suite 304
Los Angeles, CA 90025-1879
310-820-1070

Steve Sobel, *Hiring Contact*

Quicks Computer Training
991 West San Bernadino Road
Covina, CA 91722
818-966-0061

R&C Corporate Staffing
610 South Glendale Avenue
Glendale, CA 91205-2316
818-500-9016

Ray & Berndtson
2029 Century Park East, Suite 1000
Los Angeles, CA 90067
310-557-2828
Web Address: ww.rayberndtson.com

RD Solutions
4283 Empress Avenue
Encino, CA 91436
818-788-7288

Real Estate Temps
302 North El Camino Real, Suite 114A
San Clemente, CA 92672-4775
714-366-0935

Regal Personnel Services
404 West Chevy Chase Drive, Suite A
Glendale, CA 91204
818-548-5220

Reliance Staffing Services
10351 Santa Monica Boulevard, Suite 30
Los Angeles, CA 90025-6908
310-470-2648

Relis Employment
24621 Creekview Drive
Laguna Hills, CA 92653-4210
714-830-4897

Remedy Temporary Services
32122 Camino Capistrano
San Juan Capistrano, CA 92675-3717
714-661-1211

Remedy Temporary Services
32122 Camino Capistrano
San Juan Capistrano, CA 92675-3787
714-661-1211

Remedy Temporary Services
32122 Camino Capistrano
San Juan Capistrano, CA 92675-3787
714-661-1211

Remedy Temporary Services
32122 Camino Capistrano
San Juan Capistrano, CA 92675-3787
714-661-1211

Research Associates
12021 Wilshire Boulevard, Suite 229
Los Angeles, CA 90025
310-837-7241

Resource Management Group
22760 Hawthorne Boulevard, Suite 100
Torrance, CA 90505-3600
310-373-3772

RMD Technical & Management Personnel Services
27212 Soledad
Mission Viejo, CA 92691-1432
714-581-4376

Robert Half International
10877 Wilshire Boulevard, Suite 1605
Los Angeles, CA 90024
310-286-6800

Robert Half, *Hiring Contact*

Ronni Cooper Medical
1502 Wilshire Boulevard, Suite 210
Santa Monica, CA 90403
310-393-7474
Web Address: www.ronnicoopermedical.com

Royal Personnel Services
14755 Ventura Boulevard, Suite 100
Sherman Oaks, CA 91403-3669
818-981-1080

Russell Renyolds Associates
333 South Grand Avenue, 42nd Floor
Los Angeles, CA 90071
213-489-1520
Web Address: www.russreyn.com

Ryan Miller & Associates
4601 Wilshire Boulevard, Suite 225
Los Angeles, CA 90010
213-938-4768

Michael O'Connell, *Hiring Contact*

Sawyer Staffing
3825 Del Amo Boulevard, Suite 200
Torrance, CA 90503
310-376-8244

Search West
1888 Century Park East, Suite 2050
Los Angeles, CA 90067
310-284-8888

Ashton Clarke, *Hiring Contact*

Sedgwick
18201 Von Karman Avenue, Suite 800
Irvine, CA 92715-1005
714-756-3371

Select Temp
26941 Via Grande
Mission Viejo, CA 92691-6136
714-582-5848

Select Temporary Services
16525 Von Karman Avenue, Suite 3D
Irvine, CA 92714-4943
714-476-2817

Sharf, Wasson & Woodward
14640 Victory Boulevard, Suite 100
Van Nuys, CA 91411
818-898-2200

Shore Personnel Services
1301 Dove Street, Suite 650
Newport Beach, CA 92660
714-530-7191

Skills Masters
20411 South Susanna Road, Suite L
Carson, CA 90810-1508
310-884-9200

Lydia Cardenas, *Hiring Contact*

Snelling Personnel
36 Executive Park, Suite 130
Irvine, CA 92714-6744
714-252-1882

Snelling Personnel
16133 Ventura Boulevard, Suite 1245
Encino, CA 91436-2416
818-788-1608

Software Management Consultants
500 North Brand Boulevard, Suite 1090
Glendale, CA 91203
818-240-3177

Source Finance
1 Park Plaza, Suite 560
Irvine, CA 92714
714-553-8115

Source Services Corporation
2029 Century Park East, Suite 1350
Los Angeles, CA 90067-2901
310-277-8092
Web Address: www.sourcesvc.com

Lucy Yeh, *Hiring Contact*

Source Services Corporation
879 West 190th Street, Suite 250
Los Angeles, CA 90248-4220
310-323-0808
Web Address: www.wourcesvc.com

Carolyn Escobedo, *Hiring Contact*

Source Services Corporation
1 Park Plz, Suite 560
Irvine, CA 92714-5910
714-251-1335

Source Services Corporation
15260 Ventura Boulevard, Suite 220
Sherman Oaks, CA 91403-5307
818-905-1500

Staff Control Plus
12832 Valley View Street, Suite C
Garden Grove, CA 92645
714-379-5202

Staff Seekers
18062 Irvine Boulevard., Suite 105
Tustin, CA 92680
714-730-0593

Staff Source
14330 Chantry Drive
Moreno Valley, CA 92553-2948
714-242-6857

Staff Support
11835 West Olympic Boulevard, Suite 1125
Los Angeles, CA 90064-5001
310-575-3333

STAFFING 2000
540 North Azusa Avenue
West Covina, CA 91791-1146
818-331-6339

Star View Services
PO Box 6221
Huntington Beach, CA 92615-6221
714-962-0091

Stat Medical Search
2301 Dupont Drive, Suite 400
Irvine, CA 92715
714-261-0511

Stern & Associates
11260 Overland Avenue, Suite 16-A
Culver City, CA 90230-5559
310-838-0551
Web Address: www.hrconsultants.com

Anita Howe, *Hiring Contact*

Stivers Temporary Personnel
3660 Wilshire Boulevard, Suite 1150
Los Angeles, CA 90010-2756
213-386-3440
Web Address: www.stivers.com

Stivers Temporary Personnel
10880 Wilshire Boulevard, Suite 117
Los Angeles, CA 90024-4101
310-475-7700
Web Address: www.stivers.com

Diana Kay, *Hiring Contact*

Stivers Temporary Personnel
1750 Ocean Park Boulevard, Suite 206
Santa Monica, CA 90405-4950
310-392-5546
Web Address: www.stivers.com

Stivers Temporary Personnel
4040 Barranca Pky, Suite 250
Irvine, CA 92714-4766
714-857-1444

Stivers Temporary Personnel
55 South Lake Avenue, Suite 100
Pasadena, CA 91101-2626
818-796-8559

Stivers Temporary Personnel
16601 Ventura Boulevard
Encino, CA 91436-1921
818-906-1145

Strategic Staffing
3551 Camino Mira Costa, Suite M
San Clemente, CA 92672-3500
714-240-4622

Systems Experience
6033 West Century Boulevard, Suite 260
Los Angeles, CA 90045
310-215-9000

TAD Staffing Services
2540 Main Street, Suite P
Irvine, CA 92714-6241
714-250-7234

TAD Staffing Services
726-B Glendale Avenue
Glendale, CA 91206
818-265-1163

TAD Technical Services
17621 Irvine Boulevard, Suite 214
Tustin, CA 92680-3114
714-838-4380

TAD Technical Services
4552 Lincoln Avenue, Suite 105
Cypress, CA 90630-2660
714-236-2010

Talent Tree Personnel Services
30 Center Pointe Drive, Suite 11
La Palma, CA 90623
714-523-1170

Talent Tree Personnel Services
695 Town Center Drive, Suite 140
Costa Mesa, CA 92626-1924
714-850-1233

Talent Tree Personnel Services
13821 Newport Avenue, Suite 150
Tustin, CA 92680-7803
714-731-7010

Talent Tree Personnel Services
141 South Lake Avenue
Pasadena, CA 91101-2673
818-405-0101

Talent Tree Personnel Services
15490 Ventura Boulevard, Suite 105
Sherman Oaks, CA 91403-3016
818-990-0440

Talent Tree Personnel Services
17800 Castleton Street, Suite 100
Rowland Heights, CA 91748-1749
818-810-4141

Talent Tree Staffing Services
145 South State College Boulevard, Suite 1
Brea, CA 92822
714-529-8700

Tandem Staffing Services
8235 East Firestone Boulevard, Suite B
Downing, CA 90240
562-923-3077

Alex Torres, *Hiring Contact*

Taylor Dane-Personnel Services
345 North LaBrea Avenue, Suite 208
Los Angeles, CA 90036-2507
213-933-7511
Web Address: www.taylordane.com

Carolyne Holland, *Hiring Contact*

Team One
10850 Wilshire Boulevard, Suite 350
Los Angeles, CA 90024-4305
310-441-2800

Teamwork Business Services
1211 West Imperial Highway, Suite 100
Brea, CA 92621
714-773-1506

TEC Financial Corporation
3100 West Burbank Boulevard
Burbank, CA 91505-3301
818-840-0993

Tech Aid
15720 Ventura Boulevard, Suite 608
Encino, CA 91436
818-995-2910

Teleforce International
PO Box 3175
San Clemente, CA 92674-3175
714-661-3337

Temp Plus Staffing Services
3600 Wilshire Boulevard, Suite 2120
Los Angeles, CA 90010-2603
213-368-6978
Web Address: www.ontheedgeinc.com

TempChoice Personnel Services
15941 Red Hill Avenue, Suite 105
Tustin, CA 92680-7319
714-258-2110

TEMPLOY, INC.
15991 Red Hill Avenue, Suite 101
Tustin, CA 92780-7320
714-247-1100

Temporaries, Inc.
1301 Dove Street, Suite 350
Newport Beach, CA 92660-2412
714-250-1070

Temporaries, Inc.
16501 Ventura Boulevard, Suite 104
Encino, CA 91436
818-905-5522

Temporary Insurance Professionals
3821 Hendrix Street
Irvine, CA 92714-6603
714-733-2188

Temps On Time
403 East Palm
Burbank, CA 91502-1207
818-845-3030

Temps Unlimited
17411 Chatsworth Street # 103
Granada Hills, CA 91344-5718
818-363-2345

TempStaff International
21515 Hawthorne Boulevard, Suite 440
Torrance, CA 90503
310-792-5780

Tempstar Services
PO Box 81060
Rancho San Margarit, CA 92688-1060
714-457-6380

Tender Care
8001 Laurel Canyon Boulevard, Suite A
North Hollywood, CA 91605-1400
818-504-3530

The Affiliates
10887 Wilshire Boulevard, Suite 1605
Los Angeles, CA 90024
310-557-2334
Web Address: ww.roberthalf.com

Lou Salis, *Hiring Contact*

The Blue Chip Law Registry
2030 Main Street, Suite 1300
Irvine, CA 92614
714-260-4723

The Dial Group
14522 East Whitter Boulevard
Whittier, CA 90605
562-945-1071
Web Address: www.dialworks.com

Louise Douglas, *Hiring Contact*

The Employee Solution
14536 Roscoe Boulevard, Suite 112
Panorama City, CA 91402-4148
818-891-0197

The Estrin Organization
2040 Avenue of The Stars, Suite 400
Los Angeles, CA 90067
310-553-6699
Web Address: www.estrin.com

The Focus Agency
15300 Ventura Boulevard., Suite 207
Sherman Oaks, CA 91403
818-981-9519

The Party Staff
8075 West Third Street, Suite 550
Los Angeles, CA 90048
213-933-3900

The Recruiter's Recruiter
12437 Lewis Street, Suite 204
Garden Grove, CA 92640-4652
714-971-5325

The Right Connections
509 North La Cienega Boulevard
Los Angeles, CA 90048-2008
310-657-3700

The Vincam Group
2100 East Howell Avenue, Suite 108
Anaheim, CA 92806
714-634-1982

Therapists Unlimited
14241 Firestone Boulevard, Suite 200
La Mirada, CA 90638-5530
562-921-4200
Web Address: www.therapistsunlimited.com

Therapy Services Plus
5308 Perry Avenue, #K
Agoura Hills, CA 91301
818-707-2545

Thomas Staffing
24422 Avenida de la Carlota, Suite 165
Laguna Hills, CA 92653
714-380-4111

Thomas Staffing
3440 Wilshire Boulevard, Suite 1111
Los Angeles, CA 90010-2112
213-386-1700
Web Address: www.thomas-staffing.com

Leslie Robinson, *Hiring Contact*

Thomas Staffing
1990 South Bundy Drive, Suite 380
Los Angeles, CA 90025
310-442-9988
Web Address: www.thomas-staffing.com

Thomas Staffing
12750 Center Court Drive
Cerritos, CA 90703
310-869-4056
Web Address: www.thomas-staffing.com

Patty O'Connor, *Hiring Contact*

Thomas Staffing
3480 Torrance Boulevard, Suite 102
Torrance, CA 90503
310-316-8555
Web Address: www.thomas-staffing.com

Thomas Staffing
3780 Kilroy Airport Way, Suite 55
Long Beach, CA 90806
562-427-0110
Web Address: www.thomas-staffing.com

Patty O'Connor, *Hiring Contact*

Thomas Staffing
17320 Red Hill Avenue, Suite 15
Irvine, CA 92614
714-261-5400

Thomas Staffing
17320 Red Hill Avenue, Suite 140
Irvine, CA 92614
714-222-0466

Thomas Staffing
11642 Knott Street, Suite 15
Garden Grove, CA 92641
714-891-4768

Thomas Staffing
17542 East 17th Street, Suite 120
Tustin, CA 92680
714-508-1828

Thomas Staffing
377 East Chapman Avenue, Suite 220
Placentia, CA 92870-5056
714-774-9399

Thomas Staffing
3280 East Foothill Boulevard, Suite 140
Pasadena, CA 91107
818-304-9307

Thomas Staffing
100 West Broadway, Suite 720
Glendale, CA 91210
818-956-1768

Thomas Staffing
14390 Ventura Boulevard
Sherman Oaks, CA 91423
818-501-0274

Thomas Staffing
100 North Citrus, Suite 225
West Covina, CA 91791
818-967-2345

Thor Temporary Services
7334 Topanga Canyon Boulevard, Suite #113
Canoga Park, CA 91303-1268
818-710-1800

Thor Temporary Services
2500 East Colorado Boulevard, Suite #350
Pasadena, CA 91107-3701
818-795-2202

Times Personnel, Division of TRS Staffing
3353 Michelson Drive, Suite 531Y
Irvine, CA 92698
714-975-3215

Tisha Silvers Business Services
10013 South Furmont Avenue, Suite 353
Los Angeles, CA 90044
213-756-2672

Title Temps
8926 Sunland Boulevard
Sun Valley, CA 91352
818-771-0220

TLC SERVICES
1450 East 17th Street, Suite 100
Santa Ana, CA 92705-8510
714-541-5415

Tomar Enterprises
17802 Irvine Boulevard, Suite 119
Tustin, CA 92680-3241
714-573-0357

Top Tempo & Future Personnel
4727 Wilshire Boulevard, Suite 200
Los Angeles, CA 90010
213-936-1799
Web Address: www.topjobsusa.net

TPM Staffing Services
17310 Red Hill Avenue, Suite 100
Irvine, CA 92714-5642
714-852-9889

TPM Staffing Services
15375 Barranca Pky, Suite D
Irvine, CA 92718-2217
714-753-1624

TRC Staffing Services
11300 West Olympic Boulevard, Suite 780
West Los Angeles, CA 90064-1637
310-473-4161

TRC Staffing Services
17775 Main Street, Suite M
Irvine, CA 92614
714-851-5007

TRC Staffing Services
101 North Brand Boulevard, Suite 920
Glendale, CA 91203-2619
818-548-3597

TREND SERVICES
4128 West Commonwealth Avenue
Fullerton, CA 92833
714-525-0134

Ultimate Staffing
100 South State College Boulevard
Brea, CA 92821
714-990-5441

Ultimate Staffing Services
4100 Newport Place Drive, Suite 240
Newport Beach, CA 92660-2423
714-752-7373

United Source Service
28720 Canwood Street, Suite 204
Agoura Hills, CA 91301-4521
818-879-4900

US Labor
762 East Orange Grove Boulevard, Suite 7
Pasadena, CA 91104
818-793-2826

Valley Temps
601 East Glenoaks Boulevard, Suite 208
Glendale, CA 91207-1700
818-242-9585

Valley Temps
23801 Calabasas Road, Suite 1004
Calabasas, CA 91302-1547
818-223-1590

VIP Temporary Services
PO Box 18268
Anaheim, CA 92817-8268
714-632-5555

Volt Services Group
3055 Wilshire Boulevard, Suite 100
Los Angeles, CA 90010-1108
213-388-3271
Web Address: www.volt.com

Cheryl Bridges, *Hiring Contact*

Volt Services Group
12100 Wilshire Boulevard, Suite M90
Los Angeles, CA 90025-7120
310-207-0077

Sheila Harmon, *Hiring Contact*

Volt Services Group
7431 Florence Avenue
Downey, CA 90240-3608
562-806-3381

Eric Zepeda, *Hiring Contact*

Volt Services Group
500 South Douglas Street
El Segundo, CA 90245-4805
310-536-0711

Volt Services Group
3655 Torrance Boulevard, Suite 160
Torrance, CA 90503-4810
310-316-9182

Christina Harvey, *Hiring Contact*

Volt Services Group
11127 183rd Street
Cerritos, CA 90703-5415
562-809-1419

Volt Services Group
860 West Imperial Highway, Suite K
Brea, CA 92621-3810
714-529-1480

Volt Services Group
950 South Coast Drive, Suite 180
Costa Mesa, CA 92626
714-662-1988

Volt Services Group
7644 Edinger Avenue
Huntington Beach, CA 92647-3605
714-842-2166

Volt Services Group
2401 North Glassell Street
Orange, CA 92665-2705
714-921-8800

Volt Services Group
2401 North Glassell Street
Orange, CA 92665-2705
714-921-8800

Volt Services Group
2401 North Glassell Street
Orange, CA 92665-2705
714-921-8800

Volt Services Group
2401 North Glassell Street
Orange, CA 92665-2705
714-921-5481

Volt Services Group
28570 Marguerite Parkway, Suite 112
Mission Viejo, CA 92692-3713
714-364-1162

Volt Services Group
1100 East Orangethorpe Avenue, Suite 10
Anaheim, CA 92801-1161
714-879-9961

Volt Services Group
959 East Walnut Street, Suite 107A
Pasadena, CA 91106-1451
818-796-8658

Volt Services Group
21515 Vanowen Street, Suite 112
Canoga Park, CA 91303-2715
818-992-8510

Volt Services Group
150 East Olive Avenue, Suite 111
Burbank, CA 91502-1846
818-848-2000

Volt Services Group
2357 South Azusa Avenue
West Covina, CA 91792-1530
818-913-1280

Volt Services Group
950 South Coast Drive, Suite 185
Costa Mesa, CA 92626
714-549-3328

Volt Services Group
3655 Torrance Boulevard, Suite 160
Torrance, CA 90503-4810
310-316-9182

Christina Harvey, *Hiring Contact*

Wells & Associates
1225 West 190th Street, Suite 380
Gardena, CA 90248
310-323-9099
Web Address: www.welltemps.com

West Covina
541 California Avenue
West Covina, CA 91790
818-813-4440

West Covina
547 South California Avenue
West Covina, CA 91790-3640
818-814-2324

Western Staffing
11702 Imperial Highway, Suite 101
Norwalk, CA 90650-2818
310-868-8228

Western Staffing
13911 Carroll Way, Suite East
Tustin, CA 92680-1849
714-544-3033

Western Staffing
3535 Inland Empire Boulevard
Ontario, CA 91764-4908
714-941-3266

Western Staffing
2461 East Orangethorpe Avenue # 203
Fullerton, CA 92631-5302
714-879-3333

**Westways Medical Services/
Professional Staff**
7755 Center Avenue, Suite 1100
Huntington Beach, CA 92647-3007
714-372-4949

Woodbell Employment Service
10061 Talbert Avenue, Suite 200
Fountain Valley, CA 92708-5159
714-278-1330

Word Pro Personnel
3333 Michelson Drive, Suite 405
Irvine, CA 92715-1684
714-474-0200

WORLDTEC GROUP INTERNATIONAL
14150 Vine Pl
Cerritos, CA 90703-2453
562-407-3700
Web Address: www.wgis.com

Mike Cordell, *Hiring Contact*

Xtra Personnel Services
15549 Devonshire Street, Suite 4
Mission Hills, CA 91345-2648
818-891-5633

Your Staff
20300 Ventura Boulevard, Suite 150
Woodland Hills, CA 91364-2448
818-999-4100

San Diego County

Adecco
22600-C Lambert Street, Suite 902
Lake Forest, CA 92630
714-458-9331

Apple One
1295 North Euclid Street
Anaheim, CA 92801
714-956-5180

Interim Personnel
910 East Birch Street, Suite 200
Brea, CA 92621
714-990-2441

Kelly Temporary Services
5 Park Plaza, Suite 1280
Irvine, CA 92714
714-252-1755

Olsten Staffing Services
18101 Von Karman Avenue, Suite 560
Irvine, CA 92801
714-222-0966

A Plus Personnel
263 S Highway 101
Solana Beach, CA 92075
619-481-9933

ABCOW
5055 Avenida Encinas, Suite 130
Carlsbad, CA 92008-4375
619-736-3000

Abcow Services
2525 Camino del Rio S, Suite 125
San Diego, CA 92108-3717
619-291-7000

ABCOW Services
2525 Camino Del Rio South, Suite 125
San Diego, CA 92108
619-291-7000

Accountants
2011 Palomar Airport Road, Suite 30
Carlsbad, CA 92009
619-431-1101

Accountants
4225 Executive Square, Suite 1430
La Jolla, CA 92037-1487
619-452-7111

Accountemps/Office Team
409 Camino del Rio South, #305
San Diego, CA 92108
619-291-7990

Adecco
5252 Balboa Avenue, Suite 302
San Diego, CA 92117
619-560-8815

Adia Personnel Services
8304 Clairmont Mesa Boulevard
San Diego, CA 92111
619-549-0616

Aerotek
5075 Shoreham Place #220
San Diego, CA 92122
619-552-9333

Alliance Services Associates
10085 Carroll Canyon Road, Suite 110
San Diego, CA 92131-1107
619-455-2344

Alliance Staffing Associates
10951 Sorrento Valley Road, Suite 1
San Diego, CA 92121
619-623-5499

American Mobile Nurses
12730 High Bluff Drive, #400
San Diego, CA 92130
619-792-0711

Apple One Employment Services
5638 Mission Center Road, Suite 103
San Diego, CA 92108
619-542-1310

AppleOne
7420 Clairemont Mesa Boulevard, Suite 105
San Diego, CA 92111-1546
619-292-5755

B & M Associates
4180 Ruffin Road, Suite 255
San Diego, CA 92123
619-627-9675

Bank On Us
7817 Ivanhoe Avenue, Suite 300
La Jolla, CA 92037-4542
619-454-5381

BankTemps
4379 30th Street, Suite 2
San Diego, CA 92104-1323
619-584-1330

Barbachano International
660 Bay Boulevard, Suite 103
Chula Vista, CA 91910
619-427-2310

Berry Employment Services
6790 Top Gun Street, Suite 3
San Diego, CA 92121-3803
619-597-9264

Career Staff
3131 Camino del Rio North, Suite 370
San Diego, CA 92108-5701
619-285-1270

Computemp of San Diego
4350 Executive Drive, Suite 115
San Diego, CA 92121
619-597-1122

Creative Financial Staffing
2550 5th Avenue 10th Floor
San Diego, CA 92103-6612
619-702-7301

Critical Care Unlimited
41615 Morningside Court
Rancho Mirage, CA 92270-4133
619-346-6165

Culver Temporary
8885 Rio San Diego Drive, Suite 320
San Diego, CA 92108
619-297-6400

DataSkill International
12760 High Bluff Drive, Suite 210
San Diego, CA 92130
619-755-3800

Dental Statewide Staffing
8427 Cordial
El Cajon, CA 92021
619-443-7252

Desert Temps
73255 El Paseo, Suite 9
Palm Desert, CA 92260-4237
619-568-4150

eai Healthcare Staffing Solutions
1333 Camino Del Rio S, Suite 315
San Diego, CA 92108
619-299-9104

Eastridge Environmental Search
P.O. Box 33745
San Diego, CA 92163
619-260-2043

Employment Systems
11590 W Bernardo Court, Suite 211
San Diego, CA 92127-1622
619-451-0040

EXPRESS PERSONNEL SERVICES
2216 El Camino Real, Suite 208
Oceanside, CA 92054
619-966-8066

First Aid Svcs of San Diego
5907 Erlanger Street
San Diego, CA 92122-3803
619-457-5273

In Home Support Network
6114 University Avenue #33
San Diego, CA 92115
619-287-6220

Initial Staffing
9444 Balboa Avenue, Suite 175
San Diego, CA 92123
619-268-5104

Intech Summit Group
5057 Shoreham Place, Suite 280
San Diego, CA 92122
619-452-2100

Integrated Cardiovascular Systems
8555 Aero Drive
San Diego, CA 92123-1743
619-492-1115

INTERIM SERVICES
110 W C Street, Suite 1101
San Diego, CA 92101-3900
619-235-2400

INTERIM SERVICES
3131 Camino del Rio North Suite 180
San Diego, CA 92108-5701
619-624-9400

INTERIM SERVICES
9255 Towne Centre Drive, Suite 150
San Diego, CA 92121
619-458-9791

INTERIM SERVICES
5150 Murphy Canyon Road, Suite 101
San Diego, CA 92123-4361
619-268-8287

KBM Building & Security Services
3620 30th Street
San Diego, CA 92104
619-291-0404

Kelly Services
5030 Camino de la Siesta, Suite 401
San Diego, CA 92108
619-298-1631

Kirk-Mayer
5252 Balboa Avenue, Suite 502
San Diego, CA 92117-6906
619-576-6922

Lab Support
21660 East Copley Drive, Suite 330
Diamond Bar, CA 91765
909-612-1070

Labor Force
7878 Clairemont Mesa Boulevard, Suite
San Diego, CA 92111
619-560-9983

Labor Ready
1090 3rd Avenue, Suite 15
Chula Vista, CA 91911
619-425-0295

Labor Ready
1215 East Main Street
El Cajon, CA 92021-7245
619-444-7877

Labor Ready
242 W Mission Boulevard, Suite 1
Escondido, CA 92025
619-738-8355

Labor Ready
2555 Morena Boulevard
San Diego, CA 92110
619-276-7364

Legalstaff of San Diego
4250 Executive Square, Suite 520
La Jolla, CA 92037
619-597-1170

Long Term Temps
4936 Lorraine Drive
San Diego, CA 92115
619-229-8090

LP Temporaries
846 Chinquapin Avenue
Carlsbad, CA 92008-4142
619-431-9012

MacTemps
6310 Greenwich Drive, Suite 110
San Diego, CA 92122-5902
619-453-2800

MAINTENANCE MATCH
4660 La Jolla Village Drive, Suite 5
San Diego, CA 92122
619-625-4635

Manpower
101 W Broadway, Suite 1400
San Diego, CA 92101-8201
619-237-9900

Manpower Temporary Service
101 West Broadway, Suite 1400
San Diego, CA 92101
619-234-6433

Meridian Temporary Services
4320 La Jolla Village Drive, Suite 3
San Diego, CA 92122-1204
619-455-7500

Mini-Sysetms Associates
15373 Innovation Drive, Suite 301
San Diego, CA 92128
619-675-7888

New Logic Data Services
5060 Shoreham Place, Suite 200
San Diego, CA 92122
619-458-5858

Norrell Services
6480 Weathers Pl, Suite 100
San Diego, CA 92121-3911
619-452-0937

Norrell Services
73-140 Highway 111, Suite 7
Palm Desert, CA 92260
619-341-9565

Nurse's House Call
480 Camino del Rio South, Suite 206
San Diego, CA 92108-3511
619-296-1171

Office Specialists
3111 Camino del Rio North, Suite 1200
San Diego, CA 92108-5732
619-281-3200

OLSTEN STAFFING SERVICES
1450 Frazee Road, Suite 602
San Diego, CA 92108
619-688-0500

OLSTEN STAFFING SERVICES
5510 Morehouse Drive, Suite 160
San Diego, CA 92121-3721
619-693-8831

Omni Express Personnel
2185 Faraday Avenue , Suite 120
Carlsbad, CA 92008
619-438-4405

On Call Employee Solutions
5151 Shoreham Pl, Suite 110
San Diego, CA 92122
619-558-8460

On Call Temporary Mortgage Professionals
12526 High Bluff Drive, Suite 145
San Diego, CA 92130
619-794-2870

OutSource International
1010 Broadway Boulevard, Suite 1
Chula Vista, CA 91911-1867
619-476-9675

OVERFLOW Temporary staffing services
4455 Federal Boulevard, Suite 110
San Diego, CA 92102-2535
619-527-0065

PFI Personnel Service
1081 Camino del Rio South
San Diego, CA 92108-3542
619-295-1422

Physical Therapy Network
5030 Camino de La Siesta, Suite 401
San Diego, CA 92108-3116
619-581-1781

PowerTemps
1081 Camino del Rio S, Suite 110
San Diego, CA 92108-3542
619-692-3320

PowerVision Consulting
132 North El Camino Real, Box I
Encinitas, CA 92024-2801
619-597-7500

PREFERRED THERAPY REGISTRY, INC.
4655 Ruffner Street, Suite 240
San Diego, CA 92111-2226
619-505-0939

Premier Temporary Services
16476 Bernado Center Drive, Suite 127
San Diego, CA 92128
619-674-5581

Pro Tem Legal Services
110 W C Street, Suite 700
San Diego, CA 92101-3900
619-232-6191

San Diego Insurance Temps
3636 Camino Del Rio North, Suite 140
San Diego, CA 92108
619-528-8434

San Diego Personnel & Employment Agency
9474 Kearny Villa Road, Suite 105
San Diego, CA 92126
619-689-8500

Scotty's Agency
655 North Palm Canyon Drive, Suite 7
Palm Springs, CA 92262-5527
619-323-0567

Senior Design Corp
4545 Murphy Canyon Road, Suite 204
San Diego, CA 92123-4363
619-292-9010

SoCal Temps
4909 Murphy Canyon Road, Suite 405
San Diego, CA 92123-4301
619-569-7555

Source EDP
4510 Executive Drive, Suite 200
San Diego, CA 92121
619-552-0300

Source Services Corporation
4510 Executive Drive, Suite 200
San Diego, CA 92121-3021
619-552-0300

Speedy Alternatives
1502 Puls Street
Oceanside, CA 92054-2742
619-967-8339

Staffing Alternatives & Specialized Services
114 Balsam Street
Ridgecrest, CA 93555-3821
619-375-1003

State of the Art Computing Inc
480 Camino del Rio South, Suite 226
San Diego, CA 92108-3511
619-586-1858

Stellcom Technologies
10525 Vista Sorrento Parkway
San Diego, CA 92121
619-554-1400

System 1
960 Los Vallecitos Boulevard, Suite 20
San Marcos, CA 92069-1462
619-471-9200

System 1 Temps
4350 Executive Drive, Suite 100
San Diego, CA 92121-2116
619-453-1331

Talent Tree Personnel Services
9444 Balboa Avenue, Suite 175
San Diego, CA 92123-4350
619-268-5100

Technical & Office Support Services
730 North Norma Street
Ridgecrest, CA 93555-3521
619-371-7500

Technology Locator Corporation
6480 Weathers Pl, Suite 200
San Diego, CA 92121-3912
619-552-6800

Temporary Connection
3760 Convoy Street, Suite 110
San Diego, CA 92111-3742
619-268-2201

TemPro Services
7380 Clairemont Mesa Boulevard, Suite 209
San Diego, CA 92111-1115
619-268-9844

The Eastridge Group
5650 El Camino Real, Suite 101
Carlsbad, CA 92008-7124
619-438-1809

The Eastridge Group
2355 Northside Drive, Suite 100
San Diego, CA 92108-2705
619-260-2100

The Temporary Connection
334 Rancheros Drive, Suite 109
San Marcos, CA 92069-2940
619-471-8700

Therapist Unlimited
3131 Camino del Rio North, Suite 370
San Diego, CA 92108
619-285-0942

Thomas Staffing
2385 Camino Vida Roble, Suite 113
Carlsbad, CA 92009
619-930-9488

Thomas Staffing
3110 Camino del Rio S, Suite A314
San Diego, CA 92108
619-285-9800

TLC Staffing, A Lawton Company
4820 Mercury Street, Suite D
San Diego, CA 92111-2105
619-569-6260

TOPS Staffing Services
613 W Valley Parkway, Suite 210
Escondido, CA 92025-2549
619-741-1622

TOPS Staffing Services
1455 Frazee Road, Suite 102
San Diego, CA 92108-4301
619-299-8770

TOPS Staffing Services
9420 Mira Mesa Boulevard, Suite D2
San Diego, CA 92126-4848
619-566-8755

Total Quality Services
3954 Murphy Canyon Road
San Diego, CA 92123-4418
619-279-5773

TRC Staffing Services
2820 Camino Del Rio S, Suite 120
San Diego, CA 92108
619-718-6330

TriStaff Temps
4350 Executive Drive, Suite 100
San Diego, CA 92121
619-597-4000

TSA-RHO Co.
4499 Ruffin Road, Suite 150
San Diego, CA 92123-1600
619-565-4992

Uniforce Services
8840 Complex Drive, Suite 130
San Diego, CA 92123-1423
619-467-9490

Victor Valley Personnel Services
15000 7th Street, Suite 101
Victorville, CA 92392-3852
619-245-6548

Volt Services Group
8911 La Mesa Boulevard, Suite 105
La Mesa, CA 91941-4096
619-464-7081

Volt Services Group
800 Grand Avenue, Suite C-7
Carlsbad, CA 92008-1805
619-729-8916

Volt Services Group
904 W San Marcos Boulevard, Suite 10
San Marcos, CA 92069-4118
619-471-0800

Volt Services Group
7490 Opportunity Road
San Diego, CA 92111-2246
619-576-3140

Volt Services Group
8995 Mira Mesa Boulevard, Suite A
San Diego, CA 92126-2738
619-578-0920

Volt Services Group
4370 Palm Avenue, Suite J
San Diego, CA 92154-1760
619-428-7820

So. California Job Source

Employment Section

Accounting
Advertising/Marketing & Sales
Aerospace & Defense
Arts & Culture
Associations/Non-Profit & Public Interest Groups
Banking & Finance
Broadcast Media & Communications
Design & Engineering
Education
Entertainment
Healthcare
High Tech
Hospitality
Insurance
Largest & Fastest Growing Southern California Companies
Law & Lobbying
Public Relations
Real Estate
Sports & Recreation
Travel/Transportation & Utilities

Accounting

A s one of the "Big Six" certified public accounting firms, Coopers & Lybrand provides a broad range of services in the areas of accounting, auditing, taxation, management consulting, actuarial, benefits and compensation consulting. Coopers & Lybrand operates over 100 offices in the United States; 735 offices in 117 foreign locations. Common positions include: Accountant; Actuary; Computer Programmer; Economist; Financial Analyst; Statistician; Systems Analyst. Principal educational backgrounds sought: Accounting; Business Administration; Computer Science; Economics; Finance; Information Systems. Company benefits include: medical and dental insurance; pension plan; life insurance; limited tuition assistance; disability coverage; profit sharing; savings plan. Corporate headquarters is located in New York, New York.

COOPERS & LYBRAND

See Also: Banking & Finance
Insurance

Company Web Sites

ADP/Automatic Data Processing
www.adp.com
Alder Green Hasson & Janks
www.aghjcpa.com
Altschuler Melvoin and Glasser
www.amgnet.com
Arthur Andersen
www.arthurandersen.com
Bates Coughtry Reiss & Company
www.bcrcpa.aol.com
BDO Seidman
www.bdo.com
Biggs & Company
www.biggsco.com
Braverman Codron & Company
www.brav.com
Bruno Mack & Barclay
www.bmconsult.com
Cairns Haack Eng Applegate
www.cairns/haack.com
Considine & Considine
www.cccpa.com
Deloitte & Touche
www.dttus.com
Duitch, Franklin & Co.
www.dfco.com
Elliott Lewis Lieber & Stumpf
www.ellscpas.com
Ernst & Young
www.ey.com
Frazer & Torbet
www.msftllp.com
Glenn M. Gelman & Associates
www.gmgcpa.com

Good Swartz & Berns
www.gsbcpa.com
Grant Thornton
www.gt.com
Gursey Schneider & Company
www.gursey.com
Haskell & White
www.hwcpa.com
Kellogg & Andelson Accounting
www.k-a.com
KPMG Peat Marwick
www.kpmg.com
McGladrey & Pullen CPAs &
Consultants
www.mcgladrey.com
Moss Adams
www.mossadams.com
Nanas Stern Biers Neinstein & Co.
www.nsbn.com
Ozur Andersen & Radder
www.oarcpa.com/oar
Pacific Computer Systems
www.payrollservices.com
Parks Palmer Turner & Yemenidjian
www.ppty.com
Paychex
www.paychex.com
Price Waterhouse Coopers
www.pwcglobal.com
Stonefield Josephson Accounting.
www.sjaccounting.com
White Nelson & Co CPA & Conslt
www.whitenelson.com
Wiegel Szekel & Walker
www.wsw.cpa.com

ADP/Automatic Data Processing
5355 Orangethorpe Avenue
La Palma, CA 90623-1095
714-994-2000
Job Hotline: 714-994-2000
Web Address: www.adp.com
Number of Employees: 900

Frank Balog, *Division President*
Laureen Ball, *Human Resources Director*

Alder Green Hasson & Janks
10990 Wilshire Boulevard, 16th Floor
Los Angeles, CA 90024
310-873-1600
Web Address: www.aghjpa.com
Number of Employees: 60

David Green, *Managing Partner*
Elizabeth Hugh, *Office/Human Resource Manager*

Alliance of Practicing CPAs
4401 Atlantic Avenue, Suite 239
Long Beach, CA 90807
562-984-2040

Altschuler Melvoin and Glasser
2029 Century Park East, Suite 3100
Suite 3100
Los Angeles, CA 90067
310-282-8588
Web Address: www.amgnet.com
Number of Employees: 60

Maier Rosenberg, *Partner-in-charge*
Stewart Dater, *Office/Human Resource Manager*

American Express Tax / Business Services
6320 Canoga Avenue, 6th Floor
Suite 500
Woodland HIlls, CA 91367
818-710-7800
Number of Employees: 60

Les Shapiro, *Managing Director*

Arthur Andersen
701 B Street, Suite 1600
San Diego, CA 92101
619-699-6600
Job Hotline: 213-614-7579
Web Address: www.arthurandersen.com
Number of Employees: 100

Richard C. Bigelow, *Managing Partner*
Call Los Angeles for hiring contact: Ms. Jonna Jetson, Recruiting Department Assistant; 633 West 5th Street, Los Angeles, CA 90071; 213-614-8113

Bates Coughtry Reiss & Company CPAs
2600 Nutwood Avenue, Suite 200
Fullerton, CA 92831-3105
714-871-2422
Web Address: www.bcrcpa.aol.com
Number of Employees: 23

David L Bates, *Managing Partner*

BDO Seidman
3200 Bristol Street, Suite 400
Costa Mesa, CA 92626-1800
949-957-3200
Web Address: www.bdo.com
Number of Employees: 3000

Doug Naylor, *Partner*

BDO Seidman
1900 Avenue of the Stars, 11th Floor
Los Angeles, CA 90067
310-557-0300
Web Address: www.bdo.com
Number of Employees: 100

Ronald Manrinella, *Area Director*
Art Nemiroff, *Managing Director*
Patricia Chee, *Human Resource Manager*

Biggs & Company
2800 28th Street, Suite 300
Santa Monica, CA 90405
310-450-0875
Web Address: www.biggsco.com
Number of Employees: 25

Samuel R. Biggs, *Managing Partner*
Erin Rose, *Human Resource Manager*

Braverman Codron & Co.
450 North Roxbury Drive, Fourth Floor
Beverly HIlls, CA 90210
310-278-5850
Web Address: www.brav.com
Number of Employees: 55

Ward Bukofsky, *Managing Partner*
Jane Benson, *Human Resource Manager*

Brodshatzer Wallace Spoon & Yip
555 West Beech Street, Suite 400
San Diego, CA 92101
619-234-4173
Number of Employees: 20

Wayne Mushet, *Managing Partner*
Paula Kreyling, *Office Manager*

Brown Leifer Slatkin & Berns
12411 Ventura Boulevard
Studio City, CA 91604
818-760-1885
Number of Employees: 40

Eugene Brown, *Managing Partner*

Bruno Mack & Barclay
402 West Broadway, Suite 900
San Diego, CA 92101
619-687-0001
Web Address: www.bmconsult.com
Number of Employees: 40

Nick Bruno, *Managing Partner*
Karen Mcjunkin, *Hiring Contact*

Cairns Haack Eng Applegate
703 Palomar Airport Road, Suite 150
Carlsbad, CA 92009
760-438-4000
Web Address: www.cairns/haack.com
Number of Employees: 25

Michelle Santerre, *Personnel Director*

California Society of Certified Public Accountants
330 North Brand Avenue, Suite 710
Glendale, CA 91203
818-246-6000

Conrad & Associates
1100 Main Street, Suite C
Irvine, CA 92614-6730
949-474-2020
Web Address: www.conrad&associip.com
Number of Employees: 45

Ronald L Conrad, *Managing Partner*

Considine & Considine
1501 Fifth Avenue, Suite 400
San Diego, CA 92101
619-231-1977
Web Address: www.cccpa.com
Number of Employees: 35
Timothy M. Considine, *Managing Partner*
Kim Medeiros, *Hiring Manager*

Coradino Hickey & Hanson
4275 Executive Square, Suite 200
La Jolla, CA 92037
858-455-9000
Number of Employees: 16
Charles J. Coradino, *Managing Partner*
Dave Hickey, *Hiring Manager*

Corbin & Wertz
2603 Main Street, Suite 600
Irvine, CA 92614-6232
949-756-2120
Web Address: www.corbinwertz.com
Number of Employees: 40
Steven M Corbin, *Managing Partner*

Deloitte & Touche
695 Town Center Drive, Suite 1200
Costa Mesa, CA 92626-1924
949-436-7100
Web Address: www.dttus.com
Number of Employees: 18,000

Michell Farber, *Human Resources Manager*

Deloitte & Touche
701 B Street, Suite 1900
San Diego, CA 92101
619-232-6500
Web Address: www.us.deloite.com
Number of Employees: 150

Dave Hamann, *Managing Partner*
Leslie Berry, *Human Resources Manager*

Deloitte & Touche Consulting Group
1000 Wilshire Boulevard, Suite 1500
Los Angeles, CA 90071
213-688-0800
Job Hotline: 213-688-5222
Web Address: www.dttus.com
Number of Employees: 806

Lois Evans, *Managing Director*
Stacy Gannon, *Office Manager*

Derezin Breier & Company
9191 Towne Centre Drive, Suite 200
San Diego, CA 92122
858-455-6400
Number of Employees: 25

Sheldon Derezin, *Managing Partner*
Joanne Antigiovanni, *Hiring Manager*

Diehl Evans & Co
18401 Von Karman Avenue, Suite 200
Irvine, CA 92612-1542
949-757-7700
Number of Employees: 40

Michael Ludin, *General Partner*

Diehl Evans & Company
2965 Roosevelt Street
Carlsbad, CA 92008
760-729-2343
Number of Employees: 45

Philip H. Holtkamp, *Managing Partner*
Harvey Schroeder, *Personnel Manager*

Duitch, Franklin & Co.
11601 Wilshire Boulevard, Suite 2300
Los Angeles, CA 90025
310-268-2000
Web Address: www.dfco.com
Number of Employees: 85

Dennis Duitch, *Managing Partner*
Laura Sherwood, *Human Resource Manager*

Edward White & Company
21700 Oxnard Street, Suite 400
Woodland Hills, CA 91367
818-716-1120
Number of Employees: 25

Edward White, *Senior Partner*
James Conroy, *Controller*

Elliott Lewis Lieber & Stumpf
1611 East 4th Street, Suite 200
Santa Ana, CA 92701-5136
714-569-1000
Web Address: www.ellscpas.com
Number of Employees: 20

Ronald Stumpf, *President*

Ernst & Young
18400 Von Karman Avenue, Suite 800
Irvine, CA 92612-1514
949-794-2300
Number of Employees: 65000

David Bruesehoff, *Director of Human Resources*

Ernst & Young
660 Newport Center Drive, 8th Floor
Newport Beach, CA 92660-6401
949-640-5000
Web Address: www.ey.com
Number of Employees: 170

Michael Meyer, *Managing Partner*
Robin Alt, *Assistant to HR Director*

Ernst & Young
501 West Broadway, Suite 1100
San Diego, CA 92101
619-235-5000
Web Address: www.ey.com
Number of Employees: 150

Raymond V. Dittamore, *Managing Partner*
Sandy Owens, *Director of Human Resources*

Ernst & Young
515 South Flower Street, 25th Floor
Los Angeles, CA 90071
213-977-3200
Web Address: www.ey.com
Number of Employees: 1,000

Arlene Honbo, *Area Director*
Jim Freer, *Managing Partner*

Fineman West & Co.
9100 Wilshire Boulevard, Suite 200 West
Beverly Hills, CA 90212
310-888-1880
Number of Employees: 25

Harold J. West, *Managing Partner*
Janet Shaw, *Human Resource Manager*

Frankel Lodgen Lacher Golditch & Sardi
16530 Ventura Boulevard, Suite 305
Suite 305
Encino, CA 91436
818-783-0570
Number of Employees: 43

Ben Frankel, *President*

Frazer & Torbet
1199 South Fairway
Walnut, CA 91789
909-594-2713
Web Address: www.msftllp.com
Number of Employees: 55

Burke Dambly, *Managing Partner*

Gelfand Rennert & Feldman
1880 Century Park East, Suite 1600
Los Angeles, CA 90067
310-556-6606
Number of Employees: 140

Leigh Williams, *Human Resources Manager*

Glenn M. Gelman & Associates
1940 East 17th Street
Santa Ana, CA 92705
714-667-2600
Web Address: www.gmgcpa.com
Number of Employees: 30

Glenn M. Gelman, *Managing Partner*

Good Swartz & Berns
11755 Wilshire Boulevard, Suite 1700
Los Angeles, CA 90025
310-477-3722
Web Address: www.gsbcpa.com
Number of Employees: 52

Robert Golden, *Managing Partner*
Mark Burns, *Office/Human Resource Manager*

Gorelick & Uslaner CPAs
11620 Wilshire Boulevard, Suite 540
Los Angeles, CA 90025
310-444-1889
Web Address: www.gcpas.com
Number of Employees: 20

Edward Gorelick, *President*
Bill Osborn, *Director of Human Resources*

Grant Thornton
18300 Von Karmen Avenue
Irvine, CA 92612
949-553-1600
Web Address: www.gt.com
Number of Employees: 2800

Bernie Savage, *Human Resources Manager*

Grant Thornton

1000 Wilshire Boulevard, Suite 700
Los Angeles, CA 90017
213-627-1717
Web Address: www.gt.com
Number of Employees: 200

Patrick Zorsch, *Managing Partner*
Jim Hayden, *Managing Partner*
Bernice Savage, *Human Resources Director*

Grice Lund & Tarkington

144 West D Street
Encinitas, CA 92024
760-753-1157
Web Address: www.gltcpas.com
Number of Employees: 25

William F. Hatch, *Managing Partner*

Grobstein Horwath & Company

15233 Ventura Boulevard, 9th Floor
Sherman Oaks, CA 91403
818-501-5200
Number of Employees: 73

Michael Grobstein, *Managing Partner*

Gumbiner Savett Finkel Fingleson & Rose

1723 Cloverfield Boulevard
Santa Monica, CA 90404
310-828-9798
Web Address: www.gscpa.com
Number of Employees: 78

Lou Savett, *CEO*
Lynn Haque, *Human Resource Manager*

Gursey, Schneider & Company

1035 Santa Monica Boulevard, Suite 300
Los Angeles, CA 90025
310-552-0960
Job Hotline: x211
Web Address: www.gursey.com
Number of Employees: 70

Stanley Schneider, *Managing Partner*
Tracy Montague, *Human Resource Manager*

Harlan & Boettger

5415 Oberlin Drive
San Diego, CA 92121
858-535-2000
Web Address: members.aol.com/hbcpas
Number of Employees: 23

Bill Boettger, *Managing Partner*
Marshall Varano, *Hiring Manager*

Haskell & White

4901 Birch Street
Newport Beach, CA 92660-8106
949-833-8312
Web Address: www.hwcpa.com
Number of Employees: 50

Steve Haskell, *Managing Partner*

Haynie & Company CPAs

3001 Red Hill Avenue Building 4 #201
Costa Mesa, CA 92626
949-432-1880
Number of Employees: 25

Steven C Gabrielson, *President*

Holthouse Carlin & Van Trigt

11845 West Olympic Boulevard, Suite 1177
Los Angeles, CA 90064
310-477-5551
Job Hotline: x141
Web Address: www.hcvt.com
Number of Employees: 35

James Calin, *Managing Member*
Mely Soffer, *Human Resource Manager*

Horsfall Murphy & Pindroh

35 North Lake Avenue, Suite 800
Pasadena, CA 91101
626-795-5894
Web Address: www.ilmpcpas.com
Number of Employees: 50

William Horsfall, *Managing Partner*

J.H. Cohn & Co.

1420 Kettner Boulevard, Suite 411
San Diego, CA 92101
619-231-0200
Web Address: www.jhcohn.com
Number of Employees: 20

Michael J. Stewart, *Managing Partner*
Holly Hammond, *Office Manager*

Jassoy Graff & Douglas

4520 Executive Drive, Suite 350
San Diego, CA 92121
858-587-1000
Web Address: www.jgdnet.com
Number of Employees: 25

Dan Schreiber, *Managing Partner*
Debbie Isobe, *Office Manager*

Kellogg & Andelson Accounting

14724 Ventura Boulevard, 2nd Floor
Sherman Oaks, CA 91403
818-971-5100
Web Address: www.k-a.com

Tom Leaper, *President*

Kirsch Kohn Oster & Bridge
15910 Ventura Boulevard, Suite 1100
Encino, CA 91436
818-907-6500
Number of Employees: 26

Mel Kohn, *Managing Partner*

KPMG Peat Marwick
650 Town Center Drive, Suite 1000
Costa Mesa, CA 92626-1925
949-850-4300
Web Address: www.kpmg.com
Number of Employees: 350

Douglas K. Ammerman, *Managing Partner*
Cindy Patelski, *Human Resources Director*

KPMG Peat Marwick
750 B Street, Suite 1500
San Diego, CA 92101
619-233-8000
Web Address: www.kpmg.com
Number of Employees: 150

David W. Down, *Managing Partner*
Julie Stone, *Office Manager*

KPMG Peat Marwick
725 South Figueroa Street
Los Angeles, CA 90017
213-972-4000
Job Hotline: 213-955-8880 or 213-955-8454
Number of Employees: 1,000

Joseph Davis, *Managing Partner*

Kushner Smith Joanou & Gregson
2 Park Plaza, Suite 550
Irvine, CA 92614-8515
949-261-2808
Number of Employees: 25

Bob Kushner, *Managing Partner*

Lavine Lofgren Morris & Engelberg
4180 La Jolla Village Drive, Suite 300
La Jolla, CA 92037
858-455-1200
Number of Employees: 40
Shawn Goll, *Hiring Manager*

Leaf & Cole
4134 Voltaire Street
San Diego, CA 92107
619-224-2427
Number of Employees: 20

Belmore I. Thompson, *Managing Partner*
Janet Paschall, *Hiring Manager*

Lesley Thomas Schwarz & Postma
2244 West Coast Highway, Suite 100
Newport Beach, CA 92663-4724
949-650-2771
Web Address: www.ltsp@compuserv.com
Number of Employees: 28

John Postma II, *Managing Partner*

Levitz Zacks & Ciceric
701 B Street, Suite 400
San Diego, CA 92101
619-238-1077
Number of Employees: 32

Stanley A. Levitz, *Managing Partner*

Link Murrel & Company
19700 Fairchild, Suite 300
Irvine, CA 92612-2515
949-261-1120
Number of Employees: 24

Craig W Murrel, *Managing Partner*

Lipsey Millimaki & Co.
401 B Street, Suite 1140
San Diego, CA 92101
619-234-0877
Number of Employees: 25

Robert H. Lipsey, *Managing Partner*
Mike Eggart, *Hiring Manager*

Los Angeles Institute of Certified Financial Planners
8055 West Manchester Boulevard, Suite 340
Playa del Rey, CA 90293
310-821 - 2169
Web Address: www.laicfp.org

Lucas & Co. CPAs
1015 Fremont Avenue
South Pasadena, CA 91031
626+796+2727
Number of Employees: 40

William Lucas, *President*
Cindy Coulter, *Director of Human Resources*

Maginnis Knechtel & McIntyre
950 South Arroyo Parkway
Pasadena, CA 91105
626-449-3466
Number of Employees: 22

Gerald Cunha, *Partner*

Martin Werbelow & Co.
300 North Lake Avenue, Suite 930
Pasadena, CA 91101
626-577-1440
Number of Employees: 20

Steve Boyer, *Managing Partner*
Sue Applegate, *Director of Human Resources*

McGladrey & Pullen
222 South Harbor Boulevard, Suite 800
Anaheim, CA 92805
714-520-9561
Web Address: www.mcgladrey.com
Number of Employees: 75

Leroy Dennis, *Partner*

McGladrey & Pullen
3111 Camino del Rio North, Suite 1150
San Diego, CA 92108
619-280-3022
Web Address: www.mcgladreyandpullen.com
Number of Employees: 50

Patrick M. Tabor, *Managing Partner*
Stephanie Renick, *Human Resources Manager*

McGladrey & Pullen CPAs & Consultants
140 South Lake Avenue, Suite 300
Pasadena, CA 91101
626-795-7950
Web Address: www.mcgladrey.com

Ronald Barzen, *Partner-in-Charge*
Mr. Kim Carney, *Director of Human Resources*

Miller Kaplan Arase & Co.
10911 Riverside Drive
North Hollywood, CA 91602
818-769-2010
Number of Employees: 100

Mannon Kaplan, *Managing Partner*
Irv Borenzweig, *Director of Human Resources*

Moreland & Associates
1201 Dove Street, Suite 680
Newport Beach, CA 92660-2825
949-221-0025
Number of Employees: 40

Michael Moreland, *Partner*

Moss Adams
695 Town Center Drive, Suite 1550
Costa Mesa, CA 92626-1924
949-557-8344
Web Address: www.mossadams.com
Number of Employees: 14

Chris Schmidt, *Managing Partner*

Moss Adams
865 South Figueroa Street, Suite 1400
Los Angeles, CA 90017
213-680-9350
Number of Employees: 67

Robert Greenspan, *Managing Partner*

Nanas Stern Biers Neinstein & Co.
9454 Wilshire Boulevard, Suite 405
Beverly Hills, CA 90212
310-273-2501
Web Address: www.nsbn.com
Number of Employees: 60

Lawrence J. Stern, *Managing Partner*
Ken Sterlock, *Recruiter*

Nation Smith Hermes Diamond P.C.
17085 Via del Campo
San Diego, CA 92127
858-451-2452
Web Address: nshd.com
Number of Employees: 42

Paul E. Nation, *Managing Partner*
Maggie Miller, *Human Resources Manager*

National Association of Black Accountants
P.O. Box 71175
Los Angeles, CA 90071
213-665-2682

Nigro Karlin & Segal
10100 Santa Monica Boulevard, Suite 1300
Los Angeles, CA 90067
310-277-4657
Number of Employees: 130

Mickey Segal, *Managing Partner*
Nicole Katx, *Human Resource Manager*

Pacific Computer Systems
15412 Electronic Lane
Huntington Beach, CA 92649
714-891-4756
Web Address: www.payrollservices.com
Number of Employees: 45

Tim Jensen, *President*

Parks Palmer Turner & Yemenidjian
1990 South Bundy Drive, Suite 550
Los Angeles, CA 90025
310-207-2777
Web Address: www.ppty.com
Number of Employees: 50

James Parks, *Managing Partner*
Jennifer Talbert, *Office/Human Resource Manager*

Paychex
200 Sandpointe Avenue, Suite 100
Santa Ana, CA 92707-5744
714-438-4000
Web Address: www.paychex.com
Number of Employees: 4000

Louis Zimmerman, *Human Resources Manager*

Peterson & Co.
3655 Nobel Drive, Suite 500
San Diego, CA 92122
858-597-4100
Web Address: www.petersonco.com
Number of Employees: 45

Richard Evans, *Managing Partner*
Lori Marruffo, *Administrator*

Price Waterhouse Coopers
575 Anton Boulevard, Suite 1100
Costa Mesa, CA 92626
949-435-8600
Web Address: www.pwcglobal.com

Robert A. Huber, *Managing Partner*
Nancy Alvarez, *Human Resources Manager*

Price Waterhouse Coopers
402 West Broadway, Suite 1400
San Diego, CA 92101
619-525-2300
Web Address: www.pwcglobal.com
Number of Employees: 70

Bruce Blakely, *Managing Partner*

Price Waterhouse Coopers
750 B Street, Suite 2400
San Diego, CA 92101
619-231-1200
Web Address: www.pwcglobal.com
Number of Employees: 110

Thomas H. Insley, *Managing Partner*

Price Waterhouse Coopers
350 South Grand Avenue
Los Angeles, CA 90071
213-356-6000
Web Address: www.pwcglobal.com
Number of Employees: 700

G. Steve Hamm, *Managing Partner*

Price Waterhouse Coopers
400 South Hope Street, 22nd Floor
Los Angeles, CA 90071
213-236-3000
Web Address: www.pwcglobal.com
Number of Employees: 500

Kathleen Wiacek, *Managing Partner*
Greg Garrison, *Managing Partner*

Ronald Blue & Company
3000 West Macarthur Boulevard, Suite 600
Santa Ana, CA 92704-6916
714-754-1040
Number of Employees: 30

John A Laudadio, *President*

Roth Bookstein & Zaslow
11755 Wilshire Boulevard, Suite 900
Los Angeles, CA 90025
310-478-4148
Web Address: www.rbz.com
Number of Employees: 75

Thomas Schulte, *Managing Partner*

Rothstein, Kass & Company
9171 Wilshire Boulevard, Suite 512
Beverly Hills, CA 90210
310-273-2770
Web Address: www.oarcpa.com/oar
Number of Employees: 25

Thomas Andersen, *Chairman*
Linda Marquez, *Office/Human Resource Manager*

Simpson & Simpson CPAs
5750 Wilshire Boulevard, Suite 286
Los Angeles, CA 90036
213-938-3324

Brainard Simpson, *Managing Partner*

Singer Lewak Greenbaum
2700 North Main Street, Suite 200
Santa Ana, CA 92705-6638
714-953-9734
Web Address: www.sl99.com
Number of Employees: 129

David Krajanowski, *Partner*

Singer Lewak Greenbaum & Goldstein
10960 Wilshire Boulevard, Suite 1100
Los Angeles, CA 90024
310-477-3924
Web Address: www.slgg.com
Number of Employees: 100

Harvey Goldstein, *Managing Partner*
Ming Canning, *Human Resource Manager*

Sobul Primes & Schenkel
12100 Wilshire Boulevard, Suite 1150
Los Angeles, CA 90025
310-826-2060
Number of Employees: 20

Stephen Sobul, *Managing Partner*
Carol Fima, *Human Resource Manager*

Solomon Ross Grey & Co.
16633 Ventura Boulevard, Suite 600
Encino, CA 91436
818-995-0090

Drew Grey, *Partner-in-charge*

Squar Milner & Reehl
4100 Newport Place Drive, Suite 300
Newport Beach, CA 92660-2437
949-222-2999
Web Address: www.smroffice@smrinc.com
Number of Employees: 41

Naomi Hadden, *Human Resources Manager*

Sterman Higashi & Herter
335 Centennial Way
Tustin, CA 92780-3714
714-505-9000
Web Address: www.gerry@shhcpa.com
Number of Employees: 25

Gerald Herter, *President*

Stonefield Josephson Accounting.
1620 26th Street, Suite 400 South
Santa Monica, CA 90404
310-453-9400
Web Address: www.sjaccounting.com
Number of Employees: 80

Ronald Friedman, *President*
Laura Sherwood, *Human Resource*

Strabala Ramirez & Associates
19762 MacArthur Boulevard, Suite 100
Irvine, CA 92612-1591
949-852-1600
Number of Employees: 41

Manuel Ramirez, *Partner*

Tanner Mainstain Hoffer & Peyrot
10866 Wilshire Boulevard, 10th Floor
Los Angeles, CA 90024
310-446-2700
Web Address: www.tmhpcpa.com
Number of Employees: 80

Anthony Peyrot, *Managing Partner*

Turnquist, Schmitt, Kitrosser & McMahon
2550 Fifth Avenue, 10th Floor
San Diego, CA 92103
619-234-6775
Web Address: www.tskm.com
Number of Employees: 40

Edward Kitrosser, *Managing Partner*

Vasquez Farukhi & Company
510 West Sixth Street, Suite 400
Los Angeles, CA 90014
213-629-9094
Number of Employees: 30

Gilbert Vasquez, *Executive Partner*
John Menchaca, *Principal*

White Nelson & Co CPA & Conslt
2400 East Katella Avenue, Suite 900
Anaheim, CA 92806-5964
714-978-1300
Web Address: www.whitenelson.com
Number of Employees: 50

Biran Wilterink, *Managing Partner*

Wiegel Szekel & Walker
500 North State College Boulevard #1110
Orange, CA 92868-1638
714-634-8757
Web Address: www.wsw.cpa.com
Number of Employees: 20

Pam Mello, *Administrator*

WNC & Associates
3158 Red Hill Avenue, Suite 120
Costa Mesa, CA 92626-3416
949-662-5565
Number of Employees: 40

John Lester Jr, *President*

Wurth & Co
171 South Anita Drive, Suite 100
Orange, CA 92868-3300
714-634-1040
Number of Employees: 30

Larry M. Wurth, *Managing Partner*

Further References

• Associations •

American Accounting Association
5717 Bessie Drive
Sarasota, Florida 34233
941-921-7747
Web Address: www.aaa-edu.org
Promotes research and education in accounting.

American Institute of Certified Public Accountants
1455 Pennsylvania Avenue, N.W., 4th Floor
Washington, D.C. 20004
202-737-6600
Web Address: www.aicpa.org
Promotes and establishes accounting standards, education, and development.

ACCOUNTING

American Institute of Certified Public Accountants
1211 Avenue of the Americas
New York, New York 10036
212-596-6200
Web Address: aicpa.org
Promotes and establishes accounting standards, education, and development.

American Society of Women Accountants
35 E. Wacker Drive
Chicago, Illinois 60601
312-726-9030
Professional society which assists women in accounting careers.

Association of Government Accountants
2200 Mount Vernon Avenue
Alexandria, Virginia 22301
703-684-6931
Web Address: www.rutgers.edu/accounting/raw/aga/home.htm
Professional society of financial managers employed by federal, state, county, and city governments.

Institute of Internal Auditors
P. O. Box 140099
Orlando, Florida 32889
407-830-7600
Web Address: www.diia.org
Professional organization of auditors, accounting, and educators of internal auditing.

Institute of Management Accounting
10 Paragon Drive
Montvale, New Jersey 07645-1760
201-573-9000
Web Address: www.imanet.org
Conducts research on accounting methods and management applications.

National Association of Black Accountants, Inc.
7249-A Hanover Parkway
Greenbelt, MD 20770
301-474-6222
Promotes academic and professional excellence and student-professional relations.

National Association of Tax Consultants
454 North 13th Street
San Jose, California 95112
408-298-1458
Develops professional standards and ethics.

National Association of Tax Practitioners
720 Association Drive
Appleton, Wisconsin 54914
414-749-1040
Web Address: www.natptax.com
Promotes high standards and provides continuing education.

National Society of Public Accountants
1010 North Fairfax Street
Alexandria, Virginia 22314
703-549-6400
Web Address: www.nspa.org
Represents independent practitioners and conducts correspondence courses.

The EDP Auditiors Association
3701 Algonquin Road, Suite 1212
Rolling Meadows, Illinois 60008
708-253-1545
Establishes standards and systems for data processing utilization.

• Publications •

Accountants Directory
American Business Directories, Inc.

Accounting Firms Directory
American Business Directories, Inc.

Accounting Firms & Practitioners
AICPA Directory of Accounting Education
American Institute of Certified Public Accountants
Harborside Financial Center, Plaza 3
Jersey City, NJ 07311-3881
201-938-3292
Web Address: www.aicpa.org

CPA Journal
200 Park Avenue
New York, New York 10166
Referred Accounting Journal

CPA Letter
1211 Avenue of the Americas
New York, New York 10036

Management Accounting
10 Paragon Drive
Montvale, New Jersey 07645
201-573-9000
Web Address: www.imanet.org
News of Profession

National Society of Public Accountants - Yearbook
National Public Accountant
National Society of Public Accountants
1010 North Fairfax Street
Alexandria, VA 22314-1504
703-549-6400
Web Address: www.nspa.org
Association Members and Committees
Articles on Taxes and Accounting Systems

153

Advertising/Marketing

A great advantage to getting a job with an advertising firm is to have prior work experience, for example, internships or any advertising campaigns or programs you have been associated with in the past. For creative and now even account management positions, portfolios are a real plus. They should demonstrate your capabilities and past achievements. If your goal is to work in advertising, but you feel you don't have substantial prior work experience, consider traffic or administrative positions to gain experience to advance. By far the best way to get your foot in the door is to have prior work experience, so aggressively seek an internship while still in school.

DDB NEEDHAM WORLDWIDE

See also: Communications
Public Relations/Affairs

Quick Reference

Company Web Sites

AM Advertising
www.amadvertising.com
Arlen Advertising
www.arlan1.com
Asher & Partners
www.asherpartners.com
Bates USA
www.bates.com
BBDO West
www.bbdo.com
Casanova Pendrill
www.casanova.com
D'Arcy Masius Benton & Bowles
www.dmbb.com
Dailey & Associates
www.dailey&abs.com
DavisElen
www.daviselen.com
Fisher Business Communications
www.fbiz.com
Foote, Cone, & Belding
www.fcbsf.com
G2 Advertising
www.g2.com
Gavin & Gavin Advertising
www.gavinandgavin.com
Ground Zero
www.groundzero.net
Hunter Barth
www.hunterbarth.com
InterCommunications
www.intercommunications.com
Italia / Gal Advertising
www.italiagal.com

J2 Marketing Services
www.j2marketing.com
Lois / EJL
www.ejl.com
McCann-Erickson Los Angeles
www.mccann.com
Ogilvy & Mather
www.ogilvy.com
Rubin Postaer and Associates
www.rpa.com
Saatchi & Saatchi Los Angeles
www.saatchila.com
TBWA Chiat/Day
www.chiatday.com
Team One Advertising
www.teamoneadv.com
The Gallup Organization
www.gallup.com
The Townsend Agency
www.townsendagency.com
The Verity Group
www.verity-group.com
TMP Worldwide
www.tmp.com

Company Job Hotlines

DDB Needham Worldwide
310-996-5865
Rubin Postaer and Associates
310-260-4320
Saatchi & Saatchi Los Angeles
310-214-6180
TBWA Chiat/Day
310-314-6685

Ad Link
11150 Santa Monica Boulevard, Suite 1000
Los Angeles, CA 90025
310-477-3994
Web Address: www.adlink.com
Natalie Trayhnham, *Human Resource Manager*

Advertising Club of Los Angeles
6404 Wilshire Boulevard, Suite 1111
Los Angeles, CA 90048
213-782-1044
Web Address: www.ads.org

Carol Golden, *Executive Director*

Alden Design
2157 India Street
San Diego, CA 92101
619-544-9299
Web Address: adesign544@aol.com
Number of Employees: 6

Allen S. Guilmette, *Principal*
Jennifer Cavanaugh, *Production Manager*

AM Advertising
4010 Morena Boulevard, Suite 210
San Diego, CA 92117
858-490-6910
Web Address: www.amadvertising.com
Number of Employees: 20

Jim Tindaro, *Principal*

American Telemarketing Association
4605 Lankershim Boulevard, Suite 824
North Hollywood, CA 90602
800-441-3335
Web Address: www.ataconnect.org

Asher/Gould Advertising
5900 Wilshire Boulevard, 31st Floor
Los Angeles, CA 90036
323-931-4151
Web Address: www.ashergould.com
Number of Employees: 70

Joel Hochberg, *President*
Pat Pellicano, *Director of Human Resources*

Auto Pacific
12812 Panorama View
Santa Ana, CA 92705
714-838-4234

Bates USA
2010 Main Street, 7th Floor
Irvine, CA 92614-7203
949-261-0330
Web Address: www.batesusa.com
Number of Employees: 70
Timothy Hart, *President*

BBDO West
10960 Wilshire Boulevard, Suite 1600
Los Angeles, CA 90024
310-444-4500
Web Address: www.bbdo.com
Number of Employees: 150

Tom Hollerbech, *President*
Tim Wright, *Human Resource Manager*

Bozell Worldwide
535 Anton Boulevard, Suite 700
Costa Mesa, CA 92626
949-966-0200
Web Address: www.bozell.com

Campbell-Ewald Advertising
11444 West Olympic, 11th Floor
Los Angeles, CA 90064
310-914-2200
Web Address: www.campbellwald.com
Number of Employees: 400

Debra Wurgel, *Managing Director*
Lisa Rector, *Director of Human Resources*

Casanova Pendrill
3333 Michelson Drive, Suite 300
Irvine, CA 92612-1683
949-474-5001
Web Address: www.casanova.com
Number of Employees: 72

Paul Casanova, *President*

Castle & Associates
1299 Prospect Street
La Jolla, CA 92037
858-456-0708
Number of Employees: 14

David R. Castle, *Principal*

Chapman Warwick
320 Laurel Street
San Diego, CA 92101
619-232-9090
Web Address: www.chapmanwarrick.com
Number of Employees: 12

Nancy Higgins, *President*
Joanne Perkins, *Hiring Manager*

155

D'Arcy Masius Benton & Bowles
6500 Wilshire Boulevard, Suite 1000
Suite 1000
Los Angeles, CA 90048
213-658-4500
Web Address: www.dmbb.com
Number of Employees: 95

Diane Krouse, Executive VP, *Managing Director*
Eunice Chang, *Director of Human REsources*

Dailey & Associates
8687 Melrose Avenue
West Hollywood, CA 90069
213-386-7823
Web Address: www.dailey&abs.com
Number of Employees: 200

Cliff Einstein, *CEO*
Toby Burke, *Director of Personnel*

DavisElen
865 South Figueroa, 12th Floor
Los Angeles, CA 90017
213-688-7000
Web Address: www.daviselen.com
Number of Employees: 100

Mark Davis, *CEO*
Pam McCarthy, *Director of Human Resources*

DDB Needham Worldwide
11601 Wilshire Boulevard, Eighth Floor
Los Angeles, CA 90025
310-996-5700
Job Hotline: 310-996-5865
Web Address: www.ddbn.com
Number of Employees: 200

David Park, *President*
Elizabeth Gaudio, *Manager of Human Resources*

DGWB Advertising
20 Executive Park, Suite 200
Irvine, CA 92614
949-863-0404
Web Address: www.dgwb.com

Di Zinno Thompson Integrated Marketing Solutions
715 J Street, Suite 100
San Diego, CA 92101
619-237-5011
Web Address: www.dzt.com
Number of Employees: 30

Tom Di Zinno, *President*
Pati Suarez, *Special Projects Manager*

DSLV / Lawlor Advertising
777 East Walnut Street
Pasadena, CA 91101
626-449-0021

Dean Dudley, *President*

EvansGroup
5757 Wilshire Boulevard, Suite 240
Los Angeles, CA 90036
213-954-3000
Number of Employees: 10

Tom Weinberg, *Executive VP*

Fall Advertising
366 South Pierce Street
El Cajon, CA 92020
619-444-9797
Web Address: www.fallads.com
Number of Employees: 10

Donald R. Fall, *Principal*
Gina Coburn, *Hiring Manager*

Fisher Business Communications
5 Hutton Centre Drive, Suite 120
Santa Ana, CA 92707-8716
714-556-1313
Web Address: www.fbiz.com
Number of Employees: 12

Robert J Fisher, *President*

Foote, Cone, & Belding
11601 Wilshire Boulevard, 15th Floor
Los Angeles, CA 90025
310-312-7000
Web Address: www.fcb.com
Number of Employees: 70

Thom Miller, *Executive VP & General Manager*
Mary Piatti, *Director of Human Resources*

Foote Cone & Belding North America
PO Box 2505
Santa Ana, CA 92707-0505
714-662-6500
Number of Employees: 4500

Michele Anderson, *VP & Human Resources Director*

Forsythe Marcelli Johnson Advisors
800 Newport Center Drive, Suite 500
Newport Beach, CA 92660-6317
949-759-9500
Web Address: www.aforythe@fmj-adv.com
Number of Employees: 25

James Forsythe, *President*

G2 Advertising
7711 Center Avenue, Suite 400
Huntington Beach, CA 92647-3068
714-372-6600
Web Address: www.g2.com
Number of Employees: 40

David Stickles, *President*

Gavin & Gavin Advertising
9171 Towne Centre Drive, Suite 255
San Diego, CA 92122
858-457-8300
Web Address: www.gavinandgavin.com
Number of Employees: 5

Robert A. Gavin, *Principal*

Grey Advertising
6100 Wilshire Boulevard
Los Angeles, CA 90048
213-936-6060
Number of Employees: 175

Jeff Alperin, CEO, *West*
Joy Walden, *Director of Human Resources*

Ground Zero
4235 Redwod Avenue
Los Angeles, CA 90066
310-656-0050
Web Address: www.groundzero.net
Number of Employees: 60

Jim Smith, *Managing Partner*
Mary Smith, *Human Resource Manager*

Heil Brice Retail Advertising
4 Corporate Park, Suite 100
Newport Beach, CA 92660
949-644-7477
Web Address: www.hbra.com

Hunter Barth
30 Corporate Park, Suite 212
Irvine, CA 92606-5132
949-852-9800
Web Address: www.hunterbarth.com
Number of Employees: 22

Paul Barth, *President*

InterCommunications
620 Newport Center Drive, Suite 600
Newport Beach, CA 92660-6400
949-644-7520
Web Address:
www.intercommunications.com
Number of Employees: 20

Toni Alexander, *President*

Italia / Gal Advertising
5900 Wilshire Boulevard, Suite 2400
Los Angeles, CA 90036
213-934-7711
Web Address: www.italiagal.com

Kenneth Gal, *CEO*

J2 Marketing Services
505 Mercury Lane
Brea, CA 92821-4898
714-529-2527
Web Address: www.j2marketing.com
Number of Employees: 20

Jim Worthen, *President*

LAK Advertising
5520 Ruffin Road, Suite 100
San Diego, CA 92123
858-571-8535
Web Address: www.lakadv.com
Number of Employees: 17

Jim Lakdawala, *Principal*

Lambesis
100 Via de la Valle
Del Mar, CA 92014
858-794-6444
Number of Employees: 45
Eve Jimenez, *Executive Assistant*

Lois / EJL
5700 Wilshire Boulevard, Sixth Floor
Los Angeles, CA 90036
213-965-6104
Web Address: www.ejl.com
Number of Employees: 30

Dennis Coe, *President*

Los Angeles Advertising Women
P.O. Box 2073
Simi Valley, CA 93062
818-712-0802

Luth Research
1365 4th Avenue
San Diego, CA 92101
619-283-7333
Number of Employees: 45

Roseanne Luth, *Owner*
Rene Hartnett, *Human Resources Manager*

Matthews Mark
620 C Street, 6th Floor
San Diego, CA 92101
619-238-8500
Number of Employees: 70

James S. Matthews, *Principal*
Linda Wrazen, *Human Resource Director*

McCann-Erickson Los Angeles
6300 Wilshire Boulevard, Suite 2100
Los Angeles, CA 90048
213-852-5840
Web Address: www.mccann.com
Number of Employees: 170

Hank Wasiak, Executive VP, *Managing Director*
Sydney Quirk, *Director of Human Resources*

McQuerterGroup
5752 Oberlin Drive
San Diego, CA 92121
858-450-0030
Web Address: www.mcquerter.com
Number of Employees: 25

Gregory W. McQuerter, *Principal*
Jamie Blessinger, *Director of Operations*

Media Dimensions
17150 Via del Campo, Suite 303
San Diego, CA 92127
858-485-7425
Web Address: www.mdimensions.com
Number of Employees: 16

Joseph K. Piercey, *Principal*

Medical Education Products
11400 West Olympic, Suite 200
Los Angeles, CA 90064
310-820-3433
Number of Employees: 9

Phebe Nishimoto, *Executive Vice President*

Mendelsohn / Zien Advertising
11111 Santa Monica Boulevard, Suite 2150
Los Angeles, CA 90025
310-444-1990
Number of Employees: 35

Richard Zien, *President*
Andi Mitauer, *Office Manager*

Mendoza Dillon & Associados
4100 Newport Place Drive, Suite 600
Newport Beach, CA 92660-2439
949-851-1811
Number of Employees: 65

Robert Howells, *President & CEO*

Namkung Promotions
1590 Metro Drive #118
Costa Mesa, CA 92626-1427
949-432-9779
Number of Employees: 30

George Namkung, *President*

Ogilvy & Mather
11766 Wilshire Boulevard, Suite 900
Los Angeles, CA 90025
310-996-0400
Web Address: www.ogilvy.com
Number of Employees: 140

Gerald McGee, Executive VP, *Managing Director*
Elana Carreno, *Manager of Human Resources*

Oxford Group
12555 High Bluff Drive, Suite 305
San Diego, CA 92130
858-481-3446
Web Address: www.theoxfordgroup.com
Number of Employees: 5

Bill Oxford, *Owner & President*

Pacific Rim Publishing
16541 Gothard Street, Suite 101
Huntington Beach, CA 92647-4472
714-375-3900
Number of Employees: 10

Dave Daniel, *Partner*

Peryam & Kroll
4175 East La Palma Avenue, Suite 205
Anaheim, CA 92807-1842
714-572-6888
Number of Employees: 50

Catherine Crook, *Director of Human Resources*

Phillips-Ramsey
6863 Friars Road
San Diego, CA 92108
619-574-0808
Web Address: www.phillips-ramsey.com
Number of Employees: 80

Gary W. Meads, *Principal*
Ann Collins, *Hiring Manager*

Portner Novelli
One Park Plaza
Irvine, CA 92614
949-251-2100
Web Address: www.pninternational.com

Quill Communications
1010 South Coast Highway, Suite 109
Encinitas, CA 92024
760-634-1297
Web Address: www.quill.com
Number of Employees: 38

Steven F. Edwards, *Principal*
Harriet Davidson, *CFO & Director of Human Resources*

Roberts Mealer & Company
3 Hutton Centre Drive, Suite 700
Santa Ana, CA 92707-8704
714-957-1314
Number of Employees: 24

Charles Roberts, *President*

Roni Hicks & Associates
1875 Third Avenue
San Diego, CA 92101
619-238-8787
Number of Employees: 13

Jane Wheeler, *President*
Lynn Chisnell, *Director of Human Resources*

Roper Starch Worldwide
4299 MacArthur Boulevard, Suite 105
Newport Beach, CA 92660
949-756-2600
Web Address: www.roper.com

Rubin Postaer and Associates
1333 Second Street
Santa Monica, CA 90401
310-394-4000
Job Hotline: 310-917-2304
Web Address: www.rpa.com
Number of Employees: 400

Gerrold Rubin, *President*
Lark Baskerville, *VP of Human Resources*

Saatchi & Saatchi Los Angeles
3501 Sepulveda Boulevard
Torrance, CA 90505
310-214-6000
Job Hotline: 310-214-6180
Web Address: www.saatchila.com
Number of Employees: 300

Scott Gilbert, *CEO*
Karen Blakely, *Human Resource Manager*

San Diego Direct Marketing Association
6525 Seaman Street
San Diego, CA 92120
619-229-8737
Web Address: /www.sddma.org

Seiniger Advertising
9320 Wilshire Boulevard
Beverly Hills, CA 90212
310-777-6800
Web Address: www.seiniger.com
Number of Employees: 50

Tony Seiniger, *President*
Vanessa Biggs, *Human Resource Manager*

Shafer Advertising
18300 Von Karmen Avenue, Suite 800
Irvine, CA 92612
949-553-1177

Solomon Friedman Advertising
427 C Street, Suite 400
San Diego, CA 92101
619-338-0111
Web Address: www.sf-ad.com
Number of Employees: 10

Robert Solomon, *Principal*
John Masters, *Vice President*

Suissa Miller Advertising
11601 Wilshire Boulevard. 16th Floor
Los Angeles, CA 90025
310-392-9666
Number of Employees: 150

Bruce Miller, *President*
Tanya Mortazavi, *Manager of Human Resources*

Team One Advertising
1960 East Grand Avenue
El Segundo, CA 90245-5056
310-615-2000
Web Address: www.teamoneadv.com
Number of Employees: 200

Brian Sheehan, *CEO & Co-Chairman*
Ann Laygo, *Manager of Human Resources*

The Flowers Group
6244 Ferris Square
San Diego, CA 92121
858-558-6890
Web Address: www.co-opportunities.com
Number of Employees: 10

Jeff Flowers, *Principal*

The Gallup Organization
18200 Von Karman Avenue, Suite 1100
Irvine, CA 92612-1029
949-474-7900
Web Address: www.gallup.com
Number of Employees: 200

Ed Dewees, *Director of Recruiting*

The Roxburgh Agency
245 Fischer Avenue, Suite B4
Costa Mesa, CA 92626-4537
949-556-4365
Number of Employees: 12

Claudia Roxburgh, *President*

The Townsend Agency
10180 Telesis Court
San Diego, CA 92121
858-457-4888
Web Address: www.townsendagency.com
Number of Employees: 65

Jacqueline Townsend, *Principal*
Jean Concolimo, *Hiring Manager*

The Verity Group
680 Langsdorf Drive, Suite 102
Fullerton, CA 92831-3702
714-680-9611
Web Address: www.verity-group.com
Number of Employees: 450

William Matthies, *President*

ThinkTank
12396 World Trade Drive, Suite 109
San Diego, CA 92128
858-675-2570
Web Address: thinktankadv.com
Number of Employees: 7

Brian Woeller, *Principal*
Jeff Detrick, *Hiring Manager*

TMP Worldwide
500 North State College Boulevard #1470
Orange, CA 92868-1604
714-939-1867
Web Address: www.tmp.com
Number of Employees: 2200

Janet Morrison, *Diretor of Human Resources*

Wahlstrom/West
1054 Talbert Road
Santa Ana, CA 92708
714-662-2900
Number of Employees: 150

Linda Sanchez, *Director of Human Resources*

Western States Advertising Agencies Association
6404 Wilshire Boulevard, Suite 111
Los Angeles, CA 90048
213-655-1951
Web Address: www.adswest.org

Woodend Nessel & Friends
1615 Murray Canyon Road, Suite 720
San Diego, CA 92108
619-296-3101
Web Address: wnf@woodendnessel.com
Number of Employees: 7

Carl Woodend, *Principal*
Darleen Woodend, *Hiring Manager*

Links to Job Sites Worldwide, Check JobSourceNetwork.com

Further References

• Associations •

Advertising Research Foundation
641 Lexington Avenue
New York, New York 10022
212-751-5656
Web Address: www.arffice.org/arf
Promotes effectiveness of advertising.

American Advertising Federation
1101 Vermont Avenue, NW, Suite 500
Washington, D.C. 20005
202-898-0089
Web Address: www.aaf.org
Works to advance advertising.

American Association of Advertising Agencies
405 Lexington Avenue, 18th floor
New York, New York 10174
(212) 682-2500
Web Address: www.commercepark.com/AAAA
Fosters development of advertising industry.

American Marketing Association
250 South Wacker Drive, Suite 200
Chicago, Illinois 60606
312-648-0536
Web Address: www.ama.org
Supports research, seminars, and student marketing clubs.

Direct Marketing Association
1120 Avenue of the Americas
New York, NY 10036-6700
212-768-7277
www.tat-dma.org
Studies the effectiveness of direct marketing.

International Advertising Association
521 5th Avenue, Suite 1807
New York, New York 10175
212-557-1133
Web Address: www.IAAglobal.org
Demonstrates value of advertising to governments and consumers.

League of Advertising Agencies
2 South End Avenue #4C
New York, New York 10280
212-945-4991
Education in areas of agency administration.

Marketing Research Association
2189 Silas Deane Highway, Suite #5
Rocky Hill, Connecticut 06067
Organization for those involved in Marketing research.

Public Relations Society of America
33 Irving Place
New York, New York 10003
212-995-2230
Web Address: www.prsa.org
Professional development, job referral, and research information center.

The Advertising Council
261 Madison Avenue
New York, New York 10016
212-922-1500
Web Address: www.adcouncil.org
Conducts public service advertising campaigns.

World Wide Partners
2280 South Xanadu Way, Suite 300
Aurora, Colorado 80014
303-671-8551

• Publications •

AAAA Roster & Organization
666 Third Avenue, 10th Floor
New York, New York 10017
212-682-2500
Web Address: www.commercepark.com/ AAAA
Compilation of National Advertising Agencies

Ad Trends
200 North 4th, P.O. Box 1
Burlington, IA 52601-001
319-752-5415
A monthly report of advertising and merchandise ideas.

Advertising Age
Crain Communications,
740 Rush Street
Chicago, Illinois 60611
312-649-5316
Web Address: www.adage.com
News of World Advertising

Advertising Career Directory
Career Press, Inc.
Hawthorne, New Jersey

Journal of Marketing
250 South Wacker Drive, Suite 200
Chicago, Illinois 60606
312-648-0536
Web Address: www.ama.org
Advances Science and Practice of Advertising

Sales and Marketing Management
355 Park Avenue, South
New York, NY 10010-1789
212-592-6456

Standard Directory of Advertising Agencies
National Register Publishing Company
P.O. Box 31
New Providence, New York 07974
800-521-8110
Web Address: www.reedref.com

Target Marketing-Who's Who in Direct Marketing
North American Publishing Co.
Philadelphia, Pennsylvania

The Gallup Poll Monthly
47 Hulfish Street
P.O. Box 628
Princeton, NJ 08542
609-924-9600
Web Address: www.gallup.com
Source of public opinion.

The Marketing News
250 South Wacker Drive, Suite 200
Chicago, Illinois 60606
312-648-0536
Web Address: www.ama.org
Articles on Marketing in General

ADVERTISING, MAKRETING & SALES

EMPLOYMENT TIP

Starting salaries for entry-level AD/ PR hover around $25,000 but the average manager earns $44,000 and talented managers often earn much more.

Aerospace & Defense

Advanced Ground System Engineering Corporation
1265 North Kraemer Boulevard
Anaheim, CA 92806-1900
714-632-8200
Number of Employees: 100

John Marshman, *President*

Aerochem
1885 North Batavia Street
Orange, CA 92865-4190
714-637-4401
Web Address: www.aerocheminc.com
Number of Employees: 218

Jeff Abbott, *President*

Aerofit Products
6460 Dale Street
Buena Park, CA 90621-3115
714-521-5060
Web Address: www.aerofit.com
Number of Employees: 140

R F Peterjohn, *President*

Aeromil Engineering Co
2344 South Pullman Street
Santa Ana, CA 92705-5515
714-261-9963
Number of Employees: 60

George Ono, *General Manager*

Aerospace Composites
11782 Western Avenue, Suite 7
Stanton, CA 90680-1189
714-897-4654
Number of Employees: 10

Cynthia Garcia, *Owner*

Aerospace Corporation
2350 East El Segundo Boulevard
El Segundo, CA 90245
310-336-5000
Web Address: www.aero.com

Air Transport Association of America
8939 South Sepulveda, CA 90045, Suite 408
Los Angeles, CA 90045
310-670-5183
Web Address: www.air-transport.org
Number of Employees: 5

Neil Bennet, *Executive Director*

AlliedSignal Aerospace
2525 West 190th Street
Torrance, CA 90504
310-323-9500
Job Hotline: 310-512-2012
Web Address: www.alliedsignal.com
Number of Employees: 2,500

Tig Krekel, *President*
Gary Parkinson, *Human Resources Director*

Applied Data Technology
10151 Barnes Canyon Road
San Diego, CA 92121
619-450-9951

Rod Powers, *Director of Business Development*

Arden Engineering
1878 North Main Street
Orange, CA 92865-4117
714-998-6410
Web Address: www.arden-eng.com
Number of Employees: 75

John Meisenbach, *President*

Arrowhead Products
4411 Katella Avenue
Los Alamitos, CA 90720-3599
714-828-7770
Number of Employees: 600

Dale Shanahan, *President*
Carol Begley, *Human Resources Manager*

Astech
3030 Red Hill Avenue
Santa Ana, CA 92705-5823
714-250-1000
Web Address: www.astechmfg.com
Number of Employees: 200

Ross Anderson, *President*

Auger Industries
4050 East Leaverton Court
Anaheim, CA 92807-1610
714-632-8256
Number of Employees: 20

Richard Auger, *President*

Aviation Distributors Incorporated
1 Capital Drive
Lake Forest, CA 92630
714-586-7558
Web Address: www.adi-inc.com
Number of Employees: 60

Kenneth A. Lipinski, *President*
Patricia Potter, *Director of Personnel*

Bailey Industries
25256 Terreno Drive
Mission Viejo, CA 92691-5528
714-461-0807
Number of Employees: 2

Nonny K Bailey, *President*

Bay City Marine
1625 Cleveland Avenue
National City, CA 91950
619-477-3991
Number of Employees: 54

David E. Lloyd, *President*
Fred Workman, *Production Manager*

Boeing Co./Info Space & Defense
5301 Bolsa Avenue
Huntington Beach, CA 92647-2099
714-896-3311
Web Address: www.boeing.com
Number of Employees: 6,341

Victor Koman, *Secretary of Employment*
Diane Bradford, *Human Resources Director*

Boeing Co/Electro-Optical
3370 East Mira Lorna Avenue
Anaheim, CA 92803-3105
714-762-5570
Web Address: www.boeing.com
Number of Employees: 3300

Bob Pastr, *Div President*

C&D Aerospace
5412 Argosy Avenue
Huntington Beach, CA 92649-1039
714-891-1906
Number of Employees: 1600

James E Downey, *CEO*

C&D Aerospace
7330 Lincoln Way
Garden Grove, CA 92841-1427
714-891-0683
Number of Employees: 1600

Joe Moran, *President*

California Composite Design
1935 East Occidental Street
Santa Ana, CA 92705-5115
714-258-0405
Web Address: www.ccdicomposites.com
Number of Employees: 30

Fred Good, *President*

Cartwright Electronics
655 West Valencia Drive
Fullerton, CA 92832-2144
714-525-2300
Number of Employees: 105

Quinton Miller, *President*

Chen-Tech Industries
10 Autry
Irvine, CA 92618-2796
949-855-6716
Web Address: www.chentech.com
Number of Employees: 40

Shannon Ko, *President*

Composites Unlimited
16452 Construction Circle South
Irvine, CA 92606-4417
949-559-0930
Number of Employees: 60

Rolf Uitzetter, *President*

Computer Sciences Corporation
4045 Hancock Street
San Diego, CA 92110
619-225-8401

Lee Taylor, *Operations Director*

Continental Maritime of San Diego
1995 Bayfront Street
San Diego, CA 92113
619-234-8851
Number of Employees: 330

David McQueary, *President*
Maryanne Sablan, *Human Resource Manager*

Contour Aerospace
428 Berry Way
Brea, CA 92821-3114
949-990-9281
Web Address: www.ccindustries.com
Number of Employees: 444

Tom Wallace, *President & CEO*
Vicki Saurez, *Human Resources Director*

Datum Incorporated
9975 Toledo Way
Irvine, CA 92618
949-380-8880
Web Address: www.datum.com

Ducommun, Inc.
23301 South Wilmington Avenue
Carson, CA 90745
562-624-0800

Norman A. Barkeley, *Chairman*

Edler Industries
2101 Dove Street
Newport Beach, CA 92660-1998
949-252-0555
Number of Employees: 50

Vernon Edler III, *President*

Electrol Manufacturing Co
1100 East Elm Avenue
Fullerton, CA 92831-5056

714-871-6922
Web Address: www.electromfg.com
Number of Employees: 40

James M Roark, *President*

Fairchild Fasteners
190 West Crowther Avenue
Placentia, CA 92870-5639
714-524-5854
Web Address: www.fairchild.com
Number of Employees: 180

Bob Edwards, *President*

Flight Line Industries
14 Centerpointe Drive
La Palma, CA 90623-1028
714-523-9977
Number of Employees: 400

Angelica Ybarra, *Director of Human Resources*

Hawker Pacific Aerospace
11310 Sherman Way
Sun Valley, CA 91352
818-765-6201
Web Address: www.hawker.com
Number of Employees: 280

David L. Lokken, *President*
Carol Schaub, *Personnel Director*
Provider of aircraft repair services and parts for
business and government. Customers include
FedEx, US Coast Guard, and American Airlines.
Has agreement to buy British Airways' landing
gear repair operations for about $22 million.

Hughes Aircraft
1801 Hughes Drive
Fullerton, CA 92833-2249
714-732-3232
Web Address: www.hughes.com

Phil George, *President*

IDC Detector Systems
11650 Seaboard Circle
Stanton, CA 90680-3426
949-895-6366
Number of Employees: 400

Infotec Development
3611 South Harbor Boulevard
Santa Ana, CA 92704
714-549-2182

Interface Displays & Controls, Inc.
4630 North Avenue
Oceanside, CA 92056
760-945-0230
Web Address: www.interfacedisplays.com
Number of Employees: 40

Bill Lang, *President*
Sherry Scott, *Human Resources Manager*

Interstate Electronics Corp
1001 East Ball Road
Anaheim, CA 92803-3117
714-758-0500
Web Address: www.iehome.com
Number of Employees: 600

Sherry Dowe, *Human Resources Director*

J&R Engineering Co
2870 East Via Martens
Anaheim, CA 92806-1751
714-666-8084
Number of Employees: 30

Jorge Gutierrez, *President*

Jaycor
9775 Towne Centre Drive
San Diego, CA 92121
858-453-6580
Web Address: www.jaycor.com
Number of Employees: 100

Eric P. Wenaas, *President*
Thelest Stewart, *Human Resource Director*

Kaiser Electroprecision
17000 Red Hill Avenue
Irvine, CA 92614-5676
949-250-1015
Web Address: www.kaiserep.com
Number of Employees: 300

George Faulkner, *Div President*
Robert Oxley, *Human Resources Director*

Kaynar Tech/K-Fast Tooling Division
800 South State College Boulevard
Fullerton, CA 92831
714-871-1550
Web Address: www.kaynar.com
Number of Employees: 980

Jordan A. Law, *President*
Joseph F. Blomberg, *Director of Personnel*

L'Garde
15181 Woodlawn Avenue
Tustin, CA 92780-6487
714-259-0771
Web Address: www.lgarde.com
Number of Employees: 25

Gayle D Bilyeu, *CEO*
Alan Hirasuna, *Human Resources Director*

Litton Industries
21240 Burbank Boulevard
Woodland Hills, CA 91367-6675
818-598-5000
Web Address: www.littoncorp.com
Number of Employees: 3537

John M. Leonis, *Chairman*
Nancy L. Gaymon, *Director of Personnel*

Provider of aerospace, defense, and commercial electronics, mostly for the US government. The company's operations are located primarily in the US, Canada, and Western Europe.

Litton Industries
Engineering Service Center
7425 Mission Valley Road, Suite 205
San Diego, CA 92100
619-298-6408
Web Address: www.litton.com

Logicon
3701 Skypark Drive
Torrance, CA 90505
310-373-0220
Web Address: www.logicon.com
Number of Employees: 57

John R. Woodhull, *CEO*

M & M Machine & Tool Company
17800 Gothard Street
Huntington Beach, CA 92647-6259
949-841-1750
Number of Employees: 60

Robert McGuire, *President*

Marconi Integrated Systems
PO Box 509009
San Diego, CA 92150
619-573-8000
Web Address: www.marconi-is.com

Maxwell Technologies
9275 Sky Park Court
San Diego, CA 92123
619-279-5100
Web Address: www.maxwell.com
Number of Employees: 450

Kenneth F. Potashner, *CEO*
Emily Berr, *Human Resource Representative*

Megditt Defense System
2672 Dow Avenue
Tustin, CA 92780-7208
714-832-1333
Web Address: www.meggitt.com
Number of Employees: 75

Roger Brum, *President*

Merco Manufacturing Co
1927 North Glassell Street
Orange, CA 92865-4398
714-637-5500
Number of Employees: 25

Douglas R Rossman, *President*

National Steel & Shipbuilding Co.
Harbor Drive & 28th Street
San Diego, CA 92113
619-544-3400
Job Hotline: 619-544-8512
Web Address: www.nasco.com
Number of Employees: 5,000

Fred Hallett, *CFO*

Nellcor Puritan Bennett/Wemac
18475 Pacific Street
Fountain Valley, CA 92708-7004
714-962-8874
Web Address: www.nellcorpb.com
Number of Employees: 66

Trish Vance, *Director of Human Resources*

Newmar
2911 Garrey Avenue
Santa Ana, CA 92704
714-751-0488
Web Address: www.newmarpower.com
Number of Employees: 100

J. R. Johnson, *President*

Northrop Grumman Corp.
1840 Century Park East
Los Angeles, CA 90067
310-553-6262
Web Address: www.northgrum.com
Number of Employees: 14,600

Kent Kresa, *President*
Gloria Rodriguez, *Manager of Employment*

Notthoff Engineering LA
15651 Container Lane
Huntington Beach, CA 92649-1532
714-894-9802
Number of Employees: 25

Terry Caller, *President*

Omohundro Company
960 West 16th Street
Costa Mesa, CA 92627
949-631-6660
Number of Employees: 75

Mark Sparks, *President*
Allison Phillips, *Human Resources Manager*

Pacific Scientific/HTL-Kin Tech
1800 Highland Avenue
Duarte, CA 91010
626-359-9317
Number of Employees: 300
Sandi Deets, *Director of Human Resources*

Pacific Ship Repair & Fabrication
1625 Rigel Street
San Diego, CA 92113
619-232-3200

Job Hotline: 619-232-2300 x125
Number of Employees: 140
David Bain, *President*
Kathy Livingston, *Human Resource Manager*

Park Engineering Manufacturing
6430 Roland Street
Buena Park, CA 90621-3198
714-521-4660
Number of Employees: 20

Rose Marie Swanke, *President*

Parker Aerospace
18321 Jamboree Road
Irvine, CA 92612-1011
949-833-3000
Web Address: www.parker.com
Number of Employees: 3500

Stephen L. Hayes, *Group President*
Linda Walker, *Group VP for Human Resources*

Programmed Composites
250 Klug Circle
Corona, CA 92880
909-520-7300
Number of Employees: 90

Alex Roberts, *President*
Debbie Ardolino, *Human Resources Manager*

Rohr/BF Goodrich Aerospace
850 Lagoon Drive
Chula Vista, CA 91910
619-691-4111
Job Hotline: 619-691-3022
Web Address: www.rhor.com

Robert H. Rau, *President*

SEMCOR
7170 Convoy Court
San Diego, CA 92111
619-560-7233
Web Address: www.semcor.com
Number of Employees: 90

Paul Maynard, Director, *Southern California Ops.*
Tony Shea, *Human Resource Director*

Sun Eight Co
588 Porter Way
Placentia, CA 92870-6453
714-993-5600
Number of Employees: 40
Herbert E Conway, *President*

Swiss Pattern
2611 South Yale Street
Santa Ana, CA 92704-5227
714-545-8040
Number of Employees: 22
Daniel Dick, *President*

Symbolic Displays
1917 East Saint Andrew Place
Santa Ana, CA 92705-5143
714-258-2811
Number of Employees: 85
Norm Suits, *President*

Tolo Incorporated
18341 Jamboree Road
Irvine, CA 92612
949-261-8656
Web Address: www.tolo.com
Number of Employees: 260
Charles G. Cawthorne, *President*
Ken Vadofski, *Human Resources Manager*

Tri-Tech Precision
1577 North Harmony Circle
Anaheim, CA 92807-6003
714-970-1363
Web Address: www.verisurf.com
Number of Employees: 22
Ernie Husted, *President*

UCSD Office of Contract and Grant Administration
9500 Gilman Drive, Dept. 0934
La Jolla, CA 92137
619-534-3330
Robert C. Dynes, *Chancellor*

Unit Industries
1140 East Valencia Drive
Fullerton, CA 92831-4627
714-871-4161
Number of Employees: 43

John W. Abouchar, *President*

Weber Aircraft
1300 East Valencia Drive
Fullerton, CA 92831
714-449-3000
Web Address: www.weberair.com
Number of Employees: 1700

Michel Labarre, *President*
Cindy Samarin, *Human Resources Director*

Western Design Howden
16952 Millikan Avenue
Irvine, CA 92606-5014
949-863-0560
Web Address: www.wd.com
Number of Employees: 60

Michael S Quinn, *President*

Whittaker Corporation
1955 North Surveyor Avenue
Simi Valley, CA 93063
805-526-5700
Web Address: www.whittaker.com

Wills Wing
500 West Blueridge Avenue
Orange, CA 92865-4206
714-998-6359
Web Address: www.willswing.com
Number of Employees: 32

Robert T Kells Jr, *President*

Yeager Manufacturing Corp
2222 East Orangethorpe Avenue
Anaheim, CA 92806-1286
714-879-2800
Number of Employees: 35

W B Cummins, *President*

Further References

• Associations •

American Institute of Aeronautics & Astronautics
85 John Street
New York, New York 10038
212-349-1120
Web Address: www.aiaa.org
Advancement of Engineering Information

Future Aviation Professionals of America
4959 Massachusetts Avenue
Atlanta, Georgia 30337
Career Planning for Industry

National Aeronautic Association of USA
1815 North Fort Meyer Drive, Suite 700
Arlington, Virginia 22209
703-527-0226
Web Address: www.naa.ycg.org
Development of Aviation

• Publications •

Aerospace America
370 L'Enfant Promenade SW, 10th Floor
Washington, DC 20024
202-646-7400

Aviation Week & Space Technology
1120 Vermont Avenue NW, 12th Floor
Washington, DC 20005

Business & Commercial Aviation
260 Rye Brook
New York, NY 10573

Check High Tech for More Listings

AEROSPACE & DEFENSE

Arts & Culture

- Art Schools
- Galleries
- Museums
- Motion Picture Organizations
- Performing Arts Presenters
- Theaters
- Dance Companies
- Music Ensembles

There are two primary markets for arts-related employment: federal positions at institutions such as the National Endowment for the Arts, Smithsonian Institution; and jobs with local arts organizations including theaters, galleries, museums, arts schools, performing arts presenters, dance companies and music ensembles.

Jobs with larger institutions are more specialized. Entry-level positions tend to be administrative, and mid-level positions frequently require advanced degrees or technical training. At local organizations, employees tend to function more as generalists, participating in many aspects of the organization's day-to-day management.

While finding your first job in the arts is challenging, it is not impossible! Job-seekers should take advantage of resources such as the Cultural Alliance JOBank and the Smithsonian Institution Job Hotline. Joining an association such as the Alliance or attending arts events is another good way to make contacts. Finally, while you search for a job, consider doing volunteer work with an organization that interests you to build your resume and develop new skills.

**CULTURAL ALLIANCE OF
GREATER WASHINGTON**

Athena Video & New Media
6150 Lusk Boulevard, Suite B-102
San Diego, CA 92121
858-597-0099
Web Address: athenavideo.com
Number of Employees: 6

Suzanne Weast, *President*

B&B Communications
904 Second Street
Encinitas, CA 92024
760-942-2800

Gary Bulkin, *Executive Producer*
Sylvia Conley, *Hiring Manager*

Bob Hoffman Video Productions
4805 Mercury Street, Suite L
San Diego, CA 92111
858-576-0046
Web Address: bobhofmanvideo.com
Number of Employees: 9

Bob Hoffman, *CEO*

Bob Sloan Productions
9965 Business Park Avenue, Suite B
San Diego, CA 92131
858-586-0600

Robert B. Sloan, *CEO*

Broadcast Images
9340 Hazard Way, Suite B
San Diego, CA 92123
858-974-7999
Web Address: www.broadcastimages.net
Number of Employees: 7

Jeff Freeman, *Chief Executive*
Janice Takade, *Hiring Manger*

California Science Center
700 State Drive
Exposition Park
Los Angeles, CA 90037
213-744-7400
Job Hotline: 213-630-3059
Number of Employees: 130

Jeffrey Rudolph, *Director*

Center Theatre Group
135 North Grand Avenue
Los Angeles, CA 90012
213-628-2772

Christie's Los Angeles
360 North Camden Drive
Beverly Hills, CA 90210
310-385-2600
Job Hotline: 212-636-2000
Web Address: www.christies.com
Number of Employees: 35

Marsha Hobbs, *Chairman*
Dernot Chichester, *Managing Director*

Craft & Folk Art Museum
5800 Wilshire Boulevard
Los Angeles, CA 90036
213-937-4230

Ferrari Productions
11717 Sorrento Valley Road
San Diego, CA 92121
619-792-8011
Web Address: pferrari@sd.znet.com

Philip Ferrari, *Chief Executive*

Gardner & Associates
11455 Lorena Lane
El Cajon, CA 92020
619-460-1000
Web Address: twms@pacbel.net
Number of Employees: 4

Robert D. Gardner, *Chief Executive*
Terry Williams, *Vice President*

Griffith Observatory
2800 East Observatory Road
Los Angeles, CA 90027
213-664-1181
Number of Employees: 75

Hollywood Bowl
2301 North Highland Avenue
Hollywood, CA 90068
323-850-2000
Web Address: www.hollywoodbowl.org

Huntington Library, Art Collection and Botanical Gardens
1151 Oxford Road
San Marino, CA 91108
626-405-2100
Web Address: www.huntington.com

International Association for Financial Planners
1651 East 4th Street, Suite 244
Santa Ana, CA 92701-5142
714-542-0024

Jennifer Zaat, *President*

Japanese American National Museum
369 1st Street
Los Angeles, CA 90012
213-625-0414

JM Digital Works
2460 Impala Drive
Carlsbad, CA 92008
760-476-1783
Web Address: www.jmtv@jmdigitalworks.com
Number of Employees: 10

Ken Kebow, *General Manager*
Rick Colson, *Hiring Manager*

Kidspace Museum
390 South El Molino
Pasadena, CA 91101
626-449-9144
Web Address: http://home.earthlink.net/kidspacem
Number of Employees: 20

Carol Scott, *Executive Director*
Karen Rabbons, *Director of Human Resources*

Laguna Art Museum
307 Cliff Drive
Laguna Beach, CA 92651
714-494-6531

Fulton Colburn, *Director*

Lenny Magill Productions/Time Zone Video
4585 Murphy Canyon Road
San Diego, CA 92123
858-569-4000
Web Address: gunvideos@aol.com
Number of Employees: 10

Lenny Magill, *Chief Executive*

Lightning Corporation
7854 Ronson Road
San Diego, CA 92111
858-565-6494
Web Address: wedovideo@aol.com
Number of Employees: 12

Karen Larsen, *Chief Executive*

Los Angeles Children's Museum
310 North Main Street
Los Angeles, CA 90012
213-687-8801
Web Address: www.lacm.org

Candis Barret, *Executive Director*

Los Angeles County Museum of Art
5905 Wilshire Boulevard
Los Angeles, CA 90036
213-857-6111
Web Address: www.lacma.org
Number of Employees: 30

Graham Beal, *Executive Director*

Los Angeles Philharmonic
135 North Grand Avenue
Los Angeles, CA 90012
323-850-2000

Multi Image Productions
8849 Complex Drive
San Diego, CA 92123
858-560-8383
Web Address: www.multiimage.com
Number of Employees: 18

L. C. Gminski, *Chief Executive*

Museum of African American Art
4005 Crenshaw Boulevard, 3rd Floor
Los Angeles, CA 90008
213-294-7071
Number of Employees: 3

Berlinda Fonentont-Jamerson, *Chairman*

Museum of Contemporary Art
250 South Grand
Los Angeles, CA 90012
213-621-2766
Web Address: www.moca-la.org
Number of Employees: 100

Richard Coshalek, *Executive Director*

Music Center of Los Angeles County
135 North Grand Avenue
Los Angeles, CA 90012
213-972-7211

Natural History Museum, Balboa Park
1788 El Prado
San Diego, CA 92101
619-232-3821
Web Address: www.sdnhm.org
Number of Employees: 120

Dr. Michael Hager, *Executive Director*
Patricia Wolery, *Controller & Director of
Administration*

Norton Simon Museum
411 West Colorado Boulevard
Pasadena, CA 91105
626-449-6840

Old Globe Theatre
PO Box 122171
San Diego, CA 92112
619-231-1941
Number of Employees: 200

Doug Evans, *Manager*

Orange County Employees Association
830 North Ross Street
Santa Ana, CA 92701-3420
714-835-3355
Web Address: www.oceanmember.org
Number of Employees: 30

Frank Eley, *President*

Orange County Medical Association
300 South Flower Street
Orange, CA 92868-3412
714-978-1770
Web Address: www.ocma.org
Number of Employees: 30

Orange County Museum of Art
850 San Clemente Drive
Newport Beach, CA 92660
949-759-1122
Web Address: www.ocartsnet.org/ocma
Number of Employees: 45
Katherine Lee, *Director of Public Relations*

Orange County Performing Arts Center
600 Town Center Drive
Costa Mesa, CA 92626
949-556-2787

Pacific Asia Museum
46 North Los Robles Avenue
Pasadena, CA 91101
626-449-2742
Web Address: www.pacasiamuseum.aol.com
Number of Employees: 26

David Kamansky, *Executive Director*
Jim Hanley, *Personnel Director*

Richard Nixon Library/Birthplace
18001 Yorba Linda Boulevard
Yorba Linda, CA 92886-3949
714-993-5075
Web Address: www.nixonlibrary.org
Number of Employees: 30

John H. Taylor, *Executive Director*

Rueben H. Fleet Science Center
1875 El Prado, Balboa Park
San Diego, CA 92101
619-238-1233
Web Address: www.rhfleet.org

Jeff Kirsch, *Executive Director*
Candi Freed, *Human Resource Manager*

SAIC Video Productions
10260 Campus Point Drive
San Diego, CA 92121
619-546-6065
Web Address: www.saic.com
Number of Employees: 3500

Steve Hutchison, *Manager*

San Diego Museum of Art
1450 El Prado, Balboa Park
San Diego, CA 92101
619-232-7931

San Diego Museum of Contemporary Art
700 Prospect Street
La Jolla, CA 92037
619-454-3541
Web Address: www.mcsd.org
Number of Employees: 30

Hughes Davies, *Executive Director*
Jennifer Butler, *Hiring Contact*

San Diego Video & Film
1432 Union Street
San Diego, CA 92101
619-291-1645
Web Address: www.brubaker.com
Number of Employees: 10

Wayne Brubaker, *Chief Executive*

Santa Monica Museum of Art
2525 Michigan Avenue, Building G
Santa Monica, CA 90405
310-586-6488
Number of Employees: 6

Thomas Rhoads, *Executive Director*
Mary Lee Cherry, *Human Resource Manager*

Satellite Video Productions
5111 Santa Fe Street
San Diego, CA 92109
858-483-4151
Web Address: www.svpontheweb.com
Number of Employees: 6

Tom Signenio, *President*
Sandy Jack, *Hiring Manager*

Simon Wiesenthal Museum of Tolerance
9786 West Pico Boulevard
Los Angeles, CA 90035
310-553-8403
Web Address: www.wiesenthal.com
Number of Employees: 200
Ann Krall, *Human Resource Manager*

Skirball Cultural Center
2701 North Sepulveda Boulevard
Los Angeles, CA 90049
310-440-4500
Job Hotline: X 4556
Web Address: www.skirball.com
Sharon Wright, *Human Resource Manager*

Society for Vector Ecology
13001 Garden Grove Boulevard
Garden Grove, CA 92843
714-971-2421
Number of Employees: 50

Florence Cavileer, *President*

Society of Critical Care Medicine
8101 East Kaiser Boulevard
Anaheim, CA 92808-2243
714-282-6000
Web Address: www.sccm.org
Number of Employees: 37

Steve Seekins, *CEO & Exec VP*
Pat Tays, *Personnel Manager*

Solar Turbines Corp Video Communications
9250 Sky Park Court
San Diego, CA 92123
858-694-6643
Web Address: www.solar.cat.com
Number of Employees: 4

Dempsey Copeland, *Manager*

Sotheby's
9665 Wilshire, Suite 101
Beverly Hills, CA 90212
310-274-0340
Web Address: www.sothebys.com
Number of Employees: 15

Rick Wolf, *Managing Partner*
Andre Van De Kamp, *VP West Coast Operations*
Christa Gruener, *Human Resource Manager*

Southwest Museums
234 Museum Drive
Los Angeles, CA 90065
213-221-2164
Web Address: www.swmuseums@annex.com
Number of Employees: 28

Duane King, *Executive Director*

Spruce Street Producers
9450 Scranton Road, Suite 210
San Diego, CA 92121
858-695-1665
Web Address: videoadv@aol.com

J. C. Arner, *Chief Executive*

The Bowers Museum/Cultural Art
2002 North Main Street
Santa Ana, CA 92706-2731
714-567-3600
Web Address: www.bowers.org
Number of Employees: 40

Tonya Daniels, *Human Resources Manager*

UCLA/Armand Hammer Museum of Art and Cultural Center
10899 Wilshire Boulevard
Los Angeles, CA 90024
310-443-7020
Web Address: www.hammerucla.edu
Number of Employees: 50

Henry Hopkins, *Executive Director*
Roberto Salazar, *Human Resource Manager*

Utd Fed Classified Emp/Loc 14794
15744 Goldenwest Street
Huntington Beach, CA 92647-0748
714-895-8765
Number of Employees: 700

Paul Wisner, *President*

Further References

• Associations •

Academy of Motion Picture Arts and Sciences
8949 Wilshire Boulevard
Beverly Hills, CA 90211
310-247-3000
Web Address: www.ampas.org
Advancement of Arts and Sciences in Motion Pictures.

Academy of Television Arts & Sciences
5220 Lankershim Boulevard
North Hollywood, California 91601
818-754-2800
Web Address: www.emmys.org
Advancement of arts and sciences in television.

Actor's Equity Association
165 West 46th Street
New York, New York 10036
212-869-8530
Represents actors and awards excellence in theatre.

Affiliate Artists
45 West 60th Street
New York, New York 10023
Promotes career development of artists.

American Crafts Council
72 Spring Street
New York, New York 10012
212-274-0630
Works to increase appreciation of American crafts.

American Dance Guild
31 West 21st Street
New York, New York 10010
212-932-2789
Initiates programs of national signifigance.

American Federation of Musicians
1501 Broadway, Suite 600
New York, New York 10036
212-869-1330
Musicians interested in advancing music industry.

American Film Marketing Association
10850 Wilshire Boulevard, 9th Floor
Los Angeles, CA 90024-4305
310-447-1555
Web Address: www.afma.com
Involved in the production and distribution of English language films to the foreign market.

American Guild of Musical Artists
1727 Broadway
New York, New York 10019
212-265-3687
Classical and opera singers and related managers.

American Music Center
30 West 26th Street, Suite 1001
New York, New York 10010
212-366-5260
Web Address: www.amc.net/amc/
Appreciation and creation of contemporary music.

American Society of Cinematographers
1782 North Orange Drive
Hollywood, CA 90028
213-969-4333

American Society of Composers, Authors & Publishers
1 Lincoln Plaza
New York, New York 10023
212-595-3050
Web Address: www.ascap.com
Clearinghouse of music performing rights.

Americans for the Arts
1 East 53rd Street
New York, New York 10012
212-223-2787
Web Address: www.artsusa.org
Promotes arts and artists.

Dance USA
1156 15th Street N.W., Suite 820
Washington, D.C. 20005
202-833-1717
Web Address: www.danceusa.org/danceusa
Promotes dance and dance programs.

International Documentary Association
1551 South Robertson Boulevard, Suite 201
Los Angeles, CA 90035
310-284-8422
Involved in the promotion of nonfiction film and the support of nonfiction film makers.

International Television Association
6311 North O'Connor Road, Suite 230
Irving, TX 75039
972-869-1112
Web Address: www.itva.org
Working for the advancement of those working in the videotape and nonbroadcast video fields.

Motion Picture Assocation

15503 Ventura Boulevard
Encino, CA 91436
818-995-6600
Web Address: www.mpaa.org/mpa.html
Represents the American film industry internationally.

Motion Picture Association of America

1600 Eye Street, N.W.
Washington, D.C. 20006
202-293-1966
Web Address: www.mpaa.org
Represents the main U.S. distributors and producers of motion pictures domestically.

National Artists Equity Association

P.O. Box 28068, Central Station
Washington, D.C. 20038
202-628-9633
Protects rights of visual artists.

National Dance Association

1900 Association Drive
Reston, Virginia 22091
703-476-3436
Web Address: www.aahpbrd.org/nda.html
Advocate for better dance education.

National Foundation for Advancement in the Arts

3915 Biscayne Boulevard
Miami, Florida 33137
305-573-0490
Supports aspiring artists.

Producers Guild of America

400 South Beverly Drive, Suite 211
Beverly Hills, California 90212
310-557-0807
Association of movie and television producers.

Professional Arts Management Institute

408 West 57th Street
New York, New York 10019
212-245-3850
Education for management of performing arts or cultural institutions.

Screen Actors Guild

5757 Wilshire Boulevard
Hollywood, California 90036
General actor assistance.

Society of Motion Picture and Television Engineers

595 West Hartsdale Avenue
White Plains, New York 10607
914-761-1100
Web Address: www.smpte.org
Strives to advance engineering knowledge and practice for television and movies.

Stuntmen's Association of Motion Picture

4810 Whitsett Avenue
North Hollywood, CA 91607
818-766-4334
Web Address: www.stuntnet.com/organization/stmass.htm
Members of the Screen Actors Guild or the American Federation of Television and Radio Artists Association who are involved in stunt work in television or motion pictures.

Theatre Communications Group

355 Lexington Avenue
New York, New York 10017
212-697-5230
Web Address: www.tcg.org
Service organization for non-profit theatres, artists, and administrators.

Women in Film

6464 Sunset Boulevard, Suite 530
Hollywood, CA 90028
213-463-6040
Supporters of women in television and film industry.

• Publications •

American Artist

One Astor Place, 1515 Broadway
New York, New York 10036
212-764-7300
Web Address: www.cc.enews.com/magazines/ameriart
Artists, Methods, and Problems

Art Business News

Myers Publishing Company
19 Old Kings Highway South
Darien, Connecticut 06820
Fine Art and Picture Framing Industry

Artforum

65 Bleeker Street
New York, New York 10012
212-475-4000
Web Address: www.artforum.com

Artists Market

Writers Digest Books
1507 Dana Avenue
Cincinnati, Ohio 45207
513-531-2222

ArtWeek

2149 Paragon Drive, Suite 100
San Jose, California 95131
408-441-7065

Back Stage
1515 Broadway
New York, New York 10036
212-764-7300
Web Address: www.backstage.com

Billboard
1515 Broadway, 11th Floor
New York, NY 10036
212-536-5167
Web Address: www.billboard.com
Music and Home Entertainment.

Crafts Report
300 Water Street
Wilmington, Delaware 19801
302-656-2209
Web Address: www.craftsreport.com
Business News for Crafts Makers.

Creative Black Book
115 5th Avenue, 3rd Floor
New York, New York 10003

Hollywood Reporter
5055 Wilshire
Los Angeles, California 90028
213-525-2000
Web Address: www.hollywoodreporter.com

NASAA Directory
National Assembly of State Art Agencies
1010 Vermont Avenue NW
Washington, DC 20005
202-347-6352
Web Address: www.nasaa-arts.org

Players Guide
165 West 46th Street
New York, New York 10036
212-869-3570

Ross Reports Television
1515 Broadway
New York, NY 10036-8986
718-937-3990
Web Address: www.backstage.com

Television Broadcast
2 Park Avenue, Suite 1820
New York, NY 10016
212-779-1919

The Academy Players Directories
8949 Wilshire Boulevard
Beverly Hills, California 90211
310-247-3000
Web Address: www.oscar.com

Variety
475 Park Avenue South
New York, New York 10016
News of Entertainment Industry.

Women Artist News
300 Riverside Drive
New York, New York 10025
212-666-6990
News for Female Artists.

World Broadcast News
9800 Metcalf Avenue
Overland Park, KS 66212
913-341-1300
International Cable and Television News

EMPLOYMENT TIP

Jobs with larger institutions are more specialized. Entry-level positions tend to be administrative, and mid-level positions frequently require advanced degrees or technical training. At local organizations, employees tend to function more as generalists, participating in many aspects of the organization's day-to-day management.

Associations, Non-Profit & Public Interest Groups

There are three basic types of associations: Trade associations, professional societies, and philanthropic or charitable organizations. Trade associations represent a group of business firms. Businesses join their associations voluntarily and manage them cooperatively. The companies work together to accomplish goals that no single firm could reach by itself. Activities include promoting business for the industry, encouraging ethical practices in the industry, setting of industry standards, conducting research, cooperating with other organizations, and holding conventions. Trade associations provide their members with important economic and industry information which enables them to forecast their business future. Members are kept informed about current trends in their industry and in businesses across the country.

There is no specific degree needed to obtain a job in an association. Several common job functions such as accountant, account executive, journalist and salesperson, all fit into association jobs.

Every association produces some sort of newsletter or magazine, so they need writers, editors, art and production people and often advertising sales representatives.

All associations must recruit members and market their products and services to them so they need people with marketing backgrounds.

Likewise, all associations have a finance department and need accountants and other financial personnel. Most associations have a government affairs and/or public affairs, public relations department.

Very few association jobs appear in the local newspapers. Most other jobs are filled by word of mouth and networking. Now is the time to start your network. But don't tell everyone you are looking for a job because this will turn them off. Instead, tell them you are interested in, for example, writing for an association publication. Ask if they know anyone who works for an association who would be willing to take 15 minutes to talk to you about their job. Think of these conversations as "information interviews", not job interviews. You may be referred to talk to others. Eventually, you will hit upon someone who does know of an opening and will remember talking to you.

AMERICAN SOCIETY OF
ASSOCIATION EXECUTIVES

Quick Reference Web Sites

National

Aerospace Industries Association of America
www.aia-aerospace.org

Air Force Association
www.afa.org

Air Transport Association of America
www.air-transport.org

America's Community Bankers
www.acbankers.org

American Anthropological Association
www.ameranthassn.org

American Association of Homes for the Aging
www.aahfa.org

American Association of Retired Persons
www.aarp.org

American Association of School Administrators
www.aasa.org

American Association of State Colleges and Universities
www.aascu.nche.edu

American Association of University Women
www.aauw.org

American Astronomical Society
www.aas.org

American Chamber of Commerce Executives
www.acce.org

American Chemical Society
www.acs.org

American College of Cardiology
www.acc.org

American College of Health Care Administrators
www.achca.org

American Council of Life Insurance
www.acli.com

American Counseling Association
www.couseling.org

American Federation of State, County and Municipal Employees
www.afscme.org

American Federation of Teachers
www.aft.org

American Forest and Paper Association
www.afandpa.org

American Gas Association
www.aga.com

American Gastroenterological Association
www.gastro.org

American Geological Institute
www.agiweb.org

American Institute of Architects
www.aiaonline.com

American Insurance Association
www.aiadc.org

American Iron and Steel Institute
www.steel.org

American Medical Association
www.ama-assn.org

American Pharmaceutical Association
www.aphanet.org

American Physical Therapy Association
www.apta.org

American Planning Association
www.planning.org

American Podiatric Medical Association
www.apma.org

American Political Science Association
www.apsanet.org

American Production & Inventory Control Society
www.apics.org

American Psychological Association
www.apa.org

American Public Health Association
www.apha.org

American Public Transit Association
www.apta.com

American Society for Microbiology
www.asmusa.org

American Society for Training & Development
www.astd.org

American Society of Association Executives
www.asaenet.org

American Society of Hospital Pharmacists
www.ashp.com/pub/ashp/index.html

American Society of Internal Medicine
www.asim.org

American Society of Landscape Architects
www.asla.org

American Society of Travel Agents
www.astanet.com

American Sociological Association
www.asanet.org

American Trucking Association
www.trucking.org

Associated Builders & Contractors
www.abc.org

Association of American Medical Colleges
www.aamc.org

Association of American Railroads
www.aar.org

Association of Family and Consumer Science
www.aafcs.org

Association of General Contractors
www.agc.org

Association of Trial Lawyers of America
www.atlanet.org

Building Owners & Managers Association International
www.boma.org

Chamber of Commerce of the United States of America
www.uschamber.org

Chemical Manufacturers Association
www.cmahq.com

Cosmetic, Toiletry & Fragrance Association
www.ctfa.com

Council of Better Business Bureaus
www.bbb.org

Council on Foundations
www.cof.org

Electronic Industries Association
www.eia.org

Food Marketing Institute
www.fmi.org

General Federation of Women's Clubs
www.gfwc.org

Greenpeace USA
www.greenpeace.org

Grocery Manufacturers Association
www.gmabrads.com

Independent Petroleum Association of America
www.ipaa.org

International Brotherhood of Electrical
Workers
www.polarnet.com/users/gnewton/ibewihtm

International City Management Association
www.icma.org

ITAA: The Computer Software & Services
Industry Association
www.itaa.org

Mortgage Bankers Association
www.mba.org

National Assciation of Convenience Stores
www.cstorecentral.com

National Association of Broadcasters
www.nab.org

National Association of College & University
Business Officers
www.nacubo.org

National Association of Life Underwriters
www.agents-online.com

National Association of Regulatory Utility
Commissioners
www.erols.com/naruc

National Association of Securities Dealers
www.nasd.com

National Association of Social Workers
www.naswdc.org

National Automobile Dealers Association
www.nadanet.com

National Education Association
www.nea.org

National Electrical Manufacturers Association
www.nema.org

National Food Processors Association
www.nfpa-food.org

National Governor's Association
www.nga.org

National League of Cities
www.nlc.org

National Mining Association
www.nma.org

National Restaurant Association
www.restaurant.org

National Rifle Association
www.nra.org

National School Boards Association
www.nsba.org

National School Supply & Equipment Association
www.nssea.org

National Soft Drink Association
www.nsda.com

National Wildlife Federation
www.nwf.org

Pharmaceutical Manufacturers Association
www.pharma.org

Retired Officers Association
www.troa.org

Society for Human Resource Management
www.shrm.org

Society of the Plastics Industry
www.socplas.org

Special Olympics International
www.specialolympics.org

The National Committee to Preserve Social
Security and Medicare
www.ncpssm.org

The Nature Conservancy
www.tnc.org

The Newspaper Guild
www.newsguild.org

The Transportation Institute
www.trans-inst.org

United States Conference of Mayors
www.usmayors.org/uscm

Who's Who in Association Management
www.asaenet.org

Regional & Local

Beverly Hills Chamber of Commerce
www.beverlyhillscc.org

Burbank Chamber of Commerce
http://burbank.acityline.com

Catalina Island Visitors Bureau
www.catalina.com

Community Associations Institute
www.caioc.com

Culver City Chamber of Commerce
www.culvercitychamber.org

Easter Seal Society of Southern
California
www.essc.org

Hollywood Chamber of Commerce
http://chamber.hollywood.com

Industry Manufacturers Council
www.ind-chmbr.com

Italy-America Chamber of Commerce
West
www.italchambers.net

Pasadena Chamber of Commerce
www.pasadena-chamber.org

Redondo Beach Chamber of
Commerce
www.redondochamber.org

San Pedro Peninsula Chamber of
Commerce
www.sanpedrochamber.com

Santa Monica Area Chamber of
Commerce
www.smchamber.com

Torrance Area Chamber of
Commerce
www.torrancechamber.com

Westchester, LA, Marina Del Ray Chamber of
Commerce
www.wlaxmdrchamber.com

Alhambra Chamber of Commerce
104 South First Street
Alhambra, CA 91801
626-799-2933
Number of Employees: 3

Jeffrey Owen, *President*
Owen Guenthard, *Executive Director*

American Indian Chamber of Commerce
4060 30th Street
San Diego, CA 92101

American Institute of Maring Underwriters
14 Wall Street
New York, NY 10005
212-233-0550

American Insurance Association
980 9th Street, Suite 2060
Sacramento, CA 94814
916-442-7617

Elizabeth Story, *Director of Public Affairs*

American Philanthropy Association
101 Santa Barbara Plaza
Los Angeles, CA 90008
213-295-3707

Anaheim Chamber of Commerce
100 South Anaheim Boulevard, Suite 300
Anaheim, CA 92805
714-758-0222

Asian Business Association Chamber of Commerce
4350 Executive Drive Suite 236
San Diego, CA 92121
858-458-6860

Australian American Chamber of Commerce
2525 Ocean Boulevard Suite F1
Corona del Mar, CA 92625
714-675-9588
Web Address: www.anzacc.com

Alan Cameron, *Executive Director*

Australian American Chamber of Commerce
2049 Century Park East - 19th Floor
Los Angeles CA 90067
213-469-6316
Web Address: www.anzacc.com

Helen Cameron, *Executive Director*

Big Bear Chamber of Commerce
630 Bartlett Drive
Big Bear, CA 92315
909-866-4607
Web Address: www.bigbearchamber.com

Rick Herrick, *President*

Black Business Chamber of Commerce
1201 Civic Center Drive West, Suite 205
Santa Ana, CA 90062
714-547-2646

Black Chamber of Commerce
1729 North euclid Avenue
San Diego, CA 92105
619-262-2121

Brea Chamber of Commerce
1 Civic Center Circle
Brea, CA 92821
714-529-4938
Web Address: www.breachamber.com

British American Chamber of Commerce
3517 Camino Del Rio South, Suite 209
San Diego, CA 92108-4028
858-485-6843

Burbank Chamber of Commerce
200 West Magnolia Boulevard
Burbank, CA 91502
818-559-4369
Web Address: http://burbank.acityline.com
Number of Employees: 5

Sue Wyninegar, *President*
Marianne Barrios, *Executive Director of Human Resources*

Catalina Island Visitors Bureau
1 Pleasure Pier
Avalon, CA 90704
310-510-1520
Web Address: www.catalina.com
Number of Employees: 6

Wayne Griffin, *President*

Chinese-American Chamber of Commerce, Orange County
8907 Wamer Avenue, #225
Huntington Beach, CA 92647
714-848-0043

Chula Vista Chamber of Commerce
233 4th Avenue
Chula Vista, CA 91910
619-420-6602
Web Address: www.chulavistachamber.org
Number of Employees: 5

Rod Davis, *Executive Director*

Community Associations Institute
23166 Los Alisos Boulevard, Suite 244
Mission Viejo, CA 92691-2812
714-380-7360
Web Address: www.caioc.com
Number of Employees: 300

Ross Feinberg, *President*

Corona Chamber of Commerce
904 East Sixth Street
Corona, CA 91719
909-737-3350
Web Address: www.coronachamber.org

Mary Conklin, *President*

Coronado Chamber of Commerce
1224 10th Street
Coronado, CA 92118
619-435-9260
Web Address: www.coronadochamber.com
Number of Employees: 4

Sherry Hamilton, *Executive Director*

Culver City Chamber of Commerce
4249 Overland Avenue
Culver City, CA 90230
310-287-3850
Web Address: www.culvercitychamber.com
Number of Employees: 5

Steven J. Rose, *President*

Del Mar Chamber of Commerce
1104 Camino del Mar
Del Mar, CA 92014
858-793-5292
Web Address: www.delmarchamber.org
Number of Employees: 2

Susan Tipton, *Executive Director*

East County Chamber of Commerce
201 South Magnolia Avenue
El Cajon, CA 92020
619-440-6161
Web Address: www.eastchamber.org
Number of Employees: 9

Terry Saverson, *President & CEO*

Easter Seal Society of Southern California
1801 East Edinger Avenue, Suite 190
Santa Ana, CA 92705-4749
714-834-1111
Web Address: www.essc.org
Number of Employees: 300

Mark Whitley, *President*
Terry McCormick, *VP for Human Resources*

Encinitas Chamber & Visitors Center
138 Encinatas Boulevard
Encinitas, CA 92024
760-753-6041
Number of Employees: 3

Judy Cunningham, *CEO*

Escondido Chamber of Commerce
720 North Broadway
Escondido, CA 92025
760-745-2125

Web Address: www.escondidochamber.org
Number of Employees: 5
David Ish, *Executive Director*

Filipino American Chamber of Commerce
PO Box 70
Bonita, CA 91908-0070
619-421-7222

Edna Conception, *President*

Fullerton Chamber of Commerce
219 East Commonwealth Avenue
Fullerton, CA 92832-0529
714-871-3100
Web Address: www.fullerton.org

Gail S. Dixon, *President*

Glendale Chamber of Commerce
200 South Louise Street
Glendale, CA 91205
818-240-7870
Number of Employees: 5

Charles E. Fenton, *President*
Sharon Beauchamp, *Executive Vice President*

Golden Triangle Chamber of Commerce
4350 Executive Drive, Suite 200
San Diego, CA 92121
858-558-1744
Web Address:
www.goldentrianglechamber.com

Greater Los Angeles Press Club
Hollywood Roosevelt Hotel
700 Hollywood Boulevard
Hollywood, CA 90028
213-469-8180

**Greater Los Angeles Visitors &
Convention Bureau**
633 West 5th Street, Suite 6000
Los Angeles, CA 90071
213-624-7300
Web Address: www.californiasedge.com

Greater Riverside Chamber of Commerce
3685 Main Street, Suite 350
Riverside, CA 92501
909-683-7100
Web Address: www.riverside-chamber.com

Dee Gipson-Jimenez, *Director*

Greater San Diego Chamber of Commerce
402 West Broadway, Suite 1000
San Diego, CA 92101
619-232-0124

**Hispanic Chamber of Commerce of
Orange County**
116-A West 4th Street, #5
Santa Ana, CA 92701
714-953-4289

Hollywood Chamber of Commerce
7018 Hollywood Boulevard
Hollywood, CA 90028
213-469-8311
Web Address: http://chamber.hollywood.com
Number of Employees: 12

Mary Lou Dudas, *President*

Hollywood Chamber of Commerce
Web Address: http://chamber.hollywood.com/

Donald Putrimas, *President*

Huntington Beach Chamber of Commerce
Web Address: www.hbchamber.org/home.html

Industry Manufacturers Council
255 North Hacienda Boulevard, Suite 100
City of Industry, CA 91744
626-968-3737
Web Address: www.ind-chmbr.com
Number of Employees: 5

Donald Sachs, *Executive Director*
Darlene Weber, *Office Manager*

International Chamber of Commerce of San Ysidro
522 East San Ysidro Boulevard
San Diego, CA 92173
619-428-9530

Jesse Navarro, *President*

Irvindale Chamber of Commerce
Web Address: www.irwindale.org
Jacque Haines, *Executive Director*

Irvine Chamber of Commerce
17200 Jamboree Road, Suite A
Irvine, CA 92714
949-660-9112

Italy-America Chamber of Commerce West
10350 Santa Monica Boulevard, Suite 210
Los Angeles, CA 90025
557-3017826-9898
Web Address: www.italchambers.net

Giuliano Lombardi, *President*

Japanese Chamber of Commerce of South California
244 San Pedro Street, Suite 504
Los Angeles, CA, 90012
213-626-3067

Akihiko Suzuki, *President*

LA Chamber of Commerce Job Fair
Web Address: www.trexproductions.com/lainfo.htm

Laguna Niguel Chamber of Commerce
30110 Crown Valley Parkway, Suite 201
Laguna Niguel, CA 92677
949-363-0136
Web Address: http://members.tripod.com/~lagunaniguel/index.html

Luis Sanchez, *President*
Debbie Newman, *Executive Director*

League of Women Voters of Los Angeles
6030 Wilshire Boulevard, Suite 301
Los Angeles, CA 90036
213-939-3535
Web Address: www.lwv.org

Long Beach Area Chamber Of Commerce
9900 Talbert Avenue, Suite 300
Fountain Valley, CA 92708
714-378-5505

Fran Hanckel, *President*

Long Beach Chamber of Commerce
Web Address: www.lbchamber.com

Los Angeles Chamber of Commerce
350 South Bixel Street
Los Angeles, CA 90051
213-580-7500

Malibu Chamber of Commerce
23805 Stuart Ranch Road, Suite 100
Malibu, CA 90265
310-456-9025
Web Address: www.malibu.org
Number of Employees: 3

Ani Dermenjian, *President*
Mary Lou Blackwood, *Executive Vice President*

Mid Valley Chamber of Commerce
14540 Victory Boulevard, Suite 100
Van Nuys, CA 91411
818-989-0300
Number of Employees: 5

Ron Feinstein, *President*
Nancy Hoffman, *Executive Vice President*

Monterrey Park Chamber of Commerce
700 El Mercado Avenue
Monterrey Park, CA
626-570-9429
Web Address: www.montereypark.com

Lucy Kelley, *President*

Natural Resources Defense Council
6310 San Vicente Boulevard
Los Angeles, CA 90048
213-934-6900
Web Address: www.nrdc.org

ASSOCIATIONS & NON-PROFIT

181

Newport Beach Chamber of Commerce
949-729-4400

Newport Harbor Area Chamber of Commerce
1470 Jamboree Road
Newport Beach, CA 92660
Web Address: http://newportbeach.com/nhacc/ NHACC.html

Richard R. Luehrs, *President*

North Hollywood Chamber of Commerce
Web Address: www.noho.org/default.htm

Oceanside Chamber of Commerce
928 N. Coast Highway
Oceanside, CA 92054
760-722-1534
Number of Employees: 6

David Nydegger, *CEO*

Old Town San Diego Chamber of Commerce
PO Box 82686
San Diego, CA 92138
619-291-4903
Web Address: www.otsd.com

Palm Springs Chamber of Commerce
190 West Amado Road
Palm Springs, CA 92262
760-325-1577
Web Address: www.pschamber.org

Pasadena Chamber of Commerce
865 East Del Mar
Suite 100
Pasadena, CA 91101
626-795-3355
Web Address: www.pasadena-chamber.org
Number of Employees: 7

Lynn Hess, *President*
Jon Catalani, *Director of Human Resources*

Pasadena Chamber of Commerce and Civic Association
117 East Colorado Boulevard, Suite 100
Pasadena, CA 91105
818-449-5419

Poland Chamber of Commerce
3111 Camino Del Rio North
San Diego, CA 92108
619-563-7052

Rancho Cucamonga Chamber of Commerce
8280 Utica Avenue, Suite 160
Rancho Cucamonga, CA 91730
909-987-1012
Web Address: www.ranchochamber.org

Redondo Beach Chamber of Commerce
200 North Pacific Coast Highway
Redondo Beach, *CA 90277*
310-376-6911
Web Address: www.redondochamber.org
Number of Employees: 3
Tom Spiglanin President
Marna Smeltzer, *CEO*

San Diego Convention & Visitors Bureau
401 B Street, Suite 1400
San Diego, CA 92101
619-232-3101
Web Address: www.sandiego.org
Number of Employees: 100

Reint Reinders, *CEO*
Althea Salas, *Director of Human Resources*

San Diego County Hispanic Chamber of Commerce
1250 6th avenue, Suite 904
San Diego, CA 92101
619-702-0790
Web Address: www.sdchcc.com
Number of Employees: 8

San Gabriel Chamber of Commerce
401 West Las Tunas Drive
San Gabriel, California 91776
626-576-2525
Web Address: www.SGChamber.com

San Pedro Peninsula Chamber of Commerce
390 West Seventh Street
San Pedro, CA 90731
310-832-7272
Web Address: www.sanpedrochamber.com
Number of Employees: 3

James Cross, *President*
Larry Cooper, *Executive Director*

Santa Ana Chamber of Commerce
1055 North Main Street, Suite904
Santa Ana, CA 92701
714-541-5353
Web Address: www.santaanacc.com/ index2.htm

Santa Clarita Valley Chamber of Commerce
23920 Valencia Boulevard, Suite 100
Suite 100
Santa Clarita, CA 91355

Tim Burkhart, *President*

Santa Fe Springs Chamber of Commerce
12016 East Telegraph Road, Suite 100
Santa Fe Springs, CA 90670
562-944-1616
Number of Employees: 8
Susan Croswell, *President*

Sierra Club
3435 Wilshire Boulevard, Suite 320
Los Angeles, CA 90010
213-387-4287
Web Address: www.sierraclub.org

Society of Certified Insurance Counselors
3630 North Hills Drive
Austin, TX 78731
512-345-7932
Web Address: www.scic.com/alliance

Solana Beach Chamber of Commerce
210 West Plaza Street
Solana Beach, CA 92075
858-755-4775
Web Address: www.solanabeachchamber.com
Number of Employees: 1

Elaine Tippett, *Executive Director*

Southern California Association of Philanthropy
315 West 9th Street, Suite 1000
Los Angeles, CA 90015
213-489-7303

Swedish-American Chamber of Commerce
550 West C Street, 17th Floor
San Diego, CA 92101-3568
619-595-1338
Number of Employees: 2

Helena Wallentin, *President*

United Agribusiness League
54 Corporate Park
Irvine, CA 92606-5105
949-975-1424
Number of Employees: 40

Ventura Chamber of Commerce
Web Address: www.ventura-chamber.org

Vietnamese Chamber of Commerce
9938 Bossa Avenue, Suite 216
Westminster, CA 92683
714-839-2257

West Covina Chamber of Commerce
811 South Sunset Avenue
West Covina, CA 91790
626-338-8496
Web Address: www.covina.org

John Fields, *Executive Director*
Reyna Del Haro, *Director of Human Resources*

West Hollywood Chamber of Commerce
8350 Santa Monica Boulevard, Suite 111
West Hollywood, CA 90069
213-650-2688
Number of Employees: 4

Michael-Jon Smith, *President*

Westchester, LA, Marina del Rey Chamber of Commerce
9800 South Sepulveda, Suite 214
Wstchester, CA 90045
310-821-0555
Web Address: www.wlaxmdrchamber.com

Richard Musella, *Executive Director*

Western Growers Association
17620 Fitch
Irvine, CA 92614
949-863-1000
Web Address: www.wga.org
Number of Employees: 225

David Moore, *President*
Diana DeWees, *Human Resources Manager*

Yorba Linda Chamber of Commerce
17670 Yorba Linda Boulevard
Yorba Linda, CA 92886
714-993-9537

ASSOCIATIONS & NON-PROFIT

Employment Tip

Very few association jobs appear in the local newspapers. Most other jobs are filled by word of mouth and networking. Now is the time to start your network. But don't tell everyone you are looking for a job because this will turn them off. Instead, tell them you are interested in, for example, writing for an association publication.

Banking & Finance

- Banks
- Mortgage Bankers
- Securities & Investments
- Credit Unions
- S & L's
- Management Consulting

W ith the elimination of many large corporate training programs of the 80's, Citizens Bank is still one of the few banks that offer a management training program. Even though we suggest candidates for the management training program to possess a strong background in Business Administration, Accounting, Economics or Finance, opportunities are not limited to just those degrees. Several of our post-trainees graduated with liberal arts degrees and even in education. One standard requirement for the management training program is a minimum 3.0 cumulative G.P.A. Upon successfully completing the management training program, typical positions are assistant branch manager, junior loan officer or junior auditor. Compensation for entry-level positions usually starts in the mid-20's. Advancement within the bank is not just based on education but rather on performance. If you feel you have an interest in pursuing a career in banking and finance, I suggest to maximize your time in and out of school. Many of our candidates are weeded out by the achievements or extracurricular activities they were involved with during school.

CITIZENS BANK/WASHINGTON

See Also: Accounting, Government
International

Quick Reference Web Sites & Job Hotlines

Aetna Capital Company
www.aetnacapital.com
American First Federal Credit Union
www.amerfirst.org
American Management Systems
www.amsinc.com
American Pacific State Bank
www.apsb.com
Analytic TSA Global Asset Management
www.analytic-tsa.com
Andersen Consulting
www.ac.com
Arthur Andersen
www.arthurandersen.com
Asian Pacific Bank
www.traders.net
Balboa Capitol Corp
www.balboacapital.com

Bank of Commerce
www.bankofcommerce.net
Baxter Credit Union
www.bch.org
BNC Mortgage
www.lonemortgage.com
Broadway Federal Bank
www.broadwayFed.com
BTA Advisory Group
www.standel.com
Cabrillo Federal
www.cabrrillofcu.com
California Korea Bank
www.ckb.net
California State Bank
www.calstatebank.com
Capital Guardian Trust Co.
www.americanfunds.com

Capital Research & Management Company
www.americanfunds.com
Citizens Business Bank
www.cbb.com
City National Bank
www.cityntl.com
Cruttenden Roth Incorporated
www.crut.com
Domain Associates
www.dimensionfunding.com
Downey Savings & Loan
www.downeysavings.com
Drake Beam Morin
www.dbm.com
East-West Bank
www.eastwest.com
Eldorado Bank
www.eldoradobank.com

Quick Reference Web Sites & Job Hotlines

Electronic Clearing House
www.echo-inc.com
Enterprise Partners
www.ent.com
Ernst & Young
www.ey.com
Evangelical Christian Cred Union
www.eccu.com
EVEREN Securities
www.everensec.com
Executive Service Corps
www.escsc.org
Fallbrook National Bank
www.fallbrooknationalbank.com
Family Savings Bank
www.blkbusiness-expo.com
Financial Federal
www.finacial21.com
First American Trust Company
www.firstam.com
First Quadrant Corp.
www.firstquadrant.com
Foothill Independent Bancorp
www.foothillindbank.com
Gage Marketing Group
www.gage.com
Gardiner & Rauen
www.gardine-raven.com
GBS Financial
www.gbsfinancial.com
Grant Thornton
www.gt.com
Great American Credit Union
www.greatamerican.org
Grossmont Bank
www.grossmontbank.com
Home Savings of America
www.homesavings.com
Impac Funding Corp
www.impaccompanies.com
IMPAC Integrated Systems
www.impac.com
Imperial Bank
www.imperialbank.com
Imperial Thrift & Loan Association
www.imperialthrift.com
Interfirst Capital Corp
www.interfirstcap.com
Itex Corporation
www.itex.com
J.D. Power and Associates
www.jdpower.com
John Hancock Financial Services
www.jhancock.com
Kline Hawkes California LP
www.klinehawkes.com
Koll Co/Strategic HR Services
www.totalemployee.com
Lease Express
www.leasex.com
Lee Hecht Harrison
www.careerlhh.com
Los Angeles National Bank
www.lanatlbank.com
Management Action Programs
www.mapconsulting.com
Manufacturers Bank
www.maubank.com
Marine National Bank
www.marinebank.com
Marwit Capital Corp. LLC
www.marwit.com

McDonnell Douglas Federal Credit Union
www.mdwfcu.org
Media Technology Ventures
www.mtventures.com
Merrill Lynch Private Client
www.merrill-lynch-ml.com
Met Life Pensions
www.metlife.com
Miramar Federal
www.miramarfcu.org
Mission Federal
www.missionfcu.org
National Bank of Southern California
www.scbnk.com
National Pacific Mortgage Corp
www.fha203kexpert.com
Nazarene Credit Union
www.nazarene.com
NWQ Investment Management Co.
www.nwq.com
Orange County Business Council
www.ocbc.org
Orange County Federal Credit Union
www.ocfcu.org
Orange County Teachers Federal Credit Union
www.octfcu.org
Pacific Crest Capital
www.paccrest.com
Pacific National Bank
www.pacificnationalbank.com
Pacific Thrift & Loan
www.pacthrift.com
PFF Bank & Trust
www.pffb.com
PIMCO Advisors Holdings L.P.
www.pimcoadvisors.com
PLG
www.plg.com
Point Loma Federal
www.plfcu.com
Price Waterhouse Coopers Consulting
www.pwc.global.com
Provident Investment Counsel
www.provnet.com
Republic Bank California
www.rbca.com
Right Management Consultants
www.right.com
Roger Engemann & Associates
www.secapl.com/rea
Roxbury Capital Management
www.roxcap.com
San Diego County Credit Union
www.sdccu.com
San Diego Teachers' Credit Union
www.sdtcu.org
Scripps Bank
www.scrippsbank.com
Silicon Valley Bank
www.sivio.com
SM&A
www.smawins.com
Smith Barney
www.smithbarney.com
Source Consulting
www.sourcesvc.com
South Western Federal Credit Union
www.swscu.com
Southern California Bank
www.scbank.com

SunAmerica
www.sunamerica.com
Sutro & Co.
www.sutro.com
The First American Financial Corporation
www.firstam.com
The Geneva Companies
www.genevaco.com
The TCW Group
www.tcw.com
Towers Perrin
www.towers.com
U.S. Trust Company of California
www.ustrust.com
Union Bank of California
www.uboc.com

United Services of America Federal
www.fedcu.org
University & State Employees
www.webmaster.usecu.org
Valutech
www.valutech.com
Waddell & Reed
www.waddell.com
Watson Wyatt Worldwide
www.watsonwyatt.com
Wedbush Morgan Securities
www.wedbush.com
Wescom Credit Union
www.wescom.com
William M. Mercer
www.mercer.com

Company Job Hotlines

Fallbrook National Bank
888-547-5600
First National Bank
619-233-5395
Grossmont Bank
619-623-3156
Imperial Bank
310-417-5606
Marine Corps West Federal
760-430-7511 ext1058
Mission Federal
619-546-2010
North County Bank
760-737-6677
Northern Trust Bank
213-346-1300
Pacific Thrift & Loan
818-883-6893 x214
Peninsula Bank of San Diego
619-525-7819
Point Loma Federal
619-495-3400
San Diego National Bank
619-233-1234 x337
San Diego Teachers' Credit Union
619-636-4292
Scripps Bank
619-456-2265
Union Bank
619-230-3771
United Services of AmericaFederal
619-693-9360 x567
University & State Employees
619-641-7555
Valle de Oro Bank
619-615-9677

Banks

Black Business Association
3550 West Wilshire Boulevard, Suite 816
Los Angeles, CA 90062
213-299-9560

1st Business Bank
2 Park Plaza, Suite 400
Irvine, CA 92614
949-474-1133
Number of Employees: 17

Rick Arredondo, *Vice President of Operations*

1st Business Bank
601 West Fifth Street
Los Angeles, CA 90071
213-489-1000
Number of Employees: 220

R. W. Kummer Jr., *CEO*
Rick Arredondo, *VP of Operations*

American Pacific State Bank
15260 Ventura Boulevard, Suite 1600
Sherman Oaks, CA 91403
818-382-1500
Web Address: www.apsb.com
Number of Employees: 160

Frank Ures Jr., *President*
David Vendetti, *Human Resources Manager*

Bank of Commerce
9918 Hibert Street
San Diego, CA 92131
619-232-6213
Web Address: www.usbank.com
Number of Employees: 230

Toby Reschan, *Operations Manager*
Ernest Ewin, *District Sales Manager*

Borrego Springs Bank
547 Palm Canyon Drive
Borrego Springs, CA 92004
760-767-5035
Web Address: www.borregospringsbank.com
Number of Employees: 20

Frank V. Riolo, *President*
Erin Hawkins, *Hiring Manager*

California Bank & Trust
4320 La Jolla Village Drive, Suite 355
San Diego, CA 92122
858-623-3190
Job Hotline: 619-623-3156
Number of Employees: 600

Robert Sarver, *CEO*
Karen Filimon, *Senior Vice President*

California Bank & Trust
402 West Broadway, Suite 190
San Diego, CA 92102
619-557-4900
Cindy Guillen, *Customer Service Manager*

California Commerce Bank
2029 Century Park East, 42nd Floor
Los Angeles, CA 90067
800-222-1234
Job Hotline: x 75653

Salvador Villar, *President*
Dennis Campos, *Director of Human Resources*

California Korea Bank
3530 Wilshire Boulevard, Suite 1800
Suite 1800
Los Angeles, CA 90010
213-385-0909
Web Address: www.ckb.net
Number of Employees: 265

Young Yoo, *President*

California State Bank
1201 Dove Street
Newport Beach, CA 92660-2841
949-851-9900
Web Address: www.calstatebank.com
Number of Employees: 25

Margaret Turner, *Human Resources Director*

Capital Bank of North County
2602 El Camino Real
Carlsbad, CA 92008
760-434-3344

Don L. Schempp, *President*
April Jacobs, *Operations Manager*
Mark Anderson, *Vice President of Sales*

Cathay Bancorp
777 North Broadway
Los Angeles, CA 90012
213-625-4700
Web Address: www.cathaybank.com
Number of Employees: 450

Dunson Cheng, *Chairman & President*
Marina Wong, *VP of Personnel*

Citizens Business Bank
2650 East Imperial Highway
Brea, CA 92821-6103
714-996-8150
Web Address: www.cbb.com
Number of Employees: 15

Mike Thompson, *Director of Human Resources*

Citizens Business Bank
110 East Wilshire Avenue
Fullerton, CA 92832-1900
714-773-0600
Web Address: www.cbb.com
Number of Employees: 6

Mike Thompson, *Director of Human Resources*

Citizens Business Bank
1201 East Katella Avenue
Orange, CA 92867-5061
714-288-5203
Number of Employees: 127

Kenneth J. Cosgrove, *President*
Geraldine Dyke, *Director of Personnel*

Citizens Business Bank
701 North Haven Avenue, Suite 350
Ontario, CA 91764
909-980-4030

D. Linn Wiley, *President*
Mike Thompson, *Human Resources Manager*

City National Bank
4275 Executive Square, Suite 101
La Jolla, CA 92037
858-642-4900
Web Address: www.cnb.com

Russel Goldsmith, *CEO*
Karen Flanders, *Employment Manager*
Terry Cook, *Assistant Vice President*

City National Bank
400 North Roxbury Drive
Beverly Hills, CA 90210
310-888-6000
Web Address: www.cityntl.com
Number of Employees: 400

Russell Goldsmith, *CEO*
Kate Durper, *Director of Personnel*
Jan GEringer, *Branch Manager*
Karen Flanders, *Employment Manager*

Coast Federal Bank
1000 Wilshire Boulevard
Los Angeles, CA 90017
213-362-2000
Job Hotline: 818-316-8730

Community Bank
100 East Corson Street
Pasadena, CA 91103
626—577-1700
Number of Employees: 310

John Getzelman, *President*
Bill Mead, *Director of Human Resources*

Community First National Bank
1234 East Main Street
El Cajon, CA 92021
619-593-3330
Job Hotline: 619-615-9677
Number of Employees: 30

William Ehler, *CEO*
Lillie Walsh, *Assistant Vice President*

Cuyamaca Bank
9955 Mission Gorge Road
Santee, CA 92071
619-562-6400
Number of Employees: 55

Bruce Ives, *President*
Dannie Ibach, *Hiring Manager*

Dai-Ichi Kangyo Bank of Calif.
555 West Fifth Street
Los Angeles, CA 90013
213-612-2700
Number of Employees: 100

Isao Arihara, *President*
Mary Beth Sosa, *Assistant Vice President*

Dana Niguel Bank NA
34180 Pacific Coast Highway
Dana Point, CA 92629-5000
714-661-4100
Number of Employees: 25

Robert A Regan, *President*

East-West Bank
415 Huntington Drive
San Marino, CA 91108
626-799-5700
Web Address: www.eastwest.com

Dominic Ng, *President*
Silvia Ross, *Director of Human Resources*

El Dorado Bank
135 Saxony Road
Encinitas, CA 92024
760-436-5226

Robert P. Keller, *CEO*
Human Resources contact: Paula Salat; 24012 Calle de la Plata, Suite 140; Laguna Hills, CA 92653

Eldorado Bank
32221 Camino Capistrano
San Juan Capistrno, CA 92675-3721
714-248-0100
Web Address: www.eldoradobank.com
Number of Employees: 15

Paula Salat, *Director of Human Resources*

BANKING & FINANCE

187

Eldorado Bank - Corporate Headquarters
24012 Calle De La Plata #150
Laguna Hills, CA 92653-3644
714-699-4344
Web Address: www.eldoradobank.com
Number of Employees: 500

Robert Keller, *CEO*
Elaine Crouch, *Senior VP for Human Resources*

Eldorado Bank - Huntington Bch
7777 Center Avenue
Huntington Beach, CA 92647-1160
714-895-2929
Web Address: www.eldoradobank.com
Number of Employees: 20

Paula Salat, *Director of Human Resources*

Eldorado Bank - Irvine & Newport
19200 Von Karman Avenue, Suite 140
Irvine, CA 92612-1540
949-756-1919
Web Address: www.eldoradobank.com
Number of Employees: 11

Eldorado Bank - Laguna Hills
24012 Calle De La Plata #140
Laguna Hills, CA 92653-3632
714-830-7440
Web Address: www.eldoradobank.com
Number of Employees: 10

Eldorado Bank - Monarch Beach
24034 Camino Del Avion
Dana Point, CA 92629-4002
714-248-4444
Web Address: www.eldoradobank.com
Number of Employees: 10

Eldorado Bank - Orange Office
2730 East Chapman Avenue
Orange, CA 92869-3237
714-771-3300
Web Address: www.eldoradobank.com
Number of Employees: 6

Eldorado Bank - San Clemente
115 Calle De Industrias
San Clemente, CA 92672-3858
714-248-2100
Web Address: www.eldoradobank.com
Number of Employees: 10

Fallbrook National Bank
130 West Fallbrook Street
Fallbrook, CA 92028
760-723-8811
Job Hotline: 888-547-5600
Web Address: www.fallbrooknationalbank.com
Number of Employees: 65

Tom Swanson, *President*
Patty Estrada, *Hiring Manager*

Far East National Bank
350 South Grand Avenue
Los Angeles, CA 90071
213-687-1200
Number of Employees: 150

Henry Hwang, *CEO*

Farmers & Merchants Bank of Long Beach
302 Pine Avenue
Long Beach, CA 90802
562-437-0011
Web Address: www.fmb-lb.com
Number of Employees: 550

George Quinde, *Administrative Assistant*

First Bank & Trust
16531 Bolsa Chica
Huntington Beach, CA 92647-0130
714-840-4681
Number of Employees: 20

Fred Jensen, *President*

First International Bank
318 Fourth Avenue
Chula Vista, CA 91910
619-425-5000

Jim Redman, *President*

First National Bank
401 West A Street
San Diego, CA 92101
619-233-5588
Job Hotline: 619-233-5395
Web Address: www.fnbsd.net
Number of Employees: 250

Leon H. Reinhart, *President*
Nancy Mackinnon, *Hiring Manager*

First Pacific National Bank
613 West Valley Parkway
Escondido, CA 92025
760-741-3312
Number of Employees: 15

Harvey L. Williamson, *President*
Margie Hanlin, *Customer Service/Operations Manager*

Foothill Independent Bancorp
510 South Grand Avenue
Glendora, CA 91741
626-963-8551
Web Address: www.foothillindbank.com
Number of Employees: 260

George Langley, *President*
Marjorie Luftenbacher, *Director of Human Resources*

Hanmi Bank
3660 Wilshire Boulevard, Penthouse A
Los Angeles, CA 90010
213-382-2200
Number of Employees: 100

Soo Bong Min, *President*
Jo Ann Kim, *Branch Manager*

Imperial Bank
695 Town Center Drive
Costa Mesa, CA 92626-1924
949-641-2200
Web Address: www.imperialbank.com
Number of Employees: 15

Terri Stidd, *Director of Human Resources*

Imperial Bank
701 B Street, Suite 600
San Diego, CA 92101
619-338-1500
Job Hotline: 310-417-5606
Web Address: www.imperialbank.com
Number of Employees: 25-30

Dino D'Auria, *Regional Vice President*
Kelly Keene, *Branch Manager*

Imperial Thrift & Loan Association
700 NorthCentral Avenue, Suite 600
Glendale, CA 91203
818-551-0600
Web Address: www.imperialthrift.com
Number of Employees: 141

George Haligowski, *Chairman & President*
Hiroko Miyake, *Director of Human Resources*

International City Bank
4493 Ruffin Road
San Diego, CA 92123
858-292-9100
Number of Employees: 15

Jane Netherton, *CEO*
Sheryl Hegg, *Operations Officer*

Long Beach Mortgage
1100 Town And Country Road
Orange, CA 92868-4600
714-541-5378

Jack Mayesh, *CEO*

Los Angeles National Bank
7005 Orangethorpe Avenue
Buena Park, CA 90621
714-670-2400
Web Address: www.lanatlbank.com
Number of Employees: 20

Henry Chen, *President & CEO*

Manufacturers Bank
701 B. Street, Suite 100
San Diego, CA 92101
619-544-3030
Web Address: www.maubank.com
Number of Employees: 10

Steve Espino, *Senior Vice President*

Manufacturers Bank
515 South Figueroa Street
Los Angeles, CA 90071
213-489-6200
Number of Employees: 300

Masato Kaneko, *Chairman & President*
Ed James, *Branch Manager*

Marine National Bank
18401 Von Karmen Avenue, Suite 100
Irvine, CA 92612
949-553-0260
Web Address: www.marinebank.com
Number of Employees: 55

Mark E Simmons, *President & CEO*

National Bank of Southern California
4100 Newport Place Drive
Newport Beach, CA 92660
949-863-2300
Web Address: www.scbank.com
Number of Employees: 175

Mark H. Stuenkel, *President*
Cheryl Rudin, *VP for Human Resources*

North County Bank
444 South Escondido Boulevard
Escondido, CA 92025
760-743-2200
Job Hotline: 760-737-6677
Number of Employees: 245

James M. Gregg, *CEO*
Lori Woolf, *Director of Human Resources*

Northern Trust Bank
4370 La Jolla Village Drive, Suite 1000
San Diego, CA 92122
858-597-2200
Job Hotline: 213-346-1300
Number of Employees: 22

Sam Brown, *Managing Director*
Hiring contact: Mr. Pina; 355 South Grand
Avenue, Suite 2600; Los Angeles, CA 90071

Pacific National Bank
4665 Macarthur Court
Newport Beach, CA 92660-1825
949-851-1033
Web Address: www.pacificnationalbank.com
Number of Employees: 130

Alan Barbieri, *President*

Peninsula Bank of San Diego
1322 Scott Street
San Diego, CA 92106
619-226-5444
Job Hotline: 619-525-7819
Number of Employees: 238

Larry Willette, *CEO*
Kathleen Silberman, *Human Resource Manager*

Preferred Bank
601 South Figueroa Street, Suite 2000
Los Angeles, CA 90017
213-891-1188
Number of Employees: 69

Li Yu, Chaiman, *President*
Stella Chan, *Branch Manager*

Republic Bank California N.A.
445 North Bedford Drive
Beverly Hills, CA 90210
310-281-4200
Web Address: www.rbca.com

John Lam, *Chairman & President*

San Diego National Bank
1420 Kettner Boulevard
San Diego, CA 92101
619-231-4989
Job Hotline: 619-233-1234 x337
Number of Employees: 200

Robert Horsman, *President/CEO*
Connie Reckling, *Vice President of Hiring*

Sanwa Bank California
1280 Fourth Avenue
San Diego, CA 92101
619-234-3511
Web Address: www.sanwa-bank-ca.com
Number of Employees: 11

Ken Pickle, Vice President, *Manager*
Sue Mystrom, *Personnel Manager*

Sanwa Bank California
601 South Figueroa Street
Los Angeles, CA 90017
213-896-7000
Job Hotline: 213-896-7214
Web Address: www.sanwa-bank-ca.com
Number of Employees: 500

Tom Takakura, *President*
Tony Ohrt, *Branch Manager*

Scripps Bank
5787 Chesapeake Court, Suite 101
San Diego, CA 92123
858-720-7149
Number of Employees: 35

Ronald J. Carlson, *CEO*
Nona Dobson, *Human Resources Administrator*

Scripps Bank
7733 Girard Avenue
La Jolla, CA 92037
858-456-2265
Job Hotline: 619-456-2265
Web Address: www.scrippsbank.com
Number of Employees: 20

Ronald J. Carlson, *CEO*
Jan Galloway, *VP for Customer Service*

Security First Bank
141 West Bastanchury Road
Fullerton, CA 92835-2501
714-870-2100
Number of Employees: 20

Robert Cambell, *CEO*

Silicon Valley Bank
18872 Macarthur Boulevard, Suite 100
Irvine, CA 92612-1450
949-252-1300
Web Address: www.sivio.com
Number of Employees: 25

Sharon Baronessa, *Director of Human Resources*

Silicon Valley Bank
9645 Scranton Road, Suite 110
San Diego, CA 92121
858-558-3808
Web Address: www.svbank.com
Number of Employees: 16

Ken Wilcox, *CEO*
Linda LeBeau, *Senior Vice President*

Southern California Bank
30000 Town Center Drive
Laguna Niguel, CA 92677-2046
714-495-3300
Web Address: www.scbank.com
Number of Employees: 30
Terry Owens, *President*
Cheryl Rudin, *Director of Personnel*

Southern California Bank
3800 East La Palma Avenue
Anaheim, CA 92807-1713
714-630-4500
Web Address: www.scbank.com
Number of Employees: 25
Larry Hartwig, *President*
Mitch Felde, *Director of Human Resources*

Southern Pacific Bank
23530 Hawthorne Boulevard, Suite 200
Torrance, CA 90025
310-442-3300
Web Address: www.spbank.com
Number of Employees: 150
John Getzelman, *President*
Vernon Nicolas, *Branch Manager*
Dave Hourigan, *Human Resource Manager*

Sunwest Bank
535 East 1st Street
Tustin, CA 92780-3352
714-730-4441
Number of Employees: 70

James Lesieur, *President*

Tokai Bank of California
4350 LaJolla Village Drive, Suite 100
San Diego, CA 92122
619-285-8130
Web Address: www.tokaibank.com
Number of Employees: 7
Len Sanghez, *Assistant Vice President*

Tokai Bank of California
300 South Grand Avenue
Los Angeles, CA 90071
213-972-0200
Web Address: www.tokai.com
Number of Employees: 420

Hirohisa Aoki, *President*
Marei Moto, *Branch Manager*

Union Bank
530 B Street, Suite 1200
San Diego, CA 92101
619-230-3904
Job Hotline: 619-230-3771
Number of Employees: 20

Takiro Moriguchi, *CEO*
Martha Mendez, *Assistant Vice President*

Union Bank of California
18300 Von Karman Avenue
Irvine, CA 92612-1057
949-553-7124
Number of Employees: 7

Union Bank of California
500 South Main Street
Orange, CA 92868
714-565-5500
Web Address: www.uboc.com

Ted Bremner, *Manager*

United National Bank
2090 Huntington Drive
San Marino, CA 91108
626-457-8588
Number of Employees: 128

Edward Lo, *Chairman & President*
Susan Uyo, *Personnel Officer*

US Bank
1385 East Vista Way
Vista, CA 92084
760-631-2500
Web Address: usbank.com
Number of Employees: 20
Lisa Hebb, *Branch Manager*

US Bank
1251 Fourth Street
Santa Monica, CA 90401
310-394-9611
Job Hotline: Ext 1 & Ext 5

Aubrey Austin, *President*
Adella Alverez, *Human Resource Manager*

Wells Fargo Bank
401 B Street
San Diego, CA 92101
877-479-3557
Job Hotline: 800-392-4780

West Coast Bancorp
4770 Campus Drive, Suite 250
Newport Beach, CA 92660-1833
949-442-9330
Number of Employees: 5

John B. Joseph, *President*

Credit Unions

American First Federal Credit Union
700 North Harbor Boulevard
La Habra, CA 90631
562-691-1112
Web Address: www.amerfirst.org
Number of Employees: 170

Robert Street, *President & CEO*
Sandy Sam, *Human Resource Manager*

Associates Mechanical Federal
4410 Glacier Avenue, Suite 103
San Diego, CA 92120
619-282-6855
Number of Employees: 2

Patricia A. Bagalini, *CEO*

Baxter Credit Union
1452 Alton Parkway
Irvine, CA 92714
949-250-2200
Web Address: www.bch.org
Lisa Wilson, *Director of Human Resources*

El Cajon Federal
266 South Magnolia Avenue, Suite 101
El Cajon, CA 92020
619-579-0941
Number of Employees: 7
Claudia Sperry, *CEO*

Escondido Federal Credit Union
201 North Broadway
Escondido, CA 92025
760-741-4606
Number of Employees: 6
Jeanine Acevedo, *CEO*
Mary Jane Sparks, *Assistant Manager*

Evangelical Christian Cred Union

1150 North Magnolia Avenue
Anaheim, CA 92801
714-828-3228
Web Address: www.eccu.com
Number of Employees: 95

Mark Holbrook, *President*

Financial 21

440 Beech Street
San Diego, CA 92101
619-233-3101
Web Address: www.financial21.com
Number of Employees: 25

Gene Roberts, *CEO*
Jeanne O'Falon, *Human Resources Director*

Great American Credit Union

2701 Midway Drive
San Diego, CA 92110
619-224-3521
Web Address: www.greatamerican.org

Sharon Updike, *CEO*

Grossmont Schools Federal Credit Union

1069 Graves Avenue, Suite 102
El Cajon, CA 92021
619-588-1515
Web Address: www.gsfcu.org
Number of Employees: 9

Julie Glance, *CEO*

Grossmont Sharp Healthcare Federal Credit Union

9000 Wakarusa, Building H, Suite 17
La Mesa, CA 91942
619-644-4244
Number of Employees: 12

Joann Gibson, *CEO*

Kearny Mesa Federal Credit Union

4285 Ruffin Road
San Diego, CA 92123
858-292-4851

James Goulet, *CEO*

Marine Corps West Federal Credit Union

MCX Complex
Camp Pendleton, CA 92055
760-430-7511
Job Hotline: 760-430-7511 ext1058
Number of Employees: 150

L. L. De Carlo, *CEO*
Penny Sandifer, *Human Resources Administrator*

McDonnell Douglas Federal Credit Union

PO Box 1220
Huntington Beach, CA 92647-1220
714-375-8000
Web Address: www.mdwfcu.org
Number of Employees: 178

Bob Talboy, *President*
Michelle Cooper, *VP for Human Resources*

Miramar Federal Credit Union

9494 Miramar Road
San Diego, CA 92126
858-695-9494
Web Address: www.miramarfcu.org
Number of Employees: 30

Bill Moyer, *CEO*
Sissy Davis, *Human Resources Manager*

Mission Federal Credit Union

5785 Oberlin Drive
San Diego, CA 92121
858-546-2000
Job Hotline: 858-546-2010
Web Address: www.missionfcu.org
Number of Employees: 300

Ron C. Martin, *CEO*
Janet Madden, *Vice President of Human Resources*

Nazarene Credit Union

1770 East Lambert Road
Brea, CA 92822-4000
714-671-6963
Web Address: www.nazarene.com
Number of Employees: 60

Mendell Thompson, *President*
Terri Snyder, *Human Resources Manager*

North County Federal Credit Union

17045 Via del Campo
San Diego, CA 92127
858-487-1880
Web Address: www.northcountyfcu.org
Number of Employees: 20

Patricia A. Hamilton, *CEO*
Katie Denney, *Vice President of Finance*

Orange County Federal Credit Union

1211 East Dyer Road
Santa Ana, CA 92705
714-755-5900
Web Address: www.ocfcu.org
Number of Employees: 130

Judith A McCartney, *President*
Avery Robinson, *Human Resources Manager*

Orange County Teachers Federal Credit Union
2115 North Broadway
Santa Ana, CA 92706
714-258-4000
Web Address: www.octfcu.org
Number of Employees: 503

Rudy Hanley, *President*

Paradise Valley Federal Credit Union
2805 East Seventh Street
National City, CA 91950
619-475-4314
Number of Employees: 14

John G. Pressler, *CEO*
Terrie Lewis, *Operations Manager*

Point Loma Federal Credit Union
9420 Farnham Street
San Diego, CA 92123
858-495-3400
Web Address: www.plcu.com
Number of Employees: 120

Ted Dennis, *CEO*
Janet Dopp, *Human Resource Manager*

San Diego County Credit Union
9985 Pacific Heights Boulevard
San Diego, CA 92121
858-453-2112
Job Hotline: 858-453-6941
Web Address: www.sdccu.com
Number of Employees: 420

Rod Calvao, *CEO*
Jane Long, *Human Resource Manager*

San Diego Firefighters Federal Credit Union
10509 San Diego Mission Road, Suite A
San Diego, CA 92108
619-283-5477
Web Address: www.sdffcu.org/sdffcu
Number of Employees: 9

Ed Daley, *CEO*
Wendy Tanishita, *Hiring Supervisor*

San Diego Medical Federal Credit Union
2365 Northside Drive, Suite C120
San Diego, CA 92108
619-641-1100
Number of Employees: 18

Paul Lewis, *CEO*
Susanne Fawaya, *CCO*

San Diego Municipal Credit Union
5555 Mildred Street
San Diego, CA 92110
619-297-4835
Web Address: www.sdmcu.org

Number of Employees: 60
Steven M. Powell, *CEO*
Becky Romas, *Vice President of Human Resources*

San Diego Teachers' Credit Union
4545 Murphy Canyon Road
San Diego, CA 92123
858-495-1600
Job Hotline: 619-636-4292
Web Address: www.calcoastcu.org

James L. McPheters, *CEO*
Sarah Bender, *Vice President Human Resources*

Santel Federal Credit Union
5890 Pacific Center Boulevard
San Diego, CA 92111
858-450-4400
Web Address: www.santel.org

Marla K. Shepard, *CEO*
Ray Kewle, *Human Resource Manager*
Send resumes to: Attn: Ray Kewle; Santel Federal Credit Union; PO Box 919006; San Diego, CA 92191-9006

South Western Federal Credit Union
901 East Whittier
La Habra, CA 90631
562-694-8296
Web Address: www.swfcu.com
Number of Employees: 43

Laura Poore, *President*
Cathy Witt, *Personnel Manager*

United Services of America Federal Credit Union
9889 Erma Road
San Diego, CA 92131
858-693-9360
Job Hotline: 619-693-9360 x567
Web Address: www.usafedcu.org
Number of Employees: 95

Martin Cassell, *CEO*
Amanda Myers, *Human Resource Manager*

University & State Employees Credit Union
3131 Camino del Rio North, Suite 230
San Diego, CA 92108
619-641-7555
Job Hotline: 619-641-7555
Web Address: www.usecu.org
Number of Employees: 60

Linda L. Baughman, *CEO & President*
Amanda Ligato, *Assistant VP of Human Resources*

Wescom Credit Union
750 The City Drive South, Suite 140
Orange, CA 92868-4940
714-667-0426
Web Address: www.wescom.com
Number of Employees: 310

Curtis Maki, *Director of Human Resources*

Wescom Credit Union
6301 Beach Boulevard #180
Buena Park, CA 90621-2840
714-739-0712
Web Address: www.wescom.com
Number of Employees: 310

Wescom Credit Union
111 Pacifica, Suite 160
Irvine, CA 92618-3311
949-727-3770
Web Address: www.wescom.com
Number of Employees: 310

Federal Savings Bank

American Savings Bank/Washington Mutual
17877 Von Karmen Avenue
Irvine, CA 92623
949-252-4883
Number of Employees: 3

Kaerry Killinger, *President*

Broadway Federal Bank
4835 West Venice Boulevard
Los Angeles, CA 90019
213-931-1886
Web Address: www.broadwayFed.com
Number of Employees: 150

Paul Hudson, *President*
Ed Lockridge, *Branch Manager*

Community Commerce Bank
5444 East Olympic Boulevard
Los Angeles, CA 90022
213-888-0065
Number of Employees: 160

William Lasher, *President*
Peggy Vargas, *Branch Manager*

Del Amo Savings Bank FSB
3422 Carson Street
Torrance, CA 90503
310-214-1491
Job Hotline: x 386
Number of Employees: 40

Nicholas Barakonski, *President*
Patrick Mautner, *Branch Manager*
Lillian Komata, *Personnel Manager*

Downey Savings & Loan
3501 Jamboree Road
Newport Beach, CA 92660
949-854-0300
Web Address: www.downeysavings.com
Number of Employees: 600

James W. Lokey, *President*
JoLene M. Bryant, *Director of Personnel*
Lender for real estate, construction and development, educational, unsecured, and installment loans. Also provides full-service investment brokerage, trust, mortgage, and insurance -home, life, and automobile- services at 30 of its 52 retail deposit branches.

Downey Savings & Loan Assn FA
PO Box 6000
Newport Beach, CA 92658-6000
949-854-3100
Web Address: www.downeysavings.com
Number of Employees: 1316

James W Lokey, *President*
Jolene Bryant, *Human Resources Director*

Family Savings Bank
3683 Crenshaw Boulevard
Los Angeles, CA 90016
213-295-3381
Web Address: www.blkbusiness-expo.com
Number of Employees: 15

Wayne Bradshaw, *President*
Ruth Johnson, *Branch Manager*

Fidelity Federal Bank FSB
4565 Colorado Boulevard
Los Angeles, CA 90039
818-241-6215

Richard Greenwood, *CEO*
Deb Matalin, *Director of Human Resources*

First Federal Savings and Loan
225 North Barranca Avenue
West Covina, CA 91791
626-859-4200
Barrett Andersen, *President*

First Global Bank
3109 West Olympic Boulevard
Los Angeles, CA 90006
213-739-0633
Harvey Ha, *President*
Steve King, *Vice President*

FirstFed Financial Corp.
401 Wilshire Boulevard, Second Floor
Santa Monica, CA 90401
310-319-6000
Number of Employees: 500
Babette Heimbuch, *CEO*
Jacqueline Kittaka, *Director of Human Resources*

Fullerton Savings & Loan Assn
200 West Commonwealth Avenue
Fullerton, CA 92832-1837
714-447-6200
Number of Employees: 87

Carl W Gregory, *President*
Beth Hill, *Personnel Manager*

Glendale Federal Bank
201 West Lexington Drive, 1st Floor
Glendale, CA 91203
818-500-2000
Web Address: www.glendalefederal.com
Number of Employees: 3,200

Steve Trafton, *CEO*
Sharon Winston, *Director of Human Resources*

Golden Security Thrift & Loan
30 W Valley Boulevard
Alhambra, CA 91801
626-289-5788
Number of Employees: 15

William Guleserian, *CEO*
Ophelia Delos Santos, *Director of Human Resources*

Highland Federal Bank FSB
601 South Glenoaks Boulevard, Suite 200
Burbank, CA 91502
818-848-4265
Number of Employees: 130

Stephen Rippe, *President*
Patty Petrovick, *Director of Human Resources*

Malaga Bank SSB
2514 Via Tejon
Palos Verdes Estates, CA 90274
310-375-9000
Number of Employees: 42
Eric Allan, *President*
Trishia McElroy, *Branch Manager*
Alison Warren, *Human Resource Manager*

Pacific Thrift & Loan
21031 Ventura Boulevard, Suite 100
Woodland Hills, CA 91364
818-883-6893
Job Hotline: 818-883-6893 x214
Web Address: www.pacthrift.com
Number of Employees: 72
Joel Schultz, *CEO*
Cathy Carrillo, *Director of Human Resources*

People's Bank of California
5900 Wilshire Boulevard
Los Angeles, CA 90036
310-273-8750
Number of Employees: 250
Rudy Guenzel, *President*
Larissa Gudelman, *Branch Manager*
Stephanie Shaw, *Human Resource Manager*

PFF Bank & Trust
350 South Garey Avenue
Pomona, CA 91766
909-623-2323
Web Address: www.pffb.com
Number of Employees: 500

Larry Rinehart, *President*
Marty Levy, *Director of Human Resources*
Audrey Brewart, *Human Resources Manager*

Quaker City Federal S&L Assoc.
7021 Greenleaf Avenue
Whittier, CA 90602
562-907-2200
Web Address: www.quakerbank.com
Number of Employees: 185

Rick McGill, *President*
Pat Strong, *Human Resource Director*

Royal Finance & Loan
11107 West Olympic Boulevard
West Los Angeles, CA 90064
310-479-1666

John Tonoyan, *President*
Steve Duffield, *Branch/Human Resource Manager*

Standard Savings Bank
228 West Garvey Avenue
Monterey Park, CA 91754
626-280-1688

John Lee, *President*
Gorden Chen, *Branch Manager*

Trust Savings Bank
638 South Atlantic Boulevard
Monterey Park, CA 91754
626-576-8800

Marina Wang, *President*

Western Financial Savings Bank
23 Pasteur
Irvine, CA 92618
949-727-1000
Number of Employees: 1200

Ernest S. Rady, *President*
Anne Fitzgerald, *Director of Personnel*

Financial Companies

Aames Financial Corporation
350 South Grand Avenue, 42nd Floor
Los Angeles, CA 90071
888-355-7712
Web Address: www.aames.net

Aetna Capital Company
2555 East Chapman Avenue, Suite 612
Fullerton, CA 92831-3621
714-449-2095
Web Address: www.aetnacapital.com
Number of Employees: 48

American Express Financial Advisors
101 Main Street, Suite 2B
Huntington Beach, CA 92648-8118
714-536-3664
Number of Employees: 50

Julie Davis, *Project Manager*

American Express Financial Advisors
8910 University Center Lane, Suite 200
San Diego, CA 92122
858-535-1331
Web Address: www.americanexpress.com
Number of Employees: 100
Suzanne Cadwallader, *Vice President of Finance*
Danielle Flaherty, *Recruiting Manager*

American International Marketing
501 North Brookhurst Street, Suite 216
Anaheim, CA 92801-5203
714-490-7900
Web Address: www.aimassoc.com
Number of Employees: 35

Analytic TSA Global Asset Management
700 South Flower, Suite 2400
Los Angeles, CA 90017
213-688-3015
Web Address: www.analytic-tsa.com
Number of Employees: 16
Gregory McMurran, *CIO*
Susan Delasuente, *Human Resources Administrator*

Asian Pacific Bank
1221 East Dyer Road, Suite 125
Santa Ana, CA 92705-5634
714-644-5661
Web Address: www.traders.net
Number of Employees: 10
Charles Shong, *President*
Stacy Guyton, *Director of Human Resources*

Asset Exchange Network/Morris Financial
3303 Harbor Boulevard, Suite K5
Costa Mesa, CA 92626
949-374-0052
Number of Employees: 24
George Morris, *Chairman*

Balboa Capitol Corp
2010 Main Street, Suite 1150
Irvine, CA 92614-7216
949-756-0800
Web Address: www.balboacapital.com
Number of Employees: 80
Shawn Giffin, *President*

Bastion Capital Corporation
1999 Avenue of the Stars, Suite 2960
Los Angeles, CA 90067
310-788-5700
Number of Employees: 9

Daniel Villenueva, *Chairman*

BIR Business Brokers
21707 Hawthorne Boulevard, Suite 303
Torrance, CA 90503
310-316-3316
Web Address: www.businessbrokers.com
Number of Employees: 56

Henry Miller, Owner, *Manager*

BIR Business Equity Services
11500 Olympic Boulevard, Suite 400
Los Angeles, CA 90064
310-914-8350
Number of Employees: 2

Thomas C. Brafford, *President*

Bradford & Marzec
333 South Hope Street, Suite 4050
Los Angeles, CA 90071
213-687-9170
Number of Employees: 27

Ted Bradford, *CIO*
Z. Marzec, *CIO*

Brantley Venture Partners
1920 Main Street, Suite 820
Irvine, CA 92614
949-475-4242
Number of Employees: 10

Jim Bergman, *General Partner*

Brentwood Venture Capital
11150 Santa Monica Boulevard, Suite 1200
Los Angeles, CA 90025
310-477-7678
Web Address: www.brentwoodvc.com
Number of Employees: 30

G. Bradford Jones, *General Partner*
Helen Lottenberg, *Human Resource Manager*

California Business Investments
18301 Ventura Boulevard
Tarzana, CA 91356
818-345-0145
Number of Employees: 6

Bill Gordon, *President*
Jim Baker, *Vice President*

Canterbury Capital Services
660 Newport Center Drive, Suite 300
Newport Beach, CA 92660-6404
949-721-9580
Number of Employees: 35

Alan T Beimfohr, *President & CEO*

Capital Guardian Trust Co.
333 South Hope Street, 53rd Floor
Los Angeles, CA 90071
213-486-9200
Web Address: www.americanfunds.com
Number of Employees: 2,000

Richard Barker, *CIO*
Louis Weaver, *Recruiter*

CDC Small Business Finance Corp
265 South Anita Drive, Suite 130
Orange, CA 92868-3310
714-978-1182
Number of Employees: 31

Kim Buttemer, *Director of Human Resources*

Century Financial Partners
1999 Avenue of the Stars, Suite 32590
Los Angeles, CA 90067
310-277-8182
Number of Employees: 5

Russell Armstrong, *President*
Tisno Onggara, *Managing Partner*
Judy Friedman, *Human Resource Manager*

CIGNA Financial Advisors
18500 Von Karman Avenue, Suite 400
Irvine, CA 92612-0504
949-660-0661
Web Address: www.cigna.com
Number of Employees: 601

Regina Gill, *Regional Operations Supervisor*

Consolidated Funding
24332 Los Arboles Drive
Laguna Niguel, CA 92677-2195
714-363-7141
Number of Employees: 20

Kimberlee D. Feld, *President*

Cramblit & Carney
550 South Hope Street, Suite 1800
Los Angeles, CA 90071
213-614-6800
Number of Employees: 17

Ron Hartwick, *President*
Richard Carney, *CIO*

Crosspoint Venture Partners
18552 MacArthur Boulevard, Suite 400
Irvine, CA 92612
949-852-1611

Robert Hoff, *General Partner*

Delta Asset Management
333 South Grand Avenue, Suite 1450
Los Angeles, CA 90071
213-626-1300
Number of Employees: 7

Robert Sandroni, *CIO*

Dimension Funding
17748 Sky Park Circle, Suite 240
Irvine, CA 92614-6420
949-250-0585
Number of Employees: 25

Mike Wagner, *President*

Dimensional Fund Advisors
1299 Ocean Avenue, 11th Floor
Santa Monica, CA 90401
310-395-8005
Web Address: www.dfafunds.com
Number of Employees: 50

Rex Sinquefield, *CIO*
Paula Guhring, *Office/Human Resource Manager*

Domain Associates
650 Town Center Drive, Suite 1830
Costa Mesa, CA 92626
949-434-6227
Web Address: www.dimensionfunding.com

Richard Schneider, *General Partner*

Electronic Clearing House
28001 Dorothy Drive
Agoura Hills, CA 91301-2697
818-706-8999
Web Address: www.echo-inc.com
Number of Employees: 76

Joel M. Barry, *President*
Luana Jackman, *Director of Personnel*
Provider of services and equipment for credit card approval and processing to more than 14,000 commercial clients -including over 6,000 U-Haul dealers-. Also makes money-order processing terminals for a US Postal Service. Its XpressCheX subsidiary offers check guarantee services.

First American Trust Company
2161 San Joaquin Hills Road
Newport Beach, CA 92660-6596
949-719-4500
Web Address: www.firstam.com
Number of Employees: 30
Jerald Lewis, *President & CEO*
Carolyn Knandel, *Vice President for Human Resources*

First American Trust Company
421 North Main Street
Santa Ana, CA 92702-0267
714-647-6171
Web Address: www.firstam.com
Number of Employees: 30

Jerald Lewis, *President & CEO*
Carolyn Knandel, *VP for Human Resources*

First Financial Planners
17772 17th Street, Suite 108
Tustin, CA 92780-1944
714-573-8193
Number of Employees: 5

Derek McLean, *President*

First Pacific Advisors
11400 West Olympic Boulevard, Suite 1200
Los Angeles, CA 90064
310-473-0225
Job Hotline: Ext 436
Number of Employees: 20

Robert Rodriquez, *CIO*
Sherry Sasaki, *Human Resource Manager*

First Quadrant Corp.
800 East Colorado Boulevard
Pasadena, CA 91101
626-683-4172
Web Address: www.firstquadrant.com
Number of Employees: 75

Robert Arnott, *Managing Partner*
Cindy Rigney, *Director of Human Resources*

Forrest Binkley & Brown
840 Newport Center Drive, Suite 480
Newport Beach, CA 92660
949-729-3222
Number of Employees: 10

Jeffrey Brown, *Partner*

Gardiner & Rauen
2540 Huntington Drive, Suite 200
San Marino, CA 91108
213-283-7531
Web Address: www.gardine-raven.com
Number of Employees: 4

Patrick Rauen, *President*

George D. Bjurman & Associates
10100 Santa Monica Boulevard, Suite 1200
Los Angeles, CA 90067
310-553-6577
Web Address: www.bjurman.com

O. Thomas Barry III, *CIO*
Cartney Rivera, *Human Resource Manager*

German American Acquisition Group
11755 Wilshire Boulevard, Suite 1800
Los Angeles, CA 90025
818-991-1447
Number of Employees: 7

Gunter Backes, *Managing Partner*

Heller First Capital Corporation
600 Anton Boulevard, Suite 950
Costa Mesa, CA 92626-7147
949-444-9000
Number of Employees: 20

Hotchkis & Wiley
800 West Sixth Street, Fifth Floor
Los Angeles, CA 90017
213-362-8888
Number of Employees: 200

J. Hotchkis, *CIO*
Margie Callaghan, *Director of Human Resources*

J.D. Power and Associates
30401 Agoura Road
Agoura Hills, CA 91301
818-889-6330
Web Address: www.jdpower.com
Number of Employees: 400

Steve Goodall, *President*
Margie Long, *Director of Personnel*

John Hancock Financial Services
8 Corporate Park, Suite 110
Irvine, CA 92606-5117
949-474-4266
Web Address: www.jhancock.com
Number of Employees: 30

Lisa Bracie, *Recruiter*

John Hancock Financial Services
3 Imperial Promenade, Suite 100
Santa Ana, CA 92707-5901
714-557-2373
Web Address: www.jhancock.com
Number of Employees: 3000

Kayne Anderson Investment Management
1800 Avenue of the Stars, Second Floor
Los Angeles, CA 90067
310-556-2721
Number of Employees: 90

Allan Rudnick, *CIO*
Lea Leshalev, *Director of Human Resources*

Kline Hawkes California LP
11726 San Vicente Boulevard, Suite 300
Los Angeles, CA 90049
310-442-4700
Web Address: www.klinehawkes.com
Number of Employees: 20
Frank Kline Jr., *Managing Partner*
Debra Ramsey, *Human Resource Assistant*

Lauren Dahl & Associates
205 South Beverly Drive, Suite 212
Beverly Hills, CA 90212
310-275-4620
Number of Employees: 11

Stephen Dahl, *Owner*

LBA Properties
4440 Von Karman Avenue, Suite 150
Newport Beach, CA 92660
949-833-0400
Number of Employees: 15

Phil A. Belling, *President*
Karryn Anderson, *Director of Personnel*
Real estate investment trust that owns, manages, leases, and develops office and industrial properties throughout Southern California. Its portfolio includes 32 office properties, 15 industrial properties, and one retail center and is headquartered in Newport Beach, CA.

Levine Leichtman Captial Partners
345 North Maple Drive, Suite 304
Beverly Hills, CA 90210
310-275-5335
Number of Employees: 14

Arthur Levine, *General Partner*

Marwit Capital Corp.
180 Newport Center Drive, Suite 200
Newport Beach, CA 92660
949-640-6234
Web Address: www.marwit.com

Matthew L. Witte, *President*

Media Technology Ventures
746 West Adams Boulevard
Los Angeles, CA 90089
213-743-2938
Web Address: www.mtventures.com

Jonathan Funk, *General Partner*

Met Life Pensions
1 City Boulevard West, Suite 700
Orange, CA 92868-3608
714-939-4660
Web Address: www.metlife.com

Resa Teter, *Director of Human Resources*

Northern Trust Bank
355 South Grand Avenue, Suite 2600
Los Angeles, CA 90071
213-346-1300

Lynn Danielson, *CIO*

NWQ Investment Management Co.
2049 Century Park East, 4th Floor
Los Angeles, CA 90067
213-624-6700

Web Address: www.nwq.com
Number of Employees: 59
David Polak, *CIO*
Sandra Shapiro, *Corporate Administrator*

O'Connor & Company Securities
3 Civic Plaza, Suite 100
Newport Beach, CA 92660-5923
949-717-2000
Number of Employees: 20

William J O'Connor, *President*

Orange County Commercial Development Council
12640 Knott Street
Garden Grove, CA 92841-3902
714-897-6670
Number of Employees: 60

Marsie Mata, *Director of Human Resources*

Oxford Bioscience Partners
650 Town Center Drive, Suite 810
Costa Mesa, CA 92626
949-754-5719
Number of Employees: 10

Edmund Olivier, *General Partner*

Pacific Alliance Capital Management
445 Figueroa Street, Fifth Floor
Los Angeles, CA 90071
213-236-7133
Luke Mazur, *CIO*

Pacific Crest Capital
30343 Canwood Street, Suite 100
Agoura Hills, CA 91301
818-865-3300
Web Address: www.paccrest.com
Number of Employees: 62

Gary Wehrle, *President*
Naureen McMillan, *Director of Personnel*
Holding company for Pacific Crest Investment and Loan, which has 4 branches in Beverly Hills, Encino, San Diego, and San Francisco. It offers savings accounts and CDs, but not traditional banking services, such as checking accounts or safe-deposit boxes.

Pacific Financial Research
9601 Wilshire Boulevard, Suite 800
Beverly Hills, CA 90210
310-247-3939
Number of Employees: 25

James Gipson, *President*
Michael Kromm, *Operations Director*

Payden & Rygel
333 South Grand Avenue, 32nd Floor
Los Angeles, CA 90071
213-625-1900
Number of Employees: 90

John Isaacson, *CIO*
Carmen LaRue, *Operations Director*

Peregrine Ventures
12400 Wilshire Boulevard, Suite 240
Los Angeles, CA 90025
310-458-1441

Gene Miller, *General Partner*

PIMCO Advisors Holdings
800 Newport Center Drive, Suite 100
Newport Beach, CA 92660
949-717-7022
Web Address: www.pimcoadvisors.com
Number of Employees: 284

William D. Cvengros, *President*
James G. Ward, *Director of Personnel*
Provider of investment management for corporate and public pension funds, endowments, and foundations through seven financial services affiliates.

Preferred Credit Corporation
3347 Michelson, Suite 400
Irvine, CA 92612
949-474-0700
Number of Employees: 351

Todd A. Rodriguez , *President*
Allison Sardarian, *Director of Personnel*
Provident Investment Counsel
300 North Lake Avenue
Pasadena, CA 91101
626-449-8500
Web Address: www.provnet.com
Number of Employees: 150

Robert Kommerstad, *CIO*
Janet Whaley, *Director of Human Resources*

Roger Engemann & Associates
600 North Rosemead Boulevard
Pasadena, CA 91107
626-351-9686
Web Address: www.secapl.com/rea
Number of Employees: 85

Roger Engemann, *CEO*
Susan Pippert, *Human Resources Coordinator*

Roxbury Capital Management
100 Wilshire Boulevard, Suite 600
Santa Monica, CA 90401
310-917-5600
Web Address: www.roxcap.com
Number of Employees: 50
Anthony Browne, *CIO*
Phyllis Nelsen, *Human Resource Manager*

Stephen Wolff
20 Corporate Park, Suite 150
Irvine, CA 92606-5116
949-253-0928
Number of Employees: 26

Stephen Wolff, *President*

The AFP Group
5 Corporate Park, Suite 250
Irvine, CA 92606-5113
949-852-8846
Number of Employees: 180

Dora Loaiza, *Director of Human Resources*

The First American Financial Corporation
1st American Way
Santa Ana, CA 92702
714-558-3211
Web Address: www.firstam.com
Number of Employees: 50

Gary Kermotp, *President*
Carolyn Knandel, *Director of Personnel*

The TCW Group
865 South Figueroa Street, Suite 1800
Los Angeles, CA 90017
213-244-0000
Web Address: www.tcw.com
Number of Employees: 40
Thomas Larkin Jr., *CIO*

Topa Equities Ltd.
1800 Avenue of the Stars, Suite 1400
Los Angeles, CA 90067
310-203-9199
Number of Employees: 50

John Anderson, *President*
Virginia Flores, *Director of Human Resources*

Transamerica Investment Services
1150 South Olive Street
Los Angeles, CA 90015
213-742-3559
Number of Employees: 40

Gary Rolle, *CIO*
Susan Hughes, *Vice President & CFO*

Trident Capital
11150 Santa Monica Boulevard, Suite 320
Los Angeles, CA 90025
310-444-3840
Web Address: www.tridentcap.com
Number of Employees: 4

Rockwell Schnabel, *General Partner*

TriEqua Pension Services
2699 White Road, Suite 251
Irvine, CA 92614-6258
949-975-1990
Number of Employees: 20

Bryan Murphy, *President*

TVM Techno Venture Management
650 Town Center Drive, Suite 1350
Costa Mesa, CA 92626
949-545-6400

Randall Lunn, *Managing Partner*

U.S. Business Brokers
2540 Huntington Drive, Suite 109
San Marino, CA 91108
626-285-5653
Number of Employees: 7

Quinchee Leong, *CEO*
Miklos Varga, *Director of Human Resources*

U.S. Trust Company of California
515 South Flower Street, Suite 2700
Los Angeles, CA 90071
213-861-5000
Web Address: www.ustrust.com
Number of Employees: 130

Robert Raney, *CIO*
Barbara Akopian, *Manager of Human Resources*

Union Venture Corp.
445 South Figueroa Street
Los Angeles, CA 90071
213-236-4092

Robert Clarke, *President*

US Trust Co of California NA
600 Anton Boulevard, Suite 150
Costa Mesa, CA 92626-7147
949-438-3600
Number of Employees: 200

Valena Ramos, *Director of Human Resources*

Ventana
18881 Von Karman Avenue, Suite 350
Irvine, CA 92612
949-476-2204
Number of Employees: 20

Thomas O. Gephart, *Managing Partner*

Waddell & Reed
2501 East Chapman Avenue, Suite 250
Fullerton, CA 92831-3135
714-526-4674
Web Address: www.waddell.com

Bob Cohen, *Manager*

WFS Financial
23 Pasteur Road
Irvine, CA 92618
949-753-3000
Number of Employees: 1848

Ernest S. Rady, *President*
Anne Fitzgerald, *Director of Personnel*
Originator and purchaser of fixed rate consumer auto loans from over 5,000 new and used car dealers. Its primary competitors include General Motors Acceptance Corporation, Ford Motor Credit Company, and Chrysler Credit Corporation.

William E. Simon & Sons
10990 Wilshire Boulevard, Suite 500
Los Angeles, CA 90024
310-914-2410
Web Address: www.wesandsons.com
Number of Employees: 50

William E. Simon Jr., *Executive Director*

Wilshire Asset Management
1299 Ocean Avenue, Suite 700
Santa Monica, CA 90401
310-451-3051
Web Address: www.wilshire.com

Thomas Stevens, *CIO*

Worldwide Investment Network
26691 Plaza, Suite 100
Mission Viejo, CA 92691-6347
714-348-4150
Number of Employees: 50

Tony Reguero, *CEO*

Mortgage Banking

BNC Mortgage
1063 McGaw Avenue
Irvine, CA 92614
949-260-6000
Web Address: www.lonemortgage.com
Number of Employees: 30

Evan R. Buckley, *President*
Marles Crow, *Director of Personnel*
Finance company specializing in the origination and sale of subprime residential mortgages.

Columbia Mortgage Corporation
1513 East Chapman Avenue
Fullerton, CA 92834-4075
714-871-6800
Number of Employees: 24

Leo R Kubeska, *President*

Countrywide Home Loans
155 North Lake Avenue
Pasadena, CA 91101
626-304-8400
Job Hotline: 800-881-4968
Web Address: www.countrywide.com
Number of Employees: 1480

Angelo Mozilo, *CEO*

First Alliance Mortgage Company
17305 Von Karman Avenue
Irvine, CA 92614-6203
949-224-8500
Number of Employees: 450

Brian Chisick, *President*
Cindy Foster, *Director of Personnel*
Originator, purchaser, seller and servicer of non-conventional mortgage loans secured by first mortgages on single-family homes. It reaches customers through telemarketing as well as retail offices throughout the US. In addition, it has a UK subsidiary.

Impac Funding Corp
20371 Irvine Avenue, Building A
Santa Ana Heights, CA 92707-5651
714-556-0122
Web Address: www.impaccompanies.com
Number of Employees: 275

Joseph R. Tomkinson, *Chairman*
Denise Anderson, *Director of Personnel*

Long Beach Financial Corporation
1100 Town & Country Road, Suite 1600
Orange, CA 92868
714-835-5743
Number of Employees: 350

M. Jack Mayesh, *President*
Elizabeth Wood-Snell, *Director of Personnel*
Originator, purchaser, and seller of sub-prime residential mortgage loans secured by one-to-4-family residences through its wholly-owned subsidiary Long Beach Mortgage Company.

NAB Asset Corporation
19200 Von Karman Avenue, Suite 950
Irvine, CA 92618
949-475-4444
Number of Employees: 10

Charles E. Bradley Sr., *President*
Scott Kline, *Director of Personnel*
Financial services company primarily engaged in the mortgage lending and retail automobile sales businesses. The company generally deals with commercial and consumer financial services related to housing, household goods, durable goods, and automobiles.

National Pacific Mortgage Corp
2150 South Towne Center Place
Anaheim, CA 92816-6008
714-978-6762
Web Address: www.fha203kexpert.com
Number of Employees: 250

Steve Ginder, *President*

New Century Financial Corporation
18400 Von Karman Avenue, Suite 1000
Newport Beach, CA 92612
949-440-7030
Number of Employees: 462

Robert K. Cole, *President*
Gordon Shaffer, *Director of Personnel*
Provider of subprime mortgage loans through its subsidiary, New Century Mortgage. The company's retail division markets its services directly to individuals, while the wholesale division obtains loans from independent brokers.

Sea Breeze Mortgage
1973 South State College Boulevard
Anaheim, CA 92806-6115
714-634-7500
Number of Employees: 22

Len Hamilton, *President*

Temple-Inland Mortgage Corp
17731 Irvine Boulevard, Suite 110
Tustin, CA 92780-3235
714-838-6677
Web Address: www.pimc.com
Number of Employees: 842
Ellen Skaggs, *Branch Manager*

Virtual Mortgage Network
4590 MacArthur Boulevard, Suite 175
Newport Beach, CA 92660
949-252-0700
Number of Employees: 162

Michael A. Barron, *President*
Lee Shorey, *Director of Personnel*
Independent mortgage broker and mortgage bank. Provides video-conferencing systems that let home buyers shop for mortgages from real estate offices, provides credit histories, payment preferences, and completes and submits loan applications.

Securties & Investments

A.G. Edwards & Sons
8880 Rio San Diego Drive, Suite 1150
San Diego, CA 92108
619-298-9700
Web Address: www.agedwards.com

Timothy Cronin, *Corporate Vice President*
Denise Ruiz, *Human Resource Manager*

AG Edwards & Sons
19800 MacArthur Boulevard Avenue, Suite 100
Irvine, CA 92612-1566
949-756-0353
Number of Employees: 1000

Bear Stearns & Company
1999 Avenue of the Stars, 32nd Floor
Los Angeles, CA 90067
310-201-2600
Web Address: www.bearstearns.com
David Pollack, *Resident Sr. Managing Director*
Susan Mearns, *Human Resource Manager*

Charles Schwab & Company
450 A Street, Suite 1000
San Diego, CA 92101
800-435-4000
Job Hotline: 415-627-7000
Web Address: www.schwab.com
Number of Employees: 40

Charles Schwab & Company
355 South Grand Avenue, Suite 170
Los Angeles, CA 90071
800-435-4000
Web Address: www.schwab.com
John Yoshitake, *Branch Manager*

Crowell Weedon & Company
One Wilshire Boulevard, Suite 2600
Los Angeles, CA 90017
213-620-1850
Number of Employees: 200
Donald Crowell, CEO, *Managing Partner*
Steve Brixey, *Director of Retail Sales*

Cruttenden Roth Incorporated
18301 Von Karman Avenue, Suite 100
Irvine, CA 92626
949-757-5700
Web Address: www.crut.com
Number of Employees: 220

Walter Cruttenden III, *Chairman*

Dean Witter Reynolds
575 Anton Boulevard, Suite 100
Costa Mesa, CA 92626
949-241-3100
Number of Employees: 70

Brad Saunders, *Human Resources Manager*
Sam LoPresti, *Human Resources Manager*

Dean Witter Reynolds
24260 El Toro Road
Laguna Hills, CA 92654-2309
714-587-2500
Number of Employees: 50

Dean Witter Reynolds
800 Newport Center Drive, Suite 700
Newport Beach, CA 92658-8936
949-760-2400
Number of Employees: 40

Mary Ellen Pike, *Human Resources Manager*
Dee Markos, *Human Resources Manager*

Dean Witter Reynolds
1221 East Dyer Road
Santa Ana, CA 92799-5275
714-549-7400

Dean Witter Reynolds
601 South Figueroa Street, 29th Floor
Los Angeles, CA 90017
213-362-4600

Michael Noble, Sr. VP, *Regional Director*

Dreyfus Brokerage Services
6500 Wilshire Boulevard, 9th Floor
Los Angeles, CA 90048
310-276-0200
Job Hotline: 310-276-2765
Web Address: www.dreyfus.com
Number of Employees: 150

Steven Wallace, *President*
George Agyare, *Human Resource Manager*

EVEREN Securities
620 Newport Center Drive, Suite 130
Newport Beach, CA 92658-8730
949-476-5100
Web Address: www.everensec.com
Number of Employees: 50

David Hudson, *Operations Manager*

EVEREN Securities
2400 Katella Avenue, Suite 1000
Anaheim, CA 92805-2911
714-956-4230
Number of Employees: 50

Frank Munoz, *Operations Manager*

Financial Network Investment Corporation
2780 Skypark Drive, Suite 300
Torrance, CA 90505
310-326-3100
Number of Employees: 180

Miles Gordon, *President*
Kristin Quinn, *Director of Human Resources*

Frederick Capital Corporation
5000 Birch Street, Suite 3000W
Newport Beach, CA 92660-2127
949-476-3720
Number of Employees: 300

Dolliver Frederick, *President*

GBS Financial
15233 Ventura Boulevard, Suite 404
Sherman Oaks, CA 91403
818-788-6210
Web Address: www.gbsfinancial.com
Number of Employees: 2

Don Gloisten, *President*

Gilford Securities
550 Newport Center Drive #C-197
Newport Beach, CA 92660-7011
949-852-7000
Number of Employees: 150

Cynthia Brown, *Operations Manager*

Great Western Financial Securities
9301 Corbin Avenue
Northridge, CA 91324
818-725-0234

James Overholt, *President*

Imperial Capital
150 South Rodeo Drive, Suite 100
Beverly Hills, CA 90212
310-246-3700
Job Hotline: Ext 3711

Randy Wooster, *CEO*
Mark Wild, *Human Resource Manager*

Independent Advantage Financial
330 Washington Boulevard, 8th Floor
Marina del Rey, CA 90292
310-821-1600
Number of Employees: 45

Lennie Gzesh, *Sales Director*

Interfirst Capital Corp
2401 East Katella, Suite 65
Anaheim, CA 92806
714-738-5483
Web Address: www.interfirstcap.com
Number of Employees: 65

Mark Bolinger, *Manager*

JB Oxford Holdings
9665 Wilshire Boulevard
Beverly Hills, CA 90212
310-777-8888
Web Address: www.jboxford.com
Number of Employees: 400

Stephen Rubenstein, *CEO*
Maxine Woods, *Recruiter*

M.L. Stern & Co.
8350 Wilshire Boulevard
Beverly Hills, CA 90211
213-658-4400
Number of Employees: 200

Milford Stern, *President*
Maxine Stern, *Vice President*

Merrill Lynch & Co
24422 Avenue De La Carlota #400
Laguna Hills, CA 92653-3634
714-859-2950
Number of Employees: 49800

Merrill Lynch & Co
1065 North Pacificenter Drive #100
Anaheim, CA 92806-2131
714-237-7800
Number of Employees: 49800

Merrill Lynch Pierce Fenner & Smith
701 B Street, Suite 2400
San Diego, CA 92101
619-699-3700
Web Address: www.ml.com
Number of Employees: 75

Dave Cormier, *District Recruiter*

Merrill Lynch Pierce Fenner & Smith
350 South Grand Avenue, Suite 2700
Los Angeles, CA 90071
213-627-7900
Number of Employees: 150

Rod Hagenbuch, *Resident VP*
Jay Brown, *Administrative Manager*

Merrill Lynch Private Client
4695 macArthur Boulevard
Newport Beach, CA 92662-0640
949-955-6000
Number of Employees: 43300

Max Hampton, *Human Resources Manager*
Joann D'amico, *Human Resources Manager*

Merrill Lynch Private Client
3010 Old Ranch Parkway, Suite 150
Seal Beach, CA 90740-2750
562-493-1300
Web Address: www.ml.com
Number of Employees: 26

David Klmansky, *CEO*
Bill Fallon, *Branch Manager*

Merrill Lynch Private Client Group
19200 Von Karman Avenue, Suite 1000
Irvine, CA 92612-1540
949-752-7900
Number of Employees: 430

Morgan Stanley Dean Witter
2677 North Main Street
Santa Ana, CA 92705-6623
714-836-5181
Web Address: www.deanwitter.com
Number of Employees: 60

Lisa Sanchez, *Operations Manager*

Morgan Stanley Dean Witter
5297 Priestly Drive, Suite 110
Carlsbad, CA 92008
760-931-4600
Web Address: www.deanwitter.com
Number of Employees: 33

Charles Ferges, *Branch Manager*
Arlene Austreng, *Manager's Assistant*

Mutual Service Corporation
428 Greencraig Road
Los Angeles, CA 90049
310-471-4471

Larry Roberts, *Manager*

PaineWebber
4675 MacArthur Court # 100
Newport Beach, CA 92658-8050
949-752-0211
Number of Employees: 16000

PaineWebber
620 Newport Center Drive #900
Newport Beach, CA 92660-6420
949-760-5308
Number of Employees: 16000

PaineWebber
1100 West Town & Country Road #1000
Orange, CA 92868-4625
714-973-6000

PaineWebber
725 South Figueroa Street, Suite 4100
Los Angeles, CA 90017
213-972-1577

Michael Davis, *Division Manager*

Prudential Securities
4695 MacArthur Court #900
Newport Beach, CA 92658-7910
949-752-2280

Dick Donovan, *Branch Manager*

Prudential Securities
777 South Figueroa Street, 47th Floor
Los Angeles, CA 90017
213-486-5200
Number of Employees: 100

Jim Thilking, *Branch Manager*

Quick & Reilly
200 Newport Center Drive, Suite 12
Newport Beach, CA 92658-7866
949-760-1334
Number of Employees: 1100

Brian Reily, *Human Resources*

San Clemente Securities
1031 Calle Recodo, Suite B
San Clemente, CA 92673-6269
714-366-8800
Number of Employees: 20

Cooke Christopher, *President*

Sentra Securities/Spelman & Company
2355 Northside Drive, Suite 200
San Diego, CA 92108
619-640-9090
Web Address: www.sentraspelman.com
Number of Employees: 120

Richard Voltman, *CEO*
Dave Fischer, *Director of Recruiting*
Sarah Scott, *Human Resources Manager*

Smith Barney
1100 West Town & Country Road, Suite 1400
Orange, CA 92863-1493
714-835-3100
Web Address: www.smithbarney.com

Nancy Kunesh, *Branch Administrator*

Smith Barney
24022 Calle de la Plata, Suite 100
Laguna Hills, CA 92653
949-206-5000
Web Address: www.smithbarney.com

Smith Barney
15260 Ventura Boulevard, Suite 1950
Sherman Oaks, CA 91403
818-907-3700

Gerrold Eberhardt, *Division Director*
Elizabeth Fehmel, *Generalist*

SunAmerica
1 SunAmerica Center
1999 Avenue of the Stars, 37th Floor
Los Angeles, CA 90067
310-772-6000
Web Address: www.sunamerica.com
Number of Employees: 300

Eli Broad, *CEO*

BANKING & FINANCE

Sutro & Co.
11150 Santa Monica Boulevard, Suite 1500
Los Angeles, CA 90025
310-914-0718
Job Hotline: 310-914-0732
Web Address: www.sutro.com
Number of Employees: 55

Thomas Weinberger, *Executive Vice President*
Susan Stone, *Administrative Manager*

Titan Value Equities Group
8001 Irvine Center Drive, Suite 710
Irvine, CA 92618-2917
949-453-4999
Number of Employees: 70

Steven McGinnis, *President*
Jerry Duhobie, *Human Resources Director*

Wedbush Morgan Securities
1000 Wilshire Boulevard
Los Angeles, CA 90017
213-688-8000
Web Address: www.wedbush.com
Number of Employees: 400

Edward Wedbush, *President*
Jill Lance, *Director of Human Resources*

Zahorik Co.
2700 East Foothill Boulevard, Suite 201
Pasadena, CA 91107
818-792-0835
Number of Employees: 75

James Stracka, *President*

Management Consulting

American Consulting Group
3185 Airway Avenue, Suite J
Costa Mesa, CA 92626-4601
949-556-2640
Web Address: www.amergroup.com
Number of Employees: 40

Peter J. Becker, *CEO*

American Management Systems
1455 Frazee Road, Suite 315
San Diego, CA 92108
619-291-8500
Web Address: www.amsinc.com
Number of Employees: 10

American Management Systems
333 South Hope Street, Suite 110
Los Angeles, CA 90071
213-613-5400
Web Address: www.amsinc.com
Number of Employees: 60

Rob Hupp, *Vice President*
Carol Bates, *Manager of Recruiting*

Andersen Consulting
18500 Von Karman Avenue, Suite 1100
Irvine, CA 92612-0504
949-757-3500

Dale Fraza, *Managing Partner*

Andersen Consulting
3131 Camino del Rio North, Suite 400
San Diego, CA 92108
619-610-1700
Web Address: www.ac.com
Number of Employees: 35

Randy Coulfhard, *Associate Partner*
Dana Builbeux, *Human Resources Manager*
*Hiring contact: Dana Builbeux, Human Resources
Manager; 2101 Rosecranz Avenue, Suite 3300; El
Segundo, CA 90247*

Andersen Consulting
2101 Rosecrans Avenue, Suite 3300
El Segundo, CA 90245
310-726-2700
Web Address: www.ac.com
Number of Employees: 800
Douglas Cunningham, *Office Managing Partner*

Aon Consulting
707 Wilshire Boulevard, Suite 5700
Los Angeles, CA 90017
213-630-2900
William Xanthos, *Executive Vice President*

Arthur Andersen
633 West Fifth Street, Suite 3200
Los Angeles, CA 90071
213-614-6500
Job Hotline: 213-614-7579
Web Address: www.arthurandersen.com
Dick Poladian, *Managing Partner*
Gayle Montgomery, *Director of Human Resources*

AT Kearney
600 Anton Boulevard, Suite 1000
Costa Mesa, CA 92626-7147
949-445-6800

BTA Advisory Group
1001 Dove Street, Suite 240
Newport Beach, CA 92660-2815
949-833-9800
Web Address: www.standel.com
Number of Employees: 50
Jill Boocock, *Human Resources Manager*

Buck Consultants
1801 Century Park East, Suite 500
Los Angeles, CA 90067
310-282-8232
Web Address: www.buckconsultants.com
Number of Employees: 60

Jon King, *Office Manager*
Ester VArela, *Director of Human Resources*

Communispond
4665 MacArthur Court, Suite 280
Newport Beach, CA 92660-1856
949-851-9200
Number of Employees: 150

Drake Beam Morin
100 Bayview Circle, Suite 5500
Newport Beach, CA 92660-2985
949-854-2045
Web Address: www.dbm.com
Number of Employees: 200

Bill Giezendamner, *Regional Sales Manager*

Drake Beam Morin
6701 Center Drive West, Suite 1100
Los Angeles, CA 90045
310-665-1105
Web Address: www.dbm.com

Bylle Snyder, *VP Operations & Administration*
John Davis, *Sales Manager*
Lynn Farr, *Human Resource Manager*

Edu-Tech Industries
151 Kalmus Drive, Suite K-2
Costa Mesa, CA 92626
949-540-7660
Web Address: www.interliance.com
Number of Employees: 30

Gloria Kamph, *President*

Elan International
620 Newport Center Drive, 11th Floor
Newport Beach, CA 92660-6420
949-721-6644
Number of Employees: 20

Lucia DeGarcia, *President*

Employee Support Systems Co
309 North Rampart Street, Suite A
Orange, CA 92868-1857
714-978-7915
Number of Employees: 23
Norman Honeycutt, *President*

Executive Service Corps
520 South Lafayette Park Place, Suite 210
Los Angeles, CA 90057
213-381-2891
Web Address: www.escsc.org
Number of Employees: 5
Megan Cooper, *Executive Director*

Financial Strategies Group
4400 Macarthur Boulevard, 5th Floor
Newport Beach, CA 92660-2031
949-955-7959
Number of Employees: 36

Kenneth L Nicolas, *President*

Gage Marketing Group
3620 Birch Street, 1st Floor
Newport Beach, CA 92660-2624
949-553-1400
Web Address: www.gage.com
Number of Employees: 1500

Doug Reeves, *General Manager*

IMPAC Integrated Systems
3300 Irvine Avenue, Suite 308
Newport Beach, CA 92660-3108
949-724-1579
Web Address: www.impac.com
Number of Employees: 1500

Incentive Associates
22972 Mill Creek Drive
Laguna Hills, CA 92653
714-581-3708
Number of Employees: 32

Wayne Wright, *President*

Itex Corporation
2900 South Bristol, Suite C-205
Costa Mesa, CA 92626
949-437-0300
Web Address: www.itex.com
Number of Employees: 60

Lori Gaines, *Regional Manager*

Karl Newman Training Innovations
PO Box 6445
Laguna Niguel, CA 92607-6445
714-363-5275
Number of Employees: 30

Karl Newman, *President*

KForce
879 West 190th Street, Suite 300
Gardena, CA 90248
310-323-9337
Job Hotline: 813-251-1700
Web Address: www.kforce.com
Number of Employees: 30
Joseph Gendron, *Regional Vice President*

Koll Co/Strategic HR Services
5000 Birch Street, Suite 8000
Newport Beach, CA 92660-2158
949-852-9555
Web Address: www.totalemployee.com
Number of Employees: 100

John Hermann, *President HR*

Lease Express
30012 Ivy Glenn Drive, Suite 200
Laguna Niguel, CA 92677-5005
714-363-3700
Web Address: www.leasex.com
Number of Employees: 20
David Emmes, *President*

Lee Hecht Harrison
2415 Campus Drive, Suite 250
Irvine, CA 92612-1598
949-250-9541
Web Address: www.careerlhh.com
Number of Employees: 300

Lorraine Bouknight, *Office Manager*

London Associates International
18062 Irvine Boulevard, Suite 200
Tustin, CA 92780-3328
714-505-0873
Number of Employees: 25

Dr. Ray William London, *Chairman*

Louis Kravitz & Associates
15760 Ventura Boulevard, Suite 910
Encino, CA 91436-3017
818-995-6100
Number of Employees: 68

Louis Kravitz, *President*
John Clancy, *Director of Human Resources*

Management Action Programs
4725 Hazeltine Avenue
Sherman Oaks, CA 91423
818-380-1177
Web Address: www.mapconsulting.com

Jim Wichterman, *President*
Kimberly House, *Director of Human Resouces*

Maritz Performance Improvement
333 City Boulevard West, Suite 2100
Orange, CA 92868-2924
310-217-4658
Number of Employees: 7000

Mark Langan, *Director of Human Resources*

P. Murphy & Associates
4405 Riverside Drive, Suite 105
Burbank, CA 91505
818-841-2002
Number of Employees: 250

Phyliss Murphy, *President*

PLG
4590 Macarthur Boulevard, Suite 400
Newport Beach, CA 92660-2027
949-833-2020
Web Address: www.plg.com
Number of Employees: 60

Theodore U. Marston, *President*
Brandy Stone, *Office Manager*

Price Waterhouse Coopers Consulting
350 South Grand Avenue
Los Angeles, CA 90071
213-356-6224
Web Address: www.pwcglobal.com
Number of Employees: 80

James McCoy, *Partner-in-charge*

Richard Chang Associates
15265 Alton Parkway, Suite 300
Irvine, CA 92618-2320
949-727-7477
Web Address: www.richardychang.com
Number of Employees: 35

Richard Y Chang, *President & CEO*

Right Associates
2 North Lake Avenue, Suite 1030
Pasadena, CA 91101
626-577-4448
Web Address: www.right.com
Number of Employees: 12

Tim Dorman, *Executive Vice President*
Virginia Braun, *Director of Human Resources*

Right Management Consultants
3333 Michelson Drive, Suite 400
Irvine, CA 92612-1684
949-222-4000
Web Address: www.right.com
Number of Employees: 1200

Peter J Leets, *Managing Principal*

SM&A
4695 MacArthur Court, 8th Floor
Newport Beach, CA 92660
949-975-1550
Web Address: www.smawins.com
Number of Employees: 110

Steven Myers, *President & CEO*

The Geneva Companies
5 Park Plaza, 19th Floor
Irvine, CA 92623-9599
949-756-2200
Web Address: www.genevaco.com
Number of Employees: 300

Robert Kuhn, *President*
William Ricci, *Personnel Director*

Towers Perrin
2010 Main Street, Suite 1050
Irvine, CA 92614-7206
949-253-5200
Web Address: www.towers.com
Number of Employees: 4000

Lawrence A Wangler, *Principal*

Towers Perrin
1925 Century Park East, Suite 1500
Los Angeles, CA 90067
310-551-5600
Number of Employees: 300

Peter Hursh, *Managing Director*
Tina Keren, *Executive Assistant*

Valutech
30021 Tomas, Suite 250
Rch Snta Margarita, CA 92688-2128
714-888-1006
Web Address: www.valutech.com
Number of Employees: 25

Sam Wheeler, *President*

Warner Group
5950 Canoga Avenue, Suite 600
Woodland Hills, CA 91367
818-710-8855
Web Address: www.twg@warnergroup.com

Howard Goodman, *CEO*
Bende Ancurcs, *Director of Human Resources*

Watson Wyatt Worldwide
1 Park Plaza, Suite 930
Irvine, CA 92614-5999
949-474-4955
Number of Employees: 4000

Tami Lambert, *Human Resources Manager*

Watson Wyatt Worldwide
15303 Ventura Boulevard, Suite 700
Sherman Oaks, CA 91403
818-906-2631
Web Address: www.watsonwyatt.com
Number of Employees: 100

Paul Mee, *Vice President Western Region*
Tami Lambert, *Diretor of Human Resources*

William M. Mercer
1100 West Town & Country Road #1500
Orange, CA 92868-4658
714-648-3300
Web Address: www.mercer.com
Number of Employees: 7000

Barbara Slevcove, *Human Resources Director*

William M. Mercer
777 South Figueroa, Suite 2000
Los Angeles, CA 90017
213-346-2200
Web Address: www.mercer.com
Number of Employees: 200

Roy Gonella, *Office Head*
Juana Lauren, *Director of Human Resources*

California Small Business Association
5300 Beethoven Street
Los Angeles, CA 90066
310-306-4540

Orange County Business Council
2 Park Plaza, Suite 100
Irvine, CA 92614-5904
949-476-2242
Web Address: www.ocbc.org
Number of Employees: 25

Stan Oftelie, *President*

Women in Business
7060 Hollywood Boulevard, Suite 614
Los Angeles, CA 90028
213-461-2936

Further References

• Associations •

American Finance Association
44 West 4th Street, Suite 9-190
New York, NY 10012
212-998-0370
*Web Address: www.cob.ohio-state.edu/dept/
fin/journal/afabout.html*
*To study and promote the knowledge about
financial economics.*

Academy of Marketing Science
University of Miami - School of Business
Administration
Coral Gables, Florida 33124
305-284-6673
Advance knowledge and standards of marketing science.

America's Community Bankers
900 19th Street N.W. Suite 400
Washington, D.C. 23336
(202) 857-3100
Web Address: www.acbankers.org
Furthers thrift and home ownership.

American Bankers Association
1120 Connecticut Avenue, N.W.
Washington, D.C. 20036
202-663-5000
Web Address: www.naba.com
Enhance role of commercial bankers.

American Business Association
292 Madison Avenue, 4th Floor
New York, NY 10017
212-949-5900
Web Address: www.aba.org
Provides financial servies to businesses.

BANKING & FINANCE

American Business Women's Association
9100 Ward Parkway
P.O. Box 8728
Kansas City, MO 64114-0728
816-361-6621
Web Address: www.abwahq.org
Supports and promotes women in business.

American Financial Services Association
919 18th Street, 3rd Floor
Washington, D.C. 20006
202-296-5544
Web Address: www.americanfinsvcs.com
Encourages financing for useful purposes at reasonable rates.

Associated Credit Bureaus
1090 Vermont Avenue, N.W., #200
Washington, D.C. 20005-4905
202-371-0910
Web Address: www.acb-credit.com
Maintains and collects credit reports.

Association for Investment Management and Research
5 Boar's Head Lane
P.O. Box 3668
Charlottesville, VA 22903
804-977-6600
Web Address: www.aimr.com/aimr.html
Investment analysis.

Association for Management Consulting Firms
521 5th Avenue, 35th Floor
New York, New York 10175
212-697-9693
Web Address: www.amcf.org
Provides managerial services.

Bank Administration Institute
1 North Franklin
Chicago, Illinois 60606
800-323-8552
Web Address: www.bai.org
Educational and advisory services for banks.

Bank Marketing Association
1120 Connecticut Avenue, N.W.
Washington, D.C. 20036
202-663-5268
Web Address: www.bmanet.org
Provides marketing education, information, and services to financial services industry.

Banker's Association for Foreign Trade
2121 K Street, N.W., Suite 701
Washington, D.C. 20037
202-452-0952
Promotes and improves international banking and trade.

Center for International Private Enterprise
1615 H Street, N.W.
Washington, D.C. 20062
202-463-5901
Web Address: www.cipe.org
Promotes international business growth.

Chief Executives Organization
5430 Grosvenor Lane, Suite 210
Bethesda, MD 20814
301-564-9614

Consumers Bankers Association
1000 Wilson Boulevard, Suite 3012
Arlington, VA 22209-3908
703-276-1750
Web Address: www.cbanet.org
Association which sponsors a graduate school at the University of Virginia.

Electronic Funds Transfer Association (EFTA)
950 Herndon Parkway, Suite 390
Herndon, VA 22070
703-435-9800
Web Address: www.efta.org
Provide forum for those involved in Electronic Funds Transfers.

Entrepreneurship Institute
3592 Corporate Drive, Suite 101
Columbus, OH 43231
614-895-1153
Web Address: www.fsti.com/tei/
To provide opportunities for businesses to grow and expand.

Farm Credit Council
50 F Street, N.W., Suite 900
Washington, D.C. 20001
202-626-8710
Web Address: www.fccouncil.com
Makes loans to agricultural and rural America.

Financial Executives Institute
10 Madison Avenue
P.O. Box 1938
Morristown, NJ 07962-1938
201-898-4600
Web Address: www.fei.org
Sponsors financial research activities.

Institute of Certified Financial Planners
3801 East Florida Avenue, Suite 708
Denver, CO 80210-2571
303-759-4900
Web Address: www.icfp.org
Provides benefits to certified financial planner licensees nationwide.

Institute of International Bankers
299 Park Avenue, 17th Floor
New York, NY 10171
212-421-1611
Web Address: www.iib.org
Promote the improvement of knowledge in international banking.

Institute of International Finance
2000 Pennsylvania Avenue, N.W., Suite 8500
Washington, D.C. 20006-1812
202-857-3600
Web Address: www.iif.com
Seeks to improve the knowledge of financing.

International Association for Financial Planning
5775 Glenridge Drive, N.E., Suite B-300
Atlanta, GA 30328-5364
404-845-0011
Web Address: www.iafp.org
Objective is to promote the education of ethical business financial planning.

International Credit Association
243 North Linbergh Boulevard
St. Louis, MO 63141
314-991-3030
Web Address: www.ica-credit.org

International Institute of Investment and Merchant Banking
3104 Q Street, N.W.
Washington, D.C. 20007
202-835-0566
International investments to improve economic growth by eliminating investment barriers and by aiding in the cooperation of investment opportunities.

Independent Bankers Association of America
One Thomas Circle, N.W., Suite 950
Washington, D.C. 20005
202-659-8111
Web Address: www.ibaa.org
Legislative and regulatory information.

Investment Management Consultants Associations
9101 East Kenyon Avenue, Suite 3000
Denver, CO 80237
303-770-3377
Web Address: www.imca.org
To promote and protect the interests of investment consulting.

Institute of Financial Education
55 West Mineral, suite 2800
Chicago, Illinois 60603
312-364-0100
Web Address: www.ifegotheinstitute.com

Mortgage Bankers Association of America
1125 15th Street, N.W.
Washington, D.C. 20005
202-861-6500
Web Address: www.mbaa.org
Improvement in marketing and servicing of loans.

National Association of Investors Corporation
711 West 13 Mile Road
Madison Heights, MI 48071
810-583-6242
Web Address: www.better-investing.org
Independent investment groups.

National Association for Female Executives
30 Irving Place, 5th Floor
New York, NY 10003
212-477-2200
Web Address: www.nafe.com
Promotes the importance of women and their careers.

National Association of Real Estate Investment Trusts
1129 20th Street, N.W., Suite 305
Washington, D.C. 20036
202-785-8717
Web Address: www.nareit.com
Compiles statistics of real estate trusts.

National Council of Real Estate Investment Fiduciaries
180 North Stetson Avenue, Suite 2515
Chicago, IL 60601
312-819-5890
Web Address: www.ncreif.com
Analysis and assesment of investments in real estate.

National Investor Relations Institiute
8045 Leesburg Pike, Suite 600
Vienna, VA 22182
703-506-3570
Web Address: www.niri.org
Improve investment procedures and relations.

National Real Estate Investors Association
89 South Riverview Avenue
Miamiburg, OH 45342
513-866-6200
Investors in real estate.

National Association of Securities Dealers (NASD)
1735 K Street, N.W.
Washington, D.C. 20006
202-728-8000
Web Address: www.nasd.com
Self-regulatory organization for NASDAQ.

National Association of Women Business Owners
1100 Wayne Avenue, Suite 830
Silver Spring, MD 20910
301-608-2590
Web Address: www.nawbo.org/nawbo
To represent women in business and to promote women entrepreneurs.

National Venture Capital Association
1655 North Fort Myer Drive, Suite 700
Arlington, VA 22209
703-351-5269
Web Address: www.nvca.org
To improve investments in new companies.

• Publications •

AAII Journal
625 North Michigan Avenue, Suite 1900
Chicago, IL 60611
312-280-0170
Web Address: www.evensky.com/aaiipub.htm
Personal Finance and Investment.

ABA Banking Journal
1120 Connecticut Avenue, N.W.
Washington, D.C. 20036
202-663-5221
Web Address: www.aba.com
Trends and Development in Banking

American Bank Directory
6195 Crooked Creek Road
Norcross, Georgia 30092

American Banker
1 State Street Plaza
New York, NY 10004
212-934-6700
Web Address: www.americanbanker.com

American Business
80 Central Park West, Suite 16B
New York, NY 10023
212-581-2000

American Savings Directory
McFadden Business Publications
Norcross, Georgia 30092

Bank Administration
1 North Franklin
Chicago, Illinois 60606
800-323-8552
Web Address: www.bai.org

Bankers Magazine
Park Square Building
31 St. James Avenue
Boston, Massachusetts 02116
617-423-2020
Web Address: www.wgl.com
Specialized Articles on Industry

Bank Marketing Magazine
1120 Connecticut Avenue, N.W.
Washington, D.C. 20036
202-663-5378
Web Address: www.bmanet.org

Barron's National Business and Financial Weekly
World Financial Center
200 Liberty
New York, NY 10281
212-416-2700
Web Address: www.barrons.com
Issues and events which affect the financial community.

Bloomberg Magazine
100 Business Park Drive
P.O. Box 888
Princeton, NJ 08542-0888
609-252-8352
Web Address: www.bloomberg.com

Callahan's Credit Union Directory
1001 Connecticut Avenue NW, Suite 728
Washington, D.C. 20036
202-223-3920
Web Address: www.callahan.com
Directory of State and Federal Credit Unions

Directory of American Financial Institutions
McFadden Business Publications

Directory of American S&L Associations
T.K. Sanderson
Baltimore, Maryland

Economic Review
925 Grand Boulevard
Kansas City, MO 64198-0001
816-881-2683
Economic journal.

Finance & Development
700 9th Street, N.W.
Washington, D.C. 20431
202-623-8300

Financial Planning
40 West 57th Street, Suite 802
New York, NY 10019
212-765-5311
Web Address: www.fponline.com
Magazine for Finance Professionals

Financial World
1328 Broadway, 3rd Floor
New York, NY 10001-2116
212-594-5030
Web Address: www.financialworld.com
Business, economic, and social trends.

Future: The Magazine of Commodities and Options
250 South Wacker Drive, Suite 1150
Chicago, IL 60606
312-977-0999
Magazine for people interested in trading futures and options on commodities.

Institutional Investor
488 Madison Avenue
New York, NY 10022
212-303-3300
For top level business and financial professionals.

Investor's Business Daily
12655 Beatrice Avenue
Los Angeles, CA 90066
310-207-1832

Journal of Commercial Bank Lending
1 Liberty Place, 1650 Market Street, Suite 2300
Philadadelphia, Pennsylvania 19103
215-851-9100

Moneyworld
1801 Lee Road, Suite 301
Winter Park, FL 32789-2165
Web Address: www.moneyworldonline.com
Magazine for investors.

Money Market Directory
Money Market Directories
Charlottesville, Virginia

Moody's Bank & Finance Manual
99 Church Street, 1st Floor
New York, New York 10007
212-553-0300
Web Address: www.moody's.com

Mortgage Banking
1125 15th Street, N.W.
Washington, D.C. 20005
202-861-6500
Web Address: www.mbaa.org
Real estate finacning.

Polk's Bank Directory
1321 Murfree Road
Nashville, Tennessee 37217
615-889-3350

Worth Magazine
575 Lexington Avenue
New York, NY 10022
212-223-3100
Web Address: www.worth.com
Magazine for finance and investors.

EMPLOYMENT TIP

RAPIDLY CHANGING AND VERY POWERFUL, BANKING AND FINANCE OFFER EXCELLENT OPPORTUNITIES AND GOOD SALARIES. COLLEGE EDUCATION, AND OFTEN GRADUATE DEGREES, ARE A MUST TO ENTER THIS FIELD BECAUSE OF ITS TECHNICAL NATURE AND INCREASING RELIANCE ON HIGH TECHNOLOGY. STARTING SALARIES OCCASIONALLY EXCEED $30,000 BUT MOST IN THIS INDUSTRY AVERAGE BETWEEN $25,000 AND $60,000.

BANKING & FINANCE

Broadcast Media & Communications

The key to getting your foot in the door of television or radio broadcasting is experience. As an undergrad, by all means get involved with your college television or radio station or intern at a local independent station or network affiliate. It's this kind of hands-on experince that will make you a more marketable candidate for entry-level positions.

If you're presently embarking on making broadcasting your career, I suggest focusing on a small market as your launching pad. At a small station, you're more likely to play a role in every aspect of getting the product on the air, from writing and editing copy, to operating studio and field cameras, to producing and covering stories in the field.

As soon as possible, I recommend putting together a resume/audition tape. If potential employers can see and/or hear you in action, all the better.

One caveat; small market experience means small market pay. But think of the time you put in as a kind of graduate school, for it's sure to pay off down the road.

BRITT HUME

Employment Outlook

A competitive field which has good growth potential. This is also an enticing field because those involved have a chance to express themselves in creative and artistic manners which are often muted in other careers. However, this bonus is a reason for the heavy competition in the industry. College degrees and past experiences are factors not often overlooked but, candidates with natural ability are not turned away. Salaries vary widely but large market broadcasters often average around $50,000. Of course, smaller markets are easier to break into and salaries are closer to $30,000.

In addition, the onset of the Information Age is constantly creating new fields which communications specialists can exploit. Most significant of these new fields is the Internet, but even fields such as writing and reporting are changing as the almost instataneous exchange of information becomes more and more prevelant.

Quick Reference

AC Corporation
www.aaccorp.com

ABC Entertainment
www.abc.com

ACC Communications
www.workforceonline.com

Access Television Network
www.AccessTV.com

Antelope Valley Press
www.avpress.com

Applied Digital Access
www.ada.com

Atel Communications
www.atelcommunications.com

BNI Publications
www.bni-books.com

Books on Tape
www.booksontape.com

Brilliant Digital Entertainment
www.bde3.com

Claricom, Inc.
www.claricom.com

Coded Communications
Corporation
www.coded.com

ComCast Cable Ad Sales
www.comcast.com

Corridor News
www.pomeradonews.com

Creative Teaching Press
www.creativeteaching.com

Database Publishing Company
www.databasepublishing.com

Day Runner
www.dayrunner.com

Fabians Investment Resource
www.fabian.com

Frames Data
www.framesdata.com

Freedom Communications
www.freedom.com

General Instrument Corporation
www.gi.com

Haas Publishing
www.aptguides.com

Harte-Hanks Pennysaver/
Shopper
www.hhinteractive.com

Homebuyers Guide
www.hbg.com

Homes for Sale Magazine
www.homeforsale-socal.com

Installnet
www.ask-inet.com

Investor's Business Daily
www.investors.com

KABC-AM (790)
www.kabc.com

KBNT, Channel 19
www.kbnttv19.com

KBZT-FM
www.gpc.com/gpcc-job.html

KCBS-FM (93)
www.arrowfm.com

Kelley Blue Book
www.kbb.com

KEZY-FM/KORG-AM
www.kezy.com

KFMB-AM/FM & Channel 8
www.760kfmb.com (am),
www.histar.com (fm),
www.kfmbtv8.com (tv)

KFWB-AM (980)
www.kfwb.com

KGB-FM
www.101.kgb.com

KIFM-FM
www.kifm.com

KKBT-FM (92.3)
www.thebeatla.com

KLAC-AM (570)
www.kbig104.com

KLSX-FM (97.1)
www.fmtalk971.com

KMEX Channel 34
www.kmex.com

KMZT-FM (105.1)
www.kmozart.com

KNI Incorporated
www.kninc.com

Knowledge Adventure
www.adventure.com

KNSD-TV, Channel 7
www.nbc739.com

KNX-AM (1070)
www.knx1070.com

KOCE-TV Channel 50
www.koce.com

KPBS-TV, Channel 15
www.kpbs.org

KSDO-AM
www.ksdoradio.com

KTWV-FM (94.7)
www.947wave.com

KYXY-FM
www.kyxy.com

KZLA-FM (93.9)
www.kzla.com

La Opinion
www.laopinion.com

Los Angeles Times
www.latimes.com

Maranatha Music
www.maranathamusic.com

McMullen Publishing
www.mcmullenargus.com

Mitel Telephone Systems
www.mitel.com

North County Times
www.nctimes.com

Orange Coast Magazine
www.orangecoast.com

Orange County Business Journal
www.ocjournal.com

OSI COM Technologies
www.osicom.com

Poway News Chieftain
www.pomeradonews.com

RF Industries Ltd.
www.rfindustries.com

San Diego Business Journal
www.sdbj.com

San Diego Daily Transcript
www.sddt.com

Scoop
www.scoopnews.com

Sea Magazine
www.seamag.com

Siemens Business Communication
Systems
www.siemenscom.com

Sound Source Interactive
www.soundsourceinteractive.com

Standard Tel
www.standardtel.com

Surfer Publications
www.surfermag.com

Teacher Created Materials
www.teachercreated.com

Teldata Voice and Data
Communications
www.teldatausa.com

The Anaheim Bulletin
www.ocregister.com

The Orange County Register
www.ocregister.com

The San Diego Union-Tribune
www.uniontrib.com

Thomas Brothers Maps
www.thomas.com

TrialVision
www.trialvision.com

Tustin News
www.ocregister.com

TV/COM
www.tvcom.com

Volt Information Sciences
www.volt-resume.com

XHRM-FM
www.92five.com

XHTZ-FM
www.z90.com

XTRA-AM
www.xtrasports.com

XTRA-FM
www.91x.com

ABC Entertainment/KABC Channel 7
2040 Avenue of the Stars
Los Angeles, CA 90067
310-557-7777
Job Hotline: 310-557-4222
Web Address: http:www.abc.com
Number of Employees: 10,000

Jarnie Tarses, *President*

Access Television Network
2600 Michelson Drive, Suite 1650
Irvine, CA 92715
949-263-9900
Web Address: www.AccessTV.com
Number of Employees: 19

George Henry, *President*
Anna Nguyen, *Director of Personnel*
Distributor of infomercials and other advertisement to cable TV
operators. Has contracts with Tele-Communications, Time Warner,
and Continental Cablevision. Clients include Nordic Track, Health
Rider, and Lexus.

ADNET Telemanagement
14849 Firestone Boulevard
La Mirada, CA 90638-6009
714-994-4400
Number of Employees: 38

Dave Wiegand, *President*
Jean Reeves, *Director of Personnel*

Applied Digital Access
9855 Scranton Road
San Diego, CA 92121
858-623-2200
Job Hotline: 213-239-7140
Web Address: www.ada.com
Number of Employees: 150

Peter Savage, *CEO*
Candis Paul, *Human Resources Director*

Astor Broadcast Group
550 Luguna Drive, #216
Carlsbad, CA 92008
760-729-1000
Number of Employees: 25
Sandra Jennings, *Vice President & Station Manager*

AT&T
750 B Street, Suite 1400
San Diego, CA 92101
858-699-2003
Job Hotline: 213-239-7140
Number of Employees: 122
Frank Laughton, *General Manager*

Atel Communications
8447 Miramar Mall
San Diego, CA 92121
858-646-4600
Number of Employees: 25
Steven Handelman, *President*
Larry Harden, *Hiring Administrator*

Automated Interface
7121 Engineer Road
San Diego, CA 92111
858-571-3400
Number of Employees: 20

Ken Curl, *President*

Clear Channel Communications
5745 Kearny Villa Road
San Diego, CA 92123
858-565-6006
Job Hotline: 619-715-3196
Web Address: www.101kgb.com
Number of Employees: 200

Mike Glickenhaus, *Manager*
Fran Jue, *Human Resources Director*

ComCast Cable Ad Sales
1501 West Commonwealth Avenue
Fullerton, CA 92833-2799
714-525-2058
Web Address: www.comcast.com
Number of Employees: 22

Michael Szczechura, *Manager*

Communications Plus
1675 Morena Boulevard
San Diego, CA 92110
619-276-3000
Web Address: www.communicationsplus.com
Number of Employees: 22

Neil Schneider, *President*
Alan Frischman, *Vice President & General
   Manager*

Datron World Communications
3030 Enterprise Court
Vista, CA 92083
760-747-1079
Web Address: www.dtwc.com
Number of Employees: 150

Energy Communications Corporation
637 3rd Avenue
Chula Vista, CA 91912
619-585-9398
Job Hotline: 619-585-9463
Web Address: televisa.com
Number of Employees: 200

Patricia Alvarez, *President*

Golden Telecom
5751-F Palmer Way
Carlsbad, CA 92008
760-438-8383
Number of Employees: 14

Dan Golden, *CEO*

Inet
6779 Mesa Ridge Road, Suite 100
San Diego, CA 92121
858-455-7335
Job Hotline: 619-597-1864
Number of Employees: 80

Dale Stein, *CEO*
Blair Hibbard, *Human Resources Manager*

Intellicell Corp.
9314 Eton Avenue
Chatsworth, CA 91311
818-906-7777
Number of Employees: 37

Ben Neman, *President*
James E. Bunting, *Director of Personnel*
Wholesaler of wireless communications products, including cellular phones and accessories. Brands include AT&T, Ericsson, Mitsubishi, Motorola, Nokia, NEC, and Sony. Also distributes its own line of accessories including batteries, plug-in chargers, cases, and antennas.

KABC-AM -790
3321 South La Cienega Boulevard
Los Angeles, CA 90016
310-840-4900
Job Hotline: 310-557-4222
Web Address: www.kabc.com

Bill Summers, *President*

KBIG-FM -104.3- & KLAC-AM -570
7755 Sunset Boulevard
Los Angeles, CA 90046
818-546-1043
Job Hotline: 800-649-2900
Web Address: www.kbig104.com
Number of Employees: 50

Craig Wilbraham, *General Manager*
Ed Kramps, *General Manager*
Sherri Chodor, *Human Resources Manager*

KBNT, Channel 19
5770 Ruffin Road
San Diego, CA 92123
858-576-1919
Web Address: www.kbnt-tv19.com
Number of Employees: 60

Philip Wilkinson, *General Manager*
Kathy Pephens, *Human Resources Controller*

KBUE-FM -105.5
5724 Hollywood Boulevard
Hollywood, CA 90028
213-461-9300
Leonard Liberman, *Vice President*

KBZT-FM
1615 Murray Canyon Road, Suite 710
San Diego, CA 92108
619-297-9595
Job Hotline: 704-374-3875

Web Address: www.oldies949.com
Number of Employees: 100
Mike Stafford, *General Manager*
Rosemary Christman, *Human Resources Director*

KCAL Channel 9
5515 Melrose Avenue
Los Angeles, CA 90038
323-467-5459
Job Hotline: 323-960-3770
Web Address: www.ultimatetv.com

KCBS-FM -93
6121 Sunset Boulevard
Los Angeles, CA 90028
213-460-3293.
Job Hotline: 213-817-JOBS
Web Address: www.arrowfm.com
Number of Employees: 60

Dave Van Dyke, VP, *General Manager*

KCBS-TV Channel 2
7800 Beverly Boulevard
Los Angeles, CA 90036
323-852-2345
Web Address: www.channel2000.com

KCET Channel 28
4401 Sunset Boulevard
Los Angeles, CA 90027
323-666-6500
Job Hotline: 619-953-5236
Web Address: www.kcet.org

KCMG-FM -100.3
5900 Wilshire Boulevard, Suite 525
Los Angeles, CA 90036
213-931-6301
Number of Employees: 42

Bob Visotcky, *General Manager*

KCOP Channel 13
915 La Brea Avenue
Los Angeles, CA 90038
323-851-1000
Web Address: www.upn13.com

KDOC-TV
18021 Cowan
Irvine, CA 92614-6023
949-442-9800
Number of Employees: 35

KEZY-FM/KORG-AM
1190 East Ball Road
Anaheim, CA 92805-5964
714-774-9600
Web Address: www.kezy.com
Number of Employees: 50

Walter Sheltze, *Business Manager*

KFI-AM -640
610 South Ardmore Avenue
Los Angeles, CA 90005
213-385-0101
Web Address: www.kfi640.com
Number of Employees: 80

Howard Neal, *General Manager*

KFMB-AM/FM & Channel 8
7677 Engineer Road
San Diego, CA 92111
858-292-7600
Job Hotline: 858-495-8640
Web Address: www.kfmb.com
Number of Employees: 300

Ed Trimble, *General Manager*
Pamela Sanchez, *Human Resources Manager*

KFWB-AM -980
6230 Yucca Street
Los Angeles, CA 90028
213-871-4612
Job Hotline: 213-817-JOBS
Web Address: www.kfwb.com
Number of Employees: 125

Roger Nadel, VP, *General Manager*

KGTV ABC Channel 10
4600 Air Way
San Diego, CA 92102
619-237-1010
Web Address: www.kgtv.com
Number of Employees: 200

Ed Quinn, *President*
Lisa Padelford, *Human Resource Director*

KIIS-FM -102.7
3400 Riverside Drive, Suite 800
Burbank, CA 91505
818-845-1027
Web Address: www.kiis.fm.com
Number of Employees: 80

Roy Laughlin, President, *General Manager*
Brdget Aquilera, *Office Manager*

KKBT-FM -92.3
5900 Wilshire Boulevard, Suite 1900
Los Angeles, CA 90036
213-634-1800
Job Hotline: 800-649-2900
Web Address: www.thebeatla.com

Craig Wilbraham, Senior VP, *General Manager*

KLAX-FM -97.9
10281 West Pico Boulevard
Los Angeles, CA 90064
310-203-0900
Number of Employees: 50

Marie Kordus, *General Manager*
Alfonse Camacho, *Human Resource Manager*

KLOS-FM -95.5
3321 South La Cienega Boulevard
Los Angeles, CA 90016
310-840-4800
Job Hotline: 310-557-7777
Web Address: www.kabc.com
Number of Employees: 45

Maureen Lasourd, President, *General Manager*
Bill Sommers, *Personnel Manager*

KLSX-FM -97.1
3580 Wilshire Boulevard
Los Angeles, CA 90010
213-383-4222
Job Hotline: 213-817-JOBS
Web Address: www.fmtalk971.com

Robert Moore, VP, *General Manager*

KLVE-FM -107.5-, KSCA-FM -101.9- & KTNG-AM -1020
1645 North Vine Street, Suite 200
Hollywood, CA 90028
213-465-3171
Number of Employees: 130

Richard Heftel, President, *General Manager*
Elenore Smiley, *Director of Human Resources*

KMEX Channel 34
6701 Center Drive West, 15th Floor
Los Angeles, CA 90045
310-216-3434
Job Hotline: 310-348-3590
Web Address: www.kmex.com
Marilyn Davis, *Human Resource Manager*
Hispanic TV programming.

KMZT-FM -105.1
1500 Cotner Avenue
Los Angeles, CA 90025
310-478-5540
Job Hotline: Ext 239
Web Address: www.kmozart.com
Number of Employees: 50

Saul Levine, President, *General Manager*
Arline Robins, *Human Resource Manager*

KNSD-TV, Channel 7
8330 Engineer Road
San Diego, CA 92111
858-279-3939
Job Hotline: 858-467-7605
Web Address: www.nbc739.com

Neil Derrough, *General Manager*
Darcie Gulen, *Office Manager*

BROADCAST MEDIA

KNX-AM -1070
6121 Sunset Boulevard
Los Angeles, CA 90028
213-460-3321
Job Hotline: 213-817-JOBS
Web Address: www.knx1070.com
Number of Employees: 100

George Nicholaw, *VP General Manager*

KOCE-TV Channel 50
15751 Gothard Street
Huntington Beach, CA 92647-3058
714-895-5623
Web Address: www.koce.com
Number of Employees: 50

Mel Rogers, *President*

KOST-FM -103.5
610 South Ardmore Avenue
Los Angeles, CA 90005
213-427-1035
Web Address: www.klve.com
Number of Employees: 150

Howard Neal, *General Manager*
Candice Tom, *EEO Administrator*

KPBS-FM
5200 Campanile Drive
San Diego, CA 92182-5400
619-594-8100
Job Hotline: 619-594-5703
Web Address: www.kpbs.org
Number of Employees: 200

Doug Myrland, *Manager*
Cyril Sirk, *Student Assistant Coordinator*

KPLN-FM
8033 Linda Vista Road
San Diego, CA 92111
858-560-1037
Web Address: www.planetfm.com
Number of Employees: 75
Bob Bolinger, *Manager*
Chris Valentine, *Human Resource Manager*

KPOP-AM/Clear Channel Communications, KSDO-AM & KOGO-AM
5050 Murphy Canyon Road
San Diego, CA 92123
858-278-1130
Web Address: www.ksdo.com
Number of Employees: 100
Kevin McCarthy, *Manager*
Fran Jue, *Human Resource Director*

KPWR-FM -105.9
2600 West Olive Avenue, Suite 850
Burbank, CA 91505
818-953-4200
Number of Employees: 90
Marie Kordus, VP, *General Manager*

KROQ-FM -106.7
3500 West Olive Avenue, Suite 900
Burbank, CA 91505
818-567-1067
Number of Employees: 60

Trip Reeb, *General Manager*

KRTH-FM -101.1
5901 Venice Boulevard
Los Angeles, CA 90034
213-937-5230
Number of Employees: 75

Pat Duffy, *VP & General Manager*
Kristie Philips, *Office Manager*

KTBN Trinity Broadcasting
2442 Michelle Drive
Santa Ana, CA 92711-2101
714-832-2950
Number of Employees: 475

Paul F. Crouch, *President*
Ruth Brown, *Director of Personnel*

KTLA Channel 5
5100 West Sunset Boulevard
Los Angeles, CA 90028
213-460-5500
Web Address: www.ktla.com

KTTV Channel 11 - Fox
1999 South Bundy Drive
Los Angeles, CA 90025
310-584-2000
Web Address: www.fox11la.com

KTWV-FM -94.7- - WAVE
8944 Lindblade Street
Culver City, CA 90232
310-840-7112
Job Hotline: 213-817-JOBS
Web Address: www.947wave.com
Number of Employees: 50

Tim Pohlman, VP, *General Manager*
Cindy Nakano, *Human Resource Manager*

KUSI-TV, Channel 9
4575 Viewridge Avenue
San Diego, CA 92123
858-571-5151
Job Hotline: 858-645-8729
Number of Employees: 250

Michael D. McKinnon Sr., *General Manager*
Martha Flaherty, *Executive Assistant*

KWIZ Radio 1480 AM Radio Exitos
3101 West 5th Street
Santa Ana, CA 92703-1897
714-554-5000
Number of Employees: 25
Jose Lieberman, *President*
Winnie Coombs, *Operations Manager*

KYSR-FM -98.7
3500 West Olive Avenue, Suite 250
Burbank, CA 91505
818-955-7000
Number of Employees: 50

Ken Christensen, VP, *General Manager*
Karen Clark, *Administrative Assistant for Human Resources*

KYXY-FM
8033 Linda Vista Road
San Diego, CA 92111
858-571-7600
Web Address: www.kyxy.com
Number of Employees: 75

Bob Bolinger, *Manager*
Joan Rubin, *Business Manager*

KZLA-FM -93.9
7755 Sunset Boulevard
Los Angeles, CA 90046
213-882-8000
Web Address: www.kzla.com
Number of Employees: 50

Dave Irvin, *General Manager*
Terri Dorian, *Director of Human Resources*

Lantel Systems Solutions
9765 Clairemont Mesa Boulevard
San Diego, CA 92124
858-279-1330
Web Address: www.lantelsystems.com
Number of Employees: 25
Lorraine A. Nelson, *President*
Michael Nelson, *CEO*

Lucent Technologies
9645 Granite Ridge Drive, Suite 300
San Diego, CA 92123
858-874-1500
Web Address: www.lucent.com
Number of Employees: 301

Lucent Technologies
18201 Von Karman Avenue, Suite 640
Irvine, CA 92612
949-225-5700
Web Address: www.lucent.com

MCI WorldCom
19200 Von Karman Avenue, Suite 350
Irvine, CA 92612
949-756-6500
Web Address: www.mciworldcom.com

Motorola Broadband Communication
6450 Sequence Drive
San Diego, CA 92121
858-455-1500
Web Address: www.gi.com
Number of Employees: 800
Tom Linch, *General Manager*

Nextel Communication
770 The City Drive, Suite 1100
Orange, CA 92868
714-740-6500
Web Address: www.nextel.com

Orange County Newschannel
625 North Grand Avenue
Santa Ana, CA 92711-1945
714-565-3800
Number of Employees: 75

Mirverva Calzada, *Human Resources Manager*

OSI COM Technologies
9990 Mesa Rim Road
San Diego, CA 92121
858-292-0500
Web Address: www.sorrentonet.com
Number of Employees: 50

Tony Manyo, *President*
Xin Cheng, *President*

Pacific Bell
17310 Red Hill Avenue, Suite 270
Irvine, CA 92614
949-440-6640
Web Address: www.pacbell.com

Phone Systems Plus
13741 Danielson Street, Suite A
Poway, CA 92064
858-679-3900
Web Address: www.psplus.com
Number of Employees: 20

Ron Kohl, *President*
Albert Otazua, *Office Manager*
Fax resumes to 858-679-3910.

Phone Ware
5605 La Jolla Boulevard
La Jolla, CA 92037
619-459-3000
Number of Employees: 75

William J. Nassir, *President*
Sunday Dixon, *Vice President of Marketing*
Matt Harless, *Vice President of Sales*

RF Industries Ltd.
7610 Miramar Road, Building 6000
San Diego, CA 92126
858-549-6340
Web Address: www.rfindustries.com
Number of Employees: 40

Howard Hill, President, *CEO*
Terry Gross, *Human Resource Manager*

Society of Children's Book Writers
22736 Van Owens Street, Suite 106
West Hills, CA 90035
818-888-8760

Standard Tel
8375 Camino Santa Fe, Suite A
San Diego, CA 92121
858-453-7338
Web Address: www.standardtel.com
Number of Employees: 10

Ed Kershaw, *General Manager*

Staples Communication
9265 Sky Park Court, Suite 200
San Diego, CA 92123
858-565-4047
Web Address: staplescom.com
Number of Employees: 162

Mike Ferry, *Vice President of Sales*
Terry Shaw, *Hiring Manager*

STM Wireless
One Mauchly
Irvine, CA 92618
949-753-7864
Number of Employees: 128

Emil Youssefzadeh, *President*
Linda Johansen, *Director of Personnel*
Maker and installer of satellite and wireless radio communication products. Its products are designed to support data, fax, and voice and video networks requiring cost-effective connections between geographically dispersed locations.

Technical Telephone Services
1648 North Magnolia Avenue, Suite 108
El Cajon, CA 92020
619-448-6404
Number of Employees: 6

Norbert Doering, *President*

Teldata Enterprise Networks
9085 Aero Drive
San Diego, CA 92123
619-280-3400
Web Address: www.teldata-usa.com
Number of Employees: 100

David McLellan, *General Manager*

TV/COM
17066 Goldentop Road
San Diego, CA 92127
858-451-1500
Web Address: www.tvcom.com
Number of Employees: 200

Jeff Wallin, *President*
Hillary Polland, *Human Resource Manager*

ViaSat
2290 Cosmos Court
Carlsbad, CA 92009
760-438-8099
Web Address: info@viasat.com
Number of Employees: 300

Mark Dankberg, *President*
Frank Drdek, *Vice President*

Williams Communications
5810 Nancy Ridge Drive
San Diego, CA 92121
858-558-4200
Number of Employees: 75

Joe Mahoney, *Branch Manager*

Women in Communications
P.O. Box 2727
El Sugundo, CA 90245
310-640-1905

XETV Fox, Channel 6
8253 Ronson Road
San Diego, CA 92111
858-279-6666
Job Hotline: 858-279-6666 x6007
Number of Employees: 105

Joanie O'Laughlin, *General Manager*

XHKY-FM, XHTZ-FM, XLTN, XHCR-FM
1690 Frontage Road
Chula Vista, CA 91911
619-575-9090
Job Hotline: 619-575-9090
Web Address: www.z90.com, www.x99.com, www.californula.com
Number of Employees: 70

Lou Fernandez, *Manager*

XHRM-FM/Clear Channel Communications
2434 South Portway
National City, CA 91950
619-615-9570
Web Address: www.magic975.com
Number of Employees: 30

Mike Glickenhaus, *Manager*
Fran Jue, *Human Resource Director*

BROADCAST MEDIA

Further Reference

American Federation of Television & Radio Artists
260 Madison Avenue
New York, New York 10016
(212) 532-0800
Representation of Broadcasters

American Women in Radio & TV
1650 Tysons Boulevard, Suite 200
McLean, Virginia 22102
703-506-3290
Promotes Women in Broadcasting

Association of America's Public Television Stations
1350 Connecticut Avenue, N.W., Suite 200
Washington, D.C. 20036
202-887-1700
Web Address: www.universe.digex.net/~apt
Organizes Efforts of Public Television Stations.

Association of Independent Video & Filmmakers
304 Hudson Street, 6th Floor North
New York, New York 10013
212-807-1400
Champions Independent Films.

Broadcast Education Association
1771 N Street, N.W.
Washington, D.C. 20036
202-429-5355
Web Address: www.usu.edu/~bea
Promotes Broadcasting Education.

Communications Workers of America
501 3rd Street, N.W.
Washington, D.C. 20001
202-434-1444
Represents Communications Workers.

Multimedia Telecommunications Association
2500 Wilson Boulevard, Suite 3300
Arlington, VA 22201
202-296-9800
Web Address: www.mmta.org
Association of Telecommunications Providers.

National Association of Broadcasters
1771 N Street, N.W.
Washington, D.C. 20036
(202) 429-5300
Web Address: www.nab.org
Information Resource to Industry.
Job Hotline starts after 6:00 P.M.

National Association of Public Television Association
1350 Connecticut Avenue, N.W., Suite 200
Washington, D.C. 20036
202-887-1700
Web Address: www.universe.digex.net/~apts
Promotes Public Television Industry.

National Cable Television Association
1724 Massachusetts Avenue, N.W.
Washington, D.C. 20036
(202) 775-3550
Web Address: www.ncta.com
Promotes Cable Television.

National Newspaper Publishers Association
3200 13th Street, N.W.
Washington, D.C. 20010
202-588-8764
Aides Newspaper Publishers.

National Press Club
529 14th Street, N.W., 13th Floor
Washington, D.C. 20045
202-662-7500
Web Address: ntc.press.org
Organization for News Media Personnel.

Newspaper Association of America
11600 Sunrise Valley Drive
Reston, VA 22091
703-648-1000
Alliance for Free Press.

Personal Communication Industry Association
500 Montgomery Street, Suite 700
Alexandria, VA 22314-1561
703-739-0300
Web Address: www.pcia.com
Distribution of Communication and Computer Equipment.

The Newspaper Guild
8611 2nd Avenue
Silver Spring, Maryland 20910
301-585-2990
Web Address: www.newsguild.org
Retirement benefits to those in news media.

Broadcasting & Cable
1705 DeSales Street, N.W.
Washington, D.C. 20036
202-659-2340

Radio Resource
14 Inverness Drive East, Suite D-136
Englewood, CO 80112
303-792-2390
Mobile radio systems magazine.

Design & Engineering

- Architectual
- Graphic Design
- Landscape Design
- Interior Design
- Civil Engineering

A pplicants for design and engineering positions need a Bachelor's degree in interior design or architecture and experience with CAD (Intergraph or AutoCAD). A portfolio with CAD and traditional samples of work should help land an entry-level design position. Professional registration and communication skills are important for advancement in all fields. Persons with multiple disciplines have a greater chance for steady employment.

Computer productivity skills are important (word processing, spreadsheet, database) in any design position.

Typical entry-level positions are CAD architect, or CAD interior architect. Duties for these positions include working with established designers and project managers on new and existing projects and programs.

Career paths for interior architects and architects include technical, project management and general management. All involve marketing and communication skills.

SVERDRUP CORPORATION

See Also: High Tech

EMPLOYMENT OUTLOOK

A STRONG FIELD WHICH BLENDS ARTISTIC AND PROFESSIONAL ABILITIES, DESIGN AND ENGINEERING CAN BE BOTH FULFILLING AND HIGH PAYING. COLLEGE DEGREES AND AN UNDERSTANDING OF COMPUTERS ARE OFTEN NECESSARY, ESPECIALLY IN A COMPLEX FIELD SUCH AS ARCHITECTURE. SALARIES IN THIS INDUSTRY HOVER CLOSE TO $35,000 AFTER EIGHT TO TEN YEARS EXPERIENCE.

AC Martin Partners
18401 Von Karman Avenue, Suite 130
Irvine, CA 92612-1542
949-474-0101
Number of Employees: 100

Gil Thweatt, *Principal*

AC Martin Partners
811 West Seventh Street
Los Angeles, CA 90017
213-683-1900
Web Address: www.acmartin.com
Number of Employees: 100

Christopher Martin, *Managing Partner*
Corinne Yamada, *Manager of Human Resources*

Altoon & Porter Architects
5700 Wilshire Boulevard, Suite 100
Los Angeles, CA 90036
213-939-1900
Web Address: www.altoonporter.com
Number of Employees: 50

R. Altoon, *Partner*

American Institute of Architects
Los Angeles Chapter
8687 Melrose Avenue, #M-3
Los Angeles, CA 90069
310-785-1809

American Institute of Graphic Arts
116 the Plaza Pasadena
Pasadena, CA 91101
818-952-2442

American Society of Engineers and Architects
511 Garfield Avenue
South Pasadena, CA 91030
213-682-1161

Anshen & Allen
5055 Wilshire Boulevard, Suite 900
Los Angeles, CA 90036
213-525-0500
Web Address: www.anshenla.com
Number of Employees: 40

Peter Stazicker, *Senior Principal*

Anthony-Taylor Companies
2240 Vineyard Avenue, Suite B
Escondido, CA 92029
760-738-8800
Number of Employees: 50
Chris A. Post, *CEO*

Aref Associates
111 West Ocean Boulevard, Suite 1050
Long Beach, CA 90802
562-983-5811
Web Address: www.aref.com
F. Akabar-Aref, *Principal*

Asian-American Architects & Engineers
1200 Wilshire Boulevard, Suite 401
Los Angeles, CA 90017
213-386-0273
Web Address: www.aaaesc.com

Associated Architects and Planners
15260 Ventura Boulevard
Sherman Oaks, CA 91403
818-995-7484

Association for Women in Architecture
2550 Beverly Boulvard
Los Angeles, CA 90057
213-389-6490

Austin Design Group
600 West Broadway, Suite 200
San Diego, CA 92101
619-231-1960
Web Address: aurp.com
Number of Employees: 75

Douglas H. Austin, *Principal*
Chris Veum, *Principal*

Berryman & Henigar
11590 West Bernardo Court, Suite 100
San Diego, CA 92127
858-451-6100
Web Address: www.bhiinc.com
Number of Employees: 45

Ray J. Berryman, *Principal*
Mary Berryman, *Human Resources Manager*

Berryman & Henigar
2001 East 1st Street
Santa Ana, CA 92705-4020
714-568-7300
Web Address: www.bhiinc.com
Number of Employees: 320

Nancy Johnson, *Office Manager*

Brian Paul & Associates
4350 La Jolla Village Drive, Suite 130
San Diego, CA 92122
858-453-1200
Web Address:
www.brianpaulandassociates.com
Number of Employees: 25

Robert H. Mellott, *Principal*

BRW
701 B Street, Suite 530
San Diego, CA 92101
858-557-0580
Web Address: www.urscorp.com
Number of Employees: 12

James Moore, *President*
Mark Peterson, *Vice President*

BTA
1001 Westwood Boulevard
Los Angeles, CA 90024
310-208-7017
Web Address: www.btaacr.com
Number of Employees: 30

Julia Thomas, *President*
Linda Freeman, *Human Resource Manager*

Burkett & Wong Engineers
3434 Fourth Avenue, Suite 270
San Diego, CA 92103
619-299-5550
Web Address: www.burkett-wong.com
Number of Employees: 50

Timothy Yeun, *Principal*
Laura Ricker, *Human Resources Director*

Burns & Roe Enterprises
10805 Holder Street, Suite 160
Cypress, CA 90630-5145
562-944-4688
Number of Employees: 5

C&J Partners
One Colorado, 35 Hugus Alley, Suite 210
35 Hugus Alley, Suite 210
Pasadena, CA 91103
818-440-1400
Number of Employees: 30

Scott Kohno, *President*
Catherine Kuo, *Director of Human Resources*

Carmen Nordsten Igonda Design
8900 Melrose Avenue, Suite 201
Los Angeles, CA 90069
310-246-0993
Number of Employees: 12

Josephine Carmen, *President*

Carrier Johnson
1301 Third Avenue
San Diego, CA 92101
619-239-2353
Web Address: www.carrierjohnson.com
Number of Employees: 100
Gordon Carrier, *Principal*

CHCG Architects
135 West Green Street, Suite 200
Pasadena, CA 91105
626-568-1428
R. Cocke, *Principal*

City Spaces
234 East Colorado Boulevard, Suite 850
Pasadena, CA 91101
626-449-6222
Number of Employees: 20
Christie Skinner, *President*
Kurt Whitlatch, *Director of Operations*

225

Cole Martinez Curtis and Associates
310 Washington Boulevard, Suite 116
Marina del Rey, CA 90292
310-827-7200
Number of Employees: 39

Cole Martinez, *President*
Lisa Scott, *Human Resource Manager*

Coleman/Caskey Architects
100 Pacifica, Suite 300
Irvine, CA 92618
949-727-4400

Continental Graphics Holdings
4525 Wilshire Boulevard, Suite 203
Los Angeles, CA 90010
213-930-2281
Number of Employees: 13

Jerrell Shelton, *President*
Monica Desmond, *Director of Human Resources*

Daniel Mann Johnson & Mendenhall
3250 Wilshire Boulevard
Los Angeles, CA 90010
213-381-3663
Web Address: www.dmjm.com
Number of Employees: 500

Raymond Holdsworth, *President*
John Dyer, *Recruiter*

Danielian Associates
60 Corporate Park
Irvine, CA 92606-5105
949-474-6030
Web Address: www.danielian.com
Number of Employees: 45

Arthur C. Danielian, *President*

Delawie Wilkes Rodrigues Barker & Bretton
2827 Presidio Drive
San Diego, CA 92110
619-299-6690
Web Address: www.dwrbb.com
Number of Employees: 40

Michael B. Wilkes, *Principal*
Frank Ternasky, *Associate*

Design Development Company
6047 Tampa Avenue, Suite 305
Tarzana, CA 91356
818-881-8506
Number of Employees: 15

Ron Lieberman, *Owner & President*
David Liebermann, *Director of Human Resources*

DMJM Rottet
3250 Wilshire Boulevard
Los Angeles, CA 90010
213-368-2888
Web Address: www.dmjm.com
Number of Employees: 600

Lauren Rottet, *Principal*
John Dyer, *Recruiter*

Earth Tech
9675 Business Park Avenue
San Diego, CA 92131
619-536-5610
Web Address: www.earthtech.com
Number of Employees: 40

Debbie Neev, *Principal*

Edward J. Cass & Associates
3569 Fifth Avenue
San Diego, CA 92103
619-298-3480
Number of Employees: 20

Edward Cass, *Principal*

Ehrlich-Rominger Architects
5000 Birch Street, Suite 5000
Newport Beach, CA 92660-2142
949-476-4000
Web Address: www.erlich.com
Number of Employees: 500

Engineers & Architects Association
350 South Figueroa, Suite 600
Los Angeles, CA 90071
213-620-6920
Web Address: www.eaa&union.com

Environetics Group
8530 Venice Boulevard
Los Angeles, CA 90034
310-287-2180
Web Address: www.environeticsgroup.com
Number of Employees: 12
R. Lehman, *Principal*

ER+HDR
6363 Greenwich Drive, Suite 260
San Diego, CA 92122
858-623-1300
Web Address: www.hdrinc.com
Number of Employees: 15
Gregory J. Mellberg, *Principal*

Fehlman LaBarre
452 Eighth Avenue, Suite A
San Diego, CA 92101
619-234-0789
Web Address: www.FehlmanLaBarre.com
Number of Employees: 23
Mark Fehlman, *Principal*
Mike La Barre, *Principal*
Maridel Armstrong, *Office Administrator*

Fluor Corporation
3353 Michelson Drive
Irvine, CA 92698
949-975-2000
Web Address: www.fluor.com
Number of Employees: 60679

Charles J. Bradley Jr., *Vice President*
Major engineering and construction company, providing services to clients in a range of markets, including power generation, raw material processing, petroleum, and industrial markets. Subsidiaries include Fluor Daniel and A.T. Massey.

GAA Architects
4 Park Plaza, Suite 120
Irvine, CA 92614-8506
949-474-1775
Number of Employees: 21

Gilbert Aja, *President*

Gensler and Associates
2500 Broadway, Suite 300
Santa Monica, CA 90404
310-449-5600
Number of Employees: 200

Andrew P. Cohen, *Managing Principal*
Sharon Spurns, *Recruiter*

Gensler/Architects
4675 Macarthur Court, Suite 350
Newport Beach, CA 92660-1820
949-863-9434
Number of Employees: 1100

Kathy Vincent, *Human Resources Manager*

Grillias Pirc Rosier Alves
17875 Von Karman Avenue, Suite 301
Irvine, CA 92614-6257
949-250-4772
Number of Employees: 45

Sotiros P Grillias, *President*

HCA Partners
54 West Green Street
Pasadena, CA 91105
626-796-3876
Number of Employees: 15

Robert Heraldez, *President*

Hellmuth Obata & Kassabaum
1655 26th Street, Suite 200
Santa Monica, CA 90404
310-453-0100
Web Address: www.hok.com

John Conley, *Partner*
John Harmon, *Vice President*

Hirsch Bedner Associates
3216 Nebraska Avenue
Santa Monica, CA 90404
310-829-9087

Web Address: www.hbadesigns.com
Number of Employees: 50
Michael Bedner, *President*
Rene Kaerkov, *Controller*
Alex Heil, *Human Resource Manager*

HKS Architects
2440 South Sepulveda Boulevard, Suite 275
Los Angeles, CA 90064
310-966-1520
Web Address: www.hksinc.com

T. Harvey, *Principal*
Jack Price, *Principal*

HLW International
2440 South Sepulveda Boulevard, Suite 185
Los Angeles, CA 90064
310-575-3636
Web Address: hlwla@aol.com
Number of Employees: 30

Michael White, *Director*

HNTB Corp/West Division
36 Executive Park, Suite 200
Irvine, CA 92614-6744
949-752-6940
Web Address: www.hntb.com
Number of Employees: 80

Ronald L Hartje, *President*

HNTB Corporation
611 West 6th Street, Suite 1800
Los Angeles, CA 90017
213-622-4117
Web Address: www.hntb.com

Edward McSpedon, *Vice President*

Hunsaker & Associates San Diego
10179 Huennekens Street
San Diego, CA 92121
858-558-4500
Web Address: www.hunsakersd.com
Number of Employees: 76

Interior Architects
550 South Hope Street, Suite 1100
Los Angeles, CA 90071
213-623-2164
Number of Employees: 48

Leonard Scott, *Senior VP & Managing Principal*
Paula Banks, *Office Manager*

Interior Space International
10960 Wilshire Boulevard, Suite 900
Los Angeles, CA 90024
310-473-5358
Web Address: www.epstein-isi.com
Number of Employees: 29
D. Shay, *Senior Vice President*
Terry Anderson, *Office/Human Resource Manager*

DESIGN & ENGINEERING

Interni Design
115 Pine Avenue, Suite 250
Long Beach, CA 90802
562-983-0666
Web Address: http://interni.pacbell.com
Number of Employees: 8

Charles Colosimo, *President*
Marivel Tabalon, *Human Resource Manager &*
Controller

Island Architects West
7632 Herschel Avenue
La Jolla, CA 92037
858-459-9291
Number of Employees: 25

Tony Crisafi, *Principal*
Drex Patterson, *Principal*

J. Muller International
9444 Balboa Avenue, Suite 200
San Diego, CA 92123
858-974-5005
Web Address: www.jmuller.com
Number of Employees: 30
Gregory Shafer, *Principal*
Leata Griswold, *Office Manager*

J. T. Nakaoka Associates Architects
10390 Santa Monica Boulevard, Suite 370
Los Angeles, CA 90025
310-286-9375
Number of Employees: 10
James Nakaoka, *President*
Francie Stefan, *Office Manager*

James Leary Architecture & Planning
9845 Erma Road, Suite 205A
San Diego, CA 92131
858-695-0444
Number of Employees: 20
Douglas Childs, *Principal*

Janice Stevenor Dale & Associates
714 West Olympic Boulevard, Suite 1107
Los Angeles, CA 90018
213-744-0110
Web Address: www.jsda.com
Number of Employees: 10
Janice Stevenor Dale, *Principal*

Jerde Partnership
913 Ocean Front Walk
Venice, CA 90291
310-399-1558

Johnson Fain Partners
800 Wilshire Boulevard
Los Angeles, CA 90017
213-622-3500
Web Address: www.jfpartners.com
Number of Employees: 55
W. Fain Jr., *Managing Partner*

Joseph Wong Design Associates
2359 Fourth Avenue, Suite 300
San Diego, CA 92101
619-233-6777
Web Address: www.judainc.com
Number of Employees: 12

Joseph O. Wong, *Principal*

Jossy + Carrier Design Group
1520 State Street, Suite 100
San Diego, CA 92101
619-230-9211
Number of Employees: 15

Laura Banning, *CEO*

Klages Carter Vail & Partners
200 Baker Street East, Suite 201
Costa Mesa, CA 92626-4543
949-641-0191
Web Address: www.kcv.com/kcv
Number of Employees: 40

Jan Vail, *President*

KMA Architecture & Engineering
1515 Morena Boulevard
San Diego, CA 92110
619-276-7710
Web Address: kma-ae.com
Number of Employees: 33

John M. McKeown, *Principal*
Stephanie Baker, *Human Resource Manager*

KPA Associates
3033 5th Avenue, Suite 100
San Diego, CA 92103
619-725-0980
Web Address: www.kpaa.com
Number of Employees: 20

Bayless C. Tov, *Principal*

La Canada Design Group
200 East Del Mar Boulevard, Suite 108
Pasadena, CA 91105
626-795-6474
Number of Employees: 15

Lance Bird, *President*

Langdon Wilson Architects
1401 Quail Street, Suite 100
Newport Beach, CA 92660-2744
949-833-9193
Number of Employees: 78

J. Patrick Allen, *Partner*

Langdon Wilson Architectural Planning
1055 Wilshire Boulevard, Suite 1500
Suite 1500
Los Angeles, CA 90017
213-250-1186

Web Address: www.langdonwilson.com
Number of Employees: 95
Asad Khan, *Partner*
Bebble Wilkins, *Associate Partner*

Lee Burkhart Liu
2890 Colorado Avenue
Santa Monica, CA 90404
310-829-2249
Web Address: lblarch@aol.com

Kenneth Lee, *Principal*
Georgia Ford, *Associate Principal*

Lee & Sakahara
16842 Von Karman Avenue, Suite 300
Irvine, CA 92606
949-261-1100

Leidenfrost/Horowitz & Associates
1833 Victory Boulevard
Glendale, CA 91201
818-246-6050
Web Address: www.iharchitect.com
Number of Employees: 140

H. Horowitz, *Principal*
Dave Schulenberg, *Office Manager*

Leighton & Associates
3934 Murphy Canyon Road, Suite B205
San Diego, CA 92123
858-292-8030
Web Address: leightongeo.com
Number of Employees: 27

Michael R. Stewart, *Principal*
Terry Hawley, *Personnel Manager*

Leo A. Daly
911 Wilshire Boulevard, Suite 2200
Los Angeles, CA 90017
213-629-0100
Number of Employees: 50
Roy Follmuth, *Managing Principal*

LPA
17848 Sky Park Circle
Irvine, CA 92614-6401
949-261-1001
Number of Employees: 90
Dan Heinfeld, *President*

Mackler Echt + Associates
8421 Wilshire Boulevard, Suite 206
Beverly Hills, CA 90211
213-653-9551
David Mackler, *President*

Magee Architects
12121 Wilshire Boulevard, Suite 322
Los Angeles, CA 90025
310-820-4376
Number of Employees: 18
Richard Magee, *President*

MCG Architects
200 South Los Robles Avenue, Suite 300
Pasadena, CA 91101
626-793-9119
Web Address: info@mcg.com
Number of Employees: 200

Frederick Gaylord, *CEO*
Brian Arial, *Hiring Contact for Architects*
Emeline Santos, *Hiring Contact for Accountants*
Cindy Coots, *Hiring Contact for Clerical
    Personnel*

McGraw/Baldwin Architects
701 B Street, Suite 200
San Diego, CA 92101
619-231-0751
Web Address: www.mbarch.com
Number of Employees: 40

Kennon Baldwin, *Principal*
Mary Fromson, *Office Administrator*

McLarand Vasquez & Partners
1900 Main Street, 8th Floor
Irvine, CA 92612
949-809-3300
Number of Employees: 70

Carl McLarand, *President*

MCM Architects
750 B Street, Suite 1700
San Diego, CA 92101
619-233-4857
Web Address: www.mcarchitects.net
Number of Employees: 20

Joseph Martinez, *Principal*

Montgomery Watson
750 B Street, Suite 1610
San Diego, CA 92101
619-239-3888
Web Address: www.mw.com

William H. Butler, *Principal*
Harold Glaser, *Hiring Manager*

Morimoto + Widom Wein Cohen
2020 Santa Monica Boulevard, Suite 400
Santa Monica, CA 90404
310-828-0400
Number of Employees: 32

Bruce Morimoto, *Principal*

Nadel Architects
1990 South Bundy Drive, 4th Floor
Los Angeles, CA 90025
310-826-2100
Web Address: www.nadel@pronex.com
Number of Employees: 150

Herb Nadel, *President*
Maria Bracanonte, *Director of Human Resources*

Nasland Engineering
4740 Ruffner Street
San Diego, CA 92111
619-292-7770
Web Address: www.nasland.com
Number of Employees: 40

D.K. Nasland, *Principal*
Steve Nasland, *Principal*
Janene Nasland, *Hiring Manager*

Neptune-Thomas-Davis
2025 Financial Way, Suite 106
Glendora, CA 91741
626-963-1401
Web Address: www.ntd.com

Anthony O'Keefe, *President*

Nolte & Associates
15090 Avenue of Science, Suite 101
San Diego, CA 92123
858-278-9392
Web Address: www.nolte.com
Number of Employees: 30

Jon H. Walters, *Principal*
Jossie Stinchcomb, *Office Manager*

NTD Architects
4719 Viewridge Avenue, Suite 200
San Diego, CA 92123
858-277-5115
Web Address: www.ntd.com
Number of Employees: 50

Jon Baker, *Principal*
Pamela Cabaniss, *Human Resource Manager*

Parsons Brinckerhoff
1230 Columbia Street, Suite 640
San Diego, CA 92101
619-338-9376
Web Address: www.pbworld.com
Number of Employees: 5

Gordon K. Lutes, *Principal*

Perry Consulting Group
5300 Jackson Drive
La Mesa, CA 91942
619-445-6033

Robert Perry, *Principal*
Kim Perry, *Office Manager*

Project Design Consultants
701 B Street, Suite 800
San Diego, CA 92101
619-235-6471
Web Address: www.projectdesign.com
Number of Employees: 180

Douglas C. Paul, *Principal*
Irene Edwards, *Controller*

RNM Architects & Planners
4611 Teller Avenue
Newport Beach, CA 92660-2104
949-752-1800
Number of Employees: 40

Ralph J Martin, *President*

Robbins Jorgensen Christopher
660 Ninth Avenue, Suite 200
San Diego, CA 92101
619-239-9292
Web Address: www.rjcarch.com
Number of Employees: 8

James Robbins, *Principal*
Janene Christopher, *Principal & Hiring Manager*

Robert Bein, William Frost & Associates
9755 Clairemont Mesa Boulevard, Suite 100
San Diego, CA 92124
858-614-5000
Web Address: www.rbf.com
Number of Employees: 35

Richard A. Rubin, *Principal*
Diana Apodaca, *Human Resource Manager*

Rochlin Baran & Balbona
10980 Wilshire Boulevard
Los Angeles, CA 90024
310-473-3555
Web Address: www.rbbinc.colm
Number of Employees: 50

Joseph A. Balbona, *CEO*
Babara Kuklin, *Director of Personnel*

Roesling Nakamura Architects
363 Fifth Avenue, Suite 202
San Diego, CA 92101
619-233-1023
Web Address: www.rjcarch.com
Number of Employees: 22

Ralph Roseling, *Principal*
Kotaro Nakamura

RTKL Associates
333 South Hope Street, C-200
Los Angeles, CA 90017
213-627-7373
Web Address: www.rtkl.com

David Brotman, *Vice Chairman*

Salerno/Livingston Architects
363 Fifth Avenue, Third Floor
San Diego, CA 92101
619-234-7471
Web Address: www.rnparch.com
Number of Employees: 25

Stan Livingston, *Principal*
Trish Wagner, *Human Resources Director*

Schuss Clark, an Architectural Corp.
9474 Kearny Villa Road, Suite 215
San Diego, CA 92126
858-578-2950
Number of Employees: 16

Howard Schuss, *Principal*

SGPA Architecture and Planning
1545 Hotel Circle South, Suite 200
San Diego, CA 92108
619-297-0131
Number of Employees: 41

David Reinker, *Principal*
Marla Martin, *Controller*

Southern California Soil & Testing
6280 Riverdale Street
San Diego, CA 92120
619-280-4321
Web Address: scst.com
Number of Employees: 75

tBP Architecture
2300 Newport Boulevard
Newport Beach, CA 92663-3799
949-673-0300
Web Address: www.tbparch.com
Number of Employees: 45
Alan Smith, *President*

Texeira LA
717 North Cienaga Boulevard
Los Angeles, CA 90069
310-358-7280
Web Address: www.texeira-la.com
Number of Employees: 20

Glenn Texeira, *President*
Lin Kerkour, *Director of Human Resources*

The Stichler Design Group
9655 Granite Ridge Drive, Suite 400
San Diego, CA 92123
619-565-4440
Web Address: www.stichler.com
Number of Employees: 120
Ronald A. Stichler, *Principal*
Mary Wiley, *Human Resource Manager*

TSL
4465 Wilshire Boulevard, Suite 100
Los Angeles, CA 90010
213-938-3803
Number of Employees: 9
Richard Lewis, *President*

Tucker Sadler & Associates
2411 Second Avenue
San Diego, CA 92101
619-236-1662
Number of Employees: 27
Harold Sadler, *Principal*
Al Castro, *President*

URS
1615 Murray Canyon Road, Suite 1000
San Diego, CA 92108
619-294-9400
Number of Employees: 50

Michael Nienberg, *Principal*
Walleen Smith, *Personnel Manager*
Carolyn Washington, *Human Resources Manager*

Villanueva Arnoni Architects
245 Fischer Avenue, Suite A3
Costa Mesa, CA 92626-4536
949-557-7855
Number of Employees: 24

Gregory Villanueva, *President*

Walker Group/CNI
11036 Sherman Way
Sun Valley, CA 91352
818-764-9286
Number of Employees: 12

Douglas Fowler, *Project Executive*
Anoush Drboyan, *Director of Human Resources*

Ware & Malcomb Architects
18002 Cowan
Irvine, CA 92614-6812
949-660-9128
Number of Employees: 55

Lawrence Armstrong, *Partner*

William Hezmalhalch Architects
17875 Von Karman Avenue, Suite 404
Irvine, CA 92614-6256
949-250-0607
Number of Employees: 63

Bill Hezmalhalch, *Principal*

Wimberly Allison Tong & Goo
2260 University Drive
Newport Beach, CA 92660-3319
949-574-8500
Web Address: www.watg.com
Number of Employees: 105

Chuck Corwin, *Managing Principal*

Wolcott Interior Planning and Design
3859 Cardiff Avenue
Culver City, CA 90232
310-204-2290
Web Address: www.wolcottdesign.com
Number of Employees: 20

John Wolcott, *President*
Gina Nible, *Human Resource Manager*

WWTCOT Morimoto Interiors
2020 Santa Monica Boulevard, Suite 400
Santa Monica, CA 90404
310-828-0040
Web Address: www.wwcarch.com
Number of Employees: 50

Ted Widom, *Principal*

Zimmer Gunsul Frasca Partnership
333 South Grand Avenue, Suite 3600
Los Angeles, CA 90071
213-617-1901
Web Address: www.zgf.com
Number of Employees: 30

R. Doss Mabe, *Partner*
Randy Leach, *Senior Partner*

Further References

• Associations •

American Association of Engineering Societies
1111 19th Street, Suite 608
Washington, D.C. 20036
202-296-2237
Coordinates Efforts of Member Societies.

American Consulting Engineers Council
1015 15th Street, N.W.
Washington, D.C. 20005
202-347-7474
Web Address: www.acec.org
Conducts Programs.

American Institute of Architects
1735 New York Avenue, N.W.
Washington, D.C. 20006
202-626-7300
Web Address: www.aiaonline.com
Education and Training for Members.

American Society of Civil Engineers
1801 Alexander Bell Drive
Reston, VA 20191
212-705-7496
Web Address: www.asce.org
Association of Civil Engineers.

American Society of Landscape Architects
4401 Connecticut Avenue, 5th Floor
Washington, D.C. 20008
202-686-2752
Web Address: www.asla.org
Education and Training for Landscape Architects.

National Academy of Engineering
2101 Constitution Avenue, N.W.
Washington, D.C. 20418
202-334-3200
Web Address: www.nae.edu
Advises Government and Honors Excellence.

National Society of Professional Engineers
1420 King Street
Alexandria, Virginia 22314
703-684-2800
Web Address: www.nspe.org
Society of Professional Engineers.

Society of American Registered Architects
1245 South Highland Avenue
Lombard, Illinois 60148
708-932-4622

• Publications •

Architectural Record
1221 Avenue of the Americas, 41st Floor
New York, NY 10020
212-512-6229
Web Address: www.mcgraw.com
Publishes essays on architecture design and trends related to the practice of architecture.

AIA Membership Directory
1735 New York Avenue, N.W.
Washington, D.C. 20006
202-626-7300
Web Address: www.aiaonline.com

Architects Directory
5711 South 86th Circle
Omaha, Nebraska 68127

Design Quarterly
55 Hayward
Cambridge, MA 02142
612-925-9150

Education

- Public Schools
- Colleges & Universities
- Private & Preparatory

Orange County Christian-CC
www.occs.aol.com
Orange Unified School District
www.orangeusd.k12.ca.us
Our Lady Queen of Angels
www.olga.org
Pacific Christian College
www.pacificcc.edu
Page School of Costa Mesa
www.pageschool.com
Palmdale School District
www.psd.k12.ca.us
Palomar College
www.palomar.edu
Palos Verdes Peninsula Unified
School District
www.pupusd.k12.ca.us
Pasadena Area Community College
District
www.paccd.cc.ca.us
Pasadena Unified School District
www.pasadena.k12.ca.us
Pegasus
www.pegasus.pvt.k12.ca.us
Pepperdine University
www.pepperdine.edu
Placentia-Yorba Linda Unified
School District
www.plyusd.k12.ca.us
Point Loma Nazarene College
www.ptloma.edu
Pomona Unified School District
www.pomona.k12.ca.us
Prentice Day
www.prentice.org
Redondo Beach School District
www.bnet.org
Rio Hondo Community College
www.rhcc.ca.us
Saddleback College
www.saddleback.cc.ca.us
Saddleback Valley School District
www.svusd.k12.ca.us
Saint Barbara
www.saintbarbara.com
Saint Bonaventure Elementary
www.saintbonaventure.org
Saint John's Lutheran
www.stjohnsluthern.org
Saint Margaret's
www.saintmargarets.org
San Diego City College
www.sdccd.cc.ca.us
San Diego Mesa College
www.sdmesa.sdccd.cc.ca.us
San Diego State University
www.sdsu.edu
Santa Ana Unified School District
www.sausd.k12.ca.us
Santa Margarita Catholic High
www.smhs.org
Santa Monica College
www.smc.edu
Santa Monica-Malibu Unified
School District
www.smmus.org
Saugus Union School District
www.saugus.k12.ca.us
Serra Catholic Elementary
www.serraschool.org
South Orange County Community
College District
www.saddleback.cc.ca.us
Southern California College
www.sccc.edu
Southwestern College
www.swc.cc.ca.us

Sulphur Springs School District
www.ssd.k12.ca.us
The Bishop's School
www.bishops.com
Thomas Jefferson School of Law
www.jeffersonlaw.edu
United States International
University
www.usiu.edu
University of California at Los
Angeles
www.ucla.edu
University of California Irvine
www.icu.edu
University of California, San Diego
www.admissions.ucsd.edu
University of Phoenix
www.uophx.edu/sandiego
University of San Diego
www.acusd.edu
Walnut Valley Unified School District
— Personal Services
www.walnut-valley.k12.ca.us
Webster University
www.websteruniv.edu
West Los Angeles College
www.wlac.edu
Western State University/Law
www.wsulaw.edu
Westside Union School District
www.westside.k12.ca.us
Whittier Christian High
www.wchs.com
Whittier Law School
www.law.whitier.edu
William S. Hart Union High School
District
www.hart.k12.ca.us
Wilsona School District
www.wison.k12.ca.us

Job Hotlines

Arcadia Unified School District
626-821-8300 x709
Azusa Unified School District
626-858-5066
Beverly Hills Unified School
District
310-277-5900 x119
California Institute of Technology
626-395-4660
California State University
Dominguez Hills
310-243-3840
California State U., Long Beach
562-985-5491
California State University LA
213-343-3678
California State University, Northridge
818-677-2087
California State University, San Marcos
760-750-4410
Cerritos College
562-860-5042
Cerritos Community College District
562-467-5042
Compton Community College District
310-900-1605
Compton Unified School District
310-632-3764
Culver City Unified School District
310-535-6906
Cuyamaca College
619-644-7000
East Los Angeles College
213-265-8650 x8653

East Whittier City School
District
562-464-9381
El Camino College
310-660-3809
El Monte City School District
626-453-3726
Glendale Unified School District
2818-47-1384
Grossmont College
619-644-7000
Hermosa Beach City School District
310-937-5877 x281
La Canada Unified School District
818-952-8300
Las Virgenes Unified School District
818-878-5294
Long Beach CC District
562-938-4050
Long Beach Unified School District
562-491-5627
Los Alamitos Unified School District
562-799-4722
Los Angeles CC District
213-891-2099
Los Angeles County Office of Ed.
562-401-5540
Los Angeles Harbor College
310-522-8366
Los Angeles Trade Technical College
213-744-9066
Los Angeles Unified School District
213-625-5300
Manhattan Beach Unified
School District
310-546-3488 x5993
MiraCosta College
760-795-6868
National University
619-563-7198
Norwalk-La Mirada School District
562-864-3526
Palomar College
760-744-2199
Pasadena Area Community
College District
626-585-7257
Pepperdine University
310-456-4397
Point Loma Nazarene College
619-849-2212
Pomona Unified School District
909-397-4800 x3188
Rio Hondo Community College
562-692-3677
Rowland Unified School District
626-854-8553
San Diego City College
619-584-6580
San Diego Mesa College
619-584-6580
San Diego Miramar College
619-536-7235
San Diego State University
619-594-5200
Santa Monica College
310-450-5150 x9321
Santa Monica Community
College District
310-452-9336
Santa Monica-Malibu Unified
School District
310-450-8338 x993
Torrance Unified School Distric
310-328-2572

234

University of California at Los Angeles 310-825-9151 University of San Diego 619-260-4626 West Covina Unified School District 626-338-3371	West Los Angeles College 310-287-4310 Whittier Union High School District 562-698-0312

Public Schools

ABC Unified School District
16700 South Norwalk Boulevard
Cerritos, CA 90703
562-926-5566
Job Hotline: 562-802-0896
Certified- 562-802-9742
Number of Employees: 2500

Yolanda Quesada, *Director of Personnel*
Kay Jones, *Human Resource Manager*

Acton-Aguadulce Unified School District
32248 Crown Valley Road
Acton, CA 93510
805-269-0750
Number of Employees: 185

Dr. Doug Bandevas, *Superintedent*
Linda Jeffery, *Certificated Personnel*
Elvira DeJesus, *Certified Personnel*

Alhambra City Schools
15 West Alhambra Road
Alhambra, CA 91801
626-308-2233
Number of Employees: 3,500

Dr. Richard Keil Hacker, *Superintendent*
Rose B. Bard, *Assistant Superintendent of Human Resouces*

Anaheim City School District
1001 South East Street
Anaheim, CA 92805
714-517-8500
Web Address: www.acsd.k12.ca.us

Roberta A. Thompson, *District Superintendent*
Ann Beavers, *Assistant Superintendent for Human Resources*

Anaheim Union High School District
501 Crescent Way
Anaheim, CA 92803
714-999-3511
Web Address: www.auhsd.k12.ca.us

Janice Billings, *District Superintendent*
Gerald Glenn, *Assistant Superintendent of Human Resources*

Antelope Valley Union High School District
28131 Livingston Avenue
Valencia, CA 91355
805-948-7655
Web Address: www.avdistrict.org
Number of Employees: 1500

Dr. Girolamo, *Superintendent*
David Vierra, *Assistant Superintendent*
Jeanette Combs, *Certificated Personnel Technician*

Arcadia Unified School District
234 Campus Drive
Arcadia, CA 91007
626-821-6627
Job Hotline: 626-821-8300 x709

Dr. Terrence Towner, *Superintendent*
Vicki Takemura, *Director of Personnel*

Azusa Unified School District
546 South Citrus Avenue
Azusa, CA 91702
626-858-6189
Job Hotline: 626-858-5066
Web Address: www.azusa.usd.k12.ca.us

Rod Gaeta, *Superintendent*
Dave Baker, *Assistant Superintendent of Human Resources*

Baldwin Park Unified School District
3699 North Holly Avenue
Baldwin Park, CA 91706
626-962-3311
Number of Employees: 1750

Dr. Susan Parks, *Superintendent*
Janet K. Reece, *Assistant Superintendent of Personnel*

Bassett Unified School District
904 North Willow Avenue
La Puente, CA 91746-1696
626-918-3138
Number of Employees: 750
Don Samuels, *Acting Supintendent*
Juan Lopez, *Director of Human Resources*

Bellflower Unified School District
16703 South Clark Avenue
Bellflower, CA 90706
562-866-9011
Web Address: www.busd.k12.ca.us
Number of Employees: 1,000

Dr. Ed Shaw, *Assistant Superintendent of Personnel*

Bonita Unified School District
115 West Allen Avenue
San Dimas, CA 91773
909-599-6787
Web Address: www.bonita.k12.ca.us
Number of Employees: 120

Dr. Lonnie McConnell, *Assistant Superintendent of Human Resources*

Brea-Olinda Unified School District
Number One Civic Center Circle
Brea, CA 92821
714-990-7800
Web Address: www.ocde.k12.ca.us

Peggy Lynch, *District Superintendent*
Peter J. Bothroyd, *Asst. Supt. for Human Services*

Buena Park School District
6885 Orangethorpe Avenue
Buena Park, CA 90620
714-522-8412

Carol Holmes Riley, *Superintendent*
Barbara Montelongo, *Resource Specialist*

Burbank Unified School District
330 North Buena Vista Street
Burbank, CA 91505
818-558-5415
Number of Employees: 1,500

Dr. Dave Aponik, *Superintendent*
Dr. Robert Fraser, *Director of Human Resources*

Capistrano Unified School District
32972 Calle Perfecto
San Juan Capistrano, CA 92675
714-489-7000
Web Address: www.capousd.k12.ca.us

James A. Fleming, *Superintendent*
Wilma Harvey, *Executive Director for Personnel*

Castaic Union School District
28131 Livingston Avenue
Valencia, CA 91355
805-257-4500
Web Address: www.castaic.k12.ca.us
Number of Employees: 180

Dr. Alan Nioshino, *Superintendent*
Beverly Knutson, *Director of Personnel*
Carol Davis, *Secretary*

Centralia School District
6625 La Palma Avenue
Buena Park, CA 90620
714-228-3100

John Carlyle, *Superintendent*
Jean Stuesser, *Director of Human Resources*

Charter Oak Unified School District
20240 Cienega Avenue
Covina, CA 91724
626-966-8331
Web Address: www.cousd.k12.ca.us
Number of Employees: 1,200

Sue Rainey, *Superintendent*
Judy Kubicek, *Credential Technician*

Citrus Communioty College
1000 West Foothill Boulevard
Glendora, CA 91741
626-335-0521
Web Address: www.citrus.cc.ca.us
Number of Employees: 1000

Dr. Louis Zellers, *President*
Dr. Jean Malone, *Director of Personnel*

Claremont Unified School District
2080 North Mountain Avenue
Claremont, CA 91711

Ms. Devon Lingenfelter, *Assistant Superintendent of Personnel*

Compton Community College District
1111 East Artesia Boulevard
Compton, CA 90221
310-900-1600
Job Hotline: 310-900-1605
Web Address: www.compton.cc.ca.us
Number of Employees: 90
Robert Joiner, *Associate Dean & Human Resource Contact*

Compton Unified School District
604 South Tamarind Avenue
Compton, CA 90220
310-639-4321
Job Hotline: 310-632-3764
Number of Employees: 3,000

Kevin Hanks, *Director of Certificated Personnel*

Covina-Valley Unified School District
519 East Badillo Street
Covina, CA 91723
626-974-7000
Number of Employees: 2382

Dr. Jack H. Rankin, *Superintendent*
Louis A. Pappas, *Assistant Superintendent of Personnel*

Culver City Unified School District
4034 Irving Place
Culver City, CA 90232
310-842-4227
Job Hotline: 310-535-6906
Web Address: www.ccusd.ca.us
Number of Employees: 650
Gladis L. Phillips-Evans, *Human Resource Manager*

Cypress School District
9470 Moody Street
Cypress, CA 90630
714-220-6900

William D. Eller, *District Superintendent*
Dr. Elizabeth Novack, *Director of Human Resources*

Downey Unified School District
11627 Brookshire Avenue
Downey, CA 90241
562-904-3526
Web Address: www.dusd.net
Number of Employees: 1,000

Edward Potter, *Assistant Superintendent of Personnel*

Duarte Unified School District
1620 Huntington Drive
Duarte, CA 91010
626-358-1191

Kent Bechler, *Superintendent*
Dr. Johnson, *Director of Human Resources*

East Whittier City School District
14535 East Whittier Boulevard
Whittier, CA 90605
562-698-0351
Job Hotline: 562-464-9381
Number of Employees: 900

Donna Lietzau, *Administrator of Certified Personnel*
Larry Bobst, *Assistant Superintendent of Personnel*
Linda Gruttaduria, *Administrator of Classified Personnel*

Eastside Union School District
6742 East Avenue H
Lancaster, CA 93535
805-946-2813
Number of Employees: 250

Constance Webb, *Superintendent*
Diane Losey, *Personnel Technician*

El Monte City School District
3540 Lexington Avenue
El Monte, CA 91731
626-453-3700
Job Hotline: 626-453-3726

Web Address: www.emcsd.k12.ca.us
Number of Employees: 1,000
Jeff Seymour, *Superintendent*
Rich White, *Assistant Superintendent of Personnel*

El Monte Union High School District
3537 North Johnson Avenue
El Monte, CA 91731
626-444-9005
Number of Employees: 1,200

Dave Sandell, *Superintendent*
Kathy M. Furnald, *Assistant Superintendent of Personnel*

El Rancho Unified School District
9333 Loch Lomond Drive
Pico Rivera, CA 90660
562-801-5215
Web Address: www.erusd.k12.ca.us
Number of Employees: 950

Sandra M. Vasquez, *Administrator of Certified Personnel*
Alfred L. Ogas, *Director of Personnel*
Julie Goulet, *Administrator of Classified Personnel*

El Segundo Unified School District
641 Sheldon Street
El Segundo, CA 90245
310-615-2650
Number of Employees: 250

Mary Keener, *Director of Personnel*

Fountain Valley School District
17210 Oak Street
Fountain Valley, CA 92708
714-843-3200

Marc Ecker, *Superintendent*
Carl Dane, *Assistant Superintendent of Personnel*

Fullerton Joint Union High School District
780 Beechwood Avenue
Fullerton, CA 92835
714-671-4331

Michael F. Escalante, *Superintendent*
Gregory Bice, *Assistant Superintendent for Personnel*

Fullerton School District
1401 West Valencia Drive
Fullerton, CA 92833
714-447-7400
Web Address: www.fsd.k12.ca.us

Ron Cooper, *District Superintendent*
Karin Lynch, *Assistant Superintendent for Personnel*

EDUCATION

237

Garden Grove Unified School District

10331 Stanford Avenue
Garden Grove, CA 92840
714-663-6000
Web Address: www.ggusd.k12.ca.us

Ronald N. Walter, *District Superintendent*
Laura Schwalm, *Assistant Superintendent for Personnel*

Garvey School District

2730 North Del Mar
Rosemead, CA 91770
626-307-3486
Number of Employees: 900

Alex Yusem, *Superintendent*
William V. Loose, *Assistant Superintendent of Personnel*

Glendale Community College District

1500 North Verdugo Road
Glendale, CA 91208
818-551-5171
Web Address: www.glendale.cc.ca.us
Number of Employees: 900

Dr. John A. Davitt, *Superintendent*
Barbara Stepp, *Human Resources Technician*
Leticia Estrada, *Human Resources Technician*
Rima Tarverdian, *Human Resources Technician*

Glendale Unified School District

223 North Jackson Street
Glendale, CA 91206
818-241-3111
Job Hotline: 2818-47-1384
Web Address: www.gusd.jpl.nasa.gov
Number of Employees: 3,000

James Brown, *Superintendent*
Cathy McMullen, *Assistant Administrator of Personnel*

Glendora Unified School District

500 North Loraine Avenue
Glendora, CA 91741
626-963-1611
Web Address: www.glendora.k12.ca.us

Patrick Bushman, *Superintendent*
Scott Bell, *Director of Personnel*

Gorman School District

49847 Gorman School Road
Gorman, CA 93243
805-248-6441
Number of Employees: 30

Esther Pereira, *Superintendent*
Karen Kingsley, *Office Manager*

Hacienda La Puente Unified School District

15959 East Gale Avenue
City of Industry, CA 91716
626-933-1000
Web Address: www.hlpusd.k12.ca.us
Number of Employees: 2500

John Reamer, *Superintendent*
Barbara Koehler, *Assistant Superintendent of Personnel*

Hawthorne School District

14120 Hawthorne Boulevard
Hawthorne, CA 90250
310-676-2276
Web Address: www.hawthorne.k12.ca.us/
Number of Employees: 1,200

Shelley Rose, *Director of Human Resources*

Hermosa Beach City School District

1645 Valley Drive
Hermose Beach, CA 90254
310-937-5877
Job Hotline: 310-937-5877 x281
Number of Employees: 100
Nora Roque, *Executive Assistant*

Hughes-Elizabeth Lakes Union School District

16633 Elizabeth Lake Road
Lake Hughes, CA 93532
805-724-1231
Web Address: www.helus.org
Number of Employees: 22

Dr. Thomas Guthrie, *Superintendent*
Cheryl Lundgren, *Director of Personnel*

Huntington Beach City School District

20451 Craimer Lane
Huntington Beach, CA 92646
714-964-8888

Duane Dishno, *Superintendent*
Kathy Kessler, *Assistant Superintendent for Personnel*

Huntington Beach Union High School District

10251 Yorktown Avenue
Huntington Beach, CA 92646
714-964-3339
Web Address: www.hbuhsd.k12.ca.us

Ronald G. Bennett, *District Superintendent*
Susan Roper, *Assistant Superintendent for Personnel*

Inglewood Unified School District
401 South Inglewood Avenue
Inglewood, CA 90301
310-419-2748
Web Address: www.@inglewood.k12.ca.us
Number of Employees: 1,500

Sandra Black-Walker, *Acting Director of
Certificated Personnel*

Irvine Unified School District
5050 Barranca Parkway
Irvine, CA 92604
949-651-0444
Web Address: www.iusd.k12.ca.us

Susan Long, *Deputy Superintendent for Human
Resources*

Keppel Union School District
34004 128th Street East
Pearblossom, CA 93553
805-944-2155
Web Address: www.keppel.k12.ca.us
Number of Employees: 350

Dr. Jean Fuller, *Superintendent*
Dr. Joseph Cox, Jr., *Director of Personnel*

La Canada Unified School District
5039 Palm Drive
La Canada, CA 91011
818-952-8300
Job Hotline: 818-952-8300
Web Address: www.lcusd.k12.ca.us
Number of Employees: 375

Lorie Gonia, *Superintendent*
Nancy Gascich, *Director of Personnel*

La Habra City School District
500 North Walnut Street
La Habra, CA 90631
562-690-2305
Web Address: www.lhcsd.k12.ca.us
Number of Employees: 750
Richard Hermann, *District Superintendent*
Tim Harvey, *Asst Superintendent - Certified
Personnel*
Martha Bafendell, *Classified Personnel Manager*

La Puente Valley ROP
455 North Glendora
La Puente, CA 91744
626-333-3773
Number of Employees: 200
Patricia Frank, *Superintendent*
Ann Fisher, *Personnel Supervisor*

Laguna Beach Unified School District
550 Blumont Street
Laguna Beach, CA 92651
714-497-7700
Reed Montgomery, *Superintendent*
Patty Beaver, *Human Resouces Manager*

Lancaster School District
44711 North Cedar Avenue
Lancaster, CA 93534
805-948-4661
Web Address: www.lancaster.k12.ca.us
Number of Employees: 1200

Dr. Steven Gocke, *Superintendent*
James R. Schettig, *Personnel Director*

Las Virgenes Unified School District
4111 North Las Virgenes Road
Calabasas, CA 91302
818-880-4000
Job Hotline: 818-878-5294
Web Address: www.lvusd.k12.ca.us
Number of Employees: 1,038

John F. Fitzpatrick, *Superintendent*
Deborah Coleman, *Assistant Superintendent of
Personnel*

Lawndale School District
4161 West 147th Street
Lawndale, CA 90260
310-973-1300
Web Address: www.lawndale.k12.ca.us
Number of Employees: 575

Shirley Giltzow, *Director of Personnel*

Lennox School District
10319 Firmona Avenue
Lennox, CA 90304
310-673-3490
Web Address: www.lennox.k12.ca.us
Number of Employees: 1,000

Ron Chan, *Director of Personnel*
Lucian Carter, *Assistant Superintendent*

Little Lake City School District
10515 South Pioneer Boulevard
Santa Fe Springs, CA 90670
562-868-8241
Number of Employees: 300

Mike Madrid, *Assistant Superintendent of
Personnel*
Shirley Perez, *Manager of Certified Personnel*
Nydia Mendez, *Manager of Classified
Personnel*

Long Beach Community College District
4901 East Carson Street
Long Beach, CA 90808
562-938-4397
Job Hotline: 562-938-4050
Web Address: www.lbcc.cc.ca.us
Number of Employees: 1,000

John Didion, *Dean of Personnel*
Victor R. Collins, *Dean of Human Resources*

239

Long Beach Unified School District
1515 Hughes Way
Long Beach, CA 90810
562-997-8000
Job Hotline: 562-491-5627 x8108
Web Address: www.@lbusd.k12.ca.us
Number of Employees: 1050

Maggie Webster, *Director of Certificated Personnel*
Ruth Ashley, *Director of Classified Personnel*

Los Alamitos Unified School District
10293 Bloomfield Street
Los Alamitos, CA 90720
562-799-4700
Job Hotline: 562-799-4722
Web Address: www.losalusd.k12.ca.us
Number of Employees: 900

Carol Hart, *District Superintendent*
David Hatton, *Assistant Superintendent for Personnel*

Los Angeles Community College District
770 Wilshire Boulevard
Los Angeles, CA 90017
213-891-2308
Job Hotline: 213-891-2099
Web Address: www.laccd.edu
Number of Employees: 2,000

Lucian Carter, *Assistant Superintendent*

Los Angeles County Office of Education
9300 Imperial Highway
Downey, CA 90242
562-803-8577
Job Hotline: 562-401-5540
Web Address: www.lacoe.edu
Number of Employees: 2,500

Dick Lane, *Coordinator of Teacher Staffing*
Mardi Reese, *Assistant Administrator*

Los Angeles County ROP
9300 Imperial Highway
Downey, CA 90242
562-922-6842

Clell Hoffman, *Director*

Los Angeles Unified School District
450 North Grand Avenue
Los Angeles, CA 90012
213-625-5300
Job Hotline: 213-625-5300

Justo Avila, *Assistant Director of Personnel*

Los Nietos School District
8324 South Westman Avenue
Whittier, CA 90606
562-692-0271
Web Address: www.losnietos.k12.ca.us

Number of Employees: 250
Tereza Ramirez, *Assistant Supt. of Personnel Certified*
Monica Estrada, *Director of Classified Personnel*

Lowell Joint School District
11019 South Valley Home Avenue
Whittier, CA 90603
562-943-0211
Web Address: www.lsw.lacoe.edu
Number of Employees: 200

Ronald T. Randolph, *Superintendent*
Kathy Marani, *Director of Certified Personnel*
Eva Yessian, *Director of Classified Personnel*

Lynwood Unified School District
11321 Bullis Road
Lynwood, CA 90262
310-886-1646
Web Address: www.lynwood.k12.ca.us
Number of Employees: 830
Miriam Bryant, *Personnel Manager*

Magnolia School District
2705 West Orange Avenue
Anaheim, CA 92804
714-761-5533

Paul S. Mercier, *District Superintendent*
Richard Turrentine, *Assistant Superintendent for Personnel*

Manhattan Beach Unified School District
1230 Rosecrans Avenue, Suite 400
Manhattan Beach, CA 90266
310-725-9050
Job Hotline: 310-546-3488 x5993
Number of Employees: 500

Candice Peterson, *Human Resources Technician*

Monrovia Unified School District
325 East Huntington Drive
Monrovia, CA 91016
626-359-9181
Number of Employees: 770

Louise Taylor, *Superintendent*
Linda Harding, *Director of Personnel*

Montebello Unified School District
123 South Montebello Boulevard
Montebello, CA 90640
213-887-7917
Web Address: www.montebello.k12.ca.us
Number of Employees: 1,200

Carolina H. Pavia, *Director of Certificated Personnel*

Mountain View School District
3320 Gilman Road
El Monte, CA 91732
626-350-3432
Number of Employees: 1,600

Gary Rapkin, *Superintendent*
Gloria Diaz, *Director of Personnel*

Newhall School District
25375 Orchard Village Road, Suite 200
Valencia, CA 91355
805-286-2200
Number of Employees: 600

Dr. Marc Winger, *Superintendent*
Anne L. Hazlett, *Personnel Director*

Newport-Mesa Unified School District
2985-A Bear Street
Costa Mesa, CA 92626
949-424-5000
Web Address: www.nmusd.k12.ca.us

Mac Bernd, *District Superintendent*
Jack Eisner, *Director of Human Resources*

Norwalk-La Mirada Unified School District
12820 South Pioneer Boulevard
Norwalk, CA 90650
562-868-0431
Job Hotline: 562-864-3523
Web Address: www.nlmusd.k12.ca.us
Number of Employees: 3,600

Robert Diaz, *Assistant Superintendent of Personnel*

Ocean View School District
17200 Pinehurst Lane
Huntington Beach, CA 92647
714-847-2551
Web Address: www.ovsd.k12.ca.us

James R. Tarwater, *District Superintendent*
John Tennant, *Asst. Supt. for Human Resources*

Orange Unified School District
1401 North Handy Street
Orange, CA 92867
714-997-6100
Web Address: www.orangeusd.k12.ca.us

Robert L. French, *Superintendent*
Malcolm Seheult, *Asst. Supt. for Human Resources*

Palmdale School District
39139 North Tenth Street East
Palmdale, CA 93550
805-947-7191
Web Address: www.psd.k12.ca.us
Number of Employees: 2208
Nancy Smith, *Superintendent*
Ed Wohlcke, *Personnel Manager*

Palos Verdes Peninsula Unified School District
3801 Via La Selva
Palos Verdes Estates, CA 90274
310-378-9966
Web Address: www.pupusd.k12.ca.us

Ira Toibin, *Superintendent*
Pat Jacobson, *Director of Certified Personnel*

Paramount Unified School District
15110 South California Avenue
Paramount, CA 90723
562-602-6006
Number of Employees: 700

Jay Wilbur, *Assistant Supt. of Personnel*
Jack Haney, *Director of Personnel*

Pasadena Area Community College District
1570 East Colorado Boulevard
Pasadena, CA 91106
626-585-7504
Job Hotline: 626-585-7257
Web Address: www.paccd.cc.ca.us
Number of Employees: 780

Dr. james Kossler, *President*
Sandra Lindoerfer, *Director of Human Resources*

Pasadena Unified School District
351 South Hudson Avenue
Pasadena, CA 91109
626-795-6981
Web Address: www.pasadena.k12.ca.us
Number of Employees: 2200

Vera Vignes, *Superintendent*
Marietta Palmer, *Assistant Supt. of Personnel*

Placentia-Yorba Linda Unified School District
1301 East Orangethorpe Avenue
Placentia, CA 92870
714-996-2550
Web Address: www.plyusd.k12.ca.us

James O. Fleming, *Superintendent*
Timothy VanEck, *Assistant Superintendent for Personnel*

Pomona Unified School District
800 South Garey Avenue
Pomona, CA 91766
909-397-4800
Job Hotline: 909-397-4800 x3188
Web Address: www.pomona.k12.ca.us
Number of Employees: 150

Emmett L. Terrell, *Assistant Supt. Personnel*

EDUCATION

Redondo Beach Unified School District
1401 Inglewood Avenue
Redondo Beach, CA 90278
310-379-5449
Web Address: www.bnet.org
Number of Employees: 800

William Nunan, *Assistant Superintendent*
Anita Chavez, *Administrative Assistant*

Rio Hondo Community College
3600 Workman Mill Road
Whittier, CA 90601
562-908-3405
Job Hotline: 562-692-3677
Web Address: www.rh.cc.ca.us
Number of Employees: 200

Ron Catarada, *Director of Human Relations*

Rosemead School District
3907 North Rosemead Boulevard
Rosemead, CA 91770
626-312-2900
Number of Employees: 350

Dr. Richard Yodites, *Superintendent*
Carol Forgey, *Personnel Administrator*

Rowland Unified School District
1830 South Nogales Street
Rowland Heights, CA 91748
626-854-8381
Job Hotline: 626-854-8553
Number of Employees: 2,000

Ron Leon, *Superintendent*
Gail Skokan, *Personnel Technician*
Marie Domingo, *Examination AssistantClassified*

Saddleback Valley Unified School District
25631 Diseno Drive
Mission Viejo, CA 92691
714-586-1234
Web Address: www.svusd.k12.ca.us
Peter A. Hartman, *Superintendent*
Jennifer Huff, *Asst. Supt. for Personnel/ Employee Relations*

San Gabriel Unified School District
102 East Broadway
San Gabriel, CA 91776
626-285-3111
Number of Employees: 500
Dr. Gary Goodson, *Superintendent*
John Kemp, *Director of Personnel*

San Marino Unified School District
1665 West Drive
San Marino, CA 91108
626-299-7000
Number of Employees: 20
Jack R. Rose, *Superintendent*
Linda Dela Torre, *Director of Human Resources*

Santa Ana Unified School District
1601 East Chestnut Avenue
Santa Ana, CA 92701
714-558-5501
Web Address: www.sausd.k12.ca.us

Al Mijares, *Superintendent*
Winston Best, *Asst. Superintendent for Human Resources*

Santa Monica-Malibu Unified School District
1651 Sixteenth Street
Santa Monica, CA 90404
310-450-8338
Job Hotline: 310-450-8338 x993
Web Address: www.smmus.org
Number of Employees: 1,700

Joseph N. Quarles, *Assistant Supt. of Personnel*

Saugus Union School District
24930 Avenue Stanford
Santa Clarita, CA 91355
805-294-7500
Web Address: www.saugus.k12.ca.us
Number of Employees: 923
Gail Wickstrom, *Superintendent*
Jill Goldberg, *Personnel Secretary*

South Pasadena Unified School District
1020 El Centro Street
South Pasadena, CA 91030
626-441-5700
Number of Employees: 339
Dr. Leslie Addison, *Superintendent*
Richard Taver, *Director of Personnel*

South Whittier School District
10120 South Painter Avenue
Whittier, CA 90605
562-944-6231
Number of Employees: 360
Lilia B. Dickson, *Assoc. Supt. of Certified Personnel*
Dr. David Morton, *Director of Classified Personnel*

Sulphur Springs School District
17866 Sierra Highway
Canyon Country, CA 91351
805-252-5131
Web Address: www.ssd.k12.ca.us
Robert A. Nolet, *Superintendent*
Nick Teeter, *Assistant Supeintendent of Business*
Janet Ellis, *Personnel Director*

Temple City Unified School District
9516 East Longden Avenue
Temple City, CA 91780
626-285-2111
Number of Employees: 600
Clint Taylor, *Superintendent*
Bill Brod, *Assistant Supt. of Personnel*

Torrance Unified School District
2335 Plaza Del Amo
Torrance, CA 90509
310-972-6900
Job Hotline: 310-328-2572
Number of Employees: 3,300
Debbie Lee, *Certificated Personnel Technician*

Tustin Unified School District
300 South C Street
Tustin, CA 92780
714-730-7301

George W. Mannon, *District Superintendent*
Chris Davidson, *Assistant Superintendent for Personnel*

Valle Lindo School District
1431 North Central Avenue
South El Monte, CA 91733
626-580-0686
Number of Employees: 150

Mary Louise, *Superintendent*
Al Crespo, *Director of Personnel*

Walnut Valley Unified School District — Personal Services
880 South Lemon Avenue
Walnut, CA 91789
909-595-1261
Web Address: www.walnut-valley.k12.ca.us

Josie Ruvalcaba, *Personnel Clerk*

West Covina Unified School District
1717 West Merced Avenue
West Covina, CA 91790
626-939-4600
Job Hotline: 626-338-3371
Number of Employees: 800

Steven Fish, *Superintendent*
Mike Popoff, *Director of Human Resources*

Westminister School District
14121 Cedarwood Avenue
Westminster, CA 92683
714-894-7311

Barbara Winars, *Deputy Superintendent*

Westside Union School District
46809 North 70th Street, West
Lancaster, CA 93536
805-948-2669
Web Address: www.westside.k12.ca.us
Number of Employees: 650

Allen Sacks, *Superintendent*
Chartlotte Geisen, *Personnel Technician*

Whittier Area Cooperative — Special Education Program
8036 South Ocean View Avenue
Whittier, CA 90602

562-945-6431
Number of Employees: 20
John H. Hess, *Director of Human Resources*

Whittier City School District
7211 South Whittier Avenue
Whittier, CA 90602
562-698-9531
Number of Employees: 700

Kirk G. Koehler, *Assistant Supt. of Personnel*

Whittier Union High School District
9401 South Painter Avenue
Whittier, CA 90605
562-698-8121
Job Hotline: 562-698-0312
Number of Employees: 950

Elizabeth L. Johnson, *Admin. Secretary for Personnel*

William S. Hart Union High School District
21515 Redview Drive
Santa Clarita, CA 91350
805-259-0033
Web Address: www.hart.k12.ca.us
Number of Employees: 1200

Robert C. Lee, *Superintendent*
Mike VonBulow, *Personnel Director*
Juan Lopez, *Personnel Assistant*

Wilsona School District
18050 East Avenue O
Palmdale, CA 93591
805-264-1111
Web Address: www.wison.k12.ca.us
Number of Employees: 264

Mary Gerard, *Superintendent*
Diane Lupton, *Certificated Personnel Director*
Barbara Wood, *Business Services Secretary*

Wiseburn School District
13530 Aviation Boulevard
Hawthorne, CA 90250
310-643-3025
Number of Employees: 225
Don Bramm, *Human Resource Manager*

Private & Preparatory Schools

Abiding Savior Lutheran
23262 El Toro Road
Lake Forest, CA 92630
714-830-1461

Harry G. Hebel, *Minister of Education*

Academy of Our Lady of Peace
4860 Oregon Street
San Diego, CA 92116
619-297-2266
Web Address: www.olp.org
Number of Employees: 60

Sister Dolores Anchondo, *Chief Administrator*

Anaheim Discovery Christian
720 South Magniolia Avenue
Anaheim, CA 92804
714-527-8484

Carol Caltharp, *Principal*

Anneliese's Schools
758 Manzanita
Laguna Beach, CA 92651
714-494-7388

Anneliese Schimmelpfenning, *Director/Owner*

Bethany Christian Academy
13431 Edwards Street
Westminster, CA 92683
714-891-9783

Patricia Harnish, *Principal*

Bethel Baptist Church
901 South Euclid
Santa Ana, CA 92704
714-839-3600

Terry Cantrell, *Administrator*

Blessed Sacrament Elementary
14146 South Olive Street
Westminster, CA 92683
714-893-7701

Roisin McAree, *Principal*

Blessed Sacrament Parish School
4551 56th Street
San Diego, CA 92115
619-582-3862
Number of Employees: 47

Theodora Furtado, *Chief Administrator*

Brea Christian School
314 East Alder Street
Brea, CA 92821
714-529-6112

Elaine Kendrick, *Administrator*

Brea-Olinda Friends Christian
200 Associated Road
Brea, CA 92821
714-990-8780

Betty Kimes, *Administrator*

Brethren Christian Junior and Senior High Senior
5172 Orange Avenue
Cypress, CA 90630
714-952-1177

Barrett Luketic, *Administrator*

Broderick Montessori
24292 Del Prado
Dana Point, CA 92629
714-443-1193

Sharon Broderick, *Director*

Calvary Chapel
5202 Lincoln Avenue
Cypress, CA 90630
714-236-1293

Jack Stevens, *President*

Calvary Chapel High School
3800 South Fairview
Santa Ana, CA 92704
714-662-7485

Tod DiLiberto, *Principal*

Calvary Christian
18821 Yorba Linda Boulevard
Yorba Linda, CA 92886
714-777-3441

Philip Cunningham, *Administrator*

Calvary Church Christian
1010 North Tustin
Santa Ana, CA 92705
714-973-2056

Rich Gerlsen, *Administrator*

Calvary School
7111 Trask Avenue
Westminster, CA 92683
714-897-9243

Bette Mackey, *Principal*

Calvin Christian Schools
2000 North Broadway
Escondido, CA 92026
760-489-6430
Number of Employees: 40

Terry Kok, *Chief Administrator*

Capistrano Valley Christian
32032 Del Obispo Street
San Juan Capistrano, CA 92675
714-493-5683

Edward J. Carney, *Administrator*

Capo Beach Christian School
25975 Domingo Avenue
Capistrano Beach, CA 92624
714-496-3513

Frederick Lenger, Jr., *Administrator*

Carden Academy
721 Utica Avenue
Huntington Beach, CA 92648
714-536-1441

Carol Van Asten, *Principal*

Carden Hall
1541 Monrovia Avenue
Newport Beach, CA 92663
949-645-1773

Albert H. Jones, *Owner/Director*

Carden School of Fountain Valley
10460 Slater Avenue
Fountain Valley, CA 92708
714-964-5559

Linda Updegraff, *Director*

Christ Lutheran Elementary
820 West Imperial HIghway
Brea, CA 92821
714-529-0892

Deryl R. Maxwell, *Principal*

Christ Lutheran Elementary
760 Victoria Street
Costa Mesa, CA 92627
949-548-6866

Duane J. Rohmaller, *Administrator*

Christian Unified Schools of San Diego
2100 Greenfield Drive
El Cajon, CA 92019
619-441-3787
Number of Employees: 100

Barbara Benjamin, *Human Resource Manager*

Claremont High
15461 Springdale Street
Huntington Beach, CA 92649
714-379-5461

Donna Connelly, *Director*

Covenant Christian
1855 Orange - Olive Road
Orange, CA 92865
714-998-4852

Ann Samuelson, *Administrator*

Crescent Avenue Christian
5600 Crescent Avenue
Buena Park, CA 90620
714-527-6673

Loretta Scott, *Administrator*

Crystal Cathedral Academy
13280 Chapman Avenue
Garden Grove, CA 92840
714-971-4158

Sheila Coleman, *Principal*

Eastside Christian School & Pre-school
2505 Yorba Linda Boulevard
Fullerton, CA 92834
714-879-2187
Web Address: www.eastsidechristian.org

David A. Schoen, *Administrator*

Escondido Christian School
923 Idaho Avenue
Escondido, CA 92025
760-745-2071
Number of Employees: 55

Julie Evangelisto, *Chief Admin.*

Fairmont Private
121 South Citron
Anaheim, CA 92805
714-533-3930
Web Address: www.fairmontschool.org

Yvonne Conklin, *Director*

Fairmont Private
1557 West Mabel Street
Anaheim, CA 92802
714-774-1052
Web Address: www.fairmontschool.org

Jackie Kearsing, *Director*

Fairmont Private
5310 East La Palma
Anaheim, CA 92807
714-693-3812
Web Address: www.fairmontschool.org

Lynn Thatcher, *Director*

Fairmont Private
2200 Sequoia Avenue
Anaheim, CA 92801
714-999-5050
Web Address: www.fairmontschool.org

Ron Woerner, *Director*

Fairmont Private School - Edgewood Campus
12421 Newport Avenue
Santa Ana, CA 92705
714-832-4867

David Jackson, *Adminstrator*

First South Baptist Christian
10350 Ellis Avenue
Fountain Valley, CA 92708
714-962-6886

Dale E. Hickey, *Administrator*

245

Francis Parker School
6501 Linda Vista Road
San Diego, CA 92111
858-569-7900
Web Address: www.francisparker.com
Number of Employees: 250

W. Lee Pierson, *Chief Administrator*

Friends Christian
4231 Rose Drive
Yorba Linda, CA 92886
714-524-5240

Rich Kempton, *Superintendent*

Futures High School
26440 La Alameda
Mission Viejo, CA 92691
714-348-0608
*Web Address: www.geocities.com/athens/
olympus/7137*

Liz Hallasz, *Principal*

Garden Grove Christian
13201 Century Boulevard
Garden Grove, CA 92843
714-537-3774

Steve Wenning, *Principal*

Grace Christian
5100 Cerritos Avenue, Building A
Cypress, CA 90630
714-761-5200

Frank Coburn, *Principal*

Grace Lutheran Elementary
16081 Waikiki Lane
Huntington Beach, CA 92649
714-377-1500

Richard Lewis, *Principal*

Grand Avenue Christian
2121 North Grand Avenue
Santa Ana, CA 92701
714-547-5039

Maribel Allison, *Principal*

Harbor Day
3443 Pacific View Drive
Corona Del Mar, CA 92625
714-640-1410
Web Address: www.hds.pvt.k12.ca.us

Sidney I. Dupont, *Headmaster*

Hebrew Academy
14401 Willow Lane
Westminster, CA 92683
714-898-0051

Rabbi Yitchok Newman, *Dean*

Hephatha Lutheran
5900 East Santa Ana Canyon Road
Anaheim, CA 92807
714-637-4022

Mickie Reinertson, *Principal*

Heritage Oak
16971 Imperial Highway
Yorba Linda, CA 92886
714-524-1350
Web Address: www.heritageoak.pvt.k12.ca.us

Phyllis Cygan, *Adminstrator*

Hillsborough School
191 Old Springs Road
Anaheim, CA 92808
714-998-9030

Grace Blanchard, *Director*

Holy Family Cathedral School
530 South Glassell
Orange, CA 92866
714-538-6012

Lorraine Fairbairn, *Principal*

Holy Trinity School
509 Ballard Street
El Cajon, CA 92019
619-444-7529
*Web Address:
www.holytrinityschool.mswin.net*
Number of Employees: 23

Barbara Picco, *Chief Administrator*

Hope Christian Academy
14811 Monroe Street
Midway City, CA 92605
714-373-4673

Deborah Haller, *Administrator*

Huntington Christian-FCC
1207 Main Street
Huntington Beach, CA 92648
714-536-0046

Art Blietz, *Principal/Administrator*

Immaculate Heart of Mary
2204 West McFadden Avenue
Santa Ana, CA 92704
714-545-8185

Mrs. Andree Oscoff, *Principal*

Independence Christian
1820 East Meats Avenue
Orange, CA 92865
714-974-3995

Ron Cushing, *Administrator*

La Jolla Country Day School
9490 Genesee Avenue
La Jolla, CA 92037
858-453-3440
Web Address: www.jcds.org
Number of Employees: 160

John Neiswender, *Chief Administrator*
Linda Moyer, *Assistant to Headmaster*

La Purisima Elementary
18801 Spring Street
Orange, CA 92869
714-633-5411
Web Address: www.ocweb.com/lps

Sr. Ceclilia Duran, ODN, *Principal*

Liberty Christian
7661 Warner Avenue
Huntington Beach, CA 92647
714-842-5992
Web Address: www.libertychristian.org

Clark Stephens, *Principal*

Light and Life Christian School
120 North Ash Street
Escondido, CA 92027
760-745-2832
Number of Employees: 55

Al Fikse, *Chief Administrator*

Lutheran High of Orange County
2222 North Santiago Boulevard
Orange, CA 92867
714-998-5151
Web Address: www.lutheranhigh.orange.ca.us

Kenneth Ellwein, *Executive Director*

Maranatha Christian Academy
3800 South Fairview Road
Santa Ana, CA 92704
714-556-0965
Dan Kotoff, *Principal*

Marian Catholic High School
1002 18th Street
San Diego, CA 92154
619-423-2121
Number of Employees: 45
Estelle L. Kassebaum, *Principal*

Mariners Christian School
300 Fischer Avenue
Costa Mesa, CA 92626
949-437-1700
Mary Letterman, *Principal*

Mater Dei High
1202 West Edinger Avenue
Santa Ana, CA 92707
714-754-7711
Patrick Murphy, *Principal*

Mission
31641 El Camino Real
San Juan Capistrano, CA 92675
714-248-2050

Virginia Sullivan, *Principal*

Mission Hills Christian
30161 Avenida de los Banderas
Rancho Santa Margarita, CA 92688
949-589-4504

Larry Ahl, *Administrator*

Montessori on the Lake
23311 Muirlands
Lake Forest, CA 92630
714-855-5630

Sarah Smith, *Director*

Oakridge Tustin
11911 Redhill Avenue
Santa Ana, CA 92705
714-832-2461
Web Address: www.oakridgetustin.com

Patricia A. Burry, *Director*

Orange County Christian-CC
641 South Western Avenue
Anaheim, CA 92804
714-821-6227
Web Address: www.occs.aol.com

Elaine Findley, *Principal*

Orange Crescent
9802 West 13th Street
Garden Grove, CA 92844
714-531-1451

Shaukat Mela, *Principal*

Orangewood Academy
13732 Clinton Avenue
Garden Grove, CA 92843
714-534-4694
Myriam Gonzales, *Principal*

Our Lady of De Pillar
601 North Western Avenue
Santa Ana, CA 92703
714-542-5177
John F. Demor, *Principal*

Our Lady of Fatima Elementary
105 La Esperanza
San Clemente, CA 92672
714-492-7320
Sue Simmons, *Principal*

Our Lady of Grace School
2766 Navajo Road
El Cajon, CA 92020
619-466-0055
Sister Bridgette Ann Carter, *Chief Administrator*

EDUCATION

Our Lady of Guadalupe Elementary
920 West La Habra Boulevard
La Habra, CA 90631
562-697-9726
Number of Employees: 25

Sr. Kathleen Marie Pughe, *Principal*
Jeffrey Moore, *Assistant Principal*

Our Lady Queen of Angels
750 Domingo Drive
Newport Beach, CA 92660
949-644-1166
Web Address: www.olga.org

Sister Joanne Clare Gallagher, *Administrator*

Our Savior's Lutheran
200 East San Pablo
San Clemente, CA 92672
714-492-6165

Kitty Schmitt, *Principal*

Page School of Costa Mesa
657 Victoria Avenue
Costa Mesa, CA 92627
949-642-0411
Web Address: www.pageschool.com

Karen Kral, *Executive Director*

Pegasus
19692 Lexington Lane
Huntington Beach, CA 92646
714-964-1224
Web Address: www.pegasus.pvt.k12.ca.us

Laura Katz Hathaway, *Director*

Prentice Day
18341 Lassen Drive
Santa Ana, CA 92705
714-538-4511
Web Address: www.prentice.org

Nancy Royal, *Director*

Prince of Peace Lutheran
1421 West Ball Road
Anaheim, CA 92802
714-774-0993

Loren F. Haack, *Administrator*

Prince of Peace Lutheran
2987 Mesa Verde Drive East
Costa Mesa, CA 92626
949-549-0562

Ken Townsend, *Principal*

Rancho Capistrano Church
29251 Camino Capistrano
San Juan Capistrano, CA 92675
714-347-4022

John Inman, *Director*

Red Hill Lutheran
31200 Red Hill Avenue
Tustin, CA 92780
714-544-3132

Udo Schmidt, *Administrator*

Rosary High
1340 North Acacia Avenue
Fullerton, CA 92831
714-879-6302
Web Address: www.rc.net/orange/rosary.com

Trudy Mazzarella, *Adminstrator*

Saddleback Christian Academy
26571 Briarwood Lane
San Juan Capistrano, CA 92691
714-888-0380

Lori Verstegen, *Administrator*

Saint Angela Merici
575 South Walnut
Brea, CA 92821
714-529-6372

Debra Declues, *Principal*

Saint Anne School
32451 Bear Brand Road
Laguna Niguel, CA 92677
714-362-4556

Janice Stonebreaker, *Principal*

Saint Anne's School
1324 South Main Street
Santa Ana, CA 92707
714-542-9328

Sr. Delores Aguilar, ODN, *Principal*

Saint Anthony Claret
1450 East La Palma Avenue
Anaheim, CA 92805
714-535-3284

Christine Rinella, *Principal*

Saint Barbara
5306 West McFadden Avenue
Santa Ana, CA 92704
714-775-9477
Web Address: www.saintbarbara.com

Judith Bloom, *Principal*

Saint Bonaventure Elementary
16377 Bradbury Lane
Huntington Beach, CA 92647
714-846-2472
Web Address: www.saintbonaventure.org

Sr. Carmel Lynch, *Principal*

Saint Boniface Elementary
500 West Chartres Street
Anaheim, CA 92805
714-772-3060

Elizabeth Kreig, *Principal*

Saint Callistus Elementary
12901 Lewis Street
Garden Grove, CA 92840
714-971-2023

Patricia Ritter, *Principal*

Saint Catherine
3090 South Coast HIghway
Laguna Beach, CA 92651
714-494-7339

Pat Prerost, *Principal*

Saint Catherine's Military
215 North Harbor Boulevard
Aneheim, CA 92805
714-772-1363

Carolyn Marie Monahan, *Administrator*

Saint Cecilia Elementary
1311 South East Sycamore
Tustin, CA 92780
714-544-1533

Suzanne De Vaney, *Principal*

Saint Columban's Elementary
10855 Stanford Avenue
Garden Grove, CA 92840
714-534-3947

Kathleen S. Orr, *Principal*

Saint Edwards
33866 Calle La Primavera
Dana Point 92629
714-496-1241

Joe Sinacore, *Administrator*

Saint Hedwig Elementary
3591 Orangewood Avenue
Los Alamitos, CA 90720
562-431-5001

Roberta Fox, *Principal*

Saint Irenaeus Elementary
9201 Grindlay Street
Cypress, CA 90630
714-827-4500

Beverly Harrison, *Administrator*

Saint Jeanne De Lestonnac
16791 East Main Street
Tustin, CA 92780
714-542-4271

Sr. Mary of Jesus Rodriguez, ODN, *Principal*

Saint Joachim Elementary
1964 Orange Avenue
Costa Mesa, CA 92627
949-574-7411

Sr. Sharon Maria Lamprecht, ODM, *Principal*

Saint John The Baptist
1021 Baker Street
Costa Mesa, CA 92626Costa Mesa, CA 92626
949-557-5060

Sr. Mary Vianney Ennis, *Principal*

Saint John's
30382 Via Con Dios
Rancho Santa Margarita, CA 92688
949-858-5144

James Lusby, *Headmaster*

Saint John's Lutheran
515 East Almond
Orange, CA 92866
714-997-1062
Web Address: www.stjohnsluthern.org

Isabel Stuewe, *Principal*

Saint Joseph Elementary
801 North Bradford Avenue
Placentia, CA 92870
714-528-1794

Judith Johnson, *Principal*

Saint Joseph Elementary
608 Civic Center Drive East
Santa Ana, CA 92701
714-542-2704

Kurt Spanel, *Principal*

Saint Juliana Falconieri Elementary
1320 North Acacia Avenue
Fullerton, CA 92831
714-871-2829
Mary M. Santoni, *Principal*

Saint Justin Martyr Catholic
2030 West Ball Road
Anaheim, CA 92804
714-772-4902
Kathleen B. Falcone, *Principal*

Saint Margaret's
31641 Ln Novia
San Juan Capistrano, CA 92675
714-661-0108
Web Address: www.saintmargarets.org
Markham B. Campaigne, *Headmaster*

Saint Mary's Elementary
400 West Commonwealth Avenue
Fullerton, CA 92832
714-525-9689
Colette Moore, *Principal*

249

Saint Michael The Archangel Academy
6 Alameda
Irvine, CA 92620
949-730-9114

Marcia L. Neill, *Director*

Saint Norbert Elementary
300 East Taft Avenue
Orange, CA 92865
714-637-6822

Sr. Frances O'Leary, *Principal*

Saint Paul's Lutheran
901 East Helm Avenue
Orange, CA 92865
714-921-3188

James Beaudoin, *Principal*

Saint Philip Benizi
215 South Pine Drive
Fullerton, CA 92833
714-871-6121

Neil R. Donat, *Principal*

Saint Pius V Elementary
7681 Orangethorpe Avenue
Buena Park, CA 90621
714-522-5313

Lois Ann Ruso, *Administrator*

Saint Polycarp Elementary
8182 Chapman Avenue
Stanton, CA 90680
714-893-8882

Sr. Patricia Cronin, *Principal*

Saint Simon & Jude Elementary
20400 Magnolia Street
Huntington Beach, CA 92646
714-962-4451

Crystal Smith, *Principal*

Salem Lutheran
6411 East Frank Lane
Orange, CA 92869
714-639-1946

Charlotte H. Meyer, *Principal*

San Diego Academy
2700 East Fourth Street
National City, CA 91950
619-267-9550
Number of Employees: 35

Wayne Longhofer, *Chief Administrator*

San Diego Jewish Academy
8660 Gilman Drive
La Jolla, CA 92037
858-457-5155
Michael D. Kessel, *Chief Administrator*

Santa Fe Christian Schools
838 Academy Drive
Solana Beach, CA 92075
858-755-8900
Web Address: www.sfc@cts.com
Number of Employees: 100

Jeff Woodcock, *Chief Administrator*

Santa Margarita Catholic High
22062 Antonio Parkway
Rancho Santa Margarita, CA 92688
949-858-3350
Web Address: www.smhs.org

Merritt Hemenway, *Principal*

School of the Madeleine
1875 Illion Street
San Diego, CA 92110
619-276-6545
Web Address:
www.madeleine.webmailcenter.com
Number of Employees: 35

Donna M. Wittouck, *Chief Administrator*

Serra Catholic Elementary
23652 Antonio Parkway
Rancho Santa Margarita, CA 92688
949-888-1990
Web Address: www.serraschool.org

Audrey Tellers, *Principal*

Servite High
1952 West La Palma Avenue
Anaheim, CA 92801
714-774-7575

Raymond Dunne, *Administrator-Principal*

Southern California Christian School System
8612 Orange-Olive Road
Orange, CA 92865
714-974-7766

Tom Trueblood, *Principal*

St. Augustine High School
3266 Nutmeg Street
San Diego, CA 92104
619-282-2184
Web Address: www.sahs.org

John R. Sanders, *Chief Administrator*

St. Mary's Elementary
130 East 13th Avenue
Escondido, CA 92025
760-743-3431
Number of Employees: 50

Peter Navarro, *Chief Admin.*
Linda Weber, *Human Resources Adminstrator*

St. Michael School
15542 Pomerado Road
Poway, CA 92064
858-485-1303
Web Address: www.stmichaelschurch-poway.org
Number of Employees: 25

James D. Gase, *Chief Administrator*

St. Pius X School
37 East Emerson Street
Chula Vista, CA 91911
619-422-2015
Web Address: www.spx-school.com
Number of Employees: 27

Eileen Hanson, *Chief Administrator*

Stoneybrooke Christian
26300 Via Escolar
San Juan Capistrano, CA 92692
714-364-4407

Sherry L. Worel, *Principal*

Tarbut V'Torah
250 East Baker #G
Costa Mesa, CA 92626
949-509-9500

Bernice Gelman, *Administrator*

The Bishop's School
7607 La Jolla Boulevard
La Jolla, CA 92037
858-459-4021
Web Address: www.bishops.com
Number of Employees: 110

Michael Teitelman, *Chief Admin.*

The Institute for Effective Education
248 Nutmeg Street
San Diego, CA 92103
619-521-3990
Number of Employees: 118

K. L. Traupmann, *Chief Admin.*
Dr. Fitch, *Ed.D*

Tri-City Christian Schools
302 North Emerald Drive
Vista, CA 92083
760-630-8227
Web Address: www.tccs.org
Number of Employees: 120

Don Hulin, *Superintendent*

Trinity Lutheran Christian Day
4101 East Nohl Ranch Road
Anaheim, CA 92807
714-637-8370

Dennis Snyder, *Principal*

University of San Diego High School
5961 Linda Vista Road
San Diego, CA 92110
619-298-8277
Web Address: www.usdhs.org
Number of Employees: 100

Richard E. Kelly, *Chief Admin.*
Myrna Colbert, *Coordinator*

Victory Christian
227 North Magnolia Avenue
Anaheim, CA 92801
714-220-6726

James D. Arkes, *Principal*

Vineyard Christian
5340 East La Palma
Anaheim, CA 92817
714-777-5462

Richard Bannister, *Principal*

Vineyard Christian
102 East Baker
Costa Mesa, CA
949-979-2957

Michael R. Barnett, *Administrator/Principal*

Whittier Christian High
2300 West Worth Avenue
La Habra, CA 90631
562-694-3803
Web Address: www.wchs.com
Number of Employees: 32

Robert Brown, *Principal*

Zion Lutheran
1244 East Cypress
Anaheim, CA 92805
714-535-3600

Jerry Reinertson, *Principal*

Zion Lutheran School
1405 East Fallbrook Street
Fallbrook, CA 92028
760-723-3500
Number of Employees: 50

Timothy N. Timm, *Chief Admin.*

Colleges & Universities

Antelope Valley Community College
3041 West Avenue K
Lancaster, CA 93536
805-722-6300
Web Address: www.avc.edu
Number of Employees: 580
Linda Spink, *President*
Priscilla Klubescheidt, *Human Resources Technician*

Azusa Pacific University
901 East Alosta Avenue
Azusa, CA 91702-700
626-969-3434

Richard Felix, *President*
Jody Bonba, *Director of Personnel*

California Institute of Technology
1200 East California Boulevard
Pasadena, CA 91125
818-395-6326
Job Hotline: 626-395-4660
Web Address: www.caltech.edu
Number of Employees: 1,800

David Baltimore, *President*
Tom Schmitt, *Director of Human Resources*

California School of Professional Psychology
6160 Cornerstone Court East
San Diego, CA 92121
858-623-2777
Web Address: www.webcom.com

Raymond J. Trybus, *President*

California State Polytechnic University
3801 West Temple Avenue
Pomona, CA 91768
909-869-2290
Web Address: www.csupomona.edu
Number of Employees: 2,000

Bob Suzuki, *President*

California State University Dominguez Hills
1000 East Victoria Street
Carson, CA 90747
310-243-3301
Job Hotline: 310-243-3840
Web Address: www.csudu.edu
Number of Employees: 2,400

Robert Detweiler, *President*

California State University, Fullerton
800 North State College Boulevard
Fullerton, CA 92834-9480
714-278-2011
Web Address: www.fullerton.edu
Number of Employees: 2500

Milton A Gordon, *President*

California State University, Long Beach
1250 Bellflower Boulevard
Long Beach, CA 90840
562-985-4121
Job Hotline: 562-985-5491
Web Address: www.csulb.edu
Number of Employees: 1,500

Robert Maxson, *President*

California State University Los Angeles
5151 State University Drive
Los Angeles, CA 90032
213-343-3000
Job Hotline: 213-343-3678
Web Address: www.csula.edu

James Rosser, *President*

California State University, Northridge
18111 Nordhoff Street
Northridge, CA 91330-824
818-677-1200
Job Hotline: 818-677-2087
Web Address: www.hrs.csun.edu
Number of Employees: 3,300

Blenda Wilson, *President*
Steve Montgomery, *Director of Human Resources*

California State University, San Marcos
333 South Twin Oaks Valley Road
San Marcos, CA 92096
760-750-4000
Job Hotline: 760-750-4410
Web Address: www.csusm.edu/hr
Number of Employees: 800

Alexandra Gonzalez, *President*
Melodie Kessler, *Human Resources Director*

Cerritos College
11110 Alondra Boulevard
Norwalk, CA 90650
562-860-2451
Job Hotline: 562-860-5042
Web Address: www.cerritos.edu
Number of Employees: 2500
Dan O'Rourke, *Assistant Superintendent of Personnel*
Martha Contreras, *Human Resource Manager*

Chapman Univ/School of Business
One University Drive
Orange, CA 92866-1099
714-997-6684
Web Address: www.chapman.edu/sbe
Number of Employees: 32

James Doti, *President*

Chapman University
One University Drive
Orange, CA 92866-1099
714-997-6686
Web Address: www.chapman.edu
Number of Employees: 465

Ganine Dumontelle, *President*
Rebecca Anderson, *Personnel Director*

Chapman University
7460 Mission Valley Road
San Diego, CA 92108
619-296-8660
Web Address: www.chapman.edu
Number of Employees: 30

James Doti, *President*
Maria Geat, *Director*
Shelly O'Leary, *Assistant Administrator*

Christian Heritage College
2100 Greenfield Drive
El Cajon, CA 92019
619-441-2200
Web Address: www.christianheritage.edu

David Jeremiah, *President*
Romeo Boudreau, *Personnel Manager*

Coast Community College
1370 Adams Avenue
Costa Mesa, CA 92626
949-438-4600
Web Address: www.cccb.edu
Number of Employees: 2600

William M. Vega, *Chancellor*
John D. Renley, *Vice Chancellor for Human Resources*

Coastline Community College
11460 Warner Avenue
Fountain Valley, CA 92708-2597
714-546-7600
Web Address: www.coastline.cccd edu
Number of Employees: 600

Leslie Purdy, *President*

Coleman College
7380 Parkway Drive
La Mesa, CA 91942
619-465-3990
Web Address: www.coleman.edu
Number of Employees: 200

Scott Rhude, *President*

College of the Canyons
26455 Rochwell Cyn Road
Santa Clarita, CA 91355
805-259-7800
Web Address: www.coc.cc.ca.us
Number of Employees: 200

Dr. Dianne Van Hook, *President /Superintendent*
Enita Morris, *Dean of Personnel Services*

Concordia University
1530 Concordia
Irvine, CA 92612-3203
949-854-8002
Web Address: www.cui.edu
Number of Employees: 200
Ray Halm, *President*

Cuyamaca College
900 Rancho San Diego Parkway
El Cajon, CA 92019
619-670-1980
Job Hotline: 619-644-7637
Web Address: www.gcccd.cc.ca.us
Number of Employees: 400

Dr. Sherrill Amador, *President*
Lisa Scotts, *Hiring Manager -Academic Personnel only*

De Vry Institute of Technology
901 Corporate Center Drive
Pomona, CA 91768
800-243-3660

Rose Marie Dishman, *President*

East Los Angeles College
1301 Avenida Cesar Chavez
Monterey Park, CA 91754
213-265-8650
Job Hotline: 213-265-8650 x8653

Ernest Moreno, *President*

El Camino College
16007 South Crenshaw Boulevard
Torrance, CA 90506
310-532-3670
Job Hotline: 310-660-3401
Web Address: www.elcamino.cc.ca.us
Number of Employees: 1,200

Thomas Fallo, *President*
Monica Wade, *Director of Human Resources*

Fullerton College
321 East Chapman Avenue
Fullerton, CA 92832-2095
714-992-7000
Web Address: www.fullcoll.edu
Number of Employees: 1000

Vera Martinez, *President*

Glendale Community College
1500 North Verdugo Road
Glendale, CA 91208
818-240-1000

John Davitt, Superintendent, *President*

Golden Gate University
2222 Martin, Suite 100
Irvine, CA 92612-1405
949-752-1700
Web Address: www.ggu.edu
Number of Employees: 365

Dr. Tom Stafford, *President*

Golden West College

PO Box 2748
Huntington Beach, CA 92647-0748
714-892-7711
Web Address: www.gwc.ccc.edu
Number of Employees: 900
Kenneth Yglesias, *President*

Grossmont College

8800 Grossmont College Drive
El Cajon, CA 92020
619-465-1700
Job Hotline: 619-644-7637
Web Address: www.gcccd.cc.ca.us
Number of Employees: 2200
Dr. Ted Martinez Jr., *President*
Jacqueline Goff, *Senior Personnel Assistant*

Irvine Valley College

5500 Irvine Center Drive
Irvine, CA 92620-4399
949-451-5100
Web Address: www.ivc.cc.ca.us
Number of Employees: 500
Gregory Mather, *President*

ITT Technical Institute

9680 Granite Ridge Drive
San Diego, CA 92123
858-571-8500
Web Address: www.itt-tech.com
Number of Employees: 80
Jackie Parma, *College Director*
Sherly Schulgen, *Director of Recruitment*

Kelsey-Jenney College

7310 Miramar Road, Suite 300
San Diego, CA 92126
858-549-5070
Web Address: www.kelsey-jenney.com
Tom Cajke, *President*
Julie Evan, *Human Resource Officer*

Los Angeles City College

855 North Vermont Avenue
Los Angeles, CA 90029
213-953-4000
Web Address: www.lacc.cc.ca.us
Number of Employees: 1,400
Mary Spangler, *President*
Lucian Carter, *Director of Human Resources*

Los Angeles Harbor College

1111 Figueroa Place
Wilmington, CA 90744
310-522-8200
Job Hotline: 310-522-8486
Web Address: www.lahc.cc.ca.us
Number of Employees: 900
Frank Quiambao, *President*
Claudette Yousins, *Human Resource Manager*

Los Angeles Pierce College

6201 Winnetka Avenue
Woodland Hills, CA 91371
818-719-6401
E. Bing Inocencio, *President*
Joe Metscher, *Director of Human Resources*

Los Angeles Trade Technical College

400 West Washington Boulevard
Los Angeles, CA 90015
213-744-9058
Job Hotline: 213-744-9066
Web Address: www.lattc.edu
Number of Employees: 550
Hosni Nabi, *President*
Lucian Carter, *Director of Human Resources*

Los Angeles Valley College

5800 Fulton Avenue
Van Nuys, CA 91401
818-781-1200
Tyree Wieder, *President*
Joe Metscher, *Director of Human Resources*

Marymount Webster Weekend College

2300 Michelson Drive, Suite 800
Irvine, CA 92612-1336
949-263-0316
Number of Employees: 40
Dr. Thomas McFadden, *President*

MiraCosta College

One Barnard Drive
Oceanside, CA 92056
760-757-2121
Job Hotline: 760-795-6868
Web Address: www.miracosta.cc.ca.us
Number of Employees: 400
Tim Dong, *President*
Carrie Ziemak, *Human Resources Director*

Mt. San Antonio College

1100 North Grand Avenue
Walnut, CA 91789
909-594-5611
Web Address: www.mtsac.edu
Number of Employees: 1141
William Feddersen, *President*
Peter Parra, *Director of Human Resources*

National University

3390 Harbor Boulevard
Costa Mesa, CA 92626-1502
949-429-5100
Web Address: www.nu.edu
Number of Employees: 500
Jerry Lee, *President*

National University
11255 North Torrey Pines Road
La Jolla, CA 92037
619-642-8000
Job Hotline: 619-563-7198
Web Address: www.nu.edu
Number of Employees: 200

Jerry C. Lee, *President*
Bita Himida, *Human Resource Director*

Northern Orange County Community College
1000 North Lemon Street
Fullerton, CA 92832-1318
714-578-8400
Number of Employees: 2300

Ed Bush, *Human Resources Manager*

Orange Coast College
PO Box 5005
Costa Mesa, CA 92628-5005
949-432-0202
Web Address: www.occ.cc.ca.edu
Number of Employees: 1132

Margaret A. Gratton, *President*

Pacific Christian College
2500 Nutwood Avenue
Fullerton, CA 92831-3104
714-879-3901
Web Address: www.pacificcc.edu
Number of Employees: 250

LeRoy Lawson, *President*

Palomar College
1140 West Mission Road
San Marcos, CA 92069
760-744-1150
Job Hotline: 760-744-1150 x2199
Web Address: www.palomar.edu
Number of Employees: 3200

George Boggs, *President*
Jack Miyamoto, *Assistant Superintendent*

Pasadena City College
1570 East Colorado Boulevard
Pasadena, CA 91106
626-585-7123

James Kossler, Superintendent, *President*

Pepperdine University
24255 Pacific Coast Highway
Malibu, CA 90263-437
310-456-4000
Job Hotline: 310-456-4397
Web Address: www.pepperdine.edu
Number of Employees: 1,200

David Davenport, *President*

Pepperdine University/Educational Center
2151 Michelson Drive, Suite 165
Irvine, CA 92612-1380
949-223-2500
Number of Employees: 1320

Point Loma Nazarene College
3900 Lomaland Drive
San Diego, CA 92106
619-849-2200
Job Hotline: 619-849-2212
Web Address: www.ptloma.edu
Number of Employees: 535

Robert Brower, *President*
Joyce Falk, *Human Resource Director*

Saddleback College
28000 Marguerite Parkway
Mission Viejo, CA 92692-3699
714-582-4500
Web Address: www.saddleback.cc.ca.us
Number of Employees: 1600

Richard McCullough, *President*
William O. Jay, *Human Resources Manager*

San Diego City College
1313 12th Avenue
San Diego, CA 92101
619-230-2400
Job Hotline: 619-388-6580
Web Address: www.sdccd.cc.ca.us

Jerome Hunter, *President*
Wayne Murphy, *Asst. Chancellor for Human Resources*
Send resumes to: San Diego City College; 3375 Camino Del Rio South; San Diego, CA 92108

San Diego Mesa College
7250 Mesa College Drive
San Diego, CA 92111
858-627-2600
Job Hotline: 619-388-6580
Web Address: www.sdmesa.sdccd.cc.ca.us
Number of Employees: 1544

Constance M. Carroll, *President*

San Diego Miramar College
10440 Black Mountain Road
San Diego, CA 92126
858-536-7800
Job Hotline: 619-584-6580
Web Address: www.sdccd.cc.ca.us

Pat Kier, *President*

EDUCATION

San Diego State University
5500 Campanile Drive
San Diego, CA 92182
619-594-5200
Job Hotline: 619-594-5200
Web Address: www.sdsu.edu
Number of Employees: 4000
Stephen L. Weber, *President*
Sue Blair, *Personnel Director*

Santa Ana College
1530 West 17th Street
Santa Ana, CA 92706-3398
714-564-6000
Number of Employees: 1500

John Didion, *Personnel Manager*

Santa Monica College
1900 Pico Boulevard
Santa Monica, CA 90405-1628
310-434-4000
Job Hotline: 310-434-4321
Web Address: www.smc.edu
Number of Employees: 1,400
Piedad Robertson, Superintendent, *President*
Sherry Lewis, *Director of Human Resources*

Southern California College
55 Fair Drive
Costa Mesa, CA 92626-6597
949-556-3610
Web Address: www.sccu.edu
Number of Employees: 116
Wayne Kraiss, *President*

Southern California College of Optometry
2575 Yorba Linda Boulevard
Fullerton, CA 92831-1615
714-870-7226
Number of Employees: 150
Richard L Hopping, *President*
Sue Nelson, *Personnel*

Southwestern College
900 Otay Lakes Road
Chula Vista, CA 91910
619-421-6700
Web Address: www.swc.cc.ca.us
Number of Employees: 575
Serafin Zasueta, *President*

Thomas Jefferson School of Law
2121 San Diego Avenue
San Diego, CA 92110
619-297-9700
Web Address: www.tjsl.edu
Number of Employees: 100
Kenneth J. Vandevelde, *President*
Julie Miller, *Human Resource Coordinator*

United States International University
2500 Michelson Drive, Suite 400
Irvine, CA 92612-1548
949-833-2651
Web Address: www.usiu.edu
Number of Employees: 345
Dr. Garry D. Hayes, *President*

United States International University
10455 Pomerado Road
San Diego, CA 92131
858-271-4300
Web Address: www.usiu.edu
Number of Employees: 200

Garry Hays, *President*

University of California at Los Angeles
2107 Murphy Hall
Los Angeles, CA 90095
310-825-4321
Job Hotline: 310-794-0800
Web Address: www.ucla.edu
Number of Employees: 3,400

Albert Carnesale, *Chancellor*

University of California Irvine
501 Admin Building Chancellors Office
Irvine, CA 92697
949-824-5111
Web Address: www.icu.edu
Number of Employees: 10000

Richard C Atkinson, *President*

University of California, San Diego
9500 Gilman Drive
La Jolla, CA 92093
858-534-4831
Job Hotline: 619-682-1000
Web Address: www.joblink.ucsd.edu
Number of Employees: 14,000

Robert C. Dynes, *Chancellor*
Send resumes to: UCSD HR; PO Box 0967;
La Jolla, CA 92093-0967

University of La Verne-OC Center
12951 Euclid Street, Suite 100
Garden Grove, CA 92840
714-534-4860
Number of Employees: 530

Pamela Bergovoy, *Director*

University of Phoenix
10540 Talbert Avenue
Fountain Valley, CA 92708-6000
Number of Employees: 3000
Bill Gibbs, *Founder*

University of Phoenix
3890 Murphy Canyon Road
San Diego, CA 92123
800-473-4346
Web Address: www.uophx.edu/sandiego
Number of Employees: 140

Todd Nelson, *President*
Nicole Tekstra, *Human Resources Liason*

University of Redlands
9040 Friars Road, Suite 310
San Diego, CA 92108
619-284-9292
Web Address: www.redlandsuor.edu
Number of Employees: 9

James R. Appleton, *President*
Roberta Delhime, *Human Resource Director*

University of Redlands Irvine
18818 Teller Avenue, Suite 160
Irvine, CA 92612-1679
949-833-2006
Number of Employees: 300

University of San Diego
5998 Alcala Park
San Diego, CA 92110
619-260-4600
Job Hotline: 619-260-6516
Web Address: www.acusd.edu
Number of Employees: 3121

Alice B. Hayes, *President*

Webster University
6480 Weathers Place, Suite 104
San Diego, CA 92121
858-458-9310
Web Address: www.webster.edu
Number of Employees: 55

Richard A. Meyers, *President*
Tana Tucci, *Human Resource Director*

West Los Angeles College
4800 Freshman Drive
Culver City, CA 90230
310-287-4200
Job Hotline: 310-287-4310
Web Address: www.wlac.edu
Number of Employees: 200

Evelyn C. Wong, *President*
Alice Jenkins, *Director of Job Placement*

Western State University/Law
1111 North State College Boulevard
Fullerton, CA 92831-3000
714-738-1000
Web Address: www.wsulaw.edu
Number of Employees: 225

Dennis Honabach, *Dean*

Further References

• Associations •

American Association of Christian Schools
P.O. Box 2189
Independence, MO 60455
816-795-7709
Web Address: www.aacs.org
Advancement of Christian Schools.

American Federation of School Administrators
1729 21st Street, N.W.
Washington, D.C. 20009
202-986-4209
Established for administrators of education with the intent to promote quality education.

Association of American Universities
1200 New York Avenue, Suite 550
Washington, D.C. 20005
202-408-7500
Web Address: www.Tulane.edu/~aau
The association assists universities in academic research and professional education.

Cause
4840 Pearl East Circle, Suite 320E
Boulder, CO 80301
303-449-4430
Web Address: www.cause.org
Established with the intent to improve education through technology based workshops using computers.

National Association of Educational Office Professionals
P.O. Box 12619
Wichita, KS 67277
316-942-4822
To acknowlege office workers involved in education.

National Association of Women in Education
1325 18th Street, N.W., Suite 210
Washington, D.C. 20036-6511
202-659-9330
Appreciation and Advancement of Women in Education.

American Association of School Administrators
1801 North Moore Street
Arlington, Virginia 22209
703-528-0700
Web Address: www.aasa.org
Coordinates Efforts of School Administrators.

EDUCATION

American Federation of Teachers
555 New Jersey Avenue, N.W.
Washington, D.C. 20001
202-879-4400
Web Address: www.aft.com
Represents Rights of Teachers.

Association of School Business Officials
11401 North Shore Drive
Reston, Virginia 20190
703-478-0405
Web Address: www.asbointl.org
Improvement of School Business Management.

College & University Personnel Association
1233 20th Street, N.W., Suite 301
Washington, D.C. 20036
202-429-0311
Web Address: www.cupa.org
Promotes Excellence Among University Personnel.

National Association of College Admissions Counselors
1631 Prince Street
Alexandria, Virginia 22314
703-836-2222
Web Address: www.nacac.com

National Association of College & University Business Officials
1 Dupont Circle, N.W.
Washington, D.C. 20036
202-861-2500
Web Address: www.nacubo.org

National Education Association
1201 16th Street, N.W.
Washington, D.C. 20036
202-833-4000
Web Address: www.nea.org

• Publications •

American Educator
555 New Jersey Avenue, N.W.
Washington, D.C. 20001
202-879-4420
Reports educational news.

American Libraries
50 East Huron Street
Chicago, IL 60611
312-944-6780

American Teacher
555 New Jersey Avenue, N.W.
Washington, D.C. 20001
202-879-4430

Black Employment and Education Magazine
Building 56, Suite 282
2625 Piedmont Road
Atlanta, GA 30324
404-469-5891

Education Week
4301 Connecticut Avenue, N.W.
Washington, D.C. 20008
202-686-0800
Web Address: www.edweek.org
Elementary and secondary school educators.

Educational Leadership
1250 North Pitt Street
Alexandria, VA 22314-1453
703-549-9110
Magazine on curriculum and leadership in schools.

Educational Researcher
1230 17th Street, N.W.
Washington, D.C. 20036-3078
202-223-9485

Instructor
555 Broadway
New York, NY 10012
212-343-6135
Educational magazine.

Review of Educational Research
1230 17th Street, N.W.
Washington, D.C. 20036-3078
202-223-9485
Reviews of educational research literature.

Teacher Magazine
4301 Connecticut Avenue, N.W.
Washington, D.C. 20008
202-686-0800
Magazine for elementary and secondary educational instructors.

The Chronicle of Higher Education
1255 23rd Street, N.W., Suite 700
Washington, D.C. 20037
202-466-1000
Web Address: //thisweek.chronicle.com

Young Children
1509 16th Street, N.W.
Washington, D.C. 20036
202-232-8777
Educational and developmental journal about children from birth to eight years old.

Washington Higher Education Association Directory
11 Dupont Circle, Suite 400
Washington, D.C. 20036
202-328-5900
Web Address: www.case.org

Entertainment

- Studios
- Motion Picture Organizations
- Theaters
- Networks
- Agents, Directors & Producers
- Dance Companies
- Production Co's
- Music Ensembles

Quick Reference

40 Acres & A Mule Filmworks
http://40acres.com

A Band Apart
www.AandE.com

ABC Entertainment
http://abc.com

ABC Pictures
http://abc.com

Abigail Abbott Staffing Svcs
www.abigailabbott.com

Accountants Overload
www.accountantsoverload.com

Bench International
www.benchinternational.com

Buena Vista Productions
www.disney.com

Campus Crusade for Christ
www.campuscrusade.com

Caravan Pictures
www.caravan.com

Castle Rock Entertainment
www.castle-rock.com

CBS Entertainment
www.cbs.com

CDI Corporation-West
www.cdicorp.com

Columbia Pictures
www.spe.sony.com

Columbia Tristar Motion Picture Group
www.sonypicturesjobs.com

Columbia Tristar Pictures
www.spe.sony.com

Columbia Tristar Television
www.spe.sony.com

Comedy Central
comedycentral.com

Complete Post
www.completepost.com

Crest National Optical Media
www.crestnational.com

Dimension Films
www.dimensionfilms.com

Disney Channel
www.disneychannel.com

DreamWorks SKG
http://showbizjobs.com

E! Entertainment Television
www.eonline.com

Fest of Arts/Pageant of Masters
www.foapom.com

Four Media Company
www.4mc.com

Fox Broadcasting Company
www.foxworld.com

Fox Kids Network
www.foxworld.com

Harpo Films
www.oprah.com

HBO Pictures
www.hbo.com

Hearst Entertainment
www.hearst.com

HRCS
www.hrcs.com

Image Entertainment
www.image-entertainment.com

Imax Corporation
www.imax.com

Irvine Barclay Theatre Operating Company
www.irvinebarclaytheatre.com

Iwerks Entertainment
www.iwerks.com

Jim Henson Company
www.henson.com

Lifetime Television (LA)
www.lifetimetv.com

Marvel Studios
www.marvel.com

McCray & Associates
www.mccray-inc.com

Medcom Trainex
www.medcominc.com

Merv Griffen Productions
www.merv.com

Miramax Films
www.miramax.com

National Geographic Television
www.nationalgeographic.com

NBC Entertainment
http://nbc.com

Netter Digital Entertainment
www.netterdigital.com

New Line Cinema
www.newline.com

New Regency Productions
www.newregency.com

Orange County Performing Arts
www.ocartsnet.org/ocpa

Pacific Ocean Post
www.popstudios.com

Paramount Network Television
www.paramount.com

Paramount Pictures
www.paramount.com

Paramount Television Group
www.paramount.com

Playboy Entertainment Group
www.playboy.com

Polygram Filmed Entertainment
www.reellife.com\pfe

Post Group
www.postgroup.com

Ray & Berndtson
www.rayberndtson.com

Remedy Intelligent Staffing
www.remedystaff.com

Rysher Entertainment
www.rysher.com

Showtime Networks
www.showtimeonline.com

Sony Pictures Entertainment
www.spe.sony.com/

Sony Pictures Imageworks
www.spiw.com

Stanton Chase International
www.stantonchase.com

The Dial Group
www.dialworks.com

Thomas Staffing Services
www.thomas-staffing.com

TLC Services Group
www.tlcsvcsgrp.com

Turner Network Television
www.turner.com

Twentieth Century Fox
www.fox.com

United Artists Pictures
www.mgmua.com

United Paramount Network
www.upn.com

Universal Studios
www.universalstudios.com

USA Networks / Television Group
www.universalstudios.com

Walt Disney Pictures / Touchstone Pictures
www.disney.com

Warner Brothers Feature Animation,
Pictures, TV Animation & Prod.
www.warnerbros.com

Yale Video
www.yalevideo.com

Job Hotlines

ABC Entertainment
310-557-4222

ABC Pictures 310-557-4222

Castle Rock Entertainment
818-954-5400

Columbia Pictures
310-244-4436

Columbia Tristar Motion Picture Group
310-244-4436

Columbia Tristar Pictures
310-244-4436

Columbia Tristar Television
310-244-4436

Dimension Films 213-951-4331

DreamWorks SKG
818-733-6100

E! Entertainment Television
213-954-2666

Evie Kreisler & Associates
800-275-3843

Four Media Company
818-840-7378

Fox Broadcasting Company
310-369-1360

259

Fox Kids Network
310-235-9400
Iwerks Entertainment
818-955-7895
Jim Henson Company
213-960-4096
NBC Entertainment   818-840-4397
New Line Cinema   310-967-6553
North Orange County ROP
776-2170
Pacific Ocean Post   310-458-3300 x5075
Paramount Pictures & Television Group
213-956-5216
Playboy Entertainment Group
310-246-7714
Polygram Filmed Entertainment
310-385-4111
Polygram Television   310-385-4111
Showtime Networks   213-956-5216
Sony Pictures Entertainment
310-244-4436
Sony Pictures Imageworks
310-840-8546
Turner Network Television
310-788-4255
Twentieth Century Fox
310-369-1360
Twentieth Century Fox Television
310-369-1360
United Artists Pictures
310-449-3569
Universal Studios   818-777-JOBS
Viacom Productions   213-956-5216
Warner Brothers Feature Animation
818-954-5400
Warner Brothers TV Animation
818-977-8534

40 Acres & A Mule Filmworks
8899 Beverly Boulevard, Suite 401
Los Angeles, CA 90048
310-276-2116
Web Address: http://40acres.com
Number of Employees: 3

Spike Lee, *Chairman*
Sam Kitt, *President*
Glenn Gray, *Intern Coordinator*

A Band Apart
7966 Beverly Boulevard
Los Angeles, CA 90048
213-951-4600
Web Address: www.AandE.com
Number of Employees: 20

Quentin Tarantino, *Director*

Aaron & Le Duc Video
2050 Cotner Avenue
Los Angeles, CA 90025
310-268-1577
Number of Employees: 10

Greg Le Duc, *Director*

ABC Pictures
2020 Avenue of the Stars, 5th Floor
Los Angeles, CA 90067
310-557-6806
Job Hotline: 310-557-4222
Web Address: http://abc.com
Number of Employees: 2,000

Didier Pietri, *Senior Vice President*

Academy of Country Music
6255 West Sunset Boulevard, Suite 923
Los Angeles, CA 90028
213-462-2352
Web Address: www.acmcountry.com
Number of Employees: 5

Fran Boyd, *Executive Director*

Academy of Motion Picture Arts and Sciences
8949 Wilshire Boulevard
Beverly Hills, CA 90211
310-247-3000
Web Address: www.oscars.org
Number of Employees: 145

Bruce Davis, *Executive Director*

Academy of Motion Picture Arts and Sciences
8949 Wilshire Boulevard
Beverly Hills, CA 90211
310-247-3000
Number of Employees: 145

Bruce Davis, *Executive Director*

Academy of Television Arts and Sciences
5220 Lankershim Boulevard
North Hollywood, CA 90211
818-754-2800
Web Address: www.emmys.org
Number of Employees: 145

James Loper, *Executive Director*

Actors Fund of America
5410 Wilshire Boulevard, Suite 400
Los Angeles, CA 90036
213-933-9244
Number of Employees: 160

Karen Holmes, *Human Resources Director*

All Girl Productions
100 Universal Plaza, Building 507 # 4D
Universal City, CA 91608
818-777-7776
Number of Employees: 7

Bette Midler, *Producer*
Bonnie Bruckheimer, *Producer*
Yvette Taylor, *Director of Human Resources*

All Post
1133 North Hollywood Way
Burbank, CA 91505
818-556-5700
Number of Employees: 185

James Collins, *CEO*
Mary Kay Berg, *Director of Human Resources*

Alliance of Motion Picture and Television Producers
15503 Ventura Boulevard
Encino, CA 91436
818-995-3600
Number of Employees: 20

J. Nicholas Countee III, *President*
Carol Lombardini, *Vice President*

AMC Entertainment
2049 Century Park East, Suite 1020
Los Angeles, CA 90067

American Academy of Dramatic Arts/West
2550 Paloma Street
Pasadena, CA 91107
626-798-0777
Web Address: www.aada.org
Number of Employees: 17
Jean Terruso, *President*
Maguerite Argura, *Managing Director*

American Cinema Editors
1041 North Formosa Avenue
West Hollywood, CA 90046
213-850-2900
Number of Employees: 3
Tom Rolf, *Executive Director*
Jack Tucker, *Treasurer*

American Federation of Musicians
1777 Vine Street, Suite 500
Hollywood, CA 90010
213-461-3441

American Film Institute
2021 North Western Avenue
Los Angles, CA 90027
213-856-7600

American Society of Cinematographers
1782 North Orange Drive
Hollywood, CA 90028
213-876-5080
Web Address: www.cinematographer.com

American Society of Music Arrangers and Composers
P.O. Box 11
Hollywood, CA 90078
213-658-5997

American Women in Radio and TV
P.O. Box 3615
Los Angeles, CA 90028
213-964-2740

Artisan/Live Entertainment
2700 Colorado Avenue, 2nd Floor
Santa Monica, CA 90404
310-449-9200
Web Address: www.artisanpictures.com
Number of Employees: 157

Mark A. Curcio, *President*
Nancy Coleman, *Director of Personnel*
Distributor and seller of film-related entertainment products worldwide. Its largest businesses are LIVE Film and Mediaworks and LIVE International, which acquire rights to produce and distribute theatrical motion pictures, children's films, and special interest programs.

Atlantic Records
9229 Sunset Boulevard, 9th Floor
Los Angeles, CA 90069
310-205-7450
Job Hotline: 310-205-7450 x 8
Web Address: ww.atlanticrecords.com
Karen De Marr, *Director of Human Resources*

Baltimore Pictures
4000 Warner Boulevard, Building 76
Burbank, CA 91522
818-954-2666
Number of Employees: 15

Barry Levinson, *Producer*
Anne Dauchy, *Director of Human Resources*

Beacon Pictures
1041 North Formosa Avenue
Hollywood, CA 90046
213-850-2651
Number of Employees: 25

Marc Abraham, *President*
Merry Rose, *Manager of Human Resources*

Bochco Productions
10201 West Pico Boulevard, Building 1
Los Angeles, CA 90035
310-369-2400
Number of Employees: 400

Steven Bochco, *CEO*
Franklin B. Rohner, *President & CFO*
Maureen Milligan, *Vice President of Human Resources*

261

Brillstein-Grey Entertainment
9150 Wilshire Boulevard, Suite 350
Beverly Hills, CA 90212
310-275-6135
Number of Employees: 60

Lloyd Braun, *President*
Joan Geller, *Office/Human Resource Manager*

Buena Vista Pictures Distribution
3800 West Alameda Avenue
Burbank, CA 91521
818-569-7500

Phillip Barlow, *President*

Buena Vista Sound
500 South Buena Vista Street
Burbank, CA 91521
818-560-7525

Chris Carey, VP, *Post Production Svcs.*

Campus Crusade for Christ
910 Calle Negocio
San Clemente, CA 92673
714-361-7575
Web Address: www.campuscrusade.com
Number of Employees: 13000

Wayne Brink, *Human Resources Director*

Capitol Records
1750 Vine Street
Hollywood, CA 90028
213-462-6252
Job Hotline: 213-871-5763
Web Address: www.hollywoodandvine.com

Carsey-Werner Distribution
4024 Radford Avenue
Studio City, CA 91604
818-760-5598
Number of Employees: 40

Stuart Glickman, *CEO*
Caryn Mandavach, *President*
Nina Bass, *Director of Personnel*

Castle Rock Entertainment
335 North Maple Drive, Suite 135
Beverly Hills, CA 90210
310-285-2300
Job Hotline: 818-954-7143
Web Address: www.castle-rock.com
Number of Employees: 200

Alan Horn, *CEO*
Glen Padnick, *President of Castle Rock
Television*
Martin Shafer, *President of Castle Rock Pictures*
Carlos Perez, *Vice President of Administration*
Jody Horowitz, *Human Resource Director*

CBS Entertainment
7800 Beverly Boulevard
Los Angeles, CA 90036
213-852-2345
Job Hotline: 213-852-2008
Web Address: www.cbs.com
Number of Employees: 750

Leslie Moonves, *President of CBS Television*
Lucy Cavallo, *Director of Casting*
Michael A. Katcher, *Director of Casting*
Fern Orenstein, *Director of Casting*
Airi Savasta, *Intern Coordinator*

Children's Television Workshop
One Lincoln Plaza, 4th Floor
New York, NY 10023
212-595-3456
Web Address: www.ctw.org

David Britt, *President*
Jeffrey Nelson, *Executive Producer*

Cinema Products Corporation
3211 South La Cienega Boulevard
Los Angeles, CA 90016
310-836-7991
Web Address: www.steadicam.com
Christina Jancsik, *Human Resource Manager*

Cinema Ride
12001 Ventura Place, Suite 340
Studio City, CA 91604
818-761-1002
Number of Employees: 63

Mitch Francis, *CEO*

Cinergi Pictures Entertaiment
2308 Broadway
Santa Monica, CA 90404
310-315-6000

Andrew Vajna, *CEO*

City Light Films
2110 Main Street, Suite 200
Santa Monica, CA 90405
310-230-7777
Number of Employees: 6

Martin Brest, *Producer*

Columbia Tristar Television
9336 West Washington Boulevard
Culver City, CA 90232
310-202-1234
Job Hotline: 310-244-4436
Web Address: www.spe.sony.com

Eric Tannenbaum, *President*
Kathryn Brutto, *Director of Human Resources*

Comedy Central
2049 Century Park East, Suite 2295
Los Angeles, CA 90067
310-201-9500
Web Address: http://comedycentral.com
Number of Employees: 500

Doug Herzog, *President*
Beth Hisler, *Vice President for Human Resources*

Complete Post
6087 Sunset Boulevard
Hollywood, CA 90028
213-467-1244
Web Address: www.completepost.com
Number of Employees: 200

J. Klein, *Co-president*
Al Cleland, *General Manager*

Consolidated Film Industries
959 North Seward Street
Hollywood, CA 90038
213-960-7444
Number of Employees: 390

Bob Beecher, *President*
Don Robards, *VP of Human Resources*

Crest National Optical Media
1000 North Highland Avenue
Hollywood, CA 90038
213-860-1300
Web Address: www.crestnational.com
Number of Employees: 100

Ronald Stein, *President*
Lorraine Ross, *Vice President*

Davis Entertainment
2121 Avenue of the Stars, Suite 2900
Los Angeles, CA 90067
310-556-3550
Number of Employees: 15

John A. Davis, *Chairman & Human Resource Director*
Brooke Brooks, *Vice President for Administration*

Dick Clark Productions
3003 West Olive Avenue
Burbank, CA 91505
818-841-3003
Web Address: www.dickclark.com
Number of Employees: 100

Richard W. Clark, *CEO*
Bill Simmon, *Director of Personnel*

Directors Guild of America
7920 Sunset Boulevard
Los Angeles, CA 90046
310-289-2000
Web Address: www.dga.org

Disney Channel
3800 West Alameda Avenue
Burbank, CA 91505
818-569-7500
Web Address: www.disneychannel.com

Anne Sweeney, *President*
Susette Hsuing, *Vice President for Production*

DreamWorks SKG
100 Universal Plaza, Building 10
Bungalow 477
Universal City, CA 91608
818-733-7000
Job Hotline: 818-733-6100
Web Address: http://showbizjobs.com
Number of Employees: 1700

Helene Hahn, *President*
Virginia Panawong, *Director of Human Resources*
Producer of films, TV programs, interactive software, records and toys. Formed by Steven Spielberg, Jeffrey Katzenberg, and David Geffen.

Dreyfuss/James Productions
1041 Formosa Avenue, Pickford Building 104
West Hollywood, CA 90046
213-850-3140
Web Address: greg@djprods.claris.com
Number of Employees: 5

Richard Dreyfuss, *Owner*
Judith James, *Owner*

Dubs
1220 North Highland Avenue
Los Angeles, CA 90038
213-461-3726
Number of Employees: 187

Vince Lyons, *Owner*

E! Entertainment Television
5670 Wilshire Boulevard
Los Angeles, CA 90036
213-954-2400
Job Hotline: 213-954-2666
Web Address: www.eonline.com
Number of Employees: 850

Lee Masters, *President*

Entertainment Recruiting Network
7095 Hollywood Boulevard, Suite 711
Hollywood, CA 90028
Web Address: www.showbizjobs.com

Fest of Arts/Pageant of Masters
650 Laguna Canyon Road
Laguna Beach, CA 92651-1899
714-494-1145
Web Address: www.foapom.com
Number of Employees: 25

Phil Freeman, *President*

Film and Television Careers
Web Address: www.filmtvcareers.com

Foto-Kem
2800 West Olive Avenue
Burbank, CA 91505
818-846-3101

Steve Van Anda, *VP of Sales/Marketing*
Casar Corona, *Director of Human Resources*

Four Media Company
2813 West Alameda Avenue
Burbank, CA 91505-4455
818-840-7100
Job Hotline: 818-840-7378
Web Address: www.4mc.com
Number of Employees: 100

Robert T. Walston, *President*
Kristi Kleckner, *Director of Personnel*
Producer of film, video, sound, and data, including corporate promotions, music videos, infomercials, and animation for television.

Fox Kids Network
10960 Wilshire Boulevard
Los Angeles, CA 90024
310-235-9600
Job Hotline: 310-235-9400
Web Address: www.foxworld.com
Number of Employees: 650

Haim Saban, *CEO*
Wendy Hartmann, *Recruiter*

Gracie Films
10202 West Washington Boulevard
Sidney Poitier Building, 2nd Floor
Culver City, CA 90232
310-244-4222
Number of Employees: 20

James L. Brooks, *Producer*
Richard Sakai, *President*
Kely R. Kulchak, *Vice President for Production*
Denise Sirkot, *Vice President*

Greg Silverman Productions
3000 West Olympic Boulevard, Building 4
Suite 1314
Santa Monica, CA 90404
310-264-4199

Harpo Films
345 North Maple Drive, Suite 315
Beverly Hills, CA 90210
310-278-5559
Job Hotline: 312-633-1000
Web Address: www.oprah.com
Number of Employees: 6

Oprah Winfrey, *CEO*
Jeffrey Jacobs, *President*
Tim Tortora, *Director of Production*

HBO Pictures
2049 Century Park East, Suite 3600
Los Angeles, CA 90067
310-201-9200
Web Address: www.hbo.com
Number of Employees: 400

John Matoian, *President*
Carmi Zlotnik, *Senior VP for Production*
Jay Roewe, *Vice President for Production*
Alissa Katz, *Intern Cordinator & HR Manager*

Hearst Entertainment
1640 South Sepulveda Boulevard, 4th Floor
Los Angeles, CA 90025
310-478-1700
Job Hotline: Ext 197
Web Address: www.hearst.com
Number of Employees: 60

Glenda Grant, *President*
Lisa Brown, *Director of Human Resources*

Hollywood Records
500 South Buena Vista Street
Burbank, CA 90028
818-560-5670
Web Address: www.hollywoodrec.com

Horshoe Bay Productions
710 Wilshire Boulevard, Suite 600
Santa Monica, CA 90401
310-587-0787
Number of Employees: 9

Gary S. Foster, *Producer & Human Resource Director*
Chris Adams, *Intern Coordinator*

Icon Productions
4000 Warner Boulevard
Burbank, CA 91522
818-954-2960
Number of Employees: 20

Bruce Davey, *President*
Steve McEveety, *Producer*
Vicki Christianson, *Director of Human Resources*

Image Entertainment
9333 Oso Avenue
Chatsworth, CA 91311
818-407-9100
Web Address: www.image-entertainment.com
Number of Employees: 121

Martin W. Greenwald, *President*
Robin Brenner, *Director of Personnel*
The largest laserdisc licensee and distributor in the US. Has over 1,000 titles ranging from feature films and music videos to family, documentary, and special-interest programming. Releases titles from Disney's Buena Vista Home Video, Hallmark Home Entertainment, and Turner Home Entertainment.

Imax Corporation
3003 Exposition Boulevard
Santa Monica, CA 90404
310-255-5500
Web Address: www.imax.com

Andrew Gellis, *Senior VP for Film/Distribution*
Mary Sullivan, *Human Resource Director*

International Animated Film Society
P.O. Box 787
Burbank, CA 91503
818-842-8330

International Animated Film Society
P.O. Box 787
Burbank, CA 91503
818-842-8330

International Creative Training
245 Fischer Avenue, Suite B5B
Costa Mesa, CA 92626-4535
949-241-9226
Number of Employees: 35

Clark Bannert, *President*

International Stunt Association
3518 Cahuenga Boulevard, West
Los Angeles, CA 90068
213-874-3174

Irvine Barclay Theatre Operating Company
4255 Campus Drive, Suite 220
Irvine, CA 92612-2647
949-854-4646
Web Address: www.irvinebarclaytheatre.com
Number of Employees: 20

Douglas Rankin, *President*

Iwerks Entertainment
4540 West Valerio Street
Burbank, CA 91505-1046
818-841-7766
Job Hotline: 818-955-7895
Web Address: www.iwerks.com
Number of Employees: 118

Charles Goldwater, *President*
Developer of motion-simulation theaters, and giant-screen, 360-degree, and 3-D theater systems, for theme parks, clubs, and museums. Also licenses and produces films.

Jim Henson Company
5358 Melrose Avenue, Suite 300 West
Hollywood, CA 90038
213-960-4096
Job Hotline: 213-960-4096
Web Address: www.henson.com
Number of Employees: 75

Brian Henson, *President*

Katie Face Production
10202 West Washington Boulevard
D Lean # 103
Culver City, CA 90232
310-244-6788
Number of Employees: 4

Tony Danza, *Principal*
Melissa Goldsmith, *President*
Tamara Holmes, *Human Resource Manager*
George Seley, *Human Resource Manager*

King World Productions - CBS
12400 Wilshire Boulevard, Suite 1200
Los Angeles, CA 90025
310-826-1108
Web Address: www.kingworld.com
Number of Employees: 50
Roger King, *Chairman*
Michael King, *Consultant*
Brenda Young, *Human Resource Director*

Kopelson Entertainment
2121 Avenue of the Stars, Suite 1400
Los Angeles, CA 90067
310-369-7500
Number of Employees: 20
Arnold Kopelson, *CEO*
Anne Kopelson, *Producer*
Maria Norman, *Vice President for Administration*
Lara Wood, *Intern Coordinator*

Kushner Locke Co.
11601 Wilshire Boulevard, 21st Floor
Los Angeles, CA 90025
310-445-1111
Web Address: www.kushner-locke.com
Number of Employees: 90
Donald Kushner, *Co-CEO*
Sherry Mills, *Human Resources Director*

Largo Entertainment
2029 Century Park East, Suite 2500
Los Angeles, CA 90067
310-203-0055
Number of Employees: 10
Barr Potter, *CEO*
Scott Polanco, *Office Manager*

Las Vegas Entertainment
1801 Century Park East
Los Angeles, CA 90067
310-551-0011
Number of Employees: 3
Joseph A. Corazzi, *CEO*

Lifetime Television -LA
2049 Century Park East, Suite 840
Los Angeles, CA 90067
310-556-7500
Web Address: www.lifetimetv.com
Number of Employees: 25
Rick Jacobs, Head, *Talent*

Lobell-Bergman Productions
100 Universal City Plaza, # 301
Universal City, CA 91608
818-777-9944
Number of Employees: 12

Andrew Bergman, *Producer*
Mike Lobell, *Producer*

Martin Brinkerhoff Associates
17767 Mitchell North
Irvine, CA 92614-6028
949-660-9396
Number of Employees: 20

Martin Brinkerhoff, *President*

Matthews Studio Group
3111 North Kenwood Street
Burbank, CA 91505
818-525-5200
Number of Employees: 339

Carlos D. De Mattos, *President*
Pauline Williams, *Director of Personnel*
Oscar and Emmy-winning equipment producer for the movie, photography, TV, and video industries. Products include film and video cameras, lights, camera mounts and cranes, grip accessories, and tripods.

MCA Records
70 Universal Plaza
Universal City, CA 91608
818-777-4000
Job Hotline: 818-777-5627
Web Address: www.mcarecords.com

Medcom Trainex
6060 Phyllis Drive
Cypress, CA 90630-0003
714-891-1443
Web Address: www.medcominc.com
Number of Employees: 75

Larry Gorum, *President*

Melrose Productions
27420 Avenue Scott, Stage #A
Santa Clarita, CA 91355
805-295-3333

Frank South, *Executive Producer*
Terri Johnson, *Intern Coordinator*

Merv Griffin Productions
3000 31st Street
Santa Monica, CA 90405
310-664-3000
Job Hotline: Ext 3058
Web Address: www.merv.com
Number of Employees: 60

Ernest Chambers, *Senior VP for Production*
Rick Sullivan, *VP of Finance*
Annie Schindler, *Human Resource Manager*

MGM/United Artists Pictures
2500 Broadway Street, 5th Floor
Santa Monica, CA 90404
310-449-3000
Job Hotline: 310-449-3569
Web Address: www.mgmua.com

Frank Mancuso, *CEO*
Lindsay Doran, *President*
Benita Palmer, *Senior Recruiter of Administration*

Mirage Enterprises
5555 Melrose Avenue, DeMille Building
1st Floor
Los Angeles, CA 90038
213-956-5600
Number of Employees: 11

Sydney Pollack, *Producer*
William Horberg, *Producer*

Miramax Films
7920 Sunset Boulevard, Suite 230
Los Angeles, CA 90046
213-845-2000
Web Address: www.miramax.com

Neil Blatt, Executive VP, *Distribution*

Miramax Films/Dimension Films
7966 Beverly Boulevard
Los Angeles, CA 90048
213-951-4200
Web Address: www.miramax.com

Harvey Weinstein, *Co-Chairman*
Bob Weinstein, *Co-Chairman*
Paul Udouk, *Intern Coordinator*

Morgan Creek Productions
4000 Warner Boulevard, Building 76
Burbank, CA 91522
818-954-4800

James G. Robinson, *CEO*
Jonathan A. Zimbert, *President*
David Boysen, *Director of Human Resources*

Motion Picture Corporation of America
1401 Ocean Avenue, Suite 301
Santa Monica, CA 90401
310-319-9500
Number of Employees: 30

Brad Krevoy, *President*

Motion Pictures Association of America
15503 Ventura Boulevard
Encino, CA 91436
818-556-6567

MTV Films
5555 Melrose Avenue, Studio H, Suite 200
Los Angeles, CA 90038
213-956-8023
Number of Employees: 7

Van Toffler, *General Manager*
Troy Phoon, *Assistant Executive Producer*

Mutual Film Company
650 North Bronson Avenue, Clinton Building
Los Angeles, CA 90004
213-871-5690
Number of Employees: 25

Mark Gordon, *Principal*
Gary Levinsohn, *Principal*
Ed McGuire, *Director*

Naitonal Academy of Songwriters
6255 Sunset Boulevard, Suite 1023
Hollywood, CA 90028
213-463-7178

National Academy of Recording Arts
3402 Pico Boulevard
Santa Monica, CA 90405
310-392-3777
Web Address: www.grammy.com

National Associations of Composers
P.O. Box 49256
Los Angeles, CA 90049
310-541-8213

National Geographic Feature Films
4370 Tujunga Avenue, Suite 330
Studio City, CA 91604
818-506-2420
Number of Employees: 4

Hank Palmieri, *President*

National Geographic Television
4370 Tujunga Avenue, Suite 300
Studio City, CA 91604
818-506-8300
Web Address: www.nationalgeographic.com
Number of Employees: 34

Nicolas Noxon, *Executive Producer*

National Lampoon
10850 Wilshire Boulevard, Suite 1000
Los Angeles, CA 90024
310-474-5252
Web Address: www.nationallampoon.com
Number of Employees: 5
James P. Jimirro, *CEO*
Cora Asuncion, *Office/Human Resource Manager*

NBC Entertainment-KNBC Channel 4
3000 West Alameda Avenue
Burbank, CA 91523
818-840-4444
Job Hotline: 818-840-4397
Web Address: www.nbc.com
Number of Employees: 1,200
Warren Littlefield, *President*
Harold Brook, *Executive Vice President*
Faye Clark, *Employee Relations Representative*

NBC Studios
3000 West Alameda Avenue, Suite 124
Burbank, CA 91523
818-840-7500
Web Address: www.nbc.com

Harold Brook, *Executive Vice President*

Netter Digital Entertainment
5125 Lankershim Boulevard
North Hollywood, CA 91601
818-753-1990
Web Address: www.netterdigital.com
Number of Employees: 75

Douglas Netter, *President*
Producer of TV shows and movies, and provider of special-effects technology and services. Its Entertainment Production division specializes in combining live action with computer graphics

New Line Cinema
116 North Robertson Boulevard, Suite 400
Los Angeles, CA 90048
310-854-5811
Web Address: www.newline.com

Robert Shaye, *CEO*

New Regency Productions
4000 Warner Boulevard, Building 66
Burbank, CA 91522
818-954-3044
Web Address: www.newregency.com
Number of Employees: 80

Arnon Milchan, *Producer*
David Matalon, *President*
Jon Katzman, *Vice President for Television*

Northern Lights Entertainment
100 Universal City Plaza, Building 489
Universal City, CA 91608
818-777-8080
Number of Employees: 15

Ivan Reitman, *Executive Producerq*
Dan M. Goldberg, *Producer*
Terry Norton, *Director of Human Resources*

NTN Communications
5966 La Place Court, Suite 100
Carlsbad, CA 92008
760-438-7400
Web Address: www.ntn.com

Opera Pacific
9 Executive Circle, Suite 190
Irvine, CA 92614-6734
949-474-4488
Number of Employees: 21

Martin Hubbard, *Director*

Orange County Performing Arts
600 Town Center Drive
Costa Mesa, CA 92626-1997
949-556-2121
Web Address: www.ocartsnet.org/ocpa
Number of Employees: 185
Peggy Armstrong, *Personnel Director*

Pacific Ocean Post
730 Arizona Avenue
Santa Monica, CA 90401
310-458-3300
Job Hotline: 310-458-3300 x5075
Web Address: www.popstudios.com
Number of Employees: 200
Rob Walston, *President*
Lynn Cobb, *Director of Human Resources*

Pacific Title Mirage
6350 Santa Monica Boulevard
Hollywood, CA 90038
213-464-0121
Number of Employees: 80
Phil Feiner, *President*
Carol Hester, *Director of Human Resources*

Pacific Western Productions
5555 Melrose Avenue, Lubitsch Annex 119
Los Angeles, CA 90038
213-956-8601
Web Address: james_rossow@paramount.com
Number of Employees: 9
Gale Anne Hurd, *Producer*
Jake Fincioen, *Assistant Vice President*

Paramount Pictures
5555 Melrose Avenue
Los Angeles, CA 90038
213-956-5000
Job Hotline: 213-956-5216
Web Address: www.paramount.com
Number of Employees: 2,000

Sherry Lansing, *Chairman*
Garry Hart, *President of Paramount Network Television*
Harlan Goodman, *Senior VP for Music*

Pearson Television
2700 Colorado Avenue
Santa Monica, CA 90404
310-656-1100
Number of Employees: 28

Playboy Entertainment Group
9242 Beverly Boulevard, 3rd Floor
Beverly Hills, CA 90210
310-246-4000
Job Hotline: x 4602
Web Address: www.playboy.com
Number of Employees: 220
Anthony J. Lynn, *President*
Wendy Morimoto, *Human Resource Manager*

Post Group
6335 Homewood Avenue
Los Angeles, CA 90028
213-462-2300
Web Address: www.postgroup.com
Number of Employees: 150

Fred Rheinstein, *CEO*

Producers Guild of America
453 South Beverly Drive, Suite 211
Beverly Hills, CA 90212
310-557-0807

Producers Guild of America
453 South Beverly Drive, Suite 211
Beverly Hills, CA 90212
310-557-0807

Propaganda Films
940 North Mansfield Avenue
Los Angeles, CA 90038
213-462-6400
Number of Employees: 120

Steve Golin, *Chairman*
James Tauber, *President*

Quincy Jones*David Salzman Entertainment
3800 Barham Boulevard, Suite 503
Los Angeles, CA 90068
213-874-2009
Number of Employees: 9

Quincy Jones, *Co-CEO*
David Salzman, *Co-CEO*
Jay Immato, *Intern Coordinator*

Rank Video Services America
12691 Pala Drive
Garden Grove, CA 92841-3926
714-891-7306
Number of Employees: 1800

Rhino Entertainment
10635 Santa Monica Boulevard, Suite 200
Los Angeles, CA 90025
310-474-4778
Job Hotline: 310-441-6688
Web Address: www.rhino.com
Number of Employees: 150
Audra Colquitte, *Human Resource Manager*

Rysher Entertainment
2401 Colorado Avenue, Suite 200
Santa Monica, CA 90404
310-309-5200
Web Address: www.rysher.com

Tim Helfet, *President*

SAVANT Audiovisuals
801 East Chapman Avenue, #101
Fullerton, CA 92834-3670
714-870-7880
Number of Employees: 20

Howard J. Sloane, *President*

Scott Free Productions
634 North La Peer Drive
Los Angeles, CA 90069
310-360-2250
Number of Employees: 20

Ridley Scott, *Co-Chairman*
Tony Scott, *Co-Chairman*
Molly Ann Howard, *Office Manager*
Nonny Shafii, *Human Resource Manager*

Scott Rudin Productions
5555 Melrose Avene, DeMille Building
Suite 200
Los Angeles, CA 90038
213-956-4600
Number of Employees: 10

Scott Rudin, *Producer*
Adam Schroeder, *President*
Patrick Corbett, *Intern Coordinator*

Screens Actors Guild
5757 Wilshire Boulevard
Los Angeles, CA 90036
213-954-1600
Web Address: www.sag.com

Showtime Networks
10880 Wilshire Boulevard, Suite 1500 & 1600
Los Angeles, CA 90024
310-234-5200
Job Hotline: 310-234-5255
Web Address: www.showtimeonline.com
Number of Employees: 120

Jerry Offsay, *President*
Cindy Miller, *Director of Human Resources*

Society of Motion Picture and Television Art Directors
11365 Ventura Boulevard, Suite 315
Studio City, CA 91604
818-762-9995

Sony Pictures Entertainment
10202 West Washington Boulevard
Culver City, CA 90232
310-244-4000
Job Hotline: 310-244-4436
Web Address: www.sonypicturesjobs.com
Number of Employees: 1,500

Kenneth Lemberger, *President of Tristar Picture Group*
Amy Pascal, *President of Columbia Pictures*
Noel Gonzales, *Human Resource Manager*

Sony Pictures Entertainment
10202 West Washington Boulevard
Culver City, CA 90232
310-244-4000
Job Hotline: 310-244-4436
Web Address: www.spe.sony.com/
Number of Employees: 110

John Calley, *President & CEO*
Charlotte Claiborne, *Executive VP for Human Resources*

Sony Pictures Imageworks
9050 West Washington Boulevard
Culver City, CA 90232
310-840-8000
Web Address: www.spiw.com

Ken Ralston, *President*
Robin Tomkins, *Intern Coordinator & HR Manager*

South Coast Repertory
655 Towne Centre Drive
Costa Mesa, CA 92628-2197
949-957-2602
Web Address: www.theatre@scr.org/scr
Number of Employees: 67

Mark Hadley, *Business Manager*

Spelling Television
5700 Wilshire Boulevard, Suite 575
Los Angeles, CA 90036
213-965-5700
Web Address: www.viacom.com
Number of Employees: 400

Aaron Spelling, *CEO*
Jonathan C. Levin, *President*
Shauntel Hulte, *Compensation and Benefits Manager*

Technicolor, Motion Pictures Division
4050 Lankershim Boulevard
Universal City, CA 91608
818-769-8500

Ronald Jarvis, *President*
Charles Byloos, *Director of Human Resources*

The Ladd Company
5555 Melrose Avenue, Chevalier 117
Los Angeles, CA 90038
213-956-8203
Number of Employees: 11

Alan Ladd, Jr., *President*
Toby Jaffe, *Producer*
Kelliann Ladd, *Producer*

The Robert Evens Company

5555 Melrose Avenue, Lubitsch # 117
Los Angeles, CA 90038
213-956-8800
Number of Employees: 6

Robert Evans, *Chairman*
Christine Forsyth-Peters, *President*
Shannon McNulty, *Intern Cocordinator*

The Todd-AO Corp.

900 North Seward Street
Hollywood, CA 90038
213-962-4000
Number of Employees: 200

J. R. DeLang, *Senior Vice President*
Kate Reck, *VP of Human Resources*

The Walt Disney Company

500 South Buena Vista Street
Burbank, CA 91521
818-560-1000
Job Hotline: 818-558-2222
Web Address: www.disney.com

Michael D. Eisner, *CEO*
Peter Schneider, *President of Feature Animation*
Joe Roth, *Chairman of Walt Disney Studios*
Marjorie Randolf, *Vice President for Human Resources*
Kathy Nelson, *President of Music*
World's 2nd largest media conglomerate. Interests include TV & movie production (Buena Vista, Touchstone Pictures), theme parks (Disneyland, Magic Kingdom), publishing (Disney Press, Hyperion Press), and pro sports (Mighty Ducks hockey team).

TLC Entertainment

4024 Radford Avenue
Studio City, CA 91604
818-760-6155
Number of Employees: 10

George Taweel, *Producer*

Tribeca Productions

375 Greenwich Street, 8th Floor
New York, NY 10013
212-941-4040

Robert De Niro, *Chairman*
Jane Rosenthal, *President*

Trilogy Entertainment Group

2450 Broadway, Suite 675
Santa Monica, CA 90404
310-449-3095
Number of Employees: 20
Pen Densham, *Co-Chairman*
Richard Barton Lewis, *Co-Chairman*
John Watson, *Co-Chairman*
John O'Connel, *Office Manager*
Bob Webber, *VP of Corporate Affairs*

Turner Network Television

1888 Century Park East, 14th Floor
Los Angeles, CA 90067
310-551-6300
Job Hotline: 310-788-4255
Web Address: www.turner.com
Number of Employees: 150

Brad Siegel, *President*
Lynn Patterson, *Administrator of Human Resources*

Twentieth Century Fox

10201 West Pico Boulevard
Los Angeles, CA 90035
310-369-1000
Job Hotline: 310-369-1360
Web Address: www.fox.com
Number of Employees: 4,000

William Mechanic, *CEO*
Sandy Grushow, *President of Fox Television*

United Paramount Network

11800 Wilshire Boulevard
Los Angeles, CA 90025
310-575-7000
Job Hotline: 323-956-5000
Web Address: www.upn.com
Number of Employees: 300

Dean Valentine, *President*
Alice Mayer, *Manager of Administration*

Universal Studios/USA Networks

100 Universal City Plaza
Universal City, CA 91608
818-777-1000
Job Hotline: 818-777-JOBS
Web Address: www.universalstudios.com
Number of Employees: 14000

Frank J. Biondi Jr., *President*
Kenneth L. Khars, *Director of Personnel*

Viacom Productions

10880 Wilshire Boulevard, Suite 1101
Los Angeles, CA 90024
310-234-5000
Job Hotline: 213-956-5216

Perry Simon, *President*

Virgin Records

338 North Foothill Drive
Beverly Hills, CA 90210
310-278-1181
Web Address: www.virginrecords.com

ENTERTAINMENT

Warner Brothers Feature Animation
500 North Brand Boulevard, Suite 1800
Glendale, CA 91203
818-977-7707
Job Hotline: 818-954-5400
Web Address: www.warnerbros.com
Number of Employees: 300

Max Howard, *President*
Tom Knoft, *Artistic Recruiter*

Warner Brothers International TV Production
4000 West Alameda, 6th Floor
Burbank, CA 91505
818-977-5100

Catherine Malatesta, *Senior VP for International Production*
Glenda Moody, *Administrator for Human Resources*

Warner Brothers Pictures
4000 Warner Boulevard
Burbank, CA 91522
818-954-6000
Web Address: www.warnerbros.com

Robert A. Daly, *Co-CEO & Chairman*
Terry Semel, *Co-CEO & Chairman*
Gary LeMel, *President of Music*
Adrienne Gary, *Executive Vice President for Human Resources*

Warner Brothers TV Animation
15303 Ventura Boulevard, Suite 1200
Sherman Oaks, CA 91403
818-977-8700
Job Hotline: 818-977-8534
Web Address: www.warnerbros.com
Number of Employees: 900

Jean MacCurdy, *President*
Scott Sefterberg, *Director of Human Resources*

Wind Dancer Production Group
500 South Buena Vista, Production Building, 3rd Floor
Burbank, CA 91521
818-560-5715
Number of Employees: 35

Rick Leed, *President*
Pete Meserve, *Director of Human Resources*

Yale Video
1360 North Hancock Street
Anaheim, CA 92807-1921
714-693-5300
Web Address: www.yalevideo.com
Number of Employees: 30

Burt Yale, *President*

INDUSTRY OUTLOOK

The broad arts and entertainment industry is often very rewarding although high salaries are hard to find. College degrees are often necessary but are sometimes negated by talent and creativity. Starting salaries average close to $25,000 for most fields but vary greatly.

Further References

• Associations •

Academy of Motion Picture Arts and Sciences
8949 Wilshire Boulevard
Beverly Hills, CA 90211
310-247-3000
Web Address: www.ampas.org
Advancement of Arts and Sciences in Motion Pictures.

Academy of Television Arts & Sciences
5220 Lankershim Boulevard
North Hollywood, California 91601
818-754-2800
Web Address: www.emmys.org
Advancement of arts and sciences in television.

Actor's Equity Association
165 West 46th Street
New York, New York 10036
212-869-8530
Represents actors and awards excellence in theatre.

Affiliate Artists
45 West 60th Street
New York, New York 10023
Promotes career development of artists.

American Dance Guild
31 West 21st Street
New York, New York 10010
212-932-2789
Initiates programs of national significance.

American Federation of Musicians
1501 Broadway, Suite 600
New York, New York 10036
212-869-1330
Musicians interested in advancing music industry.

American Film Marketing Association
10850 Wilshire Boulevard, 9th Floor
Los Angeles, CA 90024-4305
310-447-1555
Web Address: www.afma.com
Involved in the production and distribution of English language films to the foreign market.

American Guild of Musical Artists
1727 Broadway
New York, New York 10019
212-265-3687
Classical and opera singers and related managers.

American Music Center
30 West 26th Street, Suite 1001
New York, New York 10010
212-366-5260
Web Address: www.amc.net/amc/
Appreciation and creation of contemporary music.

American Society of Cinematographers
1782 North Orange Drive
Hollywood, CA 90028
213-969-4333

American Society of Composers, Authors & Publishers
1 Lincoln Plaza
New York, New York 10023
212-595-3050
Web Address: www.ascap.com
Clearinghouse of music performing rights.

Americans for the Arts
1 East 53rd Street
New York, New York 10012
212-223-2787
Web Address: www.artsusa.org
Promotes arts and artists.

International Documentary Association
1551 South Robertson Boulevard, Suite 201
Los Angeles, CA 90035
310-284-8422
Involved in the promotion of nonfiction film and the support of nonfiction film makers.

International Television Association
6311 North O'Connor Road, Suite 230
Irving, TX 75039
972-869-1112
Web Address: www.itva.org
Working for the advancement of those working in the videotape and nonbroadcast video fields.

Motion Picture Assocation
15503 Ventura Boulevard
Encino, CA 91436
818-995-6600
Web Address: www.mpaa.org/mpa.html
Represents the American film industry internationally.

Motion Picture Association of America
1600 Eye Street, N.W.
Washington, D.C. 20006
202-293-1966
Web Address: www.mpaa.org
Represents the main U.S. distributors and producers of motion pictures domestically.

National Artists Equity Association
P.O. Box 28068, Central Station
Washington, D.C. 20038
202-628-9633
Protects rights of visual artists.

National Dance Association
1900 Association Drive
Reston, Virginia 22091
703-476-3436
Web Address: www.aahpbrd.org/nda.html
Advocate for better dance education.

National Foundation for Advancement in the Arts
3915 Biscayne Boulevard
Miami, Florida 33137
305-573-0490
Supports aspiring artists.

Producers Guild of America
400 South Beverly Drive, Suite 211
Beverly Hills, California 90212
310-557-0807
Association of movie and television producers.

Professional Arts Management Institute
408 West 57th Street
New York, New York 10019
212-245-3850
Education for management of performing arts or cultural institutions.

Screen Actors Guild
5757 Wilshire Boulevard
Hollywood, California 90036
General actor assistance.

Society of Motion Picture and Television Engineers
595 West Hartsdale Avenue
White Plains, New York 10607
914-761-1100
Web Address: www.smpte.org
Strives to advance engineering knowledge and practice for television and movies.

Stuntmen's Association of Motion Picture
4810 Whitsett Avenue
North Hollywood, CA 91607
818-766-4334
Web Address: www.stuntnet.com/organization/stmass.htm
Members of the Screen Actors Guild or the American Federation of Television and Radio Artists Association who are involved in stunt work in television or motion pictures.

Theatre Communications Group
355 Lexington Avenue
New York, New York 10017
212-697-5230
Web Address: www.tcg.org
Service organization for non-profit theatres, artists, and administrators.

Women in Film
6464 Sunset Boulevard, Suite 530
Hollywood, CA 90028
213-463-6040
Supporters of women in television and film industry.

• Publications •

American Artist
One Astor Place, 1515 Broadway
New York, New York 10036
212-764-7300
Web Address: www.cc.enews.com/magazines/ameriart
Artists, Methods, and Problems

Art Business News
Myers Publishing Company
19 Old Kings Highway South
Darien, Connecticut 06820
Fine Art and Picture Framing Industry

Artforum
65 Bleeker Street
New York, New York 10012
212-475-4000
Web Address: www.artforum.com

Artists Market
Writers Digest Books
1507 Dana Avenue
Cincinnati, Ohio 45207
513-531-2222

ArtWeek
2149 Paragon Drive, Suite 100
San Jose, California 95131
408-441-7065

Back Stage
1515 Broadway
New York, New York 10036
212-764-7300
Web Address: www.backstage.com

Billboard
1515 Broadway, 11th Floor
New York, NY 10036
212-536-5167
Web Address: www.billboard.com
Music and Home Entertainment.

Creative Black Book
115 5th Avenue, 3rd Floor
New York, New York 10003

Hollywood Reporter
5055 Wilshire
Los Angeles, California 90028
213-525-2000
Web Address: www.hollywoodreporter.com

NASAA Directory
National Assembly of State Art Agencies
1010 Vermont Avenue NW
Washington, DC 20005
202-347-6352
Web Address: www.nasaa-arts.org

Players Guide
165 West 46th Street
New York, New York 10036
212-869-3570

Ross Reports Television
1515 Broadway
New York, NY 10036-8986
718-937-3990
Web Address: www.backstage.com

Television Broadcast
2 Park Avenue, Suite 1820
New York, NY 10016
212-779-1919

The Academy Players Directories
8949 Wilshire Boulevard
Beverly Hills, California 90211
310-247-3000
Web Address: www.oscar.com

Variety
475 Park Avenue South
New York, New York 10016
News of Entertainment Industry.

Women Artist News
300 Riverside Drive
New York, New York 10025
212-666-6990
News for Female Artists.

World Broadcast News
9800 Metcalf Avenue
Overland Park, KS 66212
913-341-1300
International Cable and Television News

Healthcare

- Bio-Tech
- Hospitals
- Healthcare Companies
- Managed Care

Opportunities within the healthcare field range from entry-level accounting, claims or customer service representative positions to professional positions in nursing, data processing, actuarial and financial areas. Most entry-level positions are filled in either our customer service or claims areas which do not require a particular degree. However, positions which are more technical or specialized generally require candidates with particular degrees, professional backgrounds or expertise. For example, nurse reviewer positions are administrative positions, but require an RN (registered nurse) and at least two years of practical experience in a medical/surgical area of a hospital. Persons with an interest in accounting, actuarial, underwriting and financial areas, whether entry-level or higher, require candidates with background in those areas. Programmers are required to have several courses in data processing including COBOL, JCL and Easytrieve.

Professional skills required for customer service representative candidates include the ability to effectively communicate with internal and external customers, demonstrated analytical, organizational and time management skills and the ability to learn, retain and apply a large amount of information.

Generally, salaries for entry-level positions start around the high teens or low twenties. As with most positions, practical experience either by interning, volunteering or working with an organization in a capacity that gives a student exposure to "the workforce" while in school, can help prepare candidates when applying for positions.

BLUE CROSS AND BLUE SHIELD

Quick Reference

Aetna US HealthCare
www.aetna.com/joblink
Allergan
www.allergan.com
Alliance Imaging
www.allianceimaging.com
Applied Cardiac Systems
www.ocsholter.com
ARV Assisted Living
www.arvi.com
Baxter Healthcare Corporation
www.baxter.com
BBI-Source Scientific
www.sourcesci.com
Beckman Instruments
www.beckman.com
Beech Street Corporation
www.beechstreet.com
Beneficial Administration Company
www.bestplans.com
Bergen Brunswig Corporation
www.bergenbrunswig.com
Bio-Orthopedic Lab
www.bio-orthopedic.com
Biosite Diagnostics
www.biosite.com
Blue Cross of California
www.bluecross.ca.com
Blue Shield HMO & Preferred Plan
www.blueshieldca.com
Brea Community Hospital
www.breahospital.com
Capistrano Labs
www.capolabs.com
Capp Care
www.cappcare.com
Chapman Medical Center
www.cmclungctr.com
Chevron Petroleum Technology
www.chevron.com
Children's Hospital & Health Center
www.chsd.org
CIGNA HealthCare of San Diego
www.cigna.com
Coastal Communities Hospital
www.tenethealth.com
CoCensys
www.cocensys.com
COHR
www.cohr-inc.com
Columbia Huntington Beach Hospital
www.tenethealth.com
Columbia Mission Bay Memorial Hospital
www.columbia.com
Columbia West Anaheim Medical Center
www.columbia.net
Community Care Network
www.ccnusa.com
Community Health Group
www.chgsd.com
Comprehensive Care Corporation
http://sternco.com/pr/cmp/cmp.html
Concept Development
www.rtcgroup.com
CORE
www.coreinc.com
Cortex Pharmaceuticals
www.cortexpharm.com

Corvas International
www.corvas.com
CorVel Corporation
www.corvel.com
CR Technology
www.crtechnology.com
CRITO
www.crito.uci.edu
Del Mar Avionics
www.delmarav.com
Diagnostic Solutions
www.teststrip.com
Endocare
www.endocare.com
Energy & Enviro Research Corp
www.eercorp.com
Flex Foot
www.flexfoot.com
Foundation Health Systems
www.fhs.com
Fountain Valley Regional Hospital
www.tenethealth.com
Furon Company
www.furon.com
Garden Grove Hospital
www.tenethealth.com
Gen-Probe
www.gen-brobe.com
Gish Biomedical
www.gishbmed.com
Glidewell Laboratories
www.glidewell-lab.com
Green Hospital of Scripps Clinic
www.scrippsclinic.com
Grossmont Hospital
www.sharp.com
Health Net
www.healthnet.com
HemaCare Corporation
www.hemacare.com
Hoag Memorial Hospital Presbyterian
www.hoag.org
IBRD-Rostrum Global
www.ibrd-rostrum.com
ICN Pharmaceuticals
www.icnpharm.com
Imagyn Medical
www.imagyn.com
Innovation Sports
www.isports.com
Interpore International
www.interpore.com
Irvine Medical Center
www.tenethealth.com
J. Hewitt
www.jhewitt.com
Kaiser Permanente
www.kptx.org
Kaiser Permanente Medical Center
www.ca.kaiser.permanente.org
La Jolla Pharmaceutical Co.
www.ljpc.com
MarDx Diagnostics
www.syntron.net
MBC Applied Enviro Sciences
www.mbcnet.net
Medical Science Systems
www.medscience.com
Medstone International
www.medstone.com
Melles Griot
www.mellegriot.com
Mercy Hospital
www.scrippshealth.org

Metrolaser
www.metrolaserinc.com
Mission Hospital Regional Medical Center
www.mhrmc.com
Molecular Biosystems
www.mobi.com
NeoTherapeutics
www.neotherapeutics.com
O'Neil Product Development
www.oneilinc.com
Optimum Care Corporation
www.opmc.com
Orthomerica Products
www.orthomerica.com
Pacific Biometrics
www.pacbio.com
Pacific Mutual Holding Co.
www.pacificlife.com
PacifiCare
www.pch.com
PacifiCare Health Systems
www.pacificare.com
PharmaPrint
www.pharmaprint.com
Placentia-Linda Hospital
www.tenethealth.com/placentialinda
Pomerado Hospital
www.pphs.org
PPO Alliance/OneSource Health Network/CCN
www.ccn.us.com
Preferred Health Network
www.phn.com
Premier Laser Systems
www.premierlaser.com
Respiratory Systems
www.lifeair.com
Saddleback Memorial Medical Center
www.tenethealth.com
Safeguard Health Enterprises
www.safeguardhealth.com
Scripps Hospital-East County
www.scrippshealth.org
Scripps Memorial Hospital-Chula Vista
www.scrippshealth.org
Scripps Memorial Hospital-Encinitas
www.scrippshealth.org
Scripps Memorial Hospital-La Jolla
www.scrippshealth.org
Sentry Medical Products
www.sentrymed.com
Sharp Chula Vista Medical Center
www.sharp.com
Sharp Coronado Hospital
www.sharp.com
Sharp Metro Hospitals
www.sharp.com
SIBIA Neurosciences
www.sibia.com
SK&A Information Services
www.skainfo.com
Sorin Biomedical
www.sorinbio.com
South Coast Medical Center
www.adventisthealth.com
St. Joseph Hospital of Orange
www.saintjoseph.com
St Jude Medical Center
www.stjude.com

Quick Reference

Steri-Oss
www.steri-oss.com
Stratagene
www.stratagene.com
**Summit Care Corporation/
Fountain View**
www.sumc.com
Survivair
www.survivair.com
Syntron Bioresearch
www.syntron.net
Techniclone Corporation
www.techniclone.com
The Langer Biomechanics Group
www.langerbiomechanics.com
Toshiba America Medical Systems
www.toshiba.com
Tustin Rehabilitation Hospital
www.westernmedical.com
UCSD Medical Center
www.ucsd.edu
UniHealth
www.unihealth.org
Universal Care
www.universalcare.com
Unocal Corp/Agricultural Product
www.unocal.com
**Western Medical Center Hosp -
Anaheim**
www.westernmedical.com
WestEd Laboratories
www.wested.org
Western Medical Center Santa Ana
www.westernmedical.com
Whitewing Labs
www.whitewing.com

Company Job Hotlines
Aetna US Healthcare
619-497-4247

**Alvarado Hospital Medical
Center**
619-224-7100
Blue Shield HMO & Preferred Plan
800-408-5627
Blue Shield of California
310-670-4040
Chevron Petroleum Technology
415-894-2552
Children's Hospital & Health Center
619-576-5880
Good Samaritan Hospital
213-977-2300
Green Hospital of Scripps Clinic
619-554-5627
Grossmont Hospital
619-627-5935
Harbor - UCLA Medical Center
800-970-5478
Health Net
818-676-7236
**Hollywood Presbyterian
Medical Center**
800-426-6998
Huntington Memorial Hospital
626-397-8504
Kaiser Permanente
714-279-6080
**Kaiser Permanente Medical
Center - L.A.**
213-857-2615
**Martin Luther King Jr.- Drew
Medical Center**
213-351-5478
Mercy Hospital
619-554-8400
Mesa Vista Hospital
619-627-5935
Palomar Medical Center
760-739-3960
Paradise Valley Hospital
619-470-4422

Pomerado Hospital
619-485-4680
Prudential HealthCare
800-994-9966
San Pedro Peninsula Hospital
310-540-7373
Scripps Hospital-East County
619-554-8400
**Scripps Memorial Hospital-
Chula Vista**
619-554-8400
**Scripps Memorial Hospital-
Encinitas**
619-554-8400
Scripps Memorial Hospital-La Jolla
619-554-8400
Sharp Chula Vista Medical Center
619-627-5935
Sharp Coronado Hospital
619-627-5935
Sharp Metro Hospitals
619-627-5935
St. Mary Medical Center
562-491-9844
St. Vincent Medical Center
213-484-7032
The Immune Response Corp.
760-431-3396
Tri-City Medical Center
760-940-5002
UCLA Medical Center
310-794-0526
UCSD Medical Center
619-682-1001
UniHealth
818-238-6029
Unilab Corporation
818-996-7300 x6680
Universal Care
562-981-9064
VA Medical Center - Long Beach
562-494-5971

Healthcare Companies

Abbott Labs/Diagnostics Div
8001 Irvine Center Drive, Suite 1400
Irvine, CA 92618-2935
949-753-6040
Number of Employees: 2500

Diana Prins, *Personnel*

ADMAR Corp
1551 North Tustin Avenue, Suite 300
Santa Ana, CA 92705-8638
714-953-9600
Number of Employees: 215
Richard Toral, *CEO*
Susan Lawson, *Human Resources Manager*

Aetna US Healthcare
PO Box 1294
Orange, CA 92856-0294
714-992-3271
Web Address: www.aushc.com
Number of Employees: 40000

Aetna US Healthcare
7676 Hazard Center Drive, Suite 1400
San Diego, CA 92116
619-497-0046
Job Hotline: 619-497-4247
Web Address: www.aetna.com
Number of Employees: 400

Dean Hosmer, *General Manager*

Aetna US HealthCare
10417 Mountain View Avenue
Loma Linda, CA 92354
909-796-2000
Web Address: www.aetna.com/joblink
Number of Employees: 125

John Mayhew, *General Manager*

American Specialty Health Plans
8989 Rio San Diego Drive, Suite 250
San Diego, CA 92108
619-686-5990

George DeVries, *President*

Apria Healthcare Group
3560 Hyland Avenue
Costa Mesa, CA 92626
949-427-2000
Number of Employees: 8255

Lawrence M. Higby, *President*
Susan K. Skara, *Vice President of Human
Resources*
*Provider of home-health care (largest in the US). Operates about
350 branches in all 50 states and serves patients who have been
discharged from hospitals but still require treatment.*

Bayer Corp/Diagnostics Division
24411 Ridge Route Drive, Suite 230
Laguna Hills, CA 92653-1685
714-951-8062
Number of Employees: 25000

Beech Street Corporation
173 Technology Drive
Irvine, CA 92618-2402
949-727-9300
Web Address: www.beechstreet.com
Number of Employees: 550

George Bregante, *President*

Beneficial Administration Company
2515 McCabe Way
Irvine, CA 92614-6243
949-756-1000
Web Address: www.bestplans.com
Number of Employees: 100

James K Voegtlin, *President*

Bio-Path Medical Group
17330 Newhope Street
Fountain Valley, CA 92708
714-433-1330
Number of Employees: 30

Sheldon Barasch, *Owner*

Blue Cross of California
21555 Oxnard Street
Woodland Hills, CA 91367
818-703-2345
Web Address: www.bluecross.ca.com
Number of Employees: 10,608

Ron Williams, *President*

Blue Cross Prudent Unicare
21555 Oxnard Street Suite 6D
Woodland Hills, CA 91367
818-703-2345
Web Address: www.bluecross.ca.com
Ron Williams, *President*

Blue Shield HMO & Preferred Plan
6701 Center Drive West
Los Angeles, CA 90045
310-670-4040
Job Hotline: 800-408-5627
Web Address: www.blueshieldca.com
Number of Employees: 260

Alan Puzarne, *Sr. VP & Regional CEO*
Sharon Miller, *Manager of Human Resouces*

Blue Shield of California
625 The City Drive South, Suite 400
Orange, CA 92868-4985
714-663-4200
Number of Employees: 2800

Sharon Miller, *Human Resources Manager*

Blue Shield of California
591 Camino de la Reina, Suite 100
San Diego, CA 92108
619-686-4200
Job Hotline: 800-408-JOBS

Bruce Bodaken, *Executive Director*
Sharon Miller, *Personnel Director*
*Send resumes to: Sharon Miller; 6701 Center Drive West; Los
Angeles, CA 90045 or fax to 310-568-4631.*

BPS Healthcare
888 South Figueroa Street, Suite 1400
Los Angeles, CA 90017
213-489-2694
Number of Employees: 178

Barbara Rodin, *President*
Christine Scarus, *Director of Human Resources*

Capp Care
4000 MacArthur Boulevard, Suite 10000
Newport Beach, CA 92660-2558
949-251-2200
Web Address: www.cappcare.com

Michael E. Henry, *President*

Central Drug Scan
16560 Harbor Boulevard, Suite A
Fountain Valley, CA 92708-1382
714-418-0130
Web Address: www.centraldrugscan.com
Number of Employees: 40

Todd Horton, *Human Resouces Manager*

Chad Therapeutics
21622 Plummer Street
Chatsworth, CA 91311
818-882-0883
Number of Employees: 90

Frank Flemings, *President*
Barbara Muskin, *Director of Personnel*
*Manufacturer of portable oxygen equipment. Its products are sold
to home oxygen suppliers in Australia, Canada, Germany, Japan,
and the US.*

Cigna Healthcare of California
2400 East Katella Avenue, Suite 250-A
Anaheim, CA 92806
714-939-5858
Web Address: www.cigna.com

CIGNA HealthCare of California
505 North Brand Boulevard Suite 400
Glendale, CA 91203
818-500-6262
Web Address: www.cigna.com

Leslie Margolin, *President*

CIGNA HealthCare of San Diego
3131 Camino del Rio North, Suite 900
San Diego, CA 92108
619-641-5400
Web Address: www.cigna.com

Antonio Linares, *Medical Director*
Donna DeFrank, *General Manager*

COHR
21540 Plummer Street
Chatsworth, CA 91311
818-773-2647
Web Address: www.cohr-inc.com
Number of Employees: 500

Steve Damble, *CEO*
Bonnie Hacke, *Director of Personnel*
Provider of outsourcing services include equipment sales and servicing and group purchasing, for health providers nationwide . The company serves about 2,000 clients through more than 30 offices.

Community Care Network
5251 View Ridge
San Diego, CA 92123
619-278-2273
Web Address: www.ccnusa.com

Richard Mastaler, *Executive Director*
Donna Nagel, *Vice President of Human Resources*

Community Health Group
740 Bay Boulevard
Chula Vista, CA 91910
619-422-0422
Web Address: www.chgsd.com
Number of Employees: 150

Gabriel Arce, *CEO*
Norma Diaz, *Human Resource Manager*

Comprehensive Care Corporation
1111 Bayside Drive, Suite 100
Corona Del Mar, CA 92625
714-222-2273
Number of Employees: 303

Chriss W. Street, *President*
Brenda Gillette, *Director of Personnel*
Provider of psychiatric and substance abuse services for managed health care providers. Most services are provided under capitation agreements, in which providers pay a fixed, monthly per-member fee, regardless of utilization.

ConserviCare
5173 Waring Road
San Diego, CA 92120
619-286-7917
Number of Employees: 3

E.L. Raffetto, *Founder*

CORE
18881 Von Karman, Suite 1750
Irvine, CA 92612
949-442-2100
Web Address: www.coreinc.com
Number of Employees: 700

George C. Carpenter IV, *President*
Sara Tague, *Director of Personnel*
National provider of health care utilization management programs. Its programs provide a system of reviewing, evaluating, and monitoring the medical appropriateness of health care services prescribed for participants in health care plans.

CorVel Corporation
2010 Main Street, Suite 1020
Irvine, CA 92614
949-851-1473
Web Address: www.corvel.com
Number of Employees: 1900
V. Gordon Clemons, *President*
Cathy Casil, *Human Resources Manager*
Provider of workers' compensation medical cost containment and managed-care services. The company's services include automated medical fee auditing, utilization review, medical case management, vocational rehabilitation services, and independent medical examinations.

Foundation Health
3400 Data Drive
Rancho Cordova, CA 95670
916-631-5000
Gary Velzsquez, *President*

Foundation Health Systems
21600 Oxnard Street
Woodland Hills, CA 91367
818-676-6978
Web Address: www.fhs.com
Number of Employees: 14,000
Jay Gellert, *President*
Dan Smithson, *Director of Personnel*
Health care provider to more than six million members in 18 states, primarily in the western US. Is the fourth-largest public managed health care organization in the nation.

Furon Company
29982 Ivy Glenn Drive
Laguna Niguel, CA 92667
714-831-5350
Web Address: www.furon.com
Number of Employees: 3456

J. Michael Hagan, *President*
Kevin G. Krogmeier, *Vice President of Human Resources*
Provider of industrial products and health care supplies. Its industrial products include plastic and silicone components, products for handling fluid, release liners, and foam components.

Health Net
3187 Red Hill Avenue, Suite 200
Costa Mesa, CA 92626-3437
949-429-3100
Number of Employees: 2500

Health Net
3131 Camino del Rio North, Suite 1100
San Diego, CA 92108
619-521-4900
Job Hotline: 818-676-7236
Web Address: www.healthnet.com

David W. Anderson, *Regional Director*

Health Net
21600 Oxnard Street, 10th Floor
Woodland Hills, CA 91367
818-719-6775
Job Hotline: 818-593-7236
Number of Employees: 2,000

Arthur M. Southam, *President*
Miriam Shakter, *Director of Human Resources*

HealthCare COMPARE Corporation
3200 Highland Avenue
Downers Grove, IL 60515
714-373-8611

A. Lee Dickerson, *VP Marketing*

Homelife Staff Builders
23832 Rockfield Boulevard
Lake Forest, CA 92630-2858
714-707-3030
Number of Employees: 500

John F. Northway, *President*
Bridgett Dravitczski, *Human Resources Manager*

I-Flow Corporation
2532 White Road
Irvine, CA 92714
949-553-0888
Number of Employees: 236

Donald M. Earhart, *President*
Linda Bainbridge, *Human Resources Manager*

IBRD-Rostrum Global
PO Box 19759
Irvine, CA 92623-9759
949-476-2727
Web Address: www.ibrd-rostrum.com
Number of Employees: 100

Tom Semler, *President*

ICU Medical
951 Calle Amanecer
San Clemente, CA 92673
714-366-2183
Number of Employees: 121
George A. Lopez, *President*
Jim Reitz, *Director of Personnel*

Imagyn Medical Technologies
5 Civic Plaza, Suite 100
Newport Beach, CA 92660
949-668-5858
Number of Employees: 936

Charles A. Laverty, *President*
Cheryl Barraco, *Director of Personnel*

Inter Valley Health Plan
300 South Park Avenue
Pomona, CA 91769
909-623-6333
Number of Employees: 150

Mark C. Covington, *President*

J.F. Jelenko & Co
10005 Muirlands Boulevard, Suite G
Irvine, CA 92618-2519
949-770-0219
Number of Employees: 100

Kaiser Permanente
200 North Lewis Street
Orange, CA 92868-1538
714-748-2600
Job Hotline: 714-279-4229
Web Address: www.kptx.org
Number of Employees: 33912

Kaiser Permanente
6507 Mission Gorge Road
San Diego, CA 92120
619-528-5000
Job Hotline: 619-528-3071
Web Address: www.kpnewjobs.com
Number of Employees: 5100

Dr. Flippen, *Medical Director*
Cindy Murnane, *Area Recruitment Manager*

Kaiser Permanente
470 North Lake Avenue
Pasadena, CA 91188
626-440-0036
Web Address: www.kptx.org

Edgar Carlson, Sr. VP, *Operations Dev.*

Maxicare California
1149 South Broadway, Suite 826
Los Angeles, CA 90015
213-742-0900
Number of Employees: 500

Warren D. Foon, VP, *General Manager*
Charmaine Hancock, *Director of Human Resources*

Medical Cables
1340 Logan Avenue
Costa Mesa, CA 92626-4007
949-545-3469
Number of Employees: 20
Peter Bonin, *President*

Merry X-Ray Chemical Corporation
1130 North Citrus Street
Orange, CA 92867-3510
714-538-8801
Number of Employees: 130

Donna Atkinson, *Human Resources Manager*

Modern Medical Enterprises
25 Mauchly, Suite 321
Irvine, CA 92618-2332
949-450-0440
Number of Employees: 20

Newport Dental
1401 Dove Street, Suite 290
Newport Beach, CA 92660-2426
949-752-8522
Number of Employees: 175

Dennis Faratt, *President*

Nihon Kohden -America
2601 Campus Drive
Irvine, CA 92612-1601
949-250-3959
Number of Employees: 100

Fumio Sukuki, *President*
Christine Gonzales, *Personnel Director*

NYLCare Health Plans
800 North Brand Avenue, Suite 230
Glendale, CA 91203
818-552-6230

Bill Caswell, *Regional Executive*

Optimum Care Corporation
30011 Ivy Glenn Drive, Suite 219
Laguna Niguel, CA 92677-5018
714-495-1100
Web Address: www.opmc.com
Number of Employees: 200

Edward Johnson, *President*
Rita M. Skok, *Human Resources Director*

Pacific Foundation for Medical Care
9555 Chesapeake Drive, Suite 203
San Diego, CA 92123
858-268-7500
Web Address: whgill@king.cbs.com
Number of Employees: 25

Michael J. Ganey, *Executive Director*
Natalie Condor, *Human Resource Manager*

PacifiCare
4365 Executive Drive, Suite 500
San Diego, CA 92121
858-658-8900
Web Address: www.pacificare.com
Number of Employees: 50

PacifiCare Health Systems
3120 West Lake Center Drive
Santa Ana, CA 92704-5186
714-825-5950
Web Address: www.pacificare.com
Number of Employees: 4957

Alan R. Hoops, *President*
Wanda Lee, *Senior VP for Corporate Resources*
HMO that also operates the nation's largest Medicare HMO chain through its Secure Horizons Program. It also offers dental and vision care, laboratory and radiology services, pharmacy services, psychological counseling, and traditional indemnity insurance plans.

PacifiCare Health Systems
5995 Plaza Drive
Cypress, CA 90630-5028
714-952-1121
Web Address: www.pacificare.com
Number of Employees: 5000

Alan R. Hoops, *President & CEO*
Wanda Lee, *Senior VP for Corporate Resources*

Picker International
1 Marconi, Suite F
Irvine, CA 92618-2520
949-699-2300
Number of Employees: 2500

PPO Alliance/OneSource Health Network/CCN
5251 View Ridge Court
Suite 550
San Diego, CA 92123
800-624-9300
Job Hotline: Ext 2062
Web Address: www.ccn.usa.com

Mike Bell, *President*
Richard Mastaler, *CEO*
Donna Nagel, *Director of Human Resources*

Private Healthcare Systems
3345 Michelson Drive, Suite 200
Irvine, CA 92612
949-476-9816

Mike Hanson, *Executive Director*
Karoline Chiavetta, *Human Resources Manager*

PruCare of California
5800 Canoga Avenue
Woodland Hills, CA 91367
818-992-2000
Jeff Kamil, *President*

Prudential HealthCare
5800 Canoga Avenue
Woodland Hills, CA 91367
818-992-2000
Job Hotline: 800-994-9966
Number of Employees: 1,600
Cora Tellez, *President*
Juliana McQuillam, *Manager of Human Resources*

Quest Diagnostics
33608 Ortega Highway
San Juan Capistrno, CA 92675-2042
714-728-4000
Number of Employees: 20000

David MacDonald, *President*
Bill MacGowan, *VP for Human Resources*

Rehab Designs of America
1920 East Katella Avenue
Orange, CA 92867-5146
714-639-7422
Number of Employees: 35

Michael Martin, *President*

Safeguard Health Enterprises
505 North Euclid Street, Suite 200
Anaheim, CA 92801
714-778-1005
Web Address: www.safeguardhealth.com
Number of Employees: 307

Steven J. Baileys, *President*
Hal Netter, *Human Resources Manager*
Operator of managed dental care plans offered by employers as an alternative to or replacement of dental indemnity insurance.

Sharp Health Plan
9325 Sky Park Court, Suite 300
San Diego, CA 92123
858-637-6530
Number of Employees: 75

B. Kathlyn Mead, *President*

TKB International
760 West 16th Street, Building N
Newport Beach, CA 92658-8985
949-631-9020
Number of Employees: 20

Kirk Inoue, *President*

UHP Healthcare
3405 West Imperial Highway Suite 605
Inglewood, CA 90303
310-671-3465
Job Hotline: 213-955-6923

Clyde Oden, *President*
Madria Marshall, *VP of Personnel*

UniHealth
3400 Riverside Drive
Burbank, CA 91505
818-238-6000
Job Hotline: 818-238-6029
Web Address: www.unihealth.org
Number of Employees: 11,000
David R. Carpenter, *CEO*
Gary Leary, *President*
Barbara Cook, *Director of Personnel*
Healthcare provider which focuses on large physician practice networks. Also provides home health care services, including home infusion, dialysis, and hospice services, and care for senior citizens.

Universal Care
1600 East Hill Street
Signal Hill, CA 90806
562-424-6200
Job Hotline: 562-981-9064
Web Address: www.universalcare.com
Number of Employees: 1,200

Howard E. Davis, *President*
Tia Shiller, *Director of Human Resources*

Urosurge Medical Supplies
8 Holland
Irvine, CA 92618-2504
949-580-0930
Number of Employees: 20

Gary Schach, *President*

Vista Behavioral Health Plans
2355 Northside Drive, 3rd Floor
San Diego, CA 92108
858-521-4444
Number of Employees: 45

Ollie Landsman, *President*

Vitas Health Care Corp
333 South Anita Drive, Suite 950
Orange, CA 92868-3320
714-921-2273
Number of Employees: 2500

Carol Cavish, *Human Resources Manager*

VNA Home Health Systems
2500 Redhill Avenue, Suite 105
Santa Ana, CA 92705
949-263-4700
Number of Employees: 95

Heather Woodion, *President & CEO*
Carmella Bozulich, *VP for Human Resources*

Westcliff Medical Laboratories
361 Hospital Road, Suite 222
Newport Beach, CA 92663-3521
949-646-0216
Number of Employees: 300

Richard E. Nicholson, *Vice President*

Westcliff Medical Laboratories
13876 Harbor Boulevard Building 3B
Garden Grove, CA 92843-4028
714-554-3922
Number of Employees: 300

Richard E. Nicholson, *Vice President*

HEALTHCARE

Bio-Tech

3M/Dental Products Division
2111 McGaw Avenue
Irvine, CA 92614-0913
949-863-1360
Number of Employees: 70,000

Access Pharmaceuticals
11099 North Torrey Pines Road
La Jolla, CA 92037
858-452-6550
Number of Employees: 190

Kevin J. Kinsella, *Principal*

Advanced Tissue Sciences
10933 North Torrey Pines Road
La Jolla, CA 92037
858-657-5985
Number of Employees: 214

Art Benvenuto, *Principal*

Alcon Surgical
PO Box 19587
Irvine, CA 92623-9587
949-753-1393
Number of Employees: 550

Ann Schneider, *Human Resources Manager*

Allergan
2525 Dupont Drive
Irvine, CA 92612
949-246-4500
Web Address: www.allergan.com
Number of Employees: 6100

William C. Shepherd, *President*
Richard J. Hilles, *Vice President of Human
    Resources*
Leading maker of eye-care and skin-care products. Its eye-care
products (88% of sales) include medications, surgical equipment,
contact-lens cleaners, and intraocular lenses.

Alliance Imaging
1065 North Pacificenter Drive, Suite 200
Anaheim, CA 92806-2128
714-688-7100
Web Address: www.allianceimaging.com
Number of Employees: 300
Richard N. Zehner, *CEO*
Vincent S. Pino, *President*
C. Braun, *Personnel Manager*

Alliance Pharmaceutical Corp.
3040 Science Park Road
San Diego, CA 92121
858-558-4300
Web Address: www.allp.com
Number of Employees: 250
Duane J. Roth, *CEO*
Carol McWilson, *Human Resource Director*

Amgen
PO Box 2569
Thousand Oaks, Ca 91319
805-447-1000
Web Address: www.amgen.com

Amylin Pharmaceuticals
9373 Towne Centre Drive
San Diego, CA 92121
858-552-2200
Number of Employees: 238

Richard M. Haugen, *Principal*

Ansys
2 Goodyear
Irvine, CA 92618-2002
949-770-9381
Number of Employees: 58

Steven Schulthis, *President*

Applied Cardiac Systems
22912 El Pacifico Drive
Laguna Beach, CA 92653-1378
714-855-9366
Web Address: www.ocsholter.com
Number of Employees: 75

Danny Marcus, *CEO*

Applied Medical Resources
PO Box 3206
Mission Viejo, CA 92690-1206
714-582-6120
Number of Employees: 300

Said Hilal, *President & CEO*

ARMM
17744 Sampson Lane
Huntington Beach, CA 92647-6751
714-848-8190
Number of Employees: 25

Roger Wood, *President*

ASP-Advanced Sterilization Products
33 Technology Drive
Irvine, CA 92618-2346
949-581-5799
Number of Employees: 300

Tralance Addy, *President*
Dawn Moore, *Administrator*

Associated Laboratories
806 North Batavia Street
Orange, CA 92868-1242
714-771-6900
Number of Employees: 80

Tito L Parola, *President*
Debbie Smith, *Office Manager*

Bausch & Lomb Surgical/Chiron Vision
555 West Arrow Highway
Claremont, CA 91711
909-623-2020
Web Address: www.chironvision.com

Baxter Biotech/Immunotherapy
9 Parker
Irvine, CA 92618-1605
949-470-9011
Number of Employees: 150

John A. Osth, *Division President*
Kathy Carroll, *Human Resources Director*

Baxter Healthcare Corporation
17221 Redhill Avenue
Irvine, CA 92614
949-250-2591
Web Address: www.baxter.com
Number of Employees: 300

Baxter Healthcare/Cardiovascular Group
17221 Redhill Avenue
Irvine, CA 92614
949-250-2500
Web Address: www.baxter.com
Number of Employees: 1500

Mike Mussalem, *Group President*
Kevin Harley, *Human Resources Director*

Baxter Healthcare/IV Systems Division
PO Box 52830
Irvine, CA 92619-2830
949-851-9066
Number of Employees: 100

Vicki Hewlett, *Human Resources Manager*

BBI-Source Scientific
7390 Lincoln Way
Garden Grove, CA 92841-1437
714-898-9001
Web Address: www.sourcesci.com
Number of Employees: 65

Richard A Sullivan, *President*
Catherine Curtis, *Director*

Beckman Instruments
4300 Harbor Boulevard
Fullerton, CA 92835
714-871-4848
Web Address: www.beckman.com
Number of Employees: 11100

Jack Wareham, *President*
Amia Khalifa, *Executive VP of Personnel*
Beckman Instruments manufactures products used in laboratories, hospitals, and schools to research and diagnose disease and study biology.

Bergen Brunswig Corporation
4000 Metropolitan Drive
Orange, CA 92868-3598
714-385-4000
Web Address: www.bergenbrunswig.com
Number of Employees: 5100

Donald R. Roden, *President*
Carol E. Scherman, *Director of Personnel*
Major distributor of pharmaceuticals. Distributes drugs and medical-surgical supplies to hospitals and managed care facilities, as well as providing over-the-counter medications, and beauty products to retailers.

Bio-Orthopedic Lab
3198 Airport Loop Drive, Suite J
Costa Mesa, CA 92626-3407
949-546-6140
Web Address: www.bio-orthopedic.com
Number of Employees: 30

Richard Lowe, *Owner*

Biomerica
1533 Monrovia Avenue
Newport Beach, CA 92663
949-645-2111
Number of Employees: 80

Zake Irani, *President*
Janet Moore, *Human Resources Manager*
Maker of diagnostic tests to detect medical problems including ulcers, cancer, and diabetes.

Biosite Diagnostics
11030 Roselle Street
San Diego, CA 92121
858-455-4808
Web Address: www.biosite.com
Number of Employees: 240

Kim Blickenstaff, *Presidnet*
Julie Cunningham, *Human Resource Representative*

Byran Company
18092 Redondo Circle
Huntington Beach, CA 92648-1326
714-841-9808
Number of Employees: 60

Janell Dunagan, *President*

Canon Information Systems
3188 Pullman Street
Costa Mesa, CA 92626-3304
949-438-7100
Web Address: www.canon.com
Number of Employees: 114

Michihiko Senoh, *President*

HEALTHCARE

283

Capistrano Labs
1010 Calle Recodo
San Clemente, CA 92673-6225
714-492-0390
Web Address: www.capolabs.com
Number of Employees: 25

Ray Ryan, *President*

Cardiovascular Dynamics
13900 Alton Parkway, Suite 160
Irvine, CA 92718
949-457-9546
Number of Employees: 160

Michael R. Henson, *President*
Burgess Stockell, *Director of Human Resources*
Manufacturer medical devices— coronary catheters, coronary stents and vascular access needles. CVD sells its products in the US and Japan and distributes through 25 companies serving 41 other countries.

Champion Dental Products
1941 East Miraloma Avenue
Placentia, CA 92870-6770
714-993-3099
Number of Employees: 20

John Olson, *President*
Wendy Quandt, *Human Resources Manager*

Chevron Petroleum Technology
145 South State College Boulevard
Brea, CA 92822
714-671-3200
Web Address: www.chevron.com
Number of Employees: 250

Doug Lanier, *CEO*
Paul Gorsky, *Human Resource Manager*

Chiron Vision
9342 Jeronimo Road
Irvine, CA 92618-1903
949-768-4690
Number of Employees: 1400

Debra Parent, *Human Resources Manager*

CN Biosciences
10394 Pacific Center Court
San Diego, CA 92121
858-450-5500
Number of Employees: 100

Jim Stewart, *Principal*

Coast Medical
1060 North Batavia Street, Suite H
Orange, CA 92867-5543
714-288-4160
Number of Employees: 57

Doug Mongeon, *President*
Ron Frasco, *CFO*

CoCensys
213 Technology Drive
Irvine, CA 92718
949-753-6100
Web Address: www.cocensys.com
Number of Employees: 176

F. Richard Nichol, *President*
Janet Rhodes Randolph, *Human Resources Manager*

Concept Development
3198 Airport Loop Drive, Suite G
Costa Mesa, CA 92626-3438
949-557-1811
Web Address: www.rtcgroup.com
Number of Employees: 20

James Reardon, *President*

Cortex Pharmaceuticals
15241 Barranca Parkway
Irvine, CA 92618
949-727-3157
Web Address: www.cortexpharm.com
Number of Employees: 22

Vincent F. Simmon, *President*
Janet Ingram-Mellow, *Human Resources Manager*

Corvas International
3030 Science Park Road
San Diego, CA 92121
858-455-9800
Web Address: www.corvas.com
Number of Employees: 85

Randall E. Woods, *President*
Steve Zug, *Human Resource Director*

Cotton Buds
1921 East Miraloma Avenue, Suite B
Placentia, CA 92870-6769
714-579-0300
Number of Employees: 28

DeWitt Paul, *President*

CR Technology
27752 El Lazo #A
Laguna Niguel, CA 92677-3914
714-448-0443
Web Address: www.crtechnology.com
Number of Employees: 30

Richard E Amtower, *President*

CRITO
UCI 3200 Berkeley Pl
Irvine, CA 92697-4650
949-824-5449
Web Address: www.crito.uci.edu
Number of Employees: 20

Gina Rosis, *Administrator*

Del Mar Avionics
1621 Alton Parkway
Irvine, CA 92606-4801
949-250-3200
Web Address: www.delmarav.com
Number of Employees: 200

Bruce Del Mar, *President & CEO*
Elbert Phillips, *Personnel Manager*

Diagnostic Solutions
8 Pasteur, Suite 100
Irvine, CA 92618-3814
949-453-0540
Web Address: www.teststrip.com
Number of Employees: 35

Gary Krantz, *President*

Dresser Ind/Instrument Division
3931 Macarthur Boulevard, Suite 202
Newport Beach, CA 92660-3014
949-852-8948
Number of Employees: 1500

ENDOcare
7 Studebaker
Irvine, CA 92618
949-595-4770
Web Address: www.endocare.com
Number of Employees: 20

Paul W. Mikus, *President*
Christine Concepcion, *Human Resource Manager*
*Manufacturer of minimally invasive medical devices for the
treatment of urological diseases. It focuses on the 2 most common
diseases of the prostate, benign prostate hyperplasia (BPH) and
prostate cancer.*

Endocare
18 Technology Drive, Suite 134
Irvine, CA 92618-2311
949-450-1410
Web Address: www.endocare.com
Number of Employees: 25
Paul Mikus, *President*
Christine Concepcion, *Human Resoucres
    Manager*

Energy & Enviro Research Corp
18 Mason
Irvine, CA 92618-2798
949-859-8851
Web Address: www.eercorp.com
Number of Employees: 120
Thomas Tyson, *President*

Flex Foot
27412A Laguna Hills Drive
Aliso Viejo, CA 92656-3371
714-362-3883
Web Address: www.flexfoot.com
Number of Employees: 50
John Fosberg, *President*
Maggie Thurman, *Human Resources Director*

GE Medical Systems
7700 Irvine Center Drive, Suite 100
Irvine, CA 92618-2939
949-450-3222
Number of Employees: 15000

Gen-Probe
10210 Genetic Center Drive
San Diego, CA 92121
858-410-8000
Web Address: www.gen-brobe.com
Number of Employees: 450

Henry L. Nordhoff, *Principal*
Robin Vebova, *Personal Director*

Gish Biomedical
2681 Kelvin Avenue
Irvine, CA 92614-5821
949-756-5485
Web Address: www.gishbmed.com
Number of Employees: 235

Jack W. Brown, *President*
Jeanne M. Miller, *Human Resources Manager*
*Manufacturer of specialty medical devices for cardiovascular
surgery, orthopedic surgery and oncology. Products include
cardiovascular tubing systems, arterial filters, cardiotomy
reservoirs to recycle blood, and oxygen-saturation monitors,.*

Glidewell Laboratories
4141 Macarthur Boulevard
Newport Beach, CA 92660-2044
949-440-2600
Web Address: www.glidewell-lab.com
Number of Employees: 215

Jim Glidewell, *Owner*
Lenny La Bao, *Human Resources Manager*

HemaCare Corporation
4954 Van Nuys Boulevard
Sherman Oaks, CA 91403
818-986-3883
Web Address: www.hemacare.com
Number of Employees: 103

Hal I. Lieberman, *President*
Linda McDermott, *Director of Personnel*

Hitachi Chemical Research Center
1003 Health Sciences Road
Irvine, CA 92612-3054
949-725-2721
Number of Employees: 21

Jiro Akiba, *President & CEO*
Lisa Osborne, *Human Resources Manager*

Hycor Biomedical
18800 Von Karman Avenue
Irvine, CA 92612
949-440-2000
Number of Employees: 180

Richard D. Hamill, *President*
Cheryl Gramm, *Human Resources Manager*

I-Flow Corporation
20202 Windrow Drive
Lake Forest, CA 92630-8152
714-206-2700
Number of Employees: 83

Donald Earhart, *President*
Linda Bainbridge, *Human Resources Manager*

ICN Pharmaceuticals
3300 Hyland Avenue
Costa Mesa, CA 92626
949-545-0100
Web Address: www.icnpharm.com
Number of Employees: 12784

Milan Panic, *President*
Jack Sholl, *Human Resources Manager*
International pharmaceutical company that develops, manufactures, and markets drugs, research chemicals, and diagnostic products. Its leading product is a broad-spectrum antiviral agent, ribavirin, which is marketed in the US, Canada, and most of Europe under the name Virazole.

IDEC Pharmaceuticals Corp.
11011 Torreyana Road
San Diego, CA 92121
858-550-8500
Number of Employees: 340

William H. Rastetter, *CEO*
Jeff White, *Human Resource Director*

Imagyn Medical
27651 La Paz Road
Laguna Niguel, CA 92677-3917
714-362-2500
Web Address: www.imagyn.com
Number of Employees: 100

Frank Brown, *President*

Innovation Sports
6 Chrysler
Irvine, CA 92618-2008
949-859-4407
Web Address: www.isports.com
Number of Employees: 150

Edward Castillo, *President*
Trish Terena, *Human Resources Manager*

Interpore International
181 Technology Drive
Irvine, CA 92618-2402
949-453-3200
Web Address: www.interpore.com
Number of Employees: 87

David C. Mercer, *President*
Linda Fox, *Human Resources Manager*

J. Hewitt
6 Faraday, Suite B
Irvine, CA 92618-2770
949-855-8104

Web Address: www.jhewitt.com
Number of Employees: 20
James D. Hewitt, *President*

Kingsley Manufacturing Co
1981 Placentia
Costa Mesa, CA 92628-5010
949-645-4401
Number of Employees: 30

Jeffry G. Kingsley, *President*

La Jolla Pharmaceutical Co.
6455 Nancy Ridge Drive
San Diego, CA 92121
858-452-6600
Web Address: www.ljpc.com
Number of Employees: 65

Steve Engell, *CEO*
Teddi Reilly, *Director of Human Resources*
Fax resumes to: 858-625-0155

Lee Pharmaceuticals
1444 Santa Anita Avenue
El Monte, Ca 91733
626-442-3141
Web Address: www.leepharmaceuticals.com

Ligand Pharmaceuticals
9393 Towne Centre Drive
San Diego, CA 92121
858-535-3900
Number of Employees: 310

Davied Robinson, *President*

Liston Scientific Corp
18900 Teller Avenue
Irvine, CA 92612-1617
949-756-1632
Web Address: www.liston@earthlink.net
Number of Employees: 20

Max Liston, *President*

Luther Medical Products
14332 Chambers Road
Tustin, CA 92680
888-237-2762
Number of Employees: 62

David Rollo, *President*
Vicki Yen, *Human Resources Manager*
Luther Medical Products manufactures needles and intravascular catheters. It makes several types of catheters, as well as tracheostomy products, sold through distributors and OEMs.

MarDx Diagnostics
5919 Farnsworth Court
Carlsbad, CA 92008
760-929-0500
Web Address: www.syntron.net
Number of Employees: 60

Arnie Aquilino, *CEO/President*
Tracy Petri, *Human Resources*

Masimo
2852 Kelvin Avenue
Irvine, CA 92614
949-250-9688
Number of Employees: 25

Joe Kiani, *President*

MBC Applied Enviro Sciences
3000 Red Hill Avenue
Costa Mesa, CA 92626-4524
949-850-4830
Web Address: www.mbcnet.net
Number of Employees: 40

Charles T Mitchell, *President*

Medical Science Systems
4400 MacArthur Boulevard, Suite 980
Newport Beach, CA 92660
949-440-9730
Web Address: www.medscience.com
Number of Employees: 27

Paul J. White, *President*
*Supplier of genetic susceptibility tests to identify individuals'
chances of being affected by such treatable and preventable diseases
as periodontitis, osteoporosis, coronary artery disease, and diabetic
retinopathy (blindness associated with diabetes).*

Medstone International
100 Columbia, Suite 100
Aliso Viejo, CA 92656-4114
714-448-7700
Web Address: www.medstone.com
Number of Employees: 81

David Radlinski, *President*
Grant Lenning, *Human Resources Manager*

Medtronic Heart Valves
18011 Mitchell South
Irvine, CA 92614-6007
949-474-3943
Number of Employees: 300

Donita Assimus, *Human Resources*

Melles Griot
1770 Kettering
Irvine, CA 92614-5670
949-261-5600
Web Address: www.mellegriot.com
Number of Employees: 800

Joel Price, *Human Resources Director*

Merck Research Laboratory
505 Coast Boulevard South, Suite 300
La Jolla, CA 92037
858-452-5892
Web Address: www.merck.com
Number of Employees: 120

Jeffrey McKelvy, *President*
Lynn Alba, *Human Resources Director*

Metrolaser
18006 Sky Park Circle, Suite 108
Irvine, CA 92614-6406
949-553-0688
Web Address: www.metrolaserinc.com
Number of Employees: 35

Cecil Hess, *President*

Micro Motors
151 East Columbine Avenue
Santa Ana, CA 92707-4402
714-546-4045
Number of Employees: 105

Bill Fitzpatrick, *President*

Micro Therapeutics
1062 Calle Negocio, Suite F
San Clemente, CA 92673
714-361-0616
Number of Employees: 82

George Wallace, *President*
Sue Lyons, *Director of Personnel*
*Manufacturer of minimally invasive medical instruments for the
diagnosis and treatment of vascular diseases.*

Miravant Medical Technologies
7408 Hollister Avenue
Santa Barbara, CA 93117
805-685-9880
Web Address: www.miravant.com

Molecular Biosystems
10030 Barnes Canyon Road
San Diego, CA 92121
858-452-0681
Web Address: www.mobi.com
Number of Employees: 150

Laura Gross, *Human Resources Director*

NeoTherapeutics
157 Technology Drive
Irvine, CA 92618
949-788-6700
Web Address: www.neotherapeutics.com
Number of Employees: 9

Alvin J. Glasky, *President*
Shelton K. Stern, *Human Resources Manager*
*Biopharmaceutical R&D company. Develops drugs to treat the
central nervous system and neurodegenerative conditions such as
Alzheimer's disease, memory deficits, stroke, and spinal cord injuries.*

Newport Medical Instruments
760 West 16th Street #M
Costa Mesa, CA 92627
949-642-3910
Number of Employees: 85

Kirk Inoue, *President*

HEALTHCARE

287

NovaCare/Orthotic & Prosthetic
41 East La Palma, Suite B400
Anaheim, CA 92807
714-996-9500
Number of Employees: 1354

Richmond Taylor, *Reg President*

O'Neil Product Development
8 Mason
Irvine, CA 92618-2705
949-458-1234
Web Address: www.oneilinc.com
Number of Employees: 100

Timothy O'Neil, *Owner*
Chris McCoy, *Human Resources Specialist*

Oncotech
17500 Red Hill Avenue #100
Irvine, CA 92614-5645
949-474-9262
Number of Employees: 80

Frank Kisner, *President & CEO*
Heather Allaim, *Human Resources Manager*

Orthomerica Products
PO Box 2927
Newport Beach, CA 92659-0400
949-723-4500
Web Address: www.orthomerica.com
Number of Employees: 125

David Kerr, *President*
Geza Molnar, *Executive Vice President*

Pacific Biometrics
1370 Reynolds Avenue, Suite 119
Irvine, CA 92614
949-263-9933
Web Address: www.pacbio.com
Number of Employees: 31

Paul G. Kanan, *President*
Tanya Witsaman, *Director of Personnel*
Developer of noninvasive diagnostic products for chronic diseases.

PharmaPrint
4 Park Plaza, Suite 1900
Irvine, CA 92614
949-655-7778
Web Address: www.pharmaprint.com
Number of Employees: 12

Elliot P. Friedman, *President*

PharMingen
10975 Torreyana Road
San Diego, CA 92121
619-812-8800
Web Address: info@pharmingen.com
Number of Employees: 245

Ernest C. Huang, *Principal*

Philips Ultrasound
29 Parker, Suite A
Irvine, CA 92618-1605
949-470-1300
Number of Employees: 100

Premier Laser Systems
3 Morgan
Irvine, CA 92718
949-859-0656
Web Address: www.premierlaser.com
Number of Employees: 47

Colette Cozean, *President*
Judy McCall, *Human Resources Manager*

Racal-Datacom
160 South Old Springs Road
Anaheim, CA 92808-1246
714-998-9301
Number of Employees: 2700

Respiratory Systems
1040 East Howell Avenue
Anaheim, CA 92805-6406
714-939-0900
Web Address: www.lifeair.com
Number of Employees: 25

Jerry Tochilin, *President & GM*

Sechrist Industries
4225 East La Palma Avenue
Anaheim, CA 92807-1844
714-579-8400
Number of Employees: 90

David Bush, *President*
Rosemary Hernandez, *Human Resources
Manager*

SensorMedics Corporation
22705 Savi Ranch Parkway
Yorba Linda, CA 92887-4645
714-283-1830
Number of Employees: 250

Michelle Santamauro, *Human Resources*

Sentry Medical Products
17171 Murphy Avenue
Irvine, CA 92614-5915
949-250-0233
Web Address: www.sentrymed.com
Number of Employees: 40

Claudia Smith, *Human Resources*

Skye Pharma Inc.
10450 Science Center Drive
San Diego, CA 92121
858-625-2424
Web Address: www.skyepharma.com
Number of Employees: 149
John Longemacker, *Principal*
Sandy Ginther, *Human Resources Manager*

SmithKline Beecham Clinical
13272 Garden Grove Boulevard
Garden Grove, CA 92843-2205
714-748-5400
Number of Employees: 1000

Jodi Weinridge, *Human Resources*

Sorin Biomedical
17600 Gillette Avenue
Irvine, CA 92614-5751
949-250-0500
Web Address: www.sorinbio.com
Number of Employees: 305

Spectrum Medsystems
2166 Michelson Drive
Irvine, CA 92612-1304
949-442-8400
Number of Employees: 30

Thomas Hursman, *President*

Starkey Laboratories
2536 West Woodland Drive
Anaheim, CA 92801-2636
714-826-0824
Web Address: www.starkey.com
Number of Employees: 2500

Bernadette Lopez, *Human Resources Coordinator*

Steri-Oss
22895 Eastpark Drive
Yorba Linda, CA 92887
714-282-6515
Web Address: www.steri-oss.com
Number of Employees: 232

Kenneth A. Darienzo, *President*
Pat Bolton, *Director of Human Resources*

Stratagene
11011 North Torrey Pines Road
La Jolla, CA 92037
858-535-5400
Web Address: www.stratagene.com
Number of Employees: 240

Joseph A. Sorge, *Principal*
Dennis Ferguson, *Human Resources Director*

Surgin
14762 Bentley Circle
Tustin, CA 92780-7226
714-832-6300
Number of Employees: 43

Armand Maaskamp, *President*
Loretta Kelly, *Human Resources Manager*

Survivair
3001 South Susan Street
Santa Ana, CA 92704-6413
714-545-0410
Web Address: www.survivair.com

Number of Employees: 175
Jack Bell, *President*
Shannon Justin, *Human Resources Manager*

Syncor International Corp.
6464 Canoga Avenue
Woodland Hills, CA 91367
818-737-4000
Web Address: www.syncor.com

Robert Funari, *President*
Sheila Coop, *Vice President of Human Resources*

Syntron Bioresearch
2774 Loker Avenue West
Carlsbad, CA 92008
760-930-2200
Number of Employees: 260

Techniclone Corporation
14282 Franklin Avenue
Tustin, CA 92780-7017
714-838-0500
Web Address: www.techniclone.com
Number of Employees: 44

John Bonfiglio, *President*
Valerie Kos, *Human Resources Manager*

The Immune Response Corp.
5935 Darwin Court
Carlsbad, CA 92008
760-431-7080
Job Hotline: 760-603-3396
Web Address: www.imnr.com
Number of Employees: 125

Dennis J. Carlo, *President*
Lisa Gonzales, *Human Resources Coordinator*

The Langer Biomechanics Group
2951 Saturn Street
Brea, CA 92821-6206
714-996-0030
Web Address: www.langerbiomechanics.com
Number of Employees: 300

Kathy Parks, *Director of Personnel*

The Phoenix
27405 Puerta Real #20
Mission Viejo, CA 92691-6314
714-348-1050
Web Address: www.phoenixresearch.com
Number of Employees: 42

TKB/Newport Medical Instrmnts
760 West 16th Street, Suite M
Costa Mesa, CA 92627-4319
949-650-0430
Number of Employees: 85

Kirk Inoue, *President*

Toshiba America Medical Systems
2441 Michelle Drive
Tustin, CA 92781-2068
714-730-5000
Web Address: www.toshiba.com
Number of Employees: 1000

Masamichi Katsurada, *President*
Eric Lindgren, *Human Resources Director*

Tronomed
32921 Calle Perfecto
San Juan Capistrano, CA 92675-4705
714-240-5833
Number of Employees: 30
Tracy Hurst, *Human Resources Manager*

Unilab Corporation
18448 Oxnard Street
Tarzana, CA 91356-1504
818-996-7300
Job Hotline: 818-996-7300 x6680
Number of Employees: 2,600

David Weavil, *CEO*
Angela Bagasao, *Director of Personnel*

Unocal Corp/Agricultural Product
376 South Valencia Avenue
Brea, CA 92823
714-528-7201
Web Address: www.unocal.com
Number of Employees: 1000

Sal Sangia, *Human Resources Manager*

Vical
9373 Towne Centre Drive, Suite 100
San Diego, CA 92121
619-453-9900
Job Hotline: 619-646-1143
Number of Employees: 95

Alain B. Schreiber, *Principal*
Christine Goodall, *Human Resources Manager*

Voxel
26081 Merit Circle, Suite 117
Laguna Hills, CA 92653
714-348-3200
Web Address: www.voxel.com
Number of Employees: 24

Allan M. Wolfe, *President*

Watson Pharmaceuticals
311 Bonnie Circle
Corona, CA 91718
909-270-1400
Web Address: www.watsonpharm.com

WestEd Laboratory for Ed Res
4665 Lampson Avenue
Los Alamitos, CA 90720-5139
562-598-7661

Web Address: www.wested.org
Number of Employees: 50
Anne Williams, *Personnel Director*

Whitewing Labs
15455 San Fernando Mission Boulevard
Suite 105
Mission Hills, CA 91345
818-898-2167
Web Address: www.whitewing.com
Number of Employees: 6

Cynthia Kolke, *President*
Cynthia Kolke, *Director of Personnel*

Healthcare

Alvarado Hospital Medical Center
6655 Alvarado Road
San Diego, CA 92120
858-287-3270
Job Hotline: 858-224-7100
Number of Employees: 1160

Barry Weinbaum, *CEO*
Carolyn Stoll, *Human Resource Director*

Anaheim General Hospital
3350 West Ball Road
Anaheim, CA 92804-3799
714-827-6700
Number of Employees: 323

Reynold Welch, *CEO*
Dennis Chaney, *Human Resources Manager*

Anaheim Memorial Medical Center
1111 West La Palma Avenue
Anaheim, CA 92801-2881
714-774-1450
Number of Employees: 800

Mike Carter, *CEO*

BP Campus/Anaheim Gen Hosp
5742 Beach Boulevard
Buena Park, CA 90621-2043
714-521-4770
Number of Employees: 100

Reynold Welch, *CEO*
Dennis Chaney, *Human Resources Manager*

Brea Community Hospital
380 West Central Avenue
Brea, CA 92821-3075
714-529-0211
Web Address: www.breahospital.com
Number of Employees: 380

Gietano Zanfini, *President*
Dennis Chaney, *Human Resources Director*

Brotman Medical Center
3828 Delmas Terrace
Culver City, CA 90231
310-836-7000
Job Hotline: 310-202-4725
Web Address: www.tenethealth.com/Brotman
Number of Employees: 1,000

John Fenton, *CEO*
Paul Woerz, *Human Resource Director*

Capistrano By The Sea Hospital
34000 Capistrano By The Sea Drive
Dana Point, CA 92629-0398
714-496-5702
Number of Employees: 150

Samuel L Mayhugh, *CEO*
Sandra Parker, *Human Resources Director*

Cedars-Sinai Medical Center
8725 Alden Drive
Los Angeles, CA 90048
310-855-5000
Job Hotline: 310-967-8230
Web Address: www.csmc.edu
Number of Employees: 6100

Thomas Priselac, *President*
Jeanne Flores, *Director of Human Resources*

Chapman Medical Center
2601 East Chapman Avenue
Orange, CA 92869-3296
714-633-0011
Web Address: www.cmclungctr.com
Number of Employees: 350

Maxine Cooper, *CEO*
Cheryl Hefner, *Human Resources Director*

Charter Behavioral Health System
23228 Madero
Mission Viejo, CA 92691-2706
714-830-4800
Number of Employees: 120

Jim Plummer, *CEO*
Julie Thompson, *Human Resources Manager*

Children's Hospital & Health Center
3020 Children's Way
San Diego, CA 92123
858-576-1700
Job Hotline: 858-576-5880
Web Address: www.chsd.org
Number of Employees: 3000

Blair L. Sadler, *CEO*

Children's Hospital of Los Angeles Employment Office
4601 Sunset Boulevard
Los Angeles, CA 90027
213-660-2450
Web Address: www.childrenshospitalla.org

Children's Hospital of Orange
455 South Main Street
Orange, CA 92868-3835
714-997-3000
Web Address: www.choc.com
Number of Employees: 1400

Kim Cripe, *President & CEO*
Kelly McIntosh, *Human Resources Manager*

Coastal Communities Hospital
2701 South Bristol
Santa Ana, CA 92704
714-754-5454
Web Address: www.tenethealth.com
Number of Employees: 455

Mark Meyers, *CEO*
John Gamble, *Human Resources Director*

Columbia Huntington Beach Hospital
17772 Beach Boulevard
Huntington Beach, CA 92647-6819
714-842-1473
Web Address: www.tenethealth.com
Number of Employees: 500

Carol Freeman, *President & CEO*
Sandra Anderson, *Human Resources Director*

Columbia Mission Bay Memorial Hospital
3030 Bunker Hill Street
San Diego, CA 92109
619-274-7721
Web Address: www.columbia.com
Number of Employees: 400

Deborah K. Brehe, *CEO*
Karen Sklueff, *Human Resource Manger*

Columbia San Clemente Hospital
654 Camino De Los Mares
San Clemente, CA 92673-2876
714-496-1122
Number of Employees: 300

Tony Struthers, *CEO*
Sandra Fictor, *Human Resources Manager*

Columbia West Anaheim Medical Center
3033 West Orange Avenue
Anaheim, CA 92804-3156
714-827-3000
Web Address: www.columbia.net
Number of Employees: 3500

David Culberson, *CEO*
George Wilhelm, *Human Resources Director*

Encino Tarzana Regional Medical Center
18321 Clark Street
Tarzana, CA 91356
818-881-0800

Dale Surowitz, *CEO*
Eileen Wolf, *Recruiter*

HEALTHCARE

Fountain Care Center
1835 West La Veta Avenue
Orange, CA 92868-4132
/14-978-6800
Number of Employees: 250

Dale Ladd, *Human Resources*

Fountain Valley Regional Hospital
17100 Euclid Avenue
Fountain Valley, CA 92708
714-966-7200
Job Hotline: 714-979-8108
Web Address: www.fountainvalleyhospital.com
Number of Employees: 1600

Tim Smith, *President & CEO*
Mary Leahy, *Human Resources Director*

Friendly Hills Regional Medical Center
1251 West Lambert Road
La Habra, CA 90631-6600
562-653-7658
Job Hotline: Ext 4438
Number of Employees: 1600

Albert E. Barnett, *CEO*
Pat Murphy, *Human Resources Manager*

Garden Grove Hospital
12601 Garden Grove Boulevard
Garden Grove, CA 92843-1959
714-537-5160
Web Address: www.tenethealth.com
Number of Employees: 600

Tim Smith, *CEO*
Mary Leahy, *Human Resources Director*

Glendale Adventist Medical Center
1509 Wilson Terrace
Glendale, CA 91206
818-409-8000

David Nelson, *CEO*

Good Samaritan Hospital
1225 Wilshire Boulevard
Los Angeles, CA 90017
213-977-2121
Job Hotline: 213-977-2300
Web Address: www.goodsam.org
Number of Employees: 2,500

Andrew Leeka, *CEO*

Green Hospital of Scripps Clinic
10666 Torrey Pines Road
La Jolla, CA 92037
619-455-9100
Job Hotline: 619-554-5627
Web Address: www.scrippsclinic.com

Thomas Waltz, *CEO*
Claudia Schwartz, *Human Resource Director*

Grossmont Hospital
5555 Grossmont Center Drive
La Mesa, CA 91942
619-465-0711
Web Address: www.sharp.com
Number of Employees: 2000

Michele Tarbet, *CEO*
Ruth Shannon, *Human Resource Director*

Harbor - UCLA Medical Center
1000 West Carson Street
Torrance, CA 90509
310-222-3241
Job Hotline: 800-970-5478
Web Address: www.hr.co.la.ca.us

Tecla Mickoseff, *CEO*
Judith Hardy, *Director of Human Resources*

Hoag Memorial Hospital Presbyterian
PO Box 6100
Newport Beach, CA 92658-6100
949-645-8600
Web Address: www.hoag.org
Number of Employees: 2800

Michael Stephens, *President*
Sherry Hollingsworth, *Human Resources
    Manager*

Hollywood Presbyterian Medical Center
1300 North Vermont Avenue
Los Angeles, CA 90027
213-413-3000
Job Hotline: 800-426-6998
Number of Employees: 1,000

S. M. Graff, *CEO*
Liz Hoang, *Human Resources Recruiter*

Huntington Memorial Hospital
100 West California Boulevard
Pasadena, CA 91109
626-397-5000
Job Hotline: 626-397-8504
Web Address: www.huntingtonhospital.com
Number of Employees: 2,000

Stephen Ralph, *CEO*
Dr. Ronald Quenzer, *Hiring Contact for Doctors*
Noni chernoff, *Hiring Contact for Nurses*
Sara Keever, *Hiring Contact for General
    Personnel*

Irvine Medical Center
16200 Sand Canyon Avenue
Irvine, CA 92618-3701
949-753-2000
Web Address: www.tenethealth.com
Number of Employees: 600

Richard H. Robinson, *CEO*
Sharon McKay, *Human Resources Director*

Kaiser Foundation Hospital - Bellflower
9400 East Rosecrans Boulevard
Bellflower, CA 90706
562-461-4242
Job Hotline: 888-499-1500 x3

Timothy Reed, *CEO*

Kaiser Permanente Medical Center
441 North Lakeview Avenue
Anaheim, CA 92807-3028
714-279-4000
Web Address: www.kp.org
Number of Employees: 80609

Jean Melnikoff, *Human Resources Director*

Kaiser Permanente Medical Center - L.A.
4867 Sunset Boulevard
Los Angeles, CA 90027
213-783-4011
Job Hotline: 213-857-2615
Web Address: www.kp.org
Number of Employees: 4,500

Joseph Hummel, *CEO*
Richard Broyer, *Director of Human Resources*

L.A. County + USC Medical Center
1200 North State Street, Suite 1112
Suite 1112
Los Angeles, CA 90033
213-226-6899
Number of Employees: 7,000

Dave Runke, *CEO*
Bob Navarro, *Director of Human Resources*

La Palma Intercommunity Hospital
7901 Walker Street
La Palma, CA 90623
714-670-7400
Number of Employees: 295

Steve Dixon, *President*
Tracey Montgomery, *Human Resources Director*

Loma Linda University Medical Center
11234 Anderson Street
Loma Linda, CA 92354
909-824-0800
Web Address: www.llu.edu

Long Beach Memorial Medical Center
2801 Atlantic Avenue
Long Beach, CA 90801
562-933-2000
Job Hotline: 562-933-1288
Web Address: www.memorialcare.com
Number of Employees: 2,500

Byron Schweigert, *CEO*
Patty Ossen, *Director of Human Resources*

Los Angeles County/UCS Medical Center
1200 North State Street, Suite 1112
Los Angeles, CA 90033
213-226-2622

Martin Luther Hospital
PO Box 3304
Anaheim, CA 92803-3304
714-491-5200
Number of Employees: 675

Stephen Dixon, *President*
Laura Cato, *VP for Human Resources*

Martin Luther King Jr.- Drew Med. Ctr.
12021 South Wilmington Avenue
Los Angeles, CA 90059
310-668-5201
Number of Employees: 3,500

Randall Foster, *CEO*
Tobi Moree, *Human Resource Manager*

Mercy Hospital
4077 Fifth Avenue
San Diego, CA 92103
619-294-8111
Job Hotline: 619-554-8400
Web Address: www.scrippshealth.org
Number of Employees: 2000

Nancy Wilson, *Senior Vice President*
Cathy Fredrick, *Human Resource Director*

Mesa Vista Hospital
7850 Vista Hill Avenue
San Diego, CA 92123
619-694-8300
Job Hotline: 619-627-5935
Web Address: dallen@vistahill.org

Donald K. Allen, *CEO*
Connie Jameson, *Human Resource Director*

Mission Hospital Regional Medical Center
27700 Medical Center Road
Mission Viejo, CA 92691-6474
714-364-1400
Web Address: www.mhrmc.com
Number of Employees: 1400

Peter Bastone, *President*
Shirley Barnes, *VP for Human Resources*

Mullikin Med Center - Anaheim
2100 West Lincoln Avenue
Anaheim, CA 92801-5640
714-956-7401
Number of Employees: 2500

HEALTHCARE

Mullikin Medical Center
13950 Milton Avenue
Westminster, CA 92683-2911
714-892-0622
Number of Employees: 2500

Newport Bay Hospital
1501 East 16th Street
Newport Beach, CA 92663-5900
949-650-9750
Number of Employees: 50

Jim Burtnum, *President*

Northridge Hospital Medical Center
18300 Roscoe Boulevard
Northridge, CA 91328
818-885-8500

Roger Seaver, *CEO*
Ellen Henderson, *Nurse Coordinator*

Orange County Community Hospital
6850 Lincoln Avenue
Buena Park, CA 90620
714-827-1161

Pacifica Hospital
18800 Delaware Street
Huntington Beach, CA 92648-1959
714-596-8000
Number of Employees: 250

Michael Sussman, *CEO*
Krystal Voris, *Human Resources Manager*

Palomar Medical Center
555 East Valley Parkway
Escondido, CA 92025
760-739-3000
Job Hotline: 760-739-3960
Number of Employees: 4000

Victoria M. Penland, *CEO*
Holly Wimer, *Human Resources Director*

Paradise Valley Hospital
2400 East Fourth Street
National City, CA 91950
619-470-4321
Job Hotline: 619-470-4422
Number of Employees: 1092

Eric Martinsen, *CEO*
Alfonso Small, *Human Resource Director*

Placentia-Linda Hospital
1301 North Rose Drive
Placentia, CA 92870-3899
714-993-2000
Web Address: www.tenethealth.com/placentialinda
Number of Employees: 324

Maxine Cooper, *CEO*
Lora Leiga, *Human Resources Director*

Pomerado Hospital
15615 Pomerado Road
Poway, CA 92064
619-485-6511
Job Hotline: 619-485-4680
Web Address: www.pphs.org
Number of Employees: 584

Victoria M. Penland, *CEO*
Holly Wimer, *Human Resource Manager*

Pomona Valley Hospital Medical Center
1798 North Garey Avenue
Pomona, CA 91767
909-865-9500
Number of Employees: 2,300

Richard Yochum, *CEO*

Providence Saint Joseph Medical Center
501 South Buena Vista Street
Burbank, CA 91505
818-843-5111

Michael Madden, *CEO*
Diane Doyle, *Recruiter*
Ruth Redfern, *Recruiter*
Maria Celli, *Recruiter*

Rancho Los Amigos Medical Center
7601 East Imperial Highway
Downey, CA 90242
562-401-7022
Job Hotline: 800-970-5478
Number of Employees: 1,500

Consuelo Diaz, *CEO*
Marisa Lopez, *Human Resources Director*

Saddleback Memorial Medical Center
24451 Health Center Drive
Laguna Hills, CA 92653-3689
714-837-4500
Web Address: www.tenethealth.com
Number of Employees: 1350

Nolan G. Draney, *CEO*
Tom Miller, *Human Resources Director*

Saint John's Hospital & Health Center
1328 22nd Street
Santa Monica, CA 90404
310-829-5511
Web Address: www.stjohn.org
Number of Employees: 3,000
Lindi Funston, *Personnel Manager*

San Pedro Peninsula Hospital
1300 West Seventh Street
San Pedro, CA 90732
310-832-3311
Job Hotline: 310-540-7373
Number of Employees: 3,300

John Wilson, *CEO*
Linda Lopez, *Human Resource Manager*

Santa Ana Hospital Medical Center
1901 North Fairview Street
Santa Ana, CA 92706-2291
714-554-1653
Number of Employees: 400

Mark Meyers, *CEO*
JoAnne Gamble, *Human Resources Director*

Scripps Hospital-East County
1688 East Main Street
El Cajon, CA 92061
619-440-1122
Job Hotline: 619-554-8400
Web Address: www.scrippshealth.org
Number of Employees: 398

Ames Early, *CEO*
Claudia Mazanec, *Vice President of Human Resources*

Scripps Memorial Hospital-Chula Vista
435 H Street
Chula Vista, CA 91910
619-691-7000
Job Hotline: 619-554-8400
Web Address: www.scrippshealth.org
Number of Employees: 670

Ames Early, *CEO*
Claudia Mazanec, *Vice President of Human Resources*

Scripps Memorial Hospital-Encinitas
354 Santa Fe Drive
Encinitas, CA 92024
760-753-6501
Job Hotline: 619-554-8400
Web Address: www.scrippshealth.org
Number of Employees: 750

Ames Early, *CEO*
Sue Fitzgibbons, *Director of Human Resources*

Scripps Memorial Hospital-La Jolla
9888 Genesee Avenue
La Jolla, CA 92037
619-457-4123
Job Hotline: 619-554-8400
Web Address: www.scrippshealth.org
Number of Employees: 1500

Ames Early, *CEO*
Claudia Mezanec, *Vice President of Human Resources*

Sharp Chula Vista Medical Center
751 Medical Center Court
Chula Vista, CA 91911
619-482-5800
Job Hotline: 619-627-5935
Web Address: www.sharp.com
Number of Employees: 800

Britt Berrett, *CEO*
Diana Delaney, *Human Resource Director*

Sharp Coronado Hospital
250 Prospect Place
Coronado, CA 92118
619-522-3600
Job Hotline: 619-627-5935
Web Address: www.sharp.com
Number of Employees: 500

Marcia Hall, *CEO*
Diana Delaney, *Human Resource Director*

Sharp Metro Hospitals
7901 Frost Street
San Diego, CA 92123
619-541-3400
Job Hotline: 619-627-5935
Web Address: www.sharp.com
Number of Employees: 600

Dan Gross, *CEO*
Diana Delaney, *Human Resource Director*

South Coast Medical Center
31872 South Coast Highway
Laguna Beach, CA 92677-3290
714-499-1311
Web Address: www.adventisthealth.com
Number of Employees: 650

T. Michael Murray, *President*
Ron Oh, *Human Resources Manager*

St. Francis Medical Center
3630 East Imperial Highway
Lynwood, CA 90262
310-603-6000
Number of Employees: 1,600

Gerald T. Kozai, *CEO*
Julie Sedlacek, *Recruiter*
Laura Kato, *Human Resource Director*

St. Joseph Hospital of Orange
1100 Stewart Drive
Orange, CA 92863-5600
714-633-9111
Job Hotline: 714-744-8557
Web Address: www.stjosham.on.ca
Number of Employees: 2600

Larry Ainsworth, *President*
Jan Clardy, *Human Resources Manager*

St. Jude Medical Center
101 East Valencia Mesa Drive
Fullerton, CA 92834-4138
714-992-3000
Number of Employees: 1600

Robert J. Praschetti, *President*

St. Mary Medical Center
1050 Linden Avenue
Long Beach, CA 90801
562-491-9000

HEALTHCARE

Job Hotline: 562-491-9844 x3687
Tammie McMann Brailsford, *CEO*
Stacy Wong, *Employment Coordinator*
Tonya Houston, *Human Resource Manager*

St. Vincent Medical Center
2131 West Third Street
Los Angeles, CA 90057
213-484-7111
Job Hotline: 213-484-7032
Number of Employees: 1,110

Myda Magarian Marse, *CEO*
Theresa Lopez, *Employment Coordinator*

Tri-City Medical Center
4002 Vista Way
Oceanside, CA 92056
760-724-8411
Job Hotline: 760-940-5002
Number of Employees: 1962

John P. Lauri, *CEO*
Deborah Gac, *Human Resources Director*

Tustin Hospital/Medical Center
14662 Newport Avenue
Tustin, CA 92781-1046
714-838-9600
Number of Employees: 300

Kim Bui, *Human Resources Manager*

Tustin Rehabilitation Hospital
14851 Yorba Street
Tustin, CA 92780-2925
714-832-9200
Web Address: www.westernmedical.com
Number of Employees: 300

Gwen Chambers, *Human Resources Director*

UCI Medical Center
101 The City Drive South
Orange, CA 92868-3298
714-456-6011
Web Address: www.ucimc@uci.edu
Number of Employees: 2000

Pat Thatcher, *Human Resources Director*

UCLA Medical Center
10833 LeConte Avenue
Los Angeles, CA 90024
310-825-9111
Job Hotline: 310-794-0506
Web Address: www.amedctr.ucla.edu
Number of Employees: 4,500

Michael Karpf, *CEO*
Mark Spear, *Director of Human Resources*

UCSD Medical Center
200 West Arbor Drive
San Diego, CA 92103
619-543-6222

Job Hotline: 619-682-1001
Web Address: www.ucsd.edu
Number of Employees: 3500
Kent Sherwood, *CEO*
Ann Skinner, *Human Resource Director*

VA Medical Center - Long Beach
5901 East Seventh Street
Long Beach, CA 90822
562-494-2611
Job Hotline: Ext 5651

Jerry Boyd, *CEO*

Vencor Hospital San Diego
1940 El Cajon Boulevard
San Diego, CA 92104
619-543-4500
Number of Employees: 200

Michael Cress, *CEO*
Debbie Gainey, *Human Resource Director*

West Los Angeles - VA Medical Center
11301 Wilshire Boulevard
Los Angeles, CA 90073
310-478-3711
Number of Employees: 5,000

Kenneth Clark, *CEO*

Western Medical Center Hosp - Anaheim
1025 South Anaheim Boulevard
Anaheim, CA 92805-5806
714-533-6220
Web Address: www.westernmedical.com
Number of Employees: 480

Richard Butler, *CEO*
Gwen Chambers, *Human Resources Manager*

Western Medical Center Santa Ana
1001 North Tustin Avenue
Santa Ana, CA 92705-3577
714-835-3555
Web Address: www.westernmedical.com
Number of Employees: 1400

Lexi Schuster, *VP for Human Resources*

Managed Care

ARV Assisted Living
245 Fischer Avenue, Suite D-1
Costa Mesa, CA 92626
949-751-7400
Web Address: www.arvi.com
Number of Employees: 2600

Howard G. Phanstiel, *President*
Charlotte Deulloa, *Human Resources Manager*
Operater of about 50 assisted living facilities for the elderly in 11 states, including California, Texas, and Florida.

Further References

• Associations •

American Association of Blood Banks
8101 Glenbrook Road
Bethesda, Maryland 20814
301-907-6977
Web Address: www.aabb.org
Enhances Efforts of Blood Banks

American Association of Colleges of Pharmacy
1426 Prince Street
Alexandria, Virginia 22314
703-739-2330
Web Address: www.aacp.org
Promotes Excellence and Standards.

American Association of Dental Schools
1625 Massachusetts Avenue, N.W.
Washington, D.C. 20036
202-667-9433
Web Address: www.aads.jhu
Promotes Teaching and Research.

American Association of Health Plans
1129 20th Street, N.W., Suite 600
Washington, D.C. 20036
202-778-3200
Web Address: www.aahp.org

American Association of Medical Assistants
20 North Wacker Drive
Chicago, Illinois 60606
312-899-1500
Web Address: www.aama/ntl.org
Accreditation of One and Two Year Programs.

American Chiropractic Association
1701 Clarendon Boulevard
Arlington, Virginia 22209
703-276-8800
Web Address: www.amerchiro.org/aca
Promotes Excellence and Standards.

American College of Healthcare Executives
1 North Franklin Street, Suite 1700
Chicago, Illinois 60606-3491
312-424-2800
Web Address: www.ache.org
Updates on Trends and Issues.

American Dental Association
211 East Chicago Avenue
Chicago, Illinois 60611
312-440-2500
Web Address: www.ada.org
Resources for Dental Field.

American Health Care Association
1201 L Street, N.W.
Washington, D.C. 20005
202-842-4444
Promotes Standards and Quality Care.

American Hospital Association
1 North Franklin
Chicago, Illinois 60606
312-422-3000
Strives for Better Service to Patients.

American Nurses Association
600 Maryland Avenue, S.W.
Washington, D.C. 20024
202-554-4444
Web Address: www.nursingworld.org
Represents Registered Nurses.

American Pharmaceutical Association
2215 Constitution Avenue, N.W.
Washington, D.C. 20037
202-628-4410
Web Address: www.aphanet.org
Promotes Quality and Standards.

American Physical Therapy Association
1111 North Fairfax Street
Alexandria, Virginia 22314
703-684-2782
Web Address: www.apta.org
Promotes Innovation and Quality.

American Psychiatric Association
1400 K Street, N.W.
Washington, D.C. 20005
202-682-6000
Web Address: www.psych.org
Furthers Study of Mental Disorders.

American Psychological Association
750 First Street, N.E.
Washington, D.C. 20002
202-336-5520
Web Address: www.apa.org
Advances Psychology as a Science.

HEALTHCARE

American Society of Hospital Pharmacists
7272 Wisconsin Avenue, N.W.
Bethesda, Maryland 20814
301-657-3000
Web Address: www.ashp.org
Placement and Education for Members.

Health Industry Manufacturers Association
1200 G Street, N.W., Suite 400
Washington, D.C. 20005
202-783-8700
Web Address: www.himanet.com
Represents Domestic Manufacturers.

National Medical Association
1012 10th Street, N.W.
Washington, D.C. 20001
202-347-1895
Society of Black Physicians.

National Pharmaceutical Council
1894 Preston White Drive
Reston, Virginia 22091
703-620-6390
Professional Minority Pharmacists.

• Publications •

ADA News
211 East Chicago Avenue
Chicago, IL 60611
312-440-2791
Web Address: www.ada.org/adapco/daily/today.html
American Dental Association newspaper.

Healthcare Executive
1 North Franklin Street, Suite 1700
Chicago, IL 60611
312-424-2800
Healthcare management magazine.

Healthcare Facilities Management
737 North Michigan Avenue, Suite 700
Chicago, IL 60611
312-440-6800

Hospital Magazine
655 Avenue of the Americas
New York, NY 10010
Web Address: //hospitalmed.com
Forum for physicians.

Physician Magazine
8605 Explorer Drive
Colorado Springs, CO 80920
719-548-4575
Magazine for the medical profession.

Resident & Staff Physician
80 Shore Road
Port Washington, NY 11050
908-656-1140
Hospital based physicians with direct patient-care responsibilites.

The American Nurse
600 Maryland Avenue, S.W., Suite 100
Washington, D.C. 20024-2571
202-651-7026
Web Address: www.nursingworld.org/pub.htm
News of the Nursing Profession.

American Medical News
515 North State Street
Chicago, Illinois 60605
312-464-5000
Web Address: www.ama-assn.org

Drug Topics
5 Paragon Drive
Montvale, NJ 07645
201-358-7200
Web Address: www.medecinteract.com

Encyclopedia of Medical Organizations & Agencies
835 Penobscot Building
Detroit, Michigan 48226
313-961-2242

Health Care Executive
1 North Franklin Street, Suite 1700
Chicago, Illinois 60606-3491
312-424-2800
Web Address: www.ache.org

Managed Health Care Directory
1129 20th Street, N.W.
Washington, D.C. 20036
202-778-3200
Web Address: www.aahp.com

Modern Healthcare
740 North Rush Street
Chicago, IL 60611
312-649-5374

High Tech

- Computers - Software/Hardware
- Engineering
- Environmental Consulting
- Defense Contracting
- Information Services
- Internet Developers/Providers

*B*ooz, Allen is one of the world's largest and most respected management and technology consulting firms. We provide a broad range of analytic, engineering and technical program management services to government and commercial clients.

Generally, our entry–level openings require a technical degree (BS or MS: Engineering, Computer Science and other related disciplines), and although we do consider GPA an important criteria, we also seek individuals with some internship, co–op or other applicable work experience. In addition to technical qualifications, we require excellent oral and written communications skills.

Booz, Allen Technology Center professionals address leading edge problems encompassing information systems concepts, design, and development. We develop specialized software and integrate large scale hardware and software systems; we design telecommunications architectures and implement local area networks; we apply artificial intelligence algorithms and validate new concepts in signal processing. Booz, Allen also provides clients with expert, unbiased assistance in research, development, acquisition and operations to support advanced defense, space, environmental, healthcare, human resource and transportation systems.

I would strongly advise interested parties to seek some sort of related work experience while in school.

BOOZ, ALLEN & HAMILTON, INC.

See Also: Government

HIGH-TECH

299

3-D Instruments
www.3dinstruments.com

Able Communications
www.able.com

ACCEL Technologies
www.acceltech.com

Accurate Circuit Engineering
www.ace-pcd.com

Acucorp, Inc.
www.acucorp.com

Adaptive Information Systems
www.ais-hitachi.com

Admor Memory Corporation
www.admor.com

Advanced Industrial Systems
www.advancedindustrialsystems.com

Advanced Logic Research
www.alr.com

Advanced Media
www.advancedmedia.com

Advanced Micro Devices
www.amd.com

Advanced Technology Center
www.atc.com

Advantage Memory Corporation
www.advantagememory.com

AeroVironment
www.aerovironment.com

Airshow
www.airshowinc.com

Alpha Microsystems
www.alphamicro.com

Alpha Systems Lab
www.aslrwp.com

Alps Electric USA
www.alpsusa.com

Alton Geoscience
www.altongeo.com

Alyn Corporation
www.alyn.com

Amdahl Corporation
www.amdahl.com

American Computer Hardware
www.achc.com

American Microwave Technology
www.amtinc.com

Amplicon Financial
www.amplicon.com

Amtec Engineering Corporation
www.amtec-eng.com

Anacomp
www.anacomp.com

Anagraph
www.anagraph.com

AnaServe
www.anaserve.com

AOT Electronics
www.shortages.com

Area Electronics Systems
www.areasys.com

Arinc
www.arinc.com

Artios Corporation
www.artioslink.com

ASL Consulting Engineers
www.aslce.com

AST Research
www.ast.com

ATC Associates
www.atc-enviro.com

Aten Research
www.cliffwood.com

ATL Products
www.atlp.com

Atmel Corporation
www.atmel.com

Auspex Systems
www.auspex.com

Auto-By-Tel Corporation
www.autobytel.com

Automated Solutions Group
www.asgsoft.com

Autosplice
http://autosplice.com

Aztek
www.aztek.net

Bambeck Systems
www.bambecksystem.net

Barco Visual Systems
www.barco.com

BAS Micro Industries
www.basmicro.com

Basic Electronics
www.basicinc.com

BCM Advanced Research
www.bcmgvc.com

BE Aerospace/In-Flight Entertainment
www.bear.com

Becwar Engineering
www.becwar.com

Biolase Technology
www.biolase.com

Black & Veatch Engineers/Architects
www.bv.com

Blizzard Entertainment
www.blizzard.com

Bluebird Systems
www.bluebird.com

Boyle Engineering Corporation
www.boyleengineering.com

Broadcom Corporation
www.broadcom.com

Brown & Caldwell
www.brownandcaldwell.com

Business Automation
www.baipro.com

C Hoelzle Associates
www.chainc.com

Cabletron Systems
www.ctron.com

CACI Products Company
www.caciasl.com

Cair Systems Corporation
www.cairsystems.com

Cal Quality Electronics
www.calquality.com

Cal-Tronic's
www.caltronics.com

CalComp Technology
www.calcomp.com

California Analytical Instruments
www.gasanalyzers.com

California Economizer
www.hvaccomfort.com

California IC
www.californiaic.com

California Software Products
www.calsw.com

Calty Design Research
www.calty.com

CAM Data Systems
www.camdata.com

Cambridge Management Corporation
www.cppus.com

Camintonn Corporation
www.camintonn.com

Canon Business Machines
www.canon.com

Canon Computer Systems
www.ccsi.canon.com

CCH
www.prosystemfx.com

CDCE
www.cdce.com

Cedko Electronics
www.cedko.com

Centon Electronics
www.centon.com

Century Computer Corporation
www.centurycomputercorp.com

CET Environmental Service
www.cetenvironmental.com

CG Tech
www.cgtech.com

CH2M Hill
www.ch2m.com

ChatCom
www.jlchatcom.com

CIE America
www.citoh.com

Circuit Image Systems
www.circuitimage.com

Circuit World
www.circuit-world.com

Cirtech
www.cirtech.com

CISD International
www.cisd.com

Clayton Engineering
www.4cei.com

CLS Software
www.maisystems.com

CMD Technology
www.cmd.com

Coast Computer Products
www.purchasepro.com/coast/
computer

Coast Technologies
www.coastech.com

Colorbus
www.colorbus.com

COMARCO
www.cmro.com

Compucable Corporation
www.compucable.com

Compusource Corporation
www.compusource.com

Computer Associates International
www.cai.com

Computer Peripherals International
www.cpinternational.com

ComStream Corporation
www.comstream.com

Continuus Software Corporation
www.continuos.com

Converse Consultants Orange County
www.converseconsultants.com

Copper Clad Multilayer Products
www.ccmpinc.com

Core Dynamics Corporation
www.core-dynamics.com

Corning OCA
www.oca-inc.com

Corollary
www.corollary.com

Cosmotronic Company
www.cosmotronic.com

Coyote Network Systems
www.coyotenetworksystems.com/

Quick Reference

Creative Computer Applications
www.ccainc.com

Credentials Services International
www.credentials-net.com

CSS Labs
www.csslabs.com

CSTI
www.celeritysolutions.com

Cyberworks
www.cyberworks.net

D-Link Systems
www.dlink.com

Dainippon Screen Engineering
www.dsea.com

Daniel Measurement & Control
www.danielind.com

Data Color International
www.dci.com

Data Express
www.dataexp.com

Data General Corp/Field Sales
www.dg.com

Data Processing Design
www.dpd.com

Data Processing Resources
Corporation
www.dprc.com

Datametrics Corporation
www.datametricscorp.com

Datum
www.datum.com

Davox Corp
www.davox.com

Delphi Components
www.microwavebd.com

Dense-Pac Microsystems
www.dense-pac.com

Details
www.detailsinc.com

Diamond Technologies
www.diamondtech.com

Digital Equipment Corporation
www.digitalinfo.com

Digital West Media
www.dwmi.com

Digital Wizards
www.digwiz.com

DKS Associates
www.dksassociates.com

Document Control Solutions
www.docsolutions.com

Dynamotion
www.elc.sci.com

EIP Microwave
www.eipm.com/index.htm

Electro-Chemical Devices
www.ecdi.com

EMCON
www.emconinc.com

Emulex Corporation
www.emulex.com

Encore Computer Corporation
www.encore.com

ENSR Consulting & Engineering
www.ensr.com

Enterprise Solutions Ltd.
www.csi.esltd.com

EOS International
www.eosintl.com

EQE
www.eqe.com

Equifax National Decision Systems
www.natdecsys.com

ESI/FME
www.esifme.com

Excello Circuits
www.excello.com

Executive Software
www.execsoft.com

Exide Electronics
www.exide.com

Expersoft Corp.
www.expersoft.com

Extron Electronics
www.extron.com

FileNet Corporation
www.filenet.com

Financial Processing Systems
www.fpsnet.com

Fineline Circuits & Technology
www.finelinecircuits.com

FM Systems
www.fmsystems-inc.com

Formula Consultants
www.formula.com

FTG Data Systems
www.ftgdata.com

Future Focus
www.future-focus.com

Gage Babcock & Associates
www.gage-babcock.com

GDE Systems
www.gde.com

Geac Computers/Hotel Computer
www.hotels.geac.com

GEC Plessey Semiconductors
www.gpsemi.com

General Automation
www.genauto.com

General Instrument Corp
www.gi.com

General Monitors
www.generalmonitors.com

General Software Solutions
www.gsscorp.com

Genesis 2000
www/.genesis2000.com

Genisco Tech Corp/Solaris Sys
www.gtc.com

Genovation
www.genovation.com

Gensia Sicor
www.gensiasicor.com

GeoSyntec Consultants
www.geosynthetic.com

GERS Retail Systems
www.gers.com

Golden State Bancorp
www.glenfederal.com

Golden West Circuits
www.gwcircuits.com

Gouvis Engineering California
www.gouvisgroup.com

Graphic Resources Corporation
www.grc.com

GSI
www.gsi-inc.com

Gulton Statham Transducers
www.gulton-statham.com

Harding Lawson Assoc Group
www.harding.com

Hargis + Associates
www.lawinfo.com/biz/hargis

HDR Engineering
www.hdrinc.com

Hirsch Electronics Corporation
www.hirschelectronics.com

Holt Integrated Circuits
www.holtic.com

Horiba Instruments
www.horiba.com

Horizons Technology
www.horizons.com

Hughes Aircraft, Data Systems &
Info Tech Systems
www.hughes.com

Hughes Aircraft/Microelectron
www.raytheon.com

I/Omagic Corporation
www.iomagic.com

ICCI (Intl Circuits/Component)
www.icciusa.com

ICL Retail Systems
www.iclretail.com

Idea
http://eemonline.com/idea

Image & Signal Processing
www.cersnet.com

Imaging Tech
www.imaging.com

iMALL
www.imall.com

IMC Networks
www.imcnetworks.com

Impco Technologies
www.impcotechnologies.com

InCirT Technology
www.incirt.com

IndeNet
www.indenet.com

Infographics Systems Corp
www.infographicsystems.com

Ingram Micro
www.ingrammicro.com

Inline
www.inlineinc.com

Innovative Sensors
www.isi-ph.inter.net

InSight Health Services Corp.
www.insighthealth.com

Inspired Arts
www.inspiredarts.com

Intergraph Corporation
www.intergraph.com

Intermetrics
www.intermetrics.com

International Remote Imaging
Systems
www.proiris.com

International Sensor Technology
www.gotgas.com

International Space Optics SA
www.isorainbow.com

International Technology Corp
www.itcorporation.com

Interplay Productions
www.interplay.com

Iris www.irisnet.com

Irvine Sensors Corporation
www.irvine-sensors.com

Island Pacific Systems Corp
www.islandpacific.com

Isocor
www.isocor.com

IVID Communications
www.ivid.com

Javelin Systems
www.jvln.com

Jaycor
www.jaycor.com

Jones & McGeoy Sales
www.jonesmcgeoy.com

Jonesville Webs
www.blurtheline.com

KCA Electronics
www.kcamerica.com

KFC USA
www.smilekfc.com

Kimley-Horn & Associates
www.kimleyhorn.com

King Instrument Company
www.kinginstrument.com

Kingston Technology Company
www.kingston.com

Kleinfelder
www.kleinfelder.com

Kofax Image Products
www.kofax.com

Kor Electronics
www.korelec.com

KVB
www.kvb-cems.com

Lantronix
www.lantronix.com

Laser Industries
www.laserindustries.com

Laser Products Corp
www.laserproducts.com

Lasergraphics
www.lasergraphics.com

Leaming Industries
www.leaming.com

Lifetime Memory Products
www.lifetimememory.com

Linfinity Microelectronics
www.linfinity.com

Link SanDiego.Com.
www.sandiego.com

Litronic Industries
www.alliedsignals.com

Live Software
www.livesoftware.com

Lotus Development Corporation
www.lotus.com

MacNeal-Schwendler Corp.
www.macsch.com

Macrolink
www.macrolink.com

Madge Networks
www.madge.com

Magic Software Enterprises
www.magic-sw.com

MAI Systems Corporation
www.maisystems.com

MARCOR Mediation
www.marcor.com

Marway Power Systems
www.marway.com

McCurdy Circuits
www.mccurdy.com

McLaren/Hart
www.mclaren-hart.com

Meade Instruments Corp
www.meade.com

Medata
www.medata.com

MEI (Marcel Electronics Intl)
www.marcelelec.com

Mettler Electronics Corp
www.mettlerelec.com

MGV International
www.mgvgroup.com

Michael Brandman Associates
www.brandman.com

Micro Express
www.microexpress.net

MicroNet Technology
www.micronet.com

Microsemi Corporation
www.microsemi.com

Microsoft Corporation
www.microsoft.com

Mission Geoscience
www.cerfnet.com

Mitsubishi Electronics America
www.mea.com

Monitoring Automation Systems
www.monauto.com

Monroe Systems for Business
www.monroe-systems.com

Montgomery Watson
www.mw.com

MPI Technologies
www.mpitech.com

MTI Technology Corporation
www.mti.com

Multilayer Technology
www.multek.com

Murrietta Circuits
www.murrietta.com

Nadek Computer Systems
www.nadek.com

National Computer Systems
www.ncslink.com

National Steel & Shipbuilding Co.
www.nasco.com

National Technical Systems
www.ntscorp.com

NCCS
www.nccs.com

NCS (National Computer Systems)
www.ncs.om

Net Manage
www.aharmony.com

Network Associates
www.nai.com

Network Intensive
www.ni.net

New Dimension Software
www.ndsoft.com

New Media Corporation
www.newmediacorp.com

NewCom
www.newcominc.com

NewGen Imaging Systems
www.newgen.com

Newport Corporation
www.newport.com

Nexgen SI
www.nexgensi.com

Nichols Research Corporation
www.nichols.com

Ninyo & Moore
www.ninyoandmoore.com

Nova Logic
www.novalogic.com

Novell
www.novell.com

ObjectShare
www.objectshare.com

OC Alphanetics
www.alphanetics.com

OCE' Printing
www.oceprinting.com

Odetics
www.odetics.com

Ogden Environmental & Energy
Services Co.
www.ogdensfo.com

OnVillage Communications
www.onvillage.com

Optical Laser
www.opticallaser.com

OPTUM Software
www.optum.com

Oracle Corporation
www.us.oracle.com

Orange Micro
www.macph.com

OrCad
www.orcad.com

OWEN Group
www.owengroup.com

P&D Consultants
www.cte-eng.com

PairGain Technologies
www.pairgain.com

Palomar Systems
www.elcsci.com

Parsons Transportation Group
www.parsons.com

Pentadyne-Pentaflex
www.pentadyne-pentaflex.com

Perceptronics
www.perceptronics.com

Phase One
www.phase1.com

Phoenix Technologies Ltd.
www.phoenix.com

Photo Research
www.photoresearch.com

Pick Systems
www.picksys.com.

Pinnacle Micro
www.pinnaclemicro.com

Pioneer Circuits
www.pioneercircuits.com

Plaid Brothers Software
www.plaid.com

Plastship Logistics Intl
www.plastship.com

Platinum Software Corporation
www.platsoft.com

Power Circuits
www.powerckts.com

Powerwave Technologies
www.powerwave.com

Precision Glass & Optics
www.precision-glass.com

Presto-Tek Corporation
www.newportinc.com

Printrak International
www.printrakinternational.com

Printronix
www.printronix.com/

Prism Software
www.prism-software.com

Procom Technology
www.procom.com

Productivity Enhancement
Products
www.pepinc.com

Professional Service Industries
www.psi.com

Progen Technology
www.progen.com

PSIMED Corporation
www.psi-med.com

PsiTech
www.primenet.com/~psitech

Quick Reference

Pulse Engineering
www.pulseeng.com
Puroflow Incorporated
www.puroflow.com
QLogic
www.qlc.com
QLP Laminates
www.qlp.com
QuadraMed Corp.
www.quadramed.com
Quality Systems
www.qsii.com
Quarterdeck Corp.
www.quarterdeck.com
Quest Software
www.quests.com
QuickStart Technologies
www.quickstart.com
Radian International LLC
www.radian.com
Radiant Technology Corporation
www.radianttech.com
Rainbow Technologies
www.rainbow.com
Ram Optical Instrumentation
www.ramoptical.com
Rational Software Corporation
www.rational.com
Reedex
www.robust.com/reedex
Relsys International
www.relsys-inc.com
REMEC
www.remec.com
Research Engineers
www.reiusa.com
Risk Data Corporation
www.riskdata.com
Robert Bein William Frost & Associates
www.rbf.com
Rockwell International Corporation
www.rockwell.com
ROI Systems
www.roisysinc.com
Ross Systems
www.rossinc.com
Router Solutions
www.rsi-inc.com
Routerware
www.routerware.com
Russell Information Sciences
www.russellinfo.com
Sabtech Industries
www.sabtec.com
Safety Components International
www.safetycomponents.com
SAIC Internet Solutions
www.saic.com
SAS Institute
www.sas.com
Scantron Corporation
www.scantron.com
SCS Engineers
www.scseng.com
Seagate Technology
www.seagate.com
Secure Communication Systems
www.securecomm.com
Seimens Nixdorf Information Systems
www.intranet.sni-usa.com
Select Software Tools
www.selectst.com

SEMCOR
www.semcor.com
Semicoa
www.semicoa.com
Sensorex
www.sensorex.com
SGS Thomson Microelectronics
www.st.com
Sharp Digital Information Prod
www.sharpsdi.com
Shopping.com
www.shopping.com/ss/default.asp
Siemens Pyramid Information Systems
www.pyramid.com
Silicon Graphics Computer Systems
www.sgi.com
Silicon Systems
www.ssi1.com
Simons Li & Associates
www.simonsli.com
Simple Technology
www.simpletech.com
SimpleNet
www.simplenet.com
Simulation Sciences
www.simsci.com
Smartek Educational Technology
www.wordsmart.com
Smartflex Systems
www.smartflex.com
Smith Micro Software
www.smithmicro.com
SMK Electronics Corp USA
www.smkusa.com
SMT Dynamics Corp
www.smtblackfox.com
Soldermask
www.soldermask.com
Soligen Technologies
www.PartsNow.com
Somerset Automation
www.somersetwms.com
Sony Technology Center
www.sgo.sony.com
Source Diversified
www.sourced.com
Southland Micro Systems
www.southlandmicro.com
Space Applications Corp/Information Systems Division
www.spaceapps.com
Sparta
www.sparta.com
Speedy Circuits
www.speedycircuits.com
SRS Labs
www.srslabs.com
SRS Technologies
www.srs.com
StarBase Corporation
www.starbase.com
State of the Art
www.sota.com
Storage Concepts
www.storageconcepts.com
Storage Technology Corp
www.stortek.com
Subscriber Computing
www.subscriber.com
Sun Microsystems Computer Corp
www.sun.com

Superior Manufacturing Co
www.laxmigroup.com
Symbios Logic
www.symbios.com
Symbol Technologies
www.symbol.com
Symitar Systems
www.symitar.com
Sync Research
www.sync.com
SYS Technology
www.systechnology.com
Syspro Impact Software
www.sysprousa.com
Systems & Software
www.kaiwan.com/nssi/ssi.htmd
T-HQ
www.thq.com
Tait & Associates
www.tait.com
Tanner Research
www.tanner.com
Tayco Engineering
www.taycoeng.com
TCI Management
www.tcisolutions.com
Techmedia Computer Systems Corporation
www.techmedia.net
Technologic Software
www.technologic.com
Tekelec
www.tekelec.com
Tektronix/Color Printing
www.tek.com
Telecom Solutions
www.tsiusa.com
Tetra Tech
www.tetratech.com
The Cerplex Group
www.cerplex.com
The Flamemaster Corporation
www.flamemaster.com
The Laxmi Group
www.laxmigroup.com
The MacNeal-Schwendler Corp
www.macsch.com
The Park Corporation
www.parkenv.com
The Planning Center
www.planningcenter.com
Tone Software Corporation
www.tonesoft.com
Toshiba America Info Systems
www.toshiba.com
TouchStone Software Corporation
www.checkit.com
Transitional Technology
www.ttech.com
TRC Environmental Solutions
www.treesi.com
Tri-Star Engineered Products
www.tri-star-epi.com
Triconex Corp
www.triconex.com
TriTeal Corp.
www.triteal.com
Tutor-Saliba Corporation
www.tutorsaliba.com
Unisys Corporation
www.unisys.com
Unit Instruments
www.unit.com

Unitech Research
www.unitech.com

US Sensor Corp
www.ussensor.com

V3I Engineering
www.v3i.com

Vanguard Technology
www.vanguard.com

Velie Circuits
www.velie.com

Viking Components
www.vikingcomponents.com

Virgin Interactive Entertainment
www.vie.com

Vis-A'Vis Communications
www.weedpuller.com

VisiCom Laboratories
www.visicom.com

Vision Solutions
www.visionsolutions.com

VitalCom
www.vitalcom.com

Voice Powered Technology International
www.vpti.com

Volt Delta Resources
www.volt.com

Wahlco Environmental Systems
www.wahlco.com

Watson General Corp.
www.wgen.com

Wavefunction
www.wavefun.com

Western Data Systems
www.westdata.com

Western Digital Corporation
www.westerndigital.com

Western Pacific Data Systems
www.wpds.com

Western Telematic
www.wti.com

Willdan Associates
www.willdan.com

Wiz Technology
www.wiztech.com

Wonderware Corporation
www.wonderware.com

Woodward-Clyde Intl -Americas
www.wcc.com

Wyle Electronics
www.wyle.com

Wynns International
www.wynns.com

XCD
www.xcd.com

Xicor
www.xicor.com

Xilinx
www.xilinx.com

Xtend Micro Products
www.xmpi.com

XyberNet
www.xyber.net

Xylan Corporation
www.xylan.com

Zenographics
www.zeno.com

ZyXEL Communications
www.zyxel.om

Company Job Hotlines

Autosplice
619-535-0868

Bluebird Systems
800-669-2220

CCH
800-254-7772

Centon Electronics
714-855-2039

Continental Maritime of San Diego
619-234-8851 #3

Cubic Corporation
619-505-1540

Delta Environmental Consultants
800-988-5819

Emulex Corporation
714-513-8200

GDE Systems
800-545-0506

Ingram Micro
714-566-1000

International Technology Corp
949-660-5434

McLaren/Hart
916-638-3696

Microsoft Corporation
800-892-3181

Mitsubishi Electronics America
714-229-6565

Monroe Systems for Business
562-946-5678

National Steel & Shipbuilding Co.
619-544-8512

Pacific Ship Repair & Fabrication
619-232-2300 x125

Printronix
714-221-2828

Procom Technology
714-852-1000 x5999

SAS Institute
919-677-8000

SECOR International
619-525-5151

State of the Art
714-759-1222 x4080

The Austin Company
949-453-1000 x263

The Laxmi Group
714-903-5676 x211

Thermeon Corporation
800-232-9191

Toshiba America Info Systems
949-461-4949

TriTeal Corp.
760-827-5509

Wonderware Software Corp
714-727-3200 x7901

3-D Instruments
15542 Chemical Lane
Huntington Beach, CA 92649-1578
714-894-5351
Web Address: www.3dinstruments.com
Number of Employees: 60

Randy Heartfield, *President*
Earl Selman, *Human Resources Manager*

3E Co.
1905 Aston Avenue
Carlsbad, CA 92008
760-602-8700
Number of Employees: 200

Jess F. Kraus, *President*
Carrie McDowell, *Human Resource Director*

A+Net
5266 Eastgate Mall
San Diego, CA 92121
858-455-7709
Web Address: info@abac.com

Ivan Vachovsky, *CEO*

Able Communications
3629 West Macarthur Boulevard, Suite 210
Santa Ana, CA 92704-6844
714-979-7893
Web Address: www.able.com
Number of Employees: 15
Ken Omohundro, *President*

Abracon Corporation
125 Columbia
Laguna Hills, CA 92654-3080
714-448-7070
Number of Employees: 45
Don Bebout, *President*
Kathy Greco, *Human Resources Manager*

Accesspoint Corporation
300 Harbor Boulevard, Suite 700
Anaheim, CA 92805
714-781-2288
Web Address: www.apc.net

Accurate Circuit Engineering
3019 Kilson Drive
Santa Ana, CA 92707-4202
714-546-2162
Web Address: www.ace-pcd.com
Number of Employees: 50
Charles Lowe, *President*

Activision
3100 Ocean Park Boulevard
Santa Monica, CA 90405
310-255-2000
Web Address: www.activision.com
Number of Employees: 500
Robert A. Kotick, *CEO*
Ruth Pearson, *Human Resource Manager*

Adaptive Information Systems
26001 Pala
Mission Viejo, CA 92691-2705
714-587-9077
Web Address: www.ais-hitachi.com
Number of Employees: 40

K. Airmura, *President & CEO*

Admor Memory Corporation
217 Technology Drive #100
Irvine, CA 92618-2400
949-789-7292
Web Address: www.admor.com
Number of Employees: 100

Van Andrews, *President*
Fran Sussman, *Human Resources*

Advanced Industrial Systems
15235 Alton Parkway, Suite 200
Irvine, CA 92618-2307
949-753-1995
Web Address:
www.advancedindustrialsystems.com
Number of Employees: 22

Gene Kaplan, *President*

Advanced Kinetics
18281 Gothard Street #104
Huntington Beach, CA 92648-1205
714-848-0996
Number of Employees: 30

Francis Tran, *Director of Engineering*

Advanced Logic Research
9401 Jeronimo Road
Irvine, CA 92618
949-581-6770
Web Address: www.alr.com
Number of Employees: 450

Gene Lu, *President*
Irene Martinez, *Manager*
A subsidiary of Gateway 2000, ALR makes PCs for the client/server and desktop markets. Its products are based on Intel's Pentium and Pentium Pro processors and supports DOS, Windows, Windows 95, Windows NT, UNIX, OS/2, and Novell NetWare.

Advanced Media
695 Town Center Drive, Suite 250
Costa Mesa, CA 92626-1924
949-957-1616
Web Address: www.advancedmedia.com
Number of Employees: 40

Sam Hassabo, *General Manager*

Advanced Micro Devices
125 Pacifica, Suite 200
Irvine, CA 92618-3304
949-450-7500
Web Address: www.amd.com
Number of Employees: 12800
Sam Windick, *Vice President of Human Resources*

305

Advanced Technology Center
22982 Mill Creek Drive
Laguna Hills, CA 92653-1214
714-583-9119
Web Address: www.atc.com
Number of Employees: 25

Sahib Dudani, *President*

Advantage Memory Corporation
25 Technology Drive #A
Irvine, CA 92618-2302
949-453-8111
Web Address: www.advantagememory.com
Number of Employees: 84

John Harriman, *President*
Judy Pritz, *Human Resources Manager*

Aerospace Corporation
2350 East El Segundo Boulevard
El Segundo, CA 90245
310-336-5000
Web Address: www.aero.com

AeroVironment
222 East Huntington Drive
Monrovia, CA 91016
626-357-9983
Web Address: www.aerovironment.com
Number of Employees: 250

Paul MacCready, *Founder*
Timothy Conver, *CEO*
Cathlene Cline, *Vice President of Administration*

AETS
5202 Oceanus Drive
Huntington Beach, CA 92649-1029
714-379-6000
Number of Employees: 20

Chris Kling, *Manager*

AGRA Earth & Environmental
1290 North Hancock
Anaheim, CA 92807
714-779-2591
Number of Employees: 40

Brian Contant, *Manager*

Airshow
15222 Del Amo Avenue
Tustin, CA 92780-6414
714-669-1300
Web Address: www.airshowinc.com
Number of Employees: 120

Dennis Ferguson, *President*
Jade Orzol, *Recruiting Specialist*

AlliedSignal Aerospace
2525 West 190th Street
Torrance, CA 90504
310-323-9500

Job Hotline: 310-512-2012
Web Address: www.alliedsignal.com
Number of Employees: 2,500
Tig Krekel, *President*
Gary Parkinson, *Human Resources Director*

Almatron Electronics
644 Young Street
Santa Ana, CA 92705-5633
714-557-6000
Web Address: www.almatron@pacbell.com
Number of Employees: 50

Margarito Alvarez, *President*
Mario Mendoza, *Officer Manager*

Alpha Microsystems
2722 South Fairview
Santa Ana, CA 92704
714-957-8500
Web Address: www.alphamicro.com
Number of Employees: 191

Douglas J. Tullio, *President*
Michelle Duggin, *Director of Personnel*
Alpha Microsystems makes information technology products -
primarily Internet/intranet software-, and provides training,
consulting, maintenance, and networking services in the US and
Canada.

Alpha Systems Lab
17712 Mitchell North
Irvine, CA 92614-6013
949-622-0688
Web Address: www.aslrwp.com
Number of Employees: 60

Rose Hwang, *President*

Alps Electric USA
5301 Oceanus Drive
Huntington Beach, CA 92649-1030
714-897-1005
Web Address: www.alpsusa.com
Number of Employees: 72

Pam Hernandez, *Human Resources Manager*

Alton Geoscience
25A Technology Drive
Irvine, CA 92618-2302
949-753-0101
Web Address: www.altongeo.com
Number of Employees: 75

William T. Hunt, *President*
Ken Powers, *Human Resources Manager*

Alton Geoscience
9471 Ridgehaven Court, Suite E
San Diego, CA 92121
619-505-8881

Ronald Kofron, *Manager Technical Operations*

Alyn Corporation
16761 Hale Avenue
Irvine, CA 92606
949-475-1525
Web Address: www.alyn.com
Number of Employees: 33

Robin A. Carden, *President*
Margaret Roche, *Controller*
Developer of products using Boralyn, its patented combination of boron carbide -a ceramic that is the world's 3rd hardest material-, and aluminum. Boralyn is a strong, lightweight material, and Alyn is targeting sports equipment makers for sales.

Amdahl Corporation
770 The City Drive South, Suite 4000
Orange, CA 92868-4929
714-740-0440
Web Address: www.amdahl.com
Number of Employees: 10000

Ken Comee, *Vice President of Sales*

American Computer Hardware
2205 South Wright Street
Santa Ana, CA 92705-5319
714-549-2688
Web Address: www.achc.com
Number of Employees: 49

Ed St. Amour, *President*
Regan Dunne, *Vice President*

American Electronics Association
15300 Ventura Boulevard, Suite 226
Sherman Oaks, CA 91403
818-986-6944

American Microwave Technology
2570 East Cerritos Avenue
Anaheim, CA 92804
714-456-0777
Web Address: www.amtinc.com
Number of Employees: 50

William P. Clark, *President*
Tracy George, *Human Resources Manager*

Amplicon Financial
5 Hutton Centre Drive, Suite 500
Santa Ana, CA 92707
714-751-7551
Web Address: www.amplicon.com
Number of Employees: 220

Patrick E. Paddon, *President*
Lavone Jackson, *Director of Personnel*
Supplier of mid-range computers, peripherals, workstations, personal computer networks, telecommunications equipment, computer-aided design/computer-aided manufacturing systems, office equipment, and computer software.

Amtec Engineering Corporation
2749 Saturn
Brea, CA 92821
714-993-1900

Web Address: www.amtec-eng.com
Number of Employees: 20
Scott Kuthen, *Manager*

Anacom General Corporation
1240 South Claudina Street
Anaheim, CA 92805-6232
714-774-8080
Number of Employees: 100

William A. Haines, *President*
Jennifer Hayward, *Human Resources Manager*

Anacomp
12365 Crosthwaite Circle
Poway, CA 92064
858-679-9797
Web Address: www.anacomp.com
Number of Employees: 2000

Anagraph
3100 Pullman Street
Costa Mesa, CA 92626-4501
949-540-2400
Web Address: www.anagraph.com
Number of Employees: 40

Chase Roh, *President*

AnaServe
1300 North Bristol Street, Suite 220
Newport Beach, CA 92660-2953
949-250-7262
Web Address: www.anaserve.com
Number of Employees: 20

Paul Summers, *President*
Brad Eisenstein, *Human Resources Manager*

Anello Corp/Epsco Products
2601 Walnut Avenue
Tustin, CA 92780-7005
714-234-3030
Number of Employees: 50

Peter J. Anello, *President*
Kay Higgins, *Human Resources Manager*

Anthony-Taylor Companies
2240 Vineyard Avenue, Suite B
Suite B
Escondido, CA 92029
760-738-8800
Number of Employees: 50

Chris A. Post, *CEO*

AOT Electronics
4400 Macarthur Boulevard, Suite 790
Newport Beach, CA 92660-2060
949-852-9999
Web Address: www.shortages.com
Number of Employees: 27

A Omar Turbi, *President*

Applicon
2102 Business Center Drive #130
Irvine, CA 92612-1012
949-253-4131
Number of Employees: 300

Applied Data Technology
10151 Barnes Canyon Road
San Diego, CA 92121
619-450-9951

Rod Powers, *Director of Business Development*

Area Electronics Systems
950 Fee Ana Street, Suite A
Placentia, CA 92870-6755
714-993-0300
Web Address: www.areasys.com
Number of Employees: 35

William Hung, *President*

Arinc
100 Bayview Circle, Suite 2000
Newport Beach, CA 92660-2985
949-737-6200
Web Address: www.arinc.com
Number of Employees: 30

Chris Olsen, *Manager*

ARK Energy
27401 Los Altos, Suite 400
Mission Viejo, CA 92691-6316
714-588-3767
Number of Employees: 25

Arnold Klann, *President*

Artios Corporation
163 Technology Drive
Irvine, CA 92618-2402
949-788-7300
Web Address: www.artioslink.com
Number of Employees: 250

John Carrington, *CEO*
Michael Frue, *Human Resources Manager*

ASI Systems International
326 West Katella Avenue #4K
Orange, CA 92867-4756
714-744-1594
Number of Employees: 130

James Whatley, *President*
Renee Haas, *Director of Personnel*

ASL Consulting Engineers
1 Jenner, Suite 200
Irvine, CA 92618-3810
949-727-7099
Web Address: www.aslce.com
Number of Employees: 70

William Bennett, *Manager*

AST Research
16215 Alton Parkway
Irvine, CA 92718
949-727-4141
Web Address: www.ast.com
Number of Employees: 4151

Soon-Taek Kim, *President*
Larry Levinson, *Director of Personnel*
Maker of notebooks, PCs, and network servers that it markets through retailers and VARs. The company is a privately owned subsidiary of Samsung Electronics, the world's #1 maker of memory chips and part of the Samsung Group, one of South Korea's largest conglomerates.

Astronic
20 Mason
Irvine, CA 92618-2706
949-454-1180
Number of Employees: 90

Sang H. Choi, *President*
Dolly Carreon, *Human Resources Manager*

ATC Associates
17321 Irvine Boulevard, 2nd floor
Tustin, CA 92780-3010
714-734-0303
Web Address: www.atc-enviro.com
Number of Employees: 16

Joel Sadler, *Office Manager*

ATC Associates
50 East Foothill Boulevard
Arcadia, CA 91006
626-447-5216
Number of Employees: 50

David McElwain, *Branch Manager*
Margie Martinez, *Office Manager*

Aten Research
340 Thor Pl
Brea, CA 92821-4132
714-255-0566
Web Address: www.cliffwood.com
Number of Employees: 340

Lee Chang, *President*

ATL Products
2801 Kelvin Avenue
Irvine, CA 92614
949-774-6900
Web Address: www.atlp.com
Number of Employees: 300

Kevin C. Daly, *President*
Kathy Steger, *Director of Personnel*
Manufacturer of automated digital linear tape libraries for data backup, archival, and recovery. Products are sold in the US, Europe, and Asia through value added resellers and OEMs. DEC accounts for almost 20% of sales.

Atlantic Computer Products
10772 Noel Street
Los Alamitos, CA 90720-2548
714-952-2274
Number of Employees: 20

Benny Chu, *President*
Linda Sedky, *Human Resources Director*

Atmel Corporation
8101 East Kaiser Boulevard
Anaheim, CA 92808-2243
714-282-8080
Web Address: www.atmel.com
Number of Employees: 2978

Audient
26212 Dimension Drive, Suite 130
Lake Forest, CA 92630-7801
714-830-9412
Number of Employees: 22

Jerry Rossi, *President*

Auspex Systems
24681 La Plaza Drive, Suite 340
Dana Point, CA 92629
714-455-0424
Web Address: www.auspex.com
Number of Employees: 10

Mark Renalt, *Account Executive*

Auto-By-Tel Corporation
18872 MacArthur Boulevard, Suite 200
Irvine, CA 92612-1400
949-225-4500
Web Address: www.autobytel.com
Number of Employees: 73

Peter R. Ellis, *President*
Karen Peterson, *Human Resources Manager*
Seller of vehicles on the Internet. Consumers who visit the
company's Web site can get information about cars and light-duty
trucks and make purchases.

Automated Solutions Group
16742 Gothard Street, Suite 207
Huntington Beach, CA 92647-4567
714-375-4252
Web Address: www.asgsoft.com
Number of Employees: 20

Michael Erickson, *President*

Autosplice
10121 Barnes Canyon Road
San Diego, CA 92121
858-535-0077
Job Hotline: 619-535-0868
Web Address: http://autosplice.com
Number of Employees: 250

Irwin Zahn, *CEO*
Patricia Gallagher, *Human Resources Generalist*

Aztek
23 Spectrum Pointe, Suite 209
Lake Forest, CA 92630
714-770-8406
Web Address: www.aztek.net
Number of Employees: 20

Phillip Lippincott, *President*

Bambeck Systems
1921 Carnegie Avenue
Santa Ana, CA 92705-5510
714-250-3100
Web Address: www.bambecksystem.net
Number of Employees: 30

Robert J Bambeck, *President*

BAS Micro Industries
6 Bendix
Irvine, CA 92618-2006
949-457-8822
Web Address: www.basmicro.com
Number of Employees: 75

Basic Electronics
11371 Monarch Street
Garden Grove, CA 92841-1406
714-530-2400
Web Address: www.basicinc.com
Number of Employees: 45

Nancy Balzano, *President*

Bay City Marine
1625 Cleveland Avenue
National City, CA 91950
619-477-3991
Number of Employees: 54

David E. Lloyd, *President*
Fred Workman, *Production Manager*

BCM Advanced Research
1 Hughes
Irvine, CA 92618-2021
949-470-1888
Web Address: www.bcmgvc.com
Number of Employees: 40

Ray Wang, *President*

BE Aerospace/In-Flight Entertainment
17481 Redhill Avenue
Irvine, CA 92714
949-660-7722
Web Address: www.bear.com
Number of Employees: 550

Art Lipton, *Division President*
R. J. Landry, *Vice President for Human Resources*

HIGH-TECH

309

Becwar Engineering
7 Vanderbilt
Irvine, CA 92618-2011
949-855-2293
Web Address: www.becwar.com
Number of Employees: 58
C. P. Becwar, *President*

Bell Industries
2201 East El Segundo Boulevard
El Segundo, CA 90245
310-563-2355
Web Address: www.bellind.com

Bien Logic
2223 Avenida de la Playa, Suite 205
La Jolla, CA 92037
954-229-1950
Web Address: info@bienlogic.com
Frederic Bien, *CEO*

Bing Yen & Associates
17701 Mitchell North
Irvine, CA 92614-6029
949-757-1941
Number of Employees: 25
Bing Yen, *President*
Larry Taylor, *Human Resources Manager*

Biolase Technology
981 Calle Amanecer
San Clemente, CA 92673
714-361-1200
Web Address: www.biolase.com
Number of Employees: 21
Donald A. LaPoint, *President*
Jody Comeau, *Director of Human Resources*
Manufacturer and marketer of dental lasers and accessories.

Black & Veatch Engineers/Architects
6 Venture, Suite 315
Irvine, CA 92618-3317
949-753-0500
Web Address: www.bv.com
Number of Employees: 10
David G. Argo, *Senior Partner*
Joe Sewards, *Human Resources Manager*

Blizzard Entertainment
50 Corporate Park
Irvine, CA 92606-5105
949-955-1380
Web Address: www.blizzard.com
Number of Employees: 97
Michael Morphaime, *President*
Christina Cade, *Human Resources Manager*

Bluebird Systems
5900 La Place Court
Carlsbad, CA 92008
760-438-2220
Job Hotline: 800-669-2220

Web Address: www.bluebird.com
Number of Employees: 80
Hal Tilbury, *President*
April Juric, *Director of Human Resources*

Boyle Engineering Corporation
1501 Quail Street
Newport Beach, CA 92660
949-476-3300
Web Address: www.boyleengineering.com
Number of Employees: 500
Daniel W. Boyd, *CEO*

Boyle Engineering Corporation
7807 Convoy Court, Suite 200
San Diego, CA 92111
858-268-8080
Web Address: www.boyleengineering.com
Number of Employees: 55
Donald L. MacFarlane Jr., *Principal*
Tami Schnitzler, *Human Resource Director*

Broadcom Corporation
16251 Laguna Canyon Road
Irvine, CA 92618
949-450-8700
Web Address: www.broadcom.com
Number of Employees: 217
Henry T. Nicholas III, *President*
Candice Walsh, *Director of Human Resources*

Broadley-James Corporation
19 Thomas
Irvine, CA 92618-2704
949-829-5555
Number of Employees: 40
Leighton Broadley, *President*

Brown & Caldwell
16735 Von Karman Avenue, Suite 200
Irvine, CA 92606-4953
949-660-1070
Web Address: www.brownandcaldwell.com
Number of Employees: 45
Kristin Del Campo, *Human Resources Manager*

Brown & Caldwell
9040 Friars Road, Suite 220
San Diego, CA 92108
619-528-9090
Web Address: www.brownandcaldwell.com
Number of Employees: 60
George M. Khoury, *Vice President*

Business Automation
1572 North Main Street
Orange, CA 92867-3448
714-998-6600
Web Address: www.baipro.com
Number of Employees: 30
Doug Nation, *President*
Jennifer Elif, *Human Resources Manager*

C Hoelzle Associates
17321 Eastman
Irvine, CA 92614-5523
949-251-9000
Web Address: www.chainc.com
Number of Employees: 90

E. Chris Hoelzle, *President*
Judith Molden, *Human Resources Manager*

Cabletron Systems
2201 Dupont Drive, Suite 600
Irvine, CA 92612-7510
949-852-4126
Web Address: www.ctron.com
Number of Employees: 45

Pauline Staid, *Office Manager*

CACI Products Company
3333 North Torrey Pines Court
La Jolla, CA 92037
858-824-5200
Web Address: www.caciasl.com
Number of Employees: 50

Joe Lenz, *President*

Cair Systems Corporation
2100 Main Street, Suite 4
Irvine, CA 92614-6237
949-862-1240
Web Address: www.cairsystems.com
Number of Employees: 50

Bill Salway, *President*

Cal Quality Electronics
2700 South Fairview Street
Santa Ana, CA 92704-5947
714-545-8886
Web Address: www.calquality.com
Number of Employees: 175

Thai Nguyen, *President*
Lee Thuong, *Controller*

Cal-Flex
1255 North Knollwood Circle
Anaheim, CA 92801-1313
714-952-0373
Web Address: www.info@calflex.com
Number of Employees: 52

Wei-Cheng Chen, *President*

Cal-Tronic's
15421 Red Hill Avenue, Suite A
Tustin, CA 92780-7309
714-259-1818
Web Address: www.caltronics.com
Number of Employees: 25

Prashant Amin, *President*

CalComp Technology
2411 West La Palma Avenue
Anaheim, CA 92801
714-821-2000
Web Address: www.calcomp.com
Number of Employees: 194

John C. Batterton, *President*
Kevin Coleman, *Director of Personnel*

California Amplifier
460 Calle San Pablo
Camarillo, CA 93012
805-987-9000
Web Address: www2.calamp.com

California Analytical Instruments
1238 West Grove Avenue
Orange, CA 92865-4134
714-974-5560
Web Address: www.gasanalyzers.com
Number of Employees: 45

Roger P. Furton, *President*

California Economizer
5622 Engineer Drive
Huntington Beach, CA 92649-1124
714-898-9963
Web Address: www.hvaccomfort.com
Number of Employees: 20

Jeff A Osheroff, *President*

California IC
34 Mauchly, Suite A
Irvine, CA 92618-2357
949-453-8185
Web Address: www.californiaic.com
Number of Employees: 30

Kurtis Alderson, *Owner*

California Software Products
1221 East Dyer Road
Santa Ana, CA 92705-5600
714-435-0900
Web Address: www.calsw.com
Number of Employees: 60

Bruce Acacio, *President*

Calty Design Research
2810 Jamboree Road
Newport Beach, CA 92660-3298
949-759-1701
Web Address: www.calty.com
Number of Employees: 49

Judy Moussette, *Human Resources*

CAM Data Systems
17520 Newhope Street, Suite 100
Fountain Valley, CA 92708
714-241-9241
Web Address: www.camdata.com

Number of Employees: 145
Geoffrey D. Knapp, *President*
Nadine Arrona, *Administrator*
Provider of point-of-sale equipment and software systems, technical support and training to help retailers track sales and inventory, provide accounting and sales reports, and identify merchandise performance.

Cambridge Management Corporation
16841 Armstrong
Irvine, CA 92606-4918
949-261-8901
Web Address: www.cppus.com
Number of Employees: 25

Norton Garfinkel, *President*
Michelle Hervel, *Human Resources Manager*

Camintonn Corporation
22 Morgan
Irvine, CA 92618-2094
949-454-1500
Web Address: www.camintonn.com
Number of Employees: 55

Bosco K. Sun, *President*
Sheila Munso, *Human Resources Manager*

Camp Dresser & McKee
1925 Palomar Oaks Way, Suite 300
Carlsbad, CA 92008
760-438-7755
Number of Employees: 45

Kellene Burn-Lucht, *Principal*
Leland Womack, *Human Resources Manager*

Camp Dresser & McKee
18881 Von Karman Avenue, Suite 650
Irvine, CA 92612-1565
949-752-5452
Number of Employees: 40

Christie Weissinger, *Human Resources*

Candle Corporation
201 North Douglas Street
El Segundo, CA 90245
310-829-5800
Web Address: www.candle.com
Number of Employees: 637

Aubrey Chernick, *CEO*

Canon Business Machines
3191 Red Hill Avenue
Costa Mesa, CA 92626-3498
949-556-4700
Web Address: www.canon.com
Number of Employees: 375
Mr. Nitanda, *President*

Canon Computer Systems
2995 Red Hill Avenue
Costa Mesa, CA 92626-5984
949-438-3000
Web Address: www.ccsi.canon.com

Number of Employees: 350
Yashuhiro Tsubota, *CEO*
Lorraine Valencia, *Human Resources Director*

Capital Management Sciences
11766 Wilshire Boulevard, Suite 300
Los Angeles, CA 90025
310-479-9715
Number of Employees: 110
Laurie Adami, Executive VP, *Managing Director*
Ami Hausthor, *Director of Human Resources*

Care Computer Systems
500 South Kraemer Boulevard, Suite 307
Brea, CA 92821-6728
714-524-1165
Number of Employees: 9
Lina Nix, *Manager*

Casey-Johnston Sales
455 Los Positas, Suite B
Livermore, CA 94550
714-937-9204
Number of Employees: 28

Cash & Associates
5772 Bolsa Avenue, Suite 100
Huntington Beach, CA 92649
714-895-2072
Number of Employees: 30
Randy H. Mason, *President*

Catalina Marketing Corporation
721 East Ball Road
Anaheim, CA 92805-5935
714-956-6600
Number of Employees: 700

CCH
21250 Hawthorne Boulevard
Torrance, CA 90503
310-543-6200
Job Hotline: 800-254-7772
Web Address: www.prosystemfx.com
Number of Employees: 350
Arthur C. Ruzzano, *Executive Director*
Cyndi Andrew, *Recruiter*

CDCE
22641 Old Canal Road
Yorba Linda, CA 92887-4601
714-282-8881
Web Address: www.cdce.com
Number of Employees: 28
Carrie Solomon, *President*

Cedko Electronics
3002 Oak Street
Santa Ana, CA 92707-4291
714-540-8454
Web Address: www.cedko.com
Number of Employees: 25

Mike Mangrolia, *Owner*

Centon Electronics
20 Morgan
Irvine, CA 92718
949-855-9111
Job Hotline: 714-855-2039
Web Address: www.centon.com
Number of Employees: 70

Eugene Miscionne, *President*
Jerry Wasson, *Director of Personnel*

Century Computer Corporation
1150 West Central Avenue #B
Brea, CA 92821-2251
714-671-2800
Web Address: www.centurycomputercorp.com
Number of Employees: 10

Larry R. Fry, *President*

Century Laminators
1182 North Knollwood Circle
Anaheim, CA 92801-1333
714-828-2071
Number of Employees: 350

Gary Behunin, *President*
Cora Behunin, *Personnel*

CET Environmental Service
14761 Bentley Circle
Tustin, CA 92780-7226
714-505-1800
Web Address: www.cetenvironmental.com
Number of Employees: 45

Michelle Islas, *Office Manager*

CG Tech
15375 Barranca Parkway, Suite L
Irvine, CA 92618-2217
949-753-1050
Web Address: www.cgtech.com
Number of Employees: 45

Jon Prun, *President*

CH2M Hill
3 Heighton Center Drive, Suite 200
Santa Ana, CA 92707
714-429-2000
Web Address: www.ch2m.com
Number of Employees: 200

Jocelyn Tambio, *Human Resources Manager*

ChatCom
9600 Topanga Canyon Boulevard
Chatsworth, CA 91311-5803
818-709-1778
Web Address: www.jlchatcom.com
Number of Employees: 45

Carey Walters, *President*
Diana Saltmarch, *Director of Personnel*
ChatCom's ChatterBox products help businesses consolidate computer servers and platforms, even those using different operating systems. Products are fully scalable, use power efficiently, and have easy-to-use, functionally compatible software. The high to ultra-high density platforms fit in compact industry-standard enclosures and support standard PC technology, including Intel's Pentium and Pentium Pro. ChatterBoxes are used worldwide in a variety of applications including Internet server functions, database and groupware server systems, and intranet and Web server functions. Products are sold primarily through value-added resellers; end users include US Robotics Access, which accounts for more than 10% of sales.

CIE America
2701 Dow Avenue
Tustin, CA 92780
714-573-2942
Web Address: www.citoh.com
Number of Employees: 65

Shigeka Nishiyama, *President*
Elizabeth Mugar, *Human Resources Director*

Cinerom
2809 Main Street
Irvine, CA 92614-5901
949-660-7111
Number of Employees: 25

William Hustwit, *President*

Circuit Connection
930 West Hoover Avenue
Orange, CA 92867-3512
714-538-0023
Number of Employees: 27

Norma Sokolosky, *President*

Circuit Image Systems
870 North Eckhoff Street
Orange, CA 92868-1008
714-288-4247
Web Address: www.circuitimage.com
Number of Employees: 37

Marvin Bain, *President*

Circuit World
1470 North Batavia Street
Orange, CA 92867-3505
714-777-2480
Web Address: www.circuit-world.com
Number of Employees: 35

Kanu S. Patel, *President*

Cirtech
250 East Emerson Avenue
Orange, CA 92865-3317
714-921-0860
Web Address: www.cirtech.com
Number of Employees: 89

Brad E. Reese, *President*

CISD International
3525 Hyland Avenue, Suite 260
Costa Mesa, CA 92626
949-641-4300
Web Address: www.cisd.com
Number of Employees: 40
S. Oya, *President*
Pam Lewis, *Human Resources Manager*

CJ Rogers Electronics
326 North Katella Avenue, Suite 413
Orange, CA 92867
714-288-1144
Number of Employees: 20
Carol Rogers, *President & Owner*

Clayton Engineering
3661 Spruce Street
Newport Beach, CA 92660-2904
949-863-0202
Web Address: www.4cei.com
Number of Employees: 20
Gregory Clayton, *President*
Ron Record, *Human Resources*

CMD Technology
One Vanderbilt
Irvine, CA 92718
949-454-0800
Web Address: www.cmd.com
Number of Employees: 187
Simon Huang, *President*

Coast Computer Products
22707 La Palma Avenue
Yorba Linda, CA 92887-4772
714-694-0550
*Web Address: www.purchasepro.com/coast/
computer*
Number of Employees: 20
James Dickson, *President*

Coast Technologies
17702 Mitchell North, Suite 101
Irvine, CA 92614-6040
949-752-9520
Web Address: www.coastech.com
Number of Employees: 23
Stewart Flamm, *President*
Angela Thomas, *Human Resources Manager*

Colorbus
18261 McDurmott West
Irvine, CA 92614
949-852-1850
Web Address: www.colorbus.com
Number of Employees: 111
Paul R. Peffer, *President*
Anita Kingman, *Executive Secretary*
Developer and seller of network print servers that produce high-resolution color images from digital color copiers and large format printers.

COMARCO
22800 Savi Ranch Parkway, Suite 214
Yorba Linda, CA 92887
714-282-3832
Web Address: www.cmro.com
Number of Employees: 5
Don M. Bailey, *President*
Maker of products for the wireless communications industry. Also supplies software for military and commercial use, technology training, and technical and engineering services -information technology, test systems, weapon systems engineering-.

Comcast Online
1534 Brookhollow Drive, Suite B
Santa Ana, CA 92705
714-424-5230
Web Address: www.inorangecounty.com

Comm-Base Technologies
2302 Martin, Suite 475
Irvine, CA 92612-1449
949-252-8060
Number of Employees: 25
Paula Treece, *President*

Compucable Corporation
210 McCormick Avenue, Suite A
Costa Mesa, CA 92626-3309
949-557-5510
Web Address: www.compucable.com
Number of Employees: 26
Sharon Huang, *President*

Compusource Corporation
20 Centerpointe Drive, Suite 105
La Palma, CA 90623-1078
714-522-8300
Web Address: www.compusource.com
Number of Employees: 40
Dave Roberts, *President*

Computer Associates International
7755 Center Avenue, Suite 760
Huntington Beach, CA 92647-3007
714-895-3018
Number of Employees: 70

Computer Associates International
9740 Scranton Road #200
San Diego, CA 92027
858-452-0170
Web Address: www.cai.com
Number of Employees: 170
Charles Wang, *CEO*
Gregg Fox, *VP Research and Development*

Computer Peripherals International
7 Whatney
Irvine, CA 92618-2806
949-454-2441
Web Address: www.cpinternational.com
Number of Employees: 125
Mike Zachau, *President*

Computer Sciences Corporation
4045 Hancock Street
San Diego, CA 92110
619-225-8401

Lee Taylor, *Operations Director*

Computer Variations
2667 Camino del Rio South, Suite 308
San Diego, CA 92108
619-294-7310
Web Address: www.compuvar.com

Computing Insights
880 Gretna Green Way
Escondido, CA 92025
760-743-2556
Web Address: www.computinginsights.com
Number of Employees: 5

Thomas L. Scrivner, *CEO*

Connector Products
16721 Noyes Avenue
Irvine, CA 92606-5123
949-474-4439
Web Address: www.cosmotronic.com
Number of Employees: 50

Peter Cohen, *President*

Connector Technology
5065 East Hunter Avenue
Anaheim, CA 92807-6001
714-701-9333
Number of Employees: 47

George Dobelis, *President*

Consolidated Peritronics Medical
3200 East Birch Street
Brea, CA 92821-6258
714-572-8100
Number of Employees: 9

Carl E. Wilcox, *President*

Contel Electronics
14101 Myford Road
Tustin, CA 92780-7020
714-505-3136
Number of Employees: 150

Peiman Amoukhteh, *President*
Debbie Hughes, *Hiring Contact*

Continental Maritime of San Diego
1995 Bayfront Street
San Diego, CA 92113
619-234-8851
Number of Employees: 330

David McQueary, *President*
Maryanne Sablan, *Human Resource Manager*

Continuus Software Corporation
108 Pacifica
Irvine, CA 92618-3332
949-453-2200
Web Address: www.continuos.com
Number of Employees: 140

John Wark, *President & CEO*
Marilyn Hill, *Human Resources Manager*

Converse Consultants Orange County
185 Paularino Avenue, Suite B
Costa Mesa, CA 92626
949-444-9660
Web Address: www.converseconsultants.com
Number of Employees: 20

Richard Gilbert, *President*

Cooper Microelectronics
1671 Reynolds Avenue
Irvine, CA 92614-5709
949-553-8352
Number of Employees: 30

Ken Cooper, *President*

Copper Clad Multilayer Products
1150 North Hawk Circle
Anaheim, CA 92807-1708
714-237-1388
Web Address: www.ccmpinc.com
Number of Employees: 75

Fred Ohanian, *President*
Leah Rodriguez, *Human Resources Manager*

Core Dynamics Corporation
1 Technology Park, Building A, Suite 250
Irvine, CA 92618-2702
949-450-0188
Web Address: www.core-dynamics.com
Number of Employees: 8

Carl Perkins, *President*
Dwain Brinson, *Human Resources Manager*

Corning OCA
PO Box 3115
Garden Grove, CA 92842-3115
714-895-1667
Web Address: www.oca-inc.com
Number of Employees: 260

Michael Devlin, *President*

Corollary
Q802 Kelvin
Irvine, CA 92614
949-250-4040
Web Address: www.corollary.com
Number of Employees: 80

George P. White, *President*

Cosmotronic Company
16721 Noyes Avenue
Irvine, CA 92606-5176
949-660-0740
Web Address: www.cosmotronic.com
Number of Employees: 80

Peter Cohen, *President*

Coyote Network Systems
4360 Park Terrace Drive
Westlake Village, CA 91361
818-735-7600
Web Address: www.coyotenetworksystems.com/
Number of Employees: 80

James J. Fiedler, *CEO*
Linda Marier, *Director of Personnel & VP*
Provider of scalable public network telephony and Internet
switching equipment to communications service providers.

Creative Computer Applications
26115-A Mureau Road
Calabasas, CA 91302
818-880-6700
Web Address: www.ccainc.com
Number of Employees: 67

Steven M. Besbeck, *President*
Manufacturer of medical data information systems. Its software
helps to collect and track information about clinical tests,
treatments, outcomes, pharmaceutical inventories, radiology, and
billing.

Credentials Services International
333 City Boulevard West, 10th Floor
Orange, CA 92868
714-704-6400
Web Address: www.credentials-net.com
Number of Employees: 163

David C. Thompson, *President*
Susan Henderson, *Director of Personnel*
Provider of credit reporting information to consumers, particularly
credit inquiries and the entry of negative data.

Critical Path
3420 Ocean Park Boulevard, Suite 2010
Santa Monica, CA 90405
310-581-8100
Job Hotline: 415-808-8800
Web Address: www.@cp.net
Number of Employees: 70

Paul Giggs, *President*

CSG Visual Communication
19800 Macarthur Boulevard, Suite 500
Irvine, CA 92612-2434
949-757-4100
Number of Employees: 26

CSS Labs
1641 McGaw Avenue
Irvine, CA 92614-5631
949-852-8161

Web Address: www.csslabs.com
Number of Employees: 110
Ed Chiu, *President*
Amy Fu, *Human Resources Manager*

CSTI
13896 Harbor Boulevard #5C
Garden Grove, CA 92843-4028
714-554-1551
Web Address: www.celeritysolutions.com
Number of Employees: 3

Rick Evans, *Vice President*

CTL Environmental Services
24404 South Vermont Avenue, Suite 307
Harbor City, CA 90710
310-530-5006
Number of Employees: 44

Stuart E. Salot, *President*
Renee Ruiz, *Accounting Manager*
Martha Salot, *Human Resource Manager*

CTS Network Services
8913 Complex Drive, Suite C
San Diego, CA 92123
858-637-3600
Web Address: www.cts.com
Number of Employees: 100

Bill Blue, *Owner/CEO*
Linda Wise, *Customer Service Manager*

Cubic Corporation
9333 Balboa Avenue
San Diego, CA 92123
858-277-6780
Web Address: www.cubic.com
Number of Employees: 140

Walter J. Zable, *CEO*
Bob Stamp, *Corporate Staffing Manager*

CUC Software
19840 Pioneer Avenue
Torrance, CA 90503
310-793-0600
Job Hotline: 310-793-0599
Number of Employees: 700

Chris McLeod, *President*

Cyberg8t Internet Services
374 South Indian Hill Boulevard
Claremont, CA 91711
909-398-4638
Web Address: cyberg8t.com

Cyberworks
11555 Sorrento Valley Road, Suite F
San Diego, CA 92121
619-794-8383
Web Address: www.cyberworks.net
Number of Employees: 20
Richard T. Harrison, *President*

D-Link Systems
55 Discovery Drive
Irvine, CA 92718
949-455-1688
Web Address: www.dlink.com
Number of Employees: 120

Roger Kao, *President*
Tracy Riffel, *Hiring Contact*

Dahl Taylor & Associates
2960 Daimler Street
Santa Ana, CA 92705-5824
714-756-8654
Number of Employees: 34

Quang D Vu, *President*

Dainippon Screen Engineering
3700 West Segerstrom Avenue
Santa Ana, CA 92704-6410
714-546-9491
Web Address: www.dsea.com
Number of Employees: 41

Daniel Measurement & Control
15441 Red Hill Avenue, Suite B
Tustin, CA 92780-7304
714-259-8300
Web Address: www.danielind.com
Number of Employees: 2000

Todd Bratton, *President*

Data Color International
24022 Via Bayona
Mission Viejo, CA 92691-3624
714-461-9382
Web Address: www.dci.com
Number of Employees: 5

Data Express
12833 Monarch Street
Garden Grove, CA 92841-3921
714-895-8832
Web Address: www.dataexp.com
Number of Employees: 12

Kevin Burke, *Principal*
Greg Nohalty, *Hiring Contact*

Data General Corp/Field Sales
2603 Main Street, Suite 400
Irvine, CA 92614-6232
949-724-3500
Web Address: www.dg.com
Number of Employees: 5,000

Ron Skates, *President*
Tim Downs, *Recruiter*

Data Processing Design
1290 North Hancock Street, Suite 204
Anaheim, CA 92807-1925
714-695-1000

Web Address: www.dpd.com
Number of Employees: 15
Steve Abbott, *President*

Data Processing Resources Corporation
18301 VonKarman Avenue
Newport Beach, CA 92660
949-553-1102
Web Address: www.dprc.com
Number of Employees: 1636

Mary Ellen Weaver, *CEO*
Paulette J. Suiter, *Director of Personnel*
Information technology consultant specializing in year 2000
projects, mainframe-to-client server migration, and systems
architecture and design. Clients include Nissan, Capitol Records,
Starbucks, and Princess Cruise Lines.

Data Systems Support
1228 West Shelley Court
Orange, CA 92868-1216
714-771-0454
Number of Employees: 35

Louis Parks, *President*

Datametrics Corporation
26604 Agoura Road
Calabasas, CA 91302
818-871-0300
Web Address: www.datametricscorp.com
Number of Employees: 50

Adrien A. Maught, Jr., *President*
Kathy O'Brien, *Director of Personnel*
Developer of high speed color printers, high-resolution nonimpact
printer/plotters, and computers, printers, and workstations. Also
makes mil-spec and ruggedized compter hardware for the US
Department of Defense.

Dataram Corp
939 Glenneyre Street, Suite C
Laguna Beach, CA 92651-2706
714-955-5930
Number of Employees: 60

DataWorks
21 Technology Drive
Irvine, CA 92618-2335
949-789-2900
Number of Employees: 600

Datum
9975 Toledo Way
Irvine, CA 92618-1605
949-598-7500
Web Address: www.datum.com
Number of Employees: 665

Eric Vander Kaay, *President*
Laurie Pedroza, *Director of Personnel*
Producer of ultra-accurate timekeeping devices used in
telecommunications and enterprisewide computer systems. Its 5
largest customers, including Lucent Technologies, account for
nearly half of its sales.

Datum Incorporated
9975 Toledo Way
Irvine, CA 92618
949-380-8880
Web Address: www.datum.com

Davox Corp
18818 Teller Avenue, Suite 200
Irvine, CA 92612-1680
949-475-4401
Web Address: www.davox.com
Number of Employees: 175

Kerry Shaffin, *Manager*

DecisionOne
2929 East Imperial Highway, Suite 101
Brea, CA 92821-6729
714-572-3300
Number of Employees: 6000

Delphi Components
950 Lawrence Drive
Newburg Park, CA 91320
805-499-0410
Web Address: www.microwavebd.com
Number of Employees: 56

Lee Leong, *President*
Danny Ryan, *Human Resources Manager*

Delta Environmental Consultants
27141 Aliso Creek Road, Suite 270
Aliso Viejo, CA 92656-3360
714-362-3077
Job Hotline: 800-988-5819
Number of Employees: 20

Elaine Hedden, *Office Manager*

DeltaNet
731 East Ball Road
Anaheim, CA 92805
714-490-2000
Web Address: www.delta.net

Dense-Pac Microsystems
7321 Lincoln Way
Garden Grove, CA 92841-1428
714-898-0007
Web Address: www.dense-pac.com
Number of Employees: 106

Uri Levy, *President*
Kristi Jolliffe, *Director of Personnel*

Details
1231 North Simon Circle
Anaheim, CA 92806-1813
714-630-4077
Web Address: www.detailsinc.com
Number of Employees: 500

Bruce McMaster, *President*

DGA Consultants
2130 East 4th Street, Suite 100
Santa Ana, CA 92705-3818
714-568-0200
Number of Employees: 18

Donald D. Greek, *President*

Diamond Technologies
1275 South Lewis Street
Anaheim, CA 92805-6429
714-533-9910
Web Address: www.diamondtech.com
Number of Employees: 25

Steven Chen, *President*

Digital Equipment Corporation
24 Executive Park
Irvine, CA 92614-6738
949-261-4300
Web Address: www.digitalinfo.com
Number of Employees: 100

Alan Zimmerly, *VP for Human Resources*

Digital West Media
9190 Camino Santa Fe
San Diego, CA 92121
619-684-5246
Web Address: www.dwmi.com

James X. Bremner, *CEO*

Digital Wizards
2727 Camino del Rio South, Suite 340
San Diego, CA 92108
619-260-1100
Web Address: www.digwiz.com
Number of Employees: 100

Stephen E. Stamper, *President*
Gus Sanchez, *Human Resource Controller*

Diodes Incorporated
3050 East Hillcrest Drive, Suite 200
Westlake Village, CA 91362
805-446-4800
Web Address: www.diodes.com

DKS Associates
2700 North Main Street, Suite 900
Santa Ana, CA 92705-6636
714-543-9601
Web Address: www.dksassociates.com
Number of Employees: 7

Jeff Goldfain, *Office Manager*

DMI
2501 West Fifth Street
Santa Ana, CA 92703
714-571-1900
Number of Employees: 2

Elvin Rose, *President*

Document Control Solutions
187 West Orangethorpe Avenue, Suite 101
Placentia, CA 92870-6932
714-961-0193
Web Address: www.docsolutions.com
Number of Employees: 42

DPCS
10221 Slater Avenue
Fountain Valley, CA 92708-4748
714-964-3154
Number of Employees: 110

Dave Thomas, *CEO*

Ducommun, Inc.
23301 South Wilmington Avenue
Carson, CA 90745
562-624-0800

Norman A. Barkeley, *Chairman*

Dycam
9414 Eton Avenue
Chatsworth, CA 91311
818-998-8008
Web Address: www.dycam.com
Number of Employees: 20

John A. Edling, *President*
Dolores Delgado, *Director of Personnel*
Maker of digital cameras and support software for PCs. Also makes camera accessories including carrying cases, editing software, power supplies, cable adapters, and specialized lenses.

Dynamotion
1639 East Edinger Avenue
Santa Ana, CA 92705
714-541-2927
Web Address: www.elc.sci.com
Number of Employees: 72

Brian Meehan, *General Manager*
Helen Borden, *Director of Personnel*

Eagle Monitoring Systems
3211 South Shannon Street
Santa Ana, CA 92704-6352
714-438-9280
Number of Employees: 20

Amir Sardair, *President*

Earthlink Network
3100 New York Drive
Pasadena, CA
626-296-5681
Web Address: www.earthlink.net

EIP Microwave
4500 Campus Drive, Suite 219
Newport Beach, CA 92660
949-851-3177
Web Address: www.eipm.com/index.htm
Number of Employees: 35

J. Bradford Bishop, *President*
E. O. Bince, *Director of Personnel*
Manufacturer of microwave and radio-frequency test instruments for telecommunications and defense uses. The US government and its contractors account for some 40% of sales; about 30% of sales are foreign.

Electro-Chemical Devices
23665 Via Del Rio
Yorba Linda, CA 92887-2715
714-692-1333
Web Address: www.ecdi.com
Number of Employees: 25

Larry Berger, *President*
Marie Berger, *Human Resources Manager*

Electronic Component & Supply
6840 Orangethorpe
Buena Park, CA 90622-5567
714-522-0241
Number of Employees: 25

Susan Allen, *President*

Elexsys International
18522 Von Karman Avenue
Irvine, CA 92612-1544
949-833-0870
Number of Employees: 1000

Uri Solis, *President*
Melanie Kelly, *Human Resources Manager*

EMCON
15255 Alton Parkway, Suite 200
Irvine, CA 92618-2316
949-450-0622
Web Address: www.emconinc.com
Number of Employees: 14

Darlene Larson, *Office Manager*

Emulex Corporation
3535 Harbor Boulevard
Costa Mesa, CA 92626
949-662-5600
Job Hotline: 714-513-8200
Web Address: www.emulex.com
Number of Employees: 332

Paul F. Folino, *President*
Sadie A. Herrera, *Director of Personnel*
Emulex Corporation supplies network-access products in three distinct product groups: network-access servers, printer servers, and high-speed fibre channel products.

Encore Computer Corporation
1301 Dove Street
Newport Beach, CA 92660-2412
949-577-6713
Web Address: www.encore.com
Number of Employees: 300

EnecoTech Southwest
2535 Camino del Rio South, Suite 250
San Diego, CA 92108
619-299-0033
Number of Employees: 12
Dennis Fransway, *Vice President*

Enersource Engineering
10175 Slater Avenue, Suite 20
Fountain Valley, CA 92708-4702
909-866-2312
Number of Employees: 30
John Gray, *President*

Engineering Group of America/Orange
210 North Crescent Way, Suite A
Anaheim, CA 92801-6705
714-635-3615
Number of Employees: 20
Ray D. Glascock, *Owner*

England & Associates
15375 Barranca Parkway, Suite F106
Irvine, CA 92618-2207
949-453-8085
Number of Employees: 20
Dennis C. England, *President*

ENSR Consulting & Engineering
17952 Sky Park Circle, Suite E
Irvine, CA 92614-6411
949-752-0403
Web Address: www.ensr.com
Number of Employees: 15
Jerry Cimmerle, *Manager*

Enterprise Solutions Ltd.
31416 Agoura Road, Suite 180
Westlake Village, CA 91361
818-597-8943
Web Address: www.csi.esltd.com
Number of Employees: 25
Robert Edge, *CEO*
Cathy Russel, *Director of Personnel*

Enviro Pacifica
3934 Murphy Canyon Road, Suite B-204
San Diego, CA 92123
619-268-1320
Bruce Bossfiard, *President*

Environmental Audit
1000 Ortega Way, Suite A
Placentia, CA 92870-7162
714-632-8521
Number of Employees: 11
Steven A. Bright, *President*
Debra Bright, *Human Resources*

Environmental Business Solutions
8799 Balboa Avenue, Suite 290
San Diego, CA 92123
858-571-5500

Web Address: ebsenvironmental.com
Number of Employees: 13
Daniel E. Johnson, *President*
Lori Yefsky, *Office Manager*

EOS International
5838 Edison Place
Carlsbad, CA 92008
760-431-8400
Web Address: www.eosintl.com
Number of Employees: 70
Scot A. Cheatham, *President*
Joellen Thacker, *Human Resources Manager*

Epicure Software Corporation
5010 Wateridge Vista Drive
San Diego, CA 92121
619-546-9600
Number of Employees: 300
George Klaus, *President*
Cathy Akin, *Human Resource Manager*

EQE
4590 McArthur Boulevard, Suite 400
Newport Beach, CA 92660
949-833-3303
Web Address: www.eqe.com
Number of Employees: 90
Greg Hardy, *Manager*

Equifax National Decision Systems
5375 Mira Sorrento Place, Suite 400
San Diego, CA 92121
619-622-0800
Web Address: www.natdecsys.com
Number of Employees: 175
Bob Nascenzi, *President*
Julie Bockersman, *Human Resource Director*

ERM-EnviroClean-West
1920 Main Street, Suite 600
Irvine, CA 92614-7226
949-946-0455
Number of Employees: 25

Mark Ransom, *President*

ESI/FME
1921 Carnegie Avenue, Suite 3K
Santa Ana, CA 92705-5510
714-261-1811
Web Address: www.esifme.com
Number of Employees: 24
Dale L Forbes, *President*

Excello Circuits
1924 Nancita Circle
Placentia, CA 92870-6737
714-993-0560
Web Address: www.excello.com
Number of Employees: 30
Anal Shah, *President*

Executive Software
701 North Brand Boulevard, 6th Floor
Glendale, CA 91203
818-547-2050
Web Address: www.execsoft.com
Number of Employees: 102

Craig Jensen, *CEO*
Vicki Coleman, *Director of Human Resources*

Exide Electronics
2727 Kurtz Street
San Diego, CA 92110
619-291-4211
Web Address: www.exide.com
Number of Employees: 230

Patrick Steffen, *CEO*
Judy Michelle, *Senior Human Resource Representative*

Exodus Communications
19200 Von Karman Avenue, Suite 400
Irvine, CA 92612-1540
949-622-5434
Number of Employees: 30

Expersoft Corp.
5825 Oberlin Drive, Suite 300
San Diego, CA 92121
619-824-4100
Web Address: www.expersoft.com

Tom Greene, *COO*

Extron Electronics
1230 South Lewis Street
Anaheim, CA 92805
714-491-1500
Web Address: www.extron.com
Number of Employees: 300

Andrew Edwards, *President*
Joanne Grush, *Human Resources Manager*

Fast Point Systems
8381 Katella, Suite J
Stanton, CA 90680
714-484-6300
Web Address: www.ftgdata.com
Number of Employees: 33

Doug Lippincott, *President*

FileNet Corporation
3565 Harbor Boulevard
Costa Mesa, CA 92626-1420
949-327-3400
Web Address: www.filenet.com
Number of Employees: 800

Lee D. Roberts, *President*
Audrey N. Schaeffer, *Vice President*

Financial Processing Systems
1815 East Wilshire Avenue, Suite 910
Santa Ana, CA 92705-4646
714-953-8681
Web Address: www.fpsnet.com
Number of Employees: 40

Gary Ruhelin, *President*

Fine Pitch Technology
3200 South Susan Street
Santa Ana, CA 92704-6839
714-557-2370
Number of Employees: 190

Fineline Circuits & Technology
594 Apollo Street
Brea, CA 92821-3101
714-529-2942
Web Address: www.finelinecircuits.com
Number of Employees: 26

Rick Bajaria, *President*

Flour Daniel GTI
6450 Lusk Boulevard, Suite E208
San Diego, CA 92121
619-453-8415
Number of Employees: 7

Mike Wulff, *Operations Manager*

Fluor Daniel GTI
3353 Michelson Drive, Suite 200
Irvine, CA 92698
949-975-6480
Number of Employees: 60

Dave Backus, *Regional Manager*
Daniella Smigiel, *Human Resources Manager*

FM Systems
3877 South Main Street
Santa Ana, CA 92707-5710
714-979-3355
Web Address: www.fmsystems-inc.com
Number of Employees: 20

Francis McClatchie, *President*

Forbes Computer Group
2805 McGaw Avenue
Irvine, CA 92614-5835
949-941-9999
Number of Employees: 22

Siraj Bukhari, *President*

Formula Consultants
100 South Anaheim Boulevard, Suite 200
Anaheim, CA 92805
714-778-0123
Web Address: www.formula.com
Number of Employees: 76

R. Joseph Dale, *President*
Shirley Blan, *Human Resoures Manager*

Francais Engineering Corp
5951 Lakeshore Drive
Cypress, CA 90630-3372
714-995-1891
Number of Employees: 7

Richard K. Francais, *President*

Frederick Brown Associates
3420 Irvine Avenue, Suite 200
Newport Beach, CA 92660-3189
949-852-9995
Number of Employees: 37

Frederick R. Brown, *Principal*
Les McCrimmon, *Principal & Hiring Contact*

FT Andrews
631 South Brookhurst Street, Suite 200
Anaheim, CA 92804-3564
714-772-9193
Number of Employees: 23

Ivan R. Cranston Jr., *President*

Future Focus
9740 Scranton Road, Suite 150
San Diego, CA 92121
619-452-4365
Web Address: www.future-focus.com
Number of Employees: 15

Tim Ash, *CEO*
Robyn Goodwrich, *Hiring Manager*

Gage Babcock & Associates
1 Centerpointe Drive, Suite 240
La Palma, CA 90623-1058
714-739-3870
Web Address: www.gage-babcock.com
Number of Employees: 6

Michael J. Madden, *Principal*

GDE Systems
16550 West Bernardo Drive
San Diego, CA 92127
619-675-2600
Job Hotline: 800-545-0506
Web Address: www.gde.com
Number of Employees: 1800

Terry A. Straeter, *CEO*
Michael Brown, *Human Resource Manager*

GE Capital ITS
6490 Weathers Place
San Diego, CA 92592
619-678-1500
Web Address: www.gecits.ge.com

Geac Computers/Hotel Computer
15621 Red Hill Avenue, Suite 100
Tustin, CA 92780-7322
714-258-5800
Web Address: www.hotels.geac.com

Number of Employees: 65
Tom Martin, *General Manager*
Cynthia Phifer, *Human Resources Manager*

GEC Plessey Semiconductors
2600 Michelson Drive, Suite 830
Irvine, CA 92612-6520
949-852-3900
Web Address: www.gpsemi.com
Number of Employees: 240

Gem Products
12472 Edison Way
Garden Grove, CA 92841-2828
714-372-9619
Number of Employees: 25

John Kirtley, *President & CFO*
David Mulnard, *Human Resources Director*

General Automation
17731 Mitchell North
Irvine, CA 92614-6028
949-250-4800
Web Address: www.genauto.com
Number of Employees: 150

Jane Christie, *President*
Judy Cimorell, *Director of Personnel*
Provider of open systems and complementary software products to value-added resellers. Its services include system design, site preparation, product training, call center support, and disaster-recovery programs.

General Ceramics/Tekform Prods
2770 East Coronado Street
Anaheim, CA 92806-2401
714-630-2340
Number of Employees: 90

General Monitors
26776 Simpatica Circle
Lake Forest, CA 92630-8128
714-581-4464
Web Address: www.generalmonitors.com
Number of Employees: 110
Don Edwards, *President*
Beverly Collins, *Hiring Contact*

General Software Solutions
991 Calle Amanecer
San Clemente, CA 92673-6212
949-492-2400
Web Address: www.gsscorp.com
Number of Employees: 150
Gary Munoz, *President*

Genesis 2000
5000 North Park Way Calabasas, Suite 200
Calabasas, CA 91302
818-223-3260
Web Address: www/.genesis2000.com
Number of Employees: 36
Homy Majd, *President*
Caroline Leibow, *Director of Personnel*

Genisco Tech Corp/Solaris Sys
1620 South Sunkist Street
Anaheim, CA 92806-5811
714-938-0348
Web Address: www.gtc.com
Number of Employees: 25

Michael F. Boice, *President*

Genovation
17741 Mitchell North
Irvine, CA 92614-6028
949-833-3355
Web Address: www.genovation.com
Number of Employees: 25

Leonard Genest, *President*
Jeff Anderson, *CFO*

Gensia Sicor
19 Hughes
Irvine, CA 92618-1902
949-455-4700
Web Address: www.gensiasicor.com
Number of Employees: 250

Donald E. Panoz, *President*
Linda Hughes, *Director of Personnel*
R&D company that focuses on the discovery, development, manufacturing, and marketing of specialty pharmaceutical products for the acute care market.

Geocon Environmental Consultants
6970 Flanders Drive
San Diego, CA 92121
858-558-6100

Jim Likins, *President*
Nancy Likins, *Human Resource Manager*

Geomatrix Consultants
20201 SW Birch Street, Suite 150
Newport Beach, CA 92660-1751
949-474-9181
Number of Employees: 250

Anthony D. Daus III, *President*

GeoSoils
1446 East Chestnut Avenue
Santa Ana, CA 92701-6319
714-647-0277
Number of Employees: 30

Albert Kleist, *President*
Ed Burrows, *Vice President*

GeoSyntec Consultants
2100 Main Street, Suite 150
Huntington Beach, CA 92648-2460
714-969-0800
Web Address: www.geosynthetic.com
Number of Employees: 50

Kearny Fangelat, *Manager*

GERS Retail Systems
9725 Scranton Road, Suite C
San Diego, CA 92121
619-457-3888
Web Address: www.gers.com
Number of Employees: 250

Gary Reif, *President*

Golden West Circuits
15622 Computer Lane
Huntington Beach, CA 92649-1608
714-379-6700
Web Address: www.gwcircuits.com
Number of Employees: 12

Vijay Merchant, *President*

Golden West Tech
1180 East Valencia Drive
Fullerton, CA 92831-4627
714-738-3775
Number of Employees: 75

Dan P Rieth, *President*

Gouvis Engineering California
4400 Campus Drive #A
Newport Beach, CA 92660-1813
949-752-1612
Web Address: www.gouvisgroup.com
Number of Employees: 40

Saeed Bekam, *President & CEO*
Mike Houshand, *Human Resources*

Graphic Resources Corporation
12311 Industry Street
Garden Grove, CA 92841-2817
714-891-1003
Web Address: www.grc.com
Number of Employees: 60

Stephen Beko, *President*

Green Flash Systems
10010 Mesa Rim Road, Suite B
San Diego, CA 92121
619-452-4995
Web Address: dr@greenflash.com
Number of Employees: 6

D. R. Peck, *CEO*

GSI
17951 Sky Park Circle, Suite H
Irvine, CA 92614-6323
949-261-7949
Web Address: www.gsi-inc.com
Number of Employees: 25

Tony Goodfellow, *President*

Gulton Statham Transducers
1644 Whittier Avenue
Costa Mesa, CA 92627-4415

949-642-2400
Web Address: www.gulton-statham.com
Number of Employees: 275
Steve Pirrone, *President*
Cindy Chow, *Hiring Contact*

Hall & Foreman
203 North Golden Circle Drive, South 300
Santa Ana, CA 92705
714-664-0570
Number of Employees: 45

John Hogan, *President*

Hank Mohle & Associates
901 East Imperial Highway, Suite A
La Habra, CA 90631-7470
714-738-3471
Number of Employees: 20

R. Henry Mohle, *President*

Harding Lawson Assoc Group
30 Corporate Park, Suite 400
Irvine, CA 92606-5133
949-260-1800
Web Address: www.harding.com
Number of Employees: 930

Matt McCullough, *Office Manager*

Hargis + Associates
2223 Avenida de la Playa, Suite 300
La Jolla, CA 92037
858-454-0615
Web Address: www.lawinfo.com/biz/hargis

David R. Hargis, *President*

HDR Engineering
2600 Michelson Drive, Suite 1600
Irvine, CA 92612-1581
949-756-6800
Web Address: www.hdrinc.com
Number of Employees: 40

Eric King, *Department Manager*

Health Science Associates
10771 Noel Street
Los Alamitos, CA 90720-2547
714-220-3922
Number of Employees: 50

Howard B. Spielman, *President*
Janine Weitzel, *Human Resources Manager*

Herco Technology Corporation
13330 Evening Creek Drive
San Diego, CA 92128
619-679-2800
Number of Employees: 576

Robert Herring Sr., *CEO*
Saul Moreno, *Production Manager*

Hewlett Packard
16399 West Bernardo Drive
San Diego, CA 92127
619-655-1899
Web Address: www.hp.com

Hewlett-Packard
1421 Manhattan Avenue
Fullerton, CA 92831-5246
714-999-6700
Number of Employees: 111800

Hewlett-Packard
16399 West Bernardo Drive
San Diego, CA 92127
619-655-4100
Number of Employees: 2,212

Ray Brubaker, *CEO*

Hirsch Electronics Corporation
2941 Alton Parkway
Irvine, CA 92606-5142
949-250-8888
Web Address: www.hirschelectronics.com
Number of Employees: 47

Lawrence Midland, *President*
Diana Midland, *Hiring Contact*

HM Electronics
6675 Mesa Ridge Road
San Diego, CA 92121
619-535-6000
Number of Employees: 353

Harry Miyahira, *CEO*

Holt Integrated Circuits
45 Parker
Irvine, CA 92618-1605
949-859-8800
Web Address: www.holtic.com
Number of Employees: 25

William G. Holt, *President*

Honeywell
514 South Lyon Street
Santa Ana, CA 92701-6362
714-547-9357
Number of Employees: 65

Mike Bishop, *Business Manager*

Horiba Instruments
17671 Armstrong Avenue
Irvine, CA 92614-5701
949-250-4811
Web Address: www.horiba.com
Number of Employees: 185

Juishi Saito, *Executive Vice President*
Deanna Larcome, *Human Resources Manager*

Hughes Aircraft
3970 Sherman Street
San Diego, CA 92110
619-543-4102
Web Address: www.hughes.com
Number of Employees: 290

Ernie Tedeschi, *CEO*
Joyce Prickett, *Human Resource Director*

Hughes Aircraft/Microelectron
500 Superior Avenue
Newport Beach, CA 92663
949-759-2411
Web Address: www.raytheon.com
Number of Employees: 700

Chuck Krunm, *President*

Hughes Data Systems
2362 McGaw Avenue
Irvine, CA 92614-5832
949-253-9120
Web Address: www.hughes.com
Number of Employees: 50

Dave Davisson, *President*

Hughes Info Technology Systems
1801 Hughes Drive
Fullerton, CA 92834-2249
714-446-4336
Web Address: www.hughes.com
Number of Employees: 4500

Huitt-Zollars
15101 Red Hill Avenue
Tustin, CA 92780-6500
714-259-7900
Web Address: www.huitt-zollars.com
Number of Employees: 70

Brent Caldwell, *Office Manager*

Hunsaker & Associates Irvine
3 Hughes
Irvine, CA 92618-2021
949-583-1010
Number of Employees: 130

Richard Hunsaker, *President*

Hygienetics Environmenal Services
1920 East Warner Avenue, Suite A
Santa Ana, CA 92705-5547
714-955-0201
Number of Employees: 40
Laura Jeremias, *Office Manager*

I/Omagic Corporation
6B Autry
Irvine, CA 92618-2708
949-727-7466
Web Address: www.iomagic.com
Number of Employees: 25
Tony Shahbaz, *President*

IBM Corporation
600 Anton Boulevard
Costa Mesa, CA 92626-7147
949-438-5000
Number of Employees: 235000

ICCI -Intl Circuits/Component
3701 East Miraloma Avenue
Anaheim, CA 92806-2123
714-572-1900
Web Address: www.icciusa.com
Number of Employees: 130

Richard Cheng, *President*
Brian Meecher, *Hiring Contact*

ICL Retail Systems
9801 Muirlands Boulevard
Irvine, CA 92618-2521
949-855-5500
Web Address: www.iclretail.com
Number of Employees: 19000

Idea
1300 Pioneer Street, Suite B
Brea, CA 92821-3728
562-697-4332
Web Address: http://eemonline.com/idea
Number of Employees: 20

Maoyeh Lu, *President*
Elsie Lu, *Vice President of Administration*

Image & Signal Processing
1250 North Lakeview Avenue, Suite H
Anaheim, CA 92807-1801
714-970-0700
Web Address: www.cersnet.com
Number of Employees: 12

Lawrence Goshorn, *President*
R.J. Ghielen, *Human Resources Manager*

Imaging Tech
27122 B Paseo Espada, Suite 1023
San Juan Capistrano, CA 92675
714-960-7676
Web Address: www.imaging.com
Number of Employees: 4

Bradley Finney, *Sales Manager*

iMALL
4400 Coldwater Canyon Boulevard, Suite 200
Studio City, CA 91604
818-509-3600
Web Address: www.imall.com
Number of Employees: 115

Richard Rosenblatt, *President*
Tamar Nadell, *Director of Personnel*
Operator of a Web site which markets products and services from over 1,000 merchants. Also provides Web development and Internet consulting. iMall registers about 18 million hits each month, and includes banner advertising, classified ads, and links to other sites.

IMC Networks
16931 Millikan Avenue
Irvine, CA 92606
949-724-1070
Web Address: www.imcnetworks.com
Number of Employees: 75

Jerry Roby, *President*
Janet Thompson, *Director of Personnel*

Impco Technologies
16804 Gridley Place
Cerritos, CA 90703
562-860-6666
Web Address: www.impcotechnologies.com
Number of Employees: 380

Robert Stemmler, *CEO & President*
Martha Eoff, *Human Resource Manager*

InCirT Technology
1382 Bell Avenue
Tustin, CA 92780-6430
714-258-5650
Web Address: www.incirt.com
Number of Employees: 168

Alan L Weaver, *President*
Rhonda Barbara, *Human Resources Manager*

IndeNet
16000 Ventura Boulevard, Suite 700
Encino , CA 91436
818-461-8525
Web Address: www.indenet.com
Number of Employees: 395

Andre A. Blay, *President*
Provider of management software and systems to television and radio broadcasters, advertisers, cable TV operators, and TV programmers throughout the world. Customers include NBC and Fox.

Industrial Circuit Design
17801 Sky Park Circle
Irvine, CA 92614-6107
949-975-8511
Number of Employees: 25

Dave Masarik, *President*

Industrial Computer Source
6260 Sequence Drive
San Diego, CA 92121
619-677-0877
Web Address: sales@indocompsrc.com
Number of Employees: 285

Steven Peltier, *CEO*

Industrial Contracting Engineers
421 East Cerritos Avenue
Anaheim, CA 92805-6320
714-491-1317
Number of Employees: 200

Gerald G. Pyle, *President*

Infographics Systems Corp
4442 Corporate Center Drive
Los Alamitos, CA 90720-2539
714-220-4980
Web Address: www.infographicsystems.com
Number of Employees: 50

Terry Bain, *Personnel Manager*

Informer Computer Systems
12833 Monarch Stret
Garden Grove, CA 92841
714-891-1112
Number of Employees: 20

Edward P. Dailey, *President*

Infotec Development
3611 South Harbor Boulevard
Santa Ana, CA 92704
714-549-2182

Ingram Micro
1600 East St. Andrew Place
Santa Ana, CA 92705
714-566-1000
Job Hotline: 714-566-1000
Web Address: www.ingrammicro.com
Number of Employees: 3000

Jerre L. Stead, *President*
David M. Finley, *Director of Personnel*
Wholesale distributor of microcomputer products. It offers more than 36,000 products -including desktop and notebook PCs, servers, storage devices, CD-ROM drives, monitors, printers, and software- to 100,000 resellers in 120 countries.

Inline
22860 Savi Ranch Parkway
Yorba Linda, CA 92887-4610
714-921-4100
Web Address: www.inlineinc.com
Number of Employees: 50

Arturo Garcia, *President*
Maria Roberto, *Personnel Manager*

Innovative Sensors
4745 East Bryson Street
Anaheim, CA 92807-1993
714-779-8781
Web Address: www.isi-ph.inter.net
Number of Employees: 45
Gary L Bukaimer, *President*

InSight Health Services Corp.
4400 MacArthur Boulevard, Suite 800
Newport Beach, CA 92660
949-476-0733
Web Address: www.insighthealth.com
Number of Employees: 624
E. Larry Atkins, *President*
Cecilia A. Gusastaferro, *Director of Personnel*
Supplier of MRI and CT imaging services to hospitals and HMOs. Also offers conventional X-ray, mammogram, ultrasound, and nuclear medicine and provides such related services as marketing, scheduling, and billing.

Inspired Arts
4225 Executive Square, Suite 1160
San Diego, CA 92037
619-623-3525
Web Address: www.inspiredarts.com
Number of Employees: 18

Brian A. Kent, *CEO*
Victoria Smith, *Chief of Staff*

Intelenet Communication
18101 Von Karman Avenue, Suite 550
Irvine, CA 92612
949-851-8250
Web Address: www.intelenet.net

Interface Displays & Controls, Inc.
4630 North Avenue
Oceanside, CA 92056
760-945-0230
Web Address: www.interfacedisplays.com
Number of Employees: 40

Bill Lang, *President*
Sherry Scott, *Human Resources Manager*

Intergraph Corporation
26 Technology Drive
Irvine, CA 92618-2301
949-727-0646
Web Address: www.intergraph.com
Number of Employees: 45

Jim Meadlock, *President*

Intermec Corporation
2572 White Road
Irvine, CA 92614-5526
949-475-0900
Number of Employees: 30

Harvey Gumaer, *Manager*

Intermetrics
7755 Center Avenue, Suite 200
Huntington Beach, CA 92647
714-891-4631
Web Address: www.intermetrics.com
Number of Employees: 25

Jeff England, *Director*

International Remote Imaging Systems
9162 Eton Avenue
Chatsworth, CA 91311-5874
818-709-1244
Web Address: www.proiris.com
Number of Employees: 68

Fred H. Deindoerfer, *President*
Don Horacek, *Controller*
Manufacturer of equipment and supplies for urinalysis, for clinical laboratories and hospitals throughout the US.

International Sensor Technology
3 Whatney
Irvine, CA 92618-2824

949-452-9000
Web Address: www.gotgas.com
Number of Employees: 32
Jack C. Chou, *President*
Florence Edwards, *Human Resources Manager*

International Space Optics SA
2495 DaVinci
Irvine, CA 92614
949-898-6544
Web Address: www.isorainbow.com
Number of Employees: 25

Joanie Hamasaki, *Human Resources*

International Technology Corp
3347 Michaelson Drive, Suite 200
Irvine, CA 92612
949-261-6441
Job Hotline: 949-660-5434
Web Address: www.itcorporation.com
Number of Employees: 80

Mike Farrell, *General Manager*

Internet and Web Services Corp.
12780 High Bluff Drive, Suite 200
San Diego, CA 92130
619-794-8000
Web Address: sales@iwsc.com

Bryan Hertz, *CEO*

Interplay Productions
16815 Von Karman Avenue
Irvine, CA 92606
949-553-6655
Web Address: www.interplay.com
Number of Employees: 560

Brian Fargo, *CEO*
Lisa Fisher, *Director of Personnel*
Chris Kilpatrick, *President*
Margo Engel, *Recruiter*

Iris
1400 North Kellogg Drive, Suite F
Anaheim, CA 92807-1966
714-777-2027
Web Address: www.irisnet.com
Number of Employees: 15

Eddie Ureno, *President*

Irvine Electronics
17791 Sky Park Circle, Suite D
Irvine, CA 92614-6118
949-250-0315
Number of Employees: 50

Jane Zerounian, *President*

Irvine Sensors Corporation
3001 Redhill Avenue, Building 3, Unit 104
Costa Mesa, CA 92626-4529
949-549-8211

Web Address: www.irvine-sensors.com
Number of Employees: 65
James D. Evert, *President*
Gail Lafferty, *Director of Personnel*
Manufacturer of electro-optical equipment, infrared detector and missile seeker arrays, high-density memory chips. Researches, develops, and makes high-density microelectronics packages and imaging and sensing devices.

Island Pacific Systems Corp
19800 Macarthur Boulevard #12
Irvine, CA 92612-2421
949-476-2212
Web Address: www.islandpacific.com
Number of Employees: 100

Paul Mickelsen, *President*
Mark Woulff, *VP for Human Resources*

IT NetTrac Corp.
6120 Paseo del Norte, Suite J-2
Carlsbad, CA 92009
760-431-1982
Web Address: www.nettrac.com
Number of Employees: 10

Michael Dalsin, *CEO*

ITOCHU Technology
2701 Dow Avenue
Tustin, CA 92780-7209
714-573-2721
Number of Employees: 83

Hiro Inoue, *President*

IVID Communications
7220 Trade Street, Suite 201
San Diego, CA 92121
619-537-5000
Web Address: www.ivid.com

Jack Spiegelberg, *CEO*

J D Edwards
611 Anton Boulevard, Suite 300
Costa Mesa, CA 92626-1904
949-755-5420
Number of Employees: 50

Pam Lennon, *Office Manager*

J. L. Wood Optical Systems
1361 East Edinger Avenue
Santa Ana, CA 92705-4475
714-835-1888
Number of Employees: 20

Brian L Seaman, *President*

J-Tron
512 East Central Park Avenue South
Anaheim, CA 92802-1472
714-991-1510
Number of Employees: 13

Tillie Jones, *President*
Irma Sanchez, *Human Resources Manager*

Javelin Systems
1881 Langley Avenue
Irvine, CA 92614
949-223-5130
Web Address: www.jvln.com
Number of Employees: 35

Richard P. Stack, *President*
Shanna Campbell, *Director of Personnel*
Supplier of open-system, touch-screen, point-of-sale computers. The systems are used by the food service, retail, and industrial markets and in information-kiosk applications.

Jaycor
9775 Towne Centre Drive
San Diego, CA 92121
858-453-6580
Web Address: www.jaycor.com
Number of Employees: 100

Eric P. Wenaas, *President*
Thelest Stewart, *Human Resource Director*

JDF Enterprises
712 Dunn Way
Placentia, CA 92870-6896
714-524-1100
Number of Employees: 13

John J. Farley, *President*
Kis Converse, *Hiring Contact*

Jet Equipment Corporation
3021 Shannon Stret
Santa Ana, CA 92704-6927
714-786-3210
Number of Employees: 30

Derreck Ford, *President*

Johnson-Frank & Associates
5150 East Hunter Avenue
Anaheim, CA 92807-2049
714-777-8877
Number of Employees: 25

Roger A Frank, *President*

Jones & McGeoy Sales
5100 Campus Drive #300
Newport Beach, CA 92660-2101
949-724-8080
Web Address: www.jonesmcgeoy.com
Number of Employees: 25

Roger Jones, *President*

Jonesville Webs
4179 Third Avenue, Suite 409
San Diego, CA 92103
619-295-5512
Web Address: www.blurtheline.com
Number of Employees: 3

Arthur Jones, *CEO*

KCA Electronics
223 North Crescent Way
Anaheim, CA 92801-6704
714-239-2433
Web Address: www.kcamerica.com
Number of Employees: 400

C. W. Cho, *President*
Linda Williamson, *Human Resources Manager*

Kennedy/Jenks Consultants
2151 Michelson Drive, Suite 100
Irvine, CA 92612-1311
949-261-1577
Number of Employees: 20

Michael Greenspan, *Manager*

KFC USA
1575 Sunflower Avenue
Costa Mesa, CA 92626-1532
949-546-0336
Web Address: www.smilekfc.com
Number of Employees: 33

Yung Yu, *President*

Kimley-Horn & Associates
2100 West Orangewood Avenue, Suite 140
Orange, CA 92868-1950
714-939-1030
Web Address: www.kimleyhorn.com
Number of Employees: 10

George Feres, *Office Manager*

King Instrument Company
16792 Burke Lane
Huntington Beach, CA 92647-4559
714-841-3663
Web Address: www.kinginstrument.com
Number of Employees: 50

Clyde F. King, *President*
Carol Simpson, *General Manager*

Kingston Technology Company
17600 Newhope Street
Fountain Valley, CA 92708
714-435-2600
Web Address: www.kingston.com
Number of Employees: 900

John Tu, *President*
Daniel Hsu, *Director of Personnel*

Kleinfelder
9555 Chesapeake Drive, Suite 101
San Diego, CA 92123
858-541-1145
Web Address: www.kleinfelder.com

William Siegel, *Vice President*

Kleinfelder
1370 Valley Vista Drive, Suite 150
Diamond Bar, CA 91765

909-396-0335
Web Address: www.kleinfelder.com
Number of Employees: 50
Bartlett Patton, *Regional Manager*

Kofax Image Products
3 Jenner Street
Irvine, CA 92618
949-727-1733
Web Address: www.kofax.com
Number of Employees: 151

David S. Silver, *President*
Lynn Scheid, *Human Resources Manager*

Kor Electronics
11958 Monarch Street
Garden Grove, CA 92841-2126
714-898-8200
Web Address: www.korelec.com
Number of Employees: 50

Louis Greenbaum, *CEO*

KVB
3191 Aenita De Las Vandergs
Ranch Santa Margarita, CA 92688
949-766-4200
Web Address: www.kvb-cems.com
Number of Employees: 51

Judy Heston, *Human Resources Manager*

Kyocera America
8611 Balboa Avenue
San Diego, CA 92123
619-576-2600
Web Address: kaicorp@kyocera.com
Number of Employees: 968

David Grooms, *CEO*
Sean Ristine, *Human Resource Representative*

Lantronix
15353 Barranca Parkway
Irvine, CA 92618-2216
949-453-3990
Web Address: www.lantronix.com
Number of Employees: 70

Fred Ghiel, *President*
Karen Peterson, *Human Resources Manager*

Laser Industries
677 North Hariton Street
Orange, CA 92868-1311
714-532-3271
Web Address: www.laserindustries.com
Number of Employees: 38

John Butterly, *President*
Joe Butterly, *Hiring Contact*

HIGH-TECH

329

Laser Products Corp
18300 Mount Baldy Circle
Fountain Valley, CA 92708-6122
714-545-9444
Web Address: www.laserproducts.com
Number of Employees: 98
John Matthews, *President*
Randi Seckman, *Human Resources Manager*

Lasergraphics
20 Ada
Irvine, CA 92618-2303
949-753-8282
Web Address: www.lasergraphics.com
Number of Employees: 50
Dr. M. Demetrescu, *President*
Cindy Gruenke, *Human Resources Administrator*

Law Crandall
9177 Sky Park Court, Suite A
San Diego, CA 92123
858-278-3600
Web Address: lawco.com
Number of Employees: 80
Jack Fraser, *West Regional Manager*
Steve Brinigar, *Branch Manager*

LCOA -Laminating Co/America
7311 Doig Drive
Garden Grove, CA 92841-1893
714-891-3581
Number of Employees: 100

Leaming Industries
15339 Barranca Parkway
Irvine, CA 92618-2216
949-727-4144
Web Address: www.leaming.com
Number of Employees: 23
Robert Leaming, *President*
Peg Fallan, *Human Resources Manager*

Leighton & Associates
17781 Cowan
Irvine, CA 92614-6009
949-250-1421
Number of Employees: 100
Bruce R. Clark, *President*
Terry Hawely, *Human Resources Manager*

Level Computer
521 South State College Boulevard
Fullerton, CA 92831-5113
714-578-8800
Number of Employees: 25
Tony Wang, *President*

Levine-Fricke-Recon
1920 Main Street
Irvine, CA 92614-7209
949-955-1390
Number of Employees: 68
James D. Levine, *President*
Meredith Bernhard, *Human Resources Manager*

LG & E Power
575 Anton Boulevard, Suite 250
Costa Mesa, CA 92626-1946
949-241-4700
Number of Employees: 17
Dave Gubser, *Vice President*

Lifetime Memory Products
2505 Davinci
Irvine, CA 92614
949-444-4700
Web Address: www.lifetimememory.com
Number of Employees: 70
Paul Columbus, *Manager*

Linfinity Microelectronics
11861 Western Avenue
Garden Grove, CA 92841-2119
714-898-8121
Web Address: www.linfinity.com
Number of Employees: 240
James J. Peterson, *President*
Eileen Hardesty, *Human Resources Manager*

Link SanDiego.Com.
2251 San Diego Avenue, Suite A-141
San Diego, CA 92110
619-220-8601
Web Address: www.sandiego.com
Number of Employees: 10
Thomas R. Hillebrandt, *CEO*
Sheila Thorton, *Human Resource Manager*

LinkOnline Network
3250 Wilshire Boulevard, Suite 2150
Los Angeles, CA 90010
213-251-1500
Web Address: www.linkonline.net

Linscott Law & Greenspan
1580 Corporate Drive, Suite 122
Costa Mesa, CA 92626-1460
949-641-1587
Number of Employees: 50
Paul Wilkinson, *President*
Tamara McVey, *Human Resources*

Litronic Industries
2950 Red Hill Avenue
Costa Mesa, CA 92626-5935
949-545-6649
Web Address: www.alliedsignals.com
Number of Employees: 150
Kris Shah, *President*
Diane Hoppel, *Human Resources Manager*

Litton Industries
21240 Burbank Boulevard
Woodland Hills, CA 91367-6675
818-598-5000
Web Address: www.littoncorp.com
Number of Employees: 3537
John M. Leonis, *Chairman*
Nancy L. Gaymon, *Director of Personnel*
Provider of aerospace, defense, and commercial electronics, mostly for the US government. The company's operations are located primarily in the US, Canada, and Western Europe.

Litton Industries
Engineering Service Center
7425 Mission Valley Road, Suite 205
San Diego, CA 92100
619-298-6408
Web Address: www.litton.com

Live Software
5703 Oberline Drive
San Diego, CA 92121
619-643-1919
Web Address: www.livesoftware.com
Number of Employees: 5

Paul Colton, *CEO*
Shannon Gillikin, *Director of Operation*

Lockheed Martin Corp/IMS Div
30 Fairbanks, Suite 100
Irvine, CA 92618-1623
949-580-2100
Number of Employees: 100

Marcia Monnich, *Office Manager*

Logicon
3701 Skypark Drive
Torrance, CA 90505
310-373-0220
Web Address: www.logicon.com
Number of Employees: 57

John R. Woodhull, *CEO*

Los Angeles Computer Company
204 Technology Drive, Suite F
Irvine, CA 92618-2406
949-453-7654
Number of Employees: 15

Yusuf Motiwalla, *Owner*

Lotus Development Corporation
2010 Main Street, Suite 1100
Irvine, CA 92614-7216
949-261-2697
Web Address: www.lotus.com
Number of Employees: 20

Michelle Coffman, *Manager*

LSA Associates
1 Park Plaza, Suite 500
Irvine, CA 92614-5981

949-553-0666
Number of Employees: 45
Carolyn Lobell, *Principal*
Rob Balen, *Human Resources*

Lucas Aerospace/Cargo Systems
610 Neptune Avenue
Brea, CA 92822-2207
714-671-4500
Number of Employees: 345

Ron Yeager, *Human Resources Manager*

Lucent Technologies
18201 Von Karman Avenue, Suite 640
Irvine, CA 92612
949-225-5700
Web Address: www.lucent.com

MacDonald-Stephens Engineers
24741 Chrisanta Drive #100
Mission Viejo, CA 92691-4812
714-458-8844
Number of Employees: 18

David MacDonald, *President*

MacNeal-Schwendler Corp.
815 Colorado Boulevard
Los Angeles, CA 90041
213-258-9111
Web Address: www.macsch.com
Number of Employees: 180

Thomas Curry, *President*
Rich Lander, *Director of Human Resources*

Macrolink
1500 North Kellogg Drive
Anaheim, CA 92807-1930
714-777-8800
Web Address: www.macrolink.com
Number of Employees: 40

R. David Vednor, *President*
Melanie Hall, *Human Resources*

Madge Networks
1 Park Plaza, Suite 340
Irvine, CA 92614-8511
949-224-0400
Web Address: www.madge.com
Number of Employees: 2200

Magic Software Enterprises
1642 Kaiser Avenue
Irvine, CA 92614-5700
949-250-1718
Web Address: www.magic-sw.com
Number of Employees: 38

John O'Leary, *CEO*

Magnetic Sensors Corporation
1365 North McCan Street
Anaheim, CA 92806-1316
714-630-8380
Web Address:
www.magsensers@compuserve.com
Number of Employees: 35
Charles Boudakian, *President*

MAI Systems Corporation
9601 Jeronimo Road
Irvine, CA 92618
949-598-6000
Web Address: www.maisystems.com
Number of Employees: 551

George G. Bayz, *President*
Cheryl Moreno, *Director of Personnel*
Christine Young, *Human Resources Manager*
Distributor of information management systems designed especially for the hospitality industry and midsized process manufacturers. It operates worldwide, selling through independent distributors, resellers, and local sales agents.

Marconi Integrated Systems
PO Box 509009
San Diego, CA 92150
619-573-8000
Web Address: www.marconi-is.com

Marmac
15621 Red Hill Avenue, Suite 200
Tustin, CA 92780-7322
714-258-8500
Number of Employees: 85

Mike Hendrix, *President*

Marotz
13518 Jamul Drive
Jamul, CA 91935
619-669-3100
Web Address: info@marotz.com
Number of Employees: 60

William Roetzheim, *CEO*
Cheryl Delozier, *Human Resource Manager*

Marshall Industries
9320 Telstar Avenue
El Monte, CA 91731
626-307-6000
Web Address: www.marshall.com
Number of Employees: 1,000

Robert Rodin, *President*
Les Jones, *Director of Human Resources*

Marway Power Systems
1670 North Main Street
Orange, CA 92867-3405
714-283-4349
Web Address: www.marway.com
Number of Employees: 60

Mary Munday, *President*

Matrix
3183 Red Hill Avenue
Costa Mesa, CA 92626-3401
949-513-2266
Number of Employees: 75

Marvin Cha, *President*

Matrix Systems
17011 Beach Boulevard, Suite 900
Huntington Beach, CA 92647-5998
714-375-6693
Number of Employees: 100

Maxwell Technologies
9275 Sky Park Court
San Diego, CA 92123
619-279-5100
Web Address: www.maxwell.com
Number of Employees: 450

Kenneth F. Potashner, *CEO*
Emily Berr, *Human Resource Representative*

MCA Engineers
2960 Airway Avenue, Suite A103
Costa Mesa, CA 92626-6001
949-662-0500
Number of Employees: 50

Maxwell C. Cheung, *Owner & President*

McCurdy Circuits
1739 North Case Street
Orange, CA 92865-4292
714-974-0401
Web Address: www.mccurdy.com
Number of Employees: 180

Scott McCurdy, *President*
Pat Halay, *Human Resources Manager*

MCI WorldCom
19200 Von Karman Avenue, Suite 350
Irvine, CA 92612
949-756-6500
Web Address: www.mciworldcom.com

MCI WorldCom
700 South Flower Street, Suite 1600
Los Angeles, CA 90017
213-239-2300
Web Address: www.mciworldcom.com

McLaren/Hart
16755 Von Karman Avenue
Irvine, CA 92606-4918
949-756-2667
Job Hotline: 916-638-3696
Web Address: www.mclaren-hart.com
Number of Employees: 610

Toni Johnson, *Office Manager*

MDM Engineering
28202 Cabot Road, Suite 205
Laguna Niguel, CA 92677-1248
714-365-1350
Number of Employees: 15

Michael Flowers, *President*
Cynthia Williams, *Human Resources Manager*

MDS Consulting
17320 Red Hill Avenue, Suite 350
Irvine, CA 92614-5644
949-251-8821
Number of Employees: 58

Stanley C. Morse, *President*

Meade Instruments Corp
6001 Oak Canyon
Irvine, CA 92620
949-451-1450
Web Address: www.meade.com
Number of Employees: 260

Steve Murdock, *President*
Kristen Sumwalt, *Human Resources Manager*

MEC Analytical Systems
2433 Impala Drive
Carlsbad, CA 92008
760-931-8081
Web Address: www.mecanalytical.com
Number of Employees: 30

Arthur Barnett, *President*
Terri Sartor, *Controller*

Medata
801 Park Center Drive
Santa Ana, CA 92705-3526
714-953-1770
Web Address: www.medata.com
Number of Employees: 50

Constantine Callas, *President*
Becky Wendt, *Human Resources Manager*

MEI -Marcel Electronics Intl
130 West Bristol Lane
Orange, CA 92865-2637
714-974-8590
Web Address: www.marcelelec.com
Number of Employees: 115

Jack Evans, *President*

Memory Direct
7911 Professional Circle
Huntington Beach, CA 92648-1901
714-848-5958
Number of Employees: 35

James Marks, *President*
Steve Lane, *Human Resources Manager*

Metcalf & Eddy
701 B Street, Suite 1100
San Diego, CA 92101
619-233-7855
Web Address: www.m-e.com
Number of Employees: 30

Charles E. Pound, *Senior Vice President*

Mettler Electronics Corp
1333 South Claudina Street
Anaheim, CA 92805-6266
714-533-2221
Web Address: www.mettlerelec.com
Number of Employees: 55

Stephen C. Mettler, *President*
Suzanne Davis-Kowhal, *Human Resources Manager*

MGV International
29B Technology Drive #100
Irvine, CA 92618-2302
949-453-1965
Web Address: www.mgvgroup.com
Number of Employees: 100

Marco Ganona, *CEO*
Teresa Sisson, *Human Resources Manager*

Michael Brandman Associates
17310 Red Hill Avenue, Suite 250
Irvine, CA 92614-5642
949-250-5555
Web Address: www.brandman.com
Number of Employees: 30

Michael Brandman, *President*

MICOM Communications Corporation
4100 Los Angeles Avenue
Simi Valley, CA 93063
805-583-8600
Web Address: www.micom.com

Micro Express
1811 Kaiser Avenue
Irvine, CA 92614-5707
949-852-1400
Web Address: www.microexpress.net
Number of Employees: 25

Art Afshar, *President*

Microcadam
355 South Grand Avenue, Suite 2300
Suite 2300
Los Angeles, CA 90071
213-613-2300
Number of Employees: 60

Hiroshi Hara, *President*
Janice Heisler, *Manager of Administration*

MicroNet Technology
80 Technology Drive
Irvine, CA 92618-2301
949-453-6000
Web Address: www.micronet.com
Number of Employees: 82

Gene Sherman, *Human Resources Manager*

Microsemi Corporation
2830 South Fairview Street
Santa Ana, CA 92704
714-979-8220
Web Address: www.microsemi.com
Number of Employees: 539

Philip Frey Jr., *President*
James M. Thomas, *Director of Personnel*

Microsoft Corporation
3 Park Plaza, Suite 1800
Irvine, CA 92614-8541
949-263-0200
Job Hotline: 800-892-3181
Web Address: www.microsoft.com
Number of Employees: 65

Dave Bery, *Manager*
Jeff Bank, *Human Resources Manager*

Mintie Corp.
1114 San Fernando Road
Los Angeles, CA 90065
213-225-4111
Number of Employees: 126

Kevin Mintie, *CEO*
Colleen Cook, *Office Manager*

Mission Geoscience
1000 Quail Street, Suite 200
Newport Beach, CA 92660-2721
949-955-9086
Web Address: www.cerfnet.com
Number of Employees: 15
James R. Ashby, *President*
Abigail Abbott, *Human Resources*

Mitsubishi Electronics America
5665 Plaza Drive
Cypress, CA 90630-0007
714-220-2500
Job Hotline: 714-229-6565
Web Address: www.mea.com
Number of Employees: 300
Debbie Fudge, *Human Resources Manager*
Thelma Toribio, *Hiring Contact*

Modulink
105 North Pointe Drive
Lake Forest, CA 92630
714-859-3333
Number of Employees: 40
Ernest Shin, *President*
Helen Song, *Human Resources Manager*

Molecular Simulations
9685 Scranton Road
San Diego, CA 92121
619-458-9990
Web Address: solutions@msi.com

Mick Savage, *President*

Monarch Marking Systems
249 West Baywood Avenue, Suite A
Orange, CA 92865-2617
800-543-6650
Number of Employees: 2100

Therese Simpson, *Manager*

Monitoring Automation Systems
101 Academy, Suite 100
Irvine, CA 92612-3000
949-733-7800
Web Address: www.monauto.com
Number of Employees: 55

Steven Keefer, *President*

Monroe Systems for Business
10618 South Shoemaker
Santa Fe Springs, CA 90670
714-955-3181
Job Hotline: 562-946-5678
Web Address: www.monroe-systems.com
Number of Employees: 200

David Zuniga, *President*

Montgomery Watson
300 North Lake Avenue, Suite 1200
Pasadena, CA 91101
626-796-9141
Web Address: www.mw.com
Number of Employees: 375

Murli Tolaney, *CEO*
Gary Melillo, *Human Resources Director*

Mooney and Associates
9903-B Businesspark Avenue
San Diego, CA 92131
619-578-8964
Number of Employees: 30
Brian F. Mooney, *Senior Principal*

MOST
11205 Knott Avenue, Suite B
Cypress, CA 90630-5491
714-898-9400
Number of Employees: 145
Yas Yamazaki, *President*

MPI Technologies
4952 Warner Avenue, Suite 301
Huntington Beach, CA 92649-5506
714-840-8077
Web Address: www.mpitech.com
Number of Employees: 6
Michel Isti, *Manager*

MRV Communications
20415 Nordhoff
Chatsworth, CA 91311
818-773-9044
Web Address: www.nbase.com
Number of Employees: 54

Noam Lotan, *President*
Edmund Glazer, *Director of Personnel*
Maker of high speed network switching and fiber-optic transmission systems for data and telecommunications networks. Sells Ethernet LAN switches, hubs, fiber-optics, and related equipment for voice, data, and video transmissions.

MTI Technology Corporation
4905 East La Palma Avenue
Anaheim, CA 92807
714-970-0300
Web Address: www.mti.com
Number of Employees: 511

Earl M. Pearlman, *President*
Kathie Nichols, *Director of Personnel*
Provider of high-performance data storage products, including RAID -redundant array of independent disks- systems, high-performance storage servers that manage the recording and retrieval of data, tape library systems, and software to manage data and data storage equipment.

Multilayer Technology
16 Hammond
Irvine, CA 92618-1606
949-951-3388
Web Address: www.multek.com
Number of Employees: 1700

Tom Soderquist, *Human Resources Manager*

Murrietta Circuits
4761 East Hunter Avenue
Anaheim, CA 92807-1940
714-970-2430
Web Address: www.murrietta.com
Number of Employees: 100

Albert Murrietta, *President*
Monica Gallegos, *Human Resources Manager*

MySite
5830 Oberlin Drive, Suite 300
San Diego, CA 92121
619-625-2001
Web Address: sales@mysite.net

Bryan Hertz, *CEO*

Nadek Computer Systems
18818 Teller Avenue, Suite 100
Irvine, CA 92612-1679
949-261-1300
Web Address: www.nadek.com
Number of Employees: 35

Richard Sudek, *President*
Richard Campbell, *Hiring Contact*

National Computer Systems
23436 Madero, Suite 100
Mission Viejo, CA 92691-2773
714-455-7000
Web Address: www.ncslink.com
Number of Employees: 150

Roseann Frett, *Vice President*
Janice Chandler, *Human Resources Manager*

National Steel & Shipbuilding Co.
Harbor Drive & 28th Street
San Diego, CA 92113
619-544-3400
Job Hotline: 619-544-8512
Web Address: www.nasco.com
Number of Employees: 5,000

Fred Hallett, *CFO*

National Technical Systems
24007 Ventura Boulevard, Suite 200
Calabasas, CA 91302
818-591-0776
Web Address: www.ntscorp.com
Number of Employees: 449

Jack Lin, *President*
Linda Freeman, *Director of Personnel*
Provider of analysis, engineering, and testing equipment for motor vehicles, missiles, nuclear power, communications, and other products. Also provides technical staffing and ISO 9000 evaluation.

NCCS
2600 Michelson Drive, 17th Floor
Irvine, CA 92612-1550
949-553-1077
Web Address: www.nccs.com
Number of Employees: 20
Donald F. Schultz, *President*

NCS
23461 South Pointe Drive, Suite 200
Laguna Hills, CA 92653-1523
714-768-6000
Web Address: www.ncslink.com
Number of Employees: 75
Russell Gullotti, *President*

NCS -National Computer Systems
20 Centerpointe Drive
La Palma, CA 90623-2505
714-521-3830
Web Address: www.ncs.om
Number of Employees: 2700
Dwight Jereszek, *Manager*

Net Manage
31 Technology Drive, 2nd Floor
Irvine, CA 92618-2322
949-753-0800
Web Address: www.aharmony.com
Number of Employees: 100
Carol Carson, *Human Resources Manager*
Ruth Hughes, *Hiring Contact*

Netad Systems
6755 Mira Mesa Boulevard, Suite 123-288
San Diego, CA 92121
619-231-3773
Web Address: weast@netadsys.com

Robert East, *CEO*

Netwood Communications
11718 Barrington Court, Suite 301
Los Angeles, CA 90049
310-442-1530
Web Address: www.netwood.net
Jonas Fornander, *Manager of Human Resources*

Network Associates
1970 South Santa Cruz Street
Anaheim, CA 92805-6814
714-939-9188
Web Address: www.nai.com
Number of Employees: 15

Christine Quinlan, *Manager*

Network Intensive
8001 Irvine Center Drive, Suite 1200
Irvine, CA 92618-2933
949-450-8400
Web Address: www.ni.net
Number of Employees: 45

Edward Milstein, *President*

New Boston Systems
4400 Macarthur Boulevard, Suite 160
Newport Beach, CA 92660-2032
949-253-3050
Number of Employees: 10

Michael Mandau, *Office Manager*

New Dimension Software
18551 Von Karman Avenue #250
Irvine, CA 92612-1510
949-757-4300
Web Address: www.ndsoft.com
Number of Employees: 102

Dalia Prashker, *President*
Elaine Johnson, *Human Resources Manager*

New Media Corporation
1 Technology Drive Building A
Irvine, CA 92618-2350
949-453-0100
Web Address: www.newmediacorp.com
Number of Employees: 30

Carl Perkins, *President*
Kim Novak, *Human Resources Manager*

NewCom
31166 Via Colinas
Westlake Village, CA 91362
818-597-3200
Web Address: www.newcominc.com

Number of Employees: 73
Sultan W. Khan, *President*
Christine Lewis, *Director of Personnel*
Provider of modems and other communications products under the names NewCom, NewTalk, and WebPal. Also produces multimedia products including CD-ROM drives and sound cards.

NewGen Imaging Systems
3545 Cadillac Avenue
Costa Mesa, CA 92626-1401
949-641-8600
Web Address: www.newgen.com
Number of Employees: 20

Robin Poei, *Manager*

Newport Corporation
1791 Deere Avenue
Irvine, CA 92714
949-863-3144
Web Address: www.newport.com
Number of Employees: 500

Robert G. Duester, *President*
Ingrid Stern, *Director of Personnel*
Designer, producer, and marketer of instruments and electronic devices used by scientists, researchers, and precision manufacturers.

Newport Optical Laboratories
1633 Monrovia Avenue
Costa Mesa, CA 92627-4404
949-642-9776
Number of Employees: 40

Ray Larsen, *President*

Nexgen SI
30 Corporate Park, Suite 410
Irvine, CA 92606-5133
949-476-4097
Web Address: www.nexgensi.com
Number of Employees: 100

A Rick Dutta, *President*

Nextel Communication
770 The City Drive, Suite 1100
Orange, CA 92868
714-740-6500
Web Address: www.nextel.com

Nichols Research Corporation
3919 Westerly Pl
Newport Beach, CA 92660-2308
949-476-0800
Web Address: www.nichols.com
Number of Employees: 15

Greg McNeal, *Manager*

Ninyo & Moore
9272 Jeronimo Road, Suite 123A
Irvine, CA 92618-1914
949-472-5444
Web Address: www.ninyoandmoore.com
Number of Employees: 45
Wanda Hamilton, *Office Manager*

Ninyo & Moore
10225 Barnes Canyon Road, Suite A-112
San Diego, CA 92121
619-457-0400
Web Address: www.ninyoandmoore.com
Number of Employees: 350

Steven C. Geyer, *Principal Engineer*

Nova Logic
26010 Mureau Road, Suite 200
Calabasas, CA 91302
818-880-1997
Web Address: www.novalogic.com
Number of Employees: 65

John Garcia, *President*
Kathy Hafton, *Director of Personnel*

Novadyne Computer Systems
17771 Cowan
Irvine, CA 92614-6009
949-685-6100
Number of Employees: 750

Beverly Mattson, *Human Resources*

Novell
18101 Von Karman Avenue, Suite 500
Irvine, CA 92612-1033
949-474-2800
Web Address: www.novell.com
Number of Employees: 12

Cody Leger, *District Manager*

Nupon Computing
18102 South 3rd Street
Fountain Valley, CA 92708-4425
714-258-8622
Number of Employees: 52

Craig Lee, *President*

ObjectShare
16811 Hale Avenue
Irvine, CA 92606-5020
949-833-1122
Web Address: www.objectshare.com
Number of Employees: 169

Eugene L. Goda, *President*
Lisa Malkoff, *Director of Personnel*
Supplier of object-oriented applications development tools for
client/server applications. Also provides customer support, on-site
assistance, and training. Major clients include Electronic Data
Systems and Andersen Consulting.

OC Alphanetics
2102 West Chestnut Avenue
Santa Ana, CA 92703-4306
714-647-9750
Web Address: www.alphanetics.com
Number of Employees: 80

Francisco Lopez, *President*
Jose Lopez, *Human Resources Manager*

OCE' Printing
2530 East Cerritos Avenue
Anaheim, CA 92806-5627
714-979-2240
Web Address: www.oceprinting.com
Number of Employees: 45

Tim Crosson, *Manager*

Odetics
1515 South Manchester Avenue
Anaheim, CA 92802-2907
714-774-5000
Web Address: www.odetics.com
Number of Employees: 400

Joel Slutzky, *CEO*
Cathy Steger, *Director of Personnel*

Office Mate Software
16 Technology Drive, Suite 100
Irvine, CA 92618-2323
949-727-7080
Number of Employees: 18

Larry Roth, *President*

Ogden Environmental & Energy Services Co.
5510 Morehouse Drive
San Diego, CA 92121
619-458-9044
Web Address: www.ogdensfo.com
Number of Employees: 130

Donna J. McClay, *Vice President*
Larry Schou, *Human Resource Manager*

OMB Electrical Engineers
23412 Moulton Parkway, Suite 230
Laguna Hills, CA 92653-1732
714-830-1552
Number of Employees: 31

Jeffrey C. Overmyer, *Principal*

OnVillage Communications
26135 Mureau Road, Suite100
Calabasas, CA 91302
818-871-2800
Web Address: www.onvillage.com
Number of Employees: 23

Jack B. Tracht, *President*
Barbara Harper, *Director of Personnel*
A development stage company providing access to Internet
information as well as business advertising. Its primary product is
On'Village Yellow Pages, a national online no-fee directory that
contains more than 15 million business listings.

Optical Laser
5702 Bolsa Avenue, Suite 100
Huntington Beach, CA 92649
714-379-4400
Web Address: www.opticallaser.com
Number of Employees: 50
Michael Raab, *President*

Optimal Integrated Solutions
2260 Rutherford Road, Suite 105,#C
Carlsbad, CA 92008
760-431-6858
Web Address: www.optimalis.net
Number of Employees: 25

Ayman Suleiman, *CEO*

OPTUM Software
3330 Harbor Boulevard
Costa Mesa, CA 92626-1502
949-557-9050
Web Address: www.optum.com
Number of Employees: 165

Bill Grun, *President*
Paula Mann, *Human Resources Manager*

Oracle Corporation
600 Anton Boulevard
Costa Mesa, CA 92626-7147
949-444-8300
Web Address: www.us.oracle.com
Number of Employees: 28,000

Fran Brace, *Manager*

Orange County Restaurant Services
17320 Red Hill Avenue, Suite 190
Irvine, CA 92614-5644
949-851-9047
Number of Employees: 30

Ronald F Higgins, *President*

Orange Micro
1400 North Lakeview Avenue
Anaheim, CA 92807-1896
714-779-2772
Web Address: www.macph.com
Number of Employees: 30

Arthur Scotten, *President*

OrCad
16275 Laguna Canyon Road
Irvine, CA 92618-1624
949-770-3022
Web Address: www.orcad.com
Number of Employees: 100

Michael Bosworth, *President*
Sarah Christian, *Human Resources Manager*

Ortel Corporation
2015 West Chestnut Street
Alhambra, CA 91803
818-281-3636
Web Address: www.ortel.com

Osicom Technologies
2800 28th Avenue
Santa Monica, CA 90405
310-581-4030
Job Hotline: 858-558-3960

Web Address: www.osicom.com
Number of Employees: 15
Par Chadha, *CEO*

Oster & Associates
6225 Lusk Boulevard
San Diego, CA 92110
619-535-8101
Number of Employees: 8

Beverly Oster, *CEO*

OWEN Group
19700 Fairchild, Suite 200
Irvine, CA 92612-2514
949-756-0202
Web Address: www.owengroup.com
Number of Employees: 20

Michael Chegini, *Principal*
Shobeh Noori, *Human Resources*

P&D Consultants
999 Town & Country Road, 4th Floor
Orange, CA 92868
714-835-4447
Web Address: www.cte-eng.com
Number of Employees: 60

John L. Kinley, *President*
Grace Alexander, *Human Resources*

P&D Consultants/CTE Engineers
401 West A Street, Suite 2500
San Diego, CA 92101
619-232-4466
Number of Employees: 25

Chuck Moore, *Vice President*
Grace Alexandra, *Human Resource Director*

Pacer Infotec
3621 South Harbor Boulevard, Suite 250
Santa Ana, CA 92704-6950
714-549-0460
Number of Employees: 700

Pacer Infotec
16490 Harbor Boulevard, Suite A
Fountain Valley, CA 92708-1375
714-418-0204
Number of Employees: 700

Pacific Bell
17310 Red Hill Avenue, Suite 270
Irvine, CA 92614
949-440-6640
Web Address: www.pacbell.com

Pacific Net
19725 Sherman Way, Suite 395
Canoga Park, CA 91306
818-717-99500
Web Address: www.pacificnet.net

Pacific Scientific Co
620 Newport Center Drive, Suite 700
Newport Beach, CA 92660-8007
949-720-1714
Number of Employees: 2600

David Schlotterbeck, *President & CEO*
Thomas Griffith, *Human Resources Director*

Pacific Ship Repair & Fabrication
1625 Rigel Street
San Diego, CA 92113
619-232-3200
Job Hotline: 619-232-2300 x125
Number of Employees: 140

David Bain, *President*
Kathy Livingston, *Human Resource Manager*

PairGain Technologies
14402 Franklin Avenue
Tustin, CA 92780
714-832-9922
Web Address: www.pairgain.com
Number of Employees: 700

Charles S. Strauch, *CEO*
Charles W. McBrayer, *CFO*
S. Straight, *Hiring Contact*
Supplier of telecommunications equipment that allows copper telephone lines to transmit high-speed digital data, providing a cost-effective alternative to fiber optics while allowing services such as high-speed Internet access.

Palomar Systems
2310 Aldergrove Avenue
Escondido, CA 92029
760-741-9717
Web Address: www.elcsci.com
Number of Employees: 250

Robert Belter, *CEO*
Rich Tamburro, *Human Resources Director*

Parsons Transportation Group
2 Venture, Suite 550
Irvine, CA 92618-3335
949-453-1619
Web Address: www.parsons.com
Number of Employees: 250
Gary Adams, *Office Manager*

Parsons Transportation Group
2 Venture, Suite 250
Irvine, CA 92618-3335
949-453-0220
Web Address: www.parsons.com
Number of Employees: 1100

Pentadyne-Pentaflex
711 Fee Ana Street
Placentia, CA 92870-6706
714-528-6200
Web Address: www.pentadyne-pentaflex.com
Number of Employees: 50
Manu Patolia, *CEO*

Perceptronics
21010 Erwin Street
Woodland Hills, CA 91367
818-884-7470
Web Address: www.perceptronics.com
Number of Employees: 20

Richard Vestewig, *President*
Robert Anderson, *Director of Personnel*
Producer and marketer of computer simulations for training and decision support. Products are used in training for military and commercial equipment, vehicles, and weapons. They are also used for command and control, process modeling, and electronic products development.

Perkin-Elmer/West Coast Optics
1751 Kettering
Irvine, CA 92614-5665
949-261-5562
Number of Employees: 38

Donald Sirney, *Manager*
Bonnie Quiggle, *Human Resources Manager*

Phase One
85 Argonaut, Suite 190
Aliso Viejo, CA 92656-4105
714-457-0097
Web Address: www.phase1.com
Number of Employees: 17

Eric Kieselbach, *President*

Phoenix Technologies Ltd.
135 Technology Drive
Irvine, CA 92618-2402
949-790-2000
Web Address: www.phoenix.com
Number of Employees: 250

Stephanie Earli, *Manager*

Photo Research
9330 DeSoto Avenue
Chatsworth, CA 91311
818-341-5151
Web Address: www.photoresearch.com
Number of Employees: 39

Francis Dominic, *President*
Terri Thomas, *Director of Personnel*
The largest maker of photometers in the world. Its products are used to develop aircraft and automotive instruments and lights, movie screens, flat panel displays and CRTs, as well as in astronomical measurements and human factors testing.

Pick Systems
1691 Browning
Irvine, CA 92606-4896
949-261-7425
Web Address: www.picksys.com.
Number of Employees: 115

George Olenick, *President*
Marilyn De Angelis, *Human Resources Manager*

Pico Products

12500 Foothill Boulevard
Lakeview Terrace, CA 91342
818-897-0028
Web Address: www.piconet.com

Picofarad

237 North Euclid Way, Suite D
Anaheim, CA 92801-6768
714-533-3880
Number of Employees: 75
Henry Carr, *President*
Frank Lindquist, *Human Resources Manager*

Pinnacle Micro

19 Technology Drive
Irvine, CA 92718
949-789-3000
Web Address: www.pinnaclemicro.com
Number of Employees: 25
William F. Blum, *President*
Chuck McGee, *Director of Personnel*

Pioneer Circuits

3000 South Shannon Street
Santa Ana, CA 92704-6387
714-641-3132
Web Address: www.pioneercircuits.com
Number of Employees: 150
James Lee, *President*

Plaid Brothers Software

20 Corporate Park, Suite 300
Irvine, CA 92606-5103
949-261-7255
Web Address: www.plaid.com
Number of Employees: 80
Franks Peters, *President*

Plastship Logistics Intl

2719 White Road
Irvine, CA 92614-6261
949-221-0200
Web Address: www.plastship.com
Number of Employees: 20

C. Eugene Cook II, *Chairman*
Charlotte Newman, *Human Resources Manager*

Platinum Software Corporation

195 Technology Drive
Irvine, CA 92618-2402
949-453-4000
Web Address: www.platsoft.com
Number of Employees: 600
L. George Klaus, *President*
Nancy Orr, *Director of Personnel*
Carol Pearson, *Human Resources Manager*

Platinum Software Corporation

195 Technology Drive
Irvine, CA 92618
949-453-4000
Web Address: www.platsoft.com

Popov Engineers

19800 Macarthur Boulevard
Irvine, CA 92612-2421
949-752-0121
Number of Employees: 20

T. Robert Popov, *President*
Diane Popov, *Human Resources*

Powell Internet Consulting

2105 Garnet Avenue, Suite E
San Diego, CA 92109
619-270-2086
Web Address: info@pint.com
Number of Employees: 12

Thomas Powell, *President*
Fran Weisser, *Human Resource Director*

Power Circuits

2645 South Croddy Way
Santa Ana, CA 92704-5290
714-241-0303
Web Address: www.powerckts.com
Number of Employees: 200

James Eisenberg, *President*
Pat Schrage, *Human Resources Manager*

Power Plus!

1281 East Sunshine Way
Anaheim, CA 92806-1759
714-764-0020
Number of Employees: 180

Cathy Economy, *Human Resources Director*

Powerwave Technologies

2026 McGaw Avenue
Irvine, CA 92614
949-757-0530
Web Address: www.powerwave.com
Number of Employees: 442

Bruce C. Edwards, *President*
Mark Winters, *Director of Personnel*
Cheryl Hayes, *Human Resources Manager*
Designer and manufacturer of ultra-linear radio frequency power amplifiers used in wireless communication networks, including cellular, PCS, and air-to-ground networks.

Precision Glass & Optics

3600 West Moore Avenue
Santa Ana, CA 92704-6835
714-540-0126
Web Address: www.precision-glass.com
Number of Employees: 40

Dan Bukaty, *President*

Precision Optical Company

869 West 17th Street
Costa Mesa, CA 92627-4336
949-631-6800
Number of Employees: 75
Allen M. Lambert, *President*
Rod Randolph, *Hiring Contact*

Precision Wholesale
1430 Village Way, Suite K
Santa Ana, CA 92705-4752
714-547-9500
Number of Employees: 30

Michael Dixon, *President*
Randy Hein, *Human Resources Manager*

Presto-Tek Corporation
2229 South Yale Street
Santa Ana, CA 92704-4426
714-540-5346
Web Address: www.newportinc.com
Number of Employees: 30

Preston Scientific
1180 North Blue Gum Street
Anaheim, CA 92806-2409
714-632-3700
Number of Employees: 15

Bernard Spear, *President*

Princeton Technology
2552 White Road
Irvine, CA 92614-6236
949-851-7776
Number of Employees: 35

Nasir Javed, *President*
Dinyar Irani, *Human Resources Manager*

Printrak International
1250 North Tustin Avenue
Anaheim, CA 92807
714-238-2000
Web Address: www.printrakinternational.com
Number of Employees: 200

Richard M. Giles, *President*
Jan Peterson, *Director of Personnel*
Leah Gazaway, *Hiring Contact*

Printronix
17500 Cartwright Road
Irvine, CA 92623-9559
949-863-1900
Job Hotline: 714-221-2828
Web Address: www.printronix.com/
Number of Employees: 866

Robert A. Kleist, *President*
Juli A. Mathews, *Director of Personnel*

Prism Software
23696 Birtcher
Lake Forest, CA 92630-1769
714-855-3100
Web Address: www.prism-software.com
Number of Employees: 18

Ted Daniels, *CEO*
Dee Sharler, *Human Resources Manager*

Pro-Tech
17371 Mount Wynne Circle
Fountain Valley, CA 92708-4107
714-641-8786
Number of Employees: 125

Charles McGarry, *President*
Tom Ford, *Human Resources Manager*

Procom Technology
2181 Dupont Drive
Irvine, CA 92612
949-852-1000
Job Hotline: 714-852-1000 x5999
Web Address: www.procom.com
Number of Employees: 246

Alex Razmjoo, *President*
Atashe Aydin, *Director of Personnel*
Supplier of CD-ROM-based computer storage products. Also makes RAID -redundant arrays of independent disks- and tape backup subsystems and hard disk drive upgrade packages.

Productivity Enhancement Products
26072 Merit Circle, Suite 110
Laguna Hills, CA 92653-7015
714-348-1011
Web Address: www.pepinc.com
Number of Employees: 35

Dan Beadle, *President*
Tris Moery, *Human Resources*

Professional Service Industries
3960 Gilman Street
Long Beach, CA 90815
562-597-3977
Web Address: www.psi.com
Number of Employees: 20

Michael Mooradian, *VP*
Martin Falk, *District Manager*

Progen Technology
15501 Red Hill Avenue
Tustin, CA 92780-7302
714-566-9200
Web Address: www.progen.com
Number of Employees: 100

Jesse Lin, *President*

Provision Computers
212 Technology Drive, Suite L
Irvine, CA 92618-2418
949-453-0453
Number of Employees: 20
Ben Nejad, *President*

PSIMED Corporation
1221 East Dyer Road, Suite 260
Santa Ana, CA 92705-5635
714-979-7653
Web Address: www.psi-med.com
Number of Employees: 42
Vansel Johnson, *President*

HIGH-TECH

PsiTech

18368 Bandilier Circle
Fountain Valley, CA 92708-7001
714-964-7818
Web Address: www.primenet.com/~psitech
Number of Employees: 15

Clive Towndrow, *President*
Alice Shaw, *Personnel Manager*

Pullman Industrial Systems

23052 Alcalde Drive #A
Laguna Hills, CA 92653-1327
714-855-7510
Number of Employees: 25

Stephen Lutz, *President*

Pulse Engineering

12220 World Trade Drive
San Diego, CA 92128
619-674-8100
Web Address: www.pulseeng.com
Number of Employees: 215

John Kowalski, *CEO*
Sheila Ricks, *Human Resource Director*

Puroflow Incorporated

16559 Saticoy
Van Nuys, CA 91406
818-756-1388
Web Address: www.puroflow.com
Number of Employees: 75

Mike Figoff, *President*
Sandy Yoshisato, *Director of Personnel*

Pyramid Optical Corporation

10871 Forbes Avenue
Garden Grove, CA 92843-4978
714-265-1100
Number of Employees: 53

Takashi Imura, *President*
Lau Nguyen, *Hiring Contact*

Q-Com

17782 Cowan #A
Irvine, CA 92614-6012
949-833-1000
Number of Employees: 21

Fred Kaiser, *President*

QLogic

3545 Harbor Boulevard
Costa Mesa, CA 92626
949-438-2200
Web Address: www.qlc.com
Number of Employees: 250
H. K. Desai, *President*
Tim Ashcroft, *Director of Personnel*
Developer, manufacturer, and marketer of IC and adapter cards
used to connect peripheral devices to computer systems. Also
produces target and disk controller chips used to control inside
peripherals.

QuadraMed Corp.

20955 Warner Center Lane
Woodland Hills, CA 91367
818-598-3200
Web Address: www.quadramed.com
Number of Employees: 96

Fred Rothenberg, *President*
Marc Slipty, *Director of Human Resources*

Quality Systems

17822 East 17th Street, Suite 210
Tustin, CA 92680
714-731-7171
Web Address: www.qsii.com
Number of Employees: 110

Robert G. McGraw, *Vice President*
Ray Mead, *Director of Personnel*
System integrators for healthcare industry; software development.
Markets computerized information processing systems to medical
and dental group practices, PHOs -physician hospital
organizations-, MSOs -management service organizations-, and
HMOs -health maintenance organizations-.

Qualtech Backplane

2649 Campus Drive
Irvine, CA 92612-1601
949-660-4967
Number of Employees: 55

Steve Boot, *President*

Quest Software

610 Newport Center Drive, Suite 1400
Newport Beach, CA 92660-6465
949-720-1434
Web Address: www.quests.com
Number of Employees: 130

David Doyle, *President*
Amada Zapata, *Human Resources Manager*

QuickStart Technologies

1500 Quail Street, 6th Floor
Newport Beach, CA 92660-2732
949-476-7575
Web Address: www.quickstart.com
Number of Employees: 84

Mitchell Argon, *President*
Bill Crane, *Human Resources Manager*

Radian International

16845 Von Karman Avenue #100
Irvine, CA 92606-4920
949-261-8611
Web Address: www.radian.com
Number of Employees: 35

Anne Pena, *Office Manager*

Radiant Technology Corporation

1335 South Acacia Avenue
Fullerton, CA 92831
714-991-0200
Web Address: www.radianttech.com

Number of Employees: 50
Lawrence R. McNamee, *CEO*
Sandra Constable, *Director of Personnel*
Manufacturer and servicer of precision thermal processing systems, including conveyor belt-equiped furnaces and ovens, for manufacturers of electronic components. AMD accounts for about 35% of the firm's sales.

Radyne ComStream Corporation
6340 Sequence
San Diego, CA 92121
858-458-1800
Web Address: www.raydynecomstream.com
Mark Steinman, *CEO*
Fred Lawrence, *President*

Rainbow Technologies
50 Technology Drive
Irvine, CA 92618-
949-450-7300
Web Address: www.rainbow.com
Number of Employees: 150
Walter W. Straub, *President*
Cheryl Baffa, *Director of Personnel*
Manufacturer of software protection and encryption technology for the secure exchange of electronically distributed information. The company markets its products to software publishers including Microsoft, Aldus, and Microfocus for use with software programs selling at retail for $600 or more.

Rainbow Technologies
50 Technology Drive, W
Irvine, CA 92618
949-450-7300
Web Address: www.rainbow.com

Ram Optical Instrumentation
1791 Deer Avenue
Irvine, CA 92606
949-863-0221
Web Address: www.ramoptical.com
Number of Employees: 75

Rational Software Corporation
10 Pasteur
Irvine, CA 92618-3815
949-788-6220
Web Address: www.rational.com
Number of Employees: 550

RECON
4241 Jutland Drive, Suite 201
San Diego, CA 92117
619-270-5066
Number of Employees: 40
Charles S. Bull, *President*

Reedex
15526 Commerce Lane
Huntington Beach, CA 92649-1602
714-894-0311
Web Address: www.robust.com/reedex
Number of Employees: 40
Dan Reed, *President*
Kathy Reed, *Hiring Contact*

Relsys International
16267 Laguna Canyon Road
Irvine, CA 92619-0700
949-453-1715
Web Address: www.relsys-inc.com
Number of Employees: 80

Dave Bajaj, *President*

REMEC
9404 Chesapeake Drive
San Diego, CA 92123
858-560-1301
Web Address: www.remec.com
Number of Employees: 931

Ronald E. Ragland, *CEO*

Research Engineers
22700 Savi Ranch Parkway
Yorba Linda, CA 92687
714-974-2500
Web Address: www.reiusa.com
Number of Employees: 60

Amrit K. Das, *President*
Clara Young, *Director of Personnel*
Maker of stand-alone and network-based engineering software for architectural, transportation, and utility industries. It specializes in structural analysis and design software -STAAD III- and makes other Windows-based software for mechanical, civil, and pipe engineers.

RF Electronics
20432 Barents Sea Circle
Lake Forest, CA 92630
714-583-0808
Number of Employees: 22
R. Fred Webb, *President & CEO*
Brian Marriott, *Hiring Contact*

Risk Data Corporation
111 Pacifica, 3rd Floor
Irvine, CA 92618-3310
949-753-8010
Web Address: www.riskdata.com
Number of Employees: 95
Sean Downs, *President & CEO*

Robert Bein William Frost & Associates
14725 Alton Parkway
Irvine, CA 92618
949-472-3505
Web Address: www.rbf.com
Number of Employees: 400
S. Robert Kallenbaugh, *President*
Doug Frost, *Accounting Manager*

Rock Industries
5402 Commercial Drive
Huntington Beach, CA 92649-1232
714-891-1750
Number of Employees: 33
Charles Gifford, *President*
Vicki Morey, *Human Resources Manager*

343

Rockwell Automation/Software
25381 Groveside Lane
Lake Forest, CA 92630-2706
714-586-1571
Web Address: www.rockwell.com
Number of Employees: 25000

Rockwell International Corporation
600 Anton Boulevard, Suite 700
Costa Mesa, CA 92626-7147
949-424-4200
Web Address: www.rockwell.com
Number of Employees: 45000
Don H. Davis Jr., *President*
Joel R. Stone, *Director of Personnel*
World's #1 maker of microchips and chip sets for fax, voice, and data modems, and one of the world's largest industrial automation companies. Supplier of programmable controllers, worker-machine interface devices, industrial motors, and power transmission products.

Rockwell Semiconductor Systems
4311 Jamboree Road
Newport Beach, CA 92660-3007
949-221-4600
Web Address: www.rockwell.com
Number of Employees: 2,000

Dwight D. Decker, *President*
William C. Tipton, *VP for Human Resources*

Rohr/BF Goodrich Aerospace
850 Lagoon Drive
Chula Vista, CA 91910
619-691-4111
Job Hotline: 619-691-3022
Web Address: www.rhor.com

Robert H. Rau, *President*

ROI Systems
949 South Coast Drive, Suite 405
Costa Mesa, CA 92626-7733
949-434-0425
Web Address: www.roisysinc.com
Number of Employees: 14

Bob Garbutt, *Vice President*

Ross Systems
220 West Crest Street
Escondido, CA 92025
760-745-6006
Web Address: www.rossinc.com
Number of Employees: 20

Bryce G. Hodgson, VP, *GM for Asia*

Router Solutions
180 Newport Center Drive, Suite 240
Newport Beach, CA 92660-6915
949-721-1017
Web Address: www.rsi-inc.com
Number of Employees: 20

Dennis Webster, *General Manager*

Routerware
3961 Macarthur Boulevard, Suite 212
Newport Beach, CA 92660-3016
949-442-0770
Web Address: www.routerware.com
Number of Employees: 20

Ross L. Wheeler, *President*

Russell Information Sciences
35 Journey
Aliso Viejo, CA 92656-3333
714-362-4000
Web Address: www.russellinfo.com
Number of Employees: 25

Richard Russell, *President*

Rust Environment Infrastructure
17671 Cowan, Suite 150
Irvine, CA 92614
949-251-6400
Number of Employees: 20

Sophia Ramirez, *Office Manager*

Sabtech Industries
PO Box 1132
Yorba Linda, CA 92885-1132
714-692-3800
Web Address: www.sabtec.com
Number of Employees: 30

Rahim Sabadia, *President*
Nafees Batool, *Human Resources Manager*

Safety Components International
3190 Pullman Street
Costa Mesa, CA 92626
949-662-7756
Web Address: www.safetycomponents.com
Number of Employees: 200

Robert A. Zummo, *President*
Robert Cauble, *Human Resources Manager*
Global manufacturer of automotive air bags and supplier of a wide range of military ordnance products. Its automotive division makes air bags for General Motors, Ford, Chrysler, Toyota, Mazda, Volkswagen, and Audi.

Sage Software
56 Technology Drive
Irvine, CA 92618
949-753-1222
Web Address: www.sota.com

SAIC Internet Solutions
10260 Campus Point Drive
San Diego, CA 92121
858-546-6022
Web Address: www.saic.com
Number of Employees: 3500

Steve Hutchinson, *Manager*

SAS Institute
5 Park Plaza, Suite 900
Irvine, CA 92614-8527
949-852-8550
Job Hotline: 919-677-8000
Web Address: www.sas.com
Number of Employees: 25

Chris Hansen, *Regional Manager*

Saunders/MHP
3151 Airway Avenue, Suite N1
Costa Mesa, CA 92626-4626
949-540-7033
Number of Employees: 23

Scantron Corporation
1361 Valencia Avenue
Tustin, CA 92780-6463
714-247-2700
Web Address: www.scantron.com
Number of Employees: 230

Tom Hoag, *President*
Sherri Cox, *Human Resources Manager*

Scope Industries
233 Wilshire Boulevard
Santa Monica, CA 90401
310-458-1574
Number of Employees: 14

Meyer Luskin, *CEO*
Eleanor Smith, *Controller & Human Resource Manager*

Scrantom Engineering
3550 Cadillac Avenue
Costa Mesa, CA 92626-1415
949-979-6373
Number of Employees: 72

Charles Q. Scrantom, *President*
Heidi MacPherson, *Human Resources Manager*

SCS Engineers
3711 Long Beach Boulevard, Ninth Floor
Ninth Floor
Long Beach, CA 90807
562-426-9544
Web Address: www.scseng.com
Number of Employees: 74

Robert Stearns, *CEO & President*
Elayne Welch, *Director of Human Resources*

Seagate Technology/Recording Media
3845 East Coronado Street
Anaheim, CA 92807-1606
714-630-7573
Web Address: www.seagate.com
Number of Employees: 1,200

Jody Spence, *Director*
Kim Gardner, *Human Resouces Manager*

Seagate Technology/Tape Operations
1650 Sunflower Avenue
Costa Mesa, CA 92626-1513
949-641-1230
Web Address: www.seagate.com
Number of Employees: 400

Steve Shoda, *Human Resources Director*

SECOR International
2655 Camino del Rio North, Suite 302
San Diego, CA 92108
619-296-6195
Job Hotline: 619-525-5151
Number of Employees: 30

Craig Smith, *Principal*
Margartie Shuffleton, *Human Resource Director*

Secure Communication Systems
1507 East McFadden Avenue
Santa Ana, CA 92705-4307
714-547-1174
Web Address: www.securecomm.com
Number of Employees: 45

Allen B. Ronk, *President*
Nancy Rank, *Human Resources Manager*

Seimens Nixdorf Information Systems
2532 East Cerritos Avenue
Anaheim, CA 92806-5627
714-938-1212
Web Address: www.intranet.sni-usa.com
Number of Employees: 120

Select Software Tools
19600 Fairchild, Suite 350
Irvine, CA 92612-2511
949-477-4100
Web Address: www.selectst.com
Number of Employees: 53

Ed Holt, *President*
Stuart Frost, *Human Resources Director*

SEMCOR
7170 Convoy Court
San Diego, CA 92111
619-560-7233
Web Address: www.semcor.com
Number of Employees: 90

Paul Maynard, Director, *Southern California Ops.*
Tony Shea, *Human Resource Director*

Semi-Kinetics
22822 Granite Way #C
Laguna Hills, CA 92653-1203
714-830-7364
Number of Employees: 107

Rick Gonzalez, *President*
Thone Phaxayaseng, *Human Resources Manager*

HIGH-TECH

Semicoa
333 McCormick Avenue
Costa Mesa, CA 92626-3479
949-979-1900
Web Address: www.semicoa.com
Number of Employees: 100

Mark Kalatsky, *President*
Tricia Luna, *Human Resources Manager*

Semiconductor Components
1353 East Edinger Avenue
Santa Ana, CA 92705-4430
714-547-6059
Number of Employees: 20

A L Brainard, *President*

Sensorex
11661 Seaboard Circle
Stanton, CA 90680-3427
714-895-4344
Web Address: www.sensorex.com
Number of Employees: 36

Ted McCarthy, *President*

Sensotron
5881 Engineer Drive
Huntington Beach, CA 92649-1127
714-893-1514
Number of Employees: 35

Armen Sahagen, *CEO*

SGS Thomson Microelectonics
16350 West Bernardo Drive
San Diego, CA 92127
619-485-8900
Number of Employees: 215

Jack Mendenhall, *CEO*

SGS Thomson Microelectronics
3 Hutton Centre Drive, Suite 850
Santa Ana, CA 92707-8703
714-957-6018
Web Address: www.st.com
Number of Employees: 14000

Mike Yousef, *Manager*

Sharp Digital Information Prod
5901 Bolsa Avenue
Huntington Beach, CA 92647-2053
714-903-5000
Web Address: www.sharpsdi.com
Number of Employees: 35

Shopping.com
2101 East Coast Highway, Garden Level
Corona Del Mar, CA 92625
949-640-4393
Web Address: www.shopping.com/ss/default.asp
Number of Employees: 44

Robert J. McNulty, *President*
Michael Miramontes, *Director of Personnel*
A 24-hour, Internet-based, discount shopping mall. The company sells a wide variety of products and services at wholesale prices through its Web site, which integrates order placement, secure payment verification, inventory control, order fulfillment, and vendor invoicing.

Sidon Data Systems
2030 Main Street, 11th Floor
Irvine, CA 92614-7219
949-553-1131
Number of Employees: 20

Wael Cory, *President*

Siemens Pyramid Information Systems
100 Pacifica, Suite 160
Irvine, CA 92618-3319
949-453-3950
Web Address: www.pyramid.com
Number of Employees: 1200

Sigma Circuits
3300 Irvine Avenue, Suite 120
Newport Beach, CA 92660-3115
949-440-8123
Number of Employees: 400

Silicon Graphics Computer Systems
18201 Von Karman Avenue, Suite 100
Irvine, CA 92612-1005
949-852-1980
Web Address: www.sgi.com
Number of Employees: 30

Ron Rathman, *General Manager*

Silicon Systems
14351 Myford Road
Tustin, CA 92781-2020
714-573-6000
Web Address: www.ssil.com
Number of Employees: 550

Rick Goerner, *President*
John Holtrust, *VP for Human Resources*

Simons Li & Associates
3150 Bristol Street, Suite 500
Costa Mesa, CA 92626-3067
949-250-6788
Web Address: www.simonsli.com
Number of Employees: 47

Ruh-Ming Li, *President*
Chad Phillips, *Human Resources*

Simple Technology
3001 Daimler Street
Santa Ana, CA 92705
714-476-1180
Web Address: www.simpletech.com
Number of Employees: 300

Mike Moshnayedi, *President*
Kathy Herold, *Director of Personnel*

SimpleNet
225 Broadway, 13th Floor
San Diego, CA 92101
619-453-6511
Web Address: www.simplenet.com
Number of Employees: 30

Robert W. Bingham, *CEO*
Brian Pollard, *Human Resource Manager*

Simulation Sciences
601 Valencia Avenue, Suite 100
Brea, CA 92823
714-579-0412
Web Address: www.simsci.com
Number of Employees: 260

Charles R. Harris, *President*
Daniel T. Nichols, *Director of Personnel*
Kathy Murphy, *Human Resources Manager*

Sitelab International
2223 Avenida de la Playa, Suite 208
La Jolla, CA 92037
619-456-4720
Number of Employees: 8

Vic Spindler, *CEO*
Marlene Matheson, *Senior Accountant*

Smartek Educational Technology
7908 Convoy Court
San Diego, CA 92111
619-565-8068
Web Address: www.wordsmart.com
Number of Employees: 24

David Kay, *President*
Mike McMahan, *Sales Manager*

Smartflex Systems
14312 Franklin Avenue
Tustin, CA 92680
714-838-8737
Web Address: www.smartflex.com
Number of Employees: 1006

William L. Healey, *President*
Cheryl Moreno, *Director of Personnel*
Designer of turnkey flexible interconnect assembly manufacturing systems to producers of electronic products. It sells to OEMs such as Hewlett-Packard, Maxtor, and Quantum.

Smith Micro Software
51 Columbia
Aliso Viejo, CA 92656
714-362-5800
Web Address: www.smithmicro.com
Number of Employees: 89

William W. Smith Jr., *President*
Christine Gonzales, *Director of Personnel*
The leading provider of communication software to modem manufacturers. Its QuickLink line of data/fax software is bundled with modems from U.S. Robotics, Practical Peripherals, IBM, Hayes Microcomputer Products, Motorola, AT&T, and GVC.

Smith-Emery GeoServices
791 East Washington Boulevard
Los Angeles, CA 90021
213-745-5333
Number of Employees: 41

Scott Pearson, *Manager*

SMK Electronics Corp USA
625 Fee Ana Street
Placentia, CA 92870-6782
714-996-0960
Web Address: www.smkusa.com
Number of Employees: 62

Carol Ramsey, *Human Resources Manager*

SMT Dynamics Corp
1551 South Harris Court
Anaheim, CA 92806-5932
714-938-0133
Web Address: www.smtblackfox.com
Number of Employees: 213

Ann Lovell, *Human Resources Manager*

SMT Electronics
11820 Western Avenue
Stanton, CA 90680-3438
714-821-7393
Number of Employees: 40

Henry Tran, *Owner*

Smyth Systems
7 Mason
Irvine, CA 92618-2799
949-859-8888
Number of Employees: 28

Larry Smyth, *Manager*

Software Technologies Corp.
PO Box 661090
Arcadia, CA 91066
626-471-6000
Number of Employees: 128

James Demitriades, *President*

Soldermask
17905 Metzler Lane
Huntington Beach, CA 92647-6258
714-842-1987
Web Address: www.soldermask.com
Number of Employees: 22

Ruth Kurisu, *President*
Frank Kurisu, *Human Resources Manager*

Soligen Technologies
19408 Londelius Street
Northridge, CA 91324
818-718-1221
Web Address: www.PartsNow.com
Number of Employees: 60
Yehoram Uziel, *CEO*
Donna Shattuck, *Director of Personnel*
Manufacturer of proprietary systems to generate ceramic casting molds for metal parts and tooling equipment. Its products are use in aerospace, automotive, metal die casting, and plastic injection molding industries.

Somerset Automation
18301 Von Karman Avenue, Suite 500
Irvine, CA 92612-1009
949-260-0600
Web Address: www.somersetwms.com
Number of Employees: 30
Mike Brewer, *President*
Doug Lada, *Human Resources Manager*

Sony Technology Center
16450 West Bernardo Drive
San Diego, CA 92127
619-487-8500
Web Address: www.sgo.sony.com
Number of Employees: 4,400
Tadakatsu Hasebe, *CEO*

Source Diversified
22961 Triton Way, Suite G
Laguna Hills, CA 92653-1230
714-380-4891
Web Address: www.sourced.com
Number of Employees: 25
Alfred Ortiz, *President*

Southland Micro Systems
7 Morgan
Irvine, CA 92718
949-380-1958
Web Address: www.southlandmicro.com
Number of Employees: 300
John Meehan, *President*
Connie Cole, *Director of Personnel*

Space Applications Corp/Information Systems Division
200 Sandpointe Avenue, Suite 300
Santa Ana, CA 92707-5751
714-434-4200
Web Address: www.spaceapps.com
Number of Employees: 200

Sparta
23041 Avenue De La Carlota #325
Laguna Hills, CA 92653-1545
714-768-8161
Web Address: www.sparta.com
Number of Employees: 40
Wayne Winton, *CEO*
Debbie Henigan, *Human Resources*

Spatializer Audio Laboratories
20700 Ventura Boulevard, Suite 134
Woodland Hills, CA 91364-2357
818-227-3370
Web Address: www.spatializer.com
Number of Employees: 40
Steven D. Gershick, *President*
Scott Saso, *Controller*

Special Devices
16830 West Placentia Canyon Road
Newhall, CA 91321
805-259-0753
Web Address: www.specialdevises.aol.com
Number of Employees: 600
Thomas F. Treinen, *Chairman & President*
Arlene Balmadrid, *Human Resources Specialist*

Speedy Circuits
5292 System Drive
Huntington Beach, CA 92649-1527
714-891-9441
Web Address: www.speedycircuits.com
Number of Employees: 70
Peter Casson, *President*

Spicer America Corp
23591 El Toro Road, Suite 213
Lake Forest, CA 92630-4760
714-251-9277
Number of Employees: 100

Sprint Corporation
1025 West 190th Street, Suite 400
Gardena, CA 90248
310-515-5353
Job Hotline: 650-513-2000
Web Address: www.sprint.com

SRS Labs
2909 Daimler Street
Santa Ana, CA 92705
714-442-1070
Web Address: www.srslabs.com
Number of Employees: 27
Steven Sedmark, *President*
Nicole Morell, *Director of Personnel*
Developer of immersive audio technologies that create 3D sounds using 2 conventional speakers. Its technology has been licensed to Apple, Kenwood, Sony and others, for use in TVs, stereos, PCs, professional sound systems, and arcade and video games.

SRS Technologies
1811 Quail Street
Newport Beach, CA 92660
949-852-6900
Web Address: www.srs.com
Number of Employees: 18

M. S. Sandhu, *President*
Connie Campanile, *Human Resources Manager*

StarBase Corporation
18872 MacArthur Boulevard, Suite 300
Irvine, CA 92612-1441
949-442-4400
Web Address: www.starbase.com
Number of Employees: 77

Donald R Farrow, *President*

State of the Art
56 Technology Drive
Irvine, CA 92618-2301
949-753-1222
Job Hotline: 714-759-1222 x4080
Web Address: www.sota.com
Number of Employees: 360

David Hanna, *President*
Kelly Henry, *Human Resources Director*
Charlotte Robertson, *Recruiter*

Storage Concepts
2652 McGaw Avenue
Irvine, CA 92614-5840
949-852-8511
Web Address: www.storageconcepts.com
Number of Employees: 40

James Lizzio, *President*

Storage Technology Corp
2030 Main Street, Suite 1400
Irvine, CA 92614-7240
949-622-5151
Web Address: www.stortek.com
Number of Employees: 10500

Stracon
1672 Kaiser Avenue #1
Irvine, CA 92614-5700
949-851-2288
Number of Employees: 50

Son Pham, *President*

Structural Research & Analysis Corp.
12121 Wilshire Boulevard, Suite 700
Los Angeles, CA 90025
310-207-2800
Web Address: www.cosmosm.com
Number of Employees: 55

V. I. Weingarten, *President*
Jeff Hangen, *Human Resource Manager*

Subscriber Computing
18881 Von Karman Avenue, Suite 450
Irvine, CA 92612-1561
949-260-1500
Web Address: www.subscriber.com
Number of Employees: 160

Dennis Andrews, *CEO*
Judy Ell, *Human Resources Manager*

Sun Microsystems Computer Corp
1920 Main Street, Suite 500
Irvine, CA 92614-7225
949-833-1640
Web Address: www.sun.com
Number of Employees: 50

Marla Kopycki, *Administrative Manager*

Super Circuits
1217 Wakeham Avenue
Santa Ana, CA 92705
714-558-7528
Number of Employees: 37

Sterling R. Haight, *Owner*

Super Computer
5980 Lakeshore Drive
Cypress, CA 90630-3371
714-826-9680
Number of Employees: 15

Steven Chen, *Owner*
Sean Taniwaki, *Sales Manager*

Superior Manufacturing Co
3133 West Harvard Street
Santa Ana, CA 92704-3912
714-540-4605
Web Address: www.laxmigroup.com
Number of Employees: 250

Raymond Fung, *President*
Caroline Chain, *Human Resources Manager*

Sverdrup Corp
675 Anton Boulevard #400
Costa Mesa, CA 92626-1919
949-549-5050
Number of Employees: 5,000

Christine Lundren, *Office Manager*

Symbios Logic
3300 Irvine Avenue, Suite 255
Newport Beach, CA 92660-3107
949-474-7095
Web Address: www.symbios.com
Number of Employees: 17

Symbol Technologies
340 Fischer Avenue
Costa Mesa, CA 92626-4523
949-549-6000
Web Address: www.symbol.com
Number of Employees: 115

Christopher Vroman, *Head of Facilities*

Symitar Systems
5151 Murphy Canyon Road, Suite 300
San Diego, CA 92123
619-576-0946
Web Address: www.symitar.com

Manny Prupes, *President*

349

Sync Research
40 Parker
Irvine, CA 92718
949-588-2070
Web Address: www.sync.com
Number of Employees: 190

John H. Rademaker, *Vice Chairman*
Joan Gosewisch, *Human Resources Director*

SYS Technology
6481 Global Drive
Cypress, CA 90630-5227
714-821-3900
Web Address: www.systechnology.com
Number of Employees: 35

William Yen, *President*

Syspro Impact Software
959 South Coat Drive, Suite 100
Costa Mesa, CA 92626
949-437-1000
Web Address: www.sysprousa.com
Number of Employees: 150

Brian Stein, *President*

Systems & Software
18012 Cowan, Suite 100
Irvine, CA 92614-6809
949-833-1700
Web Address: www.kaiwan.com/nssi/ssi.htmd
Number of Employees: 25

Y P Chien, *President*

T-HQ
5016 North Parkway Calabasas, Suite 100
Calabasas, CA 91302
818-591-1310
Web Address: www.thq.com
Number of Employees: 48
Brian J. Farrell, *President*
Mary N. Garrett, *Director of Personnel*
Maker of video games for Nintendo, Sony, and SEGA systems. T-HQ's games are designed internally or by developers under contract to T-HQ. Titles include Olympic Summer Games, Disney's Toy Story, Madden '97 Football, Sim City 2000, and Super Return of the Jedi.

Tait & Associates
1100 Town & Country Road, Suite 1200
Orange, CA 92868
714-560-8200
Web Address: www.tait.com
Number of Employees: 70
Tom Tait, *President*

Tanner Research
2650 East Foothill
Pasadena, CA 91107
626-792-3000
Web Address: www.tanner.com
Number of Employees: 90
John Tanner, *President*
Linda Tanner, *Director of Human Resources*

Tayco Engineering
10874 Hope Street
Cypress, CA 90630-0034
714-952-2240
Web Address: www.taycoeng.com
Number of Employees: 160

Charles Taylor, *President*
Eddie Cline, *Human Resources Manager*

TCI Management
17752 Sky Park Circle, Suite 160
Irvine, CA 92614-6419
949-476-1122
Web Address: www.tcisolutions.com
Number of Employees: 15

Lance Jacobs, *President*

Techmedia Computer Systems Corporation
7301 Orangewood Avenue
Garden Grove, CA 92841
714-379-6677
Web Address: www.techmedia.net
Number of Employees: 100

Andrew H. Park, *President*
Pam Scott, *Director of Personnel*
Computer equipment maker and reseller. Operates worldwide and resells imported monitors, computers, and peripherals, and also assembles its own desktop computers for business and consumers in its California plant.

Technical Aid Corporation
17782 17th Street, Suite 103
Tustin, CA 92780-1947
617-969-3100
Number of Employees: 900

Technologic Software
4199 Campus Drive, Suite 400
Irvine, CA 92612-2698
949-509-5000
Web Address: www.technologic.com
Number of Employees: 80

Tom Politowski, *President & GM*

TEG/LVI Environmental
4710 South Eastern Avenue
Los Angeles, CA 90040
213-726-9696
Number of Employees: 350

M. Canessa, *Principal*
Kathy Taylor, *Human Resources Manager*

Teglvi
4710 South Eastern Avenue
Los Angeles, CA 90040
562-944-8971
Number of Employees: 200

Mark Canessa, *VP*

Tekelec
26580 West Agoura Road
Calabasas, CA 91302
818-880-5656
Web Address: www.tekelec.com
Number of Employees: 367

Michael L. Margolis, *President*
Scott Gardner, *Director of Personnel*
Designer and manufacturer of advanced communications diagnostic systems and network switching equipment. Its products are sold to telephone companies, communications manufacturers, and government agencies through direct sales and distributors including AT&T.

Tektronix/Color Printing
27 Technology Drive #110
Irvine, CA 92618-2302
949-789-7200
Web Address: www.tek.com
Number of Employees: 65

Jerry Myer, *CEO*

Telecom Solutions
20162 Windrow Drive
Lake Forest, CA 92630-8115
714-597-0100
Web Address: www.tsiusa.com
Number of Employees: 75

Amrik S. Podnian, *President*
Sheila Ollar, *Human Resources Manager*

Teletronic Laboratories
5502 Engineer Drive
Huntington Beach, CA 92649-11??
310-715-6946
Number of Employees: 32

Pablo Aguayo, *President*

Terranext
11235 Knott Avenue, Suite B
Cypress, CA 90630-5494
714-890-9133
Number of Employees: 200

Tetra Tech
591 Camino de la Reina, Suite 640
San Diego, CA 92108
619-718-9676
Web Address: www.tetratech.com
Number of Employees: 32

Roger Argus, *Area Manager*
Heather Davidson, *Human Resource Manager*

The Austin Company
27 Technology Drive
Irvine, CA 92618-2302
949-453-1000
Job Hotline: 949-453-1000 x263
Number of Employees: 110

Donna Dillon, *Human Resources*

The Cerplex Group
1382 Bell Avenue
Tustin, CA 92780
714-258-5600
Web Address: www.cerplex.com
Number of Employees: 2100

Robert P. Bunce, *Human Resources Manager*
Repairer of electronic equipment including computers, peripherals, and printed circuit board assemblies. Provides outsourced repair for OEMs such as computer companies Digital Equipment, IBM, Spectravision, and Sun Microsystems, and 3rd-party maintenance organizations such as Novadyne.

The Flamemaster Corporation
11120 Sherman Way
Sun Valley, CA 91352
818-982-1650
Web Address: www.flamemaster.com
Number of Employees: 26

Joseph Mazin, *President*
Maker of flame-retardant and heat-resistant coatings and sealants. Its products are used in aircraft fuel tanks, pressurized crew compartments, and on marine vessels. Largest customer is US General Services Administration.

The Laxmi Group
7777 Center Avenue, Suite 410
Huntington Beach, CA 92647-3067
714-903-5676
Job Hotline: 714-903-5676 x211
Web Address: www.laxmigroup.com
Number of Employees: 80

Shankar N Ram, *President*
Amy Day, *Office Manager*

The Lee Company
7711 Center Avenue, Suite 625
Huntington Beach, CA 92647-3076
714-899-2177
Number of Employees: 4

Kent Burlinson, *Manager*

The MacNeal-Schwendler Corp
2975 Red Hill Avenue
Costa Mesa, CA 92626-5923
949-540-8900
Web Address: www.macsch.com
Number of Employees: 500

Tom Curry, *President*

The Park Corporation
5360 East Hunter Avenue
Anaheim, CA 92807-2049
714-777-1001
Web Address: www.parkenv.com
Number of Employees: 20

Rick Caporale, *President*

The Planning Center
1300 Dove Street, Suite 100
Newport Beach, CA 92660-2415
949-851-9444
Web Address: www.planningcenter.com
Number of Employees: 28
Richard Ramella, *President*
Janette Caprario, *Human Resources*

Thermeon Corporation
12241 Newport Avenue
Santa Ana, CA 92705-3288
714-731-9191
Job Hotline: 800-232-9191
Number of Employees: 21
Scott L. Sampson, *President*
Sharon Miller, *Vice President of Operations*

Tivoli Industries
1513 East Saint Gertrude Place
Santa Ana, CA 92705
714-957-6101
Number of Employees: 90
Terrence C. Walsh, *President*
Margaret Lundberg, *Director of Personnel*
Maker of lighting for specialty applications including theaters,
casinos, aircraft, theme parks, and construction projects. Its
products include low-voltage tube lighting, marine and vehicular
lighting, and energy-efficient lamps.

Tone Software Corporation
1735 South Brookhurst Street
Anaheim, CA 92804-6491
714-991-9460
Web Address: www.tonesoft.com
Number of Employees: 75
John W. Hutchison, *President*
Shannon Holmes, *Director of Personnel*

Toshiba America Info Systems
9740 Irvine Boulevard
Irvine, CA 92618
949-583-3000
Job Hotline: 949-461-4949
Web Address: www.toshiba.com
Number of Employees: 2,000
Atsutoshi Nishida, *President*
Hitomi Mishinaka, *Human Resources Director*
Manufacturer of personal and desktop computers, telecommunica-
tion products, disk drive products, copiers and faxes. Also provides
systems integration, desktop engineering software development;
engineering services.

TouchStone Software Corporation
2124 Main Street, Suite 250
Huntington Beach, CA 92648
714-969-7746
Web Address: www.checkit.com
Number of Employees: 50
Larry Jordan, *President*
Shan Dabiri, *Director of Personnel*
Doreen Ritchie, *Human Resources Manager*
Developer and publisher of software used to set up and maintain
PCs. The company's products include anti-virus program,

FastMove! file transfer program-, CheckIt Diagnostic Kit and
WINCheckIt -troubleshooting utilities, and e-Support electronic
technical support network.

Tracer Environmental Sciences & Tech.
970 Los Vallecitos Boulevard, Suite 100
San Marcos, CA 92069
760-744-9611
Web Address: tjrapp@tracer-est.com
Number of Employees: 15
Thomas J. Rappolt, *President*
Jennie Koo, *Office Manager*

Trandes Corp.
9630 Ridgehaven Court, Suite A
San Diego, CA 92123
619-268-4930
Number of Employees: 130

Tom Armstedt, *Vice President*
Karen Steed, *Human Resource Manager*

Transitional Technology
5401 East La Palma Avenue
Anaheim, CA 92807-2064
714-693-1133
Web Address: www.ttech.com
Number of Employees: 55

Ernie Wassmann, *President*
Terry Glumb, *Human Resources*

TRC Environmental Solutions
21 Technology Drive, Suite 100
Irvine, CA 92618-2335
949-727-9336
Web Address: www.treesi.com
Number of Employees: 80

Richard Ellison, *President*

Tri-Star Engineered Products
351 Thor Pl
Brea, CA 92821-4133
714-671-1545
Web Address: www.tri-star-epi.com
Number of Employees: 45

James G. Natzke, *President*

TRI/Data Technologies
3940 Hancock Street
San Diego, CA 92110
619-223-5303

Scott Thornton, *CEO*

Triconex Corp
15091 Bake Parkway
Irvine, CA 92618-2501
949-768-3709
Web Address: www.triconex.com
Number of Employees: 150

H. Carr Wells, *President*
Kimberly Crowell, *Human Resources Manager*

Trident Micro Systems
17951 Lyons Circle
Huntington Beach, CA 92647-7167
714-843-9300
Number of Employees: 24

David Anderson, *President*

Trimedyne
2801 Barranca Road
Irvine, CA 92606
949-559-5300
Number of Employees: 100

Marvin Loeb, *President*
Kinair Thomas, *Human Resources Manager*

Trio-Tech International
355 Parkside Drive
San Fernando, CA 91340
818-365-9200
Web Address: www.triotech.com
Number of Employees: 40

Siew W. Yong, *President*
Maria Chittim, *Director of Personnel*
Producer of test equipment, including centrifuges, burn-in systems, and temperature sensors, for semiconductors. Its customers are IC manufacturers including Hyundai, AMD, Motorola, and Texas Instruments, with the majority of revenues coming from the Pacific Rim.

TriTeal Corp.
2011 Palomar Airport Road, Suite 200
Carlsbad, CA 92009
760-930-2077
Job Hotline: 760-827-5509
Web Address: www.triteal.com
Number of Employees: 70

Jeff Witous, President, *Chairman*
Darcy Lynn, *Director of Human Resources*

Trivec-Avant Corp
17831 Jamestown Lane
Huntington Beach, CA 92647-7136
714-841-4976
Number of Employees: 20

Dennis Freund, *President*

Tustin Electronics Company
1580 North Kellogg Drive
Anaheim, CA 92807-1902
714-777-5800
Number of Employees: 10

John R. Taylor, *President*

UCSD Office of Contract and Grant Administration
9500 Gilman Drive, Dept. 0934
La Jolla, CA 92137
619-534-3330

Robert C. Dynes, *Chancellor*

Ultra Media
6161 El Cajon Boulevard, Suite 24
San Diego, CA 92115
619-582-2172

Unique Business Systems Corp.
2901 Ocean Park Boulevard, Suite 215
Santa Monica, CA 90405
310-396-3929
Number of Employees: 50

Ravi Khatod, *National Sales Manager*
Ike Arshadi, *Executive VP*

Unisys Corporation
25725 Jeronimo Road
Mission Viejo, CA 92691-2792
714-380-5000
Web Address: www.unisys.com
Number of Employees: 1,500

Dick Ulmer, *Manager*

Unisys Corporation
25725 Jeronimo Road
Mission Viejo, CA 92691
949-380-5000
Web Address: www.unisys.com

Unit Instruments
22600 Savi Ranch Parkway
Yorba Linda, CA 92887-7027
714-921-2640
Web Address: www.unit.com
Number of Employees: 403

Michael J. Doyle, *President*
Kathryn S. Tricoli, *Director of Personnel*
Manufacturer of process control equipment. Designs and makes mass flow controllers used to precisely measure and control gas flow during the manufacturing of ICs and other semiconductor wafer fabrication equipment.

Unitech Research
100 Pacifica, Suite 450
Irvine, CA 92618-3322
949-753-1511
Web Address: www.unitech.com
Number of Employees: 35

Koichi Yokota, *President*

United Circuit Technology
18101 Mount Washington Street
Fountain Valley, CA 92708-6120
714-979-1561
Number of Employees: 45
Craig Johnson, *President*
Anita Johnson, *Human Resources Manager*

United Environmental Technologies
9838 Joe Vargas Way, Suite C
South El Monte, CA 91733
626-279-2380
Number of Employees: 100
Mary Fichter, *President*

HIGH-TECH

Universal Circuits
2249 South Yale Street
Santa Ana, CA 92704-4426
714-540-3936
Number of Employees: 103

Hal Krohn, *General Manager*

URS Greiner
1241 East Dyer Road, Suite 250
Santa Ana, CA 92705-5611
714-556-9260
Number of Employees: 50

John Masek, *Office Manager*

US Sensor Corp
1832 West Collins Avenue
Orange, CA 92867-5425
714-639-1000
Web Address: www.ussensor.com
Number of Employees: 50

Roger Dankert, *President*

V3I Engineering
24843 Del Prado, Suite 475
Dana Point, CA 92629-2852
949-248-2644
Web Address: www.v3i.com
Number of Employees: 55

Susan Torres, *President*

VAL Circuits
2221 South Anne Street
Santa Ana, CA 92704-4410
714-556-6190
Number of Employees: 60

Jess Valverde, *President*

Van Dell & Associates
17801 Cartwright Road
Irvine, CA 92614-6251
949-474-1400
Number of Employees: 30

J. E. Van Dell, *President*

Vanguard Technology
18 Technology Drive, Suite 109
Irvine, CA 92618-2309
949-453-0119
Web Address: www.vanguard.com
Number of Employees: 4

Jim Wilson, *Regional Manager*

Velie Circuits
1267 Logan Avenue
Costa Mesa, CA 92626-4098
949-751-4994
Web Address: www.velie.com
Number of Employees: 120

Larry Velie, *President*

Verio
8001 Irvine Center Drive, Suite 1200
Irvine, CA 92618
949-450-8400
Web Address: www.socal.verio.net

Vidya Media Ventures
110 West Lewis Street
San Diego, CA 92103
619-683-2624
Kim Roberts, *CEO*

Viking Components
30200 Avenida De Las Banderas
Rch Santa Margarita, CA 92688
714-643-7255
Web Address: www.vikingcomponents.com
Number of Employees: 470
Glen McCusker, *President*
Kerri Brechbiel, *Director of Personnel*

Virgin Interactive Entertainment
18061 Fitch
Irvine, CA 92614-6018
949-833-8710
Web Address: www.vie.com
Number of Employees: 200
Martin Alper, *President*

Virtual Advantage
6046 Cornerstone Court West, Suite 216
San Diego, CA 92121
619-457-3307

Vis-A'Vis Communications
18010 Sky Park Circle, Suite 155
Irvine, CA 92614-6440
949-789-5251
Web Address: www.weedpuller.com
Number of Employees: 30

Robert Allison, *President*

VisiCom Laboratories
10052 Mesa Ridge Court
San Diego, CA 92121
619-457-2111
Web Address: www.visicom.com
Number of Employees: 100
Clifton Cooke, *President*
Rob Babbush, *Human Resource Director*

Vision Solutions
17911 VonKarman
Irvine, CA 92612
949-724-5455
Web Address: www.visionsolutions.com
Number of Employees: 100
Chris Turner, *President*
Pam Schuller, *Hiring Contact*
Developer, supporter, and marketer of software for use in high
systems availability, data warehousing, and Internet and system
clustering. The company's customers have included Upjohn, UPS,
and Toyota.

VitalCom
15222 Del Amo Avenue
Tustin, CA 92780
714-546-0147
Web Address: www.vitalcom.com
Number of Employees: 200

Frank T. Sample, *President*
Albert G. Sack, *Director of Personnel*
Provider of communications networks that acquire, interpret, and distribute real-time physiologic data generated by point-of-care patient monitors located throughout a health care facility. VitalCom's products are sold to acute-care hospitals, integrated healthcare delivery networks, and OEMs.

Voice Powered Technology International
18425 Burbank Boulevard, Suite 506
Tarzana, CA 91356
818-757-1100
Web Address: www.vpti.com
Number of Employees: 12

Mitchell B. Rubin, *President*
Ellie Shams, *Director of Personnel*
Developer and seller of low-cost voice recognition and voice activated products.

Volt Delta Resources
2401 North Glassell
Orange, CA 92865
714-921-8000
Web Address: www.volt.com
Number of Employees: 200

Ingrid Kutschal, *Personnel Manager*

Wahlco Environmental Systems
3600 West Segerstrom Avenue
Santa Ana, CA 92704-6495
714-979-7300
Web Address: www.wahlco.com
Number of Employees: 75

Steven Beal, *President*
Anne L. Anderson, *Director of Personnel*
Designer, manufacturer, and marketer of air pollution control and power plant efficiency equipment. It also provides combined cycle gas turbine products and related services to electric utilities, independent power producers, cogeneration plants, and industrial manufacturers around the world.

Wang Laboratories
3150 Bristol Street, Suite 170
Costa Mesa, CA 92626-3067
949-825-1000
Number of Employees: 6500

Waste Management
9081 Tujunga Avenue
Sun Valley, CA 91352
818-767-6180
Number of Employees: 800

Greg Loughnane, *General Manager*
Michael Servantes, *Director of Personnel*

Watson General Corp.
32 Mauchly, Suite B
Irvine, CA 92618-2336
949-986-8011
Web Address: www.wgen.com
Number of Employees: 50

Ronald Crane, *President & CEO*

Wavefunction
18401 Von Karman Avenue, Suite 370
Irvine, CA 92612-1542
949-955-2120
Web Address: www.wavefun.com
Number of Employees: 20

Warren J. Hehre, *President*
Shawn Butler, *Human Resources Manager*

WebAssist
3453 Ingraham Street, Suite 530
San Diego, CA 92109
619-272-5599

Neal Hansch, *CEO*

WebNetworks International
5414 Oberlin Drive, Suite 220
San Diego, CA 92121
619-646-7070
Number of Employees: 13

Eric Wormser, *CEO*
Andrew Harby, *Hiring Contact*

Wesco Services
14712 Franklin Avenue, Suite F
Tustin, CA 92780-7223
714-832-8797
Number of Employees: 2

Larry Kinsela, *Owner*

Western Data Systems
26707 Agoura Road, Suite 200
Calabasas, CA 91302
818-880-0800
Web Address: www.westdata.com
Number of Employees: 190

Anton Rodde, *President*
Trudy Hadala, *Director of Human Resources*

Western Digital Corporation
8105 Irvine Center Drive
Irvine, CA 92718
949-932-5000
Web Address: www.westerndigital.com
Number of Employees: 13507

Charles A. Haggerty, *President*
Jack Van Berkel, *Director of Personnel*
One of the largest independent makers of PC hard disk drives. Operates in all three major segments of the hard drive market: desktop PCs, mobile PCs, and workstation and server/multiuser systems.

Western Digital Corporation
8105 Irvine Center Drive
Irvine, CA 92618
949-932-5000
Web Address: www.westerndigital.com

Western Micro Technology
10 Holland
Irvine, CA 92618-2504
949-206-2331
Number of Employees: 38

Bob O'Reilly, *Human Resources Manager*

Western Pacific Data Systems
7590 Fay Avenue
La Jolla, CA 92037
619-454-0028
Web Address: www.wpds.com

Margaret Jackson, *President*
Chris Berel, *Human Resource Manager*

Western Telematic
5 Sterling
Irvine, CA 92618-2517
949-586-9950
Web Address: www.wti.com
Number of Employees: 68

David L Morrison, *President*
Dottie Hansen, *Human Resources Manager*

White Horse Technologies
3211 South Shannon Street
Santa Ana, CA 92704-6352
714-438-9270
Number of Employees: 15

Amir Sardari, *President*

Whittaker Corporation
1955 North Surveyor Avenue
Simi Valley, CA 93063
805-526-5700
Web Address: www.whittaker.com

Willdan Associates
888 South West Street, Suite 300
Anaheim, CA 92802-1806
714-563-3200
Web Address: www.willdan.com
Number of Employees: 60

Dan Heil, *President*
Denise Placencia, *Human Resources Manager*

WIZ Technology
32951 Calle Perfecto
San Juan Capistrano, CA 92675
714-443-3000
Web Address: www.wiztech.com
Number of Employees: 30

Mar-Jeanne Tendler, *President*
Carmen Walsh, *Director of Personnel*

Supplier of low-cost computer software for home and small-business use, and intranet software for retailers, wholesalers, and OEMs. More than 85% of WIZ's sales go to eight customers, including CompUSA, Ingram-Micro, Slash, and ADTI.

Wonderware Corporation
100 Technology Drive
Irvine, CA 92618
949-727-3200
Job Hotline: 714-727-3200 x7901
Web Address: www.wonderware.com
Number of Employees: 443

Roy H. Slavin, *President*
Teresa Horton, *Director of Personnel*
Provider of industrial automation software for Windows. Its products provide dynamic, graphical representations of physical processes in a factory. Its biggest customers are as Coca-Cola, Mercedes-Benz -its largest end-use customer-, Nestle, and Texaco.

Woodward-Clyde Intl -Americas
2020 East 1st Street, Suite 400
Santa Ana, CA 92705-4032
714-835-6886
Web Address: www.wcc.com
Number of Employees: 125

John A Barneich, *Principal*
Hazel Boyd, *Human Resources Manager*

World Library
PO Box 19625
Irvine, CA 92623-9625
949-424-5100
Number of Employees: 30

William Hustwit, *President*

Worldwide/Web Spinners
4669 Murphy Canyon Road, Suite 204
San Diego, CA 92123
619-292-7706

Greg Wolf, *CEO*

Wyle Electronics
15370 Barranca Parkway
Irvine, CA 92618
949-753-9953
Web Address: www.wyle.com
Number of Employees: 1600
Mike Rohleder, *President*
Marketer of electronics products such as semiconductors, electric components, and computer systems. It stocks over 30,000 items from 50 suppliers, including Digital Equipment Corp., Intel, Motorola, and Texas Instruments.

Wynns International
500 North State College Boulevard, Suite 700
Orange, CA 92868
714-938-3700
Web Address: www.wynns.com
Number of Employees: 12
John Huber, *President*
Producer of car care products, industrial fluids, automotive chemicals, and related products for international automotive and industrial markets.

XCD
1682 Browning
Irvine, CA 92606
949-573-7055
Web Address: www.xcd.com
Number of Employees: 25

Keith Sugawara, *President*

Xicor
4100 Newport Place Drive, Suite 710
Newport Beach, CA 92660-2451
949-752-8700
Web Address: www.xicor.com
Number of Employees: 750

Xilinx
15615 Alton Parkway, Suite 280
Irvine, CA 92618-3307
949-727-0780
Web Address: www.xilinx.com
Number of Employees: 6

Melinda Reynolds, *Office Manager*

Xtend Micro Products
2 Faraday
Irvine, CA 92618-2714
949-699-1400
Web Address: www.xmpi.com
Number of Employees: 55

Mark Rappaport, *President*
Heidi Chamberlain, *Human Resources Manager*

XyberNet
10640 Scripps Ranch Boulevard
San Diego, CA 92131
619-530-1900
Web Address: www.xyber.net

Joseph Bigley, *CEO*

Xylan Corporation
26707 West Agoura Road
Calabasas, CA 91302
818-880-3500
Web Address: www.xylan.com
Number of Employees: 500

Steve Y. Kim, *President*
Andrew Jentis, *Director of Personnel*
Maker of inexpensive switches to replace hubs, bridges, and routers in communications networks. Products include OmniSwitch, AutoTracker, and OmniVision -a set of network management applications-.

Zenographics
34 Executive Park, Suite 150
Irvine, CA 92614-6721
949-851-6352
Web Address: www.zeno.com
Number of Employees: 25

Robert Romney, *President*

ZNetwork
625 Broadway, Suite 1020
San Diego, CA 92101
800-336-1862
Web Address: info@znetwork.net

Greg O. Paquette, *CEO*

ZyXEL Communications
4920 East La Palma Avenue
Anaheim, CA 92807-1912
714-693-0808
Web Address: www.zyxel.om
Number of Employees: 50

Gordon Yang, *President*
Teresa Sallamin, *Human Resources Manager*

Employment Tip

For More High-Tech

Job Sites, Visit

Job Source Network.com

Further References

• Associations •

Aerospace Industries Association of America
1250 I Street, N.W., Suite 1100
Washington, D.C. 20005
202-371-8400
Web Address: www.aia-aerospace.org
Association for Manufacturers

American Institute of Aeronautics & Astronautics
85 John Street
New York, New York 10038
212-349-1120
Web Address: www.aiaa.org
Advancement of Engineering Information

American Institute of Aeronautics & Astronauts
555 West 57th Street
New York, New York 10019
212-247-6500
Advancement of Engineering Information

Future Aviation Professionals of America
4959 Massachusetts Avenue
Atlanta, Georgia 30337
Career Planning for Industry

Information Technology Association of America
1616 North Fort Myer Drive, Suite 1300
Arlington, Virginia 22209
703-522-5055
Web Address: www.itaa.org
Companies Offering Software and Services to the Public

National Academy of Engineering
2101 Constitution Avenue, N.W.
Washington, D.C. 20418
202-334-3200
Web Address: www.nae.edu
Advises Government and Honors Excellence

National Aeronautic Association of USA
1815 North Fort Meyer Drive, Suite 700
Arlington, Virginia 22209
703-527-0226
Web Address: www.naa.ycg.org
Development of Aviation

National Society of Professional Engineers
1420 King Street
Alexandria, Virginia 22314
703-684-2800
Web Address: www.nspe.org
Society of Professional Engineers

• Publications •

Aerospace America
370 L'Enfant Promenade SW, 10th Floor
Washington, DC 20024
202-646-7400

Aviation Week & Space Technology
1120 Vermont Avenue NW, 12th Floor
Washington, DC 20005

Business & Commercial Aviation
260 Rye Brook
New York, NY 10573

Computerworld
500 Old Connecticut Path
Framingham, MA 01701
508-879-0700
Web Address: www.computerworld.com

Data Communications
1221 Avenue of the Americas
41st Floor
New York, NY 10020
212-512-2000
Web Address: www.data.com

Directory of Engineering Societies
1111 19th Street, Suite 608
Washington, D.C. 20036
202-296-2237

Directory of Engineers in Private Practice
1420 King Street
Alexandria, Virginia 22314
703-684-2800
Web Address: www.nspe.org

EDN Career News
275 Washington Street
Newton, Massachusetts 02158
617-964-3030

Engineering Times
1420 King Street
Alexandria, Virginia 22314
703-684-2800
Web Address: www.nspe.org

Information Industry Directory
835 Penobscot Building
Detroit, Michigan 48226
313-961-2242

InfoWorld
155 Bovet Road, Suite 800
San Mateo, CA 94402-3115
415-572-7341
Web Address: www.infoworld.com
A Weekly Publication.

R & D Magazine
1350 East Touhy Avenue
Des Plaines, IL 60018
847-635-8800
Reports on research and development.

Hospitality

- Catering
- Food Service
- Hotels
- Event Planning
- Resorts

A lthough many large hospitality industry companies no longer maintain the corporate management training programs that existed in the 80's, opportunities still exist for both graduates with hotel management degrees as well as those with other educational backgrounds. Individuals with previous hotel/motel/restaurant experiences may find opportunities to begin their careers in supervision while others might pursue any number of entry-level positions to act as stepping stones leading to promotional opportunities.

While the hotel industry may require flexibility in your hours of work and at times test your stamina, the rewards and opportunities toward which to work are there.

Human Resources Department
Mid-Atlantic Region
HYATT HOTELS & RESORTS

Quick Reference

Del Mar Fairgrounds
www.delmarfair.com
Disneyland Hotel
www.disneyland.com
Doubletree Hotel Anaheim/Airport
www.doubletreehotels.com
Doubletree Hotel Pasadena
www.doubletreehotel.com
Embassy Suites La Jolla
www.embassy-suites.com
Fairmont Hotel
www.fairmont.com
Hacienda Hotel
www.haciendahotel.com
Hotel Laguna
www.menubytes.com/hotellaguna
Hotel Queen Mary
www.queenmary.com
Howard Johnsons Hotel
www.hojoanaheim.com
Hyatt Newporter
www.hyatt.com
Hyatt Regency Hotels
www.hyatt.com
Irvine Marriott Hotel
www.jobshr.com
La Costa Resort, Spa and Country Club
www.lacosta.com
La Jolla Marriott
www.marriott.com
La Quinta Inn - Irvine
www.laquinta.com
Le Meridan
www.lemeridanbh.com
Loews Coronado Bay Resort
www.loewshotels.com
Marriott's Laguna Cliffs Resort
www.marriott.com

NuOasis Resorts
www.otcfn.com/nuoa
Park Hyatt Los Angeles at Century City
www.hyatt.com
Radisson Hotel
www.radisson.com
Ramada Inn - Anaheim
www.anaheimramada.com
San Diego Convention Center Corp.
www.sdccc.org
San Diego Marriott Hotels
www.marriott.com
San Diego Mission Valley Hilton
www.hilton.com
San Diego Princess Resort
www.princessresort.com/princess
Seoul Plaza Hotel
www.ramada.com
Sheraton Grande Torrey Pines
www.sheraton-tp.com
Sheraton San Diego Hotel & Marina
www.sandiego-sheraton.com
Sutton Place Hotel
www.travelweb.com/sutton.html
The Anaheim Hilton & Towers
www.hilton.com
The Atrium Hotel
www.atriumhotel.com
The Seal Beach Inn & Gardens
www.sealbeachinn.com
The Waterfront Hilton
www.hilton.com/hilton
The Westin South Coast Plaza
www.westin.com
Town & Country Resort & Conference Center
www.towncountry.com
Warner Center Marriott
www.marriot.com

Wyndham Hotel
www.wyndham.com

Company Job Hotlines
Anaheim Marriott Hotel
714-748-2482
Beverly Hilton
310-285-1340
Catamaran Resort Hotel
619-539-7733
Century Plaza Hotel & Tower
310-551-3390
Continental Plaza LA Airport Hotel
310-649-7049
Country Side Inn Suites
Costa Mesa
714-549-0300 x199
Disneyland Hotel
714-781-1600
DoubleTree Hotel/OC Airport
714-438-4963
Embassy Suites La Jolla
619-453-0400 x547
Hanalei Hotel
619-297-0268
Holiday Inn on the Bay
619-232-3861 x7766
Holiday Inn Torrance
310-781-9100 x578
Hollywood Roosevelt Hotel
213-769-7293
Hotel Inter-Continental
Los Angeles
213-356-4049
Hotel Nikko Beverly Hills
310-246-2074
Hyatt Newporter
704-759-3075
Hyatt Regency Alicante
704-740-6052

359

Quick Reference

Hyatt Regency Irvine 714-225-6716	Marina Village Conference Center 619-525-2800	San Diego Princess Resort 619-581-5902
Hyatt Regency La Jolla 619-552-6058	Marriott's Laguna Cliffs Resort 714-661-5000 x1111	Sheraton Grande Torrey Pines 619-558-8058
Hyatt Regency Long Beach 562-624-6090	Miramar Sheraton Hotel & Bungalows	Sheraton San Diego Hotel & Marina
Hyatt Regency Los Angeles 213-612-3139	310-319-3145	619-692-2793
Hyatt Regency San Diego 619-687-6000	New Otani Hotel and Garden 310-617-0368	Sutton Place Hotel 714-955-5656
International Food Service	Omni Los Angeles Hotel and Center	The Anaheim Hilton & Towers
Executives 714-846-6566	213-612-3990	714-740-4319
La Costa Resort, Spa and	Park Hyatt Los Angeles at Century City	The Atrium Hotel 714-833-2770 x448
Country Club 760-433-9675	310-284-6521	The Ritz-Carlton - Marina del Rey 310-574-4290
La Jolla Marriott	Radisson Hotel 310-348-4174	The Waterfront Hilton
619-597-6325	Radisson Wilshire Plaza Hotel	714-960-7873
Loews Coronado Bay Resort	213-368-3068	Torrance Marriott 310-792-6171
619-424-4000 x4480	Renaissance Long Beach Hotel 562-499-2518	Town & Country Resort &
Loews Santa Monica Beach Hotel 310-576-3121	Renaissance Los Angeles Hotel	Conference Center 619-299-2254
Long Beach Marriott	888-462-7746	Westin Bonaventure Hotel and
562-627-8000	San Diego Concourse 619-525-5151	Suites 213-612-4845
Los Angeles Airport Hilton &	San Diego Convention Center	Westin Horton Plaza San Diego
Towers 310-413-6111	619-525-5151	619-239-2200 x7177
Los Angeles Airport Marriott	San Diego Hilton Beach & Tennis Resort	Westin Long Beach 562-499-2056
310-621-5327	619-275-8994	Wyndham Emerald Plaza
Los Angeles Marriott Downtown	San Diego Marriott Hotel & Marina	619-515-4541
213-617-0788	619-234-1500 x8901	Wyndham Hotel at Los Angeles
Marina Beach Marriott 310-448-4850	San Diego Mission Valley Hilton 619-543-9441	Airport 310-337-6455

Anaheim Marriott Hotel
700 West Convention Way
Anaheim, CA 92802-3483
714-750-8000
Job Hotline: 714-748-2482
Web Address: www.marriott.com
Number of Employees: 800

Sharon Lockwood, *Human Resources Director*
Yolanda Quintana, *Human Resources*

Anaheim Plaza Hotel
1700 South Harbor Boulevard
Anaheim, CA 92802-2375
714-772-5900
Web Address: www.anaheimplazahotel.com
Number of Employees: 200

Raj Patel, *President & Owner*

Bahia Hotel
998 West Mission Bay Drive
San Diego, CA 92109
858-488-0551
Web Address: www.evanshotels.com
Number of Employees: 1000

Dan Fullen, *General Manager*
Carol Sullivan, *Director of Sales*
Jim Fulks, *Human Resource Director*

Bel Air Hotel
701 Stone Canyon Road
Los Angeles, CA 90077
310-472-1211
Job Hotline: Ext 570
Web Address: www.hotelbelair.com
Antoinette lara, *Human Resource Manager*

Ben Brown's Aliso Creek Inn
31106 South Coast Highway
South Laguna, CA 92677-2599
714-499-2271
Number of Employees: 75

V. T. Brown, *President*

Beverly Hilton
9876 Wilshire Boulevard
Beverly Hills, CA 90210
310-274-7777
Job Hotline: Ext 1290
Web Address: www.hilton.com
Number of Employees: 800

Peter Kretschmann, *General Manager*
Chris Crider, *General Manager*
Shawn Robertson, *Assistant General Manager*
Juana Valerio, *Human Resource Manager*

Burbank Airport Hilton & Convention Center
2500 Hollywood Boulevard
Burbank, CA 91505
818-843-6000

David Cornish, *General Manager*
Griff Gunther, *Director of Personnel*

California Restaurant Association
3435 Wilshire Boulevard, Suite 2606
Los Angeles, CA 90010
213-384-1200
Web Address: www.calrest.org

Catamaran Resort Hotel
3999 Mission Boulevard
San Diego, CA 92109
858-488-1081
Job Hotline: 858-539-7733
Number of Employees: 400

Luis Barrios, *General Manager*
Elsa Butler, *Director of Sales*
Jim Fulks, *Human Resource Director*

Century Plaza Hotel & Tower
2025 Avenue of the Stars
Los Angeles, CA 90067
310-277-2000
Job Hotline: 310-551-3311
Web Address: www.westin.com
Number of Employees: 800

Jim Petrus, *General Manager*
Edwina Morales, *Staffing Manager*
Hema Cardenas, *Human Resource Manager*

Chefs de Cuisine Association of Southern California
4580 North Figueroa Street
Los Angeles, CA 90065
818-905-1557

Continental Plaza LA Airport Hotel
9750 Airport Boulevard
Los Angeles, CA 90045
310-645-4600
Job Hotline: 310-649-7049
Number of Employees: 202

Cindy Boulton, *General Manager*

Country Side Inn Suites Costa Mesa
325 Bristol Street
Costa Mesa, CA 92626-7939
949-549-0300
Job Hotline: 714-549-0300 x199
Number of Employees: 175

Don Ayres III, *President*
Lee Wettengel, *Director of Human Resources*

Crowne Plaza Los Angeles Airport
5985 Century Boulevard
Los Angeles, CA 90045
310-642-7500
Job Hotline: Ext 1357
Number of Employees: 250

Chuck Bolyard, *General Manager*
Diane Legsage, *Director of Human Resources*

Del Mar Fairgrounds
2260 Jimmy Durante Boulevard
Del Mar, CA 92014
619-755-1161
Web Address: www.delmarfair.com
Number of Employees: 140

Char Cunningham, *Director of Sales*
Theresa Shirley, *Human Resources Clerk*

Disneyland Hotel
1150 West Cerritos Avenue
Anaheim, CA 92802
714-781-1600
Job Hotline: 714-781-1600
Web Address: www.disneyland.com
Number of Employees: 1700

Disneyland Pacific Hotel
1717 Disneyland Drive
Anaheim, CA 92802-2390
714-999-0990
Web Address: www.disneyland.com
Number of Employees: 300

Doubletree Hotel Anaheim/OC
100 The City Drive South
Orange, CA 92868-3291
714-634-4500
Web Address: www.doubletreehotels.com
Number of Employees: 250

Marty Trobich, *Human Resources Director*

Doubletree Hotel Pasadena
191 North Los Robles
Pasadena, CA 91101
626-792-2727
Web Address: www.doubletreehotel.com
Number of Employees: 200

John Lange, *General Manager*
Patrice Siffert, *Director of Human Resources*

Doubletree Hotel-Los Angeles, Westwood
10740 Wilshire Boulevard
Los Angeles, CA 90024
310-475-8711
Web Address: www.doubletree.com
Number of Employees: 130
Eddie Hartman, *Human Resource Manager*

HOSPITALITY

361

DoubleTree Hotel/OC Airport
3050 Bristol Street
Costa Mesa, CA 92626-3036
949-540-7000
Job Hotline: 714-438-4963
Web Address: www.doubletreehotels.com
Number of Employees: 350

Edith Pueblos, *Human Resources*

Embassy Suites La Jolla
4550 La Jolla Village Drive
San Diego, CA 92122
858-453-0400
Job Hotline: 619-453-0400 x547
Number of Employees: 110
Doug Ramsay, *General Manager*
Jennifer Mardon, *Hiring Contact*
Kendra Aintzen, *Human Resource Administrator*

Embassy Suites San Diego Bay
601 Pacific Highway
San Diego, CA 92101
619-239-2400
Number of Employees: 145
Ahmed Mahrous, *General Manager*
Tonya Bays, *Human Resource Director*

Four Seasons Los Angeles
300 South Doheny Drive
Los Angeles, CA 90048
310-273-2222
Web Address: www.fourseasons.com
Debra Zaharychuk, *Human Resource Manager*

Furama Hotel Los Angeles
8601 Lincoln Boulevard
Los Angeles, CA 90045
310-670-8111
Job Hotline: Ext 1999
Web Address: www.furama.hotels.com
Number of Employees: 260
Sam Ebeid, *General Manager*
Otho Bogs, *Director of Human Resources*

Hacienda Hotel
525 North Sepulveda Boulevard
El Segundo, CA 90245
310-615-0015
Job Hotline: Ext 4141
Web Address: www.haciendahotel.com
Number of Employees: 450
Frank Godoy, *General Manager*
Andy Behnky, *Director of Guest Services*
Maggie Shannon, *Human Resource Manager*

Hanalei Hotel
2270 Hotel Circle North
San Diego, CA 92108
619-297-1101
Job Hotline: 619-297-1101 x3338
Number of Employees: 260
Dennis G. Sannes, *General Manager*

Holiday Inn - Buena Park
7000 Beach Boulevard
Buena Park, CA 90620-1897
714-522-7000
Web Address: www.holiday-inn/hotels/laxbp
Number of Employees: 140

Barbara Ulrich, *Personnel Manager*

Holiday Inn Burbank
150 East Angeleno Avenue
Burbank, CA 91502
818-841-4770

Chris Haven, *General Manager*

Holiday Inn Express
1600 East 1st Street
Santa Ana, CA 92701-6317
714-835-3051
Number of Employees: 37

Mohamid Oliai, *President*

Holiday Inn Hollywood
1755 North Highland Avenue
Hollywood, CA 90028
213-462-7181
Number of Employees: 200

Tony Lovoy, *General Manager*
Martin Navarro, *Employee Services Director*

**Holiday Inn Hotel Circle Select -
San Diego**
595 Hotel Circle South
San Diego, CA 92108
619-291-5720
Number of Employees: 150

Martin Astengo, *General Manager*
Lisa Manuel, *Human Resource Coordinator*

Holiday Inn LAX
9901 La Cienega Boulevard
Los Angeles, CA 90045
310-649-5151
Job Hotline: Ext 1251
Number of Employees: 45

Pawan Deepak, *General Manager*
Arlene Glacer, *Director of Human Resources*

Holiday Inn on the Bay
1355 North Harbor Drive
San Diego, CA 92101
619-232-3861
Job Hotline: 619-232-3861 x7766
Number of Employees: 300

Al Hatfield, *General Manager*
Mary Hemus, *Director of Sales*
Daniel Maloney, *Director of Human Resource*

Holiday Inn Pasadena
303 East Cordova Street
Pasadena, CA 91101
818-449-4000

Ray Serafan, *General Manager*

Holiday Inn Torrance
19800 South Vermont Avenue
Torrance, CA 90502
310-781-9100
Job Hotline: 310-781-9100 x578
Web Address: www.basshotels.com/holidayinn
Number of Employees: 100

Michael Payton, *General Manager*
Christine Casillas, *Employee Services*

Hollywood Roosevelt Hotel
7000 Hollywood Boulevard
Hollywood, CA 90028
213-466-7000
Job Hotline: 213-769-7293
Number of Employees: 400

Melvin Choo, *General Manager*
Colleen Jimenez, *General Manager*

Hotel del Coronado
1500 Orange Avenue
Coronado, CA 92118
619-435-6611
Web Address: http://hoteldel.com
Number of Employees: 1,100

Giuseppe Lama, *General Manager*
Fernando Robles, *Human Resource Recruiting
  Assistant*

Hotel Inter-Continental Los Angeles
251 South Olive Street
Los Angeles, CA 90012
213-617-3300
Job Hotline: 213-356-4049
Number of Employees: 260
Lewis Fader, *General Manager*
Karen Devaney, *Director of Human Resources*

Hotel Laguna
425 South Coast Highway
Laguna Beach, CA 92651-2493
714-494-1151
*Web Address: www.menubytes.com/
hotellaguna*
Number of Employees: 120
Claes Anderson, *Owner*

Hotel Queen Mary
1126 Queens Highway Drive
Long Beach, CA 90802
562-435-3511
Web Address: www.queenmary.com
Number of Employees: 800
Joseph Prevratil, *General Manager*
Yvonne McGuire, *Recruiter*

Howard Johnsons Hotel
1380 South Harbor Boulevard
Anaheim, CA 92802-2396
714-776-6120
Web Address: www.hojoanaheim.com
Number of Employees: 200

James P. Edmondson, *Owner*

Hyatt Islandia
1441 Quivira Road
San Diego, CA 92109
619-224-1234
Number of Employees: 300

Jerry Westenhaver, *General Manager*
Gwen Seah, *Human Resource Director*

Hyatt Newporter
1107 Jamboree Road
Newport Beach, CA 92660-6296
949-729-1234
Job Hotline: 704-759-3075
Web Address: www.hyatt.com
Number of Employees: 300
Sara Rivera, *Human Resources Director*

Hyatt Regency Alicante
100 Plaza
Garden Grove, CA 92840
714-750-1234
Job Hotline: 704-740-6052
Web Address: www.hyatt.com
Number of Employees: 250
Ken Jasinski, *Human Resources*

Hyatt Regency Irvine
17900 Jamboree Road
Irvine, CA 92614-6288
949-975-1234
Job Hotline: 714-225-6716
Web Address: www.hyatt.com
Number of Employees: 400
Christing Anbel, *Human Resources*

Hyatt Regency La Jolla
3777 La Jolla Village Drive
San Diego, CA 92122
619-552-1234
Job Hotline: 619-552-6058
Web Address: www.hyatt.com
Number of Employees: 450
Allan Farwell, *General Manager*
Rob Stirling, *Director of Sales*
Alison McAbee, *Hiring Contact*

Hyatt Regency Long Beach
200 South Pine Avenue
Long Beach, CA 90802
562-624-6090
Job Hotline: 562-624-6090
Web Address: www.hyatt.com
Cheryl Phelps, *General Manager*
Shareen Poynter, *Employment Manager*

363

Hyatt Regency Los Angeles
711 South Hope Street
Los Angeles, CA 90017
213-683-1234
Job Hotline: 213-612-3139
Web Address: www.hyatt.com
Number of Employees: 300

Frank Lavey, *General Manager*
Margret Pock, *Employment Manager*

Hyatt Regency San Diego
One Market Place
San Diego, CA 92101
619-232-1234
Job Hotline: 619-687-6000
Web Address: www.hyatt.com
Number of Employees: 1,000

Alan Randle, *General Manager*
Scott Hermes, *Director of Sales*
Darrell Flood, *Human Resource Director*

IHOP Corp.
525 North Brand Boulevard, Third Floor
Glendale, CA 91203
818-240-6055
Web Address: www.ihop.com

Richard Herzer, *Chairman & President*
Naomi Shively, *Vice President*

Industry Hills Sheraton Resort
One Industry Hills Parkway
City of Industry, CA 91744
818-810-4455

Detlef Reck, *General Manager*
Sharon Haimowitz, *Director of Human*
  Resources

International Food Service Executives
17112A Sims Street
Huntington Beach, CA 92649
714-846-6566
Job Hotline: 714-846-6566
Number of Employees: 2,000
Hal Espy, *President*

Irvine Marriott Hotel
18000 Von Karman Avenue
Irvine, CA 92612-1096
949-553-0100
Web Address: www.jobshr.com
Number of Employees: 450
Patty Zachik, *Human Resources Director*
Fernando Rivas, *Human Resources*

Jolly Roger Inn
640 West Katella Avenue
Anaheim, CA 92802-3499
714-772-7621
Web Address: www.tarsadia.com
Number of Employees: 160
Cherry Robetson, *Human Resources*

Kona Kai Continental Plaza Resort
1551 Shelter Island Drive
San Diego, CA 92106
619-221-8000
Web Address: www.shelterpoint.com
Number of Employees: 240

John Richardson, *Director of Sales*
Sarah Kidder, *General Manager*
Kris Bautista, *Human Resource Director*

La Jolla Marriott
4240 La Jolla Village Drive
La Jolla, CA 92037
619-587-1414
Job Hotline: 619-597-6325
Web Address: www.marriott.com
Number of Employees: 360

Paul Corsinita, *General Manager*
Joan Mitchell, *Human Resource Director*

La Quinta Inn - Irvine
14972 Sand Canyon Avenue
Irvine, CA 92618-2100
949-551-0909
Web Address: www.laquinta.com
Number of Employees: 35

Beverly Yageo, *Human Resources*

Laguna Hills Lodge
23932 Paseo De Valencia
Laguna Hills, CA 92653-3146
714-830-2550
Number of Employees: 20

William J. Crawford, *Owner*

Le Meridan
465 South La Cienega Boulevard
Los Angeles, CA 90048
310-247-0400
Job Hotline: 310-246-2074
Web Address: www.lemeridanbh.com
Number of Employees: 200

Jaques Ligne, *General Manager*
Arlene Gould, *Employment Manager*

Loews Coronado Bay Resort
4000 Coronado Bay Road
Coronado, CA 92118
619-424-4000
Job Hotline: 619-424-4000 x4480
Web Address: www.loewshotels.com
Number of Employees: 500

Myraline Morris, *Director of Sales*
Marguarite Clark, *Director of Public Relations*
Rosemary Stoll, *Human Resource Director*

Loews Santa Monica Beach Hotel
1700 Ocean Avenue
Santa Monica, CA 90401

310-458-6700
Job Hotline: 310-576-3121 x3120
Web Address: www.loewshoteljobs.com
Number of Employees: 350
Dan King, *General Manager*
Serina Sager, *Director of Human Resources*

Long Beach Marriott
4700 Airport Plaza Drive
Long Beach, CA 90815
562-425-5210
Job Hotline: 562-627-8000
Number of Employees: 600

Jerry Slaton, *General Manager*
Sandra Maranon, *Director of Human Resources*

Los Angeles Airport Hilton & Towers
5711 West Century Boulevard
Los Angeles, CA 90045
310-410-4000
Job Hotline: 310-413-6111
Web Address: www.hilton.com
Number of Employees: 700

David Villarubia, *General Manager*
Debi Benitez, *Director of Human Resources*

Los Angeles Airport Marriott
5855 West Century Boulevard
Los Angeles, CA 90045
310-641-5700
Job Hotline: 310-337-5327
Number of Employees: 750

Javier Cano, *General Manager*
John Masamori, *Human Resource Manager*

Los Angeles Marriot Downtown
333 South Figueroa Street
Los Angeles, CA 90071
213-617-1133
Job Hotline: 213-617-0788

Joe Zarrahy, *General Manager*

Marina Beach Marriott
4100 Admiralty Way
Marina Del Rey, CA 90292
310-301-3000
Job Hotline: 310-448-4850
Number of Employees: 230

Susan Reardon, *General Manager*
Georgia Sandesson, *Recruiter*

Marina Inn
24800 Dana Point Harbor Drive
Dana Point, CA 92629-2919
714-496-1203
Number of Employees: 27

Marina Village Conference Center
1936 Quivira Way
San Diego, CA 92109

619-222-1620
Job Hotline: 619-525-2800
Number of Employees: 8
Camille Lutes, *Director of Sales*
Denise Huing, *Human Resource Coordinator*

Marriott's Laguna Cliffs Resort
25135 Park Lantern
Dana Point, CA 92629-2878
714-661-5000
Job Hotline: 714-661-5000 x1111
Web Address: www.marriott.com
Number of Employees: 250

Debe Cupano, *Human Resources Director*

Miramar Fairmont Hotel
101 Wilshire Boulevard
Santa Monica, CA 90401
310-576-7777
Job Hotline: 310-319-3145
Web Address: www.fairmont.coim
Number of Employees: 250

Karl Buchda, *General Manager*
Sara Rivera, *Director of Human Resources*

New Otani Hotel and Garden
120 South Los Angeles Street
Los Angeles, CA 90012
213-629-1200
Job Hotline: 310-617-0368
Number of Employees: 400

Kenji Yoshimoto, *General Manager*

NuOasis Resorts
4695 MacArthur Court, Suite 530
Newport Beach, CA 92660
949-833-5381
Web Address: www.otcfn.com/nuoa
Number of Employees: 8

Fred G. Luke, *President*
John Rif, *Office Manager*

Omni Los Angeles Hotel and Center
930 Wilshire Boulevard
Los Angeles, CA 90017
213-688-7777
Job Hotline: 213-612-3990
Number of Employees: 650

John Stoddard, *General Manager*
Joya Lee, *Employment Manager*

Orange County Airport Hilton
18800 Macarthur Boulevard
Irvine, CA 92612-1479
949-833-9999
Web Address: www.hilton.com
Number of Employees: 200

Park Hyatt Los Angeles at Century City
2151 Avenue of the Stars
Los Angeles, CA 90067
310-277-1234
Job Hotline: 310-284-6521
Web Address: www.hyatt.com
Number of Employees: 340

Cormac O'Modhrain, *General Manager*
Rhonda Vancooney, *Director of Human Resources*

Pasadena Hilton
150 South Los Robles Avenue
Pasadena, CA 91101
626-577-1000

Bob Yeoman, *General Manager*
Diane Corballey, *Director of Human Resources*

Radisson Hotel
6161 Centinela Avenue
Culver City, CA 90231
310-649-1776
Job Hotline: 310-348-4174
Web Address: www.radisson.com
Number of Employees: 200

Jim Bushey, *General Manager*
Reina Torres, *Director of Human Resources*

Radisson Hotel Harbor View-Downtown
1646 Front Street
San Diego, CA 92101
619-239-6800
Number of Employees: 150

Art Cato, *General Manager*
Kim Rebout, *Human Resource Director*

Radisson Wilshire Plaza Hotel
3515 Wilshire Boulevard
Los Angeles, CA 90010
213-381-7411
Job Hotline: 213-368-3068
Number of Employees: 250

Wayne Williams, *General Manager*
LIida Hong, *Human Resources Manager*

Ramada Inn - Anaheim
1331 East Katella Avenue
Anaheim, CA 92805-6626
714-978-8088
Web Address: www.anaheimramada.com
Number of Employees: 95

Ramada Limited
1680 Superior Avenue
Costa Mesa, CA 92627-3652
949-645-2221
Web Address: www.ramadalimitednewport.com
Number of Employees: 1,000

Red Lion Hotel
100 West Glenoaks Boulevard
Glendale, CA 91202
818-956-5466

Mike Hirsch, *General Manager*

Regal Biltmore Hotel
506 South Grand Avenue
Los Angeles, CA 90071
213-624-1011
Number of Employees: 350

Randall Villareal, *General Manager*

Renaissance Long Beach Hotel
111 East Ocean Boulevard
Long Beach, CA 90802
562-437-5900
Job Hotline: 562-499-2518
Web Address: www.ren.hotels.com
Number of Employees: 300

Joachim Ortmayer, *General Manager*

Renaissance Los Angeles Hotel
9620 Airport Boulevard
Los Angeles, CA 90045
310-337-2800
Job Hotline: 888-462-7746
Web Address: www.renaissance.com
Number of Employees: 300

Gregory Lehman, *General Manager*
Christine Korthus, *Human Resources Manager*

Ritz Carlton
33533 Ritz-Carlton Drive
Laguna Niguel, CA 92629
714-240-2000
Web Address: www.ritzcarlton.com

Ritz-Carlton Huntington Hotel
1401 South Oak Knoll Avenue
Pasadena, CA 91106
626-568-3900

Mark Hodgdon, *General Manager*
Blair Antonacci, *Director of Human Resources*

Ritz-Carlton Huntington Hotel
1401 South Oak Knoll Avenue
Pasadena, CA 91106
818-568-3900
Web Address: www.ritzcarlton.com

San Diego Concourse
202 C Street, Mail Station 57
San Diego, CA 92101
619-615-4100
Job Hotline: 619-525-5151
Number of Employees: 400

David Drummond, *Director of Sales*
Kim Calum, *Human Resource Representative*

San Diego Convention Center Corp.
111 West Harbor Drive
San Diego, CA 92101
619-525-5000
Job Hotline: 619-525-5151
Web Address: www.sdccc.org
Number of Employees: 800

Carole A. Krizmanic, *Director of Sales*
Thomas Mazzocco, *Human Resource Director*

San Diego Del Mar Hilton Hotel
15575 Jimmy Durante Boulevard
Del Mar, CA 92014
619-792-5200
Number of Employees: 185

Bette Gill, *Director of Sales*
Heather Davidson, *Human Resouce Manager*

San Diego Hilton Beach & Tennis Resort
1775 East Mission Bay Drive
San Diego, CA 92109
619-276-4010
Job Hotline: 619-275-8994
Number of Employees: 300

Patrick Duffy, *General Manager*
Kathy Kennedy, *Human Resource Director*

San Diego Marriott Hotel & Marina
333 West Harbor Drive
San Diego, CA 92101
619-234-1500
Job Hotline: 619-234-1500 x8901
Web Address: www.marriott.com
Number of Employees: 400

Ray Warren, *General Manager*
Tim Price, *Director of Sales*
Annabel Valdez, *Job Placement Coordinator*

San Diego Marriott Mission Valley
8757 Rio San Diego Drive
San Diego, CA 92018
619-692-3800
Web Address: www.marriott.com
Number of Employees: 275

Gordon Luster, *General Manager*
Liz Franzese, *Director of Sales*
Mary Staples, *Director of Human Resource*

San Diego Mission Valley Hilton
901 Camino del Rio South
San Diego, CA 92108
619-543-9000
Job Hotline: 619-543-9441
Web Address: www.hilton.com
Number of Employees: 250

Art Sapanli, *General Manager*
Peggy Johnson, *Director of Sales*
Diane Mitchell, *Director of Human Resource*

San Diego Princess Resort
1404 West Vacation Road
San Diego, CA 92109
619-274-4630
Job Hotline: 619-581-5902
Web Address: www.princessresort.com/
  princess

Thomas C. Vincent IV, *General Manager*
John Davies, *Director of Sales*
Cheri Abbot, *Director of Human Resources*

Scottish Rite Center
1895 Camino del Rio South
San Diego, CA 92108
619-297-0397
Number of Employees: 13

Pamela S. Roos, *Director of Sales & Human Resources*

Seoul Plaza Hotel
10022 Garden Grove Boulevard
Garden Grove, CA 92844-1621
714-534-1818
Web Address: www.ramada.com
Number of Employees: 30

Mr. Ding, *Owner*
Mr. Jun, *Human Resources*

Sheraton Four Points Anaheim-Fullerton
1500 South Raymond Avenue
Fullerton, CA 92831-5295
714-635-9000
Web Address: www.starwood.com
Number of Employees: 200

Steve Cabasos, *Human Resources Manager*

Sheraton Gateway Hotel LA Airport
6101 West Century Boulevard
Los Angeles, CA 90045
310-642-1111
Number of Employees: 350

Jack Ward, *General Manager*
Martha Satelo, *Human Resources Manager*

Sheraton Grande Torrey Pines
10950 North Torrey Pines Road
La Jolla, CA 92037
619-558-1500
Job Hotline: 619-558-8058
Web Address: www.sheraton-tp.com
Number of Employees: 400

Steve Gold, *General Manager*
Bill Allison, *Director of Sales*
Ann Towle-Mason, *Director of Human Resources*

HOSPITALITY

Sheraton Newport Beach Hotel
4545 Macarthur Boulevard
Newport Beach, CA 92660-2078
949-833-0570
Number of Employees: 188

Sheraton San Diego Hotel & Marina
1380 Harbor Island Drive
San Diego, CA 92101
619-291-2900
Job Hotline: 619-692-2793
Web Address: www.sandiego-sheraton.com
Number of Employees: 875

Joseph Terzi, *General Manager*
John Dean, *Director of Sales*
Sandy Grove, *Director of Human Resources*

Sheraton Universal Hotel
333 Universal Terrace Parkway
Universal City, CA 91608
818-980-1212

Reginald R. McDowell, *General Manager*
Carol Reynolds, *Director of Human Resources*

Southern California Grocers Association
100 West Broadway
Long Beach, CA 90802
562-432-8610
Web Address: http://home.earthlink.net/ ~cgasouth

Sunstone Hotel Investors
115 Calle De Industrias #201
San Clemente, CA 92672-3858
714-361-3900
Number of Employees: 75

Randy Hulce, *President*

Sutton Place Hotel
4500 Macarthur Boulevard
Newport Beach, CA 92660-2053
949-476-2001
Job Hotline: 714-955-5656
Web Address: www.travelweb.com/sutton.html
Number of Employees: 500

Cindy Lindsay, *Human Resources*

The Anaheim Hilton & Towers
777 West Convention Way
Anaheim, CA 92802-3425
714-750-4321
Job Hotline: 714-740-4319
Web Address: www.hilton.com
Number of Employees: 1250

Valerie Becker, *Human Resources Director*
Joanne Leith, *Human Resources*

The Atrium Hotel
18700 Macarthur Boulevard
Irvine, CA 92612-1478

949-833-2770
Job Hotline: 714-833-2770 x448
Web Address: www.atriumhotel.com
Number of Employees: 105
Nancy Munt, *Human Resources Director*

The Ritz-Carlton - Marina del Rey
4375 Admiralty Way
Marina del Rey, CA 90292
310-823-1700
Job Hotline: 310-574-4290
Web Address: www.ritz.com
Number of Employees: 450

Charles De Foucault, *General Manager*
Cheryl Magdaleno, *Director of Human Resources*

The Seal Beach Inn & Gardens
212 5th Street
Seal Beach, CA 90740-6115
562-493-2416
Web Address: www.sealbeachinn.com
Number of Employees: 23

Marjorie F Bettenhausen, *Owner*

The Waterfront Hilton
21100 Pacific Coast Highway
Huntington Beach, CA 92648-5307
714-960-7873
Job Hotline: 714-960-7873
Web Address: www.hilton.com/hilton
Number of Employees: 350

Lauray Hollandleis, *Human Resources Director*

The Westin South Coast Plaza
686 Anton Boulevard
Costa Mesa, CA 92626-1988
949-540-2500
Web Address: www.westin.com
Number of Employees: 300

Maria Corpeno, *Human Resources*

Torrance Hilton at South Bay
21333 Hawthorne Boulevard
Torrance, CA 90503
310-540-0500
Job Hotline: Ext 3136
Number of Employees: 200

Yair Eldar, *General Manager*
Chris Baldanado, *Director of Human Resources*

Torrance Marriott
3635 Fashion Way
Torrance, CA 90503
310-316-3636
Job Hotline: 310-792-6171 x6152
Number of Employees: 331

Mr. Gunderson, *General Manager*
Renee Licona, *Director of Human Resources*

Town & Country Resort & Conference Center
500 Hotel Circle North
San Diego, CA 92108
619-291-7131
Job Hotline: 619-299-2254
Web Address: www.towncountry.com
Number of Employees: 2,000

Duke Sobek, *General Manager*
James Johnson, *Director of Sales*
Alma Gonzales, *Director of Human Resources*

Travelodge-Orange County Airport
1400 SE Bristol Street
Santa Ana, CA 92707-5397
714-557-8700
Number of Employees: 45

Sam Khamneian, *President & GM*

U.S. Grant
326 Broadway
San Diego, CA 92101
619-232-3121
Web Address: www.grandheritage.com
Number of Employees: 310

Norma J. Wilt, *Director of Sales*
Tina Allen, *Director of Human Resources*

Universal City Hilton & Towers
555 Universal Terrace Parkway
Universal City, CA 91608
818-506-2500

Juan Aquinde, *General Manager*
Susan Caplin, *Director of Human Resources*

Warner Center Marriott
21850 Oxnard Street
Woodland Hills, CA 91367
818-887-4800
Web Address: www.marriot.com

Allen Kramme, *General Manager*
Debbi Lee, *Director of Human Resources*

Waterfront Hilton Beach Resort
PO Box 8680
Newport Beach, CA 92658-8680
949-759-8091
Web Address: www.hilton.com
Number of Employees: 300

Stephen K. Bone, *President*

West Coast Anaheim Hotels
1855 South Harbor Boulevard
Anaheim, CA 92802-3509
714-750-1811
Web Address:
www.westcoastanaheimhotel.com
Number of Employees: 243

John Lesko, *Personnel Director*

Westin Bonaventure Hotel and Suites
404 South Figueroa Street
Los Angeles, CA 90071
213-624-1000
Job Hotline: 213-612-4845

Bob Graney, *General Manager*
Aleea Algeyer, *Human Resources Coordinator*

Westin Horton Plaza San Diego
910 Broadway Circle
San Diego, CA 92101
619-239-2200
Job Hotline: 619-239-2200 x7177
Number of Employees: 330

Edward Netzhammer, *General Manager*
Linda Gutierrez, *Director of Human Resource*

Westin Long Beach
333 East Ocean Boulevard
Long Beach, CA 90802
562-436-3000
Job Hotline: 562-499-2056 x2041
Web Address: www.westin.com
Number of Employees: 327

Linda O'Toole, *General Manager*
Liz Gray, *Human Resource Manager*

Woodland Hills Hilton & Towers
6360 Canoga Avenue
Woodland Hills, CA 91367
818-595-1000

Ed deVries, *General Manager*
Francine Schuster, *Director of Human Resources*

Wyndham Emerald Plaza
400 West Broadway
San Diego, CA 92101
619-239-4500
Job Hotline: 619-515-4541
Number of Employees: 325

Jay Best, *Regional Director of Marketing*
Peter Cipkins, *Director of Sales*
Kris Campiglia, *Director of Human Resources*

Wyndham Hotel at Los Angeles Airport
6225 West Century Boulevard
Los Angeles, CA 90045
310-670-9000
Job Hotline: 310-337-6455
Web Address: www.wyndham.com
Number of Employees: 300

Jack Highsmith, *General Manager*
Wilmer Baliton, *Director of Human Resources*

Further References

• Associations •

American Bed and Breakfast Association
P.O. Box 1387
Midlothian, VA 23113-8387
804-379-2222
Web Address: www.abba.com

American Hotel & Motel Association
1201 New York Avenue, N.W., Suite 600
Washington, D.C. 20005
202-289-3100
Web Address: www.ahma.com

American Resort Development Association (ARDA)
1220 L Street, N.W., Suite 510
Washington, D.C. 20005
202-371-6700
Web Address: www.arda.org

Association of Meeting Professionals
212 South Henry Street
Alexandria, VA 22314-3522
703-549-0900

Council of Hotel, Restaurant & Institutional Education
1200 17th Street, N.W.
Washington, D.C. 20036
202-331-5990

Hospitality Sales & Marketing Association International
1300 L Street, N.W., Suite 800
Washington, D.C. 20005
202-789-0089

National Restaurant Association (NRA)
1200 17th Street, N.W.
Washington, D.C. 20036
202-331-5900
Web Address: www.restaurant.org

• Publications •

Hotels
1350 East Touhy Avenue
Des Plaines, IL 60018
847-390-2139

Lodging Magazine
1201 New York Avenue, Suite 600
Washington, D.C. 20005-3931
202-289-3100
Web Address: www.lodgingmagazine.com

Restaurant Hospitality
1100 Superior Avenue
Cleveland, OH 44114
216-696-7000

Insurance

Insurance and Financial Service Companies in California are actively seeking quality individuals to join their sales force as Agents and/or Registered Representatives. No specific degree in the field is required but we strongly recommend that candidates for a representative position be self-employed, competitive, well-disciplined, business oriented and have a desire to be an entrepreneur. Individuals should possess excellent use of time management and outstanding written and verbal skills.

To become an Agent and/or Registered Representative a candidate must first obtain a resident state license for Life and Health Insurance. Additional licensing may be required prior to a hire date or in a given time from the hire date, including: Series 6 & 63. Upon successfully obtaining a license, most Insurance and Financial Service Companies offer in-house training to be a qualified Trainer, Sales Manager, Managing Partner or General Manager.

Duties include marketing a variety of products to individuals and businesses, fact-finding, developing solutions, making recommendations and servicing existing clients. Candidates should be prepared for a lot of travel because most all reputable Insurance and Financial Service Companies pride themselves on face-to-face interaction with clients.

Compensation usually provides a Training Allowance plus commissions with potential expense allowances. A great advantage to working in the Insurance and Financial Services field is that your profit potential is solely based on your motivation for success.

Michael Gore, LUTCF
Partner
MINNESOTA LIFE

20th Century Insurance Group
6301 Owensmouth Avenue
Woodland Hills, CA 91367
818-704-3000
Job Hotline: 818-704-3760
Number of Employees: 1,500
William Mellick, *President*

ABD Financial Insurance Services
21250 Hawthorne Boulevard, Suite 600
Suite 600
Torrance, CA 90503
310-543-9995
Job Hotline: Ext 190
Web Address: abdi.com
Number of Employees: 45
Jim Hall, *President*
Phyllis Kaethea, *Director of Human Resources*

Acordia Benefit Services of Southern California
828 West Taft Avenue
Orange, CA 92865-4232
949-225-6900
Number of Employees: 200

AIG Aviation Insurance Services
5700 Wilshire Boulevard, Suite 456E
Los Angeles, CA 90036
213-965-5250
Number of Employees: 22

John Grob, *Manager*

Alliance of American Insurers
1501 East Woodfield Road, Suite 400W
Schaumburg, IL 60173
847-330-8500

Allianz Insurance Company
3400 Riverside Drive, Suite 300
Burbank, CA 91510
818-972-8000
Number of Employees: 380

Wolfgang Schlink, *CEO*
Terri Legard, *Director of Human Resources*

INSURANCE

Allmarket Insurance Services of California
1601 Dove, Suite 260
Newport Beach, CA 92660
949-862-5450
Web Address: www.allmarketinsurance.com
Number of Employees: 4

Sherry Allder, *President*

Allstate Insurance Group
725 West Town & Country Road
Suite 700
Orange, CA 92868
714-667-6507
Web Address: www.allstate.com
Number of Employees: 160

Franklin Millar, *Regional VP Southern Calif.*
Bob Wicks, *Human Resources*

American Academy of Actuaries
1100 17th Street, Suite 700
Washington, DC 20036
202-223-8196

American Arbitration Association
140 West 51st Street
New York, NY 10020
212-484-4000

American Association of Crop Insurers - AACI
1 Massachusetts Avenue NW, Suite 800
Washington, DC 20001
202-789-4100
Web Address: www.aginsurance.org

American Association of Insurance Services -AAIS
1035 South York Road
Bensenville, IL 60106
630-595-3225

American Institute for Chartered Property and Casualty Underwriters
PO Box 3016
Malvern, PA 19355
610-644-2100
Web Address: www.aicpcu.org

American Institute of Maring Underwriters
14 Wall Street
New York, NY 10005
212-233-0550

American Insurance Association
980 9th Street, Suite 2060
Sacramento, CA 94814
916-442-7617

Elizabeth Story, *Director of Public Affairs*

American International Group
777 South Figueroa Street
Los Angeles, CA 90017
213-689-3500
Number of Employees: 400

Vincent J. Masucci, *Senior Executive*
Celia Young, *Director of Human Resources*

American Reinsurance Company
333 City Boulevard West, Suite 1900
Orange, CA 92668
714-634-2233
Web Address: www.amre.com
Number of Employees: 20

Dennis Doyle, *Western Regional Manager*
Iris Cruz, *Human Resources Manager*

American Special Risk Insurance Service
6400 Canoga Avenue, Suite 265
Woodland Hills, CA 91367
818-887-7711
Number of Employees: 8

Harris Rutsky, *President*

American Sterling Corporation
9800 Muirlands Boulevard
Irvine, CA 92618-2515
949-206-6200
Web Address: www.americansterling.com
Number of Employees: 7

Mike Thompson, *President*

Amwest Insurance Group
5230 LasVirgenes Road
Calabasas, CA 91302
818-704-1111
Web Address: www.farwestservices.com
Number of Employees: 600
Richard H. Savage, *Chairman*
Barbara Allen, *Director of Personnel*
Holding company that underwrites specialty bonds. Offers a wide range of surety bonds, and provides specialty property and casualty coverage such as auto liability, homeowner, and physical-damage coverage. Markets its products through independent agents and brokers.

Anderson & Murison
800 West Colorado Boulevard
Los Angeles, CA 90041
213-255-2333
Number of Employees: 40
D.F. Anderson, *CEO*
Horst Lechler, *President*

Anserv Insurance Services
3900 Harney Street, Suite 250
San Diego, CA 92110
619-296-4706
Number of Employees: 20
Brian Harnes, *CEO*
Judith Conway, *Manager*

Aon Risk Services

707 Wilshire Boulevard, Suite 6000
Irvine, CA 90017
949-630-3347
Web Address: www.aainsure.com
Number of Employees: 107

Robert M. Anderson, *President*

Aon Risk Services of Southern California

707 Wilshire Boulevard
Suite 700
Los Angeles, CA 90017
213-630-3200
Number of Employees: 450

Doug Brown, *President*
Debbie Redmund, *Director of Human Resources*

Appleby & Sterling

30851 West Agoura Road, Suite 203
Agoura Hills, CA 91301
818-707-3488
Number of Employees: 8

Walter M. Maurer, *President*

Argonaut Insurance

5757 Wilshire Boulevard, Suite 200
Los Angeles, CA 90036
213-937-0400
Web Address: www.argonautgroup.com
Number of Employees: 50

Bill Courtney, *Vice President*
Jeanne Mayoral, *Human Resources Manager*

Argonaut Insurance Company

120 South State College Boulevard #100
Brea, CA 92821-5806
213-937-0400
Number of Employees: 150

Aris Insurance Services

5038 North Parkway Calabasas, Suite 400
Calabasas, CA 91372
800-894-2747
Joyce Weckerly, *Personnel Manager*

Armstrong/Robitaille Insurance Services

17501 East 17th Street, Suite 200
Tustin, CA 92780
714-832-5500
Web Address: www.arinsurance.com
Number of Employees: 120

Frank Robitaille, *President*
Bob Dennerline, *Human Resources*

Arrowhead Group of Companies

6055 Lusk Boulevard
San Diego, CA 92121
619-658-6000
Job Hotline: 619-677-5299

Web Address: www.arrowhead.org
Number of Employees: 630
Karen Sweeney, *Senior Vice President*
Mark Sciarretta, *Director of Human Resources*

Arthur J. Gallagher & Company

2030 Main Street, Suite 1100
Irvine, CA 92714
949-756-8500
Number of Employees: 50

Dennis O'Hara, *Area President*

Assocation of California Surety Companies

925 L Street, Suite 220
Sacramento, CA 95814
916-441-4166

Associated Aviation Underwriters

21650 Oxnard, Suite 1550
Woodland Hills, CA 91367
818-883-4100
Number of Employees: 17

Richard Davis, *Western Regional Manager*
Heather Belger, *Director of Human Resources*

Association Life & Health Administrators

7798 Starling Drive, Suite 307
San Diego, CA 92123
858-277-3926
Number of Employees: 40

Douglas Edwards, *President & Human Resource Contact*

Association of California Insurance Companies

1121 L Street, Suite 510
Sacramento, CA 95814
916-442-4581

Barry Carmody, *President*

Auto Club

33 Fairview Road
Costa Mesa, CA 92626
949-741-3427
Number of Employees: 5,000

Thomas V. McKernan Jr., *President*
Diane Grice, *Human Resources Manager*

Balboa Life & Casualty

PO Box 19702
Irvine, CA 92623-9702
949-553-0700
Job Hotline: 800-654-2826
Web Address: www.avco-textron.com
Number of Employees: 1,100

John Spence, *Division President*
Neil Aton, *Manager*

Barney & Barney
9171 Towne Centre Drive, Suite 200
San Diego, CA 92122
858-457-3414
Web Address: www.barney&barney.com
Number of Employees: 130

Lawrence W. Shea, *Managing Partner*
Dennis Pierce, *Director of Human Resource*

Best Life Assurance Company of California
2505 McCabe Way
Irvine, CA 92614-6243
949-253-4080
Number of Employees: 60

Thomas J. Cahill, *President*
Carolyn Johnson, *Human Resources Manager*

Bliss & Glennon
435 North Pacific Coast Highway, Suite 200
Redondo Beach, CA 90277
800-829-7330
Web Address: www.bgsurplus.com
Number of Employees: 35

Robert Abramson, *President*
Joanna Farmer, *Human Resource Manager*

Bolton/RGV Insurance Brokers
1100 El Centro Street
South Pasadena, CA 91030
626-799-7000
Web Address: http://boltonco.com

William Bolton, *CEO*
Karlene Wallwork, *Director of Human Resources*

Brakke Schafnitz Insurance Brokers
28202 Cabot Road, Suite 500
Laguna Niguel, CA 92677-1259
714-365-5100
Number of Employees: 65

James G. Brakke, *President*
Steve Wood, *Human Resources Manager*

Brown & Riding Insurance Services
777 South Figueroa, Suite 2550
Los Angeles, CA 90017
213-452-7060
Web Address: www.brownandriding.com
Number of Employees: 25

Christopher A. Brown, *President*
Cedric Snow, *Human Resources Manager*

Burns & Wilcox Insurance Services
2650 Camino del Rio North, Suite 308
San Diego, CA 92108
619-688-7920
Number of Employees: 14

Bonnie Frank, *Branch Manager*

CA. Corp. Benefits Insurance Services
16955 Via del Campo, Suite 250
San Diego, CA 92127
858-487-4125
Number of Employees: 12

Robert E. Recchia, *President*
Mary Formosa, *Office Manager & Human Resources Assistant*

Cal-Surance Associates
333 City Boulevard West
Orange, CA 92868
714-939-0800
Number of Employees: 120

Donald E. Martin, *CEO*

California Association of Independent Insurance Adjusters
PO Box 3159
Napa, CA 94558
707-258-2530

Gene Riggs, *Executive Director*

California Association of Life Underwriters
70 Washington, Suite 325
Oakland, CA 94607
510-834-2258

Anne K. Scully, *Executive Vice President*

California Auto Assigned Risk Plan
120 Montgomery Street, Suite 325
San Francisco, CA 94120
415-765-6767

Richard Manning, *Regional Manager*

California Casualty Insurance Group
1900 Alameda de las Pulgas
San Mateo, CA 94402
415-572-4342
Ed McKoon, *VP for Corporate Development*

California Casualty Management
700 North Brand Boulevard, Suite 700
Glendale, CA 91209
818-956-1960
Number of Employees: 30
Charles Gross, *Sales Manager*

California Department of Forestry and Fire Protection
1416 9th Street
Sacramento, CA 95814
916-653-7097
Ronny J. Coleman, *State Fire Marshall*

California Fair Plan Association
PO Box 76924
Los Angeles, CA 90076
213-487-0111
Stuart M. Wilkinson, *President*

California Insurance Group
2300 East Katella Avenue, Suite 400
Anaheim, CA 92806
714-712-9000
Number of Employees: 15

Marta Greger, *Branch Manager*
Merle Malland, *Claim Branch Manager*

California Worker's Compensation Institute
120 Montgomery Street, Suite 1300
San Francisco, CA 94104
415-981-2107
Web Address: www.csci.org

Edward C. Woodward, *President*

Cannon Insurance Service
9171 Wilshire Boulevard, Suite 509
Beverly Hills, CA 90210
310-859-8600
Number of Employees: 10

Andrew B. Rosenfeld, *President*

Carnet Insurance Agency
690 Knox, Suite 100
Torrance, CA 90502
310-323-7500
Web Address: www.thecarnet.com
Number of Employees: 60

Michael York, *President*
Maxine Toler, *Human Resource Manager*

Casualty Actuarial Society -CAS
1100 North Glebe Road, Suite 600
Arlington, VA 22201
703-276-3100

Cavignac & Associates
501 West Broadway, Suite 1340
San Diego, CA 92101
619-234-6848
Number of Employees: 17

Jeff Cavignac, *President*
Sue Marberry, *Office Manager*

Century-National Insurance Company
12200 Sylvan Street
North Hollywood, CA 91606
818-760-0880
Number of Employees: 300

Weldon Wilson, *President*
Nancy Skarie, *Director of Human Resources*

Chubb & Son
801 South Figueroa, Suite 2400
Los Angeles, CA 90017
213-612-0880
Number of Employees: 65

Walter Guzzo, *Managing Director*
Mary Scelba, *Director of Human Resources*

Cigna Group
725 South Figueroa Street, Suite 2050
Los Angeles, CA 90017
213-932-6600
Web Address: www.cigna.com

Janice Yoshimura, *Field Operations Manager*
Myra McMillian, *Special Operations*

Claim Net
9 Corporate Park, Suite 200
Irvine, CA 92606-5129
949-263-1353
Web Address: www.claimnet.com
Number of Employees: 15

Jary Danible, *President*
Amy Clem, *Human Resources*

CNA Insurance Companies
2165 Oxnard Street, Suite 600
Woodland Hills, CA 91367
818-226-5101

Ken Lauber, *Branch Manager*
Karen Benson, *Director of Human Resources*

CNA International
500 North Central Avenue, Suite 900
Glendale, CA 91203
800-262-8714
Job Hotline: 800-351-9440
Web Address: www.cnaworldwide.com

Brian Murphy, *Vice President*

Coastal Brokers Insurance Service
130 North Brand Boulevard, Suite 200
Glendale, CA 91203
818-549-0794
Number of Employees: 4

Gary Gibson, *President*
Marcy Williams, *Director of Human Resources*

Commercial Associates Insurance
4226 East La Palma Avenue
Anaheim, CA 92807-1816
714-524-4949
Number of Employees: 13

Ralph Eidem Jr, *President*
Jennifer Smith, *Human Resources*

Dodge Warren & Peters Insurance
3625 Del Amo Boulevard, Suite 300
Torrance, CA 90503
310-542-4370
Web Address: www.dwanp.com
Number of Employees: 70

David Warren, *President*
Debbie Rogister, *Operations Manager*

INSURANCE

Dodge Warren Peters Insurance Services
765 The City Drive South, Suite 300
Orange, CA 92868-4974
714-748-0464
Number of Employees: 25

Debbie Rogistes, *Office Manager*

E.J. Phelps & Company
3636 Nobel Drive, Suite 410
San Diego, CA 92122
619-455-5580
Number of Employees: 20

E. Jack Phelps, *President*
Kim Webster, *Vice President of Administration*

El Camino Insurance Agency
1365 West Vista Way
Vista, CA 92083
760-726-3232
Web Address: ecins@aol.com
Number of Employees: 25

George A. Porter, *President*
Dianne Sommer, *Office Manager*

Employee Benefit Planning Asociation
714 West Olympic Boulevard, Suite 710
Los Angeles, CA 90015
213-742-0756
Number of Employees: 2

Betty L. Tellefsen, *Executive Director*

Explorer Insurance Company
303 North Glenoaks Boulevard, Suite 1000
Burbank, CA 91502
818-558-1700
Number of Employees: 200

Fred B. Tisovic, *Senior Vice President*
Dave Geier, *Director of Marketing*
Rich Jacobs, *Director of Human Resources*

Farmers Insurance Group of Cos.
4680 Wilshire Boulevard
Los Angeles, CA 90010
213-932-3200
Number of Employees: 18

Martin Feinstein, *President*
Dennis Wilde, *Human Resources Manager*

Financial Advisory Services
12555 High Bluff Drive, Suite 333
San Diego, CA 92130
858-792-1400
Web Address: faseda.com
Number of Employees: 15

Thomas Freismoth, *President*
Melissa Brean, *Office Manager*

Fireman's Fund Insurance Companies
17542 East 17th
Tustin, CA 92780
714-669-0911
Number of Employees: 350

Eddy Laugle, *Senior Vice President*

Five Star Insurance Company
2400 Main Street, Suite 100
Irvine, CA 92714
949-474-7500
Number of Employees: 50

George McNamee, *CEO*
Ken Guillaume, *Director of Marketing*

Fremont Compensation Insurance
500 North Brand, Suite 700
Glendale, CA 91203
818-549-4600
Job Hotline: 800-646-4478
Number of Employees: 550

James Little, *President*
Mary Wilkman, *Sr. VP of Human Resources*

Fremont Life Insurance Company
725 Town & Country Road, Suite 500
Orange, CA 92868
714-750-7900
Number of Employees: 7

Robert Tfeil, *Office Manager*

G.S. Levine Insurance Services
12555 High Bluff Drive, Suite 310
San Diego, CA 92130
619-481-8692
Number of Employees: 23

Gary S. Levine, *President*
Judy King, *Office Manager*

GAB Robins
3230 East Imperial Highway, Suite 312
Brea, CA 92821-6746
714-528-5300
Number of Employees: 7

Ed Buchner, *Branch Manager*

Gateway Excess & Surplus Lines
21820 Burbank Boulevard, Suite 270
Woodland Hills, CA 91367
818-226-9788
Web Address: www.gateway.com
Number of Employees: 25

Robert Iritano, *President*
Melissa Carmichael, *Office Manager*

General American Life Insurance Company
4100 Newport Place Drive, Suite 840
Newport Beach, CA 92660-2442
949-474-7060
Number of Employees: 6

Rhonda Marenburg, *Office Manager*

General Reinsurance Corporation
550 South Hope Street, Suite 600
Los Angeles, CA 90071
213-630-1900
Number of Employees: 24

M. Colleen Carey, *Vice President*
Sari Alcot, *Human Resource Director*

Golden Bear Insurance Company
709 North Center
Stockton, CA 95201
209-948-8191
Web Address: www.goldenbear.com
Michael Hall, *President*

Golden Pacific Insurance Service
3280 East Foothill Boulevard, Suite 100
Suite 100
Pasadena, CA 91107
818-583-1900
Number of Employees: 60
Fritz Mutter, *President*
Mary Mussili, *Director of Human Resources*

Goreham Moore & Associates
1231 Morena Boulevard, Suite 300
San Diego, CA 92110
619-275-6191
Number of Employees: 20

Barry K. Moore, *President*
Terry Lawson, *Office Manager*

Hewitt Associates
100 Bayview Circle
Newport Beach, CA 92660-2983
949-725-4500
Web Address: www.hewittassoc.com
Number of Employees: 230
Carol Compton, *Office Manager*

Independent Insurance Agents & Brokers of California
101 Market Street, Suite 702
San Francisco, CA 94105
415-957-1212

Independent Insurance Agents & Brokers of Los Angeles
550 North Brand Boulevard, suite 1030
Glendale, CA 91203
818-244-7509
Number of Employees: 3
Andrew Valdivia, *President*
Ann Oliver, *Executive Director*

Independent Insurance Agents of America
127 South Peyton Street
Alexandria, VA 22314
703-683-4422
Web Address: iiaa.iix.com

Insurance Brokers & Agents of San Fernando Valley
2331 Honolulu Avenue, Suite E
Montrose, CA 91020
818-248-9705

Viviane Furlong, *Executive Director*

Insurance Data Management Association
85 John Street
New York, NY 10038
212-669-0496

Insurance Educational Association
1201 Dove Street, Suite 570
Newport Beach, CA 92660
949-833-8784
Web Address: www.iea.com
Number of Employees: 8

Barbara Robertson, *Office Manager*

Insurance Fraud Management Committee
700 New Brunswick Avenue
Rahway, NJ 07065
732-388-5700

Insurance Institute for Highway Safety
1005 North Glebe Road, Suite 800
Arlington, VA 22201
703-247-1500

Insurance Institute of America
720 Providence Road
Malvern, PA 19355
610-644-2100

Insurance Service Office
450 Sansome Street, Suite 1500
San Francisco, CA 94111
415-439-4660

John Stephen Spellman, *Vice President*

Insurance Unlimited Group
9699 Tierra Grande, Suite 202
San Diego, CA 92130
619-877-2170
Number of Employees: 15

Robert M. Hamzey Jr., *President & Human Resource Contact*

International Insurance Council
900 19th Street NW, Suite 250
Washington, DC 20006
202-682-2345

INSURANCE

Interstate Specialty Marketing
17722 Irvine Boulevard
Tustin, CA 92780-3220
714-505-1100
Number of Employees: 20

Gary Hendricks, *President*

ISU Insurance Group
3750 East Foothill Boulevard
Pasadena, CA 91107
626-440-0262

Donald Anderson, *President*

ITT/Hartford Insurance Group
One Pointe Drive
Brea, CA 92822
714-257-7500
Number of Employees: 300

Mark S. Dobrzenski, *General Manager*
John Preston, *Personnel Manager*

J&H Marsh & McLennan
4695 McArthur Court, Suite 700
Newport Beach, CA 92660
949-641-8899
Number of Employees: 700

John Burnham & Co.
610 West Ash Street
San Diego, CA 92101
619-231-1010
Number of Employees: 400

Brad Orr, *President*
Denise Hujing, *Director of Human Resources*

John Burnham & Company
2 Park Plaza, Suite 700
Irvine, CA 92614
949-833-2462
Number of Employees: 32

Nancy Green, *Office Manager*

Johnson Higgins, Marsh & McClennan
2029 Century Park East, Suite 2400
Los Angeles, CA 90067
213-624-5555
Number of Employees: 600

James McElvany, *Chairman*
Rebecca Merrit, *Vice President*

Keenan & Associates
2355 Crenshaw Boulevard, Suite 200
Torrance, CA 90501
310-212-3344
Web Address: www.keenanassociates.com
Number of Employees: 600

John Keenan, *CEO*
Pam Rhoden, *Human Resources Director*

Kemper Insurance Companies
2677 North Main Street
Santa Ana, CA 92705
714-480-3300
Number of Employees: 45

Debbie Seniff, *Office Manager*

Kemper Insurance Companies
17800 Castleton Street, Suite 300
City of Industry, CA 91748
626-369-7700
Web Address: www.kemperinsurance.com
Number of Employees: 100

Bert Moses, *Resident Vice President*
Al Yochen, *Director of Human Resources*

Liability Insurance Research Bureau
1501 Woodfield Road, Suite 400W
Schaumburg, IL 60173
847-330-8647

Liberty Mutual
6006 Wilshire Boulevard
Los Angeles, CA 90036
818-502-1500

Jim Caswell, *Regional Sales Manager*

Life Underwriters Association of Los Angeles
2 North Lake Avenue, Suite 250
Pasadena, CA 91101
626-584-6298

Barton R. Bruttig, *President*

Lincoln Financial Advisors
5 Hutton Centre Drive, Suite 700
Santa Ana, CA 92707-8715
714-754-1900
Number of Employees: 50

Jerry Boucher, *Regional President*
Peggy Taylor, *Human Resources*

Lockton Insurance Brokers
725 South Figueroa Street, 35th Floor
Los Angeles, CA 90017
213-689-0065
Number of Employees: 70

Frederick Toland, *CEO*
Eilene Bacon, *Office Administrator*

London American General Agency
10085 Carroll Canyon Road, Suite 100
San Diego, CA 92131
619-547-9000
Number of Employees: 15

Edward J. Maucere, *President*
Manual Martinez, *Vice President*

Los Angeles General Agents & Managers Association
235 North Lake Avenue, Suite 600
Pasadena, CA 91101
818-795-1500

Anita Bergsten, *President*

M.J. Hall & Company
5950 Canoga Avenue, Suite 530
Woodland Hills, CA 91367
818-888-9828
Number of Employees: 9

Steve Stern, *Branch Manager*
Jennifer Soper, *Office Manager*

Marine Office of America Corporation
500 North Central Avenue, Suite 910
Glendale, CA 91203
818-551-6350
Web Address: www.moac.com
Number of Employees: 2

James A. Thompson, *Branch Manager*

Marine Underwriters of Southern California/Kemper
17800 Castleton, Suite 300
City of Industry, CA 91748
626-369-8860

Kathy Daniels, *President*

Murria & Frick Insurance Agency
380 Stevens Avenue, First Floor
Solana Beach, CA 92075
619-259-5800
Web Address: www.ideafit.com
Number of Employees: 30

Joseph V. Murria, *CEO*
Deborah Grady, *Director of Human Resources*

Mutual of Omaha Group Operation
500 North Brand Boulevard, Suite 1000
Glendale, CA 91203
714-475-4550
Number of Employees: 12

Charles Russell, *Office Manager*

National Association of Casualty & Surety Agents
701 Pennsylvania Avenue NW, Suite 750
Washington, DC 20004
202-783-4400
Web Address: www.ciab.com

National Association of Health Underwriters
1000 Connecticut Avenue NW, Suite 810
Washington, DC 20004
202-223-5533

National Association of Independent Insurers
980 Ninth Street, Suite 1600
Sacramento, CA 95814
916-446-2009

Sam Sorich, *Assistant Vice President*

National Association of Insurance Brokers
1300 I Street NW, Suite 490E
Washington, DC 20005
202-628-6700

National Association of Insurance Commissioners
120 West 12th Street, Suite 1100
Kansas City, MO 64105
816-842-3600
Web Address: www.nahu.org

National Association of Insurance Women
PO Box 4410
Tulsa OK, 74159
918-744-5195
Web Address: www.naiw.org

National Association of Mutual Insurance Companies
PO Box 68700
Indianapolis, IN 46286
317-875-5250
Web Address: www.namic.org

National Association of Professional Insurance Agents
400 North Washington
Alexandria, VA 22314
703-836-9340

National Association of Surety Bond Producers
5225 Wisconsin Avenue NW, Suite 600
Washington, DC 20015
202-686-3700
Web Address: www.nasbp.org

National Automobile & Casualty Insurance
257 South Fair Oaks Avenue
Pasadena, CA 91105
626-577-0600
Number of Employees: 70

James V. O'Donnell, *President*
Raymond McMannis, *Director of Human Resources*

National Crop Insurance Services
7201 West 129th Street, Suite 200
Overland Park, KS 66213
913-685-2767
Web Address: www.ag-risk.org

National Fire Protection Association
1 Battery March Park
Quincy, MA 02269
617-770-3000
Web Address: www.nfpa.org

National Flood Insurance Program
PO Box 6465
Rocklin, MD 20849
800-611-6123

New York Life Insurance Co
2677 North Main Street, Suite 700
Santa Ana, CA 92705-6629
714-560-7800
Number of Employees: 7

John Chisam, *Managing Partner*
Eric Smith, *Office Manager*

Nico Insurance Services
7290 Navajo Road, Suite 111
San Diego, CA 92119
619-667-2111

Phillip D. Nico, *President*
Gail Seeman, *Hiring Contact*

Pacific Indemnity Group
801 South Figueroa, Suite 2400
Los Angeles, CA 90017
213-612-0880
Number of Employees: 95

William F. Mitchell, *Senior Vice President*
Michelle Scott, *Human Resources Manager*

Pacific Life Insurance Company
700 Newport Centre Drive
Newport Beach, CA 92660
949-640-3011
Job Hotline: 714-721-5050
Web Address: www.pacificlife.com
Number of Employees: 2500

Glenn Schafer, *President*
Anthony Bonno, *VP for Human Resources*

Pacific Natl/Vik Brothers Insurance
1561 Red Hill Avenue, Suite 100
Tustin, CA 92780
714-259-5700
Number of Employees: 20

Jo Jo McPherson, *Office Manager*

Personal Insurance Federation of California
980 9th Street, Suite 2030
Sacramento, CA 95814
916-442-6646

Dan C. Dunmoyer, *President*

Petersen International Insurance Brokers
23929 Valencia Boulevard, Suite 215
Valencia, CA 91355
805-254-0006
Web Address: www.picu.org
Number of Employees: 9

Thomas Petersen, *CEO*
Mike Petersen, *Hiring Manager*

PHD Insurance Brokers
12966 Euclid, Suite 495
Garden Grove, CA 92842
714-534-6310
Web Address: www.phdins.com
Number of Employees: 17

Howard Lewis, *President*

Pickering Insurance Services
1011 South Santa Fe Avenue, Suite K
Vista, CA 92083
760-758-9800
Web Address: pikins@aol.com
Number of Employees: 6

Randy Pickering, *President*

Professional Insurance Agents Association of California
101 South 1st Street, Suite 304
Burnak, CA 91502
818-973-4800

Professional Insurance Agents of California & Nevada
1315 I Street, Suite 200
Sacramento, CA 95814
916-443-4221

Alan A. Smith, Jr., *Executive Vice President*

Progressive Group
11010 Whiterock Road
Rancho Cordova, CA 95741
916-638-5212
Mike Niehaus, *General Manager*

Public Risk Management Association
1815 North Fortmeyer Drive, Suite 1020
Arlington, VA 22209
703-528-7701
Web Address: www.rims.org

Reinsurance Association of America
1301 Pennsylania Avenue NW, Suite 900
Washington, DC 20004
202-638-3690

Reliance Insurance Group
700 North Brand Boulevard
Glendale, CA 91203
818-507-9333
Number of Employees: 50
Scott Keller, *Region Vice President*

Republic Indemnity of America
15821 Ventura Boulevard, Suite 370
Encino, CA 91436
818-990-9860
Web Address: www.ri-net.com

David Mitchell, *Senior Vice President*
Mindy Kreger, *Director of Human Resources*

Risk and Insurance Management Society
655 3rd Avenue, Suite 200
New York, NY 10017
212-286-9292
Web Address: www.rims.org

Robert F. Driver Co.
1620 Fifth Avenue
San Diego, CA 92101
619-238-1828
Web Address: www.rfdriver.com
Number of Employees: 220

Thomas W. Corbett, *CEO*
Barbara Weiland, *Director of Human Resources*

Royal Insurance
801 North Brand Boulevard, Suite 500
Glendale, CA 91203
818-241-5212
Number of Employees: 70

John Norfleet, *Resident Vice President*
Harvard Auger, *Director of Human Resources*

Rubin Insurance Agency
6363 Greenwich Drive, Suite 120
San Diego, CA 92122
619-457-5720
Number of Employees: 7

Stuart Rubin, *President & Hiring Contact*

Safeco Insurance
330 North Brand Boulevard, Ninth Floor
Glendale, CA 91203
818-956-4200

Don Chambers, *Branch VP*
Dorothy Papazian, *Director of Human Resources*

San Diego Associates
3550 Camino del Rio North, Suite 206
San Diego, CA 92108
619-283-7800
Number of Employees: 6

David N. Peterson, *President & Hiring Contact*

Sherwood Insurance Services
21650 Oxnard, Suite 1400
Woodland Hills, CA 91367
818-593-2008
Number of Employees: 80

Curt L. Biersch, *President*
Nelly C. Luciano, *Branch Administrative Manager*

Society of Certified Insurance Counselors
3630 North Hills Drive
Austin, TX 78731
512-345-7932
Web Address: www.scic.com/alliance

Society of Insurance Research
691 Crossfire Ridge
Marietta, GA 30064
770-426-9270
Web Address: www.connetyou.com/sir/

Society of Insurance Trainers & Educators
2120 Market Street, Suite 108
San Francisco, CA 94114
415-621-2830

Lois A. Markovich, *Executive Director*

Society of Risk Management Consultants
300 Park Avenue, Suite 1700
New York, NY 10022
800-765-7762

State Compensation Insurance
1750 East Fourth Street
Santa Ana, CA 92705
714-565-5000
Number of Employees: 200

Liz Glaidden, *Office Manager*

State Farm Group
31303 Agoura Road
Westlake Village, CA 91363
818-707-5858

Greg Jones, *Regional Vice President*
Kevin McKay, *Director of Human Resources*

Stewart Smith West
550 North Brand Boulevard, Suite 200
Glendale, CA 91203
818-265-0860
Number of Employees: 30

Fred Anderson, *CEO*
Marion Patino, *Administrative Vice President*

Sullivan & Curits Insurance
2100 Main Street
Irvine, CA 92614
949-250-7172
Web Address: www.sullivan-curtis.com
Number of Employees: 65

Bill Curtis, *President*
Pam Bracini, *Director of Human Resources*

Superior Pacific Insurance
26601 Agoura Road
Calabasas, CA 91302
818-880-1600
Web Address: www.superior.com
Number of Employees: 355

William L. Gentz, *President*
Curtis H. Carson, *Director of Personnel*
Provider of worker's compensation insurance to businesses in California and Arizona. Focuses on smaller accounts in agriculture and hospitality. Subsidiaries provide data processing, vocational rehabilitation, legal, and paralegal services in-house.

Superior Pacific Insurance Company - Southern California Regional Office
5200 Canoga Avenue
Woodland Hills, CA 91367
818-226-6200

James L. Cinney, *Vice President*
Marcia Sutton, *Manager of Human Resources*

Surety Association of America
100 Wood Avenue South
Iselin, NJ 08830
908-494-7600

Swett & Crawford
515 South Figueroa, Suite 600
Los Angeles, CA 90071
213-439-3400
Number of Employees: 34

Daniel V. Colacurcio, *Executive Vice President*
Lori Hunter, *Branch Manager*

Teague Insurance Agency
5550 Baltimore Drive, Suite 100
La Mesa, CA 91942
619-464-6851

Walter Johnston Jr., *President*
Elizabeth Bonilla, *Office Manager*

TG International Insurance Brokerage
27352 Calle Regal
San Juan Capistrno, CA 92675
714-661-6019
Number of Employees: 20

W. W. Nevitt, *President*

The Atlantic Mutual Companies
770 The City Drive South, Suite 5000
Orange, CA 92868
714-740-0888
Web Address:
www.atlanticmutualcompanies.com
Number of Employees: 40

Robert F. Bell, *Marketing Center Manager*

The Centris Group
650 Town Center Drive, Suite 1600
Costa Mesa, CA 92626
949-549-1600
Web Address: www.centrisgroup.com
Number of Employees: 135

David L. Cargile, *President*
Patricia S. Boisseranc, *Director of Personnel*
A specialty insurance and reinsurance group.

The Council of Insurance Agents & Brokers
701 Pennsylvania Avenue NW, Suite 750
Washington, DC 20004
202-783-4400
Web Address: www.ciab.com

The David Companies
1940 Fifth Avenue, Suite 200
San Diego, CA 92101
619-230-8850
Number of Employees: 5

James H. David, *President*
Rita David, *Vice President & Hiring Contact*

The Grant Nelson Group
3131 Camino del Rio North, Suite 350
San Diego, CA 92108
619-521-5710

Michael Meehan, *Regional Vice President*
Ronnie Adair, *Regional Manager*

TIG Holding
5205 North OΔConnor Boulevard
Irving, TX 75039
972-831-5000

Don Hutson, *President*

Timothy S. Mills Insurance Services
4365 Executive Drive, Suite 1400
San Diego, CA 92121
619-535-1800
Number of Employees: 17

Thomas A. James, *President & Hiring Contact*

Tokio Marine & Fire Insurance Company
800 East Colorado Boulevard
Pasadena, CA 91101
626-568-7600
Number of Employees: 220

Jim Nomura, *General Manager*
Don Diamond, *Assistant Manager*

Topa Insurance Company
1800 Avenue of the Stars, Suite 1200
Los Angeles, CA 90067
310-201-0451
Web Address: www.topains.com
Number of Employees: 80

Nosh Marfatia, *President*
Janet Toma, *Human Resources Administrator*

Total Financial & Insurance Services
11835 West Olympic Boulevard, Suite 600
Los Angeles, CA 90064
310-477-7500
Web Address: www.totalfinancial.com
Number of Employees: 30

Martin Greenberg, *President*
Kevin Oliphant, *Human Resource Manager*

Travelers Insurance Company
145 South State College Boulevard
Brea, CA 92621
714-671-8000
Number of Employees: 340

Austin Lewis, *Office Manager*

Travelers Insurance Group
P.O. Box 1903
Van Nuys, CA 91408-190
818-778-0600

Beverly Ellis, *Manager*

TriWest Insurance Services
14140 Ventura Boulevard, Third Floor
Sherman Oaks, CA 91423
818-906-3350
Number of Employees: 159

Paul Bronow, *President*
Miriam Saliter, *Director of Human Resources*

Unicare Insurance Company
3070 Bristol Street, Suite 300
Costa Mesa, CA 92626
949-429-2400
Number of Employees: 157

Norma Velasco, *Office Manager*

Unico American Corporation
23251 Mulholland Drive
Woodland Hills, CA 91364
818-591-9800
Number of Employees: 139

Cari Cheldin, *President*
Stacy Kroll, *Director of Personnel*
Seller of property and casualty, health, and life insurance. Also provides insurance claim adjusting services and premium financing to insurance purchasers, as well as individual and group medical, dental, life, and accidental death and dismemberment insurance.

US Pension Services
3030 Old Ranch, Suite 400
Seal Beach, CA 90740
562-799-6333
Job Hotline: Ext 255
Number of Employees: 45
Cicely McKinney, *Human Resource Manager*

USAA Group
2241 Harvard Street
Sacramento, CA 95815
916-921-6366

Richard Fowler, *Senior VP & General Manager*

Wateridge Insurance Services
10525 Vista Sorrento Parkway, Suite 300
San Diego, CA 92121
619-452-2200
Number of Employees: 25

Jeffrey H. Byroads, *Managing General Partner*
John Clanton, *Vice President*

WEB Consultants
12832 Valley View Street, Suite 208
Garden Grove, CA 92845-2514
714-379-2424
Number of Employees: 42

Mr. Irwin, *President*

Western Insurance Information Service
3530 Wilshire Boulevard, Suite 1610
Los Angeles, CA 90010
213-738-5333
Web Address: www.wiis.org
Number of Employees: 3

Candysse Miller, *Director*

Western Security Surplus Insurance
790 East Colorado Boulevard, Suite 700
Pasadena, CA 91101
626-584-0110
Web Address: www.wssib.com
Number of Employees: 17

Richard L. Polizzi, *President*
Georgina Polizzi, *Director of Human Resources*

William J. King & Associates
5120 Avenida Encinas #A
Carlsbad, CA 92008
760-438-8850
Number of Employees: 6

William J. King, *President*
Beth Goldfarb, *Office Manager*

Willis Corroon Corp. of Los Angeles
801 North Brand Boulevard, Suite 400
Glendale, CA 91203
818-548-7500
Number of Employees: 85

Annette Zideam, *Director of Human Resources*

Willis Corroon Corp. of Orange County
1551 North Tustin Avene, Suite 1000
Santa Ana, CA 92705
714-953-9521
Number of Employees: 45
Kevin Reed, *CEO*

Willis Corroon Corp. of San Diego
1615 Murray Canyon Road, Suite 905
San Diego, CA 92108
619-297-7111
M. Monte Richardson, *President*
Linda Madsen, *Vice President & Hiring Contact*

Wood Gutmann Insurance Brokers
3100 Bristol Street, Suite 390
Costa Mesa, CA 92626-3096
949-557-0800
Number of Employees: 50
Donald L. Wood, *Partner*
Kathryn Stjernstrom, *Director of Human Resources*

Zurich-America Insurance Group
770 The City Drive South, Suite 8500
Suite 8500
Orange, CA 92868
818-500-4700

Pam Rygiel, *Territorial Executive*

Further References

• Associations •

America Insurance Association
1130 Connecticut Avenue, N.W., Suite 1000
Washington, D.C. 20036
202-828-7100
Web Address: www.aiadc.org
Represents Property and Casualty Insurance Providers.

American Council of Life Insurance
1001 Pennsylvania Avenue, N.W., 5th Floor
Washington, D.C. 20004
202-624-2000
Advancement of Industry

Insurance Information Institute
110 William Street, 24th Floor
New York, NY 10038
212-669-9200
Web Address: www.iii.org
Information and Mass Media for Industry

National Association of Life Underwriters
1922 F Street, N.W.
Washington, D.C. 20006
202-331-6000
Web Address: www.agents-online.com
Promotes Ethical Standards and Goodwill

• Publications •

American Agent & Broker
330 North 4th Street
St. Louis, MO 63102
314-421-5445
Magazine covering independent insurance agencies in fire, casualty, or surety.

Business Insurance
740 North Rush Street
Chicago, IL 60611-2590
312-649-5350

Independent Agent
127 South Peyton Street
Alexandria, VA 22310
703-683-4422
Magazine covering both property/casualty and life/health insurance agencies.

Largest & Fastest Growing Companies

Aames Financial Corporation
www.aamesfinancial.com
Ace Parking Management
www.aceparking.com
Activision
www.activision.com
Advanced Access
www.advaccess.com
Advanced Marketing Services
www.admsweb.com
AECOM Technology Corp.
www.dmjm.com
Agouron Pharmaceuticals
www.agouron.com
Alaris Medical Systems
www.alarismed.com
Align-Rite International
www.align-rite.com
AlliedSignal Aerospace
www.alliedsignal.com
American Suzuki Motor
Corporation
www.suzuki.com
Ameron International Corporation
www.ameron-intl.com
Andataco
www.andataco.com
Anderson Lithograph Company
www.andlitho.com
Applied Micro Circuits
Corporation
www.amcc.com
ARB
www.arbinc.com
Artisan
www.artisanpictures.com
Ashworth
www.ashworthinc.com
Atlantic Richfield Company
www.arco.com
Aura Systems
www.aurasystems.com
Balboa Travel
www.balboatravel.com
Barnes Wholesale
www.barneswholesale.com
Bason Computer
www.basoncomputer.com
Belkin Components
www.belkin.com
Bell Industries
www.bellind.com
Big 5 Corp.
www.big5sportinggoods.com
Bob Baker Enterprises
www.bobbaker.com
Bonded Motors
www.bondedmotors.com
Breath Asure
www.breathasure.com
Burnham Pacific Properties
www.bpac.com
Callaway Golf Company
www.callawaygolf.com

CalMat Company
www.calmart.com
Candle Corporation
www.candle.com
CareAmerica Health Plans
www.careamerica.com
COA
www.coaster.com
Compu-D International
www.compu-d.com
Comtrade Electronic
www.comtrade.com
Conterm Consolidation Services
USA
www.conterm.com
Countrywide Credit Industries
www.countrywide.com
Coverall Cleaning Concepts
www.coverall.com
CyberMedia
www.cybermedia.com
Dames & Moore
www.dames.com
Dataworks
www.interactive-group.com
DataWorks Corporation
www.dataworks.com
Datron World Communications
www.dtsi.com
DH Technology
www.axiohm.com
Diagnostic Products Corporation
www.dpc.web.com
Dick Clark Productions
www.dickclark.com
Dirt Cheap Car Rental
www.w3m.com/dirtcheap.com
Dole Food Company
www.dole.com
Dura Pharmaceuticals
www.durapharm.com
Dycam
www.dycam.com
EarthLink Network
www.earthlink.net
Easton Sports
www.eastonsports.com
Edison International
www.sce.com
Electro Rent Corp.
www.electrorent.com
En Pointe Technologies
www.enpointe.com
ENCAD
www.encad.com
Epic Solutions
www.epicsolutions.com
Executive Car Leasing
www.executivecarleasing.com
Fedco
www.fedco.com
First Consulting Group
www.scgnet.com

Foodmaker
www.jackinthebox.com
Fountainview
www.sunc.com
FPA Medical Management
www.fpamm.com
Galpin Motors
www.gogalphin.com
Gensia Sicor
www.gensiasicor.com
Glacier Water Services
www.glacierwater.com
Goldmine Software Corporation
www.goldminesw.com
Gray Cary Ware & Freidenrich
www.gcwp.com
Guitar Center
www.musician.com
H.F. Ahmanson & Company
www.homewsavings.com
Hilton Hotels Corp.
www.hilton.com
HNC Software
www.hnc.com
Hughes Electronics Commerce
www.hughes.com
IHOP Corp.
www.ihop.com
Imperial Bancorp
www.imperialbank.com
INCOMNET
www.incomnet.com
Infonet Services
www.infonet.com
Insurance Auto Auctions
www.iaa.com
Interactive Group
www.interactive-group.com
IT NetTrac Corp.
www.nettrac.com
Jenny Craig
www.jennycraig.com
K-Swiss
www.kswiss.com
Kennedy-Wilson
www.kennedywilson.com
Kett Engineering Corp.
www.ketteng.com
Kinetics Technology International
Corp.
www.kticorp.com
Koo Koo Roo
www.kookooroo.com
Kushner Locke Co.
www.kushnerlocke.com
Learning Tree International
www.learningtree.com
Liquid Investments
www.mesadistributing.com
Lithographix
www.lithographix.com
Litton Industries
www.littoncorp.com

Quick Reference

Logicon
www.logicon.com
Machinery Sales Co.
www.mchysales.com
Mail Boxes Etc.
www.mbc.com
Marshall Industries
www.marshall.com
Mattel
www.mattel.com
Maxwell Technologies
www.maxwell.com
Mazda Motor of America
www.mazdausa.com
Midern Computer
www.sagernotebook.com
MiniMed
www.minimed.com
Mitake
www.mitake.com
Mitsuba Corp.
www.mitsuba.com
Modern Mold International
www.pens.com
Morrow-Meadows Corp.
www.morrow-meadows.com
MRV Communications
www.nbase.com
Natural Alternatives International
www.nai.online.com
Nestle USA
www.nestle.com
New Century BMW
www.ncbmw.com
New Star Media
www.doveaudio.com
Norm Reeves Honda
www.normreeves.com
NTN Communications
www.ntn.com
O'Melveny & Myers
www.omm.com
Optimal Integrated Solutions
www.optimslis.net
Oriental Motor USA Corp.
www.omusa.com
Osicom Technologies
www.osicom.com
Pacific Theatres Corp.
www.pacifictheatres.com
Pearson Ford Co.
www.pearsonford.com
Peerless Systems Corp.
www.peerless.com
Pinkerton's
www.pinkertons.com
PinnacleOne
www.pinnacle.com
PMR Corp.
www.pmrcorp.com
Pollution Research & Control Corp.
www.dasibi.com
Public Storage
www.publicstorage.com
Qualcomm
www.qualcomm.com
Quidel Corp.
www.quidel.com
R.J. Gordon & Co.
www.rjgordon.com
Realty Income Corp.
www.realtyincome.com
Reliance Steel & Aluminum Co.
www.rsac.com
Rohr
www.rhor.com
Ryan Herco Products Co.
www.ryanherco.com

San Diego Travel Group
www.sdtg.com
Science Applications International Corp.
www.saic.com
Signature Resorts
www.sunterra.com
Software Dynamics
www.sdinc.com
Software Technologies Corp.
www.stc.com
Southern California Water Co.
www.scwater.com
Southland Industries
www.southlandind.com
Space Electronics
www.spaceelectronics.com
Spatializer Audio Laboratories
www.spatializer.com
Special Devices
www.specialdevises.aol.com
Stac
www.stac.com
Sunkist Growers
www.sunkist.com
Sunrise Medical
www.sunrisemedical.com
Superior Industries International
www.superiorindustries.com
Systems Engineering Associates
www.sea.com
Tetra Tech
www.tetratech.com
The National Dispatch Center
www.ndcwireless.com
The Titan Corp.
www.titan.com
The Walt Disney Company
www.disney.com
ThermoTrex Corp.
www.thermo.com
Ticketmaster Group
www.ticketmaster.com
Times Mirror Co.
www.latimes.com
TransWestern Publishing
www.transwesterpub.com
Trillium Digital Systems
www.trillium.com
TRW Space & Electronics Group
www.trw.com
TV/COM International
www.tvcom.com
University of Southern California
www.usc.edu
Utility Trailer Manufacturing Co.
www.utilitytrailer.com
Ventura Foods LLC
www.venturafood.com
ViewSonic
www.viewsonic.com
Wavetek Instruments
www.wavetek.com
Webb Automotive Group
www.toyotacerritos.com
WellPoint Health Networks
www.wellpoint.com
Western Atlas
www.univa.com
WGI Solutions
www.wgis.com
Wheb Systems
www.whebsys.com
Xerox
www.zero.com
Xpedx
www.xpedx.com
Zenith National Insurance Corp.
www.znic.com

SEARCHING FOR JOBS OVER THE INTERNET

JobSourceNetwork.com

LARGEST COMPANIES

20th Century Insurance
6301 Owensmouth Avenue
Woodland Hills, CA 91367
818-704-3700
Web Address: www.20thcenturyinsurance.com
Number of Employees: 1615

William L. Mellick, *President*

Aames Financial Corporation
350 South Grand Avenue
Los Angeles, CA 90071
213-640-5000
Job Hotline: 213-210-5554
Web Address: www.aamesfinancial.com
Number of Employees: 1385

Cary H. Thompson, *President*
Patrick Genyea, *Director of Personnel*
Katherine Tober, *Human Resources Director*
Provider, purchaser, seller, and servicer of mortgages and home
equity loans. Aames, together with subsidiary One Stop Mortgage,
has about 100 retail loan offices across the country.

Ace Parking Management
645 Ash Street
San Diego, CA 92101
619-233-6624
Job Hotline: 619-231-9501
Web Address: www.aceparking.com
Number of Employees: 4,000

Scott A. Jones, *CEO*
Preston Carpenter, *Human Resource & Office
    Manager*

Advanced Access
9395 Cabot Drive
San Diego, CA 92126
619-693-1200
Job Hotline: 619-693-1200 x1195
Web Address: www.advaccess.com

James B. Warburton, *CEO*
Leigh Jenkins, *Human Resource Administrator*

Advanced Aerodynamics & Structures
3205 Lakewood Boulevard
Long Beach, CA 90808
562-938-8618
Web Address: www.aasiaircraft.com
Number of Employees: 95

Carl Leei Chen, *CEO*
Karen Kimber, *Human Resource Manager*

Advanced Marketing Services
5880 Oberlin Drive, Suite 400
San Diego, CA 92121
858-457-2500
Web Address: www.admsweb.com
Number of Employees: 200

Michael Nicita, *President*
Alisa Judge, *Vice President for Human Resources*

AECOM Technology Corp.
3250 Wilshire Boulevard
Los Angeles, CA 90010
213-381-3612
Web Address: www.dmjm.com
Number of Employees: 500

Richard Newman, *CEO*
John Dyer, *Recruiting Director*

Agouron Pharmaceuticals
10350 North Torrey Pines Road
La Jolla, CA 92037
619-622-3000
Web Address: www.agouron.com
Number of Employees: 537

Peter Johnson, *President*

Aircraft Engineering Corp.
15500 Texaco Avenue
Paramount, CA 90723
562-634-2401
Number of Employees: 110

E. T. Warner, *CEO & President*
Gary Petrilla, *Human Resources Manager*

Aisin World Corp. of America
24330 Garnier Street
Torrance, CA 90505
310-326-8681
Web Address: www.aircrafteng.com
Number of Employees: 20

Tetsuro Senga, *President*
Andy Tsui, *Controller & Human Resource
    Manager*

Alaris Medical Systems
10221 Wateridge Circle
San Diego, CA 92121
619-458-7000
Web Address: www.alarismed.com
Number of Employees: 3,000

William J. Mercer, *President*

Aldila
15822 Bernardo Center Drive
San Diego, CA 92127
619-592-0404
Number of Employees: 500

Gary T. Barbera, *CEO*
Mary Ann Jacobs, *Personnel Representative*

Align-Rite International
2428 Ontario Street
Burbank, CA 91504
818-843-7220
Web Address: www.align-rite.com
Number of Employees: 258

James L. MacDonald, *President*
Liz Ashual, *Director of Personnel*

American Suzuki Motor Corporation
3251 East Imperial Highway
Brea, CA 92821
714-996-7040
Web Address: www.suzuki.com

Masao Nagura, *President*
Ahmad Tarzi, *Director of Personnel*

Ameron International Corporation
245 South Los Robles Avenue
Pasadena, CA 91101
818-683-4000
Web Address: www.ameron-intl.com
Number of Employees: 50

James Marlen, *President*
Terry O'Shea, *Director of Human Resources*

Andataco
10140 Mesa Rim Road
San Diego, CA 92121
619-453-9191
Web Address: www.andataco.com
Number of Employees: 150

David Sykes, *President*
Ligaya, *Office Manager*

Anderson Lithograph Company
3217 South Garfield Avenue
Los Angeles, CA 90040
213-727-7767
Web Address: www.andlitho.com
Number of Employees: 400

John Fosmire, *President*
Betty Miyahira, *Human Resources Director*

Applause Enterprises
6101 Variel Avenue
Woodland Hills, CA 91367
818-595-2690

Melvyn Gagerman, *CEO*

Applied Micro Circuits Corporation
6290 Sequence Drive
San Diego, CA 92121
858-450-9333
Web Address: www.amcc.com
Number of Employees: 325

Dave Rickey, *President*
Candace Kilborn, *Director of Human Resources*

Arden Group
2020 South Central Avenue
Compton, CA 90220
310-638-2842
Web Address: www.gelsons.com

Bernard Briskin, *Chairman & President*

Arden Realty Group
11601 Wilshire Boulevard, 9th Floor
Los Angeles, CA 90025
310-271-8600
Number of Employees: 150

Richard S. Ziman, *CEO*
Joyce Sotero, *Human Resources Administrator*

Argonaut Group
1800 Avenue of the Stars, Suite 1175
Los Angeles, CA 90067
310-553-0561
Job Hotline: 650-326-0900
Web Address: www.argonautgroup.com
Number of Employees: 200

Marla Watson, *President*

Ashworth
2791 Loker Avenue West
Carlsbad, CA 92008
760-438-6610
Web Address: www.ashworthinc.com
Number of Employees: 300

Randall L. Herrel, *President*
Stacey Knepper, *Director of Human Resources*

Assael BMW
1451 South Mountain Avenue
Monrovia, CA 91016
626-358-4269

Dennis Assael, *President*
Jeffrey Tamanski, *Director of Humn Resources*

Atlantic Richfield Company
515 South Flower Street, 46th Floor
Los Angeles, CA 90071
213-486-3511
Web Address: www.arco.com
Number of Employees: 2891

Mike Bowlin, *CEO*

Aura Systems
2335 Alaska Avenue
El Segundo, CA 90245
310-643-5300
Web Address: www.aurasystems.com
Number of Employees: 200

Zvi Kurtzman, *President*
Melinda Chestney, *Human Resources Manager*

Avery Dennison
150 North Orange Grove Boulevard
Pasadena, CA 91103
626-304-2000
Number of Employees: 200

Charles Miller, *Chairman*
Joyce Murdock, *Director of Human Resources*

Balboa Travel

5414 Oberlin Drive
San Diego, CA 92121
619-678-3300
Job Hotline: 619-678-3470
Web Address: www.balboatravel.com
Number of Employees: 200

Joe da Rosa, *CEO*
Katie O'Grady, *Personnel Administrator*

Bank of America

450 B Street
San Diego, CA 92101
619-515-7575
Job Hotline: 619-515-5514
Number of Employees: 50

Doug Sawyer, *Executive Vice President*
Maria Bouer, *Human Resource Manager*

Bank of America

555 South Flower Street
Los Angeles, CA 90071
213-228-4567
Number of Employees: 7360

R. Thomas Decker, *Executive Vice President*
Maria Garcia, *Recruiter*

Barnes Wholesale

740 Glasgow Avenue
Inglewood, CA 90301
310-641-1885
Web Address: www.barneswholesale.com

Bob Schwartz, *CEO*
Dave Thomas, *Human Resources Manager*

Bason Computer

20130 Plummer Street
Chatsworth, CA 91311
818-725-9704
Web Address: www.basoncomputer.com

R. J. Yeh, *President*
H. J. Yeh, *Director of Human Resources*

Belkin Components

501 West Walnut Street
Compton, CA 90220
310-898-1100
Web Address: www.belkin.com
Number of Employees: 400

Chester Pipkin, *CEO*
Donna Pierson, *Director of Human Resoucres*

Ben Myerson Candy Company

928 Towne Avenue
Los Angeles, CA 90021
213-623-6266
Number of Employees: 300

Robert Myerson, *Chairman*
Shala Weaver, *Human Resources Manager*

Big 5 Corp.

2525 East El Segundo Boulevard
El Segundo, CA 90245
310-536-0611
Web Address: www.big5sportinggoods.com
Number of Employees: 95

Robert Miller, *CEO*
Jeff Fraley, *Director of Human Resources*

Bob Baker Enterprises

591 Camino de la Reina, Suite 1100
San Diego, CA 92108
858-297-1001
Web Address: www.bobbaker.com
Number of Employees: 800

Robert H. Baker, *President*

Bocchi Laboratories

20465 East Walnut Drive
Walnut, CA 91789
909-598-1951
Number of Employees: 100

Robert Bocchi, *President*

Boeing Corp.

3855 Lakewood Boulevard
Long Beach, CA 90846
562-593-5511
Web Address: www.boeing.com
Number of Employees: 20,000

W. J. Orlowski, *President*

Boeing North American

6633 Canoga Avenue
Canoga Park, CA 91303
818-586-1000
Job Hotline: 818-586-2834
Number of Employees: 8250

Ruff Turner, *President of Rocketdyne Division*
Janet Saltemier, *Director of Human Resources*

Bonded Motors

7522 South Maie Avenue
Los Angeles, CA 90001
213-583-8631
Web Address: www.bondedmotors.com
Number of Employees: 400

Aaron Landon, *CEO*
Paul Lim, *Director of Human Resources*

Breath Asure

26025 Mureau Road
Calabasas, CA 91302
818-878-0011
Web Address: www.breathasure.com
Number of Employees: 45

Lauren Raissen, *President*
Janet Gallagher, *Director of Human Resources*

Burnham Pacific Properties
110 West A Street, Suite 900
San Diego, CA 92101
619-652-4700
Web Address: www.bpac.com
Number of Employees: 60

J. David Martin, *President*
Donna Godbout, *Director of Human Resources*
Robyn Lamb, *Office Manager*

BW/IP
200 Oceangate, Suite 900
Long Beach, CA 90802
562-435-3700
Number of Employees: 130

Bernard G. Rethore, *Chairman & President*

Cacique
14940 Proctor Avenue
City of Industry, CA 91744
626-961-3399
Number of Employees: 320

Gillbert D. Cardenas, *President*
Maria Pineda, *Director of Human Resources*

California Dairies
11709 East Artesia Boulevard
Artesia, CA 90701
562-865-1291
Number of Employees: 100

Gary Korsmeier, *CEO*

California State Bank
100 North Barranca Street
West Covina, CA 91791
626-915-4424
Number of Employees: 150

Thomas A. Bishop, *CEO*
Margaret Tunner, *Director of Human Resources*

Callaway Golf Company
2285 Rutherford Road
Carlsbad, CA 92008
760-931-1771
Web Address: www.callawaygolf.com
Number of Employees: 2500

Donald H. Dye, *President*
Elizabeth O'Mea, *SVP of Human Resources*
Sheri Wright, *Human Resources Manager*

CalMat Company
3200 San Fernando Road
Los Angeles, CA 90065
213-258-2777
Web Address: www.calmart.com
Number of Employees: 1,800

A. Frederick Gerstell, *CEO*
Karen Elston, *Recruiter*

Carbite Golf Company
6330 Nancy Ridge Drive, Suite 107
San Diego, CA 92121
619-625-0065
Number of Employees: 100

Mike Spacciapolli, *CEO & Hiring Contact*

CareAmerica Health Plans
6300 Canoga Avenue
Woodland Hills, CA 91367
818-598-8000
Job Hotline: 818-228-2400
Web Address: www.careamerica.com

Robert P. White, *President*

Carlton Forge Works
7743 Adams Street
Paramount, CA 90723
562-633-1131
Number of Employees: 200

Allan Carlton, *Chairman*

Cedarwood-Young Co.
14620 Joanbridge Street
Baldwin Park, CA 91706
626-962-4047
Number of Employees: 150

Stephen Young, *President*
Joe Pearson, *Director of Human Resources*

Central Financial Acceptance
5480 East Ferguson Drive
Commerce, CA 90022
213-720-8600
Number of Employees: 2,000

Gary M. Cypres, *President*
Marilyn Ogella, *Employee Benefits Manager*

Certified Grocers of California
2601 South Eastern Avenue
Los Angeles, CA 90040
213-723-7476
Number of Employees: 2,400

Alfred Plamann, *President*
Ray Cook, *Human Resource Administrator*

Charlotte Russe
4645 Morena Boulevard
San Diego, CA 92117
619-587-1500
Number of Employees: 300

Bernie Zeichner, *President*
Sue Penn, *Human Resource Manager*

Chart House Enterprises
115 South Acacia Avenue
Solana Beach, CA 92075
619-755-8281

Cheesecake Factory

26950 Agoura Road
Calabasas Hills, CA 91301
818-880-9323
Number of Employees: 200
David Overton, *President*
Jennifer Jackson, *Director of Human Resources*

Children's Wonderland

28310 Roadside Drive
Agoura, CA 91301
818-865-1306
Kenneth W. Bitticks, *Chairman*
Cynthia Batastini, *Director of Human Resources*

Chorus Line

4505 Bandini Boulevard
Vernon, CA 90040
213-881-3200
Number of Employees: 500
Barry Sacks, *Chairman*
Robert Ranieri, *Director of Human Resources*

City Chevrolet

2111 Morena Boulevard
San Diego, CA 92110
619-276-6171

Kenneth Nieman, *President*
Tina Alo, *Human Resource Manager*

Clougherty Packing/Farmer John

3049 East Vernon Avenue
Los Angeles, CA 90058
213-583-4621
Number of Employees: 2,300

Joseph Clougherty, *President*
Jose Torres, *Director of Personnel*

Coast Savings Financial

1000 Wilshire Boulevard
Los Angeles, CA 90017
213-316-8635

Ray Martin, *President*

Coastcast Corporation

3025 East Victoria Street
Rancho Dominguez, CA 90221
310-638-0595
Web Address: www.coastcast.com
Number of Employees: 900

Hans H. Buehler, *CEO*
Bob Roman, *Director of Human Resources*

Coaster Company

12928 Sandoval Street
Santa Fe Springs, CA 90670
562-944-7899
Web Address: www.coaster.com
Number of Employees: 350
Michael Yeh, *President*
Matthew Chen, *VP of Human Resources*

Cohu

5755 Kearny Villa Road
San Diego, CA 92123
858-277-6700
Web Address: cohu.com
Number of Employees: 200

Charles A. Schwan, *CEO*
Linda Jacobson, *Human Resource Manager*

Color Systems

5648 Copley Drive
San Diego, CA 92111
619-560-8900

Gary Lavin, *CEO*
Lisa Lavin, *Human Resource Director*

Commerce Casino

6131 East Telegraph Road
City of Commerce, CA 90040
213-721-2100
Job Hotline: 213-838-3399
Number of Employees: 2,000

George Tumanjan, *President*
Susan Holyfield, *Director of Human Resources*

Compu-D International

6741 Van Nuys Boulevard
Van Nuys, CA 91405
818-787-3282
Web Address: www.compu-d.com

Mike Dardashti, *CEO*

Computer Sciences Corporation

2100 East Grand Avenue
El Segundo, CA 90245
310-615-0311
Job Hotline: 310-615-1785
Web Address: www.csc.com
Number of Employees: 4,500

Van Honeycutt, *CEO*
Marv Pulliam, *Director of Human Resources*
Fredrick Wallrath, *Human Resource Manager*
Fredrick Wallrath, Human Resource Manager: 310-615-1785

Comtrade Electronic

1215 Bixby Drive
City of Industry, CA 91745
626-961-6688
Web Address: www.comtrade.com
Number of Employees: 100

Christopher Luke, *President*
Jerry Chen, *Director of Human Resources*

Consolidated Electrical Distributors

31356 Via Colinas
Westlake Village, CA 91362
818-991-9000

Keith Colburn, *President*

Conterm Consolidation Services USA
555 East Ocean Boulevard, Suite 700
Long Beach, CA 90802
562-432-8755
Job Hotline: Ext 217
Web Address: www.conterm.com
Number of Employees: 20

Bob Hackett, *President*
Iris Strom, *Human Resource Manager*

Cosmetic Group U.S.A.
11312 Penrose Street
Sun Valley, CA 91352
818-767-2889
Number of Employees: 250

Michael Baker, *President*
Carol Wong, *Director of Human Resources*

Coverall Cleaning Concepts
3111 Camino del Rio North, Ninth Floor
San Diego, CA 92108
619-584-1911
Web Address: www.coverall.com
Number of Employees: 50

Alex Roudi, *CEO*
Rachele Hershkowitz, *Human Resource Manager*

Crest Beverage Company
7598 Trade Street
San Diego, CA 92121
619-566-1800
Number of Employees: 162

Steven S. Sourapas, *President*

CU Bancorp
16030 Ventura Boulevard
Encino, CA 91436
818-907-9122
Number of Employees: 65

Dave Ranier, *CEO*
Emily Hamilton, *Manager of Human Resources*

Cush Automotive Group
1700 Auto Parkway North
Escondido, CA 92029
760-737-3200
Number of Employees: 350

Stephen P. Cushman, *President*

Dames & Moore
6 Hutton Centre Drive, Suite 700
Santa Ana, CA 92707-5755
714-433-2000
Web Address: www.dames.com
Number of Employees: 90

Roy Patterson, *Managing Principal*

Dames & Moore
9665 Chesapeake Drive, Suite 201
San Diego, CA 92123
619-541-0833
Web Address: www.dames.com
Number of Employees: 30

Michael W. Nienberg, *Managing Principal*
Caroline Washington, *Human Resource Manager*

Daou Systems
5120 Shoreham Place
San Diego, CA 92122
858-452-2221
Web Address: www.daou.com
Number of Employees: 500

Larry Grandia, *CEO*
Lou Bon, *Director of Recruitment*

Datron World Communications
3030 Enterprise Court
Vista, CA 92083
760-747-1079
Web Address: www.dtwc.com
Number of Employees: 150

Decore-Ative Specialties
4414 North Azusa Canyon Road
Irwindale, CA 91706
626-960-7731

Jack Lansford, *CEO*
Carmen Paz, *Director of Human Resources*

DEP Corporation
2101 East Via Arado Avenue
Rancho Dominguez, CA 90220
310-604-0777
Number of Employees: 300

Robert Berglass, *Chairman & President*
Pat Allen, *Human Resources Manager*

Design Collection
2209 South Santa Fe Avenue
Los Angeles, CA 90058
213-277-9200
Number of Employees: 40

Simon Barlava, *President*
Mire Byrne, *Director of Personnel*

DH Technology
15070 Avenue of Science
San Diego, CA 92128
619-451-3485
Web Address: www.axiohm.com
Number of Employees: 70

Nicolas Dourassoff, *CEO*
Geri Weftberg, *Human Resource Manager*

Diagnostic Products Corporation
5700 West 96th Street
Los Angeles, CA 90045
213-776-0180
Job Hotline: 213-776-2609
Web Address: www.dpc.web.com
Number of Employees: 70

Sigi Ziering, *CEO*
Ava Sedgwick, *Director of Human Resources*

Directed Electronics
1 Viper Way
Vista, CA 92083
760-598-6200
Web Address: www.directed.com
Number of Employees: 250

Darrell E. Issa, *President*
Steven Boykin, *Human Resources Manager*

DMX
11400 West Olympic Boulevard
Los Angeles, CA 90064
310-444-1744
Number of Employees: 120
Jerold Rubinstein, *CEO*
Kathy Carpal, *Human Resources Director*

Docusource
7040 Hayvenhurst Avenue
Van Nuys, CA 91406
818-904-3944
Number of Employees: 60
Lester Walker, *President*
Randa Huleis, *Director of Human Resources*

Dole Food Company
31365 Oak Crest Drive
Westlake Village, CA 91361
818-879-6600
Job Hotline: 818-874-4999
Web Address: www.dole.com
Number of Employees: 46000
David H. Murdock, *CEO*
Sue Hagen, *Director of Personnel*
World's largest producer of fresh fruits and vegetables, as well as canned fruits and juices.

Don Kott Auto Center
21212 South Avalon Boulevard
Carson, CA 90745
310-816-2600
Number of Employees: 150
Margaret Kott, *President*
Jim MIller, *Human Resources Director*

Douglas E. Barnhart
16981 Via Tazon, Suite H
San Diego, CA 92128
858-487-1101
Number of Employees: 250

Douglas E. Barnhart, *Managing Principal*
Amy Williams, *Human Resource Manager*

Drew Ford Volkswagen Hyundai
8970 La Mesa Boulevard
La Mesa, CA 91941
619-464-7777
Number of Employees: 400

Joe Drew, *President*

Dunn-Edwards Corp.
4885 East 52nd Place
Los Angeles, CA 90046
213-771-3330
Number of Employees: 175

Robert Mitchell, *Chairman*
Jack Slagle, *Director of Human Resources*

Dura Pharmaceuticals
5880 Pacific Center Boulevard
San Diego, CA 92121
619-457-2553
Web Address: www.durapharm.com
Number of Employees: 238

Cam L. Garner, *President*

EarthLink Network
3100 New York Drive
Pasadena, CA 91107
626-296-2400
Web Address: www.earthlink.net

C. Garry Betty, *President*
Michael Ihole, *Director of Human Resources*

Easton Sports
7855 Haskell Avenue
Van Nuys, CA 91406
818-782-6445
Web Address: www.eastonsports.com
Number of Employees: 1,000

Jim Easton, *CEO*
Michelle Cenal, *Director of Human Resources*

Edison International
2244 Walnut Grove Avenue
Rosemead, CA 91770
626-302-1212?
Job Hotline: 626-302-9850
Web Address: www.sce.com
Number of Employees: 13,000

John Bryson, *CEO*
Lilian Gorman, *Director of Human Resources*

Electro Rent Corp.
6060 Sepulveda Boulevard
Van Nuys, CA 91411
818-786-2525
Web Address: www.electrorent.com
Number of Employees: 300

Daniel Greenberg, *CEO*
Peter Shapiro, *Director of Human Resources*

Elite Show Services
2878 Camino del Rio South, Suite 260
San Diego, CA 92108
619-574-1589
Number of Employees: 1,500

Gus Kontopuls, *CEO*
Ken Mickelsen, *Human Resource Manager*

Ellison Machinery
9912 Pioneer Boulevard
Santa Fe Springs, CA 90670
562-949-8311
Job Hotline: Ext 553
Number of Employees: 100

W. Ellison, *CEO*
Jo Ellen Hagerty, *Director of Human Resources*

En Pointe Technologies
100 North Sepulveda Boulevard
El Segundo, CA 90245
310-725-1157
Web Address: www.enpointe.com
Number of Employees: 500

Attiazaz Din, *President*
Robert Chilman, *Human Resource Director*

ENCAD
6059 Cornerstone Court West
San Diego, CA 92121
858-452-0882
Web Address: www.encad.com
Number of Employees: 400

David A. Purcell, *CEO*
Simon Meth, *Human Resources Director*

Epic Solutions
10907 Technology Place
San Diego, CA 92127
858-675-3525
Web Address: www.epicsolutions.com
Number of Employees: 65

John Gledson, *CEO*

Equity Marketing
6330 San Vicente Boulevard
Los Angeles, CA 90048
310-887-4300
Number of Employees: 100

S. P. Robeck, *Chairman*
Samantha Martin, *Director of Human Resources*
Liz Dellums, *Human Resource Manager*

Ernest Paper Products
2727 East Vernon Avenue
Los Angeles, CA 90058
213-583-6561
Number of Employees: 100

A. Wilson, *Chairman*
Bob Salvador, *Director of Human Resources*

Excel Realty Trust
17140 Bernardo Center Drive, Suite 300
San Diego, CA 92128
619-485-9400
Web Address: excelegacy.com
Number of Employees: 45

Gary B. Sabin, *President*
Dianne Lyman, *Human Resource Manager*

Executive Car Leasing
7807 Santa Monica Boulevard
Los Angeles, CA 90046
213-654-5000
Web Address: www.executivecarleasing.com
Number of Employees: 100

Sam Goldman, *President*
Bob Salvador, *Director of Human Resources*

Film Roman
12020 Chandler Boulevard, Suite 200
North Hollywood, CA 91607
818-761-2544
Number of Employees: 363

David B. Pritchard, *President*
Genny Sanchez, *Director of Personnel*
*Independent animation studio that creates family-oriented animated
television programming. Its animated series and specials air on
broadcast and cable networks such as CBS, Fox, and USA Network.*

Finishmaster
4553 Glencoe Avenue
Marina del Ray, CA 90292
310-306-7112
Web Address: www.finishmaster.com
Number of Employees: 400

Tom Young, *President*
Bob Pruim, *Director of Personnel*

First Consulting Group
111 West Ocean Boulevard, 4th Floor
Long Beach, CA 90802
562-624-5200
Web Address: www.scgnet.com
Number of Employees: 700

James Reep, *CEO*
Leslie Hollingsworth, *Human Resource Manager*

Foodmaker
9330 Balboa Avenue
San Diego, CA 92123
619-571-2121
Job Hotline: 619-571-2200
Web Address: www.jackinthebox.com
Number of Employees: 500

Robert J. Nugent, *President*
Linda Jeffrey, *Human Resource Manager*

FPA Medical Management
3636 Nobel Drive, 2nd Floor
San Diego, CA 92122
619-453-1000
Web Address: www.fpamm.com
Number of Employees: 300

Seth Flam, *President*
Tanisha Bowadan, *Human Resource Manager*

Frederick's of Hollywood
6608 Hollywood Boulevard
Los Angeles, CA 90028
213-466-5151
Number of Employees: 200

Terri Patterson, *Chairman & President*

Fremont General Corporation
2020 Santa Monica Boulevard, Suite 600
Santa Monica, CA 90404
310-315-5500
Number of Employees: 200

Louis Rampano, *CEO*
David Krebs, *Director of Human Resources*

Friedman Bag Company
801 East Commercial Street
Los Angeles, CA 90012
213-628-2341
Number of Employees: 250

Alvin Lanfeld, *President*
Richard Olmstead, *Director of Human Resources*

Galpin Motors
15505 Roscoe Boulevard
North Hills, CA 91343
818-787-3800
Web Address: www.gogalphin.com
Number of Employees: 600

H. F. Boeckmann II, *Owner & President*
Joyce McNeely, *Director of Human Resources*

GBC Bancorp
800 West Sixth Street
Los Angeles, CA 90017
213-683-8338
Number of Employees: 350

Li Pei Wu, *President*
Bill Adams, *Director of Human Resources*

Gemstar International Group
135 North Los Robles Avenue, Suite 800
Pasadena, CA 91101
626-792-5700
Number of Employees: 40

Thomas Luen-Hung Lau, *Chairman*
Stacey Wong, *Director of Human Resources*

Glacier Water Services
2261 Cosmos Court
Carlsbad, CA 92009
760-930-2420
Web Address: www.glacierwater.com
Number of Employees: 300

Jerry A. Gordon, *President*
Luz Gonzales, *Vice President of Human Resources*

Goldberg & Solovy Foods
5925 Alcoa Avenue
Los Angeles, CA 90058
213-581-6161
Number of Employees: 300

Earl Goldberg, *President*
Edgar Medina, *Human Resource Contact*

Goldmine Software Corporation
17383 Sunset Boulevard, Suite B301
Pacific Palisades, CA 90272
310-454-6800
Web Address: www.goldminesw.com
Number of Employees: 100

Elan Susser, *President*
Jon Ferrara, *Executive VP*
Laquita WAshington, *Human Resources Manager*

Grand Havana Enterprises
1990 Westwood Boulevard
Los Angeles, CA 90025
310-475-5600
Web Address: www.grandhavana.com

Harry Shuster, *CEO*
Lori Rhees, *Director of Human Resources*

Gray Cary Ware & Freidenrich
401 B Street, Suite 1700
San Diego, CA 92101
619-699-2700
Web Address: www.gcwf.com
Number of Employees: 300

J. Terrence O'Malley, *CEO*
Andrea Cline, *Human Resource Manager*

Greenorange Designs
6031 Malburg Way
Los Angeles, CA 90058
213-582-0702
Number of Employees: 110

Vafa Farmanara, *CEO*
Elizabeth Lanzaro, *Personnel Manager*

GTE California
1 GTE Place
Thousand Oaks, CA 91362
800-227-5556
Number of Employees: 4934

M. L. Keith Jr., *President*

GTI Corporation
9715 Business Park Avenue
San Diego, CA 92131
619-537-2500
Number of Employees: 150

Albert J. Hugo-Martinez, *President*
Penny Letwin, *Manager of Human Resources*

Guild Mortgage Company
9160 Gramercy Drive
San Diego, CA 92123
858-560-6330
Web Address: www.guildmortgage.com
Number of Employees: 300

MaryAnn McCarry, *COO*
Theresa Jong, *Director of Human Resources*

Guitar Center
5155 Clareton Drive
Agoura Hills, CA 91301
818-735-8800
Web Address: www.musician.com
Number of Employees: 150

Larry Thomas, *CEO*
Virginia Owens, *Director of Human Resources*

Harbor Distributing
16407 South Main Street
Gardena, CA 90248
310-538-5483
Number of Employees: 30

David Reyes, *President*
Amy Mason, *Human Resources Manager*

Hawthorne Financial Corporation
2381 Rosecrans Avenue, 2nd Floor
El Segundo, CA 90245
310-725-5000
Job Hotline: Ext 5668
Number of Employees: 236

Scott Braly, *President*
Cindy Morales, *Director of Human Resources*

Hawthorne Machinery Corporation
16945 Camino San Bernardo
San Diego, CA 92127
858-674-7000
Web Address: www.hawthorne.com
Number of Employees: 550

James T. Hawthorne, *CEO*
Phil Zamora, *Human Resources Director*

Health Care Property Investors
10990 Wilshire Boulevard, Suite 1200
Los Angeles, CA 90024
714-221-0600

Kenneth Roath, *Chairman & President*
Kathleen O'Brian, *Human Resources*

Herbalife International
1800 Century Park East
Los Angeles, CA 90067
310-410-9600
Job Hotline: Ext 22908
Number of Employees: 1,500

Chris Pair, *President*
Florence Reynolds, *Human Resources Manager*

Hilton Hotels Corp.
9336 Civic Center Drive
Beverly Hills, CA 90210
310-278-4321
Job Hotline: 310-205-7692
Web Address: www.hilton.com

Stephen Bollenback, *President*

Hoffman Travel
5670 Wilshire Boulevard, Suite 800
Suite 800
Los Angeles, CA 90036
213-954-5400
Number of Employees: 185

Carol Dunn, *President*
Eileen Jacobs, *Human Resources Director*

Hughes Electronics Commerce
7200 Hughes Terrace
Los Angeles, CA 90045
805-726-3516
Web Address: www.hughes.com
Number of Employees: 22,000

C. Michael Armstrong, *CEO*

Hughes Markets
14005 Live Oak
Irwindale, CA 91706
626-856-6580
Number of Employees: 1,143

Roger K. Hughes, *CEO*

Imperial Bancorp
9920 South La Cienega Boulevard
Inglewood, CA 90301
310-417-5600
Web Address: www.imperialbank.com
Number of Employees: 1,200

George Graziadio Jr., *Chairman*
Richard Barkley, *Director of Human Resources*

Imperial Credit Industries
23550 Hawthorne Boulevard
Torrance, CA 90505
310-791-8020
Job Hotline: 310-791-8075
Web Address: www.icii.com
Number of Employees: 300

H. Wayne Snavely, *CEO*
Cindy Rosenburg, *Human Resources Director*

INCOMNET
21031 Ventura Boulevard, Suite 1100
Woodland Hills, CA 91364
818-887-3400
Web Address: www.incomnet.com
Number of Employees: 288

Melvyn Reznick, *CEO*
Helen Mulliner, *Director of Personnel*

Infonet Services
2100 East Grand Avenue
El Segundo, CA 90245
310-335-2600
Job Hotline: Ext 1073
Web Address: www.infonet.com
Number of Employees: 500

Jose Collazo, *Chairman*
Ken Montgomery, *Human Resource Manager*

Insurance Auto Auctions
7245 Laurel Canyon Boulevard
North Hollywood, CA 91605
818-786-2220
Web Address: www.iaa.com

Linda Larrabee, *CEO*
David Rodgers, *Director of Human Resources*

Interactive Group
21 Technology Drive
Irvine, CA 92618
949-788-5000
Web Address: www.interactive-group.com
Number of Employees: 350

Internal and External Communication
12910 Culver Boulevard, Suite A
Los Angeles, CA 90066
310-827-4464
Web Address: www.iec.com
Number of Employees: 440

Alexandra Rand, *CEO*
Lynn Matsunami Human Resources Director

International Aluminum Corp.
767 Monterey Pass Road
Monterey Park, CA 91754
213-264-1670
Number of Employees: 2,000

John Cunningham, *President*
Michael Snodgrass, *Human Resources Director*

International Rectifier
222 Kansas Street
El Segundo, CA 90245
310-726-8000
Number of Employees: 1,000

Eric Lidow, *Chairman*
Dennis Taylor, *Director of Human Resources*

ITWCIP Stamping
11525 Shoemaker Avenue
Santa Fe Springs, CA 90670
562-941-3281
Job Hotline: Ext 271
Number of Employees: 250

Dick Munce, *President*
Norbert Markl, *General Manager*
Jim Tembruell, *Human Resource Manager*

Jacobs Engineering Group
1111 South Arroyo Parkway
Pasadena, CA 91105
626-449-2171
Number of Employees: 286

Noel Watson, *President*
William Gebhardt, *Director of Human Resources*

JB Dental Supply Co.
3515 Eastham Drive
Culver City, CA 90232
213-935-7141
Number of Employees: 300

Joseph Berman, *President*
Helen Ojeda, *Human Resources Director*

JB Research
9062 Rosecrans Avenue
Bellflower, CA 90706
562-790-2400
Number of Employees: 90

Dorothy Lorentz, *CEO*
Cynthia Saavedro Director of Human Resources

Jefferies Group
11100 Santa Monica Boulevard
Los Angeles, CA 90025
310-445-1199
Job Hotline: Ext 1095
Web Address: www.jefco.com

Frank Baxter, *CEO*
Mel Locke, *Human Resource Manager*

Jenny Craig
11355 North Torrey Pines Road
La Jolla, CA 92037
619-812-7000
Web Address: www.jennycraig.com
Number of Employees: 200

Jenny Craig, *President*
Sid Craig, *CEO*

Jerry Leigh of California
671 South Rio Street
Los Angeles, CA 90023
213-268-6177

Jerry Leigh, *CEO*
Greg Campbell, *Human Resources Director*

K-2
4900 South Eastern Avenue, Suite 200
Los Angeles, CA 90040
213-724-2800

Richard M. Rodstein, *President*
Ellen Mochizuki, *Controller*

K-Swiss
20664 Bahama Street
Chatsworth, CA 91311
818-998-3388
Web Address: www.kswiss.com
Number of Employees: 235

Steven Nichols, *President*
Lorena Agraz, *Director of Personnel*
Designer of athletic footwear, and marketer of apparel and accessories, including tennis warm-ups, skirts, shorts, and shirts; fleece tops and pants; and T-shirts, caps, duffel bags, and socks.

Kajima Engineering & Construction
200 South Los Robles Avenue, Suite 400
Pasadena, CA 91101
626-440-0033
Number of Employees: 70

Atsushi Seki, *Partner*
Masayoshi Kamiya, *President*
Nancy Osa, *Director of Human Resources*

Kearny Mesa Toyota
5090 Kearny Mesa Road
San Diego, CA 92111
619-279-8151
Number of Employees: 150
Francois Chaker, *New Car Manager*

Kennedy-Wilson
530 Wilshire Boulevard
Santa Monica, CA 90401
310-314-8400
Web Address: www.kennedywilson.com
Number of Employees: 40

William J. McMorrow, *CEO*
Jim Ozello, *Director of Human Resources*

Kent & Spiegel Direct
6133 Bristol Parkway, Suite 150
Culver City, CA 90230
310-337-1010
Number of Employees: 85

Marsha Kent, *President*
Emelia Prim, *Human Resources Director*

Kett Engineering Corp.
15500 Erwin Street, Suite 1029
Van Nuys, CA 91411
818-908-5388
Web Address: www.ketteng.com
Number of Employees: 1,000

E. Stromsborg, *President*
Danny Gast, *Director of Human Resources*

Keymarc Electronics
478 Amapola Avenue
Torrance, CA 90501
310-783-5475
Job Hotline: 310-783-5475

Yoshio Terajima, *President*
Kaori Mogi, *Human Resource Manager*

Kinetics Technology International Corp.
650 West Cienega Avenue
San Dimas, CA 91773
909-592-4455
Web Address: www.kticorp.com
Number of Employees: 320

David Baker, *President*

King Meat
4215 Exchange Avenue
Los Angeles, CA 90058
213-582-7401
Job Hotline: 213-582-1813
Number of Employees: 50

William Hughes, *President*

Koos Manufacturing
2741 Seminole Avenue
South Gate, CA 90280
213-564-2100
Number of Employees: 1,200

Ku Yul, *President*
Ann Kim, *Controller*

Korn/Ferry International
1800 Century Park East, Suite 900
Los Angeles, CA 90067
310-552-1834
Web Address: www.kornferry.com
Number of Employees: 150

Richard Ferry, *Chairman*
John Moxley III, *Managing Vice President*
Lauren Hydeman, *Director of Human Resources*

Kraco Enterprises
505 East Euclid Avenue
Compton, CA 90224
213-774-2550
Number of Employees: 230

Lawrence Kraines, *President*
Michael De South, *Director of Human Resources*

KV Mart Co.
1245 East Watson Center Road
Carson, CA 90745
310-816-0200
Job Hotline: Ext 794
Number of Employees: 1,300

Darioush Khaledi, *CEO*
Bonnie Shoemaker, *Human Resources Director*

399

LA Gear
2850 Ocean Park Boulevard
Santa Monica, CA 90405
310-452-4327

Bruce MacGregor, *President*

LCA Intimates
6100 South Malt Avenue
Commerce, CA 90040
213-278-9999
Number of Employees: 90

J. Zarabi, *Chairman*
JoAnn Gilmartin, *Vice President of Human Relations*

Learning Tree International
6053 West Century Boulevard
Los Angeles, CA 90045
310-417-9700
Web Address: www.learningtree.com
Number of Employees: 150

David C. Collins, *CEO*
Angela Sherd, *Director of Human Resources*
Lori Shelton, *Human Resource Manager*

Leo Hoffman Chevrolet
15432 Nelson Avenue
City of Industry, CA 91744
626-968-8411
Number of Employees: 130

Thomas Hoffman, *President*
Gary Campbell, *Director of Human Resources*

Linsco Private Ledger Corp.
5935 Cornerstone Court West
San Diego, CA 92121
619-450-9606
Number of Employees: 300

Todd A. Robinson, *CEO*
Robin Coberg, *Human Resource Assistant*

Liquid Investments
8870 Liquid Court
San Diego, CA 92121
619-452-2300
Web Address: www.mesadistributing.com
Number of Employees: 500

Ron. L. Fowler, *President*
Laura Boyd, *Director of Human Resources*

Lithographix
13500 South Figueroa Street
Los Angeles, CA 90061
213-770-1000
Web Address: www.lithographix.com
Number of Employees: 300

Herb Zebrack, *Owner & President*
Karen Milke, *Director of Human Resources*

Lockheed Martin Corp.
310 North Westlake Boulevard, Suite 200
Westlake Village, CA 91362
805-381-1480
Number of Employees: 50

David Claus, *VP Ethics and Business Conduct*
Dale Truskett, *Office Manager*

Lorber Industries of California
17908 South Figueroa Street
Gardena, CA 90248
213-321-8450
Number of Employees: 500

Arnold Lorber, *President*
Ester Layman, *Human Resources Director*

Lubricating Specialties Co.
8015 Paramount Boulevard
Pico Rivera, CA 90660
562-928-3311
Number of Employees: 100

M. Delaney, *President*
Pat Mangiamely, *Human Resource Manager*

Maas-Hansen Steel Corp.
2435 East Vernon
Los Angeles, CA 90058
213-583-6321
Number of Employees: 95

Leon Banks, *President*
Carlin Warner, *Controller*

Mac Frugal's Bargains Close-outs
2430 East Del Amo Boulevard
Dominguez, CA 90220
310-537-9220
Job Hotline: 800-877-1253
Number of Employees: 2,200

Machinery Sales Co.
4400 South Soto Street
Los Angeles, CA 90058
213-588-8111
Web Address: www.mchysales.com
Number of Employees: 84

Richard Rivett, *Chairman*
John Ramsey, *Director of Human Resources*

Mail Boxes Etc.
6060 Cornerstone Court West
San Diego, CA 92121
858-455-8800
Job Hotline: 619-597-8526
Web Address: www.mbe.com
Number of Employees: 250

James Amos, *CEO*
Doug Miller, *Senior Manager*
Melissa Cogan, *Recruiter*

Manhattan Motors
1500 North Sepulveda Boulevard
Manhattan Beach, CA 90266
310-546-4646
Number of Employees: 40

William Adkins, *President*
Kathy Stone, *Human Resources Manager*

Marvin Engineering Co.
260 West Beach Avenue
Inglewood, CA 90302
310-674-5030
Number of Employees: 300

Marvin Gussman, *President*
Carrie Shalling, *Director of Human Resources*

Mattel
333 Continental Boulevard
El Segundo, CA 90245
310-252-2000
Job Hotline: Ext 4520
Web Address: www.mattel.com
Number of Employees: 1,500
Cheryl Nishimura, *Human Resource Manager*

Maxicare Health Plans
1149 South Broadway, Suite 923
Los Angeles, CA 90015
213-765-2000
Number of Employees: 1,000

Peter Ratican, *Chairman & President*

Mazda Motor of America
7755 Irvine Center Drive
Irvine, CA 97218
949-727-1990
Web Address: www.mazdausa.com

Richard N. Beattie, *President*
Andrea Kelly, *Director of Personnel*

Mercury Air Group
5456 McConnell Avenue
Los Angeles, CA 90066
310-827-2737
Job Hotline: Ext 156
Number of Employees: 600

Seymour Kahn, *Chairman*
Steve Antonoff, *Director of Human Resources*

Mercury General Corp.
4484 Wilshire Boulevard
Los Angeles, CA 90010
213-937-1060
Job Hotline: 213-857-7198
Number of Employees: 2,103

George Joseph, *CEO*
Michael Curtius, *President*
Michael Turney, *Human Resources Director*

Merisel
200 Continental Boulevard
El Segundo, CA 90245
310-615-3080
Web Address: www.merisel.com
Number of Employees: 1,500

Dwight Steffensen, *CEO*
Christina Cameron, *Assistant for Human Resources*

MiniMed
12744 San Fernando Road
Sylmar, CA 91342
818-362-5958
Web Address: www.minimed.com
Number of Employees: 373

Allfred E. Mann, *President*
Linda Whitney, *Director of Personnel*
Manufacturer of insulin pumps for treating diabetes. Provider of external pumps and related equipment that are designed to deliver small quantities of insulin.

Mitsuba Corp.
1925 Wright Avenue
La Verne, CA 91750
909-392-2000
Web Address: www.mitsuba.com
Number of Employees: 75

James Chen, *President*

MMC
8797 Beverly Boulevard, 2nd Floor
Los Angeles, CA 90048
310-659-3835
Web Address: www.mmchr.com

Mashi Rahmani, *Executive Director*
Annette Kathlin, *Human Resources*

Montrose Travel
2355 Honolulu Avenue
Montrose, CA 91020
818-553-3210
Number of Employees: 101

A. McClure, *Co-president*
J. McClure, *Co-president*
Steve Steller, *Director of Human Resources*

Motorcar Parts & Accessories
2727 Maricopa Street
Torrance, CA 90503
310-212-7910
Job Hotline: 310-782-3260
Web Address: www.mpaa-inc.com

Mel Marks, *CEO*
Maria Madueno, *Human Resource Manager*

Mycogen Corp.
5501 Oberlin Drive
San Diego, CA 92121
619-453-8030
Number of Employees: 107

Jerry D. Caulder, *CEO*
Carl Eibl, *Principal*
Suzanne Rhinehart, *Hiring Contact*

Natural Alternatives International
1185 Linda Vista Drive
San Marcos, CA 92069
760-744-7340
Web Address: www.nai-online.com
Number of Employees: 130

Mark A. Le Doux, *CEO*
Jo Phillipe, *Human Resource Director*

Nestle USA
800 North Brand Boulevard
Glendale, CA 91203
818-549-6000
Web Address: www.nestle.com

Joe Weller, *CEO*
Cam Starrett, *Director of Human Resources*

New Century BMW
3001 West Main Street
Alhambra, CA 91801
626-570-8444
Web Address: www.ncbmw.com
Number of Employees: 80

Frank Lin, *President*
Robin Milligan, *Director of Human Resources*

New Star Media
8955 Beverly Boulevard
Los Angeles, CA 90048
310-786-1600
Job Hotline: Ext 611
Web Address: www.newstarmedia.com
Number of Employees: 60

Ronald Lightstone, *President & CEO*
Jan Kalajian, *Director of Human Resources*

Nitches
10280 Camino Santa Fe
San Diego, CA 92121
858-625-2633
Job Hotline: 619-625-6230
Number of Employees: 55

Arjun C. Waney, *Chairman*
Glenda Bomze, *Human Resource Manager*

Norm Reeves Honda
18500 South Studebaker Road
Cerritos, CA 90703
562-402-3844
Web Address: www.normreeves.com

Number of Employees: 300
David Conant, *Owner & President*
Mary Beth Rosson, *Training Coordinator*

NTN Communications
5966 La Place Court, Suite 100
Carlsbad, CA 92008
760-438-7400
Web Address: www.ntn.com
Number of Employees: 250

Bob Anderson, *President*
Sandra McCart, *Human Resources Manager*

O'Melveny & Myers
400 South Hope Street, Suite 1060
Los Angeles, CA 90071
213-669-6000
Web Address: www.omm.com
Number of Employees: 400

Charles Bender, *Managing Partner*

Occidental Petroleum Corp.
10889 Wilshire Boulevard
Los Angeles, CA 90024
310-208-8800
Web Address: ww.oxy.com
Number of Employees: 300

Ray Irani, *CEO*
Richard Hallock, *Executive VP & HR Director*

Oltmans Construction Co.
10005 Mission Mill Road
Whittier, CA 90608
562-948-4242
Job Hotline: Ext 3402
Web Address: www.oltmans.com
Number of Employees: 500

R. M. Holmes, *Chairman*
Vicki Hermstad, *Human Resource Manager*

Optimal Integrated Solutions
2260 Rutherford Road, Suite 105
Carlsbad, CA 92008
760-431-6858
Web Address: www.optimalis.net
Number of Employees: 25

Ayman Suleiman, *CEO*

Oriental Motor USA Corp.
2580 West 237th Street
Torrance, CA 90505
310-515-2264
Web Address: www.omusa.com
Number of Employees: 80

Mike Tatsuya, *President*
Bob Purcell, *Human Resources Manager*

Outrigger Lodging Services
16000 Ventura Boulevard, Suite 1010
Encino, CA 91436
818-905-8280
Number of Employees: 3,000

John Fitts, *President*
Sarie Mannoja, *Director of Human Resources*

Pacific Enterprises
555 West Fifth Street, Suite 2900
Los Angeles, CA 90013
213-895-5000
Number of Employees: 5,800

Willis Wood Jr., *CEO*

Pacific Holding
10900 Wilshire Boulevard, 16th Floor
Los Angeles, CA 90024
310-208-6055
Job Hotline: 818-847-4999
Number of Employees: 15

David Murdock, *CEO*
Evelyn Lauchenauer, *Director of Human Resources*

Pacific Pioneer Corp.
18300 Pioneer Boulevard
Artesia, CA 90702
310-865-7134
Number of Employees: 325

Lin Wu Lan, *CEO*
Matt Stevens, *Human Resources Director*

Pacific Theatres Corp.
120 North Robertson Boulevard
Los Angeles, CA 90048
310-657-8420
Web Address: www.pacifictheatres.com
Number of Employees: 5,000

Jerome Foreman, *President*
Donald Troudy, *Director of Human Resources*

Panavision
6219 De Soto Avenue
Woodland Hills, CA 91367
818-316-1000
Number of Employees: 805

John Farrand, *President*
Sheri Sasaki, *Director of Personnel*
Maker of TV and movie production equipment. Its products, including cameras, lenses, and accessories, are available only by rental from the company and its agents.

Parsons Corp.
100 West Walnut Street
Pasadena, CA 91124
626-440-2000
Number of Employees: 305

James McNulty, *President*
Eric Miski, *Director of Human Resources*

PDI Enterprises
26245 Technology Drive
Valencia, CA 91355
805-294-8200
Number of Employees: 50

Irwin Schaeffer, *Chairman*
Linda New, *Director of Human Resources*

Pearson Ford Co.
4300 El Cajon Boulevard
San Diego, CA 92105
619-283-7181
Web Address: www.pearsonford.com
Number of Employees: 250

John B. McCallan Jr., *Owner*

Peerless Systems Corp.
2381 Rosecrans Avenue, Suite 400
El Segundo, CA 90245
310-536-0908
Web Address: www.peerless.com

Edward A. Gavaldon, *CEO*
Michelle Foster, *Human Resources Manager*

Petco Animal Supplies
9125 Rehco Road
San Diego, CA 92121
619-453-7845
Number of Employees: 8,000

Brian K. Devine, President, *Chairman*
Tom Roh, *Hiring Contact*

Pinkerton's
15910 Ventura Boulevard
Encino, CA 91436
818-380-8800
Web Address: www.pinkertons.com
Number of Employees: 2,500
Denis Brown, *President*
Melinda Joe, *Recruiter*

PinnacleOne
225 Broadway, Suite 2200
San Diego, CA 92101
619-230-0336
Web Address: www.pinnacle.com
Number of Employees: 150
Gene Bennett, *President*
Stephanie Keiserman, *Director of Human Resources*

PMC Global
12243 Branford Street
Sun Valley, CA 91352
818-896-1101
Number of Employees: 4299
Philip E. Kamins, *President*
Karen Ferguson, *Director of Personnel*
Manufacturer of chemical products including packaging, plastics-molding equipment, food dyes, drugs, paint, and varnish. The company also makes military instruments and neurosurgical devices.

PMR Corp.
501 Washington Street, 5th Floor
San Diego, CA 92103
619-610-4001
Job Hotline: 800-866-7677
Web Address: www.pmrcorp.com
Number of Employees: 1,100

Allen Tepper, *CEO*
Michael Goldberg, *Staffing Manager*

Pollution Research & Control Corp.
506 Paula Avenue
Glendale, CA 91201
818-247-7601
Web Address: www.dasibi.com
Number of Employees: 115

Albert E. Gosselin Jr., *President*
Marcia Smith, *Director of Personnel*

Potential Industries
922 East E Street
Wilmington, CA 90744
310-549-5901
Number of Employees: 100

Henry Chen, *President*
Jessica Chen, *Director of Personnel*

Power Lift Corp.
8314 East Slauson Avenue
Pico Rivera, CA 90660
562-949-1000
Web Address: www.powerlift.com
Number of Employees: 300

Richard Cowan, *President*
Mason Dickerson, *Human Resources Manager*

Power-Sonic Corp.
9163-A Siempre Viva Road
San Diego, CA 92173
619-661-2020
Number of Employees: 75
Guy C. Clum, *President*
Kim Tran, *Human Resource Manager*

Protection One
6011 Bristol Parkway
Culver City, CA 90230
310-338-6930
Number of Employees: 1,000
Annette Beck, *President*
Linda Brown, *Human Resources Director*

Public Storage
600 North Brand Boulevard
Glendale, CA 91203
818-244-8080
Job Hotline: 1-888-477-5627
Web Address: www.publicstorage.com
Number of Employees: 600
Wayne Hughes, *CEO*
Ed Stapleton, *Director of Human Resources*

Qualcomm
5775 Morehouse Drive
San Diego, CA 92121
858-587-1121
Job Hotline: 858-658-5627
Web Address: www.qualcomm.com
Number of Employees: 8,000

Irwin M. Jacobs, *CEO*
Fax resumes to: 858-658-2110

Quidel Corp.
10165 McKellar Court
San Diego, CA 92121
619-552-1100
Web Address: www.quidel.com
Number of Employees: 263

Andre De Bruin, *President*
Dena Purvis, *Director of Human Resources*

R.J. Gordon & Co.
9200 Sunset Boulevard, Suite 515
Los Angeles, CA 90069
310-724-6000
Job Hotline: 310-724-6530
Web Address: www.creditcards.com
Number of Employees: 86

Richard Gordon, *Chairman*
Conrad Frankowski, *Human Resource Manager*

Ralphs Grocery/Food 4 Less
1100 West Artesia Boulevard
Compton, CA 90220
310-884-9000
Job Hotline: 310-884-4642
Web Address: www.ralphs.com
Number of Employees: 5,558

George Golleher, *CEO*
Sheri Meek, *VP of Human Resources*

Randall Foods
4901 South Boyle Avenue
Vernon, CA 90058
213-587-2383
Number of Employees: 400

Stan Bloom, *President*
Evelyn Cherne, *Director of Personnel*

Realty Income Corp.
220 West Crest Street
Escondido, CA 92025
760-741-2111
Web Address: www.realtyincome.com
Number of Employees: 45

Tom Lewis, *CEO*
Teresa Glenn, *Hiring Manager*

Reliance Steel & Aluminum Co.
2550 East 25th Street
Los Angeles, CA 90058
213-582-2272
Web Address: www.rsac.com
Number of Employees: 35

Joe Crider, *CEO*
Terry Deichman, *Director of Personnel*

Revatex
1013 South Los Angeles Street, 3rd Floor
Los Angeles, CA 90015
213-747-9283
Number of Employees: 50

Haim Revah, *Chairman*

Ryan Herco Products Co.
3010 North San Fernando Boulevard
Burbank, CA 91504
818-841-1141
Job Hotline: 1-800-597-1141 x569
Web Address: www.ryanherco.com
Number of Employees: 124

Frank Gibbs, *President*
Linda Kass, *Director of Human Resources*

Safeskin Corp.
12671 High Bluff Drive
San Diego, CA 92130
619-794-8111

Richard Jaffe, *President*
Kathy Jane, *Human Resource Representative*

Salick Health Care
8201 Beverly Boulevard
Los Angeles, CA 90048
213-966-3400
Number of Employees: 800

Bernard Salick, *CEO*
Joe Tomsack, *Recruiter*

San Diego Travel Group
9710 Scranton Road, Suite 300
San Diego, CA 92121
619-450-4060
Web Address: www.sdtg.com
Number of Employees: 100

Nicole Del Festo, *Director of Operation*

Santa Monica Ford Corp.
1230 Santa Monica Boulevard
Santa Monica, CA 90404
310-451-1588
Number of Employees: 100

R. Karlin, *President*
Ricky Berargi, *Director of Human Resources*

Sasco Electric
12900 Alondra Boulevard
Cerritos, CA 90703
562-926-0900
Web Address: www.sasco.com
Number of Employees: 150

Scott Eaton, *President*
Gordon Westerling, *Partner*

SBC Communications
1010 Wilshire Boulevard, 16th Floor
Los Angeles, CA 90017
213-975-4900
Number of Employees: 9533

Cindy Brinkley, *Vice President*

Science Applications International Corp.
10260 Campus Point Drive
San Diego, CA 92121
619-546-6000
Web Address: www.saic.com
Number of Employees: 3,843

J. R. Beyster, *CEO*
Gary D. Jones, *Vice President*
Barnie Theule, *Human Resource Manager*

Seda Specialty Packaging
2501 West Rosecrans Avenue
Los Angeles, CA 90059
310-635-4444
Web Address: www.cclcontainer.com
Number of Employees: 300

Shawn Sedaghat, *CEO*
Rita Bates, *Personnel Manager*

Shapell Industries
8383 Wilshire Boulevard, Suite 700
Beverly Hills, CA 90211
213-655-7330
Number of Employees: 80

Nathan Shapell, *President*
Lynn Muzingo, *Personnel Director*

Sizzler International
6101 Centinela, Suite 200
Culver City CA 90230
310-568-0135
Number of Employees: 80

James Collins, *Chairman*
Mabel Woods, *Human Resources Manager*

Smart & Final
4700 South Boyle Avenue
Los Angeles, CA 90058
213-589-1054
Job Hotline: 800-995-4630

Robert Emmons, *President*
Sasha Lee, *Director of Personnel*

Software Dynamics

9400 Topanga Canyon Boulevard, Suite 200
Chatsworth, CA 91311
818-773-0330
Web Address: www.sdinc.com
Number of Employees: 200

Tom Shen, *President*
Susan Ryan, *Director of Human Resources*

Southern California Edison

8631 Rush Street
Rosemead, CA 91770
626-302-1212
Number of Employees: 12,000

John Bryson, *CEO*
Lilian Gorman, *Vice President of Human
    Resources*

Southland Industries

1661 East 32nd Street
Long Beach, CA 90807
562-424-8638
Job Hotline: 949-440-5023
Web Address: www.southlandind.com
Number of Employees: 500

Michael Moore, *Chairman*

Southwest Marine

Foot of Sampson Street
San Diego, CA 92113
619-238-1000
Job Hotline: 619-557-4277
Number of Employees: 1,400

B. Edward Ewing, *CEO*
Vicky Shane, *Human Resource Supervisor*

Space Electronics

4031 Sorrento Valley Boulevard
San Diego, CA 92121
619-452-4167
Web Address: www.spaceelectronics.com
Number of Employees: 100

Robert Czajkowski, *CEO*
Dana Beall, *Manager of Human Resources*

Stac

12636 High Bluff Drive, 4th Floor
San Diego, CA 92130
619-794-4300
Job Hotline: 619-794-4576
Web Address: www.stac.com
Number of Employees: 80

Gary W. Clow, *CEO*
Susan Brown, *Human Resource Supervisor*

StyleClick.com

3861 Sepulveda Boulevard
Culver City, CA 90230
310-312-9826
Web Address: www.style.com
Number of Employees: 90

Joyce Freedman, *President*
Deirdra Abbot, *Recruiter*

Sunkist Growers

14130 Riverside Drive
Sherman Oaks, CA 91423-2392
818-986-4800
Job Hotline: 818-379-7390
Web Address: www.sunkist.com
Number of Employees: 813

Russell L. Hanlin, *President*
John R. McGovern, *Director of Personnel*
Adrienne Scanlon, *Recruiter*
*Cooperative owned by citrus farmers in California and Arizona.
Markets fresh fruit and produces processed products, such as fruit
juices and oils.*

Sunrise Medical

2382 Faraday Avenue, Suite 200
Carlsbad, CA 92008
760-930-1570
Job Hotline: 760-930-1596
Web Address: www.sunrisemedical.com
Number of Employees: 40

Richard H. Chandler, Chairman, *President*
Deborah Beasley, *Human Resources Administrator*

Superior Industries International

7800 Woodley Avenue
Van Nuys, CA 91406-1788
818-781-4973
Web Address: www.superiorindustries.com
Number of Employees: 4500
Louis L. Borick, *President*
Jim Walker, *Director of Personnel*
*International manufacturer of cast aluminum wheels and automotive
accessories. Products are installed on vehicles manufactured by
Ford, General Motors, Chrysler, BMW, Jaguar, Toyota, Mazda, and
Nissan.*

Swatfame

16425 Gale Avenue
City of Industry, CA 91745
626-961-7928
Job Hotline: 626-961-7928 x193
Number of Employees: 300
Bruce Stern, *CEO*
Fran Coye, *Director of Human Resources*

Systems Engineering Associates

2851 Camino del Rio South, Suite 410
San Diego, CA 92108
619-681-1828
Web Address: www.sea.com
Judy Weaver, *CEO*
Brian Cooper, *Director of Human Resources*

Ta Chen International Corp.
5855 Obispo Avenue
Long Beach, CA 90805
562-630-8793
Job Hotline: 800-364-8389
Number of Employees: 30

Robert Shieh, *President*
Lynn Shieh, *Human Resources Manager*

Tecstar
15251 Don Julian Road
City of Industry, CA 91745
626-968-6581
Number of Employees: 500

David Van Buren, *President*
Jim Littrell, *Director of Human Resources*

Tetra Tech
670 North Rosemead Boulevard
Pasadena, CA 91107
626-351-4664
Web Address: www.tetratech.com
Number of Employees: 116

Li-San Hwang, *President*

The Corky McMillin Companies
2727 Hoover Avenue
National City, CA 91950
619-477-4117
Web Address: www.mcmillin.com
Number of Employees: 160

Corky McMillin, *CEO*
Mark McMillin, *President*
Judy Webster, *Human Resource Director*

The National Dispatch Center
8911 Balboa Avenue
San Diego, CA 92123
619-654-9000
Job Hotline: 800-439-1896
Web Address: www.ndcwireless.com
Number of Employees: 100

John MacLeod, *CEO*
Deborah Lettper, *Director of Human Resources*

The Titan Corp.
3033 Science Park Road
San Diego, CA 92121
619-552-9500
Web Address: www.titan.com
Number of Employees: 450

Gene W. Ray, *CEO*
Mike Fowler, *Vice President*
Diane Scott, *Vice President of Human Resources*

The Weekend Exercise Company
8960 Carroll Way
San Diego, CA 92121
619-537-5300

Number of Employees: 100
Arthur Levinson, *CEO*
Michelle Perry, *Payroll Manager*

ThermoTrex Corp.
10455 Pacific Center Court
San Diego, CA 92121
619-646-5300
Web Address: www.thermo.com
Number of Employees: 160

Gary S. Weinstein, *CEO*
Kenneth Y. Tang, *Senior Vice President*
Allen Wolski, *Director of Human Resources*

Ticketmaster Group
8800 Sunset Boulevard
West Hollywood, CA 90069
213-639-6100
Job Hotline: 310-360-6057
Web Address: www.ticketmaster.com
Number of Employees: 1,200

Fredric D. Rosen, *President*
Rick Karkora, *Employment Coordinator*

Todd Pipe & Supply
4828 West 145th Street
Hawthorne, CA 90251
310-970-0007
Web Address: www.toddpipe.com
Number of Employees: 250

Steve Owen, *Vice President*
Lorraine Shotsline, *Human Resources Manager*

Todd-AO Corp.
900 North Seward Street
Hollywood, CA 90038
213-962-5304
Number of Employees: 75

Solah M. Hassanein, *President*

Total Renal Care Holdings
21250 Hawthorne Boulevard
Torrance, CA 90503
310-792-2600
Number of Employees: 70

Victor M. Chaltiel, *President*
Rosa Johnson, *Director of Human Resources*

Toyota of Cerritos
18700 Studebaker Road
Cerritos, CA 90703
562-860-6561
Web Address: www.toyotacerritos.com
Number of Employees: 200

Brad Kyle, *General Manager*

Toyota of North Hollywood
4606 Lankershim Boulevard
North Hollywood, CA 91602
818-508-2900
Number of Employees: 200

Don Hankey, *Chairman*
Sheryl Herd, *Director of Human Resources*

Trader Joe's Co.
538 Mission Street
South Pasadena, CA 91030
818-441-1177

John Shields, *CEO*
Rosella Moore, *Director of Human Resources*

TransWestern Publishing
8344 Clairemont Mesa Boulevard
San Diego, CA 92111
619-467-2800
Job Hotline: 619-467-6067
Web Address: www.transwesterpub.com
Number of Employees: 700

Rick Puente, *President*
Penny Bly, *Senior Human Resource Manager*

Trikon Technologies
9255 Deering Avenue
Chatsworth, CA 91311
818-886-8000
Number of Employees: 678

Christopher D. Dobson, *CEO*
Supplier of equipment to semiconductor and flat-panel display manufacturers. The company specializes in etching equipment used to make advanced integrated circuits.

Trillium Digital Systems
12100 Wilshire Boulevard, Suite 1800
Los Angeles, CA 90025
310-442-9222
Web Address: www.trillium.com
Number of Employees: 120

Jeff Lawrence, Chairman, *President*
Gina Park, *Recruiter*

TRW Space & Electronics Group
One Space Park, Building E-1, Room 3010
Redondo Beach, CA 90278
310-812-4321
Job Hotline: 310-814-7500
Web Address: www.trw.com
Number of Employees: 10045

Timothy Hannemann, Executive VP, *General Manager*

United Television
132 South Rodeo Drive, Fourth Floor
Beverly Hills, CA 90212
310-281-4844

Evan Thompson, *President*
Tom Muir, *Controller*

University of Southern California
3620 South Vermont Avenue, KAP 246
Los Angeles, CA 90089
213-740-5371
Web Address: www.usc.edu
Number of Employees: 8199

Steven Sample, *President*
Dennis Dougherty, *VP of Administration*

Univision Communications
1999 Avenue of the Stars, Suite 3050
Los Angeles, CA 90067
310-556-7676

A. Jerrold Perenchio, *CEO*
Norma Hanley, *Director of Personnel*

Utility Trailer Manufacturing Co.
17295 East Railroad Street
City of Industry, CA 91749
626-965-1541
Web Address: www.utilitytrailer.com
Number of Employees: 350

Paul Bennett, *CEO*
John Stanton, *Director of Human Resources*

VDI Media
6920 Sunset Boulevard
Hollywood, CA 90028
213-957-5500
Number of Employees: 325

R. Luke Stefanko, *President*
Terry Ramos, *Director of Personnel*

Veterinary Centers of America
3420 Ocean Park Boulevard
Santa Monica, CA 90405
310-392-9599
Number of Employees: 75

Robert L. Antin, *CEO*

Viking Office Products
950 West 190th Street
Torrance, CA 90502
310-225-4500
Number of Employees: 1,400

Irwin Helford, *CEO*
Geri Rivers, *Director of Human Resources*

Viking Office Products
13809 South Figueroa Street
Los Angeles, CA 90061
213-321-4493
Number of Employees: 1,400

Irwin Helford, *CEO*
Geri Rivers, *Director of Human Resources*

Virco Manufacturing Corp.
2027 Harpers Way
Torrance, CA 90501
310-533-0474
Job Hotline: 310-533-0474 x220
Number of Employees: 650
Robert Virtue, *CEO*
Angelica Gamble, *Director of Personnel*

Wareforce
2361 Rosecrans Avenue
El Segundo, CA 90245
310-725-5555
Number of Employees: 90
Anita Gabriel, *CEO*
Rebecca L., *Director of Human Resources*

Wavetek Instruments
9145 Balboa Avenue
San Diego, CA 92123
619-279-2200
Web Address: www.wavetek.com
Number of Employees: 100
Derek Morikawa, *President*
Marcia Garceau, *Manager of Human Resources*

WD-40 Co.
1061 Cudahy Place
San Diego, CA 92110
619-275-1400
Number of Employees: 40
Garry Ridge, *President*
Mary Rudy, *Director of Corporate Human Resources*

Web Vision
19950 Mariner Avenue
Torrance, CA 90503
310-214-4200
Job Hotline: 310-793-4522
Web Address: www.webvision.com
Number of Employees: 300
Zeb Bhatti, *CEO*
Joan Bibb, *Director of Human Resources*

Weber Distribution Warehouses
13530 Rosecrans Avenue
Santa Fe Springs, CA 90670
562-802-8802
Web Address: www.weberdistribution.com
Number of Employees: 100
Nicholas Weber, *President*
Mike Serchia, *Director of Human Resources*

Weber Metals
16706 Garfield Avenue
Paramount, CA 90723
213-636-1285
Number of Employees: 250
Leon Kranz, *CEO*
Doilly Griarte, *Human Resources Contact*

Welk Resort Center
8860 Lawrence Welk Drive
Escondido, CA 92026
760-749-3000
Job Hotline: 760-749-3182
Web Address: welk2@aol.com
Number of Employees: 400

Mario Trejo, *General Manager*
Maribel Fuentes, *Hiring Manager*

WellPoint Health Networks
21555 Oxnard Street
Woodland Hills, CA 91367
818-703-4000
Job Hotline: 818-703-3181
Web Address: www.wellpoint.com
Number of Employees: 10,641

Leonard D. Schaeffer, *CEO*
Tom Van Berkem, *Senior VP & Director of Personnel*
Healthcare provider which serves more than 4.5 million members in its medical plans, including HMOs, PPOs, and specialty networks such as dental, workers' compensation, and mental health plans.

West Covina Toyota
1800 East Garvey Avenue
West Covina, CA 91791
626-859-7400

Mike Salta, *President*
Rachel Powers, *Business Manager*

Westfield America
11601 Wilshire Boulevard, Suite 1200
Los Angeles, CA 90025
310-478-4456

Frank P. Lowy, *Chairman*
Susan Nisbet, *Human Resources Director*

Wheb Systems
10125 Mesa Rim Road
San Diego, CA 92121
619-586-7885
Web Address: www.whebsys.com
Number of Employees: 100

Randy Hawks, *CEO*
Becky Jagger, *Human Resources Assistant*

Wherehouse Entertainment
19701 Hamilton Avenue, Suite 200
Torrance, CA 90502
310-538-2314
Number of Employees: 158

Tony Alvarez, *CEO*
Racheal Centeno, *Risk Manager*
Chris Gehrke, *Human Resource Manager*

409

World Oil Co.
9302 Garfield Avenue
South Gate, CA 90280
562-928-0100
Number of Employees: 40

Bernard Roth, *CEO*
Tosh Chan, *Office Manager*

Xerox
700 South Flower Street, Suite 700
Los Angeles, CA 90017
213-614-0271
Job Hotline: 800-423-3868
Web Address: www.zero.com
Number of Employees: 21

W. R. Ernisse, *VP General Manager*
Javene Black, *Human Resources Director*

Xpedx
17411 Valley Boulevard
City of Industry, CA 91744
626-854-5400
Web Address: www.xpedx.com
Number of Employees: 450

Dennis Bigs, *Vice President*
Lorraine Barannello, *Director of Human Resources*

Zacky Farms
2000 North Tyler Avenue
El Monte, CA 91733
818-443-9351
Number of Employees: 250

Robert Zacky, *President*
Steve Leonard, *Director of Human Resources*

Zenith National Insurance Corp.
21255 Califa Street
Woodland Hills, CA 91367-5021
818-713-1000
Web Address: www.znic.com
Number of Employees: 1,500

Stanley Zax, *President*
Norm Baker, *Director of Human Resources*
Provider of workers' compensation insurance, annuities, health and life insurance, auto, homeowners, farmowners, and other coverages in California and Texas.

ZERO Corp.
444 South Flower Street, Suite 2100
Los Angeles, CA 90071
213-629-7000

Wilford Godbold Jr., *President*
Fran Boyd, *Executive Director*

Law & Lobbying

Many law firms hire recent college graduates to assist attorneys in the delivery of legal services. Some law firms hire individuals as legal assistants, others as litigation clerks or project assistants. The differences in the positions depend on the firm's philosophy about legal assistants. Some firms hire only trained legal assistants (those who have completed a legal assistant certificate program) while others hire only college graduates and train them in house. The firms that hire certified legal assistants will hire college graduates as project assistants or litigation clerks. Regardless of the title, the work will be comparable.

Individuals in these positions can assist attorneys or experienced legal assistants with document work in litigation; monitoring legislation, assisting with administrative practice areas (immigration, patent, pension, corporate, real estate, and bankruptcy) to complete government-required filings; and assisting in regulatory practice areas (environmental, communication, energy, and labor) to include monitoring changes in federal and state policies and procedures.

Entry-level salaries will range between the low-to-mid-20's. Firms look for bright, aggressive, professional, flexible and well-organized individuals to fill these positions. While individuals with strong research and writing skills are sought after, one will typically not use these skills on the job. Instead, applicants will generally have an interest in pursuing law school and therefore learning about the practice of law.

The best way to start one's job search is to send out resumes beginning in early May and seek assistance from college alums who may be practicing at a particular firm. Most firms do their hiring in either June or September, so don't think that if you take the summer off that you will have necessarily missed an opportunity. Another bit of advice law firms are reluctant to hire people who haven't relocated so it is best to begin one's search after having moved.

Joni Chizzonite
Director of Legal Assistants
HOGAN & HARTSON L.L.P.

See Also: Government
Associations/Non-Profit/Public Interest

Allen Matkins Leck Gamble & Mallory
18400 Von Karman Avenue, 4th Floor
Irvine, CA 92715
949-553-1313

Allen Matkins Leck Gamble & Mallory
515 South Figueroa Street, Suite 800
Los Angeles, CA 90071
213-622-5555
Number of Employees: 100

Brian Leck, *Managing Partner*

Alschuler, Grossman, Stein & Kahn
2049 Century Park East, 39th Floor
Los Angeles, CA 90067
310-277-1226
Web Address: www.agplaw.com
Number of Employees: 115

Dana Levitt, *Managing Partner*
Amber Graves, *Recruiting Coordinator for Lawyers*
Ruth Kawamoto, *Recruiting Coordinator*
Sally Postelle, *Human Resource Manager*

American College of Trust and Estate Counsel -ACTEC
3415 South Sepulveda Boulevard, Suite 330
Los Angeles, California 90034
310-398-1888
Web Address: www.actec.org

Arter & Hadden
5 Park Plaza, Suite 1000
Irvine, CA 92614-8528
949-252-7500
Number of Employees: 40

Randolf W. Katz, *Managing Partner*

Ault Deuprey Jones & Gorman
1320 Columbia Street, Suite 200
San Diego, CA 92101
619-544-8300
Number of Employees: 25

Thomas H. Ault, *Manageing Partner*
Douglas Hiatt, *Executive Administrator and Hiring Contact*

Baker & Hostetler
600 Wilshire Boulevard, Suite 1200
Los Angeles, CA 90017
213-624-2400
Number of Employees: 105

Sheldon Gebb, *Managing Partner*
Angela Agrusa, *Hiring Contact for Lawyers*
Clark Carlson, *Hiring Contact*

Baker & McKenzie
101 West Broadway, Suite 1200
San Diego, CA 92101
619-236-1441
Web Address: www.bakernet.com
Number of Employees: 100

Abby Silverman, *Managing Partner*
Kristen Cooke, *Human Resource Administrator*

Berger Kahn Shafton, Moss, Figler, Simon
4215 Glencoe Avenue, 2nd Floor
Marina del Rey, CA 90292
714-474-1880
Job Hotline: 310-821-9000
Number of Employees: 100

Craig Simon, *Managing Partner*
Elaine Bramen, *Office Manager*

Beverly Hills Bar Association
300 South Beverly Drive, Suite 200
Beverly Hills, CA 90212
310-553-6644
Web Address: www.bhba.org

Black Women Lawyers Association
3870 Crenshaw Boulevard, Suite 818
Los Angeles, CA 90008
213-292-6547

Bonne Bridges Mueller O'Keefe & Nichols
3699 Wilshire Boulevard, 10th Floor
Los Angeles, CA 90010
213-480-1900
Number of Employees: 170

Jeff Moffat, *Managing Partner*
Ann Harvey, *Hiring Contact for Lawyers*
Rose Bazan, *Hiring Contact*

Brobeck Phleger & Harrison
38 Technology Drive
Irvine, CA 92618
949-752-7535
Web Address: www.brobeck.com
Number of Employees: 80

Bruce R. Hallett Esq, *Partner*
Jeannie Cabell, *Human Resources Manager*

Brobeck Phleger & Harrison
550 West C Street, Suite 1300
San Diego, CA 92101
619-234-1966
Web Address: www.brobeck.com
Number of Employees: 100

Todd J. Anson, *Managing Partner*
Andrea Uy, *Human Resource Manager*

Brobeck Phleger & Harrison
550 South Hope Street, Suite 2100
Los Angeles, CA 90071
213-489-4060
Web Address: www.brobeck.com
Number of Employees: 250

Thomas P. Burke, *Managing Partner*
Ellen Zuckerman, *Hiring Contact for Lawyers and Paralegals*
Melissa Appleby, *Hiring Contact*

Brown Pistone Hurley VanVlear
8001 Irvine Center Drive, Suite 900
Irvine, CA 92618-2921
949-727-0559
Web Address: www.brownpistone.com
Number of Employees: 15

Ernest C. Brown, *Managing Partner*
Karen Emma, *Human Resources*

Bryan Cave
18881 Von Karman Avenue, Suite 1500
Irvine, CA 92612-1582
949-223-7000
Number of Employees: 35

Andrea Bryant, *Manager Administration*

Bryan Cave
120 Broadway, Suite 300
Santa Monica, CA 90401
213-243-4300
Web Address: www.bryancavellp.com

Steven Sunshine, *Managing Partner*
Louise Kaplan, *Administrative Director*

Buchalter Nemer Fields & Younger
19100 Von Karmen, Suite 300
Irvine, CA 92612
949-760-1121
Web Address: www.buchalter.com
Number of Employees: 15

Clifford J. Mayer, *Managing Partner*
Tammy Curtis, *Human Resources*

Buchalter Nemer Fields & Younger
601 South Figueroa Street, Suite 2400
Los Angeles, CA 90017
213-891-0700
Number of Employees: 250

Richard Jay Goldstein, *Managing Partner*

California Organizations of Police and Sheriffs
175 East Olive Avenue, Suite 400
Burbank, CA 91502
818-841-2222

Call Clayton & Jensen
610 Newport Center Drive, Suite 700
Newport Beach, CA 92660-6498
949-717-3000
Web Address: www.ccjlaw.com
Number of Employees: 18

Wayne W. Call, *Managing Shareholder*
Bobbie Harker, *Human Resources Manager*

Callahan McCune & Willis
111 Fashion Lane
Tustin, CA 92780-3397
714-730-5700
Number of Employees: 150
Peter Callahan, *Partner*

Case Knowlson Mobley Burnett
5 Park Plaza, Suite 800
Irvine, CA 92614-8501
949-552-2766
Number of Employees: 29
Michael W. Burnett, *Managing Partner*

Center for Law In the Public Interest
10951 West Pico Boulevard, Third Floor
Los Angeles, CA 90064-2126
310-470-3000

Chapin Fleming Winet McNitt Shea & Carter
501 West Broadway, 15th Floor
San Diego, CA 92101
619-232-4261
Number of Employees: 90
Edward D. Chapin, *Managing Partner*
Jerry Harken, *Director of Human Resources*

Christensen Miller Fink Jacobs Glaser Weil & Shapiro
2121 Avenue of the Stars, 18th Floor
Los Angeles, CA 90067
310-553-3000
Web Address: www.chrismill.com
Number of Employees: 200
Terry Christensen, *Managing Partner*
Nancy Venturine, *Hiring Contact for Lawyers*
Terry Avchen, *Hiring Contact for Paralegals*
Emily Mersler, *Human Resource Manager*

Citizens Against Lawsuit Abuse -CALA
3128 Pacific Coast Highway, Suite 15
Torrance, CA 90505
213-630-1176
Web Address: www.cala.org
Number of Employees: 5
John Hilbert, *Chairman*

Cooksey Howard Martin
535 Anton Boulevard, 10th Floor
Costa Mesa, CA 92626
949-431-1100

Cooley Godward
4365 Executive Drive, Suite 1100
San Diego, CA 92121
858-550-6000
Web Address: www.cooley.com
Number of Employees: 200

Fred Muto, *Managing Partner*
Heather Brown, *Administrative Assistant*

Cotkin & Collins
200 West Santa Ana Boulevard, Suite 800
Santa Ana, CA 92701-4155
714-835-2330
Web Address: www.cotkincollins.com
Number of Employees: 20

James Colins, *Manager*

Cox Castle & Nicholson
19800 Macarthur Boulevard, Suite 600
Irvine, CA 92612-2435
949-476-2111
Number of Employees: 35

Arthur Spaulding, *Managing Partner*
Mark McClanahan, *Office Manager*

Cox Castle & Nicholson
2049 Century Park East, 2800
Los Angeles, CA 90067
310-277-4222
Web Address: http://ccnlaw.com
Number of Employees: 215

Mario Camara, *Managing Partner*
Jeanie Flynn, *Recruiting Coordinator*

Cummins & White
2424 SE Bristol Street, Suite 300
Newport Beach, CA 92660-0757
949-852-1800
Number of Employees: 100
Larry M. Arnold, *Senior Partner*
Donna Tsuma, *Human Resources*

Drummy King White & Gire
3200 Park Centre Drive, Suite 1000
Costa Mesa, CA 92626
949-850-1800
Number of Employees: 40
Alan I. White, *Managing Partner*

Duckor Spradling & Metzger
401 West A Street, Suite 2400
San Diego, CA 92101
619-231-3666
Number of Employees: 50
Michael Duckor, *Managing Partner*
John Balha, *Director of Administration*

Early Maslach Price & Baukol
4751 Wilshire Boulevard, Suite 140
Los Angeles, CA 90010
213-932-3721
Job Hotline: 213-964-8832

Marcus Baukol, *Managing Partner*
Ken Olsen, *Human Resource Specialist*

Edwards Sooy & Byron
101 West Broadway, 9th Floor
San Diego, CA 92101
619-231-1500
Number of Employees: 80

Thomas Byron, *Managing Partner*
Bob Schweda, *Director of Administration*

Fisher & Phillips
4675 Macarthur Court, Suite 550
Newport Beach, CA 92660-1839
949-851-2424
Number of Employees: 40

Robert J. Bekken, *Managing Partner*

Gibson Dunn & Crutcher
4 Park Plaza
Irvine, CA 92714
949-451-3800
Web Address: www.gdclaw.com

Gibson Dunn & Crutcher
333 South Grand Avenue, 47th Floor
Los Angeles, CA 90071
213-229-7000
Web Address: http:www.gdclaw.com
Number of Employees: 150

Ronald Beard, *Managing Partner*
Kathy Kennedy, *Hiring Contact for Lawyers*
Jeanine McKeown, *Hiring Contact for
  Paralegals*
Dianne Carroll, *Hiring Contact*

Good Wildman Hegness & Walley
5000 Campus Drive
Newport Beach, CA 92660-2181
949-955-1100
Number of Employees: 25

Paul Hegness, *Senior Partner*

Graham & James
801 South Figueroa Street, 14th Floor
Los Angeles, CA 90017
213-624-2500
Web Address: www.gj.com
Number of Employees: 300

Derrick Takeuchi, *Managing Partner*
Maria Michel, *Hiring Contact for Lawyers*
Gloria McMullen, *Hiring Contact*

Greenberg Glusker Fields Claman & Machtinger
1900 Avenue of the Stars, Suite 2100
Los Angeles, CA 90067
310-553-3610
Web Address: www.ggfcm.com
Number of Employees: 200

Norm Levine, *Managing Partner*
Patricia Patrick, *Recruiting Coordinator*
Leesa McNamee, *Hiring Contact for Paralegals*
Monique Moffitt, *Human Resource Manager*

Hart King & Coldren
200 Sandpointe Avenue, 4th Floor
Santa Ana, CA 92707-5751
714-432-8700
Number of Employees: 45

William R. Hart, *Managing Partner*

Heller Ehrman White & McAuliffe
601 South Figueroa Street, 40th Floor
Los Angeles, CA 90017
213-689-0200
Number of Employees: 140
Melissa Katz, *Hiring Contact for Lawyers*
Linda Prutow, *Hiring Contact for Paralegals*
Susan Wade, *Human Resource Manager*

Higgs Fletcher & Mack
401 West A Street, Suite 2000
San Diego, CA 92101
619-236-1551
Web Address: www.higgslaw.com

Steven H. Kruis, *Managing Partner*
Mary Wright, *Office Manager*

Hill Farrer & Burrill
445 South Figueroa Street, 35th Floor
Los Angeles, CA 90071
213-620-0460
Web Address: www.hf&bllp.com
Number of Employees: 100

Scott Gilmore, *Managing Partner*
Ian Green, *Hiring Contact for Lawyers*
Dalia Cleveland, *Hiring Contact*

Hinchy Witte Wood Anderson & Hodges
1901 1st Avenue
San Diego, CA 92101
619-239-1901

Hollins Schechter & Feinstein
505 South Main Street, 12th Floor
Orange, CA 92868
714-558-9119
Number of Employees: 55

Marc Feinstein, *Managing Partner*
Steve Morris, *Administrator*

Howard Rice Nemerovski Canady
610 Newport Center Drive, Suite 450
Newport Beach, CA 92660-6435
949-721-6900
Number of Employees: 25

Kenx So-Cuerdo, *Office Manager*

Irell & Manella
840 Newport Center Drive, Suite 400
Newport Beach, CA 92660-6324
949-760-0991
Web Address: www.elibirell.com
Number of Employees: 50

Robert W. Stedman, *Partner*

Irell & Manella
1800 Avenue of the Stars, Suite 900
Los Angeles, CA 90067
310-277-1010
Web Address: www.irell.com
Number of Employees: 1,500
Jeanne Walker, *Executive Director*
Karen Wilson, *Human Resource Manager*

Jackson DeMarco & Peckenpaugh
4 Park Plaza, 16th Floor
Irvine, CA 92614
949-752-8585
Number of Employees: 60

F. Scott Jackson, *Partner*
Laben DeGrau, *Office Administrator*

Jeffer Mangels Butler & Marmaro
2121 Avenue of the Stars, 10th Floor
Los Angeles, CA 90067
310-203-8080
Web Address: www.jmbm.com
Number of Employees: 350

Bruce Jeffer, *Managing Partner*
Laura Bethke, *Hiring Contact*
Leslie Drago, *Hiring Contact for Paralegals*

John F. Evans Attorney at Law
4000 Macarthur Boulevard #6000
Newport Beach, CA 92660-2516
949-722-9810
Number of Employees: 20

Jones Day Reavis & Pogue
South Park Plaza, Suite 1100
Irvine, CA 92614
949-851-3939
Number of Employees: 25

Thomas R. Malcolm, *Partner*

Jones Day Reavis & Pogue
555 West 5th Street, Suite 4600
Los Angeles, CA 90013
213-489-3939
Number of Employees: 250

Rick McKnight, *Managing Partner*
Anna Lynn Godwin, *Hiring Contact for Lawyers*
George Marinelli, *Hiring Contact for Paralegals*
Patricia Hamp, *Hiring Contact*

Katten Muchin & Zavis
1999 Avenue of the Stars, Suite 1400
Los Angeles, CA 90067
310-788-4700

Gail Migdal Title, *Managing Partner*

Knobbe Martens Olson & Bear
620 Newport Center Drive, 16th Floor
Newport Beach, CA 92660-6420
949-760-0404
Web Address: www.kmob.com
Number of Employees: 200

James Bear, *Managing Partner*

Latham & Watkins
701 B Street, Suite 2100
San Diego, CA 92101
619-236-1234
Web Address: www.lw.com
Number of Employees: 300

Donald P. Newell, *Managing Partner*
Terry Davey, *Personnel Manager*

Latham & Watkins
650 Town Centre Drive, 20th Floor
Costa Mesa, CA 92626
949-540-1235

Latham & Watkins
633 West 5th Street, Suite 400
Los Angeles, CA 90071
213-485-1234
Web Address: www.lw.com
Number of Employees: 300

Martha Jordan, *Managing Partner*
Kathy Jaffe, *Hiring Contact for Lawyers*
Beverly Gifford, *Hiring Contact for Paralegals*
Julie Lugo, *Hiring Contact*

Lawyers Club of Los Angeles County
P.O. Box 71525
Los Angeles, CA 90071
213-624-2525

Lewis D'Amato Brisbois & Bisgaard
550 West C Street, Suite 800
San Diego, CA 92101
619-233-1006
Number of Employees: 80

R. Gaylord Smith, *Managing Partner*
Karla Anderson, *Office Manager*

Lewis D'Amato Brisbois & Bisgaard
650 Town Centre Drive
Costa Mesa, CA 92626
949-545-9200

Lewis D'Amato Brisbois & Bisgaard
221 North Figueroa Street, Suite 1200
Los Angeles, CA 90012
213-250-1800
Number of Employees: 117

Christopher Bisgaard, *Managing Partner*
Carla Macias, *Hiring Contact*

Littler Mendelson Fastiff Ticky & Mathiason
701 B Street, 13th Floor
San Diego, CA 92101
619-232-0441
Web Address: www.littler.com

Lobel & Opera
19800 McArthur, Suite 1100
Irvine, CA 92612
949-476-7400
Number of Employees: 40

William N. Lobel, *Managing Partner*
Judith A. Finnegan, *Human Resources Manager*

Loeb & Loeb
1000 Wilshire Boulevard, Suite 1800
Los Angeles, CA 90017
213-688-3400
Web Address: www.loeb.com
Number of Employees: 200

David Carlin, *Managing Partner*
Celia Toll, *Hiring Contact for Lawyers*
Gina Wiblen, *Hiring Contact*

Lorenz Alhadeff Cannon & Rose
550 West C Street, 19th Floor
San Diego, CA 92101
619-321-8700
Web Address: www.lorenzlaw.com

Los Angeles County Bar Association
617 South Olive Street
Los Angeles, CA 90014
213-627-2727
Web Address: www.laba.org

Luce Forward Hamilton & Scripps
600 West Broadway, Suite 2600
San Diego, CA 92101
619-236-1414
Web Address: www.luce.com

Scott W. Sonne, *Managing Partner*
Ann Bryant, *Hiring Contact*

Manatt Phelps & Phillips
11355 West Olympic Boulevard
Los Angeles, CA 90064
310-312-4000
Job Hotline: 310-231-5670
Web Address: www.manatt.com
Number of Employees: 300

Gordon Bava, *Managing Partner*
Kimberly Ferment, *Hiring Contact*

Marshack & Shulman
6 Hutton Centre Drive, Suite 900
Santa Ana, CA 92707-5761
714-540-5400
Web Address: www.mglaw.com
Number of Employees: 45

Martin Wilson Erickson/MacDowell
6 Hutton Centre Drive
Santa Ana, CA 92707-5745
714-972-1200
Number of Employees: 19

Thomas L Wilson, *Managing Partner*

McDermott Will & Emery
2049 Century Park East, 34th Floor
Los Angeles, CA 90067
310-277-4110
Web Address: www.mwe.com
Number of Employees: 178

Don Goldman, *Managing Partner*
Murray Heltzer, *Human Resource Manager*

McInnis Fitzgerald Rees & Sharkey
1230 Columbia Street, Suite 800
San Diego, CA 92101
619-236-1711
Number of Employees: 100

William M. Low, *Managing Partner*
Dave Whitson, *Administration*

McKenna & Cuneo
444 South Flower Street, 8th Floor
Los Angeles, CA 90071
213-688-1000
Web Address: www.mckennacuneo.com
Number of Employees: 200

Michael Kavanaugh, *Managing Partner*
Julie Noainouye, *Hiring Contact for Lawyers*
Ged Jackson, *Hiring Contact*

Meserve Mumper & Hughes
2301 Dupont Drive, Suite 410
Irvine, CA 92612
949-474-8995
Number of Employees: 50

E. Avery Crary, *Partner*

LAW & LOBBYING

Milbank Tweed Hadley & McCloy
601 South Figueroa Street, 30th Floor
Los Angeles, CA 90017
213-892-4000
Web Address: www.milbank.com
Number of Employees: 100

Edwin Feo, *Managing Partner*
Judith Wollan, *Hiring Contact for Paralegals*
Barbara Bruce, *Hiring Contact*

Milberg Weiss Bershad Hynes & Lerach
600 West Broadway, Suite 1800
San Diego, CA 92101
619-231-1058
Web Address: www.milberg.com
Number of Employees: 200

Bill Lerach, *Managing Partner*
Kathy Strozza, *Office Manager*

Mitchell Silberberg & Knupp
11377 West Olympic Boulevard, 8th Floor
Los Angeles, CA 90064
310-312-2000
Web Address: www.msk.com
Number of Employees: 200

Deborah Koessler, *Managing Partner*
Laurel Travers, *Hiring Contact for Lawyers*
Johna Machak, *Hiring Contact for Paralegals*
Kathy Letizia, *Hiring Contact*

Morgan Lewis & Bockius
300 South Grand Avenue, 22nd Floor
Los Angeles, CA 90071
213-612-2500
Web Address: www.mlb.com
Number of Employees: 175

John Hartigan, *Managing Partner*
Cheryl Yoshitake, *Hiring Contact for Lawyers*
Thomas Taylor, *Hiring Contact for Paralegals*
Cheryl Weaver, *Hiring Contact*

Morrison and Foerster
19900 MacArthur Boulevard, 12th Floor
Irvine, CA 92715
949-251-7500
Web Address: www.mofo.com

Morrison & Foerster
555 West Fifth Street, Suite 3500
Suite 3500
Los Angeles, CA 90013-1024
213-892-5200
Web Address: www.mofo.com
Number of Employees: 300

David Babbe, *Managing Partner*
Jeanette Lyon, *Hiring Contact for Lawyers*
Suzanne Morradian, *Hiring Contact for
   Paralegals*
Alisha Lang, *Hiring Contact*

Mulvaney Kahan & Barry
401 West A Street, 17th Floor
San Diego, CA 92101
619-238-1010
Number of Employees: 35

Lawrence Kahan, *Managing Partner*
Leigh Broussard, *Director of Administration*

Munger Tolles & Olson
355 South Grand Avenue, 35th Floor
Los Angeles, CA 90071
213-683-9100
Number of Employees: 300

Gregory Stone, *Managing Partner*
Kevin Villard, *Hiring Contact for lawyers*
Amy Harada, *Hiring Contact*

Murchison & Cumming
801 South Grand Avenue, 9th Floor
Los Angeles, CA 90017
213-623-7400
Number of Employees: 90

Friedrich W. Seitz, *Managing Partner*
Guy Gruppie, *Hiring Contact for Lawyers and
Paralegals*
Lynn Maria Bazan, *Hiring Contact*

Murtaugh Miller Meyer & Nelson
2603 Main Street, 9th Floor
Irvine, CA 92614
949-513-6800
Number of Employees: 60

Mark Himmelstein, *Managing Partner*

Musick Peeler & Garrett
624 South Grand Avenue, Suite 2000
Los Angeles, CA 90017
213-629-7600
Number of Employees: 200

R. Joseph DeBriyn, *Managing Partner*
Beverly Donatone, *Hiring Contact for Lawyers*
Joanne Jordan, *Hiring Contact*

Neil Dymott Perkins Brown & Frank
1010 Second Avenue, Suite 2500
San Diego, CA 92101
619-238-1712
Web Address: www.neil-dymott.com

Michael I. Neil, *Managing Partner*

Newmeyer & Dillion
3501 Jamboree Road, Suite 6000
Newport Beach, CA 92660-2960
949-854-7000
Number of Employees: 33

Tom Newmeyer, *Partner*

Nossaman Guthner Knox & Elliott
18101 Von Karman Avenue, Suite 1800
Irvine, CA 92612-1047
949-833-7800
Number of Employees: 60

Howard Harrison, *Admin Partner*

O'Melveny & Myers
610 Newport Center Drive, 17th Floor
Newport Beach, CA 92660-6419
949-760-9600
Job Hotline: 213-669-6662
Web Address: www.omm.com
Number of Employees: 1,400

Jerry Carlton, *Managing Partner*
Carolyn Berger, *Office Administrator*

O'Melvny & Myers
400 South Hope Street
Los Angeles, CA 90071
323-669-6093

Oppenheimer, Wolff & Donneley
500 Newport Center Drive, Suite 700
Newport Beach, CA 92660-7007
949-719-6000
Web Address: www.bruckperry.com
Number of Employees: 20

David Perry, *CEO*
Judy Oku, *Office Manager*

Orange County Bar Association
601 Civic Center Drive West
Santa Ana, CA 92701
714-440-6700
Web Address: www.ocbar.org

Palmieri Tyler Wiener Wilhelm
2603 Main Street, Suite 1300
Irvine, CA 92614
949-851-9400
Number of Employees: 100

Dennis Tyler, *Partner*

Paone Callahan McHolm & Winton
19100 Von Karman Avenue, 8th Floor
Irvine, CA 92612-1539
949-955-2900
Web Address: www.paone.com
Number of Employees: 40

Donna Williams, *Office Manager*

Paul Hastings Janofsky & Walker
695 Town Center Drive, 17th Floor
Costa Mesa, CA 92626-1924
949-668-6200
Job Hotline: 213-683-5015
Web Address: www.phjw.com
Number of Employees: 100

Marilyn Radley, *Human Resources*

Paul Hastings Janofsky & Walker
555 South Flower Street, 23rd Floor
Los Angeles, CA 90071
213-683-6000
Job Hotline: 213-683-5015
Web Address: www.phjw.com

Donald Daucher, *Managing Partner*
Joy McCarthy, *Hiring Contact for Lawyers*
Nancy Marine, *Hiring Contact for Paralegals*
Jacqulyn Kozar, *Hiring Contact*

Pillsbury Madison & Sutro
650 Town Center Drive, 7th Floor
Costa Mesa, CA 92626
949-436-6800
Web Address: www.pillsburylaw.com
Number of Employees: 1,285

Richard S. Ruben, *Managing Partner*

Pillsbury Madison & Sutro
101 West Broadway, Suite 1800
San Diego, CA 92101
619-234-5000
Web Address: www.pillsburylaw.com

Sue J. Hodges, *Manageing Partner*
Katie Dixon, *Human Resource Manager*

Pillsbury Madison & Sutro
725 South Figueroa Street, Suite 1200
Los Angeles, CA 90017
213-488-7100
Web Address: www.pillsburylaw.com
Number of Employees: 200

Robert Wallan, *Hiring Contact for Lawyers*
Carolyn Huestis, *Hiring Contact for Lawyers*
Mary Ellen Hatch, *Hiring Contact*

Pinto & Dubia
2 Park Plaza, Suite 300
Irvine, CA 92614-8513
949-955-1177
Number of Employees: 30

Christian F. Dubia Jr., *Partner*

Pivo & Halbreich Law Partnership
1920 Main Street, Suite 800
Irvine, CA 92614-7227
949-253-2000
Number of Employees: 25

Eva Halbreich, *Partner*

Post Kirby Noonan & Sweat
600 West Broadway, Suite 1100
San Diego, CA 92101
619-231-8666
Number of Employees: 80

Tom Bettles, *Managing Partner*
Kathy Pugh, *Human Resource Manager*

Procopio Cory Hargreaves & Savitch
530 B Street, Suite 2100
San Diego, CA 92101
619-238-1900
Web Address: www.procopio.com
Number of Employees: 128

Steven Untiedt, *Managing Partner*
John Bhrnantrout, *Director of Human Resources*

Quinn Emanuel Urquhart Oliver & Hedges
865 South Figueroa Street, 10th Floor
10th Floor
Los Angeles, CA 90017
213-624-7707
Number of Employees: 200
John Quinn, *Managing Partner*
Dave Henry, *Hiring Contact for Lawyers*
Rebecca Harpster, *Hiring Contact*

Richards Watson & Gershon
333 South Hope Street, 38th Floor
Los Angeles, CA 90071
213-626-8484
Number of Employees: 180

Gregory Stepanicich, *Managing Partner*
Mitchell Abbott, *Hiring Contact*

Riordan & McKinzie
695 Town Center Drive, Suite 1500
Costa Mesa, CA 92626-1924
949-433-2600
Web Address: www.riordan.com
Number of Employees: 30
Becky Fernandez, *Office Manager*

Riordan & McKinzie
300 South Grand Avenue, Suite 2900
Los Angeles, CA 90071
213-229-8510
Number of Employees: 150
Richard Welch, *Managing Partner*
Lance Bacarsley, *Hiring Contact for Lawyers*
Elizabeth Moran, *Hiring Contact*

Rosenfeld Meyer & Susman
9601 Wilshire Boulevard, 4th Floor
Beverly Hills, CA 90210
310-858-7700
Web Address: www.rmslaw.com
Number of Employees: 200
David Wexler, *Managing Partner*
Debbie Klaegar, *Director of Human Resources*

Rutan & Tucker
611 Anton Boulevard, Suite 1400
Costa Mesa, CA 92626
949-641-5100
Web Address: www.rutan.com
Number of Employees: 220
Jeffery Oderman, *Managing Partner*

San Diego CountyBar Association
1333 Seventh Avenue
San Diego, California 92101
619-231-0781
Web Address: www.sdcba.org

Sedgwick Detert Moran & Arnold
3 Park Plaza
Irvine, CA 92614-8505
949-852-8200
Number of Employees: 50

Gregory Halliday, *Managing Partner*

Sedgwick Detert Moran & Arnold
801 South Figueroa Street, 18th Floor
Los Angeles, CA 90017
213-426-6900
Number of Employees: 116

Lane Ashley, *Managing Partner*
Wendy Martinez, *Recruiting Coordinator*

Seltzer Caplan Wilkins & McMahon
750 B Street, Suite 2100
San Diego, CA 92101
619-685-3003
Job Hotline: 619-685-3127
Web Address: www.scwm.com
Number of Employees: 200

Norman T. Seltzer, *Managing Partner*
Lucy Frederick, *Recruitment Adminstrator*

Seyfarth Shaw
2029 Century Park East, Suite 3300
Suite 3300
Los Angeles, CA 90067
310-277-7200
Web Address: www.seyfarth.com

George Preonas, *Managing Partner*
Monica Perez, *Recruiting Coordinator*

Sheppard Mullin Richter & Hampton
501 West Broadway, 19th Floor
San Diego, CA 92101
619-338-6500
Web Address: www.smrh.com
Number of Employees: 75

Michael J. Changaris, *Managing Partner*
Tiffany Skinner, *Admnistrative Assistant*

Sheppard Mullin Richter & Hampton
333 South Hope Street, 48th Floor
Los Angeles,, CA 90071
213-620-1780
Web Address: www.smrh.com
Number of Employees: 350

Richard Brunette, *Managing Partner*
Sally Bucklin, *Professional Staff Cordinator*
Julie Penney, *Hiring Contact*

Sheppard Mullin Ritchter Hampton
650 Town Center Drive, 4th Floor
Costa Mesa, CA 92626-1925
949-513-5100
Web Address: www.smrh.com
Number of Employees: 50

Finley L. Taylor, *Partner*

Shifflet Walters Kane & Konoske
750 B Street, 26th Floor
San Diego, CA 92101
619-239-0871
Number of Employees: 30

Gregory Kane, *Managing Partner*

Sidley & Austin
555 West 5th Street, Suite 4000
Los Angeles, CA 90013
213-896-6000
Web Address: www.sidley.com
Number of Employees: 235

Theodore Miller, *Managing Partner*
Susan McGrady, *Hiring Contact for Lawyers &
    Paralegals*
Laura Maher, *Hiring Contact*

Skadden Arps Slate Meagher & Flom
300 South Grand Avenue, Suite 3400
Los Angeles, CA 90071
213-687-5000
Number of Employees: 275

Rand April, *Managing Partner*
Nicole Adams, *Hiring Contact for Lawyers*
Cecile Kelley, *Hiring Contact*

Smith Brennan & Dickerson
19900 Macarthur Boulevard, Suite 750
Irvine, CA 92612-2445
949-442-1500
Number of Employees: 27

Joseph G. Harraka Jr., *Partner*

Snell & Wilmer
1920 Main Street, Suite 1200
Irvine, CA 92614
949-253-2700
Web Address: www.swlaw.com
Number of Employees: 75

William O'Hare, *Managing Partner*

Sonnenschein Nath & Rosenthal
601 South Figueroa Street, Suite 1500
Los Angeles, CA 90017
213-623-9300
Number of Employees: 100

Robert Scoular, *Managing Partner*
Ron Kent, *Hiring Contact for Lawyers*
Laura Petroff, *Hiring Contact for Paralegals*
Sharon Atkinson, *Hiring Contact*

Spray Gould & Bowers
17592 17th Street, 3rd Floor
Tustin, CA 92780-7917
714-544-7200
Number of Employees: 20

Robert Dean, *President*

State Bar of California
1149 South Hill
Los Angeles, CA 90015
213-765-1000

Stevens Kramer and Harris
18400 Von Karman Avenue, Suite 615
Irvine, CA 92612-1514
949-253-9553
Number of Employees: 10

Bonita Danser, *Office Manager*

Stradling Yocca Carlson & Rauth
660 Newport Center Drive
Newport Beach, CA 92660-6401
949-725-4000
Number of Employees: 150

Nick Yocca, *President*

Tuttle & Taylor
355 South Grand Avenue, 40th Floor
Los Angeles, CA 90071
213-683-0600
Number of Employees: 110

Douglas Beck, *Managing Partner*
Diane Kim, *Partner*

Walsworth Franklin Bevins/McCall
1 City Boulevard West, Suite 308
Orange, CA 92868-3604
714-634-2522
Web Address: www.wfbm.com
Number of Employees: 45

Jeffrey P. Walsworth, *Sr Partner*

White & Case
633 West 5th Street
Los Angeles, CA 90071
213-620-7700
Number of Employees: 82

John Sturgeon, *Executive Partner*
Lorraine Rivera, *Hiring Contact for Lawyers*
Linda Shield, *Hiring Contact*

White & Resnick A Partnership
PO Box 7849
Newport Beach, CA 92658-7849
949-851-9001
Number of Employees: 15

Barnet Resnick, *Partner*

Further References

• Associations •

American Bar Association
750 North Lake Shore Drive
Chicago, IL 60611
312-988-5000
Web Address: www.fabnet.org

Federal Bar Association
1815 H Street, N.W., Suite 400
Washington, D.C. 20006
202-638-0252
Web Address: www.fedbar.org
Private and government lawyers and judges involved in federal practice

Federal Communications Bar Association
1722 Eye Street, N.W., Suite 300
Washington, D.C. 20006
202-736-8640

National Association of Black Women Attorneys
724 9th Street, N.W., Suite 206
Washington, D.C. 20001
202-637-3570
Black women who are members of the bar

National Association of Legal Assistants
1516 South Boston, Suite 200
Tulsa, OK 74119
918-587-6828
Web Address: www.nala.org

National Bar Association (Minority Attorneys)
1255 11th Street, N.W.
Washington, D.C. 20001
202-842-3900
Web Address: www.nelanet.com/nba

National Conference of Black Lawyers
2 West 125th Street
New York, NY 10027
212-864-4000
Attorneys who represent residents of black and poor communities

National Lawyers Guild
126 University Place
New York, NY 10003-4538
212-627-2656
Web Address: www.masdef.org/serv/nlg.html
National bar association for legal workers.

• Publications •

ABA Journal
750 North Lake Shore Drive
Chicago, IL 60611-4497
312-988-6076
Web Address: //dev.abanet.org/journal
American Bar Association legal magazine.

Corporate Legal Times
3 East Huron Street
Chicago, IL 60611
312-654-3500

Environmental Law & Management
605 3rd Avenue
New York, NY 10158
212-850-6000
Environmental law and management journal.

National Trial Lawyer Magazine
212 East Vine Street
P.O. Box 1217
Millville, NJ 08332-8217
609-825-5900
Legal magazine.

The American Lawyer
600 3rd Avenue, 2nd Floor
New York, NY 10016
212-973-2800
Legal magazine.

The Washington Lawyer
1707 L Street, N.W.
Washington, D.C. 20036
202-331-7700
Legal magazine for the Washington area.

Trial
1050 31st Street, N.W.
Washington, D.C. 20007-4499
202-965-3500
Legal magazine.

Print Media

- Local & National Newspapers & Magazines
- Trade Journals   • Printers   • Publishers

To obtain a position at a large or small news corporation, college graduates should have some journalism experience, either at a college newspaper or as an intern, combined with a solid educational foundation and sharp writing skills. In this age of specialization, if students can double major in business, for example, if they plan to become a business or financial reporter, they will be able to set themselves apart from other budding reporters.

I recommend becoming familiar with the Internet. A wide variety of jobs are emerging in the new online services arena, which requires tight writing as well as experience in database searches, designing web sites and other online skills. The media industry is growing to include television, print, online services, radio and newsletters, Adaptability in this ever-changing environment is the key to success.

It also may be necessary to take a test that will assess your abilities and competence. Most managers are looking for people with experience, not always people with a high G.P.A.

Kathleen Silvassy
UNITED PRESS INTERNATIONAL

PRINT MEDIA

Quick Reference

Company Web Sites

Antelope Valley Press
www.avpress.com
Applied Digital Access
www.ada.com
BNI Publications
www.bni-books.com
Books on Tape
www.booksontape.com
Brilliant Digital Entertainment
www.bde3.com
Claricom, Inc.
www.claricom.com
Coded Communications Corporation
www.coded.com
Corridor News
www.pomeradonews.com

Creative Teaching Press
www.creativeteaching.com
Database Publishing Company
www.databasepublishing.com
Day Runner
www.dayrunner.com
Haas Publishing
www.aptguides.com
Harte-Hanks Pennysaver/Shopper
www.hhinteractive.com
Homebuyers Guide
www.hbg.com
Homes for Sale Magazine
www.homeforsale-socal.com
Investor's Business Daily
www.investors.com
Kelley Blue Book
www.kbb.com

AAC Corporation
18300 Von Karman Avenue, Suite 850
Irvine, CA 92612-1053
949-756-2700
Web Address: www.aaccorp.com
Number of Employees: 80

Ricardo G Brutocao, *President*

ACC Communications
PO Box 2440
Costa Mesa, CA 92628-2440
949-751-1883
Web Address: www.workforceonline.com
Number of Employees: 25

Margaret Magnus, *President*

Adweek Magazine
BPI Communications
5055 Wilshire Boulevard
Los Angeles, CA 90036

American Foreign Language Newspapers Association
8530 Wilshire Boulevard, Suite 404
Beverly Hills, CA 90211
213-656-4935

Antelope Valley Press
37404 Sierra Highway
Palmdale, CA 93550
805-273-2700
Web Address: www.avpress.com
Number of Employees: 293

William Markham, *CEO*
Wendy Stigge, *Personnel Manager*

Back Stage West
BPI Communications
5055 Wilshire Boulevard
Los Angeles, CA 90036
213-525-2356
Web Address: www.backstagecasting.com

Billboard
BPI Communications
5055 Wilshire Boulevard
Los Angeles, CA 90036
213-525-2270
Web Address: www.billboard.com

BNI Publications
1612 South Clementine Street
Anaheim, CA 92802-2901
714-517-0970
Web Address: www.bni-books.com
Number of Employees: 25

William D. Mohoney, *President*

Books on Tape
729 Farad
Costa Mesa, CA 92626
949-548-5525
Web Address: www.booksontape.com
Number of Employees: 84

Duvall Hecht, *President*
Jo Bradley, *Director of Human Resources*

Brilliant Digital Entertainment
6355 Topanga Canyon Boulevard, Suite 120
Woodland Hills, CA 91367
818-346-3653
Web Address: www.bde3.com
Number of Employees: 80

Mark Dyne, *CEO*
Producer of interactive CD-ROM titles mainly for children -including the KidStory Series-. Also develops Multipath Movies: animated stories with plot alternatives that can be influenced by the viewer. Has an agreement to distribute Internet-enabled CD-ROMs with Packard Bell NEC computers.

California Newspaper Service Bureau
600 West Santa Ana Boulevard, Suite 205
Santa Ana, CA 92701-4026
714-972-2672
Number of Employees: 350

Pat Johnson, *Office Manager*

Canon Communications
11444 West Olympic Boulevard, Suite 700
Los Angeles, CA 90064
310-445-4200
Web Address: www.devicelink.com
Sheba Kane, *Human Resource Manager*

Coast Magazine
3111 Second Avenue
Corona del Mar, CA 92625
949-644-4700
Web Address: www.coastmagazine.com

Copley Press
7776 Ivanhoe Avenue
La Jolla, CA 92037
858-454-0411
Web Address: www.uniontribune.com

David Copley, *President*
Jan Jackson, *Recruiter*

Corridor News & Poway News Chieftain & Rancho Bernardo News Journal
13247 Poway Road
Poway, CA 92064
858-748-2311
Web Address: www.pomeradonews.com
Number of Employees: 50

David Calvert, *Publisher*
Karen Osborne, *Office Manager*

Creative Teaching Press
10701 Holder
Cypress, CA 90630-0017
714-895-5047
Web Address: www.creativeteaching.com
Number of Employees: 100

James Connelly, *President*
Mary Ayers, *Executive Secretary*

Daily Breeze
5215 Torrance Boulevard
Torrance, CA 90509
310-540-5511
Job Hotline: Ext 454
Number of Employees: 600

Thomas J. Wafer Jr., *Publisher*
Caryn Ratcliff, *Human Resource Manager*

Daily Journal Corporation
915 East 1st Street
Los Angeles, CA 90012
213-229-5300
Web Address: www.dailyjournal.com

Daily News
21221 Oxnard Street
Woodland Hills, CA 91367
818-713-3000
Job Hotline: 818-713-3093
Number of Employees: 800

Ike Massey, *CEO*
Jim Janiga, *Vice President for Human Resources*
Danice Heckathorn, *Human Resources Manager*

Day Runner
2750 Moore Avenue
Fullerton, CA 92833-2565
714-680-3500
Web Address: www.dayrunner.com
Number of Employees: 400

James E. Freeman Jr, *President*
Karen Marshall, *Human Resources Manager*

Diamond Entertainment Corporation
3961 Miraloma Avenue
Anaheim, CA 92806
714-693-3399
Number of Employees: 28

James K. T. Lu, *President*

Donnelley & Sons
2030 Main Street
Irvine, CA 92614
949-833-1533
Web Address: www.rrdonnelley.com

Donnelley & Sons
333 South Grand Avenue, Suite 5150
Los Angeles, CA 90071
213-620-8500
Web Address: www.rrdonnelley.com

Entertainment Publications
151 Kalmus Drive, Suite L-5
Costa Mesa, CA 92626-5973
949-662-2020
Number of Employees: 5000

Carla Bray, *Office Manager*

F W Dodge/McGraw-Hill
2150 South Towne Centre Place, Suite 100
Anaheim, CA 92806-6125
714-937-0831
Number of Employees: 96

Fabians Investment Resource
2100 Main Street, Suite 300
Huntington Beach, CA 92648-2489
714-536-1931
Web Address: www.fabian.com
Number of Employees: 25
Douglas Fabian, *President*

Fancy Publications
2401 Beverly Boulevard
Los Angeles, CA 90057
213-385-2222

Frames Data
16269 Laguna Canyon Road #100
Irvine, CA 92618-3603
949-788-0150
Web Address: www.framesdata.com
Number of Employees: 35
Skip Johnson, *President*
Fariba Williams, *Human Resources Director*

Freedom Communications

17666 Fitch Avenue
Irvine, CA 92714
949-553-9292
Web Address: www.freedom.com
Number of Employees: 6900

James N. Rosse, *President*
Mark Ernst, *Vice President of Human Resources*
Owner of about 60 daily and weekly newspapers. It entered the TV market in 1981 and launched the 24-hour Orange County NewsChannel in 1990 - sold to an LA cable company in 1996-.

Fullerton Observer

PO Box 7051
Fullerton, CA 92834-7051
714-525-6402
Number of Employees: 25

Ralph Kennedy, *President*

Gick Publishing

9 Studebaker
Irvine, CA 92618-2091
949-581-5830
Number of Employees: 35

James Gick, *President & Owner*
Brian Parley, *Office Manager*

Glencoe/McGraw Hill Education Division

21600 Oxnard Street, Suite 500
Woodland Hills, CA 91367
818-615-2600
Web Address: www.glencoe.com

GTE Directories Corporation

3131 Katella Avenue
Los Alamitos, CA 90720-2399
562-594-5101
Number of Employees: 500

Bob Wilson, *Human Resources Manager*
Arlene Delossantos, *Hiring Contact*

Haas Publishing

1300 Dove Street, Suite 105
Newport Beach, CA 92660-2415
949-221-0525
Web Address: www.aptguides.com
Number of Employees: 700

Hachette-Filipacci Magazines

5670 Wilshire Boulevard, Suite 500
Los Angeles, Ca 90036
323-954-0500

Harcourt Brace & Company/Academic Press

525 B Street, Suite 1900
San Diego, CA 92101
619-231-6616
Job Hotline: 619-699-6562
Web Address: www.harcourt.com

Number of Employees: 390
Peter Bowman, *CEO*
Marilyn Bailin, *Human Resources Director*

Harte-Hanks Pennysaver/Shopper

1261 East Dyer Road #100
Santa Ana, CA 92705-5605
714-241-6700
Web Address: www.hhinteractive.com
Number of Employees: 1000

Gayle Pitt, *Human Resources Manager*

Harte-Hanks Pennysaver/Shopper

2830 Orbitor
Brea, CA 92821
714-996-8900
Web Address: www.hhinteractive.com
Number of Employees: 1000

Pete Gorman, *President*
Gayle Pitt, *Human Resources Manager*

Hollywood Reporter

5055 Wilshire Boulevard, Suite 600
Los Angeles, CA 90036
213-876-1000
Web Address: www.hollywoodreporter.com

Homebuyers Guide

17780 Fitch, Suite 195
Irvine, CA 92614-6038
949-476-3055
Web Address: www.hbg.com
Number of Employees: 26

Walter Crowell, *President*

Homes for Sale Magazine

15 Studebaker
Irvine, CA 92618-2013
949-951-4663
Web Address: www.homeforsale-socal.com
Number of Employees: 25

Gary Campbell, *President & CEO*

Inland Empire Business Journal

8560 Vineyard Avenue, Suite 306
Rancho Cucamonga, CA 91730
909-484-9765
Web Address: www.busjournal.com

Inland Valley Daily Bulletin

2041 East 4th Street
Ontario, CA 91764
909-987-6397
Web Address: www.dailybulletin.com

Inter-Tel Technologies

1667 North Batavia Street
Orange, CA 92867-3508
714-283-1600
Number of Employees: 1200

Maria Cesaro, *Human Resouces Manager*

Intervisual Books
2716 Ocean Park Bouelvard, Suite 2020
Santa Monica, CA 90405
310-396-8708
Gail Thornhill, *Controller & Human Resource Manager*

Investor's Business Daily
12655 Beatrice Street
Los Angeles, CA 90066
310-448-6000
Web Address: www.investors.com
Number of Employees: 700

William O'Neil, *Publisher*

Irvine World News
2712 McGaw
Irvine, CA 92614
949-261-2435
Number of Employees: 31

Brien Manning, *President*

Kelley Blue Book
PO Box 19691
Irvine, CA 92623-9691
949-770-7704
Web Address: www.kbb.com
Number of Employees: 54

Robert S Kelley, *Publisher*

KNI Incorporated
1261 South State College Parkway
Anaheim, CA 92806 5240
714-956-7300
Web Address: www.kninc.com
Number of Employees: 90

Jerry R Bernstein, *President*

Knowledge Adventure
1311 Grand Central Avenue
Glendale, CA 91201
818-246-4400
Job Hotline: 313-793-0599
Web Address: www.adventure.com
Number of Employees: 115
Larry Gross, *President*
Lonna Lynn, *Director of Personnel*
Maker of award-winning multimedia educational software for children. Its products include the JumpStart and Adventure Series -3-D Dinosaur and 3-D Body-, Steven Spielberg's Director's Chair, and software based on characters created by Marvel Entertainment Group and DC Comics.

La Opinion
411 West 5th Street
Los Angeles, CA 90013
213-896-2152
Web Address: www.laopinion.com
Jose Lozano, *Publisher*
Richard Cabada, *Recruiter*

Long Beach Press-Telegram
604 Pine Avenue
Long Beach, CA 90844
562-435-1161
Web Address: www.ptconnect.com
Shari Wright, *Human Resource Director*

Los Angeles Times
1375 Sunflower Avenue
Costa Mesa, CA 92626-1697
949-966-5600
Web Address: www.latimes.com
Number of Employees: 10,000

Kathy Joyce, *Human Resources Manager*

Los Angeles Times
Times Mirror Square
Los Angeles, CA 90053
213-237-5000
Job Hotline: 213-237-5700
Web Address: www.latimes.com

Mark Willes, *Publisher*

Los Angeles Weekly
6715 Sunset Boulevard
Los Angeles, CA 90028
213-465-9909
Web Address: www.laweekly.com

Maranatha Music
30230 Rancho Viejo
San Juan Capistrano, CA 92654-1050
714-248-4000
Web Address: www.maranathamusic.com
Number of Employees: 30

Tom Vegh, *President*

McMullen Publishing
774 South Placentia Avenue
Placentia, CA 92870-6846
714-572-2255
Web Address: www.mcmullenargus.com
Number of Employees: 225

Bill Porter, *CEO*

National Education Corporation
2601 Main Street, Suite 700
Irvine, CA 92614
949-474-9400
Number of Employees: 2700

Sam Yau, *President*
Lori Grigg, *Director of Personnel*
Provider of multimedia products and services for education and training. Operates ICS Learning Systems, with correspondence courses including degree programs in business and technology, and training in paraprofessional and occupational fields.

PRINT MEDIA

North County Times
207 East Pennsylvania Avenue
Escondido, CA 92025
760-839-3333
Web Address: www.nctimes.com
Number of Employees: 500

Richard High, *Publisher*
Peggy Chapman, *Director of Human Resources*

Orange Coast Magazine
3701 Birch Street, Suite 100
Newport Beach, CA 92660-2618
949-862-1133
Web Address: www.orangecoast.com
Number of Employees: 28

Ruth Ko, *Publisher*

Orange County Business Journal
4590 Macarthur Boulevard, Suite 100
Newport Beach, CA 92660-2024
949-833-8373
Web Address: www.ocjournal.com
Number of Employees: 35

Richard Reisman, *President/Publisher*

Orange County Register
625 Grand Avenue
Santa Ana, CA 92701
714-835-1234
Web Address: www.ocregister.com

Pacific MultiMedia
2477 East Orangethorpe Avenue
Fullerton, CA 92831
714-441-0782
Number of Employees: 7

James E. Campbell, *President*
Full-service audio and video production company offering on and off-site recording and duplication of spoken-word personal and professional improvement material in health, business, music, and religion.

Panorama International Productions
4988 Gold Leaf Drive
Mariposa, CA 95338
209-966-5071
Web Address: www.siepress@yosemite.net
Number of Employees: 14

Jim Wilson, *President*
Producer of videotape and photo books for tourism. Has over 40 titles, including US National Parks, such as such as Yellowstone, Yosemite, and the Grand Canyon, and theme parks. Its products are marketed to National Parks, concessionaires, retailers, and souvenir shops.

Pasadena Star-News
911 Colorado Boulevard
Pasadena, CA 91109
626-578-6300

Peterson Publishing Companies
6420 Wilshire Boulevard, 2nd Floor
Los Angeles, CA 90048
323-782-2000
Web Address: www.petersenco.com

Pfanner Communications
1371 Warner Avenue, Suite E
Tustin, CA 92780-6448
714-259-8240
Number of Employees: 20

Paul Pfanner, *President*

San Diego Business Journal
4909 Murphy Canyon Road, Suite 200
San Diego, CA 92123
858-277-6359
Web Address: www.sdbj.com
Number of Employees: 38

Ted Owen, *Publisher*
Laura Marquez, *Human Resources Director*

San Diego Commerce
2652 Fourth Avenue, Suite 200
San Diego, CA 92103
619-232-3486
Web Address: sdcommerce@adnc.com
Number of Employees: 4

Don Parret, *Publisher*
Yolanda Dominguez, *Manager*

San Diego Daily Transcript
2131 Third Avenue
San Diego, CA 92101
619-232-4381
Web Address: www.sddt.com
Number of Employees: 75

Bob Loomis, *CEO*
Adriana Gutierrez, *Human Resource Manager*

San Diego Jewish Times
4731 Palm Avenue
La Mesa, CA 91941
619-463-5515
Web Address: jewishtimes@msn.com
Number of Employees: 11

Garry Rosenberg, *Publisher*
Collenn Silea, *Associate Publisher*

San Diego Magazine
401 West A Street, Suite 250
San Diego, CA 92101
619-230-9292
Number of Employees: 25

James Fitzpatrick, *CEO/Publisher*

San Diego Voice & Viewpoint
1729 North Euclid Avenue
San Diego, CA 92105
619-266-2233
Web Address: gwarren@electriciti.com
Number of Employees: 20

John Warren, *Publisher*
Ms. Gerri Warren, *Co-Publisher*

San Gabriel Valley Tribune
1210 North Azusa Canyon Road
West Covina, CA 91790
626-962-8811

Ike Massey, *CEO*
Tim Sowecke, *Publisher*
Andrew Hernandez, *Director of Human Resources*

Scoop
2540 Redhill Avenue, Suite 100
Santa Ana, CA 92705
714-453-8383
Web Address: www.scoopnews.com
Number of Employees: 28

Rand Bleimeister, *President*
Provider of custom-order reprint services primarily for publications. Also creates genuine-looking magazine articles for display.

Sea Magazine
17782 Cowan
Irvine, CA 92614-6012
949-660-6150
Web Address: www.seamag.com
Number of Employees: 20

Duncan McIntosh, *President*

Sound Source Interactive
26115 Mureau Road, Suite B
Calabasas, CA 91302-3126
818-878-0505
Web Address: www.soundsourceinteractive.com
Number of Employees: 50

Vincent J. Bitetti, *President*
George Chong, *Corporate Controller*
Marja Reed, *CEO's Assistant*
Producer of interactive educational and entertainment software for children and adults.

Star-News -Pasadena
1210 North Azusa Canyon Road
West Covina, CA 91790
818-962-8811

Sun Newspapers
216 Main Street
Seal Beach, CA 90740-0755
562-430-7555
Number of Employees: 12

Mels Fisher, *Publisher*
Melissa Hobbs, *Hiring Contact*
Beth Yates, *Business Manager*

Surfer Publications
33046 Calle Aviador
San Juan Capistrano, CA 92675
714-496-5922
Web Address: www.surfermag.com
Number of Employees: 50

Danna Lewis-Gordon, *President*

Teacher Created Materials
6421 Industry Way
Westminster, CA 92683-3652
714-891-7895
Web Address: www.teachercreated.com
Number of Employees: 150

Rochelle Coombs, *President*
Tal Frank, *Human Resources Manager*

The Anaheim Bulletin
1771 South Lewis Street
Anaheim, CA 92805-6439
714-634-1567
Web Address: www.ocregister.com
Number of Employees: 85

Peggy Castellano, *Vice President for Human Resources*

The Orange County Register
PO Box 3629
Mission Viejo, CA 92690-1629
714-768-3631
Web Address: www.ocregister.com
Number of Employees: 3000

Peggy Castellano, *Vice President for Human Resources*

The Orange County Register
625 North Grand Avenue
Santa Ana, CA 92711-1626
714-835-1234
Web Address: www.ocregister.com
Number of Employees: 3000

R. D. Threshie, *Publisher*
Peggy Castellano, *VP for Human Resources*

The Orange County Register
1771 South Lewis Street
Anaheim, CA 92805-6439
714-704-5800
Web Address: www.ocregister.com
Number of Employees: 3000

The Signal
2400 Creek Side Road
Valencia, CA 91355
805-259-1234
Number of Employees: 125
William Fleet, *CEO*

429

Thomas Brothers Maps
17731 Cowan
Irvine, CA 92614-6065
949-863-1984
Web Address: www.thomas.com
Number of Employees: 245

Robert Foster, *President & COO*
Janice Jalosky, *Human Resources Director*

Times Mirror Co.
Times Mirror Square
Los Angeles, CA 90053
213-237-3700
Job Hotline: 213-237-6687
Web Address: www.latimes.com
Number of Employees: 3,000

Mark Willes, *Chairman & President*
Elizabeth Crewry, *Director of Personnel*

TrialVision
4100 Newport Place Drive, Suite 520
Newport Beach, CA 92660-2451
949-852-9200
Web Address: www.trialvision.com
Number of Employees: 20

Gerry Klein Esq, *President*

Tustin News
625 North Grand Avenue
Santa Ana, CA 92701
714-454-7332
Web Address: www.ocregister.com
Number of Employees: 100

Variety & Daily Variety
5700 Wilshire Boulevard, Suite 120
Los Angeles, CA 90036
213-857-6600
Web Address: www.variety.com

Volt Information Sciences
2401 North Glassell Avenue
Orange, CA 92857-8500
714-921-8800
Web Address: www.volt-resume.com
Number of Employees: 6800

Sharon Brookes, *Director*

Weider Health & Fitness
21100 Erwin Street
Woodland Hills, CA 91367
818-884-6800
Web Address: www.fitnessonline.com

Western Outdoors Publications
3197 Airport Loop Drive, Suite E
Costa Mesa, CA 92626-3470
949-546-4370
Number of Employees: 34

Robert Twilegar, *President*

Further Reference

• Associations •

Multimedia Telecommunications Association
2500 Wilson Boulevard, Suite 3300
Arlington, VA 22201
202-296-9800
Web Address: www.mmta.org
Association of Telecommunications Providers.

National Newspaper Publishers Association
3200 13th Street, N.W.
Washington, D.C. 20010
202-588-8764
Aides Newspaper Publishers.

National Press Club
529 14th Street, N.W., 13th Floor
Washington, D.C. 20045
202-662-7500
Web Address: ntc.press.org
Organization for News Media Personnel.

Newspaper Association of America
11600 Sunrise Valley Drive
Reston, VA 22091
703-648-1000
Alliance for Free Press.

The Newspaper Guild
8611 2nd Avenue
Silver Spring, Maryland 20910
301-585-2990
Web Address: www.newsguild.org
Retirement benefits to those in news media.

EMPLOYMENT TIP

The media industry is growing to include television, print, online services, radio and newsletters, Adaptability in this ever-changing environment is the key to success.

Public Relations

Like advertising, public relations/affairs involves promoting either a product or service. In public affairs, the product is not a consumer good, but rather a policy position. In public relations, it's market products and services

Ogilvy Adams & Rinehart looks for individuals with college degrees, although we do not place a premium on graduate degrees. Similarly, it is not necessary for an employee to have a PR background when that person shows an affinity for marketing or public issues. Instead we ask questions such as;

- Does the candidate understand how a bill becomes a law?
- Does a candidate have an understanding of the media?
- Does the candidate have expertise in an product area ?
- Does the candidate have experience with promoting and enhancing the image of products and services?

A support position is generally the only available option for a recent graduate. Account work is assigned only to "second career" staff (those from the hill or the media). However, support staff is exposed to a great deal of client related work in a short period of time.

The interviewing process can be long, but a graduate with a strong writing/policy background—experience with corporate products or with a newspaper—can expect to have an advantage.

Ogilvy Adams & Rinehart

See Also: Advertising & Public Interest Groups

Amies Communications
18552 MacArthur Boulevard, Suite 390
Irvine, CA 92612
949-863-1910

Bailey/Gardiner Creative Communications
416 University Avenue, Suite 200
San Diego, CA 92103
619-298-9300
Web Address: baileygardiner.com
Number of Employees: 20

Jonathan Bailey, *President/CEO*

Beck-Ellman Agency
4700 Spring Street
La Mesa, CA 91941
619-469-3500

Beverly Ellman, *Hiring Contact*
Dennis Ellman, *Hiring Contact*

Bender Goldman & Helper
11500 West Olympic Boulevard, Suite 655
Los Angeles, CA 90064
310-473-4147
Web Address: www.bhimpact.com
Number of Employees: 45

Lee Helper, *President*
Beverly Brown, *Human Resource Manager*

Benjamin Group
1851 East 1st Street, Suite 1200
Santa Ana, CA 92705
Web Address: www.benjamingroup.com

Berkman Marketing Group
401 West A Street, Suite 260
San Diego, CA 92101
619-231-9977
Web Address: berkmanpr.com
Number of Employees: 9

Jack Berkman, *President & Hiring Contact*

Bragman Nyman Cafarelli
9171 Wilshire Boulevard, Suite 300
Beverly Hills,, CA 90210
310-274-7800
Number of Employees: 45

Howard Bragman, *Principal*
Barbara Wardell, *Human Resource Manager*

Burson-Marsteller
1800 Century Park East, Suite 200
Los Angeles, CA 90067
310-226-3000
Web Address: www.bm.com

California Apparel News
Apparel News Group
110 East 9th Street, Suite A-777
Los Angeles, CA 90079
213-627-3737
Web Address: www.apparelnews.net

Cerrell Associates
320 North Larchmont Boulevard, Second Floor
Los Angeles, CA 90004
213-466-3445
Number of Employees: 30

Joseph Cerrell, *Chairman*
Steve Bullock, *Hiring Contact*

Cohn & Wolfe
1840 Century Park East, Suite 750
Century City, CA 90067
310-226-3035
Job Hotline: 310-226-3015
Number of Employees: 30

Chris Wildermuth, *Senior VP & General Manager*
Linda Herrera, *Director of Human Resources*

Cooper/Iverson Marketing
8334 Clairemont Mesa Boulevard, Suite 214
San Diego, CA 92111
619-292-7400
Web Address: www.cooperiver.com
Number of Employees: 9

Lorraine Iverson, *Principal & Hiring Contact*

Creative Communications Services
2385 Camino Vida Roble, Suite 205
Carlsbad, CA 92009
760-438-5250
Web Address: www.ccspr.com
Number of Employees: 10

Robert Fisher, *President*
Barbara Carothers, *Human Resources Manager*

Dolphin Group
10866 Wilshire Boulevard, Suite 550
Los Angeles, CA 90024
310-446-4800
Number of Employees: 16

Lee Stitzenberger, *CEO*

Drasnin Communications
2002 Jimmy Durante Boulevard, Suite 420
Del Mar, CA 92014
619-792-9994
Number of Employees: 4

Ray Drasnin, *Principal and Hiring Contact*

Edelman Public Relations Worldwide
5670 Wilshire Boulevard, Suite 1500
Los Angeles, CA 90036
213-857-9100
Web Address: www.edelman.com
Number of Employees: 25

George Drucker, *Executive VP & General Manager*
Raquel Rodriguez, *Office Manager*

Financial Relations Board
12121 Wilshire Boulevard, Suite 401
Los Angeles, CA 90025
310-442-0599
Web Address: www.frbinc.com
Number of Employees: 50

T. Kent, *Managing Partner & HR Director*

Fischer & Partners
4640 Admiralty Way, Suite 800
Marina del Rey, CA 90292
310-577-7870
Number of Employees: 25

Roger Fischer, *President*
Alex Halbur, *Hiring Contact*

Fisher Business Communications
5 Hutton Centre Drive, Suite 120
Santa Ana, CA 92707
714-556-1010
Web Address: www.fbiz.com

Fleishman-Hillard
515 South Flower Street, Seventh Floor
Los Angeles, CA 90071
213-629-4974
Web Address: www.fleishman.com

Sheena Hengs, *Senior Partner & General Manager*

Freeman/McCue Public Relations
3 Hutton Centre Drive #880
Santa Ana, CA 92707-5781
714-557-3663
Number of Employees: 22

Doug Freeman, *Partner*
Anice Katz, *Partner*

GCI Los Angeles
6100 Wilshire Boulevard, Suite 840
Los Angeles, CA 90048
213-930-0811

Michelle Jordan, *President*
Jeri Gardner, *Hiring Contact*

Gladstone International
18101 Von Karman Avenue, Suite 1280
Irvine, CA 92612
949-955-5252
Web Address: www.gladstone.com

Golin/Harris Communications
601 West Fifth Street, Suite 400
Los Angeles, CA 90071
213-623-4200
Web Address: www.golinharris.com
Number of Employees: 60

Fred Cook, *General Manager*
Jan Cox, *Office Manager*

Hill & Knowlton
19800 Macarthur Boulevard, Suite 950
Irvine, CA 92612-2438
949-752-1106
Web Address: www.hill&knowlton.com
Number of Employees: 17

Anne Romero, *Manager*

Hill & Knowlton
6500 Wilshire Boulevard, 21st Floor
Los Angeles, CA 90048
213-966-5700
Web Address: www.hillandknowlton.com
Number of Employees: 50

M. A. Hartwig, *Executive VP*
Karen Joyce, *Hiring Contact*

Katz & Associates
4275 Executive Square, Suite 530
La Jolla, CA 92037
619-452-0031
Number of Employees: 17

Sara Katz, *President*
Susan Piotrowski, *Administrative Manager*

Lippin Group
6100 Wilshire Boulevard, Suite 400
Los Angeles, CA 90048
213-965-1990

Manning Selvage & Lee
6500 Wilshire Boulevard, Suite 1900
Los Angeles, CA 90048
213-782-6600
Number of Employees: 52

Jill Farwell, *Managing Director*
Sophia Vegas, *Office Manager*

Maples Communications
2201 Dupont Drive, Suite 740
Irvine, CA 92612
949-253-8737

Matthews Mark
620 C Street, 6th Floor
San Diego, CA 92101
619-238-8500
Number of Employees: 70

James S. Matthews, *Principal*
Linda Wrazen, *Human Resource Director*

Matthews Mark MacCracken & McGaugh
750 B Street, Suite 1950
San Diego, CA 92101
619-238-8511
Number of Employees: 80

Jim Matthews, *President*
Linda Wrazen, *Human Resource Manager*

Miller/Shandwick Technologies
1888 Century Park East, Suite 920
Los Angeles, CA 90067
310-203-0550
Job Hotline: 310-201-8800
Web Address: www.shandwick.com
Number of Employees: 17

Frank Pollare, *Senior VP & General Manager*
Robin Tucker, *Human Resource Manager*

Nelson Communications Corporation
18401 Von Karman Avenue, Suite 120
Irvine, CA 92612
949-222-5400
Web Address: www.nelsongroup.com

Nelson Communications Group
402 West Broadway, Suite 2000
San Diego, CA 92101
619-687-7000
Web Address: www.nelsongroup.com
Number of Employees: 20

Karen D. Hutchens, *Principal*
Jim Bartel, *Vice President & Hiring Contact*

Nuffer, Smith Tucker
3170 Fourth Avenue, Suite 300
San Diego, CA 92103
619-296-0605
Web Address: www.nstpr.com
Number of Employees: 15

Kerry Tucker, *President & Hiring Contact*

Pacific Gateway Group
450 A Street, Suite 500
San Diego, CA 92101
619-234-3491
Number of Employees: 12

Doug Perkins, *President*
Carol Kaiser, *Office Manager*

Pacific Visions Communications
9000 Sunset Boulevard, Suite 700
Los Angeles, CA 90069
310-274-8787
Web Address: www.pacificvisions.com
Number of Employees: 12

Valsin Marmillion, *President*
David Sabikan, *Director of Operations*

Pacific West Communications Group
3435 Wilshire Bouelvard, Suite 2850
Los Angeles, CA 90010
213-487-0830

Paine & Associates
535 Anton Boulevard, Suite 450
Costa Mesa, CA 92626-1977
949-755-0400
Job Hotline: 714-755-0400
Number of Employees: 35

David Paine, *President*
Stephanie Harrel, *Human Resources Manager*

Pondel Parsons & Wilkinson
12100 Wilshire Boulevard, Suite 400
Los Angeles, CA 90025
310-207-9300
Web Address: www.pondel.com
Number of Employees: 20

Roger Pondel, *President*
Judy Sfetcu, *Hiring Contact*

Porter/Novelli
10960 Wilshire Boulevard, Suite 1750
Los Angeles, CA 90024
310-444-7000
Web Address: www.porternovelli.com
Number of Employees: 36

Barbara Parsky, *Executive VP & General Manager*
Linda Frankel, *Director of Human Resources*

Public Relations Society of America, Los Angeles Chapter
7060 Hollywood Boulevard, Suite 614
Los Angeles, CA 90028
213-461-4595
Web Address: www.prsa-la.org

Rogers & Associates
1875 Century Park East, Suite 300
Los Angeles, CA 90067
310-552-6922

Ron Rogers, *President*
Liz Warren, *Office Manager*

Rogers & Cowan
1888 Century Park East, Suite 500
Los Angeles, CA 90067
310-201-8800
Number of Employees: 60

Thomas Tardio, *President*
Robin Tucker, *Hiring Contact*

Scribe Communications
5090 Shoreham Place, Suite 108
San Diego, CA 92122
619-452-8958
Number of Employees: 3

Jan Percival, *President & Hiring Contact*

Shafer Public Relations
18200 Von Karman Avenue, Suite 800
Irvine, CA 92612-1029
949-553-1177
Web Address: www.shafer.net
Number of Employees: 55

Andrew Getsey, *President*
Dawngreen, *Human Resources Manager*

Stock/Alper & Associates
408 Nutmeg Street
San Diego, CA 92103
619-296-8221
Web Address: www.stockalper.com
Number of Employees: 15

Mickey Stockalper, *President & Hiring Contact*

Stoorza Ziegaus Metzger
355 South Grand Avenue, Suite 2800
Los Angeles, CA 90071
213-891-2822

Number of Employees: 15
Cathy Ann Connelly, *President & General Manager*
Patty Siqueiros, *Hiring Contact*

Stoorza, Ziegaus & Metzger, Inc.
225 Broadway, Suite 1800
San Diego, CA 92101
619-236-1332
Web Address: www.szmi.com
Number of Employees: 100

David De Pinto, *President*
Joni Sloan, *Human Resource Manager*

The Ardell Group
2002 Jimmy Durante Boulevard, Suite 410
Del Mar, CA 92014
619-792-7964
Number of Employees: 50

David Stowe, *President & Hiring Contact*

The Bohle Company
1999 Avenue of the Stars, Suite 550
Los Angeles, CA 90067
310-785-0515
Web Address: www.bohle.com
Number of Employees: 45

Sue Bohle, *President*

The Flannery Group
402 West Broadway, Suite 1150
San Diego, CA 92101
619-239-5558
Number of Employees: 100

Joyce Flannery, *President*
Richard Flannery, *Vice President of Human Resources*

The Gable Group
701 B Street, Suite 1400
San Diego, CA 92101
619-234-1300
Web Address: www.gablegroup.com
Number of Employees: 25

Joseph Charest, *President & Hiring Contact*

The Grove Agency
591 Camino de la Reina, Suite 600
San Diego, CA 92108
619-299-8595
Number of Employees: 6

Sandra K. Grove, *President & Hiring Contact*

The McRae Agency
835 Fifth Avenue, Suite 306
San Diego, CA 92101
619-230-1282

Elizabeth McRae, *Principal*

The Olguin Co.
662 Ninth Avenue, Suite 100
San Diego, CA 92101
619-234-0345
Number of Employees: 5

Michael A. Olguin, *Principal*
Jody Wikheim, *Office Accountant*

Tom Jones Productions
13071 Kerry Street
Garden Grove, CA 92844-1638
714-636-9909
Number of Employees: 20

Thomas G. Jones, *President*

Vista Group
805 South San Fernando Boulevard
Burbank, CA 91502
818-840-6789
Web Address: www.vistagroupUSA.com
Number of Employees: 15

Eric Dahlquist, *President*
Susan Frederick, *Director of Human Resources*

Further References

• Associations •

Public Relations Society of America
33 Irving Place
New York, New York 10003
212-995-2230
Web Address: www.prsa.org
Professional development, job referral, and research information center.

• Publications •

O'Dwyer's Directory of Public Relations Firms
271 Madison Avenue, Suite 600
New York, NY 10016
212-679-2471

Public Relations Consultants Directory
835 Penobscat Building
Detroit, MI 48226-4094
313-961-2242

Public Relations Journal Register Issue
33 Irving Place
New York, New York 10003
212-995-2230
Web Address: www.prsa.org

Public Relations News
7811 Montrose Road
Potomac, MD 20854
301-340-2100

Real Estate

- Construction
- General Contractors
- Title Insurance
- Developers
- Property Management
- Commercial & Residential Sales

Quick Reference

Alpha Construction Co.
www.alpha.com
Anastasi Construction Company
www.anastasi.com
Asset Management Group
www.assetmanagement.com
Birtcher Real Estate Group
www.birtcher.com
Brock Homes, Ryland Company
www.ryland.com
Business Real Estate Brokerage Company
www.brecommercial.com
California Pacific Homes
www.calpacific.com
Cannon Constructors
www.cannongroup.com
Capital Commercial/NAI
www.capitalcomm.com
Capital Pacific Holdings
www.cph-inc.com
CB Commercial Real Estate Group
www.cbrichardellis.com
CB Richard Ellis
www.cbc.com
Century 21 All Service Realtors
www.c21asr.com
Century 21 All Star Realty
www.century21allstar.com
Century 21 Award
www.century21award.com
Century 21/Superstars
www.c21superstars.com
Chicago Title Insurance Company
www.chicagotitle.com
Coldwell Banker Corp/Southern California
www.coldwellbanker.com
Colliers Iliff Thorn
www.colliers.com
Collins Commercial Corporation
www.collinsve.com
Commonwealth Land Title Company
www.chicagotitle.com
Continental Homes
www.continentalhomes.com
Crown Pacific
www.crownpacific.com
Cushman & Wakefield of California
www.cushwake.com
DAUM Cemmercial Real Estate Services
www.daum1904.com
Donahue-Schriber
www.donahueschriber.com
Equitable Management/Consulting
www.emcco.com
Fidelity National Financial
www.fnf.com

Fidelity National Title Insurance Company
www.f&f.com
Fieldstone Communities
www.uniontrib.com
First American Title Company of Los Angeles
www.fatcola.com
Fu-Lyons Associates
www.fulyons.com
Goldrich & Kest Industries
www.gkind.com
Grant General Contractors
www.grantgc.com
Grubb & Ellis Company
www.grubb-ellis.com
Hanson Realty
www.hansonrealty.com
Holmes & Narver
www.hninc.com
Insignia Commercial Group
www.unitas.net
James Crone & Associates
www.drhorton.com
Janez Properties
www.janezprop.com
John Aaroe & Associates
www.johnarroe.com
John Burnham & Co.
www.johnburnham.com
Koll Construction Co.
www.koll.com
Lyle Parks, Jr.
www.lpj.com
Majestic Realty Co.
www.majesticrealty.com
Marcus & Millichap
www.mmeribc.com
Marcus & Millichap Corp R/E Services
www.mmreibc.com
MBK Real Estate, Ltd.
www.mbk.com
McCarthy Brothers Company
www.mccarthybldrs.com
Morley Builders
www.morleybuilders.com
Nielsen Dillingham Builders
www.nielsendillingham.com
Nourmand & Associates Realtors
www.nourmand.com
Orange Coast Title Co.
www.octitle.com
Pacific Bay Homes.
www.pacbayhomes.com
Pacific Southwest Realty Services
www.psrs.com
Peck Jones Construction
www.peckjones.com

PM Realty Group
www.pmrg.com
Podley Doan
www.podley.com
Presley Companies
www.presleyhomes.com
Prudential California Realty
www.prudentialcalif.com
R & B Realty Group
www.oakwood.com
R. D. Olson Construction
www.rdolson.com
RE/MAX Executives
www.sandiego-executive.com
RE/MAX of Valencia
http://remax-scv.com
Real Estate Disposition Corp
www.classifiedad.com
Realty Executives Santa Clarita
www.realtyExecs-scv.com
Shea Homes
www.sheahomes.com
Sperry Van Ness
www.svn.com
Standard Pacific Corp
www.dallas.net/~stanpac
Swinerton & Walberg
www.swbuilders.com
Tarbell Realtors
www.tarbell.com
Terra Universal
www.terrauni.com
The 1st American Financial Corp
www.firstam.com
The Eastlake Company
www.eastlakehomes.com
The Irvine Company
www.irvineco.com
The Irving Hughes Group
www.irvinghughes.com
The Mills Corporation
www.millscorp.com
The Prudential-Dunn, REALTORS
www.prudential.com
The Rreef Funds
www.rreff.com
Trammell Crow So. Calif.
www.trammellcrow.com
Turner Construction Co.
www.turnerconstruction.com
Voit Companies
www.voitco.com
Warmington Homes
www.warmingtonhomes.com
Watson Land Co.
www.watsonlandcompany.com
White House Properties
www.whitehouseproperties.com
Willis M. Allen Co.
www.willisallen.com

437

Construction Companies

ARB
26000 Commerce Center Drive
Lake Forest, CA 92630
310-630-5801
Web Address: www.arbinc.com
Number of Employees: 90

Brian Pratt, *President*
Lorrie Valerio, *Human Resources Director*

Bernards Brothers Construction
610 Ilex Street
San Fernando, CA 91340
818-898-1521
Number of Employees: 60

Douglas D. Bernards, *President*
Anita Shald, *Director of Human Resources*

Bycor General Contractors
6490 Mar Industry Place
San Diego, CA 92121
858-587-1901
Number of Employees: 80

Scott Kaats, *President*
Maryanne Lamoureux, *Office Manager*

C.E. Wylie Construction Company
3777 Ruffin Road
San Diego, CA 92123
619-571-4911

C. E. Wylie, *Owner*
Ed Wylie, *President & Hiring Contact*

C.W. Driver Contractors
7442 North Figueroa Street
Los Angeles, CA 90041
213-258-8600
Number of Employees: 50

Dana Roberts, *President*

Cannon Constructors
600 Corporate Point, Suite 250
Culver City, CA 90230
310-342-9800
Web Address: www.cannongroup.com
Number of Employees: 80

Jim Williams, *President*
Mike Stieger, *CFO & Hiring Contact*

Charles Pankow Builders Ltd.
2476 North Lake Avenue
Altadena, CA 91001
213-684-2320
Number of Employees: 30

Charles Pankow, *CEO*

Clark-Porche Construction Company
PO Box 3925
El Monte, CA 91733-0925
626-443-0151
Number of Employees: 55

Collins General Contractors
11750 Sorrento Valley Road
San Diego, CA 92121
858-481-7700
Number of Employees: 50

Mickey Carhart, *Managing Principal*
Barbara Woodward, *Office Manager*

Del Amo Construction
23840 Madison Street
Torrance, CA 90505
310-378-6203
Number of Employees: 60

Jerry Donahue, *President*
Mack McLaughlin, *Controller*
Ed Hong, *Human Resource Manager*

Dinwiddie Construction Company
1145 Wilshire Boulevard, Suite 200
Los Angeles, CA 90017
213-482-1900
Number of Employees: 25

Bill Van Leuven, *Vice President*

DPR Construction
6333 Greenwich Drive, Suite 170
San Diego, CA 92122
858-597-7070
Web Address: www.dprinc.com
Number of Employees: 37

Peter A. Salvati, *Managing Principal*
Cristy Daly, *Hiring Contact*

Dumarc Corporation
187 West Orangethorpe Avenue, Suite R
Placentia, CA 92870-6932
714-993-0909
Number of Employees: 15

Valente C. Morales, *President*

Environmental Industries
24121 Ventura Boulevard
Calabasas, CA 91302
818-223-8500
Job Hotline: 800-224-1024
Number of Employees: 5,000

Burton Sperber, *President*
Phil Young, *Director of Human Resources*

REAL ESTATE

Good & Roberts
1090 Joshua Way
Vista, CA 92083
760-598-7614

Jack Good, *Managing Principal*

Grant General Contractors
5051 Avenida Encinas
Carlsbad, CA 92008
760-438-7500
Web Address: www.grantgc.com
Number of Employees: 20

W. T. Grant, *Managing Principal*

HBI Construction
4921 Birch, Suite 1
Newport Beach, CA 92660
949-851-2211
Number of Employees: 35

Peter J. Last, *CEO*

Hensel Phelps Construction Company
2415 Campus Drive, Suite 100
Irvine, CA 92612-1596
949-852-0111
Number of Employees: 2,800

Hensel Phelps Construction Company
2415 Campus Drive, Suite 100
Irvine, CA 92612
949-852-0111

Wayne Lindholm, *Managing Principal*
Jasmin Orchard, *Office Manager*

Holmes & Narver
999 Town & Country Road
Orange, CA 92868
949-567-2400
Web Address: www.hninc.com
Number of Employees: 250

Jearl Joslin, *Human Resources Manager*

Howard Building Corp.
100 West Broadway, Suite 800
Glendale, CA 91210
818-549-1850

Gary Conrad, *President*
Jan Di-bias, *Director of Human Resources*

J. Ray Construction Company
2699 White Road, Suite 150
Irvine, CA 92614-6258
949-660-8888
Number of Employees: 25

James Ray, *President*

Johnson & Jennings General Contracting
6165 Greenwich Drive, Suite 180
San Diego, CA 92122
619-623-1100

Number of Employees: 26
Jackie Jennings, *Managing Principal*
Keith Shonewill, *Operations Manager*

Kajima Construction Services
901 Corporate Center Drive, Third Floor
Monterey Park, CA 91754
213-269-0020
Number of Employees: 100

Shogo Matsuoka, *Senior Vice President*

Keller Construction Co. Ltd.
9950 East Baldwin Place
El Monte, CA 91731
626-443-6633
Number of Employees: 38

Paul Keller, *Managing Partner*
Shurina Wilkins, *Director of Human Resources*

Kemp Brothers Construction
6321 South Hoover Street
Whittier, CA 90601
562-692-7716

John Espino, *President*

Koll Construction Co.
7330 Engineer Road
San Diego, CA 92111
619-292-5550
Web Address: www.koll.com
Number of Employees: 45

Greg Motschenbacker, *Managing Principal*

Lusardi Construction Co.
1570 Linda Vista Drive
San Marcos, CA 92069
760-744-3133
Number of Employees: 450

Scott Free, *President*
Bill Tirschsield, *Director of Human Resources*

Lyle Parks, Jr.
4001 East La Palma Avenue
Anaheim, CA 92807
714-632-3210
Web Address: www.lpj.com
Number of Employees: 30

Lyle Parks Jr., *President*

McCarthy Brothers Company
100 Bayview Circle #3000
Newport Beach, CA 92660-2985
949-854-8383
Web Address: www.mccarthybldrs.com
Number of Employees: 40

Michael D. Bolen, *President*

McCormick Construction Co.
2507 Empire Avenue
Burbank, CA 91504
818 843 2010
Number of Employees: 50

Michael McCormick, *President*
Alice McCaskill, *Director of Human Resources*

Millie & Severson
3601 Serpentine Drive
Los Alamitos, CA 90720
562-493-3611
Number of Employees: 50

Jonathan E. Severson, *President*

Morley Builders
2901 28th Street, Suite 100
Santa Monica, CA 90405
310-399-1600
Web Address: www.morleybuilders.com
Number of Employees: 60

Mark Benjamin, *CEO*
Cheryl Pohjola, *Executive Administrator & HR Director*

Nielsen Dillingham Builders
3127 Jefferson Street
San Diego, CA 92110
619-291-6330
Web Address: www.nielsendillingham.com
Number of Employees: 25

Stephen C. Marble, *Managing Principal*
Denise Howe, *Manager of Human Resources*

Nielsen Dillingham Builders
3950 Paramount Boulevard, Suite 100
Lakewood, CA 90712
310-952-8880
Job Hotline: 619-291-6330
Web Address: www.nielsendillingham.com
Number of Employees: 15

Tim R. Murphy, *VP & Regional Manager*

Ninteman Construction Co.
4375 Jutland Drive, Suite 200
San Diego, CA 92117
619-490-6800
Job Hotline: 619-294-4474
Number of Employees: 55

Thomas R. Remensperger, *Managing Principal*
Mona Joseph, *Employment Administrator*

Peck/Jones Construction
10866 Wilshire Boulevard, Suite 700
Los Angeles, CA 90024
310-470-1885
Web Address: www.peckjones.com
Number of Employees: 137
Dan Penn, *President*
Susan Schmid, *Hiring Contact*

Pepper Construction
17941 Fitch
Irvine, CA 92614-6016
949-261-7080
Number of Employees: 40

Stanley Pepper, *President*

Peterbuilt Corp.
6235 Lusk Boulevard
San Diego, CA 92121
619-597-8800
Number of Employees: 30

Peter Lasensky, *Managing Principal*
Judy Kreisberg, *Corporate Development*

Pozzo Construction Co.
2894 Rowena Avenue
Los Angeles, CA 90039
213-666-5440
Number of Employees: 50

Victor Pozzo, *President*
Larry Salyer, *Executive Administrator*

Prizio Construction
1533 South Grand Avenue
Santa Ana, CA 92705-4410
714-543-3366
Number of Employees: 26

David P. Prizio, *CEO*

Quest Const. Engineering & Mgmt.
7556 Trade Street
San Diego, CA 92121
619-689-8770
Number of Employees: 20

Leslie B. Schotz, *Managing Principal*

R. D. Olson Construction
2955 Main Street, 3rd Floor
Irvine, CA 92614
949-474-2001
Web Address: www.rdolson.com
Number of Employees: 50

Robert D. Olson, *President*

R.G. Petty Construction
6650 Flanders Drive, Suite J
San Diego, CA 92121
619-458-9440
Number of Employees: 20

Bert Petty, *Managing Principal & Hiring Contact*

Ray Wilson Co.
199 South Los Robles Avenue, Suite 250
Pasadena, CA 91101
626-795-7900
Number of Employees: 200

K. C. Gopal, *President*

Raytheon Engineers & Constructors
500 Superior Avenue, Room A1135
Newpor Beach, CA 92663
949-759-2403
Number of Employees: 8

Rich Roda, *Human Resources Manager*
Len Marino, *Vice President*

Riha Construction Co.
8173 Commercial Street
La Mesa, CA 91942
619-469-2177
Number of Employees: 6

Kenneth J. Riha, *Managing Principal & Hiring Contact*

S. J. Amoroso Construction
7 Corporate Park, Suite 200
Irvine, CA 92606-5107
949-852-2363
Number of Employees: 8

Rich Armsworthy, *Chief Estimator*

Snyder Langston Real Estate
17962 Cowan
Irvine, CA 92614-6036
949-863-9200
Job Hotline: 714-863-9200
Number of Employees: 100

Stephen Jones, *President*

Soltek of San Diogo
2424 Congress Street, Suite A
San Diego, CA 92110
619-296-6247

Stephen W. Thompson, *Managing Principal*

Standard Pacific Corp
1565 MacArthur Boulevard
Costa Mesa, CA 92626-1407
949-789-1600
Web Address: www.dallas.net/~stanpac
Number of Employees: 80

Steve Scarborough, *President*

Swinerton & Walberg
9255 Towne Centre Drive, Suite 225
San Diego, CA 92121
619-622-4040
Web Address: www.swbuilders.com
Number of Employees: 15

Bill Marcotte, *Managing Principal*
Deanna Takato, *Office Manager*

Swinerton & Walberg
865 South Figueroa Street, Suite 3000
Los Angeles, CA 90017
213-896-3400
Web Address: www.swbuilders.com

Number of Employees: 150
Gary Rafferty, *Sr. VP & Division Manager*
Maja Damerjian, *Human Resources*

T.B. Penick & Sons
9747 Olson Drive
San Diego, CA 92121
619-558-1800
Number of Employees: 102

Thomas L. Penick, *Managing Principal*
Rich Robertson, *Superintendent*

Taslimi Construction Co.
12400 Wilshire Boulevard, Suite 1000
Suite 820
Los Angeles, CA 90025
310-447-3000
Number of Employees: 50

Shidan Taslimi, *President*

Taylor Ball
7777 Alvarado Road, Suite 501
La Mesa, CA 91941
619-697-8401

Jim Frager, *Vice President*
Rae Krushenskin, *Office Manager*

Terra Universal
700 North Harbor Boulevard
Anaheim, CA 92805-2553
949-635-3700
Web Address: www.terrauni.com
Number of Employees: 250

George Sadaghiani, *President*

Turner Construction Co.
555 West Fifth Street, Suite 3700
Los Angeles, CA 90013
213-891-3000
Web Address: www.turnerconstruction.com

Bill Cody, *VP & General Manager*
Tom Turner, *Human Resources Director*

Turner Construction Company
36 Executive Park, Suite 150
Irvine, CA 92614-6744
949-798-8100
Number of Employees: 50

David Seastrom, *Regional Manager*

Tutor-Saliba Corporation
15901 Olden Street
Sylmar, CA 91342
818-362-8391
Web Address: www.tutorsaliba.com
Number of Employees: 2,200

Ronald Tutor, *President*
Brenda Baczkowski, *Payroll Manager*

Property Management Firms

Asset Management Group
11750 Sorrento Valley Road
San Diego, CA 92121
858-481-7767
Web Address:
www.assetmanagementgroup.com
Number of Employees: 37

Bob Petersen, *President*
Brandy Obler, *Human Resource Manager*

Business Real Estate Management Company
703 Palomar Airport Road, Suite 250
Carlsbad, CA 92009
760-931-1134
Web Address: www.bremc@pacbell.net
Number of Employees: 4

Brent R. Covey, *President*
Tammy Richkas, *Senior Accountant*

Capital Growth Properties
1120 Silverado Street
La Jolla, CA 92037
619-454-8857
Number of Employees: 40

John Michaelsen, *President*
Renee Savage, *Property Manager*

CB Richard Ellis, Inc.
600 West Broadway, Suite 2100
San Diego, CA 92101
619-236-1231
Web Address: www.cbrichardellis.com
Number of Employees: 16

Joseph A. Winkler, Director, *Management Services*
Cindy Hodge, *Human Resource Contact*

CB/Richard Ellis
400 South Hope Street, Suite 1900
Los Angeles, CA 90071
213-362-6904
Number of Employees: 8,000

Jana Turner, *President for Los Angeles*
Karen Whitney, *Human Resources Director*

Charles Dunn Company
800 West 6th Street, Suite 600
Los Angeles, CA 90017
213-683-0500
Number of Employees: 90

Walter Conn, *CEO*

Colliers International
610 West Ash Street, Suite 1400
San Diego, CA 92101
619-231-9606
Number of Employees: 9

Jack A. Naliboff, *President*
Michelle Ramsey, *Project Accountant*

Commercial Facilities
10951 Sorrento Valley Road, Suite 2A
San Diego, CA 92121
619-452-1231

Julius Paeske, *President*

Compass Management & Leasing
19800 MacArthur, Suite 850
Irvine, CA 92619
949-222-1022

David L. Russell, *Vice President*
Barbara Wallace, *Hiring Contact*

ECP Commercial Property Management
1069 Graves Avenue, Suite 100
El Cajon, CA 92021
619-442-9200
Number of Employees: 15
Robert Phillips, *President*
Jay Jackson, *Controller*

Harman Asset Management
7835 Ivanhoe Avenue
La Jolla, CA 92037
619-454-0101
Number of Employees: 6
Athena Z. Harman, *President & Hiring Contact*

Heitman
9601 Wilshire Boulevard, Suite 200
Suite 200
Beverly Hills, CA 90210
310-550-7100
Number of Employees: 30

Hines Interests LP
601 South Figueroa Street, Suite 3690
Los Angeles, CA 90017
213-629-5200
Colin Shephard, *Senior Vice President*

Insignia Commerical Group
3655 Nobel Drive, Suite 510
San Diego, CA 92122
619-657-9900
Stephen M. Willmore, *Managing Director*

Investment Development Services
888 West 6th Street, 9th Floor
Los Angeles, CA 90017
213-362-9300
Number of Employees: 60
D. Mgrublian, *Managing Director*
Rebecca Perkins, *Director of Human Resources*

Janez Properties
12520 High Bluff Drive, Suite 100
San Diego, CA 92130
619-481-5693
Web Address: www.janezprop.com
Number of Employees: 13

John I. Kocmur, *President*
Renee Cameron, *Hiring Contact*

John Burnham & Co.
610 West Ash Street
San Diego, CA 92101
619-236-1555
Job Hotline: 619-525-2994
Web Address: www.johnburnham.com
Number of Employees: 250

Dennis Cruzan, *President*
Denise Huging, *Human Resource Manager*

Jones Lang LaSalle
19900 MacArthur Boulevard, Suite 250
Irvine, CA 92612-2445
949-222-1022
Number of Employees: 40

Koll, The Real Estate Services Co.
4275 Executive Square, Suite 215
La Jolla, CA 92037
619-597-2900
Number of Employees: 4

Joe Newman, *Senior Vice President*
Jennifer Renfro, *Senior Manager*

La Cagnina/Riley Associates
16027 Ventura Boulevard, Suite 400
Encino, CA 91436
818-788-8080

Victor La Cagnina, *President*

La Salle Partners
355 South Grand Avenue, Suite 4280
Los Angeles, CA 90071
213-680-7900
Number of Employees: 45
Brian Ross, *Executive Vice President*
Billie Yoder, *Executive Administrator*

Legacy Partners
30 Executive Park, Suite 100
Irvine, CA 92614
949-261-2100
Web Address: www.lincolnwest.com
Number of Employees: 100
Terry Thompson, *Vice President of Operations*

Meissner Jacquet Real Estate Mgmt. Group
3870 Murphy Canyon Road, Suite 300
San Diego, CA 92123
619-576-1665
Jerry H. Jacquet, *Principal*

Morlin Management Corp.
444 South Flower Street, Suite 500
Los Angeles, CA 90071
213-622-4442
Number of Employees: 16

J. Randall Moore, *President*
Julie Griess, *Office Manager*

Nationwide Health Properties
610 Newport Center Drive, #1150
Newport Beach, CA 92660
949-251-1211
Number of Employees: 12

R. Bruce Andrews, *President*
Real estate investment trust that specializes in investing in and providing financing for health care facilities. The company has investments in more than 260 facilities in 30 states, including long-term health care facilities and assisted-living facilities and rehabilitation hospitals.

Pacific Gulf Properties
4220 Von Karman, 2nd Floor
Newport Beach, CA 92660-2002
949-223-5000
Number of Employees: 30

Glenn L. Carpenter, *President*
Pam Laipple, *Director of Personnel*
Self-administered equity real estate investment trust that owns, operates, develops, and leases industrial and multifamily properties in California, Nevada, Oregon, and Washington. It owns more than 25 multifamily properties containing some 4,800 apartments.

Pacific Southwest Realty Services
2655 Camino del Rio North, Suite 100
San Diego, CA 92108
619-298-9200
Web Address: www.psrs.com
Number of Employees: 30

Daniel F. Mulvihill, *CEO*
Gloria Respa, *Human Resource Manager*

PM Realty Group
1010 Second Avenue, Suite 2250
San Diego, CA 92101
619-239-1500
Web Address: www.pmrg.com
Number of Employees: 10

H. Peter Tietz, *Regional Manager & Hiring Contact*

PM Realty Group
811 Wilshire Boulevard, Suite 1650
Los Angeles, CA 90071
213-229-4430

Ernest Johnson, President, *West*

Prentiss Properties
5050 Avenida Encinas, Suite 350
Carlsbad, CA 92008
760-438-4242
Number of Employees: 20

Mike Prentiss, *President*

R & B Realty Group
2222 Corinth Avenue
Los Angeles, CA 90064
310-478-1021
Web Address: www.oakwood.com
Number of Employees: 3,000

Howard Ruby, *Chairman*
Michael Fletcher, *Human Resources Director*
Sarah Albright, *West Coast Recruiting*

Radelow Gittins Real Property Mgmt.
438 Camino del Rio South, Suite 203
San Diego, CA 92108
619-279-0668

Larry L. Gittins, *President*

Sentre Partners
225 Broadway, Suite 1700
San Diego, CA 92101
619-234-5600
Number of Employees: 50

Michael Peckham, *Partner*

Spectrum Property Management, AMO
8799 Balboa Avenue, Suite 260
San Diego, CA 92123
619-569-8799
Number of Employees: 14

Brenda K. Pancioli, *President*
Trisha Voekel, *Accounting Supervisor*

Sudberry Properties
5465 Morehouse Drive, Suite 260
San Diego, CA 92121
619-546-3000
Number of Employees: 13

Tom Sudberry, *President*

The Carlson Co.
23353 Mulholland Drive
Woodland Hills, CA 91364
818-974-0408

Sandra Van Western, *Area Manager*

The Irvine Company
550 Newport Center Drive
Newport Beach, CA 92658
949-720-2000
Web Address: www.irvineco.com
Number of Employees: 280

Donald L. Bren, *President*
Bruce Endsley, *Director of Personnel*

Developer and manager of residential and commercial real estate in Southern California. With 54,000 acres of prime Orange County real estate, the firm develops -and sometimes manages- hotels, industrial real estate, land, office buildings, and retail and residential real estate.

Tooley & Co.
9171 Towne Centre Drive, Suite 190
San Diego, CA 92122
619-455-5151
Number of Employees: 13
Craig Ruth, *President*

Trammel Crow Company
11150 Santa Monica Boulevard, Suite 200
Los Angeles, CA 90025
310-473-9505
Web Address: www.trammellcrow.com
Number of Employees: 200
Robert Ruth, *President*
Mimi Mellett, *Hiring Contact*

Trammell Crow Co.
3570 Camino del Rio North, Suite 100
San Diego, CA 92108
619-624-2727
Number of Employees: 8
Christopher F. Wood, *Senior Vice President*

Trammell Crow So. Calif.
5801 South Eastern Avenue, Suite 100
Los Angeles, CA 90040
213-724-2246
Web Address: www.trammellcrow.com
Number of Employees: 80
E. Stevenson Belcher, *President*
Lin McAtee, *Human Resources Director*

Transwestern Property Co.
550 South Hope Street, Suite 1125
Los Angeles, CA 90071
213-683-8300
Number of Employees: 15
Paul Lentz, *President/Western Division*
David Rock, *Senior VP for Property Management*

TrizecHahn Centers
4350 La Jolla Village Drive, Suite 400
San Diego, CA 92122
619-546-1001
Number of Employees: 250
Lee H. Wagman, *President*
Mike Croll, *Human Resource Manager*

Watt Management Co.
2716 Ocean Park Boulevard, Suite 3040
Santa Monica, CA 90405
310-314-2430
Web Address: www.@wattcommercial.com
Number of Employees: 50
James Maginn, *President*
Jennifer Anni, *Human Resources Manager*

Residential Sales

Bailes & Associates
11601 Wilshire Boulevard, Suite 1900
Los Angeles, CA 90025
310-445-4300
Number of Employees: 11

Leonard Bailes, *President*

Baldwin Real Estate Services
900 South First Avenue
Arcadia, CA 91007
626-447-0858

Gordon Maddock, *President*

Beitler Commercial Realty Services
825 South Barrington Avenue
Los Angeles, CA 90049
310-820-2955
Web Address: www.beitler.com
Number of Employees: 60

Barry Beitler, *President*
Carla Victor, *Office Manager*

Capital Commercial/NAI
16000 Ventura Boulevard, Suite 900
Encino, CA 91436
818-905-2400
Web Address: www.capitalcomm.com
Number of Employees: 100

Michael Zugsmith, *Chairman*
Nancy Finkler, *Director of Human Resources*

Century 21 All Service Realtors
1076 Broadway
El Cajon, CA 92019
619-440-2020
Web Address: www.c21asr.com
Number of Employees: 6

George Serochi, *Owner*
Joe Garzanelli, *Owner*
Allan Arthur, *Manager*

Century 21 All Star Realty
13161 Black Mountain Road, Suite 9
San Diego, CA 92129
619-484-1189
Web Address: www.century21allstar.com
Number of Employees: 15

Rick Jorgensen, *Owner*
Steve Whitson, *Hiring Contact*

Century 21 Award
5640 Baltimore Drive
La Mesa, CA 91942
619-463-5000

Web Address: www.century21award.com
Number of Employees: 140
Rick Jorgensen, *President*
Steve Whitson, *Hiring Contact*

Century 21 E-N Realty
1081 South Grand Avenue, Suite A
Diamond Bar, CA 91765
909-861-2800
Number of Employees: 65

John Newe, *President*

Century 21 Eagle Realty
14757 Pomerado Road
Poway, CA 92064
619-748-5545

David Prewett, *President*

Century 21 First Choice Realty
3020 Clairemont Drive
San Diego, CA 92117
619-276-1111
Web Address: http://member.aol.com/c21choice
Number of Employees: 65

Steve Ring, *Broker/Owner*

Century 21 Klowden-Forness
7439 Jackson Drive
San Diego, CA 92119
619-462-4300
Number of Employees: 50

Century 21 Regents Properties
3202 Governor Drive, Suite 100
San Diego, CA 92122
619-450-2100

Century 21 Sparrow Realty
6615 East Pacific Coast Highway, Suite 140
Long Beach, CA 90803
562-493-6555
Number of Employees: 5

Randy Smith, *President*

Charles Dunn Co.
10990 Wilshire Boulevard, Suite 400
Los Angeles, CA 90024
310-277-3900
Number of Employees: 35

Darrell Levonian, *Chairman*
Francesca Luteraan, *Human Resource Manager*

Coldwell Banker
1660 Hotel Circle North, Suite 109
San Diego, CA 92108
619-574-5100

Roger Ewing, *Senior VP*

Coldwell Banker
9988 Hibert Street, Suite 100
San Diego, CA 92131
619-578-5510
Number of Employees: 24

Rick Hoffman, *President & Hiring Contact*

Coldwell Banker Corp/Southern California
27271 Las Ramblas
Mission Viejo, CA 92691-6392
714-367-2123
Web Address: www.coldwellbanker.com
Number of Employees: 700

Bob LeFever, *President*
Linda Berg, *Senior Vice President*

Dilbeck Realtors
1030 Foothill Boulevard
La Canada Flintridge, CA 91011
818-790-6774

Mike Silvas, *President*

Dyson & Dyson Real Estate Associates
437 South Highway 101, Suite 101
Solana Beach, CA 92075
619-755-0500
Number of Employees: 15

Robert A. Dyson Jr., *President*
Diane Seddersohn, *Human Resource Manager*

ERA Eagle Estates Realty
9906 Carmel Mountain Road
San Diego, CA 92129
858-484-2930
Web Address: www.eraeagle.com
Number of Employees: 50

Don McGuiness, *Co-owner*
Fred Bradley, *Broker*

ERA Property Movers
1802 South Escondido Boulevard, Suite C
Escondido, CA 92025
760-489-0800
Faye Hines, *President*

First Property Realty Corp.
1930 Century Park West, Suite 333
Los Angeles, CA 90067
310-208-4400
Web Address: www.firstproperty.com
Number of Employees: 17
Jeffrey Resnick, *President*
Monica Vermilya, *Office Manager*

Fred Sands Realtors
11611 San Vicente Boulevard, 9th Floor
Los Angeles, CA 90049
310-820-6811
Web Address: www.fredsands.com
Fred Sands, *President*
Linda Kay, *Human Resource Manager*

Grubb & Ellis Company
19191 South Vermont Avenue, Suite 600
Torrance, CA 90502
310-538-9620
Web Address: www.grubb-ellis.com
Number of Employees: 35

Robert Osbrink, *Senior VP LA County Regional Manager*
Mike Grabendike, *Hiring Contact for Agents*
Barbara Kennedy, *Hiring Contact*

Hanson Realty
633 North Escondido Boulevard
Escondido, CA 92025
760-745-3366
Web Address: www.hansonrealty.com

Paul Van Elderen, *President*

John Aaroe & Associates
250 North Canon Drive
Beverly Hills, CA 90210
310-777-7800
Job Hotline: 310-479-8788
Web Address: www.prudentialjohnaaroe.com
Number of Employees: 60

Steve Gomes, *President*
Annette Mott, *Manager*

John Alle Co.
3201 Wilshire Boulevard, Suite 100
Santa Monica, CA 90403
310-319-1511
Number of Employees: 2

John Alle, *President*

Julien J. Studley, Inc.
10960 Wilshire Boulevard, Suite 1500
Los Angeles, CA 90024
310-444-1000
Web Address: www.studley.com
Number of Employees: 15

Howard Sadowsky, *Executive Vice President*
April Acosta, *Office Manager*

Klabin Co.
6601 Center Drive West, Suite 300
Los Angeles, CA 90045
310-337-7000
Web Address: www.klabin.com
Number of Employees: 40

David Prior, *President*
Kathy Muno, *Principal & Hiring Contact*

Lambert Smith Hampton
9701 Wilshire Boulevard, Suite 1200
Beverly Hills, CA 90212
310-273-2999
Number of Employees: 10

Sonny Astani, *President*

Lee & Associates
500 Citadel Drive, Suite 140
Commerce, CA 90040
213-720-8484
Number of Employees: 26

Bill Lee, *Founder*
Ed Indvik, *President & Hiring Contact for Brokers*
Karen Schneider, *Office Manager & Hiring Contact*

Leo Nordine Realtors
211 Yacht Club Way
Redondo Beach, CA 90277
310-379-8800
Web Address: www.nordine.com
Number of Employees: 5

Leo Nordine, *Owner*
Molly Nordine, *Human Resource Manager*

MacGregor Realty
845 Foothill Boulevard
La Canada Flintridge, CA 91011
818-790-8300
Number of Employees: 40

Dan MacGregor, *President*
Lesli Rogers, *Director of Human Resources*

Marcus & Millichap
16501 Ventura Boulevard, Suite 103
Encino, CA 91436
818-907-0600
Web Address: www.mmeribc.com
Number of Employees: 75

Harvey Green, *COO*
Alesia Daniels, *Office Manager*

Matlow Kennedy
4510 East Pacific Coast Highway, Suite 100
Long Beach, CA 90804
562-498-8889
Number of Employees: 35

Kimball Wasich, *President*
Janice Robinson, *Office Manager*

Metrospace/CRESA
11726 San Vicente Boulevard, Suite 500
Los Angeles, CA 90049
310-207-1700
Number of Employees: 30
Gerald Porter, *President & Hiring Contact for Brokers*

Moore and Associates Realtors
2700 Pacific Coast Highway
Torrance, CA 90505
310-326-9383
Number of Employees: 100
Larry Moore, *President*
Nancy Indiere, *Operations Manager*

Muselli Commercial Realtors
501 Santa Monica Boulevard, Suite 702
Santa Monica, CA 90401
310-458-4100
Number of Employees: 10

Vincent Muselli, *President*
Barbara Muselli, *Human Resource Manager*

Nelson, Shelton, and Associates
355 North Canon Drive
Beverly Hills, CA 90210
310-271-2229
Number of Employees: 300

E. Nelson, *Vice President*

Nourmand & Associates Realtors
210 North Canon Drive
Beverly Hills, CA 90210
310-274-4000
Web Address: www.nourmand.com
Number of Employees: 45

Stephen Nourmand, *President*
Rose Borve, *VP & Sales Manager*
Florence Caraco, *Human Resource Manager*

One Source Realty-Better Homes & Gardens
2655 Camino del Rio North, Suite 450
San Diego, CA 92108
619-296-9055
Web Address: www.onesourcerealty.com
Number of Employees: 9

Gregg C. Seaman, *President*
Sara Cien, *Vice President*

Park Regency
10146 Balboa Boulevard
Granada Hills, CA 91344
818-363-6116

Joe Alexander, *President*

Pinnacle Estate Properties
9137 Reseda Boulevard
Northridge, CA 91324
818-993-7370
Number of Employees: 70

Dana Potter, *President*
Barbara Mims, *Director of Human Resources*

Podley Doan
300 West Colorado Boulevard
Pasadena, CA 91105
626-793-9291
Web Address: www.podley.com

William Podley, *President*
Lynwen Hughes-Bowmen, *Director of Human Resources*

Prudential California Realty
3790 Via de la Valle, Suite 311
Del Mar, CA 92014
619-792-6085
Web Address: www.prudentialcalif.com

Stephen C. Games, *President*
Nikki Sandoval, *Human Resource Manager*

Prudential California Realty
1650 Ximeno Avenue, Suite 120
Long Beach, CA 90804
562-494-4600
Web Address: www.prudentialcalif.com
Number of Employees: 90

Rosemary Voss-Jones, *CEO*

RE/MAX Associates
4747 Morena Boulevard, Suite 200
San Diego, CA 92117
619-272-6000
Number of Employees: 40

Geoffrey Mountain, *President*
Tim Hintz, *Office Manager*

RE/MAX Beach Cities Realty
225 South Sepulveda Boulevard, Suite 250
Manhattan Beach, CA 90266
310-376-2225
Number of Employees: 150

Kelly Amundson, *President*

RE/MAX Enterprises
629 Third Avenue, Suite A
Chula Vista, CA 91910
619-476-3030
Number of Employees: 10

Daniel Guefen, *President*

RE/MAX Executives
9840 Carmel Mountain Road
San Diego, CA 92129
619-484-5500
Web Address: www.sandiego-executive.com

Tom Perri, Broker, *Owner*

RE/MAX of Valencia
23822 Valencia Boulevard, Suite 101
Valencia, CA 91355
805-255-2650
Web Address: http://remax-scv.com
John O'Hare, *President*
Pat Turner, *Manager*

RE/MAX on the Boulevard
14242 Ventura Boulevard
Sherman Oaks, CA 91423
818-789-7117
Number of Employees: 5
Jay Belson, *President*
Melissa Farnsworth, *Director of Human Resources*

RE/MAX Palos Verdes Realty
63 Malaga Cove Plaza
Palos Verdes, CA 90274
310-378-9494
Web Address: www.pvhomes.com
Number of Employees: 30

Sandra Sanders, Owner, *Broker*

RE/MAX Rancho Bernardo
16730 Bernardo Center Drive
San Diego, CA 92128
619-485-1700

William Simmons, *Owner & Broker*

RE/MAX United
10650 Scripps Ranch Boulevard, Suite 112
San Diego, CA 92131
619-549-2700

Fred Christiansen, *Owner/Broker*

Realty Executives
5850 Avenida Encinas, Suite B
Carlsbad, CA 92008
760-603-7100
Number of Employees: 30

J. Ward Lewis III, *President*
Madeline Harless, *Director of Human Resources*

Realty Executives Santa Clarita
24106 Lyons Avenue
Newhall, CA 91321
805-286-8600
Web Address: www.realtyExecs-scv.com
Number of Employees: 125

Jim Tanner, *President*

Realty Executives Vista
911 Hacienda Drive
Vista, CA 92083
760-758-2300
Web Address: www.cronecos@.com
Number of Employees: 20

Bill Clark, *Broker*

Scheid Realty
9454 Wilshire Boulevard, Sixth Floor
Beverly Hills, CA 90212
310-278-9606

Phillip Scheid, *President*

Seeley Co.
444 South Flower Street, Suite 2200
Los Angeles, CA 90071
213-627-1214
Number of Employees: 40

Jay Haskell, *President*
Carol McConnel, *Human Resources Manager*

Southern California Job Source

Shorewood Realtors
1050 Duncan Avenue, Suite L
Manhattan Beach, CA 90266
310-376-8021
Web Address: www.sherwood.com

Arnold Goldstein, *President*
Laura Banta, *Human Resources*

Soboroff Partners
1101 Montana Avenue, Suite A
Santa Monica, CA 90403
310-451-9877
Number of Employees: 5

Steven Soboroff, *Managing Partner*

South Bay Brokers
2501 North Sepulveda Boulevard, 2nd Floor
Manhattan Beach, CA 90266
310-546-7611
Web Address: www.southbaybrokers.com
Number of Employees: 70

Jack Gillespie, *President*
Sunnie Manly, *Office Administrator*

Sperry Van Ness
16255 Ventura Boulevard, Suite 625
Encino, CA 91436
818-386-6888
Web Address: www.svn.com
Number of Employees: 30

Raffi Krikorian, *Managing Partner*
Patricia Padgett, *Office Administrator*

The Prudential-Dunn, REALTORS
4538 Cass Street
San Diego, CA 92109
619-274-3866
Web Address: www.prudential.com
Number of Employees: 65

Patrick J. Park, *President*

Travers Realty Corporation
4675 Macarthur Court, Suite 1210
Newport Beach, CA 92660-1849
949-756-5900
Number of Employees: 8

Anita Fox, *Office Manager*

Westcord Commercial Group
16461 Sherman Way, Suite 230
Van Nuys, CA 91406
818-785-6709

Joe Lopez, *President*

Westmac Commercial Brokerage Co.
1517 South Sepulveda Boulevard
Los Angeles, CA 90025
310-478-7700
Web Address: www.westmac.com

Number of Employees: 18
Timothy Macker, *President*
Lucy Ceballos, *Human Resource Manager*

White House Properties
22151 Ventura Boulevard
Woodland Hills, CA 91364
818-999-3100
Web Address: www.whitehouseproperties.com
Number of Employees: 35

Marty Williams, *President*
Angela Boester, *Director of Human Resources*

Willis M. Allen Co.
1131 Wall Street
La Jolla, CA 92037
619-459-4033
Web Address: www.willisallen.com
Number of Employees: 50

Andrew E. Nelson, *President*
Bud Clark, *Manager*

Commercial Sales

ACI Commercial
2635 Camino del Rio South, Suite 200
San Diego, CA 92108
619-299-3000
Number of Employees: 15

Chuck Hoffman, *President*
Karen Buteyn, *Hiring Contact*

Birtcher Real Estate Group
27611 La Pz Road
Laguna Niguel, CA 92677
714-643-7700
Web Address: www.birtcher.com
Number of Employees: 80

Becky Rodarte, *Director of Human Resources*

Business Real Estate Brokerage Company
4380 La Jolla Village Drive, Suite 200
San Diego, CA 92122
858-546-5400
Web Address: www.brecommercial.com
Number of Employees: 60

Ted Phoenix, *President*
Nica Knite, *Administrative Manager*

CB Commercial Real Estate Group
3501 Jamboree Road, Suite 100
Newport Beach, CA 92806
949-725-8500
Web Address: www.cbrichardellis.com
Number of Employees: 350

Helen Carter, *Office Manager*

CB Commercial Real Estate Group
2400 East Katella, 7th Floor
Anaheim, CA 92806
714-939-2100
Web Address: www.cbrichardellis.com
Number of Employees: 150
Sandy Herring, *Office Manager*

CB Richard Ellis
4365 Executive Drive, Suite 900
San Diego, CA 92121
858-546-4600
Web Address: cbrichardellis.com
Number of Employees: 150

Mark Read, *Principal Executive*
Sue King, *Administrative Assistant*

CB Richard Ellis
533 South Fremont Avenue
Los Angeles, CA 90071
213-613-3123
Web Address: www.cbc.com
Number of Employees: 8,000

James Didion, *CEO*
Charles McBride, *Senior Executive VP*
Nancy Morris, *Human Resources Director*

Century 21/Superstars
19768 Yorba Linda Boulevard
Yorba Linda, CA 92886-2800
714-779-8344
Job Hotline: 800-890-7653
Web Address: www.c21superstars.com
Number of Employees: 130

Helga Bonfils, *Owner*

Colliers Iliff Thorn
4660 La Jolla Village Drive, Suite 200
San Diego, CA 92122
619-455-1515
Web Address: www.colliers.com
Number of Employees: 50

Richard B. Bradley, *President*
Debbie Acuna, *Administrative Manager*

Collins Commercial Corporation
5000 Birch Street, Suite 1400
Newport Beach, CA 92660-2138
949-851-2300
Web Address: www.collinsve.com
Number of Employees: 23

J. Michael Collins, *President*

Crown Pacific
5252 Argosy Avenue
Huntington Beach, CA 92649-1074
714-898-0955
Web Address: www.crownpacific.com
Number of Employees: 60
James Thompson, *President*

Cushman Realty Corporation
750 B Street, Suite 3401
San Diego, CA 92101
619-696-1212
Number of Employees: 5

Dennis Hearst, *Hiring Contact*

Cushman & Wakefield of California
1920 Main Street, Suite 100
Irvine, CA 92614-7244
949-474-4004
Web Address: www.cushwake.com
Number of Employees: 2000

Cushman & Wakefield of California
1 City Boulevard West, Suite 1130
Orange, CA 92868-3612
714-634-8500
Web Address: www.cushwake.com
Number of Employees: 45

Chuck Hunt, *Office Manager*

Cushman & Wakefield of California
555 South Flower Street, Suite 4200
Los Angeles, CA 90071
213-955-5100
Web Address: www.cushwake.com
Number of Employees: 125

Richard Davis, *Senior Managing Director &*
Hiring Contact for Brokers
William Durslag, *Director of Asset Services*
Mindie Galgoul, *Hiring Contact*

DAUM Commercial Real Estate Services
2300 East Katella Avenue, Suite 100
Anaheim, CA 92806-6046
714-385-1801
Web Address: www.daum1904.com
Number of Employees: 12

Lisa Griffin, *Branch Administrator*

DAUM Commercial Real Estate Services
4695 Macarthur Court, Suite 250
Newport Beach, CA 92660-1857
949-724-1900
Web Address: www.daum1904.com
Number of Employees: 4

Russ Johnson, *Office Manager*

DAUM Commercial Real Estate Services
123 South Figueroa Street, Suite 400
Los Angeles, CA 90012
213-625-3286
Web Address: www.daum1904.com
Number of Employees: 25

Michael Nubel, *CEO*
Chris Ngai, *CFO & Hiring Contact*

Equitable Management/Consulting
12460 Euclid Street, Suite 203
Garden Grove, CA 92840-3351
714-534-7116
Web Address: www.emcco.com
Number of Employees: 29

Jerry Milos, *President*

Flocke & Avoyer Commercial Real Estate
3131 Camino del Rio North, Suite 190
San Diego, CA 92108
619-280-2600

K. James Flocke, *Principal*
Galz Courtney, *Vice President*

Golden Rain Foundation/Leisure World
13533 Seal Beach Boulevard
Seal Beach, CA 90740
562-431-6586
Number of Employees: 90

Mildred Tuttle, *President*
Eliz Leydon, *Personnel Manager*

Goldman Ferguson Partners
750 B Street, Suite 1850
San Diego, CA 92101
619-232-0026

Ronald E. Goldman, *Principal*

Grubb & Ellis Company
500 North State College Boulevard #100
Orange, CA 92868-1605
714-937-0881
Number of Employees: 30

Lila Rodriguera, *Office Manager*

Grubb & Ellis Company
8880 Rio San Diego Drive, Suite 200
San Diego, CA 92108
619-297-5500
Web Address: www.grubb-ellis.com

Curt Stephenson Sr., *District Manager*
Cheryl Young, *Hiring Contact*

Insignia Commercial Group
1 Technology Drive #G
Irvine, CA 92618-2339
949-788-3000
Web Address: www.unitas.net
Number of Employees: 150

John G. Combs, *President*

IPC Commercial Real Estate
4275 Executive Square, Suite 100
La Jolla, CA 92037
619-450-3000
Web Address: Akvargas@aol.com

Eugene F. Diskin Jr., *Local Principal*

James Crone & Associates
101 North Broadway
Escondido, CA 92025
760-480-8888
Web Address: www.drhorton.com
Number of Employees: 25

James A. Crone III, *President*

John Burnham & Co.
610 West Ash Street
San Diego, CA 92101
619-236-1557
Job Hotline: 619-525-2994
Number of Employees: 249

Dennis Cruzan, *President*
Denise Hujing, *Assistant Vice President*

Lee & Associates
15615 Alton Parkway, Suite 150
Irvine, CA 92618-3307
949-727-1200
Number of Employees: 250

Bart Pitzer, *President*

Lowe Enterprises
11777 San Vicente Boulevard, Suite 90
Los Angeles, CA 90049
310-820-6661
Web Address: www.loweenterprises.com

Robert J. Lowe, *CEO*
Suzanne Snell, *Hiring Contact*

Marcus & Millichap
9255 Towne Centre Drive, Suite 110
San Diego, CA 92121
619-452-8300
Number of Employees: 30

John Smelter, *Regional Manager & Hiring Contact*

Marcus & Millichap Corp R/E Services
19800 Macarthur Boulevard, Suite 150
Irvine, CA 92612-2420
949-851-3030
Web Address: www.mmreibc.com
Number of Employees: 50
Julie Rosas, *Office Manager*

Prudential California Realty
8898 Rio San Diego Drive
San Diego, CA 92108
619-294-3113
Web Address: www.prudentialcalif.com
Stephen C. Games, *Principal Executive*

R. B. Allen Commercial
695 Town Center Drive, Suite 110
Costa Mesa, CA 92626-1924
949-966-9494
Number of Employees: 15
Rex B. Allen, *President*

Real Estate Disposition Corp
9 Goodyear #200
Irvine, CA 92618-2001
949-583-1000
Web Address: www.classifiedad.com
Number of Employees: 60

Robert D. Friedman, *President*

REO Advisors
4320 Viewridge Avenue, Suite D
San Diego, CA 92123
619-541-7144

Tom R. McCormack, *Vice President*

Retail Properties Group
3252 Holiday Court, Suite 110
La Jolla, CA 92037
619-453-9990
Number of Employees: 20

Joseph A. Balla, *President*
Julie Dodd, *Office Manager*

Sperry Van Ness Investment Real Estate
8910 University Center Lane, Suite 100
San Diego, CA 92122
619-452-9100
Number of Employees: 30

Jim Brady, *Regional Manager*

Spring Mountain Escrow
2955 Main Street, Suite 100
Irvine, CA 92614-5909
949-930-2320
Number of Employees: 75

Jill Howes, *Office Manager*

Sure Investments
9666 Business Park Avenue, Suite 202
San Diego, CA 92131
619-281-8285

Steven Huffman, *President & Hiring Contact*

Tarbell Realtors
1403 North Tustin Avenue #380
Santa Ana, CA 92705-8620
714-972-0988
Web Address: www.tarbell.com
Number of Employees: 50

Don Tarbell, *President*
Kathy Dutton, *Human Resources Manager*

TD Service Financial Corp
1750 East 4th Street #800
Santa Ana, CA 92705-3909
714-543-8372
Number of Employees: 160

Patrick J. Dobiesz, *President*

The Carlson Company
125 East Baker Street, Suite 230
Costa Mesa, CA 92626
949-445-0280
Number of Employees: 96

Terry Barringer, *President*

The Irving Hughes Group
501 West Broadway, Suite 2020
San Diego, CA 92101
619-238-4393
Web Address: www.irvinghughes.com
Number of Employees: 16

Craig Irving, *President*
Jason Hughes, *President*
Maureen Macleann, *Office Manager & Hiring Contact*

The Rreef Funds
1630 South Sunkist Street, Suite A
Anaheim, CA 92806-5816
714-634-4664
Web Address: www.rreff.com
Number of Employees: 13

Mike Kent, *District Manager*

The Seeley Company
1 Park Plaza, Suite 1200
Irvine, CA 92614-8509
949-474-0707
Number of Employees: 20

Torie Udomsilta, *Office Manager*

The Seeley Company
2400 East Katella Avenue, Suite 950
Anaheim, CA 92806-5964
714-634-4050
Number of Employees: 20

Angela Castro, *Office Manager*

Voit Commercial Brokerage
18500 Von Karman Avenue, Suite 150
Irvine, CA 92612-0504
949-851-5110
Web Address: www.voitco.com
Number of Employees: 50

Debbie Milby, *Office Manager*

Voit Commercial Brokerage
2099 South State College Boulevard, Suite 100
Anaheim, CA 92806
714-978-7880
Job Hotline: 714-978-7880
Number of Employees: 36

John M. Owen III, *Managing Partner*

Voit Commercial Brokerage
4370 La Jolla Village Drive, Suite 990
San Diego, CA 92122
619-453-0505
Number of Employees: 30

Linda Dunfee, *Managing Partner & Hiring Contact for Agents*
Tammy Brown, *Hiring Contact*

Western Mutual Corporation
2244 West Coast Highway, Suite 100
Newport Beach, CA 92663-4724
949-642-4100
Number of Employees: 100

Larry O'Rourke, *President*

Developers

Alpha Construction Co.
6060 Sepulveda Boulevard, Suite 206
Van Nuys, CA 91411
818-779-3000
Web Address: www.alpha.com
Number of Employees: 15
Irvin Laxineta, *President*
Phillip Quezada, *Director of Human Resources*

Amcal Diversified
5743 Corsa Avenue, Suite 208
Westlake Village, CA 91362
818-706-0694
Number of Employees: 10
Percival Vaz, *President*
Luxmi Vaz, *Personnel Director*

Anastasi Construction Company
1200 Aviation Boulevard, Suite 100
Redondo Beach, CA 90278
310-376-8077
Web Address: www.anastasi.com
Number of Employees: 30
Wayne Anastasi, *President*
Tom Patty, *Vice President & Hiring Contact*

Bixby Ranch Company
3010 Old Ranch Parkway, Suite 100
Seal Beach, CA 90740-2750
562-493-1475
Number of Employees: 200
Chase Morgan, *President & CEO*
Suzanne Harris, *Manager of Personnel Administration*

Braemar Homes
30495 Canwood Street, Suite 200
Agoura Hills, CA 91301
818-889-6302
L. Maler, *Principal*
Cindy Dinow, *Principal*
Nancy Doolan, *Director of Human Resources*

Brock Homes, Ryland Company
21800 Burbank Boulevard, 3rd Floor
Woodland Hills, CA 91387
818-598-4400
Web Address: www.ryland.com

Frank Scardina, *President*
Bob Cunnion, *Director of Human Resources*

Brookfield Homes - San Diego
12865 Pointe Del Mar, Suite 200
Del Mar, CA 92014
619-481-8500

Steve Doyle, *President*

Buie Communities
380 Stevens Avenue, Suite 305
Solana Beach, CA 92075
858-794-2400
Number of Employees: 16

Robert F. Buie, *President*

C. J. Segerstrom & Sons
3315 Fairview Road
Costa Mesa, CA 92626
949-546-0110
Number of Employees: 65

Henry Segerstrom, *Managing Partner*

Cal-Coast Homes
27520 Hawthorne Boulevard, Suite 250
Rolling Hills, CA 90274
310-544-5900
Number of Employees: 30

Edward Miller, *President*
Kathy Curtis, *Office Manager*

California Pacific Homes
38 Executive Park, Suite 200
Irvine, CA 92614
949-833-6000
Web Address: www.calpacific.com
Number of Employees: 60

Cery Bren, *President*

California Traditions
12526 High Bluff Drive, Suite 100
San Diego, CA 92130
619-793-2622
Number of Employees: 30

William F. Miller Jr., *President*

Calprop Corporation
13160 Mindanao Way, Suite 180
Marina Del Rey, CA 90292
310-306-4314
Number of Employees: 10

Victor Zaccaglin, *CEO*
Dori Baron, *Office Manager*

Capital Pacific Holdings
4100 McArthur Boulevard, Suite 200
Newport Beach, CA 92660
949-622-8400
Web Address: www.cph-inc.com
Number of Employees: 35

Dell Dowers, *President*
Kathy Smith, *Director of Personnel*

Catellus Development Corp.
304 South Broadway, 4th Floor
Los Angeles, CA 90013
213-625-5865
Number of Employees: 80

Nelson Rising, *CEO*
Jaine GErtmenian, *VP for Human Resources*

Continental Development Corporation
2041 Rosecrans Avenue, Suite 200
El Segundo, CA 90245
310-640-1520
Number of Employees: 45

Richard Lundquist, *President*
Marsha Murray, *VP for Administration & HR*

Continental Homes
12636 High Bluff Drive, Suite 300
San Diego, CA 92130
858-793-2580
Web Address: www.continentalhomes.com
Number of Employees: 60

Christopher J. Chambers, *Division President*
Don Makay, *Vice President*

Cornerstone Communities Corporation
4365 Executive Drive, Suite 600
San Diego, CA 92121
858-458-9700
Number of Employees: 20

Micheal Sabourin, *Vice President*

Costain Homes
620 Newport Center Drive, Suite 400
Newport Beach, CA 92660-6434
949-760-1455
Number of Employees: 32

Julie Hill, *President & CEO*

D.R. Horton - San Diego
1010 South Coast Highway #101
Encinitas, CA 92024
760-634-6700
Number of Employees: 16

Jay Kerr, *Division President*

Donahue-Schriber
3501 Jamboree Road, South Tower, Suite 300
Newport Beach, CA 92660
949-854-2100

Web Address: www.donahueschriber.com
Number of Employees: 80
Thomas L. Schriber, *President*
Raven Lafitte, *Personnel Director*

Eric Friedman Development
9440 Telstar Avenue, Suite 201
El Monte, CA 91731
626-442-4070

Eric Friedman, *President*

Fieldstone Communities
14 Corporate Plaza Drive
Newport Beach, CA 92660-7913
949-640-9090
Number of Employees: 80

Keith Johnson, *President*
Don Hendricks, *Human Resources Manager*

Fieldstone Communities
5465 Morehouse Drive, Suite 250
San Diego, CA 92121
858-546-8081
Web Address: www.uniontrib.com
Number of Employees: 11

Jim Hansen, *Regional Manager*

Forest City Development
949 South Hope Street, Suite 100
Suite 100
Los Angeles, CA 90015
213-488-0010
Number of Employees: 60

Gregory M. Vilkin, *President*
Tania Thrashm, *Office Administrator*

Fu-Lyons Associates
15125 Garfield Avenue
Paramount, CA 90723
562-531-1000
Web Address: www.fulyons.com
Number of Employees: 4

Charles Lyons III, *Owner*

Goldrich & Kest Industries
5150 Overland Avenue
Culver City, CA 90230
310-204-2050
Web Address: www.gkind.com
Number of Employees: 600

Jona Goldrich, *General Partner*
Karen Eisenberg, *Human Resources Manager*

Greystone Homes
5973 Avenida Encinas, Suite 101
Carlsbad, CA 92008
760-804-7700
Number of Employees: 30

Todd Palmer, *Division President*

Southern California Job Source

Greystone Homes
6767 Forest Lawn Drive, Suite 300
Los Angeles, CA 90068
213-436-6300
Number of Employees: 500

Jack Harter, *CEO*
Peter Kieseckee, *Senior Vice Presiodent*
Jeri Dixon, *Director of Personnel*
Linda Kelly, *Human Resources Director*

Haagen Properties
23456 Hawthorne Boulevard, Suite 120
Torrance, CA 90505
310-375-0900
Number of Employees: 10

Christopher Fahey, *CEO Human Resources Director*

Held Properties
1880 Century Park East, Suite 508
Los Angeles, CA 90067
310-474-1414
Number of Employees: 30

Robert Held, *President*
Parvin Mavadaap, *Human Resource Manager*

Home Craftsmen
740 East Colorado, Suite 203
Pasadena, CA 91101
626-584-6535

Ed Kronz, *President*

J.H. Snyder Co.
5757 Wilshire Boulevard, Penthouse 30
Los Angeles, CA 90036
213-857-5546
Number of Employees: 35

Jerome Snyder, *Managing Partner*

JCC Homes
3480 Torrance Boulevard, Suite 300
Torrance, CA 90503
310-540-3990
Number of Employees: 30

Gregory Delgado, *President*
Alex Wong, *Human Resource Manager*

John Laing Homes
19600 Fairchild, Suite 150
Irvine, CA 92612-2509
949-476-9090
Number of Employees: 130

L. J. Edgecombe, *President*
Barbara Williamson, *Human Resource Manager*

Katell Properties
11999 San Vicente Boulevard, Suite 200
Los Angeles, CA 90049
310-459-7200

Number of Employees: 3
Gerald Katell, *President*
James Smith, *Vice President*

Kaufman and Broad Home Corp.
10990 Wilshire Boulevard, 7th Floor
Los Angeles, CA 90024
310-231-4000
Job Hotline: 310-231-4000
Web Address: www.kaufmanandbroad.com
Number of Employees: 150

Bruce Karatz, *CEO*
Gary Ray, *Human Resources Director*

Kaufman & Broad Coastal
12626 High Bluff Drive, Suite 400
San Diego, CA 92130
619-259-6000
Number of Employees: 49

Bill Cardon, *President*

Keystone Communities
9683 Tierra Grande, Suite 201
San Diego, CA 92126
619-549-1195

Kilroy Realty Corp.
2250 East Imperial Highway, Suite 1200
El Segundo, CA 90245
213-772-1193
Number of Employees: 110

John B. Kilroy Jr., *CEO & President*
Pauline Orris, *Human Resources Director*

Koll Real Estate Group
4343 Von Karman Avenue
Newport Beach, CA 92660
949-833-3030
Number of Employees: 125

Raymond E. Wirta, *President*
Lynda Lane, *Director of Personnel*
Real estate developer which obtains zoning and other entitlements for land it owns and sells it to other developers, homebuilders, or investors. The company also provides commercial, industrial, retail, and residential real estate development services to 3rd parties.

Koll Real Estate Group
10559 Holman Avenue
Los Angeles, CA 90024
310-470-3461

Jack Hileman, *Senior Vice President*

La Caze Development Co.
2601 Airport Drive, Suite 300
Torrance, CA 90505
310-534-0411
Number of Employees: 7

Norman La Caze, *Owner*

Larwin Co.
16633 Ventura Boulevard, Suite1300
Encino, CA 91436
818-986-8890
Number of Employees: 50

Michael Keston, *CEO*
Jean Turkish, *Director of Human Resources*

Lowe Enterprises
145 South State College Boulevard #145
Brea, CA 92821-5824
714-671-2133
Number of Employees: 40

Karen Tomita, *Property Development Manager*

Maguire Thomas Partners
355 South Grand Avenue, Suite 4500
Los Angeles, CA 90071
213-626-3300
Number of Employees: 60

Robert F. Maguire III, *Managing Partner*
Jesse Maemori, *Human Resources Manager*

Majestic Realty Co.
13191 Crossroads Parkway North, 6th Floor
City of Industry, CA 91746
562-692-9581
Web Address: www.majesticrealty.com
Number of Employees: 200

Edward Roski Jr., *President*
Mike Durham, *Controller*
Gail Kiralla, *Human Resource Manager*

Malcolm Riley Companies
11640 San Vicente Boulevard, Suite 202
Los Angeles, CA 90049
310-820-5891
Number of Employees: 6
Malcolm Riley, *President*

Manulife Real Estate
865 South Figueroa Street, Suite 2300
Los Angeles, CA 90017
213-689-0813
Number of Employees: 12
Thomas Patton, *Area VP & Regional Director*
Elysa Williams, *Executive Administrator*

MBK Real Estate, Ltd.
175 Technology Drive
Irvine, CA 92719
949-789-8300
Web Address: www.mbk.com
Number of Employees: 150
Michael H. Voss, *President*

Mika Co.
837 Traction Avenue, Suite 400
Los Angeles, CA 90013
213-680-1230
S. Schwartz, *Principal*

Mission Viejo Company
26137 La Paz Road
Mission Viejo, CA 92691-5387
714-837-6050
Number of Employees: 45

Sue Rounds, *Human Resource Manager*

MWH Development Corp.
828 Moraga Drive, Second Floor
Belair, CA 90049
818-757-8979
Number of Employees: 30

Mark Handel, *President*

New Urban West
520 Broadway Street, Suite 100
Santa Monica, CA 90401
310-394-3379
Number of Employees: 30

Stephen D. Gunther, *President*
Teri Kaldhusdal, *Office Manager*
Makiko Kato, *Human Resource Manager*

Newhall Land & Farming Co.
23823 West Valencia Boulevard
Valencia, CA 91355
805-255-4000
Job Hotline: 805-255-4442

Thomas L. Lee, *CEO*
Mike Whaling, *Director of Human Resources*

Overton Moore & Associates
1125 West 190th Street, Suite 200
Gardena, CA 90248
310-323-9100
Number of Employees: 25

Stanley Moore, *President*
Christina Seltzer, *Office/Human Resources Manager*

Pacific Bay Homes.
23770 Valencia Boulevard, Suite 200
Santa Clarita, CA 91355
805-260-1700
Web Address: www.pacbayhomes.com
Number of Employees: 6

Dick Hamm, *Division Manager*
Susan Gardner, *Director of Human Resources*

Pacific Gateway Homes
85 Argonaut, Suite 200
Aliso Viejo, CA 92656-4105
714-859-1000
Number of Employees: 36

Rita T. Lamkin, *President*

Pardee Homes
110 West C Street, Suite 2200
San Diego, CA 92101
619-525-7240

Mike Madigan, *Senior Vice President*

Pardee Homes
10880 Wilshire Boulevard, Suite 1900
Los Angeles, CA 90024
310-475-3525
Web Address: www.pardeehomes.com
Number of Employees: 120

Mike McGee, *President*
Melinda Junger, *Human Resources Representative*

Presley Companies
19 Corporate Plaza
Newport Beach, CA 92660
949-640-6400
Web Address: www.presleyhomes.com
Number of Employees: 70

Wade H. Cable, *President*
Linda Foster, *Vice President of Administration*
Developer of single-family detached and attached homes in California, with additional operations in Arizona and New Mexico. The company primarily targets entry-level and move-up buyers, with prices ranging from $80,000 to $480,000 and averaging about $175,000.

Presley Homes
15373 Innovation Drive, Suite 380
San Diego, CA 92128
619-451-6300

Larry Smith, *Vice President*

Rancho Vista Development Co.
40701 Rancho Vista Boulevard, Suite 360
Palmdale, CA 93551
805-943-2533
Number of Employees: 8

R. Gregg Anderson, *General Partner*
Roy Migita, *Vice President*

Recreactions Group of Cos -RGC
20 Corporate Plaza Drive
Newport Beach, CA 92660-7921
949-720-9881
Number of Employees: 20

Hal Lynch, *President*

RWR Development
16461 Sherman Way Suite 325
Van Nuys, CA 91406
818-780-3334

Bill Rheinschild, *CEO*

Ryland Homes
15373 Innovation Drive
San Diego, CA 92128
619-675-0800

Chris Beucler, *President*

Shea Homes
10721 Treena Street, Suite 200
San Diego, CA 92131
619-549-3156
Web Address: www.sheahomes.com
Number of Employees: 80

Mark Brock, *President*
Leilani Lemarre, *Human Resource Manager*

Shea Homes
655 Brea Canyon Road
Walnut, CA 91789
909-598-1841
Web Address: www.sheahomes.com
Number of Employees: 50

Roy Humphreys, *President*

Standard Pacific Homes
9335 Chesapeake Drive
San Diego, CA 92123
619-292-2200
Number of Employees: 27

Ken Cablay, *President*
Allen Willingham, *Hiring Contact*

Surf Management
357 Van Ness Way, Suite 100
Torrance, CA 90501
310-533-5900
Number of Employees: 12

Steve Fechner, *President & Owner*
Rolanda Yee, *Office Manager*

The Eastlake Company
900 Lane Avenue, Suite 100
Chula Vista, CA 91914
619-421-0127
Web Address: www.eastlakehomes.com
Number of Employees: 22

Paul G. Nieto, *CEO*
Silvanna Brazell, *Administrator*

The Lusk Company
16592 Hale Avenue
Irvine, CA 92606-5005
949-757-6000
Number of Employees: 28

Jim D. Johnson, *President*

The Mills Corporation
1 City Boulevard West, Suite 1700
Orange, CA 92868-3617
714-704-1175

Web Address: www.millscorp.com
Number of Employees: 40
Marcia Peddicord, *Office Manager*

The Olen Companies
7 Corporate Plaza
Newport Beach, CA 92660
949-644-6536
Number of Employees: 55

Igor M. Olenicoff, *President*
Bobbi Baker, *Human Resources*

The Price REIT
145 South Fairfax Avenue, 4th Floor
Los Angeles, CA 90036
213-937-8200
Number of Employees: 60

Joseph Kornwasser, *CEO & President*
Karen Meyerson, *Human Resources Director*

Transpacific Development Co.
2377 Crenshaw Boulevard, Suite 300
Torrance, CA 90501
310-618-3600
Number of Employees: 27

Thomas G. Irish, *President*
Amy Fuermann-Sapien, *Administrative Assistant for Personnel*

Vintage Communities
600 Anton Boulevard, Suite 1350
Costa Mesa, CA 92626-7147
949-825-1750
Number of Employees: 21

Matthew Osgood, *President*

Voit Companies
21600 Oxnard Street, Suite 300
Woodland Hills, CA 91367
818-593-6200
Web Address: www.voitco.com
Number of Employees: 75

Robert D. Voit, *President*
M. Marx, *Senior Vice President*
Jackie Deimel, *Director of Human Resources*

Warmington Homes
3090 Pullman Street
Costa Mesa, CA 92626
949-557-5511
Web Address: www.warmingtonhomes.com
Number of Employees: 251

Jim Warmington, *CEO*
Sara Strange, *Director of Personnel*

Watson Land Co.
22010 South Wilmington Avenue, Suite 400
Carson, CA 90745
310-952-6400
Web Address: www.watsonlandcompany.com

Number of Employees: 30
W. Huston, *Chairman*
Roger Vonting, *Controller*
Kelly Justiniane, *Human Resource Manager*

Western Pacific Housing
2385 Camino Vida Roble, Suite 107
Carlsbad, CA 92009
760-929-1600
Number of Employees: 16

Lance Waite, *President of S.D. Division*

Title Insurance

American Title Company
700 North Brand Avenue, Suite 200
Glendale, CA 91203
818-265-0370
Number of Employees: 40

Christopher White, *Branch Manager*

Chicago Title Insurance Company
245 South Los Robles Avenue, Suite 105
Rosemead, CA 91101
626-432-7600
Web Address: www.chicagotitle.com
Number of Employees: 200

William Halvorsen, Senior V. P., *Western Divi. Manager*
Anne Kulinski, *Director of Human Resources*

Commonwealth Land Title Company
801 North Brand Boulevard, Suite 1200
Glendale, CA 91203
818-552-7000
Web Address: www.chicagotitle.com
Number of Employees: 100

Glen Nelson, *County Manager*
Lorna Freeman, *Director of Human Resources*

Continental Lawyers Title Company
55 South Lake Avenue, Suite 600
Pasadena, CA 91101
626-304-2700
Number of Employees: 150

Edward Zerwekh, *President*
Rosanna Zalarde, *Director of Human Resources*

Equity Title Co.
425 West Broadway, Suite 30
Glendale, CA 91204
310-470-1007
Web Address: www.equitytitle.com
Number of Employees: 40

Robert Neville, *President*
Harriet Moretzsky, *Office/Human Resources Manager*

Fidelity National Financial
17911 Van Karman Avenue, Suite 500
Irvine, CA 92614
949-622-5000
Web Address: www.fnf.com
Number of Employees: 4500

William P. Foley II, *President*
Ann Russell, *Director of Personnel*
Title insurance company which primarily operates in the residential arena but is increasingly targeting complex commercial transactions. Issues title insurance and performs title-related services including escrow, collection and trust, closing, and real estate information and technology services.

Fidelity National Title Insurance Company
2510 Red Hill Avenue
Santa Ana, CA 92705-5542
714-852-9770
Web Address: www.f&f.com
Number of Employees: 4,700

Rada Shepherd, *Office Manager*

Fidelity National Title Insurance Company
19019 Ventura Boulevard
Tarzana, CA 91356
818-881-7800

Cindy Fried, *County Manager*
Noel Albi, *Director of Human Resources*

First American Title Company of Los Angeles
520 North Central Avenue
Glendale, CA 91203
818-242-5800
Web Address: www.fatcola.com
Number of Employees: 300

Tom Kelley, *President*
Ann Spalding, *Director of Human Resources*

Gateway Title Company
100 North First Street
Burbank, CA 91506
818-953-2300

Martin Evans, *Owner*
Ruth Brown, *Director of Human Resources*

Investors Title Co.
3055 Wilshire Boulevard, Third Floor
Los Angeles, CA 90010
213-380-1080
Number of Employees: 100

Robert Snell, *President*
Cheri Parker, *Human Resources Manager*

North American Title Co.
520 North Brand Boulevard
Glendale, CA 91203
818-240-4912

Joel Phillips, *Vice President*

Old Republic Title Co.
101 East Glenoaks Boulevard
Glendale, CA 91207
818-247-2917
Number of Employees: 160

Dick Lisi, *Executive Vice President*
Betty Egoian, *Director of Human Resources*

Orange Coast Title Co.
640 North Tustin Avenue, Suite 106
Santa Ana, CA 92705
714-558-2836
Web Address: www.octitle.com
Number of Employees: 80

John Marconi, *President*

Southland Title Corp.
7530 North Glenoaks Boulevard, Suite 202
Burbank, CA 91504
818-767-2000
Number of Employees: 500

David Cronenbold Jr., *President*
Ellie Oshiro, *Director of Human Resources*

Stewart Title Co.
505 North Brand Boulevard, Suite 1200
Glendale, CA 91203
818-502-2700
Number of Employees: 240

Nick Pappas, *Division President*
Millie Posas, *Director of Human Resources*

United Title Co.
514 Shatto Place
Los Angeles, CA 90020
213-385-3600

Henri Van Hirtum, *President*

American Constructor Inspectors Association
P.O. Box 10579
San Bernardino, CA 92423
909-594-4914

Associated General Contractors of California, Los Angeles
1255 Corporate Center Drive, Suite 100
Monteray Park, CA 91754
213-263-1500

San Diego Association of Realtors
4845 Ronson Court
San Diego, CA 92111
619-715-8000

Further References

• Associations •

Building Owners and Managers Association International (BOMA)
1201 New York Avenue, N.W., Suite 300
Washington, D.C. 20005
202-408-2662

Commercial Investment Real Estate Institute (CIREI)
430 North Michigan Avenue
Chicago, IL 60611
312-321-4460
Web Address: www.ccim.com

Institute of Real Estate Management (IREM)
430 North Michigan Avenue
Chicago, IL 60611-4090
312-329-6000
Web Address: www.irem.org

International Association for Financial Planning
5775 Glenridge Drive, N.E., Suite B-300
Atlanta, GA 30328-5364
404-845-0011
Web Address: www.iafp.org
Objective is to promote the education of ethical business financial planning.

International Real Estate Institue (IREI)
8383 East Evans Road
Scottsdale, AZ 85260
602-998-8267
Web Address: www.iami.org/irei.html

Nacore International
440 Columbia Drive, Suite 100
West Palm Beach, FL 33409
561-683-8111
Web Address: www.nacore.org

National Apartment Association (NAA)
201 North Union Street, Suite 200
Alexandria, VA 22314
703-513-6141

National Association of Industrial and Office Properties
2201 Cooperative Way, Woodland Park
Herndon, VA 22071
703-904-7100
Web Address: www.naiop.org

National Association of Real Estate Brokers
1629 K Street, N.W., Suite 602
Washington, D.C. 20006
202-785-4477
Web Address: www.nareb.org

National Association of Real Estate Investment Trusts
1129 20th Street, N.W., Suite 305
Washington, D.C. 20036
202-785-8717
Web Address: www.nareit.com

National Council of Real Estate Investment Fiduciaries
180 North Stetson Avenue, Suite 2515
Chicago, IL 60601
312-819-5890
Web Address: www.ncreif.com
Analysis and assessment of investments in real estate

National Investor Relations Institute
8045 Leesburg Pike, Suite 600
Vienna, VA 22182
703-506-3570
Web Address: www.niri.org
Improve investment procedures and relations.

National Real Estate Investors Association
89 South Riverview Avenue
Miamiburg, OH 45342
513-866-6200
Investors in real estate.

Property Management Association (PMA)
8811 Colesville Road, Suite G106
Silver Spring, MD 20910
301-657-9200
Web Address: www.reji.com/reji/associations/ pma/non-member/data
Promotes the interest and welfare of property owners.

National Association of Realtors
430 North Michigan Avenue
Chicago, IL 60611
312-329-8200
Web Address: www.realtor.com

• Publications •

Real Estate Business
P.O. Box 300
Wheaton, IL 60189
708-752-0500

Real Estate Today
430 North Michigan Avenue
Chicago, IL 60611-4087
312-329-8200

Realtor News
700 11 Street
Washington, D.C. 20001
202-383-1193

Today's Realtor -*Real estate magazine.*
700 11th Street, N.W.
Washington, D.C. 20001-4507
202-383-1193

Sports & Recreation

- Sports Management & Marketing
- Golf & Country Clubs
- Professional & College Athletics
- Health Clubs
- Parks & Recreation

Most entry level positions in Sports Marketing are filled by individuals who either have prior work experience as an intern or previous association with clients involved in Sports Marketing. Candidates for entry-level positions should possess a degree in sports marketing/management in addition to prior work experience.

Typical entry-level positions are in management. Duties include coordinating, planning and assisting project managers with up-coming events. Mobility within sports marketing firms is evaluated on performance and history.

If you are serious about becoming associated with a sports marketing firm, plan early in your undergraduate or masters program to actively seek an internship. You will find that a majority of all employees with any sports affiliated organization have had prior work experience as an intern before getting their first sports marketing position.

DELWILBER + ASSOCIATES

Quick Reference

Aftco Manufacturing Co
www.aftco.com
AMP Research
www.amp-research.com
Anaheim Mighty Ducks
www.nhl.com/teams/ana/index.htm
Anaheim Sports
www.anaheimangels.com
Balboa Bay Club
www.balboabayclub.com
Bally's Total Fitness
www.ballyfitness.com
Buck Knives
www.buckknives.com
Callaway Golf Company
www.callawaygolf.com
City of Coronado Municipal Golf Course
www.coronado.ca.us
Cubic Balance Golf Technology
www.cubicbalance.com

Disneyland
www.disney.com
El Camino Country Club
www.coblestone.com
Four Seasons Resort Aviara
www.fhr.com
GT Bicycles
www.gtbicycles.com
Heart Rate
www.heartrateinc.com
Knott's Berry Farm
www.knotts.com
La Costa Resort, Spa and Country Club
www.lacosta.com
Los Alamitos Race Course
www.losalamitos.com
Marksman Products
www.beeman.com
Master Industries
www.masterindustries.com

Oakley
www.oakley.com
Pala Mesa Resort
www.palamesa.com
Pelican Hill Golf Club
www.pelicanhill.com
Steele Canyon Golf & Country Club
www.steelecanyon.com
Taylor Made Golf Co.
www.taylormadegolf.com
Tectrix Fitness Equipment
www.tectrix.com
The California Angels
www.majorleaguebaseball.com/al/cal
Unisen
www.startrack.com
Warner Springs Ranch
www.wsranchaol.com
Yamaha Corporation of America
www.yamaha.com

Aftco Manufacturing Co
17351 Murphy Avenue
Irvine, CA 92614-5919
949-660-8757
Web Address: www.aftco.com
Number of Employees: 10

Bill Shedd, *President*

American Graphite Technology
210 West Baywood Avenue
Orange, CA 92865-2603
714-282-0137
Number of Employees: 200

Richard Tcheng, *President*

AMP Research
23531 Ridge Road
Laguna Hills, CA 92653
714-461-5990
Web Address: www.amp-research.com
Number of Employees: 38

Horst Leitner, *President*

Anaheim Angels
200 Gene Autry Way
Anaheim, CA 92806
800-796-4256
Web Address: www.majorleaguebaseball.com

Anaheim Mighty Ducks
2695 Katella Avenue
Anaheim, CA 92806
714-704-2700
Web Address: www.mightyducks.com
Number of Employees: 100

Tony Tavares, *President*

Ashworth
2791 Loker Avenue West
Carlsbad, CA 92008
760-438-6610
Web Address: www.ashworthinc.com
Number of Employees: 300

Randall L. Herrel, *President*
Stacey Knepper, *Director of Human Resources*

Balboa Bay Club
1221 West Coast Highway
Newport Beach, CA 92663-5026
949-645-5000
Web Address: www.balboabayclub.com
Number of Employees: 280

Henry Schielein, *President*
Lynn Rice, *Human Resources Director*

Balboa Golf Course
2600 Golf Course Drive
San Diego, CA 92102
619-235-1184

Michael Jory, *Pro*

Bally's Total Fitness
7755 Center Avenue, Suite 400
Huntington Beach, CA 92647-3007
714-892-5800
Web Address: www.ballyfitness.com
Number of Employees: 8,000

Lynnette Walker, *Manager*

Bernardo Heights Country Club
16066 Bernardo Heights Parkway
San Diego, CA 92128
619-487-3440

Russ Bloom, *Pro*

Betterline Products
1101 East Elm Avenue
Fullerton, CA 92831
714-526-7063
Number of Employees: 20

Byron Berkes, *President*

Bonita Golf Club
5540 Sweetwater Road
Bonita, CA 91902
619-267-1103

James P. Crockett, *Pro*
Bob Scribner, *Manager*

Buck Knives
1900 Weld Boulevard
El Cajon, CA 92020
619-449-1100
Job Hotline: 619-449-1162
Web Address: www.buckknives.com
Number of Employees: 450

Charles T. Buck, *President*
Joe Anasagasti, *Manager*

California Speedway
PO Box 9300
Fontana, CA 92443
888-849-7223
Web Address: www.racingwest.com

Callaway Golf Company
2285 Rutherford Road
Carlsbad, CA 92008
760-931-1771
Web Address: www.callawaygolf.com
Number of Employees: 2,500

Donald H. Dye, *President*
Elizabeth O'Mea, *SVP of Human Resources*
Sheri Wright, *Human Resources Manager*

Carlton Oaks Country Club
9200 Inwood Drive
Santee, CA 92071
619-448-4242

Rex Cole, *Pro*

Carmel Mountain Ranch Country Club
14050 Carmel Ridge Road
San Diego, CA 92128
619-487-9224
Number of Employees: 30

Michael Winn, *Pro*

Center City Golf Course
2323 Greenbrier Drive
Oceanside, CA 92054
760-433-8590
Number of Employees: 25
Ludwig Keehn, *Pro*

Chopra Center for Well Being
7630 Fay Avenue
La Jolla, CA 92037
619-551-7788
Web Address: www.chopra.com

City of Coronado Municipal Golf Course
2000 Visalia Row
Coronado, CA 92118
619-522-7373
Job Hotline: 619-522-7300
Web Address: www.coronado.ca.us
Ron Yarbrough, *Pro*
Dianna Axley, *Personnel Analyst*

Cubic Balance Golf Technology
30231 Tomas
Rch Santa Margarita, CA 92688-2123
714-858-0707
Web Address: www.cubicbalance.com
Number of Employees: 80
Lawrence Igarashi, *President*

Daiwa Corporation
PO Box 3235
Garden Grove, CA 92842-3235
562-802-9589
Number of Employees: 155
Tad Suzuki, *President*
Bunny Holloway, *Human Resources Manager*

Del Mar Country Club
6001 Clubhouse Drive
Rancho Santa Fe, CA 92067
619-759-5900
Tim Moher, *Pro*

Del Mar Race Track
Jimmy Durante Boulevard at Fairgrounds
Del Mar, CA 92014
619-755-1141

Disneyland
1313 South Harbor
Anaheim, CA 92803-3232
714-781-4000
Job Hotline: 714-781-4407
Web Address: www.disney.com
Number of Employees: 12,000

Dave Cox, *VP for Human Resources*

Doubletree Carmel Highlands Resort
14455 Penasquitos Drive
San Diego, CA 92129
619-672-9100
Number of Employees: 200

Michael Flanagan, *Pro*
Ann Buffington, *Human Resource Manager*

El Camino Country Club
3202 Vista Way
Oceanside, CA 92056
760-757-2100
Web Address: www.coblestone.com
Number of Employees: 40

Michael Facon, *Pro*

Elysian Park
929 Academy Road
Los Angeles, CA 90012
323-226-1402

Emerald Isle Golf Course
660 South El Camino Real
Oceanside, CA 92054
760-721-4700
Number of Employees: 8

Jeff Sampson, *Pro*
Al Meddings, *Manager of Human Resources*

Escondido Country Club
1800 Country Club Lane
Escondido, CA 92026
760-743-3301
Number of Employees: 65

Ben Dobbs, *Pro*

Fairbanks Ranch Country Club
15150 San Dieguito Road
Rancho Santa Fe, CA 92067
619-259-8811
Number of Employees: 150

Richard Merritt, *Pro*
Henny Deckman, *Human Resource Director*

Fallbrook Golf Club
2757 Gird Road
Fallbrook, CA 92088
760-728 8334
Number of Employees: 60

Mike O'Leary, *Pro*
Stacey O'Leary, *Director of Human Resources*

Fountains Executive Course
8860 Lawrence Welk Drive
Escondido, CA 92026
760-749-3225
Job Hotline: 760-749-3182
Number of Employees: 470

Ron Cropley, *Pro*
Maribell Fuentes, *Human Resources Manager*

Four Seasons Resort Aviara
7100 Four Seasons Point
Carlsbad, CA 92009
760-929-0077
Job Hotline: 760-603-6949
Web Address: www.fhr.com
Number of Employees: 900

Bill Crist, *Pro*
Ellie Dahl, *Director of Human Resources*

Golden Door Fitness Resort
77 Deer Springs Road
San Marcos, CA 92069
760-744-5777
Web Address: www.thegoldendoor.com

Goldwin Golf
2460 Impala Drive
Carlsbad, CA 92008
760-930-0077
Number of Employees: 75

Sam Nakashima, *CEO*
Shelley Devlin, *Director of Human Resources*

Graffalloy
1020 North Marshall Avenue
El Cajon, CA 92020
619-562-1020

Bill Gerhart, *President*

Great Western Forum
3900 West Manchester Boulevard
Inglewood, CA 90305
310-419-3100
Job Hotline: 213-742-7100
Number of Employees: 320

Joan McLaughlin, *Director of Human Resources*

Griffith Park
4730 Crystal Springs Drive
Los Angeles, CA 90027
323-665-5100

GT Bicycles
2001 East Dyer Road
Santa Ana, CA 92704
714-481-7100
Web Address: www.gtbicycles.com
Number of Employees: 734

Michael Haynes, *President*
Virginia Valdez, *Director of Personnel*
Designer of mid- to premium-priced mountain and juvenile BMX bicycles. The company offers more than 100 models, including its GT All Terra brand mountain bikes; GT, Dyno, Robinson, and Powerlite brand juvenile BMX models; and road and specialty models.

Heart Rate
3190 Building E Airport Loop
Costa Mesa, CA 92626-4652
949-850-9716
Web Address: www.heartrateinc.com
Number of Employees: 50

Richard Charnitski, *President*

Hollywood Park
1050 South Prairie Avenue
Inglewood, CA 90301
310-419-1500
Number of Employees: 3500

G. Michael Finnigan, *Executive VP*
Patty Boggs, *Human Resources*

Hurlbut Amusement Company
7860 Western Avenue
Buena Park, CA 90620-2627
714-523-1060
Number of Employees: 350

Wendell Hurlbut, *President*

Jazzercise International Headquarters
9235 Activity Road
San Diego, CA 92126
619-695-1503
Web Address: www.jazzercise.com

Knott's Berry Farm
8039 Beach Boulevard
Buena Park, CA 90620-3225
714-827-1776
Job Hotline: 714-995-6688
Web Address: www.knotts.com
Number of Employees: 3500

Terry E Van Gorder, *President*
Jeff Whynot, *VP for Human Resources*

La Costa Resort, Spa and Country Club
2100 Costa del Mar Road
Carlsbad, CA 92009
760-438-9111
Job Hotline: 760-433-9675
Web Address: www.lacosta.com

Number of Employees: 1000

John Peto, *General Manager*

Bill Parr, *Director of Sales*

Kristie Whitman, *Director of Human Resources*

LA Fitness
100 Bayview Circle, Suite 4100
Newport Beach, CA 92660-2985
949-509-2555
Number of Employees: 500

Louis Welch, *President*

Theresa Haty, *VP for Human Resources*

LA Fitness - Irvine
17850 Sky Park Circle
Irvine, CA 92614-6492
949-261-7500
Number of Employees: 20

Theresa Haty, *Vice President for Human Resources*

La Jolla Club Golf Co.
2445 Cades Way
Vista, CA 92083
760-599-9400
Web Address: golf4kids@aol.com
Number of Employees: 50

Steven Cade, *CEO*

La Jolla Country Club
7301 High Avenue
La Jolla, CA 92037
619-454-9601

Pete Coe, *Pro*

Lake San Marcos Country Club
1750 San Pablo Drive
San Marcos, CA 92069
760-744-1310
Number of Employees: 200

Randy Olson, *Pro*

Ms. Andrews, *Controller*

Long Beach Aquarium of the Pacific
100 Aquarium Way
Long Beach, CA
562-590-3100
Web Address: www.aquariumofthepacific.org

Los Alamitos Race Course
4961 Katella Avenue
Los Alamitos, CA 90720-2799
714-995-1234
Web Address: www.losalamitos.com
Number of Employees: 100

Rick Henson, *President*

Frank Sabato, *Vice President*

Los Angeles Athletic Club
431 West 7th Street
Los Angeles, CA 90014
213-625-2211

Los Angeles Clippers
3939 South Figueroa Street
Los Angeles, CA 90037
213-748-8000

Los Angeles Dodgers
1000 Elysian Park Avenue
Los Angeles, CA 90012
213-224-1500
Web Address: www.dodgers.com

Los Angeles Kings
Great Western Forum
3900 West Manchester Boulevard
Inglewood, CA 90305
310-419-3182
Web Address: www.lakings.com

Los Angeles Lakers
Great Western Forum
3900 West Manchester Boulevard
Inglewood, CA 90305
310-419-3182
Web Address: www.nba.com/lakers

Los Angeles Zoo
5333 Zoo Drive
Los Angeles, CA 90027
323-644-4200
Web Address: www.lazoo.org

Los Caballeros Racquet & Sports
17272 Newhope Street
Fountain Valley, CA 92708-4210
714-546-8560
Number of Employees: 120

Jack Cameron, *Owner*

Julie Fry, *Manager*

Marksman Products
5482 Argosy Avenue
Huntington Beach, CA 92649-1059
714-898-7535
Web Address: www.beeman.com
Number of Employees: 100

Robert A. Eck, *President*

Master Industries
14420 Myford Road, Building 2C
Irvine, CA 92606
949-660-0644
Web Address: www.masterindustries.com
Number of Employees: 45

Steve Norman, *President*

Meadowlake Golf Course
10333 Meadow Glen Way East
Escondido, CA 92026
760-749-1620
Number of Employees: 40

Brad Van Horn, *Pro*

Mesa Verde Country Club
3000 Clubhouse Road
Costa Mesa, CA 92626-3599
949-549-0377
Number of Employees: 100

Kim Porter, *Manager*

Mission Roller Hockey
1801 South Standard
Santa Ana, CA 92707-5715
714-556-8856
Number of Employees: 80

Thomas Wilder, *President*

Mission Trails Golf Course
7380 Golfcrest Place
San Diego, CA 92119
619-460-5400

Walt Willows, *Pro*

Mission Viejo Country Club
26200 Country Club Drive
Mission Viejo, CA 92691-5905
714-582-1550
Number of Employees: 115

Russ Disbro, *President*

Montecito Sportswear Corp.
5121 Santa Fe Street, Suite F
San Diego, CA 92109
619-490-5200
James Saxon, *President*

Morgan Run Resort & Club
5690 Cancha de Golf
Rancho Santa Fe, CA 92091
858-756-2471
Number of Employees: 160
Ray Metz, *Pro*

National Golf Properties
2951 28th Street
Santa Monica, CA 90405
310-664-4100
Number of Employees: 11
James Stanich, *President*
Bill Reagan, *Controller*

Newport Beach Golf Course
3100 Irvine Avenue
Newport Beach, CA 92660-3104
949-852-8681
Number of Employees: 20
Steven G. Lane, *Partner*

Oakley
One Icon
Foothill Ranch, CA 92610
714-951-0991
Web Address: www.oakley.com
Number of Employees: 1,180

Link Newcomb, *CEO*
Darlene Kennedy, *Director of Personnel*
Manufacturer of high-performance sunglasses and goggles for the sports and fashion sunglasses markets worldwide. Its products feature high-tech designs, including interchangeable, high-optical clarity lenses and damage resistance.

Pala Mesa Resort
2001 Old Highway 395
Fallbrook, CA 92028
760-728-5881
Job Hotline: 760-731-6814
Web Address: www.palamesa.com
Number of Employees: 200

Todd Keefer, *Pro*
Connie Herrera, *Director of Human Resources*

Pauma Valley Country Club
Highway 76 and Pauma Valley Drive
San Diego, CA 92061
619-742-3721

Mark Preister, *Pro*

Pelican Hill Golf Club
26651 Pelican Hill Road South
Newport Beach, CA 92657-2001
949-760-0707
Web Address: www.pelicanhill.com
Number of Employees: 120

Robert Ford, *President*

Pinseeker Golf
1956 East McFadden Avenue
Santa Ana, CA 92705-4706
714-979-4500
Number of Employees: 60

Tom Eastman, *Manager*

Rancho Bernardo Golf Club
12280 Greens East Road
San Diego, CA 92128
619-487-1134

Brad Lancaster, *Pro*

Rancho Carlsbad Country Club
5200 El Camino Real
Carlsbad, CA 92008
760-438-1772
Number of Employees: 15

Howard T. Fujimoto, *Pro*

Ray Cook Golf Co.
1396 Poinsettia Avenue
Vista, CA 92083
760-599-8000

Bob Bauer, *President*

RC Designs International
17391 Murphy Avenue
Irvine, CA 92614-5919
949-474-7272
Number of Employees: 75

Raul Rubalcava, *President*

Renaissance Golf Products
5812 Machine Drive
Huntington Beach, CA 92649
801-501-0200
Number of Employees: 15

Ken Craig, *President*
Janet Gardner, *Director of Personnel*

San Diego Chargers
9449 Friars Road
San Diego, CA 92108
619-280-2111
Web Address: www.nfl.com/chargers

San Diego Chargers Football
9449 Friars Road
Jack Murphy Stadium
San Diego, CA 92108
619-280-2111

San Diego Country Club
88 L Street
Chula Vista, CA 91911
619-422-8895
Number of Employees: 70

Tom Hust, *Pro*
Steve Nordstrom, *General Manager*

San Diego Padres
P.O. Box 2000
San Diego, CA 92108
619-283-4494

San Diego Padres Baseball Club
PO Box 122000
San Diego, CA 92112
619-283-4494
Web Address: www.padres.com
Eva Altamirano, *Human Resource Manager*

San Diego Zoo/Wild Animal Park
2920 Zoo Drive
San Diego, CA 92103
619-231-1515
Job Hotline: 619-557-3968
Web Address: www.sandiegozoo.org
Number of Employees: 1600

Doug Meyers, *Executive Director*

Jo Dean Parish, *Employment Administrator*
Send resumes to: PO Box 120551; San Diego, CA 92112-0551

San Luis Rey Downs Country Club
31474 Golf Club Drive
Bonsall, CA 92003
760-758-9699
Number of Employees: 200
Greg Milligan, *Pro*

San Vicente Inn & Golf Club
24157 San Vicente Road
Ramona, CA 92065
760-789-3477
Number of Employees: 65

Bob Harchut, *Pro*
Sandy Law, *Human Resources Manager*

Santa Anita Racetrack
285 West Huntington Drive
Arcadia, CA 91007
818-574-7223
Web Address: www.santaanita.com

Sea World
500 Sea World Drive
San Diego, CA 92109
619-226-3901
Job Hotline: 619-226-3861
Web Address: www.seaworld.com
Bill Davis, *General Manager*
Elizabeth Tolmei, *Employment Supervisor*

Shadowridge Country Club
1980 Gateway Drive
Vista, CA 92083
760-727-7700
Number of Employees: 150
Jim LeTouneau, *Pro*
Joan Pruett, *Human Resources Manger*

Singing Hills Country Club & Resort
3007 Dehesa Road
El Cajon, CA 92019
619-442-3425
Number of Employees: 250
Tom Addis III, *Pro*
Harry Argerenos, *Human Resource Supervisor*

Six Flags Magic Mountain
26101 Magic Mountain Parkway
Valencia, CA 91385
805-255-4100
Job Hotline: 805-255-4800
Web Address: www.sixflags.com

Slotline Golf
5252 McFadden Avenue
Huntington Beach, CA 92649
714-898-2888
Number of Employees: 30
Clovis Duclos, *President*

Steele Canyon Golf & Country Club
3199 Stonefield Drive
Jamul, CA 91935
619-441-6900
Web Address: www.steelecanyon.com
Number of Employees: 55

Sue Allan, *Pro*
Buzz Colton, *Office Manager*

Stewart Surfboards
2102 South El Camino Real
San Clemente, CA 92672-3250
714-492-1151
Number of Employees: 20

Bill Stewart, *Co-Owner*

Stoneridge Country Club
17166 Stoneridge Country Club Lane
Poway, CA 92064
858-487-2117
Number of Employees: 90

Ben Stewart, *Pro & Hiring Contact*
Human Resources: 858-487-2138

Taylor Made Adidas Golf
5545 Fermi Court
Carlsbad, CA 92008
760-931-1991
Web Address: www.taylormadegolf.com
Number of Employees: 400

Mark King, *President*
Jan Strickland, *Director of Human Resources*

Tectrix Fitness Equipment
68 Fairbanks
Irvine, CA 92618-1602
949-380-8082
Web Address: www.tectrix.com
Number of Employees: 131

Mike Benjamin, *President & COO*

The California Angels
2000 Gene Autry Way, Anaheim Stadium
Anaheim, CA 92806
949-940-2000
Job Hotline: 818-558-2222
Web Address: www.anaheimangels.com
Number of Employees: 200

Tony Tavares, *President*
Jenny Price, *Director of Personnel*

The Vineyard at Escondido
925 San Pasqual Road
Escondido, CA 92025
760-735-9545
Number of Employees: 60

Kevin Barry, *Pro*
Mark Hoesing, *General Manager*

Titleist - Golf Club Operations
1021 West Mission
Escondido, CA 92025
Web Address: www.titleist.com

Torrey Pines Golf Course
11480 North Torrey Pines Road
La Jolla, CA 92037
619-552-1784
Job Hotline: 619-236-6467
Number of Employees: 70

Joe DeBock, *Pro & Hiring Contact*

Unifiber Corp.
3855 Ruffin Road
San Diego, CA 92123
619-576-8080

Richard L. Tennent, *CEO*

Unisen
14410 Myford Road
Irvine, CA 92606
949-669-1660
Web Address: www.startrack.com
Number of Employees: 200

James McPartland, *President*

United Leisure Corporation
1081 Magnolia
Fountain Valley, CA 92708
714-837-1200
Number of Employees: 15

Harry Shuster, *President*

Universal Studios Hollywood theme Park
100 Universal City Plaza
Universal City, CA 91608
818-508-9600
Web Address: www.universalstudios.com

University Athletic Club
1701 Quail Street
Newport Beach, CA 92660-2753
949-752-7903
Number of Employees: 30

Clark Graves, *President*

US Diversified
PO Box 6476
Laguna Niguel, CA 92607-6476
714-661-8200
Number of Employees: 87

Jeff Shirkani, *President*

Vista Valley Country Club
29354 Vista Valley Drive
Vista, CA 92084
760-758-5275
Number of Employees: 50
Grant Garrison, *Pro*
John Sullivan, *General manager*

Warner Springs Ranch
31652 Highway 79
Warner Springs, CA 92086
760-782-4200
Job Hotline: 760-782-4234
Web Address: www.wsranchaol.com
Number of Employees: 120
Dave Waymire, *General Manager*
Kimberly Stanley, *Director of Human Resources*

Wild Rivers Waterpark
8770 Irvine Center Drive
Irvine, CA 92618-4200
949-768-6014
Number of Employees: 350
Dale Dawes, *CEO*

Yamaha Corporation of America
6600 Orangethorpe Avenue
Buena Park, CA 90620-1396
714-522-9011
Web Address: www.yamaha.com
Number of Employees: 300
Noriyuki Egawa, *President*
Gil Honeycutt, *Director of Personnel*

Further References

• Associations •

American Football Coaches Association
5900 Old McGregor Road
Waco, TX 76712
817-776-5900

American Golf Association
P.O. Box 8606
Lexington, KY 40533
606-278-7095

American Junior Golf Association
2415 Steeplechase Lane
Roswell, GA 30076
404-998-4653
Web Address: www.igolf.com

American Resort Development Association (ARDA)
1220 L Street, N.W., Suite 510
Washington, D.C. 20005
202-371-6700
Web Address: www.arda.org

American Ski Association
P.O. Box 480067
910 15th Street, Suite 500
Denver, CO 80202
303-629-7669

Atlantic Coast Conference (ACC)
P.O. Drawer ACC
Greensboro, NC 27419-6199
919-854-8787
Web Address: www.theacc.com

Big East Conference
56 Exchange Terrace
Providence, RI 02903
401-272-9108
Represents and sponsors athletes in the Big East region.

Big Eight Conference
104 West 9th Street, Suite 408
Kansas City, MO 64105
816-471-5088
Represents and sponsors athletes in the Big Eight Conference.

Big Ten Conference
1500 West Higgins Road
Park Ridge, IL 60068
847-696-1010
Web Address: www.bigten.org
Represents and sponsors athletes in the Big Ten Conference.

Big West Conference
2 Corporate Park, Suite 206
Irvine, CA 92714
714-261-2525
Represents and sponsors athletes in the Big West Conference.

College Football Association
6688 Gunpark Drive, Suite 201
Boulder, CO 80301
303-530-5566
Web Address:
www.chili.collegesports.news.com

Continental Basketball Association
701 Market Street, Suite 140
St. Louis, MO 63101-1824
303-331-0404

Eastern College Athletic Conference
1311 Craigville Beach Road
P.O. Box 3
Centerville, MA 02632
508-771-5060
Web Address: www.ecac.org
Represents and sponsors athletes in the mid-atlantic states and in the District of Columbia.

International Golf Association
7442 Jagger Court
Cincinnati, OH 45230
513-624-2100

International Lacrosse Federation
P.O. Box 1373
Piscataway, NJ 08854
908-445-4211

Ladies Professional Golf Association
2570 West International Speedway Boulevard
Suite B
Daytona Beach, FL 32114
904-254-8800
Web Address: www.lpga.com
Professional women golfers.

Metropolitan Collegiate Athletic Conference
2 Ravinia Drive, Suite 220
Atlanta, GA 30346
404-395-6444
Represents and sponsors athletes.

National Association of Basketball Coaches of the United States
9300 West 110th Street, Suite 640
Overland Park, KS 66210-1486
913-469-1001
College, university, junior college, and high school level baketball coaches

National Association of Intercollegiate Athletics
6120 South Yale, Suite 1450
Tulsa, OK 74136
918-494-8828
Web Address: www.naia.org
Promotes devlopment of intercollegiate athletic programs.

National Basketball Association
645 5th Avenue, 10th Floor
New York, NY 10022
212-826-7000
Web Address: www.nba.com
Professional Basketball teams.

National Collegiate Athletic Association (NCAA)
6201 College Boulevard
Overland Park, KS 66211
913-339-1906
Web Address: www.ncaa.org

National Football Foundation and Hall of Fame
1865 Palmer Avenue
Larchmont, NY 10538
914-834-0474
Honors the achievements of football players and coaches

National Football League
410 Park Avenue
New York, NY 10022
212-758-1500
Web Address: www.nfl.com

National Football League Alumni
6550 North Federal Highway, Suite 400
Fort Lauderdale, FL 33308-1400
305-492-1220
Web Address: www.nflalumni.com
Coaches, players and administrators who were involved with profesional football and who support and contribute time and money to communities and their youth programs.

National Football League Players Association
2021 L Street, N.W., 6th Floor
Washington, D.C. 20036
202-463-2200
Web Address: www.sigsysinc.com/refnfl.htm

National Recreation and Park Association
2775 South Quincy Street, Suite 300
Arlington, VA 22206
703-820-4940
Web Address: www.nrpa.org

Pacific 10 Conference
800 South Broadway, Suite 400
Walnut Creek, CA 94596
510-932-4411
Web Address: www.pac-10.org
Represents and sponsers athletes in the PAC 10 Conference.

Professional Golfers' Association of America (PGA)
100 Avenue of Champions
Palm Beach Gardens, FL 33418
407-624-8400
Web Address: www.pga.cpm
Associated with professional golfers, tournaments, clubs, and courses.

Southeastern Conference (SEC)
2201 Civic Center Boulevard
Birmingham, AL 35203
205-458-3000
Web Address: www.sec.org
Represents and sponsers athletes in the SEC region.

Southern Conference
1 West Pack Square, NO. 1508
Asheville, NC 28801-3401
704-255-7872
Web Address: www.socon.org
Represents and sponsors athletes in the SC region.

Southwest Athletic Conference
P.O. Box 569420
Dallas, TX 75356
214-634-7353
Represents and sponsors athletes in the SWC region.

U.S.A. Basketball
5465 Mark Dabling Boulevard
Colorado Springs, CO 80918-3842
719-590-4800
Web Address: www.usabasketball.com

U.S. Skiing
P.O. Box 100
Park City, UT 84060
801-649-9090
Official organization for the governing of skiing within the U.S.

United States Club Lacrosse Association
2600 Whitney Avenue
Baltimore, MD 21215
410-235-8532

United States Golf Association (USGA)
P.O. Box 708
Far Hills, NJ 07931
908-234-2300
Web Address: www.usga.org
Acts as the governing organization for golf within the United States and conducts thirteen national championships annually.

United States Intercollegiate Lacrosse Association
P.O. Box 928
Lexington, VA 24450

United States Professional Tennis Association
1 USPTA Center
3535 Briarpark Drive
Houston, TX 77042
713-978-7782
Web Address: www.uspta.org
To promote tennis instruction in the U.S. whether professional or collegiate.

United States Tennis Association
70 West Red Oak Lane
White Plains, NY 80604
914-696-7000
Web Address: www.usta.com
Seeks to promote the development of tennis throughout the U.S.

United States Women's Lacrosse Association
P.O. Box 2178
Amherst, MA 01004
413-253-0328
Promotion of women lacrosse players

University Athletic Association
668 Mount Hope Avenue
Rochester, NY 14620
716-273-5881
Promotes athletic competition for Division III colleges and universities.

Western Athletic Conference
P.O. Box 372850
Denver, CO 80237-6850
303-795-1962
Web Address: www.wac.org
Represents collegiate athletes in WAC region.

Women's Basketball Coaches Association
4646 B Lawrenceville Highway
Lilburn, GA 30247
404-279-8027
Leader's in women's basketball, developed to promote a respectable and positive image.

World Amateur Golf Council (WAGC)
P.O. Box 708
Far Hills, NJ 07931-0708
908-234-2300

WTA Tour Players Association
133 1st Street, N.E.
St. Petersburg, FL 33701
813-895-5000

Travel, Transportation & Utilities

- Airline Companies
- Travel Agencies
- Shipping/Maritime
- Ground Transportation
- Utilities & Natural Resources
- Rail

Quick Reference

Air New Zealand
www.airnz.com

American Airlines
www.aa.com

Associated Travel International
www.traveltron.com

Australian New Zealand Direct Line
www.anzdl.com

Automobile Club of Southern California
www.aaa-calif.com

Burlington Air Express
www.baxworld.com

Carlson Wagonlit Travel
www.cwtonthegotravel.com

Circle International
www.circleintl.com

Comtrans
www.comtrans.com

Continental Airlines
www.flycontinental.com

First Class Travel Management
www.fctravel.com

Fullerton Municipal Airport
www.ci.fullerton.ca.us

Interstate Consolidation
www.icsla.com

Irvine Ranch Water District
www.irwd.com

Korean Air
www.koreanair.com

Maritz Travel Co.
www.maritz.com

Moulton Niguel Water District
www.mnwd.com

Municipal Water District of OC
www.mwdoc.com

Orange County Water District
www.ocwd.com

Plaza Travel
www.plazatravel.com

Pleasant Holidays
www.pleasantholidays.com

QST Travel
www.qsttravel.com

Service By Air
www.servicebyair.com

Southern California Edison
www.edisonx.com

Southern California Water Company
www.thegasco.com

Southwest Airlines
www.southwest.com

STA Travel
www.statravel.com

Sundance Travel
www.sundancetravel.com

Travel Store
www.travelstore.com

Uniglobe In-World Travel
www.uniglobe.com

World Travel Bureau
www.wtbtvl.com

20th Century Insurance
www.20thcenturyinsurance.com

Company Job Hotlines

Alaska Airlines
206-433-3230

Associated Travel International
800-969-255 x222

Automobile Club of Southern California
714-850-2888

Continental Airlines
800-444-8414 x6952

Delta Airlines
404-715-2501

Southern California Gas Co
909-394-3600

Southwest Airlines
602-389-3738

Trans World Airlines
757-892-8052

United Airlines
888-825-5627

US Airways
703-872-7499

AEI
8500 Osage Avenue
Los Angeles, CA 90045
310-216-6600
Job Hotline: 203-655-7900
Number of Employees: 200

Gary Butts, *Regional Manager*

Aer Travel
5465 Morehouse Drive, Suite 160
San Diego, CA 92121
619-455-5773

Gil Saidy, *President & Hiring Contact*

Aeromexico Airlines
3665 North Harbor Drive
San Diego, CA 92101
800-237-6639

Patricia Shaikh, *Station Manager*

Air Canada
5761 West Imperial Highway, Second Floor
Los Angeles, CA 90045
310-646-7470
Job Hotline: Ext 210
Number of Employees: 250

L. Miller, *Regional Sales Manager*
Ann Gordon, *Human Resources Representative*

Air New Zealand
1960 East Grand Avenue, Suite 900
El Segundo, CA 90245
310-648-7000
Job Hotline: 310-648-7110
Web Address: www.airnz.com
Number of Employees: 200

Peter Burn, *Regional Manager - Cargo*
Anne Cruti, *Human Resource Manager*

Air-Sea Forwarders
9009 La Cienega Boulevard
Inglewood, CA 90301
213-776-1611
Web Address: www.airseainc.com
Number of Employees: 60

Erwin Rautenberg, *President*

Alaska Airlines
3665 North Harbor Drive
San Diego, CA 92101
800-426-0333

Rick Hines, *Station Manager*

Alaska Airlines
6033 West Century Boulevard, Suite 985
Los Angeles, CA 90045
310-337-9512
Job Hotline: 206-433-3230
LaRue Sume, *District Sales Manager*

Albert Rebel & Associates
166 University Parkway
Pomona, CA 91768
909-594-6777
Number of Employees: 25

Carl A. Telles, *President*

All Around Travel
9050 Friars Road, Suite 101
San Diego, CA 92108
619-282-3030
Web Address: www.allaroundtravel.com
Number of Employees: 11

Leslie Johnson, *Branch Manager & Hiring Contact*

Alliance Logistics Resources
347 North Oak Street
Inglewood, CA 90302
310-412-1402
Number of Employees: 19

Sanford Forman, *President*
Sue Rubin, *Office Manager*

Altour International
11661 San Vincente Boulevard, Suite 900
Los Angeles,, CA 90049
310-571-3151
Number of Employees: 40

Barry Noskeau, *Executive VP*
Julie Valentine, *Manager*

America West Airlines
3665 North Harbor Drive
San Diego, CA 92101
800-235-9292

Murray Bauer, *Station Manager*

America West Airlines
4440 Von Karman Avenue
Newport Beach, CA 92660
949-548-8969
Web Address: www.americawest.com

American Airlines
222 North Sepulveda Boulevard, Suite 2100
El Segundo, CA 90245
310-648-6431
Job Hotline: 310-648-6320
Web Address: www.aa.com
Number of Employees: 300

William Kramer, *Regional Sales Manager*
Chris Ryan, *Director of Human Resources*

American Airlines/American Eagle
3707 North Harbor Drive
San Diego, CA 92101
800-433-7300

Noel Magee, *Station Manager*

American Chemical Society
Southern California Chapters
14934 South Figueroa Street
Gardena, CA 90248
310-327-1216

American Express Corporate Services
9191 Towne Centre Drive
San Diego, CA 92122
619-488-0326

Jennifer DeSanti, *Hiring Contact*

American Society of Travel Agents
7060 Hollywood Boulevard, Suite 614
Los Angeles, CA 90028
213-466-7717

American Trans Air
333 Hergenberger Road, Suite 515
Oakland, CA 94621
510-635-5866

Jack O'Brien, VP of Sales, *West Region*

American Travel Service
316 Mission Avenue
Oceanside, CA 92054
760-722-1218
Web Address: tvldave@axisinternet.com
Number of Employees: 5

David Hadsell, *President*

AmericanTours International
6053 West Century Boulevard, Suite 700
Los Angeles, CA 90045
310-641-9953
Job Hotline: Ext 312
Web Address: www.americantours.com
Number of Employees: 390

Noel Irwin-Hentschel, *CEO*
Jose Garcia, *Human Resource Director*

ANA Hallo Tours -USA
707 Wilshire Boulevard, Suite 4750
Los Angeles, CA 90017
213-622-0186
Number of Employees: 30

Yuichi Kobayashi, *Executive VP*
Jeannie Kasahara, *Director of Human Resources*

Andante Travel of Newport
120 Newport Center Drive, Suite 140
Newport Beach, CA 92660-6909
949-759-1471
Eugene E. Koch, *President*

APA Travel Center
9300 Wilshire Boulevard
Beverly Hills, CA 90212
310-246-5900
Number of Employees: 49
Karen Canter, *Executive VP & Co-owner*

Ashland Chemical Company
6608 East 26th Street
Los Angeles, CA 90040
213-724-2440
Web Address: www.ashchem.com

Associated Travel International
1241 East Dyer Road, Suite 110
Irvine, CA 92705
949-549-2552
Job Hotline: 800-969-255 x222
Web Address: www.traveltron.com
Number of Employees: 75

Thom Nulty, *President*
Diana Stacey, *Human Resources Director*

Associated Travel International
5880 Oberlin Drive, Suite 101
San Diego, CA 92121
619-457-3350
Number of Employees: 240

Jaime Jecker, *Sales Manager*

Australian New Zealand Direct Line
3601 South Harbor Boulevard
Santa Ana, CA 92704-6947
714-424-0400
Web Address: www.anzdl.com
Number of Employees: 150

Automobile Club of Southern California
3333 Fairview Road
Costa Mesa, CA 92626
949-741-3111
Job Hotline: 714-850-2888
Web Address: www.aaa-calif.com
Number of Employees: 2,000

Thomas McKernan Jr., *President*
Diane Grice, *Human Resources Manager*

Boeing Travel Co.
3855 Lakewood Boulevard
Long Beach, CA 90846
562-593-4361
Number of Employees: 47

Dennis Hextell, *VP Business Development*

Bonneville Travel
3901 Westerly Place, Suite 101
Newport Beach, CA 92660-2306
949-476-8383
Number of Employees: 50

Gwen Henstredge, *Manager*

Branson Travel
1356 South Mission Road
Fallbrook, CA 92028
760-728-0444
Number of Employees: 10

Regina Grevatt, *Manager*

British Airways
841 Apollo Street, Suite 450
El Segundo, CA 90245
800-654-6132

Jake Warren, *VP of Sales, West*

BTI Americas
2100 West Orangewood Avenue, Suite 150
Orange, CA 92868-1950
619-702-9818
Number of Employees: 4000

BTI Americas
350 South Grand Avenue, Suite 3570
Los Angeles, CA 90071
213-626-2335
Number of Employees: 10

Phil Gaskins, *Vice President*
Mary Smith, *Office Manager*

Burlington Air Express
16808 Armstrong Avenue
Irvine, CA 92606
949-752-1212
Web Address: www.baxworld.com
Number of Employees: 5,200

Dennis Eittreim, *President*

Burlington Air Express
5500 West Century Boulevard
Los Angeles, CA 90045
Number of Employees: 170

S. Zarnowski, *Regional Director*

Cabrillo Travel Service
1357 Rosecrans Street
San Diego, CA 92106
619-224-2821
Number of Employees: 7
John L. Bateman, *President*

Carefree Travel
321 E Street
Chula Vista, CA 91910
619-426-6080

Carlson Wagonlit Travel
2107 North Broadway, Suite 309
Santa Ana, CA 92706-2634
714-834-1066
Web Address: www.cwtonthegotravel.com
Number of Employees: 15
George P. Kingston, *President*

Carlson Wagonlit Travel
10880 Wilshire Boulevard, Suite 1450
Los Angeles, CA 90027
310-786-7598
Number of Employees: 25
Jim Day, *Vice President*
Heidi Lasky, *Human Resource Representative*

Carlson Wagonlit Travel
2616 Hyperion Avenue
Los Angeles, CA 90027
909-476-0153
Number of Employees: 54

Colleen King, *Sales Manager*

Carlston Waserly Travel
5 Park Plaza
Irvine, CA 92614-5995
949-450-8550
Number of Employees: 36

Linda S. McIntosh, *CEO*

Circle International
901 West Hillcrest Boulevard
Inglewood, CA 90301
310-337-8100
Job Hotline: Ext 8101
Web Address: www.circleintl.com
Number of Employees: 90

Keith Dayton, *General Manager*
Patricia Shinn, *Human Resources Manager*

Classic Cruise & Travel
19720 Ventura Boulevard, Suite A
Woodland Hills, CA 91364
818-346-8747
Number of Employees: 40

Penny Entin, *President*
Susan Voss, *Office Manager*

Classic Travels
936 North Brand Boulevard
Glendale, CA 91202
818-240-3313
Number of Employees: 9

Jennifer Herzer, *President*
Dana Gerken, *Office Manager*

Comtrans
20651 Prism Place
Lake Forest, CA 92630-7803
714-455-9890
Web Address: www.comtrans.com
Number of Employees: 20

Wayne M. Curtis, *President*

Continental Airlines
3665 North Harbor Drive
San Diego, CA 92101
619-232-9155
Job Hotline: 800-444-8414 x6952
Web Address: www.flycontinental.com
Number of Employees: 2,000

Dave Freeland, *Station Manager*

Continental Airlines
7300 World Way West, Suite G130
Los Angeles, CA 90045
310-271-8733
Job Hotline: 713-324-5000
Web Address: www.continental.com

Ted Brady, *Divisional Sales Director*
Corporate Headquarters: 1600 Smith; PO Box 4607; Houston, TX 77002

Coppersmith
2041 Rosecrans Avenue, Suite 300
El Segundo, CA 90245
310-607-8000
Web Address: www.coppersmith.com
Number of Employees: 55

Lew Coppersmith, *CEO*
Jeff Coppersmith, *President*
Carla Bletterman, *Administrative Assistant*

Costa Travel
10150 Sorrento Valley Road, Suite 312
San Diego, CA 92121
619-453-7747

Danzas Corporation
3700 Redondo Beach Avenue
Redondo Beach, CA 90278
310-643-2727
Number of Employees: 84

Steve Olsen, *Regional Vice President*
Leesa Lehua, *Office Manager*

Delta Air Lines
3707 North Harbor Drive
San Diego, CA 92101
800-221-1212

Bill Myers, *Station Manager*

Delta Air Lines
18601 Airport Way #211
Santa Ana, CA 92707-5200
949-252-5911
Number of Employees: 60000
Renae Ruso, *Human Resources Manager*

Delta Airlines
6150 West Century Boulevard
Los Angeles, CA 90045
310-216-2200
Job Hotline: 404-715-2501
Kevin Smith, *Regional Director of Sales*

Dependable Hawaiian Express
19201 Susana Road
Rancho Dominguez, CA 90220
310-537-2000
Number of Employees: 250
Brad Dechter, *President*
Anthony Culpepper, *Controller*
Lawanza Norris, *Human Resource Manager*

DHL Worldwide Express
17102 Newhope Street
Fountain Valley, CA 92708-4200
714-241-7421
Number of Employees: 10,000

Direct Travel of California
800 South Figueroa Street, Suite 600
Los Angeles, CA 90017
213-688-1105
Number of Employees: 5

Michael Edwards, *West Region VP of Operations*

Edison International
2244 Walnut Grove Avenue
Rosemead, CA 91770
818-302-2222
Web Address: www.sce.com

El Toro Water District
24251 Los Alisos Boulevard
Lake Forest, CA 92630
714-837-0660
Number of Employees: 59

William M. Semple, *Board Member*

Elsinore Aerospace Services
PO Box 2188
Santa Ana, CA 92707
714-263-5750
Number of Employees: 700

Pat Kenna, *President & CEO*
Maria Ortega, *Human Resources Director*

Emery Worldwide
3600 West Century Boulevard
Inglewood, CA 90303
310-672-8964
Web Address: www.emeryworld.com

Enserch Development Corp
611 Anton Boulevard #811
Costa Mesa, CA 92626
949-673-1317
Number of Employees: 40

EVA Airways
12440 East Imperial Highway, Suite 250
Norwalk, CA 90650
562-565-6000
Web Address: www.evair.com
Number of Employees: 341
William Pu, *Manager*
Chester Wang, *Human Resources Manager*

Expeditors International
5200 West Century Boulevard, 6th Floor
El Segundo, CA 90045
310-343-6200
Web Address: www.exp2.com
Number of Employees: 195
Eugene Alger, *Regional Vice President*

Exxon Corporation
225 West Hillcrest Drive
Thousand Oaks, CA 91360
805-494-2000
Web Address: www.exxon.com

Federal Express
9192 Kearney Villa
San Diego, CA 92123
619-295-5545
Web Address: www.fedex.com

Federal Express
333 South Grand Avenue
Los Angeles, CA 90007
213-687-9161
Web Address: www.fedex.com

First Class Travel Management
27156 Burbank
Foothill Ranch, CA 92610
949-829-5300
Web Address: www.fctravel.com
Number of Employees: 32

Steve Sedgwick, *President*

Fritz Companies
9800 La Cienega Boulevard, 12th Floor
Inglewood, CA 90301
310-410-6530
Job Hotline: 415-538-0383
Number of Employees: 219

Betty Burghard, *Senior Director*
Michelle Chavez, *Human Resources Manager*

Fullerton Municipal Airport
4011 West Commonwealth Avenue
Fullerton, CA 92833-2537
714-738-6323
Web Address: www.ci.fullerton.ca.us
Number of Employees: 5

Rod Probst, *Airport Manager*

Global Transportation Services
2641 Manhattan Beach Boulevard
Redondo Beach, CA 90278
310-536-9033
Web Address: www.global.com
Number of Employees: 36

W. Guy Fox, *Chairman*
Carl Livingston, *General Manager*
Sane Cabral, *Human Resource Manager*

Hawaiian Airlines
6033 West Century Boulevard, Suite 810
Los Angeles, CA 90045
310-215-1866

Glen Stewart, *VP of Sales and Marketing*

Interconex
17120 Valley View Avenue
La Mirada, CA 90638
562-921-0939
Number of Employees: 25

Joel Mariano, *General Manager*

Interstate Consolidation
5800 East Sheila Street
Commerce, CA 90040
213-720-1771
Web Address: www.icsla.com
Number of Employees: 110

G. Goldfein, *President*
Patricia Hamrick, *Human Resources Director*

Irvine Ranch Water District
PO Box 57000
Irvine, CA 92619-7000
949-453-5300
Web Address: www.irwd.com
Number of Employees: 230

Janet Wells, *Personnel Director*

It's A Small World Travel
7744 Fay Avenue
La Jolla, CA 92037
619-459-0681

Joan Elder, *Hiring Contact*

Japan Airlines
300 Continental Boulevard, Suite 402
El Segundo, CA 90245
310-607-2300
Number of Employees: 160

Kohei Nishikawa, *Regional Manager*
Teruhisa Ishizawa, *Administrative Manager*

Japan Travel Bureau International
777 South Figueroa Street, Suite 4100
Los Angeles, CA 90017
213-687-9881
Number of Employees: 150

Takashi Murakami, *General Manager*
Alicia Turner, *Human Resources Supervisor*

JNR
2603 Main Street, 2nd Floor
Irvine, CA 92614-6232
949-476-2788
Number of Employees: 50

James G. Jalet, *President*

John Wayne Airport
3151 Airway Avenue, Suite K101
Costa Mesa, CA 92626-4625
949-252-5171
Number of Employees: 135

O.B. Schooley, *Airport Director*

Kahala Travel
3838 Camino del Rio North, Suite 300
San Diego, CA 92108
619-282-8300

Joyce L. Dent, *Hiring Contact*
Nancy Makay, *Hiring Contact*

Korean Air
6101 West Imperial Highway
Los Angeles, CA 90045
310-417-5200
Web Address: www.koreanair.com
Number of Employees: 300

J.J. Achoi, Senior VP, *North America*
K.S. Lee, *Vice President & General Manager*

Los Angeles County Metropolitan Transportaion Authority
425 South Main Street
Los Angeles, CA 90013
213-972-6000
Web Address: www.mta.net

Maritz Travel Co.
1515 West 190th Street, Suite 310
Gardena, CA 90248
310-217-4700
Job Hotline: 818-226-3006
Web Address: www.maritz.com
Number of Employees: 20

Steve Olman, *VP & General Manager*
Thersa Wray, *Office Administrator*

Maritz Travel Co.
6330 Variel Avenue, Suite 201
Woodland Hills, CA 91367
818-226-3000
Web Address: www.maritz.com
Number of Employees: 20

Steve Olman, *VP & General Manager*
Thersa Wray, *Office Administrator*

Metalclad Corporation
2 Corporate Plaza, Suite 125
Newport Beach, CA 92660
949-719-1234
Number of Employees: 75

Grant S. Kesler, *President*
Heather McGuigan, *Director of Personnel*
Environmental company which conducts waste treatment operations in Mexico and asbestos removal and insulation installation in the US. In a joint venture with Browning-Ferris' -BFI- BFI-Omega, Metalclad collects, transports, and treats waste in Guadalajara, Mexico City, Veracruz, and other Mexican cities.

Mexicana Airlines
9841 Airport Boulevard, Suite 220
Los Angeles, CA 90045

310-646-0401
Job Hotline: 31-258-03801
Web Address: www.mexicana.com
Number of Employees: 225
Carlos De Uriarte, *V. P., West Region*
Lourdes Richter, *Personnel Manager*

Mill-Run Travel
1801 Avenue of the Stars, Suite 1001
Los Angeles, CA 90067
310-553-2602
Number of Employees: 8

Bichara Accad, *Manager*

Moulton Niguel Water District
27500 La Paz Road
Laguna Niguel, CA 92677
949-831-2500
Web Address: www.mnwd.com
Number of Employees: 100

Larry R. Lizotte, *President*

Municipal Water District of OC
10500 Ellis Avenue
Fountain Valley, CA 92728-0895
714-963-3058
Web Address: www.mwdoc.com
Number of Employees: 25

Dee Wennerstrom, *Manager*

National Association of Business Travel Agents
3255 Wilshire Boulevard, Suite 1514
Los Angeles, CA 90010
213-382-3355

Nippon Express USA
970 Francisco Street
Torrance, CA 90502
310-532-6300
Number of Employees: 52

K. Kumagai, *Regional VP*
Larry Okasaki, *Human Resources Manager*

Norman Krieger
5761 West Imperial Highway
Los Angeles, CA 90045
310-215-0071
Web Address: www.nki.com
Number of Employees: 50

Robert Krieger, *President*
Bridgette Hanna, *Human Resource Manager*

Northwest Airlines
3707 North Harbor Drive
San Diego, CA 92101
800-225-2525

Cyndi Sticka, *Station Manager*

Northwest Airlines
11101 Aviation Boulevard, Suite 200
Los Angeles, CA 90045
310-646-0766

Fred Arnold, *Regional Director of Sales*

Occidental Petroleum
10889 Wilshire Boulevard
Los Angeles, CA 90024
213-879-1700
Web Address: www.oxy.com

Omega World Travel
13191 Crossroads Parkway North, Suite 145
Concourse Level
City of Industry, CA 91746
562-692-1313
Web Address: www.owt.net
Number of Employees: 9

De Anna Wertz, *West Coast Region Manager*

Orange County Transportion Authority
550 South Main Street
Orange, CA 92613
714-560-6282
Web Address: www.octa.net

Orange County Water District
10500 Ellis Avenue
Fountain Valley, CA 92708
714-378-3200
Web Address: www.ocwd.com
Number of Employees: 190

Phillip L. Anthony, *President*

Plaza Travel
16545 Ventura Boulevard, Suite 17
Encino,, CA 91436
818-990-4053
Web Address: www.plazatravel.com
Number of Employees: 39

Nobby Orens, *President*
Steve Orens, *Human Resources Manager*
Carol Orens, *Human Resources Manager*

Pleasant Holidays
2404 Townsgate Road
Westlake Village, CA 91361
818-991-3390
Web Address: www.pleasantholidays.com
Number of Employees: 350

Edward Hogan, *CEO*
Ronald Heuer, *President*
Christine Bogdan, *Senior Director of Personnel*

Qantas Airways
841 Apollo Street, Suite 400
El Segundo, CA 90245
310-726-1431

Job Hotline: Ext 11462
Number of Employees: 200
Scott Merrin, *Manager/Western USA*
Wally Mariani, *Regional General Manager*
Marie Quarles, *Human Resource Manager*

QST Travel
17890 Sky Park Circle
Irvine, CA 92614-6401
949-660-9200
Web Address: www.qsttravel.com
Number of Employees: 100

Mike Dorman, *Owner*

Rainbow Travel
5500 Grossmont Center Drive
La Mesa, CA 92071
619-464-5345

Phyllis Dorfman, *Hiring Contact*

Reno Air
3707 North Harbor Drive, Suite 102
San Diego, CA 92101
619-231-7355

G. Dan McCauley, Sales Manager, *Southern California*

Rosenbluth International
300 North Continental Boulevard, Suite 450
El Segundo, CA 90245
310-535-2900
Job Hotline: 909-471-5299
Web Address: www.rosenbluth.com
Number of Employees: 18

Mike Difisso, *General Manager*
Scott Mazo, *Human Resources Manager*

San Diego Gas & Elecric Company
8306 Century Park Court
San Diego, CA 92123
619-696-2034
Job Hotline: 858-654-1600
Web Address: www.sdge.com
Number of Employees: 3200
Fax resumes to: 858-654-1515

San Diego Gas & Electric Co
662 Camino De Los Mares
San Clemente, CA 92673-2827
714-361-8014
Number of Employees: 3900

San Diego Transit Corporation
100 16th Street
San Diego, CA 92101
619-238-0100

Santa Fe Pacific Pipeline
1350 North Main Street
Orange, CA 92867-3435
714-538-5227
Number of Employees: 439

Santa Margarita Water District
26111 Antonio Parkway
Rancho Santa Margarita, CA 92688-5505
949-459-6400
Number of Employees: 115

Betty Johnson, *Human Resource Manager*

Schenker International
600 Allied Way
El Segundo, CA 90245
310-607-2054
Web Address: www.shenkerusa.com
Number of Employees: 31

Luis Rodrigues, *Branch Manager*

Seino America
8728 Aviation Boulevard
Inglewood, CA 90301
310-215-0500
Job Hotline: 310-337-3639
Number of Employees: 28

Morcuni Fuma, *President*
Rose Bush, *Human Resource Manager*

Service By Air
5343 West Imperial Highway, Suite 500
Los Angeles, CA 90045
310-419-1000
Job Hotline: 800-243-5545
Web Address: www.servicebyair.com
Number of Employees: 30

Bryan Hicks, *VP Corporate Development*

Singapore Airlines
5670 Wilshire Boulevard, Suite 1800
Los Angeles, CA 90036
213-934-8833
Number of Employees: 150

Lean Kian Hai, VP, *Southwest*
Jullian Meddian, *Human Resources Manager*

Skywest
600 World Way
Los Angeles, CA 90045
310-646-0096
Job Hotline: 800-443-4952 x3370
Number of Employees: 160

Terry Bais, *Station Manager*
Kara Lee, *Human Resource Director*

SkyWest Airlines
3707 North Harbor Drive
San Diego, CA 92101
800-453-9417

Julie Asing, *Station Manager*

South Coast Water District
PO Box 30205
Laguna Niguel, CA 92607-0205

949-499-4555
Number of Employees: 46
Eric Jessen, *President*

Southern California Edison
14155 Bake Parkway
Irvine, CA 92618-1818
949-458-4413
Web Address: www.edisonx.com
Number of Employees: 17,000

Southern California Edison
1325 South Grand Avenue
Santa Ana, CA 92705-4406
714-973-5633
Number of Employees: 17000

Southern California Gas Co
PO Box 3334
Anaheim, CA 92803-3334
714-634-3106
Job Hotline: 909-394-3600
Number of Employees: 8000

Southern California Gas Company
555 West 5th Street
Los Angeles, CA 90013
213-244-1200
Job Hotline: 213-244-1234
Web Address: www.socalgas.com

Southern California Water Co.
630 East Foothill Boulevard
San Dimas, CA 91773
909-394-3600
Job Hotline: 909-394-3600
Web Address: www.scwater.com
Number of Employees: 70

Floyd Wicks, *President*

Southern California Water Company
1920 West Corporate Way
Anaheim, CA 92801-5373
714-535-7711
Web Address: www.thegasco.com
Number of Employees: 368

Southwest Airlines
1081 Camino del Rio South, Suite 223
San Diego, CA 92108
800-435-9792

Bruce Bennett, *Station Manager*

Southwest Airlines
265 South Randolph Avenue, Suite 125
Brea, CA 92821-5754
714-256-4911
Web Address: www.iflyswa.com

Sue Rosales, *Manager*

Southwest Airlines
5777 West Century Boulevard, Suite 1190
Los Angeles, CA 90045
310-215-5829
Job Hotline: 602-304-3900
Web Address: www.southwest.com

Anastasia Albanese-O'Neill, *District Marketing Manager*

STA Travel
5900 Wilshire Boulevard, Suite 2100
Los Angeles, CA 90036
213-937-1150
Web Address: www.statravel.com
Number of Employees: 35

Nick Thomas, *President*
Julie Bartholic, *Human Resources Director*

Sundance Travel
19800 Macarthur Boulevard, Suite 100
Irvine, CA 92612-2426
949-453-8687
Web Address: www.sundancetravel.com
Number of Employees: 200
Scott H. Shadrick, *President*
Judy Graven, *Human Resources Manager*

Sundance Travel
8935 Towne Center Drive, Suite 107
La Jolla, CA 92122
858-457-0991
Web Address: www.sundance.com
Number of Employees: 8
Cheri Saunders, *Director of Human Resources*
Tom Livermore, *President*

Target Airfreight
3460 Wilshire Boulevard, Suite 700
Los Angeles, CA 90010
213-387-6666
Web Address: www.ipacsnet.com/target

Texaco
9966 San Diego Mission Road
San Diego, CA 92108
619-283-7376
Web Address: www.texaco.com

The Gas Company
PO Box 3334
Anaheim, CA 92803-3334
714-634-3202
Job Hotline: 213-244-1234
Number of Employees: 710

The Travel Group
928 Fort Stockton Drive
San Diego, CA 92103
619-220-0880
Number of Employees: 15
Ron Baker, *Owner*
Thelma Rickett, *Manager*

Top Flight Travel
2707 Congress Street, Suite 1-H
San Diego, CA 92110
619-299-3005
Web Address: www.etopflight.com
Number of Employees: 12

Scott Borden, *Hiring Contact/Owner*
Vivian Kennson, *Human Resource Manager*

Total Transportation Concept
813 Arbor Vitae
Inglewood, CA 90301
310-337-0515
Number of Employees: 10

James DeArruda, *President*

Trans World Airlines
3665 North Harbor Drive
San Diego, CA 92101
800-221-2000

Don Liebbrandt, *Station Manager*

Trans World Airlines
7001 World Way West, Suite 311
Los Angeles, CA 90009
310-646-3440
Web Address: www.twa.com
Number of Employees: 200

Dale Faulstich, *Station Manager*

Travel 800/1-800-FLY CHEAP
3530 Camino del Rio North, Suite 300
San Diego, CA 92108
619-624-2000
Number of Employees: 200

Susan Parker, *President & Hiring Contact*

Travel Connection
485 East 17th Street, Suite 102
Costa Mesa, CA 92627-3265
949-631-5240
Number of Employees: 40

Travel Connoisseur
1011 Camino del Rio South, Suite 100
San Diego, CA 92108
619-294-2444
Number of Employees: 125

Laurence Skelly, *President & Hiring Contact*

Travel Headquarters
9665 Chesapeake Drive, Suite 360
San Diego, CA 92123
619-541-1710
Number of Employees: 10

James McCormack, *Owner*
Diane Mack, *Office Manager*

Travel Store
11601 Wilshire Boulevard
Los Angeles, CA 90025
310-575-5540
Job Hotline: Ext 9150
Web Address: www.travelstore.com
Number of Employees: 40
Wido Schaefer, *President*
Osvaldo Ramos, *Human Resource Director*

Traveltrust Corp.
973-A Loma Santa Fe Drive
Solana Beach, CA 92075
619-792-4600
Number of Employees: 50
Richard Meyerson, *Owner*
Jill Orr, *General Manager*

Tri-Marine International
150 West 7th Street, Suite 205
San Pedro, CA 90731
310-548-6245
Number of Employees: 23
Renato Curto, *President*
Rene Avendano, *Vice President & Director of Personnel*

Tricor America/Tricor International
12441 Eucalyptus Avenue
Hawthorne, CA 90250
310-215-5600
Number of Employees: 101
C. Johnson, *Sales Executive*
Sherry Lopez, *Office Manager*

Uniglobe In-World Travel
15901 Hawthorne Boulevard, Suite 120
Lawndale, CA 90260
714-891-8200
Web Address: www.uniglobe.com
Number of Employees: 20

Jay C. Risher, *President*

Uniglobe Vinyard Travel
1310 East Valley Parkway, Suite A-2
Escondido, CA 92027
760-741-6667
Web Address: www.vinyard@uniglobe.com
Number of Employees: 20
John Nigro, *President*

Union Carbide Corporation
PO Box 5068
Costa Mesa, CA 92628
949-662-4300
Web Address: www.unioncarbide.com

United Airlines
3665 North Harbor Drive #223
San Diego, CA 92101
800-241-6522

Jill Sheffield, *Station Manager*

United Airlines
18601 Airport Way #235
Santa Ana, CA 92707-5200
714-252-5700
Number of Employees: 82,160

United Parcel Service
1331 Vernon Avenue
Anaheim, CA 92805
714-491-7000
Web Address: www.ups.com

Unitrans International Corp.
709 South Hindry Avenue
Inglewood, CA 90301
310-410-7676
Number of Employees: 35
Fred Saxer, *President*

Unocal Corp.
2141 Rosecrans Avenue, Suite 4000
El Segundo, CA 90245
310-726-7600
Job Hotline: Ext 7637
Web Address: www.unocal.com
Number of Employees: 1,500
Roger Beach, *CEO*
David Duamont, *VP of Human Relations*
Carl McAulay, *Human Resource Manager*

USAirways
3665 North Harbor Drive
San Diego, CA 92101
800-428-4322
Nancie Carroll, *Station Manager*

Vandair Freight Systems
201 West Carob Street
Compton CA 90220
310-322-8242
Web Address: www.targetlogistics.com
Number of Employees: 5
Marcel van der Sluys, *President*
Rosalie Costales, *Human Resource Manager*

West Coast Charters
19711 Campus Drive #200
Santa Ana, CA 92707-5203
949-852-8340
Number of Employees: 45
Gary Standel, *President*

Yellow Freight Systems
1955 East Washington Boulevard
Los Angeles, CA 90021
213-742-0511
Web Address: www.yellowfreight.com

Yorba Linda Water District
4622 Plumosa Drive
Yorba Linda, CA 92886-0309
714-777-3018
Number of Employees: 54
Sterling Fox, *President*

Southern California Job Source

OFFERS THOUSANDS OF WEB SITES

FOR ADDITIONAL

INDUSTRY ASSOCIATIONS &

PUBLICATIONS WITH

WEB SITE ADDRESSES

& JOB HOTLINES, VISIT

www.JobSourceNetwork.com

Benjamin Scott Publishing
Pasadena, California

Further References

• Associations •

Air Transport Association of America
1301 Pennsylvania Avenue, N.W., Suite 1100
Washington, D.C. 20004
202-626-4000
Web Address: www.air-transport.org

Airline Pilots Association
1625 Massachusetts Avenue, N.W.
Washington, D.C. 20003
202-797-4033
Web Address: www.alpa.org

American Bus Association
1100 New York Avenue, N.W., Suite 1050
Washington, D.C. 20005
202-842-1645

American International Automotive Dealers Association
99 Canal Center Plaza, Suite 500
Alexandria, Virginia 22314
703-519-7800
Web Address: www.aiada.org
Works to preserve free market for automobiles and promote industry.

American Public Gas Association
11094D Lee Highway
Fairfax, Virginia 22030
703-352-3890
Web Address: www.apga.org
Association of public gas providers.

American Public Power Association
2301 M Street, N.W.
Washington, D.C. 20037
202-467-2900
Web Address: www.appanet.org
Association of municipally owned utilities.

American Resort Development Association (ARDA)
1220 L Street, N.W., Suite 510
Washington, D.C. 20005
202-371-6700
Web Address: www.arda.org

American Society of Travel Agents
1101 King Street
Alexandria, Virginia 22314
703-739-2782
Web Address: www.astanet.com
Promotes travel and image of agents.

American Trucking Association
2200 Mill Road
Alexandria, Virginia 22314
703-838-1700
Web Address: www.truckline.com
Works to influence government decisions and promote efficiency.

Aviation Maintenance Foundation
P.O. Box 2826
Redmond, Washington 98073
206-828-3917
Improvement of industry through education and research.

Institute of Transportation Engineers
525 School Street, S.W., Suite 410
Washington, D.C. 20024
202-554-8050
Web Address: www.ite.org
Representation and education of transport engineers.

National Air Transportation Association
4226 King Street
Alexandria, Virginia 22302
703-845-9000
Represents interests of general aviation companies.

National Motor Freight Traffic Association
2200 Mill Road
Alexandria, Virginia 22314
703-838-1810
Web Address: www.-erols.com/nmfta
Promotes professionalism and safety.

Professional Aviation Maintenance Association
500 NW Plaza, Suite 1016
St. Ann, Missouri 63074
Pursues safety and professionalism.

Travel Industry Association of America
1100 New York Avenue, NW, Suite 450
Washington, D.C. 20006
202-408-8422
Web Address: www.tia.org
Representation and promotion of travel industry.

• Publications •

Business Travel News
1515 Broadway, 32nd Floor
Manhasset, NY 11030
212-869-1300
Business travel newspaper.

Corporate Meetings & Incentives
80 Main Street
Maynard, MA 01754
508-897-5552
Web Address: www.aip.com
Aimed at senior level executives and meeting professionals in corporate America.

Moody's Transportation Manual
99 Church Street
New York, NY 10007
212-553-0300
Web Address: www.moody's.com

Successful Meetings
355 Park Avenue South
New York, NY 10010
212-592-6403
Web Address: www.successmtgs.com
Information on meetings, conventions, and travel industries.

Tour & Travel News
600 Community Drive
Manhasset, NY 11030
516-562-5000

Traffic World Magazine
1230 National Press Building
Washington, D.C. 20045
202-783-1101

Travel Agent
801 2nd Avenue, 12th Floor
New York, NY 10017
212-370-5050
Travel magazine.

Travel Weekly
500 Plaza Drive
Secaucus, NJ 07096
201-902-2000
Travel weekly.

Travelhost
10701 Stemmons Freeway
Dallas, TX 75220
214-556-0541
Web Address: www.travelhost.com
Magazine for business and vacation travelers.

Government

- **Federal**
- **State**
- **Local**

Southern California Job Source

Federal Government

- Action
- Administrative Office of the U.S. Courts
- Agency for International Development
- Central Intelligence Agency (CIA)
- Commission of Civil Rights
- Commodity Futures Trading Commission
- Consumer Product Safety Commission
- Department of Agriculture
- Department of Commerce
- Department of Defense
- Department of Education
- Department of Energy
- Department of Health & Human Services
- Department of Housing & Urban Development
- Department of Justice
- Department of Labor
- Department of State
- Department of Transportation
- Department of Treasury
- Department of Veterans Affairs
- Environmental Protection Agency
- Equal Employment Opportunity Commission
- Executive Office of the President
- Export-Import Bank of the United States
- Farm Credit Administration
- Federal Bureau of Investigation (FBI)
- Federal Communications Commission (FCC)
- Federal Deposit Insurance Corporation (FDIC)
- Federal Emergency Management Agency (FEMA)
- Federal Maritime Commission
- Federal Reserve
- Federal Retirement Thrift Investment Board
- Federal Trade Commission
- General Accounting Office (GAO)
- General Services Administration (GSA)
- Government Printing Office
- International Trade Commission
- Library of Congress
- National Aeronautics & Space Administration (NASA)
- National Archives & Records Administration
- National Credit Union Administration
- National Endowment for the Humanities
- National Labor Relations Board
- National Science Foundation
- National Security Agency
- Nuclear Regulatory Commission
- Office of Personnel Management
- Peace Corps
- Securities & Exchange Commission (SEC)
- Selective Service System
- Small Business Administration (SBA)
- Smithsonian Institution
- U.S. Information Agency
- Voice of America
- U.S. Postal Service

Federal Government

Today, more than ever before, it has become crucial that this country have the brightest, most talented and most committed leadership. The Federal Government, America's largest employer, hires more than 300,000 people each year across the Nation. No other employer can offer you the variety of career opportunities that are available in the Federal Government.

RICHARD B. POST, DIRECTOR
U.S. OFFICE OF PERSONNEL MANAGEMENT

Finding a Federal job resembles finding employment in the private sector. You need to look for a job in a field that interests you and then apply for that position. Although it may seem difficult in today's competitive job market, there are avenues for you to explore that can help you in the process of finding employment. If you are planning on pursuing a career in chemistry, engineering, or nursing, you are in luck because the Government is experiencing a shortage of these workers.

Where to start? Finding a job with the federal government has been greatly simplified in the past year. The first step is to find an opening which suits you. And with the help of a phone or the Internet, finding an opening is not a problem.

FINDING AN OPENING

Find a computer with Internet access and visit the job site of the Office of Personnel Management: www.usajobs.opm.gov. This site lists all available government jobs by category based upon the input you supply about yourself.

This input includes expected salary, experience, and desired geographic area. Click on one the available positions to get all the information you should need.

If no computer is available, pick up a phone and call the Career America Connection at (912) 757-3000. This service provides the same information through an electronic telephone system.

OBTAINING A VACANCY ANNOUNCEMENT

After finding an interesting opening, download the vacancy announcement on the website or leave your name and address on the telephone system to have the announcement mailed to you. The announcement will outline all relevant information about the position.

COMPLETING THE APPLICATION

You may apply for most jobs with a resume but the Optional Application for Federal Employment(OF-612) may also be used. The OF-612 may be downloaded from www.usajobs.opm.gov or ordered from the Career America Connection.

Follow all instructions if using the OF-612. And don't forget that this application may be filled out on-line. All the information needed is on the web site.

If sending your resume is easiest, include the following information:

1)Job Information-Announcement number, title, and grade

2)Personal Information-Complete name, social security number, address, day and evening phone numbers, and country of citizenship. Plus, include veterans' preference, reinstatement eligibility, and highest federal civilian grade held.

3)Education-Names, cities, and states of all high schools, colleges, and universities attended as well as degree information.

4)Work Experience-Title, duties, and employer information including salary and supervisory names.

5)Other Qualifications-Relevant courses and skills.

SALARY?

Federal Employees are paid in a number of different ways. Usually, the salary corresponds to the degree of skill and difficulty of the position and the GS-level assigned by the Government. The government tries to mirror private industry in its wage rates and tries to remain competitive by adjusting wage rates according to trends in the job market and cost of living.

A large percentage of Federal Government wages are set and outlined in the "general schedule (GS)," which covers most white-collar jobs listed from grades GS-1 to GS-15, each with a corresponding salary. Most entry-level candidates should expect to be hired at the GS-5 or GS-7 pay levels with a baccalaureate degree (see GS salary scale on page 240). With a Master's degree, you can possibly start as high as GS-9, with a doctorate, GS-11. With the approval of a manager within a respective agency, a Federal employee can make additional money working overtime, "premium pay" on holidays, and on weekends and nights.

BENEFITS?

Vacation & Sick Days: Paid vacation days are earned according to the length of time you've been with the Federal Government.

You earn 13 days a year for the first 3 years, 20 days a year for the next 12 years, and 26 days a year after 15 years, in addition to the 10 paid national holidays. 13 days of sick leave can also be earned each year with no limitation on the total accumulation.

HEALTH INSURANCE?

Federal employees are offered a variety of subsidized health plans administered by private insurers. Employees get to choose a plan which suits them best. Retirement Savings: The Government's pension program, the Federal Employees Retirement System matches employee's contributions up to 5% of their base pay.

WORK SCHEDULES

With management approval, Federal employees can choose from 4 types of work schedules; full-time, part-time, flexitime, and compressed. Flexitime allows employees to vary their arrival and departure times. This is a very popular choice in the summer. Compressed schedules allow employees to complete a work requirement of 80 hours in a two-week period in less than 10 working days.

JOB SEARCH AND STRATEGY

Many recent college graduates find employment with the Federal Government through the Administrative Careers with America Program (ACWA). This program offers over 100 different occupations in areas of varying interest.

Since many recent grads use this program to enter the Federal service, it is important to recognize the impact that your cumulative undergraduate GPS (grade point average) has on your hiring. A high graduating GPA (3.5 or better) will open many doors and in most be more lucrative for an applicant. There are certain occupations under ACWA, however, that do not require a written test, but rather specific college courses, such as economics and archaeology. There are fourteen other "non-test" occupations available. If you apply for "specialized occupations" for example engineering, you must complete a degree before you are hired.

In many cases, the Government agency you are applying to will make a background check of your personal history. Agencies that deal with highly classified information usually are the strictest about background checks. The Central Intelligence Agency, which works with issues involving defense and security, runs extensive tests on physical and psychiatric well-being, in addition to other background checks. The Defense Intelligence Agency also conducts thorough background checks.

A good way to get a position you are interested in is to have or make contacts who can help de-mystify the process of entering the civil service. Remember, it is important for anyone seeking Federal employment to get in touch with these contacts as they can help you with any questions or concerns that might arise.

CAREER OPTIONS

The Federal Government is always hiring, and looking for quality candidates. There are special programs, however, that promote job opportunities to special groups through affirmative action. One program that the Federal Government offers is the Federal Dual Opportunity Recruitment Program. This program works to incorporate qualified Hispanics, women, African Americans, Asians and others traditionally under-represented in the workplace. Another special program is the Hispanic Employment Program which helps Hispanics utilize their bilingual capabilities and other strengths in a career setting.

The Federal Women's Program helps to promote the role of women in the civil service. Veterans often receive preferential treatment in job placement and appointments under the Disabled Veterans' Program, which seeks to place veterans in the Federal service. In addition, the Federal Government actively seeks to place disabled persons in the workplace. In the cases of disabled candidates, special application and requirement standards may be used by the prospective agency.

The Federal Government also offers programs created to serve the needs of students. The Cooperative Education Program offers student employment opportunities to high school and college students.

The Cooperative Education Program combines periods of work with periods of study. You receive on-the-job work experience directly relating to your major and may be offered the opportunity to convert to a permanent position after graduation. If you are in the co-op program, you can choose from over 200 occupations.

Another interesting option available is the Federal Junior Fellowship Program. In this program, you are chosen directly out of high school to earn money for college while learning about careers through work experience. You are chosen based on several things: a high school diploma, a good record in school, financial need and the commitment to continue education through a bachelor's program or a community college/associate program. Most junior fellows work part-time during the year and full-time during vacations and summers. Pay, in most cases, is based on education and prior employment. Many junior fellows receive the same benefits as government employees: health insurance, training, financial aid for education and paid vacation days.

Another program available is the Student Volunteer Program. Students participating in this program utilize their volunteer work to gain contacts and acquire first-hand knowledge of the Federal service. It allows you the opportunity to explore careers choices. Requirements include enrollment in high school/trade school, college, or other recognized educational institutions and suitability for present job needs.

Designed for students finishing their graduate degrees, the Presidential Management Intern Program is a prestigious program offered by the Federal Government for those seeking a full-time career with the government. You must have a graduate degree and possess a strong interest in government and public service. The program requires that you be nominated by the dean of your graduate school and complete an application and participate in a series of interviews. If chosen as a finalist, you will serve for two years with a Federal agency after graduation, during which time you have the opportunity to take advantage of career development and rotational assignments, and are eligible for promotion and conversion to a permanent job.

The Federal Government also offers many job opportunities in the summer; These positions begin in the middle of May and are usually finished by the end of September.

FEDERAL GOVERNMENT PERSONNEL 24 HOUR HOTLINES

In addition to the FJIC, most all federal government agencies/excepted services offer their own job vacancy 24 Hour Hotlines. The Hotlines are as follows:

Agency for International Development
(202) 663-1396

Department of Agriculture
Agriculture Research Service
(301) 344-2288
Farmers Home Administration
(202) 245-5561
Food & Nutrition Service
(703) 756-3351
Forest-Service Management Staff
(703) 235-2730
Soil Conservation Service
(202) 720-6365

Department of Commerce
Office of the Secretary
(202) 482-5138
Bureau of The Census
TTD (301) 763-4944
International Trade Administration
(202) 482-5138
Nat'l Inst. of Standards & Technology
(301) 926-4851
TDD (301) 975-2039
Nat'l Oceanic & Atmospheric Ad.
(301) 713-0677
Office of Inspector General
TDD (202) 377-5897

Patent & Trademark Office
(703) 305-4221
TDD (703) 305-8586

Central Intelligence Agency (CIA)
(703) 351-2028

Department of Defense
Andrews AFB
(301) 981-5431
Department of the Army
(202) 695-9028
Consolidated Civilian Personnel Office
(202) 433-4931
Defense Investigative Service
(703) 325-6186
Department of the Navy
(703) 697-6181
Marine Corps Combat Dev. Command
(703) 640-2048
Naval Air Station
(301) 863-3545/3591
Naval Research Laboratory
(202) 767-3030
Defense Logistics Agency
(703) 274-7088
Defense Mapping Agency
(800) 777-6104

Department of Education
(202) 401-0559

Department of Energy
(202) 586-4333

Department of Labor
(202)219-8858

Department of Treasury
(202)622-1029

Environmental Protection Agency
(202) 260-5055

Equal Employment Opportunity
Commission
(202) 663-4264

Export-Import Bank
(202) 565-3946, #3

Federal Bureau of Investigation (FBI)
(202) 324-3674

Federal Communications Commission
(202) 418-0101

Federal Deposit Insurance Corporation
(202) 942-3428

Federal Emergency Management Agency
(202) 566-1600

Federal Energy Regulatory Commission
(202) 291-2990

Federal Labor Relations Authority
(202) 482-6690

Federal Trade Commission
(202) 326-2020

General Accounting Office
(202) 512-6092

General Services Administration
(202) 273-3524

Government Printing Office
(202) 512-0000

Department of Health & Human Services
Personnel   (202) 619-0257
Substance Abuse & Mental Health
  Services Administration
                   (301) 443-2282
Food & Drug Administration
                   (301) 443-1969

National Institute of Health
                   (301) 496-2403

Social Security Administration
(800) 772-1213

Department of Housing & Urban Development
(202) 708-3203

Department of Interior
Minerals Management Service
                   (703) 787-1402
National Park Service

(202) 619-7256
U. S. Geological Survey
                   (703) 648-7676

Department of Justice
Personnel   (202) 514-6818
Bureau of Prisons(202) 307-3135
Drug Enforcement Administration
                   (202) 307-4055
Immigration & Naturalization Service
                   (202) 514-2530
U.S. Marshals Service
                   (202) 307-9630

International Trade Commission
(202) 205-2651

Surface Transportation Board
(202) 565-1694

Merit Systems Protection Board
(202) 254-8013

NASA
Goddard Space Flight Center
                   (301) 286-5326

National Archives & Records Administration   (301) 713-6760

National Endowment for the Arts
(202) 682-5405

National Endowment for the Humanities
(202) 606-8281

National Labor Relations Board
(202) 273-3980

National Library of Medicine
(202) 496-6095

National Office of Management & Budget
(202) 395-5892

National Science Foundation
(703) 306-0080

Office of Personnel Management
(202) 606-2424

Peace Corps   (202) 818-9579
Securities & Exchange Commission
(202) 942-4150

Small Business Administration
(202) 205-6600

Smithsonian Institution
(202) 287-3102

U.S. Information Agency
(202) 619-4539

U.S. Postal Service
(800) 562-8777

Other institutions you might want to consider during your Federal Government job search are organizations and associations, for example:

American Federation of Government Employees
80 F Street, N.W.
Washington, D.C. 20001
(202) 737-8700

American Society for Public Administration
1120 G Street, N.W.
Washington, D.C. 20005
(202) 393-7878

Assembly of Governmental Employees
655 15th Street, N.W.
Washington, D.C. 20005
(202) 371-11123

Federally Employed Women
1400 I Street, N.W. Suite 425
Washington, D.C. 20005
(202) 898-0994

Federal Women's Interagency Board
P.O. Box 14166
Washington, D.C. 20005
(202) 267-3884

National Association of Government Employees
1313 L Street, N.W.
Washington, D.C. 20005
(202) 371-6644

National Federation of Federal Employees
1016 16th Street, N.W.
Washington, D.C. 20036
(202) 862-4400

Even though you automatically think the only place to find out about Federal jobs in is Washington, the OPM also has regional offices across the country which can give you information about jobs in other areas of the nation. To contact one nearest you, call or write to the following:

ATLANTA:
Office of Personnel Management
75 Spring Street
Atlanta, GA 30303-3109
(404) 331-3459

DALLAS:
Office of Personnel Management
1100 Commerce
Dallas, Texas 75250

PHILADELPHIA:
Office of Personnel Management
600 Arch Street
Philadelphia, PA 19106
(215) 597-4543

The only difference between applying to a federal job in Washington, D.C. and a ferderal job in California is the application process.

SALARY TABLE 2000-GS

2000 GENERAL SCHEDULE
INCORPORATING A 3.80% GENERAL INCREASE
Effective January 2000

Annual Rates by Grade and Step

	1	2	3	4	5	6	7	8	9	10	Within-Grade Increase Amounts
GS-1	$13,870	$14,332	$14,794	$15,252	$15,715	$15,986	$16,440	$16,900	$16,918	$17,351	VARIES
2	15,594	15,964	16,481	16,918	17,107	17,610	18,113	18,616	19,119	19,622	VARIES
3	17,015	17,582	18,149	18,716	19,283	19,850	20,417	20,984	21,551	22,118	$567
4	19,100	19,737	20,374	21,011	21,648	22,285	22,922	23,559	24,196	24,833	$637
5	21,370	22,082	22,794	23,506	24,218	24,930	25,642	26,354	27,066	27,778	$712
6	23,820	24,614	25,408	26,202	26,996	27,790	28,584	29,378	30,172	30,966	$794
7	26,470	27,352	28,234	29,116	29,998	30,880	31,762	32,644	33,526	34,408	$882
8	29,315	30,292	31,269	32,246	33,223	34,200	35,177	36,154	37,131	38,108	$977
9	32,380	33,459	34,538	35,617	36,696	37,775	38,854	39,933	41,012	42,091	$1,079
10	35,658	36,847	38,036	39,225	40,414	41,603	42,792	43,981	45,170	46,359	$1,189
11	39,178	40,484	41,790	43,096	44,402	45,708	47,014	48,320	49,626	50,932	$1,306
12	46,955	48,520	50,085	51,650	53,215	54,780	56,345	57,910	59,475	61,040	$1,565
13	55,837	57,698	59,559	61,420	63,281	65,142	67,003	68,864	70,725	72,586	$1,861
14	65,983	68,182	70,381	72,580	74,779	76,978	79,177	81,376	83,575	85,774	$2,199
15	77,614	80,201	82,788	85,375	87,962	90,549	93,136	95,723	98,310	100,897	$2,587

Federal Government Regional Offices

Bureau of Export Administration
3300 Irvine Avenue, Suite 345
Newport Beach, CA 92660

Bureau of the Census
15350 Sherman Way, Suite 300
Van Nuys, CA 91406

Defense Contract Audit Agency
16700 Valley View Avenue, Suite 300
La Mirada, CA 90638
714-228-7001

Robert W. Matter, *Director*

Department of Labor - Office of the Solicitor
300 North Los Angeles Street
Los Angeles, CA 90012

John C. Nangle, *Solicitor*

Department of Labor - Pension and Welfare Benefits Administration
790 East Colorado Boulevard
Pasadena, CA 91101

David Ganz, *Director*

Department of Labor - Worker's Compensation Programs
401 East Ocean Boulevard
Long Beach, CA 90807

Joyce Terry, *Director*

Department of State - Passport Office
11000 Wilshire Boulevard
Los Angeles, CA 90024
310-575-7070

Department of the Treasury - Internal Revenue Service
24000 Avila Road
Laguna Niguel, CA 92677

Jesse Cota, *Director*

Department of the Treasury - Internal Revenue Service
300 North Los Angeles Street
Los Angeles, CA 90012

Richard Orosco, *Director*

Department of the Treasury - Office of Enforcement
350 South Figueroa Street, Suite 800
Los Angeles, CA 90071

George Rodriguez, *Special Agent in Charge*

Department of the Treasury - US Customs Service
1 World Trade Center, Suite 705
Long Beach, CA 90831
310-980-3100

Rudy Camacho, *Director of Field Operations*

Department of the Treasury - US Customs Service
300 South Ferry Street
San Pedro, CA 90731
310-514-6001

John Heinrich, *Officer*

Department of the Treasury - US Customs Service
880 Front Street
San Diego, CA 92188
619-557-5455

Rudy Camacho, *Director of Field Operations*

Department of Transportation - Office of Hazardous Materials Safety
3200 Inland Empire Boulevard, Suite 230
Ontario, CA 91764

Anthony Smialek, *Director*

Department of Veteran's Affairs
11000 Wilshire Boulevard
Los Angeles, CA 90024

Stewart F. Liff, *Director*

Department of Veteran's Affairs
2022 Camino Del Rio North
San Diego, CA 92108

Patrick Nappi, *Director*

Department of Veteran's Affairs - Medical Center
2615 Clinton Avenue
Fresno, CA 93703

James DeNiro, *Director*

495

Department of Veteran's Affairs - Medical Center
5901 East 7th Street
Long Beach, CA 90822

Jerry Boyd, *Director*

Department of Veteran's Affairs - Medical Center
3350 La Jolla Village Drive
San Diego, CA 92161

Leonard C. Rogers, *Director*

Department of Veteran's Affairs - Outpatient Clinic
425 South Hill Street
Los Angeles, CA 90013

Lee Nackman, *Director*

Economic Development Office
11000 Wilshire Boulevard, Room 11105
Los Angeles, CA 90024

Equal Employment Opportunity Commission
1265 West Shaw Avenue, Suite 103
Fresno, CA 93711
559-487-5793

David Rodriguez, *Director*

Equal Employment Opportunity Commission
255 East Temple Street, 4th Floor
Los Angeles, CA 90012
213-894-1000

Dorothy Porter, *Director*

Equal Employment Opportunity Commission
401 B Street, Suite 1550
San Diego, CA 92101
619-557-7235

Patrick Matarazzo, *Director*

Export-Import Bank of the United States
1 World Trade Center, Suite 1670
Long Beach, CA 90831
310-498-0141

Federal Communications Commission
1800 Studebaker Road, Room 660
Cerritos, CA 90701

James R. Zoulek, *Engineer in Charge*

Federal Communications Commission
4542 Ruffner Street, Rom 370
San Diego, CA 92111

William H. Grisby, *Engineer in Charge*

Federal Deposit Insurance Corporation
4 Park Plaza, Jamboree Center
Irvine, CA 92714
714-263-7765

Sandra Waldrop, *Director*

Federal Maritime Commission
11 Golden Shore, Suite 270
Long Beach, CA 90802

Michael A. Murphy, *Officer in Charge*

Federal Mediation and Conciliation Service
225 West Broadway, Suite 610
Glendale, CA 91204
323-965-3814

Joseph E. Medina, *Director*

Federal Trade Commission
11000 Wilshire Boulevard, Suite 13209
Los Angeles, CA 90024

Sue L. Frauens, *Director*

Food and Drug Administration - Public Affairs Office
14900 MacArthur Boulevard, Suite 300
Irvine, CA
714-796-7600

Government Printing Office Bookstore
505 South Flower Street, ARCO Plaza, C-Level
Los Angeles, CA
213-239-9844

International Trade Administration
11150 West Olympic Boulevard, Suite 975
Los Angeles, CA 90064
310-235-7104

Julie Anne Hennessy, *Director*

International Trade Administration
6363 Greenwich Drive, Suite 230
San Diego, CA 92122
619-557-5395

Matt Anderson, *Director*

Jerry L. Pettis Memorial Veterans Hospital
11201 Benton Street
Loma Linda, CA 92357

Dean R. Stordahl, *Director*

Minerals Management Service
770 Paseo Camarillo
Camarillo, CA 93010
805-369-7502

**Minority Business
Development Agency**
9660 Flair Drive, Suite 455
El Monte, CA 91713
818-453-8636

Joseph Galindo, *Director*

**National Archives and Records
Administration - Federal Records
Centers**
24000 Avila Road
Laguna Niguel, CA 92677
714-643-4220

Sharon L. Roadway, *Director*

**National Archives and Records
Administration - Regional Archives**
24000 Avila Road
Laguna Higuel, CA 92677
714-643-44241

Diane Nixon, *Director*

National Labor Relations Board
11000 Wilshire Boulevard
Los Angeles, CA 90024
310-575-7352

James J. McDermott, *Director*

National Labor Relations Board
888 Figueroa Street
Los Angeles, CA 90017
213-894-5200

Victoria E. Aguayo, *Director*

National Labor Relations Board
555 West Beech Street
San Diego, CA 92101
619-557-6184

Claude R. Marston, *Director*

**National Transportation Safety Board -
Aviation**
1515 West 190th Street, Suite 555
Gardena, CA 90248

Gary Mucho, *Officer*

**National Transportation Safety Board -
Highway**
1515 West 190th Street, Suite 555
Gardena, CA 90248

Ronald Robinson, *Officer*

**National Transportation Safety
Board - Railroad**
1515 West 190th Street, Suite 555
Gardena, CA 90248

Dave Watson, *Officer*

Peace Corps
11000 Wilshire Boulevard, Suite 8104
Los Angeles, CA 90024
310-235-7444

Ronald Reagan Library
Simi Valley, CA 93065
805-522-8444

R. Duke Blackwood, *Director*

Securities and Exchange Commission
5670 Wilshire Boulevard, Suite 1100
Los Angeles, CA 90036
213-965-3998

Valerie Caproni, *Director*

Small Business Administration
330 North Brand Boulevard, Suite 1200
Glendale, CA 91203
213-894-2956

Alberto Alvarado, *Officer in Charge*

Small Business Administration
550 West C Street, Suite 550
San Diego, CA 92101
619-557-7252

George P. Chandler, Jr., *District Director*

Small Business Administration
901 West Civic Center Drive, Suite 160
Santa Ana, CA Suite 160
714-836-2494

John S. Waddell, *Officer in Charge*

Small Business Administration
6477 Telephone Road, Suite 10
Ventura, CA 93003
805-642-1866

Teddy Lutz, *Officer in Charge*

**United States Commission on
Civil Rights**
3660 Wilshire Boulevard, Room 810
Los Angeles, CA 90010
213-894-3437

**United States Postal Service - Postal
Inspection Office**
PO Box 2000
Pasadena, CA 91102
818-405-1200

United States Postal Service - Postal Inspection Service
PO Box 2110
San Diego, CA 92112
619-233-0610

US Coast Guard
400 Oceangate Boulevard
Long Beach, CA 90822
310-980-4300

Richard A. Applebaum, *Commander*

US Marine Corps
3704 Hochmuth Avenue
San Diego, CA 92140
619-542-5570

US Secret Service
5701 Truxton Avenue, Suite 190
Bakersfield, CA 93309
805-861-4112

US Secret Service
255 East Temple Street, Roybal Federal Building, 17th Floor
Los Angeles, CA 90012
213-894-4830

US Secret Service
550 West C Street, Suite 660
San Diego, CA 92101
619-557-5640

US Secret Service
200 West Santa Ana Boulevard, Suite 500
Santa Ana, CA 92701
714-836-2805

EMPLOYMENT TIP

Today, more than ever before, it has become crucial that this country have the brightest, most talented and most committed leadership. The Federal Government, America's largest employer, hires more than 300,000 people each year across the Nation. No other employer can offer you the variety of career opportunities that are available in the Federal Government.

California State Government

STATE AGENCY WEB SITES

Administrative Law
www.oal.ca.gov/
Aging
www.aging.state.ca.us
Agricultural Export Program
www.atinet.org/aep/
Agricultural Statistics Service
www.cdfa.ca.gov/cass/
Agriculture
www.cdfa.ca.gov/
Air Resources Board
www.arb.ca.gov
Alcohol and Drug Programs
www.adp.cahwnet.gov/
Alcoholic Beverage Control
www.abc.ca.gov/
Allocation Board
www.dgs.ca.gov/opsc/sab.htm
Animal Industry
www.cdfa.ca.gov/animal/
ApprenticeshipCouncil
www.dir.ca.gov/DIR/Apprenticeship/CAC/cac.html
ApprenticeshipStandards
www.dir.ca.gov/DIR/Apprenticeship/DAS/das.html
Architect
www.dsa.ca.gov/
Architectural Examiners
www.cbae.cahwnet.gov/
Archives
www.ss.ca.gov/archives/archives_home.htm
Arts Council
www.cac.ca.gov
Assembly
www.assembly.ca.gov
Attorney General
http://caag.state.ca.us/
Audits
www.bsa.ca.gov/bsa/
Automotive Repair
www.smogcheck.ca.gov
Behavioral Science Examiners
www.bbs.ca.gov/
Board of Prison Terms
www.bpt.ca.gov
Board of Vocational Nurse &
Psychiatric Technician Examiners
www.bvnpt.ca.gov
Boating and Waterways
www.dbw.ca.gov
Boating and WaterwaysCommission
www.dbw.ca.gov/commissi.html
Braille andTalking Book Library
http://library.ca.gov/pubser/pubser05.html
Building Standards Commission
www.bsc.ca.gov/bsc/
Bureau of State Audits
www.bsa.ca.gov/bsa/
Business, Transportation and HousingAgency
www.bth.ca.gov/
Department of Financial Institutions
www.dfi.ca.gov/
Department of Corporations
www.corp.ca.gov/
California Highway Patrol
www.chp.ca.gov/

Department of Housing and Community Development
http://housing.hcd.ca.gov
California Housing FinanceAgency
www.chfa.ca.gov/
Department of Motor Vehicles
www.dmv.ca.gov/
Department of Real Estate
www.dre.cahwnet.gov/
Department of Transportation
www.dot.ca.gov
CalEPA (Environmental Protection Agency)
www.calepa.ca.gov/
California African-American Museum
www.caam.ca.gov/
California Board of Corrections
www.bdcorr.ca.gov
California Department of Corrections
www.cdc.state.ca.us
California Department of Forestryand Fire Protection
www.fire.ca.gov
California Governor's Council on Physical Fitness & Sports
www.calfit.ca.gov/
California Highway Patrol
www.chp.ca.gov/
California Public Employees'Retirement System
www.calpers.ca.gov/
CaliforniaState Archives
www.ss.ca.gov/archives/archives_home.htm
California State University
www.calstate.edu/
CaliforniaState University Board of Trustees
www.co.calstate.edu/PublicAffairs/overview/BOT.html
California State University Institute
www.co.calstate.edu/CSUI/
California Youth Authority
www.cya.ca.gov
California Youth and Adult Correctional Agency
www.yaca.state.ca.us
Cal/OSHA
www.dir.ca.gov/DIR/OS&H/DOSH/dosh1.html
Caltrans
www.dot.ca.gov/
CalVETs
www.ns.net/cadva/
CEDAR (California Economic Diversification and Revitalization)
www.cedar.ca.gov/
Child Development Policy AdvisoryCommittee
www.cdpac.ca.gov
Child Support (Office ofChild Support)
www.childsup.cahwnet.gov/
CHP (California HighwayPatrol)
www.chp.ca.gov
CMECC(Military Environmental Coordination Committee
www.cedar.ca.gov/military/cmecc/cmecc.html
Coastal Commission(California Coastal Commission)
www.ceres.ca.gov/coastalcomm/web/
COICC (California Occupational Information Coordinating Committee)
www.soicc.ca.gov/
Commission on Improving Life Through Service
www.cilts.ca.gov/
Commission on State Mandates
www.csm.ca.gov/
Commission on TeacherCredentialing
www.ctc.ca.gov/
Community Colleges Board ofGovernors
www.cerritos.edu/cccco/

499

Compensation Insurance Fund
www.dir.ca.gov/DIR/Workers'_Compensation/SCIF/
scif.html
Conservation
www.consrv.ca.gov
Conservation Corps
www.ccc.ca.gov
Consumer Affairs
www.dca.ca.gov
Controller's Office
www.sco.ca.gov
Corporations (Department of Corporations)
www.corp.ca.gov
Corrections (Department of Corrections)
www.cdc.state.ca.us
Council on CriminalJustice
www.ocjp.ca.gov/cmmttees.html
Courts
www.courtinfo.ca.gov/aoc/aoc.htm
Criminal Justice Planning
www.ocjp.ca.gov/
Criminal Justice
www.dof.ca.gov/html/budgt6-7/LOCGOVT.HTM
CSGNet
www.teale.ca.gov/services/home.html
CYA (Department of Youth Authority)
www.cya.ca.gov
Defense Conversion
http://commerce.ca.gov/business/select/defense/
Democratic Caucus (Assembly)
http://Councildemocrats.assembly.ca.gov
Demographic Research Unit
www.dof.ca.gov/html/Demograp/druhpar.htm
Developmental Disabilities, AreaBoards on
www.ns.net/OAB/
Developmental Services
www.dds.cahwnet.gov/
DOIT (Department of InformationTechnology)
www.doit.ca.gov/
DMV (Department of MotorVehicles)
www.dmv.ca.gov/
Economic Development Division, Trade and
Commerce Agency
http://commerce.ca.gov/business/ed_home.html
Economic Diversification and Revitalization
www.cedar.ca.gov/
EDD (Employment Development Department)
www.edd.cahwnet.gov
Education Facilities Authority
www.treasurer.ca.gov/stocefa.htm
Emergency Medical Services Authority
www.emsa.cahwnet.gov/
Emergency Medical Services Commission
www.emsa.cahwnet.gov/def_comm.htm
Emergency Services
www.oes.ca.gov
Employment Development Departmen
www.edd.cahwnet.gov
Employment of Disabled Persons
www.edd.cahwnet.gov/gcedpind.htm
Employment Training Panel
www.etp.cahwnet.gov
Energy Assessments
www.dgs.ca.gov/OEA/
Energy Commission
www.energy.ca.gov/
Environmental Protection Agency
www.calepa.ca.gov/
Environmental Technology Center
http://sio.ucsd.edu/sp_progs/cetc/cetc.html
Environmental HealthHazard Assessment
www.calepa.cahwnet.gov/oehha/
Fair Political Practices Commission
http://infra1.dgs.ca.gov/fppc/
Film Commission
http://commerce.ca.gov/business/select/film/
Finance (Department of Finance)
www.dof.ca.gov/

Financial Institutions
www.dfi.ca.gov/
Fire Marshal
www.saic.com/firesafe/csfm.dir.html
Fish and Game
www.dfg.ca.gov/
Fish and Game Commission
www.dfg.ca.gov/mtgsnew.html
Food and Agriculture
www.cdfa.ca.gov/
Forestry and Fire Protection
www.fire.ca.gov
Franchise Tax Board
www.ftb.ca.gov/
General Services
www.dgs.ca.gov/
Government Claims Program
www.boc.cahwnet.gov/GovClms.htm
Government Organization andEconomy Commission
www.lhc.ca.gov/lhc.html
Governor's School to CareerTask Force
www.stc.cahwnet.gov/
Governor's Committee for Employment of
Disabled Persons
www.edd.cahwnet.gov/gcedpind.htm
Health and Safety
www.dir.ca.gov/DIR/OS&H/CHSWC/chswc.html
Job ServicesDivision
www.edd.cahwnet.gov/jsind.htm
Labor Market Information Division
www.calmis.cahwnet.gov/
Unemployment Insurance Division
www.edd.cahwnet.gov/uiind.htm
Health and Welfare Data Center
www.hwdc.cahwnet.gov/
Health Information for Policy Project
www.chipp.cahwnet.gov/
Health Planning and Development
www.oshpd.cahwnet.gov/
HealthPolicy and Data Advisory Commission
www.oshpd.cahwnet.gov/chpdac/CHPDACA.HTM
Health Services
www.dhs.cahwnet.gov/
Highway Patrol
www.chp.ca.gov
HistoricPreservation
http://cal-parks.ca.gov/programs/ohp/ohpindex.htm
Horse Racing Board
www.chrb.ca.gov/
Housing Finance Agency
www.chfa.ca.gov/
Industrial Relations
www.dir.ca.gov/
Industrial Medical Council
www.dir.ca.gov/DIR/Workers'_Compensation/IMC/
imc.html
Industrial Welfare Commission
www.dir.ca.gov/DIR/Labor_Law/IWC/iwc.html
InfoPeople
http://infopeople.berkeley.edu:8000/index.html
Information Center for the Environment
http://ice.ucdavis.edu:80/
Information Services, Department of General Services
www.dgs.ca.gov/intsvgrp/default.htm
Information Systems and Services Office
www.water.ca.gov/DWR.ISSO.Home.html
Information Technology
www.doit.ca.gov/
Insurance
www.insurance.ca.gov/docs/index.html
Insurance Commissioner
www.insurance.ca.gov/docs/Idcommis.htm
Integrated Waste Management Board
www.ciwmb.ca.gov/
Internet Services Group, Department of General Services
www.dgs.ca.gov/intsvgrp/default.htm

ITEC (Information Technology and Education Center, Dept. of General Services)
www.dgs.ca.gov/itec/index.htm
Job Services Division, EDD
www.edd.cahwnet.gov/jsind.htm
Job Training Coordinating Council
www.sjtcc.cahwnet.gov/
Judicial Council of California
www.courtinfo.ca.gov/judicialcouncil/
Judicial Branch
www.courtinfo.ca.gov/
Justice (Department of Justice)
http://caag.state.ca.us/
LEAD (Licensee Education on Alcohol and Drugs)
www.abc.ca.gov/programs/LEAD/LEAD_MENU.html
Labor Market Information Division
www.calmis.cahwnet.gov/
Labor Standards Enforcement
www.dir.ca.gov/DIR/Labor_Law/DLSE/dlse.html
Land Use Planning Information Network
www.ceres.ca.gov/planning/
Lands Commission
www.slc.ca.gov/
Law Revision Commission
www.clrc.ca.gov/
Legislative Analyst's Office
www.lao.ca.gov/
Legislative BlackCaucus
www.assembly.ca.gov/lbcweb/
Legislative Counsel
www.leginfo.ca.gov/legcnsl.html
Legislature — StateAssembly
www.assembly.ca.gov/
Legislature — State Senate
www.sen.ca.gov/
License Board
www.cslb.ca.gov/
Little Hoover Commission
www.lhc.ca.gov/lhc.html
Local Investment Advisory Board
www.treasurer.ca.gov/stolf.htm
Managed Health Care Improvement Task Force
www.chipp.cahwnet.gov/mctf/front.htm
Managed Risk Medical Insurance Board
www.mrmib.ca.gov/
Mandate Commission
www.csm.ca.gov/
Mediation & Conciliation Service
www.dir.ca.gov/DIR/M&C/SMCS/smcs.html
Medical Board of California
www.medbd.ca.gov/
Mental Health
www.dmh.cahwnet.gov
National Guard
www.calguard.ca.gov/
Parks and Recreation
http://cal-parks.ca.gov/
Peace Officer Standards and Training
www.post.ca.gov/
PERS (Public Employees' Retirement System)
www.calpers.ca.gov
Personnel Administration
www.dpa.ca.gov/
Personnel Board
www.spb.ca.gov/
Pollution Control Financing Authority
www.treasurer.ca.gov/cpcfa.htm
Pooled Money Investment Board
www.dof.ca.gov/html/deptinfo/RD_HOME.HTM
Postsecondary Education Commission
www.cpec.ca.gov/
Printing (Office of Publishing)
www.osp.ca.gov/main.htm
Prison Industry Authority
www.pia.ca.gov/
Public Defender
www.ospd.ca.gov/

Public Employees' Retirement System
www.calpers.ca.gov
Public Utilities Commission
www.cpuc.ca.gov/
Railroad Museum
www.csrmf.org
Real Estate Appraisers
www.orea.cahwnet.gov/
Real Estate
www.dre.cahwnet.gov/
Registered Veterinary Technician Examining Committee
www.vmb.ca.gov
Rehabilitation
www.rehab.cahwnet.gov/
Risk and Insurance Management
www.orim.ca.gov/
Rural Health Policy Coucil
www.ruralhealth.cahwnet.gov/
School to Career Task Force
www.stc.cahwnet.gov/
Science and Industry
www.usc.edu/CMSI/CMSI.shtml
Scripps Institute of Oceanography, UC San Diego
www.-sio.ucsd.edu
Secretary of State
www.ss.ca.gov/
Senate (State Senate)
www.sen.ca.gov
Small and Minority Business
www.osmb.dgs.ca.gov
Small Business Office
www.commerce.ca.gov
Social Services
www.dss.cahwnet.gov/
State Bar of California
www.calbar.org/
State Personnel Board
www.spb.ca.gov/
State Summer School for the Arts
www.csssa.org/
State Teachers' Retirement System
www.strs.ca.gov/
Superintendent of Public Instruction
http://goldmine.cde.ca.gov/executive/exechome.html
Teacher Credentialing
www.ctc.ca.gov/
Teachers' Retirement System
www.strs.ca.gov/
Teale Data Center
www.teale.ca.gov/
Trade and Commerce Agency
www.commerce.ca.gov
Trade Policy and Research
www.commerce.ca.gov
Transportation
www.dot.ca.gov
Treasurer
www.treasurer.ca.gov/
U.S. Congress — House of Representatives
www.house.gov/
U.S. Congress — Senate
www.senate.gov/
University of California
www.ucop.edu/
Veterans Affairs
www.ns.net/cadva/
Veterinary Medical Board and Registered Veterinary Technician Examining Committee
www.vmb.ca.gov
Vocational Nurse & PsychiatricTechnician Examiners
www.bvnpt.ca.gov
Management Board)
www.ciwmb.ca.gov
Wildlife ConservationBoard
www.dfg.ca.gov/mtgsnew.html
Wildlife Protection Division,
www.dfg.ca.gov/wpd/index.htm

Arts Council
1300 I Street, Suite 930
Sacramento, CA 95814
916-322-6555

Barry Hessenius, *Director*

Attorney General's Office
1300 I Street
Sacramento, CA 95814
916-322-3360

Bill Rocker, *Attorney General*

Board of Prison Terms
428 J Street, Suite 600
Sacramento, CA 95814

Jim Nielsen, *Chairman*

Bureau of State Audits
660 J Street, Suite 300
Sacramento, CA 95814
916-445-0255

Kurt R. Sjobert, *State Auditor*

California Office of the Governor
State Capitol, 1st Floor
Sacramento, CA 95814
916-445-2841

Gray Davis, *Governor*

Cash Management Division
915 Capitol Mall, Room 107
Sacramento, CA 95814
916-653-3601

Bruce VanHouten, *Deputy Director*

Chief Information Officer
801 K Street, Suite 2100
Sacramento, CA 95814
916-657-0318

John Thomas Flynn, *Chief Information Officer*

VISIT

CALJOBS.CA.GOV

FOR LISTINGS OF

STATE JOBS

Chief of Staff
State Capitol
Sacramento, CA 95814
916-445-2864

Lynn Schenk, *Chief of Staff*

Coastal Commission
Resources Agency
45 Fremont, Suite 2000
San Francisco, CA 94105
415-904-5200

Peter R. Douglas, *Executive Director*

Commission on the Status of Women
1303 J Street, Suite 400
Sacramento, CA 95814
916-445-3173

Iola Gold, *Executive Director*

Controller
300 Capitol Mall, 18th Floor
Sacramento, CA 94250
916-445-2636

Kathleen Connell, *Controller*

Criminal Justice Planning Office
1130 K Street, Suite 300
Sacramento, CA 95814
916-324-9140

Ray Johnson, *Executive Director*

Department of Aging
1600 K Street
Sacramento, CA 95814
916-322-5290

Dixon Arnett, *Director*

Department of Alcohol & Drug Programs
1700 K Street
Sacramento, CA 95814
916-445-0834

Elaine Bush, *Chief Deputy Director*

Department of Alcoholic Beverage Control
3801 Rosin Court, Suite 150
Sacramento, CA 95834
916-445-3221

Jay R. Stroh, *Director*

Department of Boating & Waterways
1629 S Street
Sacramento, CA 95814
916-322-1821

Ron Principe, *Director*

Department of Conservation
801 K Street
Sacramento, CA 95814
916-322-1080

Darryl Young, *Director*

Department of Conservation - Division of Mines & Geology
801 K Street, 12th Floor
Sacramento, CA 95814
916-445-1923

James F. Davis, *State Geologist*

Department of Conservation - Division of Oil & Gas
801 K Street, 20th Floor
Sacramento, CA 95814
916-323-1777

William F. Guerard, *Supervisor*

Department of Conservation- Office of Mine Reclamation
801 K Street, 12th Floor
Sacramento, CA 95814
916-323-9198

Dennis O'Bryant, *Assistant Director*

Department of Conservation - Recycling Division
801 K Street, MS20-58
Sacramento, CA 95814
916-323-3836

Jane Irwin, *Director*

Department of Consumer Affairs
400 R Street, Room 1060
Sacramento, CA 95814
916-445-4465

Kathleen Hamilton, *Director*

Department of Developmental Services
1600 9th Street, Room 240
Sacramento, CA 95814
916-654-1897

Dennis G. Amundson, *Director*

Department of Education
721 Capitol Mall, Room 524
Sacramento, CA 95814
916-657-4766

Delaine Eastin, *State Superintendent of Public Instruction*

Department of Education - Division of Vocational Education
721 Capitol Mall, 4th Floor
Sacramento, CA 95814
916-657-2532

Susan Reese, *State Director*

Department of Education - Special Schools & Services
721 Capitol Mall, Room 616
Sacramento, CA 94244
916-657-2642

Ron Kadish, *Director*

Department of Employment Development
800 Capitol Mall, Room 5000
Sacramento, CA 95814
916-654-8210

Al Lee, *Chief Deputy Director*

Department of Finance
State Capitol, 1st Floor
Sacramento, CA 95814
916-445-4141

Tim Gage, *Director*

Department of Finance - Demographic Research
915 L Street
Sacramento, CA 95814
916-322-4651

Linda Gage, *Chief*

Department of Fish & Game
1416 9th Street, 12th Floor
Sacramento, CA 95814
916-653-7667

Jacqueline Schafer, *Director*

STATE GOVERNMENT

Department of Food & Agriculture
PO Box 942871
Sacramento, CA 94271
916-654-0433

William J. Lyons Jr., *Secretary*

**Department of Food & Agriculture -
Bureau of Animal Health**
1220 N Street, Room A107
Sacramento, CA 95814
916-654-0881

Kenneth Tomazin, *Chief*

**Department of Food & Agriculture -
Measurement Standards Division**
8500 Fruitridge Road
Sacramento, CA 95826
916-229-3000

Darrell A. Guensler, *Director*

Department of Forestry & Fire Protection
PO Box 944246
Sacramento, CA 94244
916-653-7772

Richard A. Wilson, *Director*

Department of General Services
1325 J Street, Suite 1910
Sacramento, CA 95814
916-445-3441

Barry Keene, *Director*
Dennis Dunne, *Special Asst. to The Director*

Department of General Services
1823 14th Street
Sacramento, CA 95814
916-323-8289

Barry Keene, *Director*

Department of General Services
4675 Watt Avenue
North Highlands, CA 95660
916-574-2255

Dale Garrett, *Deputy Director of Procurement*

**Department of General Services -
Office of Buildings & Grounds**
1304 O Street
Sacramento, CA 95814
916-327-6224

Rosamond Bolden, *Chief*

**Department of General Services -
Office of Fleet Administration**
802 Q Street
Sacramento, CA 95814
916-327-2007

Timothy Bow, *Chief*

**Department of General Services -
Office of Information Services**
1500 5th Street, Suite 116
Sacramento, CA 95814
916-445-2294

Don Hallberg, *Presiding Chief*

Department of Health Services
714 P Street, Room 1253
Sacramento, CA 95814
916-657-1425

Diana Bonta, *Director*

Department of Health Services
PO Box 942732
Sacramento, CA 95814
916-657-1282

Virgil J. Toney, *Chief*

**Department of Health Services -
Division of Drinking Water &
Environment**
PO Box 942732, MS 396
Sacramento, CA 94234
916-322-2308

David P. Spath, *Chief*

**Department of Health Services -
Vital Statistics Branch**
PO Box 730241
Sacramento, CA 94244
916-445-1719

Michael Davis, *Chief*

Department of Highway Patrol
2555 First Avenue
Sacramento, CA 95818
916-657-7261

Dwight Helmick, Jr., *Commissioner*

**Department of Housing & Community
Development - Community Affairs**
1800 Third Street, Suite 390
Sacramento, CA 95814
916-322-1560

Duncan Howard, *Deputy Chief*

**Department of Industrial Relations -
Division of Workers Compensation**
45 Fremont Street, Suite 3160
San Francisco, CA 94105
415-975-0700

Casey Young, *Administrative Director*

**Department of Justice -
Criminal Identification**
4949 Broadway
Sacramento, CA 95820
916-227-3844

Jack Scheidegger, *Chief*

Department of Mental Health
1600 9th Street
Sacramento, CA 95814
916-654-2309

Stephen Mayberg, *Director*

Department of Military
9800 Goethe Road
Sacramento, CA 95826
916-854-3500

Tandy Bozeman, *Adjutant General*

**Department of Motor Vehicles -
Headquarters Operation**
PO Box 932328
Sacramento, CA 94232
916-657-6940

Dorothy L. Hunter, *Division Chief*

Department of Parks & Recreation
PO Box 942896
Sacramento, CA 94296
916-653-8380

Rusty Areais, *Director*

**Department of Parks & Recreation -
Office of State Historic Preservation**
PO Box 942896
Sacramento, CA 94296
916-653-6624

Cherilyn Widell, *Historic Preservation
   Officer*

Department of Personnel Administration
1515 S Street, North Building, Suite 400
Sacramento, CA 95814
916-322-5193

Marty Morgenstern, *Director*

**Department of Personnel Administration
- Training & Development**
1515 S Street, North Building, Suite 105
Sacramento, CA 95814
916-445-5121

Mary Fernandez, *Division Chief*

Department of Rehabilitation
830 K Street Mall, Room 322
Sacramento, CA 95814
530-541-3226

Catherine Campisi, *Director*

Department of Savings & loan
300 South Spring Street, Suite 16502
Los Angeles, CA 90012
213-897-8242

Keith Paul Bishop, *Commissioner*

Department of Social Services
744 P Street, MS 17-11
Sacramento, CA 95814
916-657-2598

Rita Saenz, *Director*

**Department of Social Services -
Child Support Program Branch**
744 P Street, MS 17-11
Sacramento, CA 95814
916-654-1556

Leslie Frye, *Chief*

**Department of Social Services -
Children & Family Services Division**
744 P Street, MS 9-100
Sacramento, CA 95814
916-657-2614

Marjorie Kelly, *Deputy Director*

Department of Financial Institutions
111 Pine Street, Suite 1100
San Francisco, CA 94111
415-288-8811

Donald Meyer, *Superintendent*

Department of Transportation
1120 N Street, Suite 1100
Sacramento, CA 95814
916-654-5267

James W. Van Loben Sels, *Director*

**Department of Transportation -
Aeronautics Program**
PO Box 942874
Sacramento, CA 94274
809-729-8806

Marlin Beckwith, *Program Manager*

STATE GOVERNMENT

505

Department of Transportation - Division of Highways
1120 N Street, Room 440
Sacramento, CA 95814
916-654-6228

Martha Glass, *Chief*

Department of Veterans Affairs
1227 O Street, Suite 300
Sacramento, CA 95814
916-653-2158

Jay R. Vargas, *Secretary*

Department of Water Resources
1416 Ninth Street
Sacramento, CA 95814
916-653-7007

Tom Hannegan, *Director*

Department of Youth Authority
4241 Williamsborough Drive, Suite 201
Sacramento, CA 95823
916-262-1467

Francisco J. Alarcon, *Director*

Division of Occupational Safety & Health
455 Golden Gate Avenue, Suite 5202
San Francisco, CA 94102
415-972-8500

John Howard, *Chief*

Energy Commission
1516 9th Street
Sacramento, CA 95814
916-654-5000

Winston Hickox, *Chairman*

Environmental Protection Agency
555 Capitol Mall, Suite 525
Sacramento, CA 95814
916-445-3846

James M. Strock, *Secretary*

Environmental Protection Agency - Air Resources Board
PO Box 2815
Sacramento, CA 95812
916-322-5840

John Dunlap, III, *Chairman*

Exposition & State Fair
1600 Exposition Boulevard
Sacramento, CA 95815
916-263-3000

Norbert Bartosik, *General Manager*

Fair Employment & Housing
2014 T Street, Suite 210
Sacramento, CA 95814
916-227-2873

Dennis Hyashi, *Director*

Fair Political Practices Commission
428 J Street, Suite 600
Sacramento, CA 95804
916-322-5660

Ravi Mehta, *Chairman*

Franchise Tax Board
Po Box 1468
Sacramento, CA 95812
916-845-4543

Gerald Goldberg, *Executive Officer*

Health & Welfare Agency
1600 9th Street, Room 460
Sacramento, CA 95814
916-445-6951

Sandra R. Smoley, *Secretary*

Horse Racing Board
1010 Hurley Way, Room 190
Sacramento, CA 95825
916-920-7178

Ralph Scurfield, *Chairman*

Housing & Community Development Department - Division of Codes & Standards
PO Box 1407
Sacramento, CA 95812
916-445-9471

Travis Oitts, *Deputy Director*

Housing Finance Agency
1121 L Street, 7th Floor
Sacramento, CA 95814
916-322-3991

Theresa Parker, *Executive Director*

Information Systems
801 K Street, Suite 2100
Sacramento, CA 95814
916-657-0318

John Thomas Flynn, *Chief Information Officer*

Insurance Commissoner
300 Capitol Mall, Suite 1500
Sacramento, CA 95814
916-445-5544

Charles W. Quackenbush

Integrated Waste Management Board
8800 California Center Drive
Sacramento, CA 95826
916-255-2151

Linda Moulton-Patterson, *Chairman*

Judicial Council - Administration
Office of the Courts
303 Second Street
San Francisco, CA 94107
415-396-9100

William C. Vickrey, *Director*

Lieutenant Governor
State Capitol, Room 1114
Sacramento, *CA 95814*
916-445-8994

Lottery Commission
600 North 10th Street
Sacramento, CA 95814
916-324-2025

William Popejoy, *Interim Director*

Native American Heritage Commission
915 Capitol Mall, Room 288
Sacramento, CA 95814
916-322-7791

Larry Myers, *Executive Secretary*

Office of Community Relations
18952 MacArthur Boulevard
Irvine, CA 92715
714-553-3566

Suzanna Tashiro, *Director*

Office of Emergency Services
2800 Meadowview Road
Sacramento, CA 95832
916-262-1816

Dallas Jones, *Director*

Office of Planning and Research
1400 10th Street
Sacramento, CA 95814
916-322-2318

Steve Nissen, *Director*

Office of Secretary of State - Corporate Filing Division
1230 J Street
Sacramento, CA 95814
916-653-6564

Jim Clevenger, *Chief*

Office of Secretary of State - Elections Division
1230 J Street
Sacramento, CA 95814
916-657-2166

John Mott-Smith, *Chief*

Office of State Printing
344 North 7th Street
Sacramento, CA 95814
916-445-9110

Jim Davis, *State Printer*

Office of State Public Defender
801 K Street, Suite 000
Sacramento, CA 95814
916-322-2676

Fern M. Laethem, *Public Defender*

Office of the Controller - Division of Unclaimed Property
300 Capitol Mall, Suite 801
Sacramento, CA 95814
916-323-2843

Barbara Reagan, *Chief*

Office of the Governor
444 North Capitol Street, NW
Hall of the States, Suite 134
Washington, DC 20001
202-624-5270

Olivia Morgan, *Director*

Office of the Secretary of State
1500 11th Street
Sacramento, CA 95814
916-653-7244

Bill Jones, *Secretary of State*

Office of the Secretary of State - Political Reform Division
1500 11th Street, Room 495
Sacramento, CA 95814
916-653-5943

Robert Steele, *Chief*

Office of Tourism
801 K Street, Suite 1600
Sacramento, CA 95814
916-322-5639

John Poimiroo, *Director*

Post-Secondary Education Commission
1303 J Street, Suite 500
Sacramento, CA 95814
916-445-1000

Warren H. Fox, *Executive Director*

Press Secretary
State Capitol
Sacramento, CA 95814
916-445-4571

Steven Maviglio, *Press Secretary*

Public Employment Retirement System
400 P Street
Sacramento, CA 95814
916-326-3829

Jim Burton, *CEO*

Public Utilities Commission
505 Van Ness Avenue, Room 5218
San Francisco, CA 94102
415-703-2440

Loretta Lynch, *President*

Rail & Transit
980 9th Street, Suite 2450
Sacramento, CA 95814
916-327-2892

Kenneth E. Bosanko, *Deputy Secretary*

Resources Agency
1416 9th Street, Room 1311
Sacramento, CA 95814
916-653-5656

Douglas Wheeler, *Secretary*

State Archives
1020 O Street
Sacramento, CA 95814
916-653-7715

Walter Gray, *State Archivist*

State Board of Control
PO Box 48
Sacramento, CA 95812
916-323-3432

Austin Eaton, *Executive Officer*

State Fire Marshall
PO Box 944246
Sacramento, CA 94244
916-262-1883

State Lands Commission
100 Howe Avenue
Sacramento, CA 95825
916-574 1800

Robert Hight, *Executive Officer*

State Library
900 N Street
Sacramento, CA 95814
916-654-0174

Kevin Starr, *State Librarian*

State Library - Information Reference Center
900 N Street
Sacramento, CA 95814
916-654-0261

Kevin Starr, *State Librarian*

State of California - Insurance Department
300 South Spring, 14th Floor
Los Angeles, CA 90013
213-346-6400
Web Address: www.insurance.ca.gov

Chuck Quackenbush, *Insurance Commissioner*

State Treasurer
915 Capitol Mall, Room 110
Sacramento, CA 95814
916-653-2995

Philip Angelidas, *State Treasurer*

Supreme Court
350 McAlister Street, Room 1295
San Francisco, CA 94102
415-865-7000

Ronald M. George, *Chief Justice*
Frederick K. Ohlrich, *Clerk*
Fran Jones, *Law Librarian*
Edward Jesson, *Reporter of Decisions*

Teachers Retirement System
7667 Folsom Boulevard, Suite 300
Sacramento, CA 95851
916-229-3870

James D. Mosman, *CEO*

Teale Data Center
PO Box 13436
Sacramento, CA 95813
916-263-1886

Randy Moory, *Branch Manager*

Toxic Substance Control
400 P Street, 4th Floor
Sacramento, CA 95812
916-323-9723

Edwin Lowry, *Director*

Trade & Commerce Agency
801 K Street, Suite 1700
Sacramento, CA 95814
916-322-3962

Lon Hatamiya, *Secretary*

**Trade & Commerce Agency-
Office of Small Business**
801 K Street, Suite 1700
Sacramento, CA 85814
916-322-3596

Denise Arend, *Executive Director*

Water Resources Control Board
PO Box 944213
Sacramento, CA 94244
916-657-2399

Arthur G. Baggett, *Chairman*

Youth & Adult Corrections Agency
1100 11th Street
Sacramento, CA 95814
916-323-6001

Joe Sandoval, *Secretary*

Local Government City & County

Beverly Hills City Hall
455 North Rexford Drive
Beverly Hills, CA 90210

Chula Vista
276 Fourth Avenue
Chula Vista, CA 91910
619-691-5044

Dave Rowlands, *City Manager*
Candy Emerson, *Director of Personnel*

City of Oceanside
300 North Coast Highway
Oceanside, CA 92054
760-966-4410
Job Hotline: 760-966-4499
Web Address: www.ci.oceanside.ca.us
Number of Employees: 125

Thomas J. Wilson, *City Manager*
Collen McCloud, *Administrator of Human Resources*

City of Vista
600 Eucalyptus Avenue
Vista, CA 92084
760-726-1340
Job Hotline: 760-639-6147
Number of Employees: 110

Rita Gilbert, *City Manager*
Sab Pedrod, *Assistant Personnel Manager*

City of Agoura Hills
30101 Agoura Court, #102
Agoura Hills CA 91301
818-597-7300

City of Anaheim
200 South Anaheim Boulevard
Anaheim, CA 92805
714-765-5162

City of Carlsbad
1635 Faraday Avenue
Carlsbad, CA 92008
760-602-2440
Job Hotline: 760-602-2480
Number of Employees: 528

Ray Patchett, *City Manager*
Ann Cheverton, *Director of Human Resources*

City of Encinitas
505 South Vulcan Avenue
Encinitas, CA 92024
760-633-2600
Job Hotline: 633-2726
Number of Employees: 125

Kerry Miller, *City Manager*
Tom Beckord, *Pesonnel Officer*

City of Escondido
201 North Broadway
Escondido, CA 92025
760-839-4641
Job Hotline: 760-839-4585
Web Address: www.ci.escondido.ca.us
Number of Employees: 800

Rolf Gumerson, *City Manager*
Jane Paradowski, *Hiring Manger*

City of Fullerton Personnel Department
303 West Commonwealth
Fullerton, CA 92832
714-738-6378
Job Hotline: 714-738-6378
Web Address: www.ci.fullerton.ca.us/ noframes/personnel

City of Glendale
P.O. Box 9653
Glendale 91206-9653
818-548-4844
Web Address: http://glendale-online.com/ index.html

Dave Weaver, *Mayor*

Glendale Office of Personnel & Employee Relations
613 East Broadway, Suite 100
Glendale, CA 91206-4392
818-548-2168

John F. Hoffman, *Director*

City of Long Beach
333 West Ocean Boulevard, 14th floor
Long Beach, California 90802
562-570-6801

Beverly O'Neill, *Mayor*

City of Los Angeles
200 North Spring Street
Los Angeles, CA 90012
213-485-5708
Web Address: www.ci.la.ca.us

City of Newport Beach
3300 Newport Boulevard
Newport Beach, CA 92663-3884
949-644-3309
Web Address: www.city.newport-beach.ca.us

City of Pasadena - Human Resources Department
100 North Garfield Avenue, Room 146
Pasadena, California 91109-7215
626-744-4366
Job Hotline: 626-744-4600

Robert Person, *Director*
Dorothy Kirkland, *Human Resources Manager*
Deborah Simms, *Human Resources Manager*

City of San Diego
202 C Street, 11th Floor
San Diego, CA 92101
619-236-6330
Web Address: www.sannet.gov

City of Santa Monica Personnel Department
1685 Main Street, Room 101
Santa Monica, CA 90401
Job Hotline: 310-458-8697
Web Address: www.ci.santa-monica.ca.us/personnel/

City of Torrance
Job Hotline: 310-618-2969

City of West Hollywood
8300 Santa Monica Boulevard
West Hollywood, CA 90069
213-848-6400
Web Address: www.ci.west-hollywood.ca.us/

Coronado
1825 Strand Way
Coronado, CA 92118
619-522-7320

Mark Ochenduszko, *City Manager*
Jack Van Sam Beek, *Director of Personnel*

County of San Bernardino Human Resources Department
157 West Fifth Street
San Bernardino, CA 92415-0440
909-387-8304

Del Mar
1050 Camino Del Mar
Del Mar, CA 92014
858-755-9313

Lauraine Brekke-Esparza, *City Manager*
Joe Hoefgen, *Director of Personnel*

El Cajon
200 East Main Street
El Cajon, CA 92020
619-441-1776

Bill Garrett, *City Manager*
Mary Kaerth, *Director of Personnel*

Huntington Beach Personnel Division
2000 Main Street
Huntington Beach, CA 92648
714-536-5492
Job Hotline: 714-374-1570

Imperial Beach
825 Imperial Beach Boulevard
Imperial Beach, CA 91932
619-338-4331

Barry Johnson, *City Manager*
Linda Leichtle, *Director of Personnel*

La Mesa
8130 Allison Avenue
La Mesa, CA 91941
619-667-1105

David N. Wear, *City Manager*
Marsha Arskin, *Human Resources Manager*

Lemon Grove
3232 Main Street
Lemon Grove, CA 91945
619-464-6934

Bob Richardson, *City Manager*
Betty Russell, *Director of Personnel*

Los Angeles County
500 West Temple Street
Los Angeles, CA 90012
213-974-1311
Web Address: www.co.la.ca.us

National City
1243 National City Boulevard
National City, CA 91950
619-336-4200

Tom G. McCabe, *City Manager*

Orange County
10 Civic Center Plaza
Santa Ana, CA 92702
714-834-2200
Web Address: www.oc.ca.gov

Pomona Department of Human Resources
909-620-2291

Riverside County
4080 Lemon Street
Riverside, CA 92501
909-275-1100
Web Address: www.co.riverside.ca.us

San Bernardino County
351 North Arrowhead Street, 5th Floor
San Bernardino, CA 92415
909-387-3922
Web Address: www.co.san-bernardino.ca.us

San Diego
202 C Street
San Diego, CA 92101
619-236-5555
Web Address: www.sannet.gov

Michael Uberuaga, *City Manager*
Rich Snapper, *Director of Personnel*

San Diego County
401 West Broadway Street, Suite 1000
San Diego, CA 92101
619-232-0124

San Diego County - Administrative Center
1600 Pacific Highway
San Diego, CA 92101
Job Hotline: 619-236-2191
Web Address: www.co.san-diego.ca.us

San Diego County - Employee Assistance Division
444 West Beech Street, 3rd Floor
San Diego, CA 92101
619-236-4051

San Diego County - Office of Training and Development
3989 Ruffin Road
San Diego, CA 92123
619-694-8770
Job Hotline: 619-236-2191
Web Address: www.co.san-diego.ca.us/cnty/ cntydepts/general/human_resources

San Marcos
1 Civic Center Drive
San Marcos, CA 92069
760-744-1050
Job Hotline: 760-744-1050

R. W. Gittings, *City Manager*
Lois Navolt, *Personnel Manager*

Santa Monica City Hall
1685 Main Street
Santa Monica, CA 90401

Santee
10601 Magnolia Avenue
Santee, CA 92071
619-258-4100

George E. Tockstein, *City Manager*
Richard Thaler, *Director of Administration*

Solana Beach
635 South Highway 101
Solana Beach, CA 92075
858-755-2998

Robert Semple, *City Manager*
Luci Serlet, *Assistant City Manager*

EMPLOYMENT TIP

To Apply and Search

for Jobs with the

California

State Government,

Visit Caljobs.ca.gov

Index

N

P

S

X

Y

Z

Free Company Listing

IN THE NEXT EDITION OF THE
SOUTHERN CALIFORNIA JOB SOURCE

To maintain our position as the leader in Career Publishing, Benjamin Scott Publishing annually updates our database of over 50,000 companies nationwide. We continually make every effort to keep up with changes within and around companies, but we also recognize that sometimes we miss something, so if your company would like to be listed in the next edition of the *Southern California Job Source* or has any changes with a current listing, please fill out the employer profile below and either fax or send it to us by November of each year. Questions, call 800-488-4959

◼ EMPLOYER PROFILE ◼

INDUSTRY:_____ **example:** Law, Banking or Manufacturing

Company Name _____

Address _____

_____

City, State, Zip _____

Phone ( ) _____ Fax ( ) _____

Web Address _____

Number of Employees (Local) _____ (Worldwide) _____

President/CEO _____

H.R. Contact _____ Title _____

Intern Coordinator _____

Company Description _____

_____

_____

**Fax Employer Profiles
to 626-449-1389**

or send to: Benjamin Scott Publishing
20 East Colorado Boulevard, #202
Pasadena, CA 91105

Job Source Series

The Only Source You Need to Land the Internship,
Entry-Level or Middle Management Job of Your Choice

CURRENT & FUTURE TITLES

- **Baltimore Job Source (Spring 2001)**   **$18.95**
  Covers the Entire Baltimore Metropolitan Area plus parts of Western and Eastern Maryland

- **South Flroida Job Source (New)**   **$18.95**
  Covers all of South Florida including Broward, Brevard, Dade and Palm Beach Counties

- **Pittsburgh Job Source (Spring 2001)**   **$18.95**
  Covers the Entire Pittsburgh Metropolitan Area plus Western Pennsylvania

- **San Francisco Job Source (New)**   **$18.95**
  Covers the Entire San Francisco Metropolitan Area plus Oakland/East Bay and San Jose/Silicon Valley

- **Southern California Job Source (New)**   **$18.95**
  Covers all of Southern California - Los Angeles, San Diego & Orange County plus San Bernardino, Riverside and Ventura Counties

- **Washington Job Source-5th Edition (Spring 2001)**   **$18.95**
  Covers the Entire Washington, D.C. Metropolitan Area plus Northern Virginia & Suburban Maryland

**To Learn More or Buy Any Job Source Title,
Visit Your Favorite Bookstore,
Amazon.com, barnesandnoble.com, JobSourceNetwork.com
or Call 800-488-4959**

JobSource**Network.com**

Links to Thousands of Job and Career Web Sites Worldwide

THE 1ST PLACE TO START YOUR INTERNET JOB SEARCH

- and -

**The Internet's Premiere Web Directory to the
Most Popular, Unique and Specialized
Job and Career Web Sites on the Internet**

**Search Thousands
of Job Sites by**

- **LEVEL OF JOB**
- **TYPE OF JOB**
- **INDUSTRY**
- **CITY OR STATE**

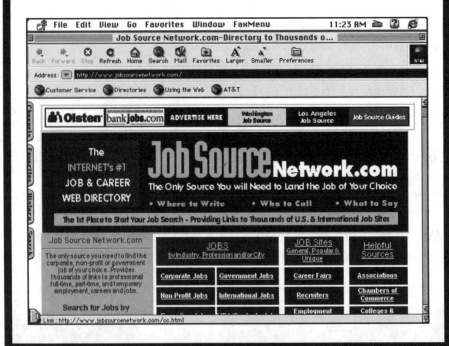

www.JobSourceNetwork.com